The University Wine Course

The University Wine Course

by

Marian W. Baldy, Ph.D.

Published by The Wine Appreciation Guild

Third Edition - Fourth Printing 2004
Copyright © 1997 Marian W. Baldy, Ph.D.
Chapter 11 Copyright © 1997 Richard W. Baldy, Ph.D.

Library of Congress Cataloging-in-Publication Data

Baldy, Marian W., 1944–
    The university wine course / by Marian W. Baldy. — 1st ed.
    426pp. 21.59 x 27.94 cm
    Includes bibliography references and index.
    ISBN 0-932664-69-5 (pbk.)
    1. Wine and wine making. I. Title.
TP548.B245 1993   92-50668
641.2'2 — dc20   CIP

Published by The Wine Appreciation Guild
360 Swift Ave.
South San Francisco, CA 94080
(650) 866-3020

FAX: (650) 866-3523

EMAIL: WWW WINEAPPRECIATION. COM

Editors
Mary Van Steenbergh
Eve Kushner

Design & Typesetting
Shahasp Herardian

Indexer
Susan De Renee Coerr

Cover Photo
Polaroid Transfer onto Oak Panel
by Paul J. Mackey and Mark Madeo

A companion Teacher's Manual is available for this book and
quantity discount for classes and educational organizations.

ISBN # 0-932664-69-5

Printed in the United States of America

This book has been bound using new OTABIND® technology. The book lies open flat, regardless of page. The spine is 5 times stronger than conventional binding and floats freely and remains crease free even with repeated use.

Foreword

The mystique of wine is the reason so many people over the centuries have been fascinated with it. However, mystique is a double-edged sword. The mysteriousness of wine often is made into a threatening aspect by the esoteric jargon of "wine experts" which intimidates consumers. Professor Marian Baldy has written a book that will introduce the neophyte to wine in a way that demystifies it, yet keeps alive the joy in discovering the world of wines. THE UNIVERSITY WINE COURSE is an easy-reading introduction to all aspects of wine of interest to the consumer, from the vineyard, through the winery to tasting the finished product. She introduces each topic at an informative level which does not require previous scientific background to understand, yet is sufficiently detailed to provide valuable material.

The best way to increase one's knowledge of wine is by tasting extensively and by describing each wine in as detailed a manner as possible. This helps provide information for us to catalogue the wines in our "mental wine aroma libraries" for future reference. With this text, the interested enophile is guided in tasting exercises which are designed to show how to learn to describe wine flavor and point out important characteristics to look for. Detailed descriptions of tasting sessions are provided so that the reader can select wines which will demonstrate specific aromas and make standards which define these aroma notes.

Among the plethora of texts on wine, this one conducts a wonderful fact-laden but scenic wine tour which provides the reader with solid information about how to learn about wine through tasting, and to appreciate the role of each factor in the vineyard through each step in winemaking in affecting the final sensory properties of the wine.

A. C. Noble
University of California, Davis

Acknowledgments

My journey toward writing this book began in 1964 when my college roommate Carol Lyons introduced me to the delights of Napa Valley Cabernet Sauvignon — selling then for $1.79 a bottle! — and wound its way through an eventful five years as a part-time commercial winemaker and 20 years of university teaching which included an introductory wine appreciation course almost every semester. Conversations along the way with students and the eager support of lab technicians John Koos and Diane Ikeda helped shape the course's wine tastings into a logical sequence of sensory evaluation exercises which introduced novice wine lovers to the odors, tastes, and varietal characteristics of the world's most important wine types. With the addition of a Macintosh to the front bedroom I refined these exercises and other course materials into THE WINE STUDENTS' BIBLE, and for several years my students and local wine aficionados bought this text at a downtown copy shop. In the fall of 1990, the Wine Appreciation Guild expressed interest in publishing a book "like" THE WINE STUDENTS' BIBLE, and I was granted a sabbatical leave for the following academic year. In July 1991, the book-writing began in earnest. Thanks to my year away from the classroom and plenty of hard work by key people, you can now enjoy the fruit of our labors: THE UNIVERSITY WINE COURSE.

Although drafting a manuscript is solitary work, creating a book depends on a cast of players with widely different talents, including the visionary publisher, the exacting editor, the inventive designer, the eagle-eyed proofreader, and the expert co-author. I now raise my glass to salute my publisher, who saw the possibilities; editor Mary Van Steenbergh, who insisted on logic and precision and helped me to achieve both; designer Shahasp Herardian, who transformed the ungainly manuscript into an attractive book; proofreader Kim Weir, who offered a fresh set of eyes and a beginner's perspective; and my co-author husband Dick Baldy, who not only wrote the chapter on grape-growing and kept the Macintosh humming along happily, but also provided crucial support, from gastronomic to moral.

In addition to the principals, every book has a large and invaluable supporting cast. Let's pour another toast of thanks to Debby Dohner for her daily faithfulness with secretarial tasks and to the "word processing SWAT team" of Lara Packwood, Jennifer Bales, Becky Hyde, Kathy Proud, Suzanne Meyer, and Cathy Pollock, who worked quickly and cheerfully to meet the final deadline. Another libation must to be raised to the technical advisers who each helped with part of the manuscript: Jane Armstrong, Linda Bartoshuk, Maryanne Bertram, John Buechsenstein, Pat Cooley, Beverly Cowart, Barry Dohner, Dean Donaldson, Roy Ekland, Richard Gahagan, Karen Keehn, Marcia Pelchat, Mary Murphy-Waldorf, and Leon Sobon.

Writing a book has made me keenly aware of the intellectual tradition I have inherited from my teachers, especially my professors in the biological sciences at the University of California at Davis. In the enological realm, I propose a special toast to Cornelius Ough, Maynard Amerine, and the late Harold Berg.

Finally, I'd like to thank my students, whose enthusiasm for the course and willingness to suggest improvements has made "Introduction to Wine" one of the most popular elective classes at Chico State. This book is dedicated to them and to the other wine enthusiasts — inside and outside official classrooms — who will use this book to enrich their lives through an increased understanding of wines.

A SPECIAL THANKS — TO SOME OF CALIFORNIA'S FINEST

Many California wineries and vineyards have supported my wine appreciation courses over the years by hosting us for field trips, donating wine, and/or providing guest speakers. I offer my thanks to Amador Foothill Winery, Beaulieu Vineyard, Beringer Vineyards, Bouchaine Vineyards, Buena Vista Winery, Burgess Cellars, Callaway Vineyards and Winery, Carmenet Vineyard, Carneros Creek Winery, Caymus Vineyards, Domaine Chandon, Chappellet Winery, Chateau Chevre, Chateau Montelena, Chateau St. Jean, Chico Cellars, The Christian Brothers, Clos du Bois, Concannon Vineyard, Cosentino Winery, Cresta Blanca Winery, Cuvaison, Dry Creek Vineyard, Eastside Winery, Edmeades Vineyards, Far Niente Winery, Fetzer Vineyards, Field Stone Winery, Franciscan Vineyards, Freemark Abbey, and E & J Gallo Winery.

I extend my genuine gratitude too, to Grand Cru Vineyards, Grgich Hills Cellar, Guenoc Winery, Guild Winery and Distillery, Gundlach-Bundschu Winery, Harbor Winery, Heitz Wine Cellars, Hop Kiln Winery, Husch Vineyards, Inglenook-Napa Valley, Johnson's Alexander Valley Wines, Frank Johnson Vineyards, Jordan Vineyard and Winery, Karly Winery, Kendall-Jackson Vineyards, Kenwood Vineyards, Kenworthy Cellars, Konocti Winery, F. Korbel Champagne Cellars, Hanns Kornell Champagne Cellars, Charles Krug Winery, Landmark Vineyards, The Lucas Winery, Markham Winery, Mark West Vineyards, Louis M. Martini Winery, Mayacaymas Vineyards, McDowell Valley Vineyards, Robert Mondavi Winery, Robert Mondavi Woodbridge, and Monteviña Wines.

The list is long, but I can't end without also offering heartfelt appreciation to Navarro Vineyards, Newton Vineyard, Nichelini Winery, Parducci Winery, Joseph Phelps Vineyards, Piper Sonoma Cellars, Prager Port Works, Quady Winery, Red Barn Ranch, Renaissance Vineyard and Winery, Ridge Vineyards and Winery, Rutherford Hill Winery, Santino Wines, Schramsberg Vineyards, Schumacher Cellars, Sebastiani Vineyards, Shenandoah Vineyards (Sobon Estate), Silver Oak Wine Cellars, Simi Winery, Spring Mountain Vineyards, John Stanton, Sterling Vineyards, Stevenot Winery, Stonegate Winery, Stony Hill Vineyard, Rodney Strong Vineyards, Stuermer Winery, Sutter Home Winery, Trefethen Vineyards, Vichon Winery, Villa Mt. Eden Winery, Wente Brothers, William Wheeler Winery, White Oak Vineyards, and Yverdon Vineyards. Also, we can't forget the following who read galleys and provided valuable input: Brother Myron Collins of St. Mary's College Moraga, Michelle Doyle of Melbourne Australia, Fred McMillin, Bruce Cass, Charles Sullivan, Greg Imbach, G.M. Pooch Puchilowski, Joe Formica, Jim Holsing, Harvey E. Finkel and Julius Wile.

And if I've missed anyone, please let me know.

THE UNITED STATES DEPARTMENT OF AGRICULTURE
EXCELLENCE IN COLLEGE AND UNIVERSITY TEACHING AWARDS

DR. MARIAN W. BALDY was recognized as one of the top two university professors of agriculture in the U.S. by being selected as a national award winner. Her selection was based on her contributions to the field of enology. The acclaim received by **THE UNIVERSITY WINE COURSE** since its recent publication, her active involvement in wine education, and her 20 year record of popularity as a teacher at California State University, Chico, contributed to her selection. She is the first Californian and the first female agriculture professor to receive the national award.

Abbreviated Contents

Detailed Table of Contents

Contents

Contents

Introduction

This book was originally developed for students taking an introductory wine appreciation course at California State University, Chico. It is intended to be used by anyone who wants to learn about wine — at home with a group of friends, in a winetasting club, or in a classroom.

This book will teach you how to enjoy wines by helping you

1. learn about your senses and how to use them
2. learn to describe wines precisely
3. practice tasting a variety of wine types
4. learn how to judge good and bad wines
5. understand how a wine's sensory characteristics are created in the vineyard and in the winery
6. experiment with some wine and food combinations.

The arrangement of topics in this book reflects my belief that from the start aspiring winetasters should have information they can use in everyday life. The result is a pragmatic presentation of material in an order geared toward the development of winetasting skills. Principles of winetasting (more properly called sensory evaluation), the production and sensory evaluation of white and red table wines, sparkling wines, and dessert wines, and grape growing are discussed in turn. A glossary, quick reference guide to varietal wines, and appendices on label reading and combining wine with food are available for independent reference.

The chapter on white table wine production explains the winemaking process and defines its terminology, which is then used to describe the production of red table wines, sparkling wines, and dessert wines. Each sequence of sensory evaluation exercises first introduces you to the aromas and structure of a group of wines, then acquaints you with commercial wines, and finally provides you with an opportunity to design your own tasting. To test your knowledge — both intellectual and gustatory   there are review questions at the end of every chapter and a review tasting at the conclusion of each series of sensory evaluation exercises. The book's last chapter gives you a chance to test your tasting skills on some "mystery wines" and to link your sensory impressions with your knowledge of winemaking and grapegrowing.

FOR APPETIZERS — SOME DEFINITIONS

Wine is a beverage produced by fermentation of the juice of grapes, mostly of the species *Vitis vinifera*. The scientific study of wines and winemaking is called enology. Winetasting is a branch of enology and is more correctly called sensory evaluation: the use of the senses of sight, smell, taste, and touch in a disciplined, systematic way to learn about some of the chemical and physical properties of wine. Those chemical and physical attributes of food and wine that affect our senses are called organoleptic characteristics, and sensory evaluation is sometimes called organoleptic evaluation. I will use the terms winetasting, sensory evaluation, and organoleptic evaluation interchangeably in this book. Because the organoleptic characteristics of a wine begin to develop in the vineyard, this text includes a chapter on viticulture — the science of grape growing.

A serious sensory evaluation involves more than just the interaction between the wine and our senses. After our senses tell us what's in a wine, our brains must analyze the information. Then we can record our tasting notes or talk to someone about the wine. If what we think about the wine is simply "I really like it!" or "That stuff is terrible!" we've made a purely subjective response — the kind that most of us start with as we begin to learn about wines. By reading this book and doing the exercises in it, however, you will learn to understand and much more precisely communicate your impressions of wines in terms of a number of distinguishable attributes. As a trained sensory evaluator you will be able to augment your subjective impressions of wines with more precise, objective analyses such as: "This 2-year-old Cabernet Sauvignon has a medium red color and a typical herbaceous, green-olive aroma balanced nicely with an oak-aging bouquet. It is dry, tart, and of medium body and has moderately rough astringency. I like this wine now, but I believe it will improve with another 5 years of bottle aging under proper cellar conditions." This book will give you both a theoretical and practical introduction to the objective, analytical approach to sensory evaluation, show how subjective impressions fit with this approach for a complete sensory evaluation, and explain how winemaking and grape growing influence wine quality. The Gary Larson cartoon below illustrates the combination of a subjective impression — "I don't like that at all" — with an objective analysis — "Too many legs" — to make a complete sensory evaluation.

THE FAR SIDE

© 1980 Chronicle Features
Distributed by Universal Press Syndicate

"Mmmmmm . . . nope . . . nope . . . I don't like that at all . . .
Too many legs."

Gary Larson's Invertebrate Taste Test — An Example of the Subjective and Objective in Sensory Evaluation

Most of us start our serious education in winetasting when we begin to wonder "What is it about this wine that makes me like it?" As we expand our knowledge of enology and viticulture and come to understand why certain wines are pleasing and others are not, we are increasingly able to make refined, consistent judgements of taste and informed wine purchases. In short, we are on the road to becoming connoisseurs. This text is a guidebook for that journey. To taste wines effectively requires technical knowledge of our senses and of tasting methods and a command of precise descriptive language as well as a systematic exposure to wine's organoleptic characteristics, all of which — except the actual wine samples! — are provided by this text. Given a situation in which the wines *are* provided, you'll have to add a disciplined concentration and memory, a willingness to practice, and the motivation of a love of wine.

THE WINETASTING EXERCISES

Each sensory evaluation exercise starts out with a reading assignment to prepare you for the tasting, and several exercises also have "sensory homework" that lets you preview some of the odors or tastes that you will be working with during the exercise. For sensory homework you will need ordinary household items like glasses and measuring cups and spoons and common beverages and foods such as tea and coffee, condiments, spices, fruits, and vegetables. Each tasting exercise contains objectives, instructions, questions, and a wine evaluation form for recording your impressions of the wines and taking notes. You will find no scorecards in the tasting exercises. Given the limited time I have to work with my students, I prefer to use the tasting periods to help them develop accurate verbal descriptions of the wines rather than discussing how to assign numerical points. If you are interested in exploring the design and use of scorecards, a variety of them can be found in other books on winetasting.[1] After you have completed a tasting you may want to refer to the "Information for the Post-Tasting Discussion" for that exercise in Appendix D to find out how previous students have described the wines or answered the questions.

APPENDIX D, "DO IT YOURSELF"

The "Do It Yourself" Appendix was written to guide wine-club members and anyone else who wants to learn about wine at home or in an informal setting. It tells you what supplies and equipment you will need to do the winetasting exercises, explains how to set up each tasting, and provides specific guidelines for buying, presenting, and discussing the wines. This book emphasizes California varietal wines for both practical and pedagogical reasons: it is easy for the students in my courses at California State University, Chico, to find California wines to do their homework assignments, and, more importantly, learning about varietal wine character-istics builds a solid foundation for understanding all the great wines of the world. I realize that California wines may not be as readily available in your area, however, and for this reason I have included information about appropriate similar wines from other regions in Appendix A, the Quick Reference Guide to Varietal Wines. This information and the wine-buying guidelines in Appendix D should make it easy for you to shop successfully for the wines for each tasting.

IF YOU ARE A WINE EDUCATOR

Because many wine textbooks begin with a discussion of grape growing, you may be surprised that the chapter on viticulture is at the end of this book. This organization is based on my experience over the years with my students: I have found that most beginning students are not very interested in grape growing or winemaking at first. They have enrolled in my class be-cause they like wine, because they know someone who enjoyed the course, or because they want to be able to talk about wine with a knowledgeable friend or relative. Typical students will only become curious about how wine is made and how grapes are grown later on, after they have become more familiar with wine characteristics and have learned that the flavors they enjoy originate in the wine cellar and the vineyard. To develop their motivation to learn about enology and viticulture, I lecture first about wine types, sensory evaluation, and wine and food combining, address winemaking in the middle of the term, and conclude with grapegrowing. Talking about winemaking in the middle of the term also allows me to cultivate their curiosity in the tasting laboratory before introducing ideas in lecture. For example, after doing some careful smelling in Exercise 4.1, students find the lecture information on olfactory adaptation to have real personal relevance. After tasting a very tart wine in Exercise 4.2, a discussion of the effect of cool ripening conditions on grape composition makes more sense — as does a description of how the malolactic fermentation can be used to reduce acidity. As for covering viticulture at the end of the term, students who have tasted Cabernet Sauvignon will be more interested in the lecture segment on how its vegetative flavors can be reduced by letting more sunlight into the vines, and if they have savored a *Botrytis*-affected sweet wine, a description of how vineyard management can promote the growth of *Botrytis* will mean more to them. Because I have found that this approach allows me to foster my students' natural inquisitiveness, this book is organized along similar lines; however, you should feel free to adapt it to your needs and use the chapters in the order that you find most effective. For this reason, Chapter 11 has been carefully designed to stand alone so that you could use it first. There is also specific information about grapegrowing as related to winemaking in Chapters 3, 5, and 9.

If you are planning to teach a wine course in a more formal setting with classes of fifteen or more students in which you will lecture and give exams, you may want to order the companion publication to this book, **THE TEACHER'S MANUAL** for THE UNIVERSITY WINE COURSE. This is a teacher's manual that contains sample quizzes and ideas that I have found useful for designing specific lessons and instructing my wine course. It is available from the Wine Appreciation Guild in San Francisco.

A PERSONAL NOTE

I have devoted about half of my professional life to teaching wine appreciation. Why? Yes, I do like both wine and students, but that's only part of it. Winetasting fascinates me because it constantly challenges my intellect in different ways. To study and teach it I must reach across traditional disciplinary boundaries to learn about geography, marketing, psychology, and philosophy, in addition to the biology and chemistry in which I was formally trained. Teaching enology and viticulture also requires that I close the gap between theory and practice — something I have always enjoyed and especially took pleasure in as a commercial winemaker for six years. The act of winetasting itself draws me back repeatedly because it combines the intellectual appreciation of wine with the sensuous and aesthetic experience it creates. When I play my guitar something similar happens: I experience visual delight as I take my instrument out of its case and tactile pleasure as I hold it and feel its vibrations when it responds to my touch; I hear the music I create and understand its place in a particular musical tradition; if I play well enough, I might experience an aesthetic response to my efforts. For me, winetasting and wine appreciation unite the sensuous, intellectual, and aesthetic much as music appreciation does. My involvement is both subjective and objective with wine and music: the subjective awe I experience tasting a fine wine or hearing a musical masterpiece well performed can be enhanced and shared through objective analysis. Of course, an objective analysis can never fully account for the pleasure and awe such artworks can inspire in a trained observer.

REVIEW QUESTIONS

For items 1-5 match the terms on the left with the definitions on the right:

_____ 1. Wine

_____ 2. Enology

_____ 3. Sensory evaluation

_____ 4. Organoleptic characteristics

_____ 5. Viticulture

A. Those chemical and physical characteristics of food and wine that affect our senses.

B. The scientific study of wines and wine-making.

C. The science of grape growing.

D. A beverage produced by the fermentation of grapes.

E. The use of the senses of sight, smell, taste, and touch to learn about wine.

6. The species of grapes from which most wines are made is. _____

ANSWERS TO THE REVIEW QUESTIONS

1. D
2. B
3. E
4. A
5. C
6. *Vitis vinifera*

ENDNOTE

[1] See Amerine, Maynard A., and Edward B. Roessler, WINES, THEIR SENSORY EVALUATION, Second Edition, W. H. Freeman, New York, 1983, and Alan Young, MAKING SENSE OF WINE, Greenhouse Publications, Richmond, Australia, 1986.

1

THE DELIGHTS AND REWARDS OF WINE STUDY

Wine is a nutritious, physiologically active, complex beverage that can feed our bodies, influence our health and behavior, and engage our intellects. It has a long history of production, sacramental and mealtime use, and connoisseurship in Mediterranean cultures. To study wine appreciation in a broad sense is to embark on a journey that is at once highly intimate, giving you a better understanding of your own senses and the influence of wine on your well-being, and expansive, taking you back in time to the ancient civilizations that invented wine and, perhaps, around the globe to see its modern regions of production. Let me briefly describe some of the delights and rewards of the study on which you are about to embark.

WINETASTING — A Way to Learn More about Ourselves and Our World

In addition to satisfying our natural intellectual curiosity, studying fine art or music transforms our use of our senses of sight or hearing, enabling us to focus our attention on and perceive entirely new visual or auditory worlds. This is analogous to the way in which skiing or playing tennis or soccer helps us appreciate the subtle nuances in the skill of accomplished athletes and heightens our enjoyment of the drama when we watch the Olympic Games, Wimbledon, or the World Cup. According to French enologist Pierre Poupon, developing skill in winetasting can have a similar effect: "Tasting is a way of life. We taste everything that comes into contact with our senses, be it works of art, the present moment, the reality of existence; objects, people, the arts, love, life."[1] As a discipline that has developed techniques to heighten our perceptions and increase our ability to articulate them, winetasting can transform our awareness and understanding of both our inner and outer worlds, creating a state of mind that is constantly receptive to the sensations in our surroundings.

WINE LINKS US TO MEDITERRANEAN TRADITIONS

Knowledge of wine also connects us with the Mediterranean component of our cultural heritage — its religious traditions and its modern-day custom of enjoying wine with food in a convivial, often family, atmosphere. Wine was the drink first of the priesthood and then of the wealthy in ancient Mediterranean civilizations because it brought man "closer to the gods" by removing him from his everyday existence through the effects of its alcohol. Until the last century, it was also widely used in medicine: in pharmacy to dissolve medicinal herbs, in surgery as an antiseptic, and to purify water mixed with it.[2] For centuries, wine has been an important sacramental beverage in both Judaism and Christianity: like the bread that accompanies it in communion, it is both consumed as daily sustenance and celebrated as a powerful religious symbol. In everyday life in Italy, Spain, Greece, Portugal, and France, wine is on the table at mealtimes to be enjoyed in moderation with food. Those Mediterraneans who have grown up with wine always available in their homes and who learned to drink it with their families have very different attitudes about wine than most Americans, with our national heritage of Prohibition and its legacy: most of us acquire our knowledge of the (not very proper) use of alcoholic drinks by surreptitiously drinking with our peers. When we become twenty-one years old — the legal drinking age — we are suddenly allowed to consume a heretofore forbidden drink that our parents could not legally serve us at home. Although many wise parents disregard the law in an effort to teach their children about the proper use of alcohol, most Americans are not educated about using alcoholic beverages in their families. It is worth noting that many scholars who have studied the origins of alcohol abuse believe that the American pattern of withholding alcoholic beverages until "adulthood" is not an effective way to prevent their abuse. These scholars have concluded that introducing children to the appropriate use of alcohol — by allowing them small quantities of watered wine with family meals — within the context of a society that disapproves of drunkenness is very good protection against alcohol abuse by these children later in life.[3]

I am a product of the American system of haphazard indoctrination in the "use" of wine, and when I first travelled in Europe I was surprised to see Spaniards leaving half-full carafes of wine on restaurant tables. I was even more amazed at the sobriety — not to be confused with dullness or seriousness — of the citizens of Tavarnelle Val de Pesa when I attended their annual vintage celebration in 1984. For a week during September this medium-sized country town celebrates the Chianti harvest. Each day one of the neighborhoods hosts the rest of the town — and anyone else who cares to join in — for dinner and all the wine they want to drink. Let's pause for a moment to contemplate this. Can you imagine the scene in your town if everyone were offered all the wine they wanted to drink? I know what I could expect in my hometown in California, and the scene I witnessed in Tavarnelle could not have been more different. People were strolling along the street, picking up the food that was set out in a blocks-long informal buffet, talking with their friends, drinking wine, keeping an eye on the children who scampered about — in short, enjoying the crisp autumn evening and their neighbors' companionship. The only people who appeared (from their prone positions on the sidewalk) to be drunk were a few young Germans visiting from Tavarnelle's sister city on the Rhine. The overwhelming majority of the people in the streets were enjoying the wine and food and conversation.

These two observations brought home to me the dramatic differences in attitudes about wine use in Spain and Italy as compared to my homeland. Another scene that was repeated throughout the Mediterranean was the amazed and puzzled expression that crept across the face of the Spaniard, Frenchman, or Italian I was talking with whenever the topic of our National Prohibition came up. For people who have been raised with wine it is impossible to understand how our nation could have made that everyday beverage illegal for thirteen years. Many Americans who enjoy wine are equally dismayed by the apparent return of prohibitionist sentiment as an unfortunate by-product of worthwhile efforts to decrease drunk driving and alcohol abuse. Speculation about why prohibitionist thinking is still part of our national character and why a more informed and tolerant philosophy of "moderation in all things" — coupled with a direct attack on the health and social problems caused by alcohol abusers — has not taken hold in our land would take this discussion far beyond my expertise. I suggest that a few of us get together with an anthropologist, a sociologist, a political scientist, and a historian to share a bottle of good wine and talk this over.

WINE AND THE GOOD LIFE

Americans associate wine with a gracious, more relaxed, sociable life-style, and demographic studies have shown that wine drinkers in the U.S. are better educated and earn more than non-wine drinkers.[4] Most of my students want to know more about wine for both social and professional reasons. They want to be able to discuss wine intelligently with friends or relatives who love wine. They know that wine knowledge is a valuable social skill and that in business a knowledge of and appreciation for good food and wine is considered an asset.[5] The vast majority of my students have been content to become "just" educated consumers, but some have entered the wine industry and are pursuing careers in vineyard management, winemaking, and wine marketing. Others are using their wine knowledge in such fields as restaurant or hotel management, public relations, nutrition, or medicine.

When we think of wine in social settings, we can all fondly remember occasions when wine has worked its magic and — though perhaps not putting us in direct communication with the gods — helped create a convivial conversational atmosphere after a busy day of work or play. Emile Peynaud, author of THE TASTE OF WINE, an important modern French treatise on sensory evaluation, muses about the paradox that alcohol is known to dull our senses, yet drinking wine is exhilarating: "What interests me is the effect on the emotions, the happy state of mind that wine causes even before it is drunk. The prospect of wine is so pleasant that it relaxes the face muscles and makes one's eyes light up. Even before the cork is drawn, a good bottle induces a festive atmosphere of good humor and relaxation."[6] Moving from the psychological to the physiological, we know that the pleasant relaxing effects of wine can continue throughout the evening when wine is enjoyed in moderate amounts and with a meal. This is because when wine is consumed with food, its alcohol enters our bloodstream relatively slowly. If we continue to drink slowly with an awareness of the amount we are consuming — one or two glasses per hour for most people — we can keep our blood alcohol concentration at around 0.05%, the level at which most of us perceive the maximum relaxation.[7] This level of blood alcohol is consistent both with a pleasant social evening and the ability to enjoy the subtleties of fine wine and food. Winetasting is separated from wine drinking by its requirement that we engage our minds in tasting. Peynaud notes that "to be appreciated wine demands attention and contemplation; the appeal of tasting is enhanced if one can analyze it. Countless pleasures are wasted through ignorance and want of skill and attention." Winetasting encourages moderation by its demand for attention: it demands keen senses to perceive the wine's stimuli and a sharp mind to analyze what the senses send.[8] Connoisseurship both encourages and benefits from moderation.

WINE AND NUTRITION

Wine plays three main roles in nutrition: first, as a food; second, as an aid to the absorption of minerals; and third, as an appetite stimulant. The main nutrients in wine are the simple carbohydrates ethyl alcohol, glucose, and fructose. The glass of white wine shown among the beverages on Lynda J. Barry's whimsical version of the Four Basic Food Groups (Figure 1.1) will provide about 100 calories per four-ounce serving — slightly more if it contains residual sugar or is a higher-alcohol white wine such as Chardonnay.[9] It has been suggested that a reasonable estimate of a safe limit of alcohol consumption for healthy people — the amount that would not displace essential nutrients — is ten percent of the total energy intake necessary to maintain ideal body weight.[10] A person of average weight can maintain themselves on about 2000-3000 calories per day, which would mean that two or three four-ounce glasses of wine is a safe limit. This nutritional estimate agrees nicely with research on the benefits of moderate alcohol consumption for cardiovascular health to be discussed later in this chapter.

Both red and white wines contain iron and also appear to increase the absorption of iron from other foods.[11] Wine can be an appetite stimulant. Many of us have had our good intentions of "not eating very much tonight" melt away after drinking a glass or two of wine with our dinner. While this may not be a desirable effect for people who are trying to lose weight, it can be a life-giving adjunct to therapies that include low-salt or other bland and uninteresting diets. A 1985 survey of metropolitan hospitals in the U.S. found that about half of them offered a wine service to their patients, citing its importance as an appetite stimulant in addition to its general therapeutic value and its utility as a substitute for tranquilizers.[12] Wine's 4000-year history of therapeutic use makes its medicinal properties nearly legendary. Medical research is still finding specific areas where moderate amounts of wine can enhance our health, and in some cases it has discovered the specific mechanisms by which tiny amounts of biologically active compounds in wines accomplish these therapeutic effects. Some of these are described later in this chapter.

Speaking of tiny amounts of chemicals in wine, concerns were raised in the early 1980s about the levels of sulfites in wine and more recently about possible excess levels of lead. Publicity about

Figure 1.1
Lynda J. Barry's
"The Four Basic
Food Groups"
Reprinted from BIG IDEAS,
© Lynda Barry 1983, first Harper
Perennial edition published 1992,
By permission, The Real Comet Press,
Seattle WA

rare adverse effects of sulfites resulted in a federal requirement that the words "contains sulfites" appear on all wine labels. Should this be of concern to you? No, not unless you are one of an estimated 50,000-100,000 steroid-dependent asthmatics in the U.S. who are very sensitive to sulfites.[13] What about lead? This could be a problem if you drink very large amounts of old red wines directly out of bottles whose corks have leaked and allowed some of the lead from the protective capsule to become dissolved. If your drinking habits are different — for example, if you wipe off the top of the bottle before you pull out the cork — it is extremely unlikely that lead in wine will pose any threat to you. Furthermore, wineries are phasing out lead capsules to meet landfill requirements. Although lead from capsules could be a problem in some instances, lead in wine poses a negligible danger: the average lead content of 436 samples of California wine analyzed in 1991 was 30 parts per billion, while the standard for lead in U.S. drinking water is 50 parts per billion.[14] Most of us — wine-lovers though we may be — drink a lot more water than wine, so it seems highly unlikely that we are in danger of vinous lead poisoning. The sixteenth-century Swiss physician Paracelsus is credited with the observation that "the dose makes the poison," and this principle should be kept in mind the next time you see a headline alerting you to yet another trace hazard in your water, food, or wine.

WINE AND GOOD HEALTH — What Does Medical Research Reveal?

If we were to base our decisions about healthy eating or drinking on the conflicting newspaper headlines we see with confounding regularity, we really would not know what to do about drinking coffee, eating bran, and the like. This situation seems unlikely to change, given the newsworthiness of medical research findings and the inherent conflict between the need of the daily newspapers for eye-catching headlines and that of the scientific research process for time-consuming, methodical repetition of experiments and verification or contradiction of data and theories. One scientific study does not determine "the truth" or even "the facts" but just adds another piece of information to the compendium. To evaluate the state of research in a particular area we must rely on individual experts to review the literature in that field. As a nation, we depend upon groups of experts such as the American Medical Association or the American Council on Science and Health to evaluate scientific data and make policy recommendations.

So where are we today on the question of the effect of wine on health? We're right in the middle of the process I just described: between the continual assault of contradictory news items and a potential recommendation by the U.S. Government that a glass of Zinfandel be added to the daily diet of every American. As a means of analyzing the current state of research in this area, medical epidemiologist Dr. Keith Marton recently undertook a systematic and exhaustive review of medical research findings on the effect of moderate alcohol consumption on longevity. (Medical researchers define moderate alcohol consumption as an average of two drinks or less — about two four-ounce glasses of wine — daily.) He presented his results in June 1989 to the International Council on Alcohol and Addiction. To assemble information for the review, Dr. Marton's research team made a computerized literature search for all epidemiological studies — investigations of the occurrence of a disease in human populations — published in English that investigated the relationship between alcohol consumption and health. They included in the review only those studies that 1. adequately described the study population in terms of sample size, sex, and age; 2. adequately described the means of ascertaining alcohol consumption; and 3. used an independently determined, valid measure of health outcome — hospitalization, surgery, or death, for example.[15] After applying these criteria, Dr. Marton found that research on the relationship between moderate alcohol consumption and health has focused primarily on cardiovascular mortality and morbidity and on breast cancer. What were the results?

Moderate Drinking and Heart Disease

Twenty-two studies reviewed by Marton evaluated the relationship between alcohol consumption and cardiovascular mortality. The vast majority of the study subjects were men. Nearly all the studies demonstrated increased mortality with heavy alcohol use, and the majority showed that moderate drinkers have a relative risk of cardiovascular mortality of 0.5 to 0.7 compared to non-drinkers. In other words, when compared to a population of non-drinkers, the population of moderate drinkers had 30% to 50% fewer deaths due to cardiovascular disease. The notion that moderate alcohol consumption exerts a protective effect in cardiovascular disease is supported both by that fact that these results have been replicated in a wide variety of studies and by the discovery of a plausible mechanism for this effect: moderate alcohol consumption raises the blood's concentration of high-density lipoproteins — the "good cholesterols" that help reduce the accumulation of fat in the arteries.

One criticism of studies showing that men who drink moderately live longer and are healthier than men who abstain has been a suggestion

Figure 1.2
The J-shaped Curve
Chart prepared by AWARE based on data presented by P. Boffetta and L. Garfinkel (1990).

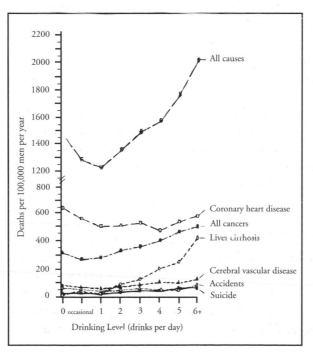

that the populations of non-drinkers studied may have included "hidden" sick people who quit drinking because of health problems.[16] Since Dr. Marton did his literature review in 1989, three significant studies have been published that were carefully controlled for pre-existing disease. All three have confirmed that men who drink moderately reduce their risk of death from coronary heart disease compared to men who abstain from alcohol.[17]

Let's take a look at the data from one of these recent studies: that of Boffetta and Garfinkel, who followed 276,000 U.S. men aged 40-59 for twelve years. Their data, summarized in Figure 1.2, is typical of the information from which epidemiologists derive the idea that moderate drinking reduces the risk of death from coronary heart disease.[18] The graph reflects the fact that the rate of deaths from all causes and from each of the four leading causes of death (coronary heart disease, cancers, cerebrovascular disease, and accidents) is lower for individuals reporting "occasional" drinking or one drink per day than the rate for non-drinkers. For deaths from all causes and from coronary heart disease, the rate remains lower for drinkers through two drinks per day, while for cancers and liver cirrhosis the death rate for non-drinkers and drinkers are about the same at two drinks per day. With the apparent exception of coronary heart disease, at three or more drinks per day there are increases in the risk of death. The increase is particularly sharp for liver cirrhosis.

Moderate Alcohol Consumption and Breast Cancer

Medical research has found an increased risk of liver, breast, esophageal, and oral-cavity cancer in heavy drinkers and an increased risk of breast cancer in women who consume moderate amounts of alcohol. When writing his review of current knowledge on the relationship between alcohol consumption and longevity, Dr. Marton took a close look at 23 studies of the relationship between breast cancer and alcohol consumption. He found 16 studies that showed a positive correlation between alcohol consumption and breast cancer, indicating a relative risk of about 1.5 (a 50% increase) for moderate drinkers compared to non-drinkers. In addition, a threshold effect was demonstrated in these studies, with the increased risk occurring only at or above two drinks per day. Nine of the studies showed no increased risk of breast cancer with moderate alcohol consumption, and the data from the last two could not be analyzed. Unlike the investigations that have shown a protective effect of moderate alcohol consumption on cardiovascular morbidity and mortality, the research data suggesting that moderate drinking leads to an increased risk of breast cancer is relatively inconsistent and weak — though the best-designed studies do show the strongest, most consistent relationship. No mechanism has been identified to explain how alcohol could cause breast cancer. Furthermore, because we know less about the factors that contribute to breast cancer than about those related to heart disease, it is harder to design experiments that exclude these variables.[19] So there are a number of reasons why the situation with breast cancer is less clear than that for cardiovascular disease, and we will have to await further research in this area. Since Dr. Marton reviewed the literature in 1989, no new studies have been published on the relationship between moderate alcohol consumption and breast cancer.[20]

The Effect of Maternal Alcohol Use on Fetal Health

What about the effect of maternal alcohol use on fetal health? Fetal alcohol syndrome (FAS) was first described clinically in the early 1970s and is defined as a group of symptoms — including mental retardation, small head size and stature, and wide-set eyes — occurring in the children of mothers who have consumed large amounts of alcohol during pregnancy. About one out of ten women who are active alcoholics during pregnancy will deliver a child who clearly suffers from FAS; FAS has not been identified in the children of any women who were not active alcoholics during pregnancy.[21] Dr. Marton's review of the dozens of studies designed to measure the effects of moderate alcohol consumption on fetal development revealed that the majority of the studies showed no differences between the children of non-drinkers and those of women who consume one to two drinks per day. However, a few studies found slightly lower birth weights among the children of moderate drinkers compared to non-drinkers.[22] Many physicians currently recommend that no alcohol be consumed during pregnancy.

What's the "Bottom Line"?
Does Medical Research Tell Us to Drink?

Dr. Marton concludes from his review that the health evidence in itself is not clear-cut enough that it should influence anyone's decision about whether or not to drink. He regards the benefits to cardiac health as a pleasant bonus for men who drink in moderation. For women the choice is not so clear, except that safe levels of alcohol intake may be lower than they are for men.[23]

The medical research reviewed by Dr. Marton shows that women in particular have to think about more than one risk at a time. Dr. Marton gives the example of a hypothetical woman in her thirties who is looking only at the data about the effect of moderate wine consumption on breast cancer and cardiovascular mortality. She has to weigh an increase of from 6-8% to 9-12% in her lifetime risk of breast cancer against the fact that the same alcohol consumption will decrease her chances of having a heart attack from 35% to 25%.[24] Each woman has to decide such health matters by taking into account her own family medical history and her personal tolerance for risk and uncertainty.

Given the same information, we will all take risks into account in a different manner, using our own personal scale to weigh the risks of drinking as we understand them against the pleasure we derive from wine. Each of us will decide how important the health research data is in a different way. Some of us will design our decisions to minimize risk and possible later regret — "I can live without wine for nine months, just in case . . ." — while others will be comfortable with greater risks in the face of what they believe are greater present benefits — "I can drink moderately while pregnant. After all, only one heavy drinker in ten has an FAS child. Besides, I enjoy relaxing with a glass of wine with dinner, and medical research cannot measure the health benefits I derive from the feeling of well-being I enjoy from serving and drinking wine." In this chapter I have provided the latest data on the health effects of moderate drinking. Each reader must evaluate it and take his or her own course of action.

So, if you are a man who drinks moderately, you can enjoy a decreased risk of coronary heart disease along with your Cabernet Sauvignon. This may also be true for women, but there is much less data on women and heart disease and the information on breast cancer is not complete, so medical research is not as useful at this time in providing guidance about the potential benefits and risks of moderate drinking. As for me, I'll take a swim or bicycle each day to help raise my HDL level, get my mammograms, continue to spurn cigarettes, wear a seat belt, and raise my glass of Zinfandel with pasta and Chardonnay with salmon in the belief that moderation in all things is probably as good a rule now as it was when my grandfather practiced medicine in rural Ohio and lived by that belief — and prescribed wine for his patients.

Does Medical Research Tell Us What to Drink?

In addition to the paucity of data about women, there is very limited epidemiological data available that distinguishes between various kinds of alcoholic beverages in health studies. We do know that persons who prefer wine are more likely to be women, temperate drinkers, young or middle-aged, non-smokers, and better educated compared to persons who prefer liquor.[25] Because many of these factors associated with wine drinking also contribute to better overall health, it is hard to design an epidemiological study to examine only the influence of wine, beer, or liquor consumption on health. We'll have to look to the experimental scientists rather than the epidemiologists for answers to this question.

Stay Tuned for Future Developments — The French Paradox, Resveratrol, and Quercetin

The research plans of a Boston epidemiologist and two recent biochemical research findings make intriguing current reading and give us a tantalizing glimpse into the future of two areas of medical research involving grapes and wine.

Dr. Curtis Ellison, an epidemiologist in the department of medicine at Boston University, is intrigued by the apparent paradox of the French, who eat a diet high in fat and cholesterol and yet enjoy a rate of heart disease lower than that of the United States population. Ellison wonders if the amounts and patterns of French wine consumption play a role in creating this "paradox." He plans to study the long-term health consequences of introducing wine into the diet early in life by comparing the dietary intakes — including alcohol, fat, cholesterol, and other nutrients— of children and adults in the U.S. and France.[26] Moving from Ellison's proposed macro-scale study of wine and cardiovascular health (comparing populations of wine drinking adults in different cultures) to a sub-microscopic investigation of the same topic, Cornell Pomologist Leroy Creasy has suggested that a substance called resveratrol may be the compound that explains how red wine can increase the level of high-density lipoproteins in the bloodstream.[27] Resveratrol is the active ingredient in a traditional Japanese folk remedy for "cleansing the blood" using knotweed, and it is present in the skins of grapes — where it helps fight fungal disease — and in wines, especially lightly processed red wines. The stage appears to be set for future studies to investigate the possible medical benefits of resveratrol and to discover whether it is indeed the solution to the French paradox that intrigues Dr. Ellison.

Studies begun several years ago by Professor Terrance Leighton of the University of California, Berkeley, were designed to solve another riddle: why did red wine, unlike an equivalent dose of pure ethanol, not increase the incidence of mammary cancer in mice? Dr. Leighton's research led to the identification of quercetin, a cancer-preventative compound, in red wines. It was further shown that quercetin appears in wine after the alcoholic fermentation, apparently from the conversion of precursors in the grapes. Bacteria in our intestines can also perform this conversion, which explains how eating grapes or drinking wine — both of which, along with broccoli, garlic, onions, and squash, contain quercetin or its precursors — can benefit our health by providing us with this cancer-inhibiting compound. Further studies are under way to figure out just how quercetin is formed in winemaking, how viticultural practices can influence the amount of quercetin precursors in grapes, and whether quercetin plays a role in the relationship between dietary factors and colon cancer.[28]

It's a safe bet that future developments on the French Paradox, resveratrol, and quercetin will be heralded by our local newspapers and popular magazines. Often their reports on wine and health are short and designed more to catch our attention than to inform us, and yet we all want to know if we really do need to change our diets, drinking habits, or life-styles for better health. What is the health-conscious news reader to do? I recommend two sources of guidance: 1. to help you critique health news as it breaks, check into *In Health* magazine's recently published guidelines for evaluating news reports of health research,[29] and 2. to provide yourself with an unbiased scientifically sound assessment of contemporary health issues contact the American Council on Science and Health.[30]

REVIEW QUESTIONS

Instructions: You might want to use a separate sheet of paper to answer the following review questions. In that way you can use the questions to check your knowledge of this chapter more than once. You may, for example, want to re-test yourself on items that you have missed or use the "Review Questions" to test your knowledge before you read a chapter. For the True or False items, answer "True" if the statement is accurate or "False" if the statement is incorrect. If you determine that a statement is false make a note explaining why. For the multiple choice items pick the best alternative. Check your answers after you have completed all the questions.

1. True or false: In the earliest, ancient Mediterranean civilizations wine was the first drink of the common citizen. _____

2. True or false: Scholars who have studied the origins of alcohol abuse agree that the American pattern of prohibiting exposure to alcoholic beverages until age 21 is one of the most effective ways to prevent alcohol abuse. _____

3. True or false: Demographic studies have shown that wine drinkers are better educated and earn more than non-wine drinkers. _____

4. At what blood alcohol concentration do most people perceive the maximum relaxation?
   A. .001%   B. .01%   C. .05%   D. .10%   E. .15%

5. Wine provides about how many calories per four-ounce serving?
   A. 50   B. 100   C. 200   D. 500   E. 1000

6. True or false: Although wine has a 4000-year history of therapeutic use, it is not considered useful in today's hospital setting in the U.S. _____

7. True or false: The people who should be most concerned about sulfites in wines are sulfite-sensitive, steroid-dependent asthmatics. _____

8. Medical researchers define moderate alcohol consumption as about how many four-ounce glasses of wine daily?
   A. 0   B. 1-2   C. 3-4   D. 5-6   E. 7-8

9. True or false: The research reviewed by Dr. Keith Marton showed that cardiovascular mortality increased with heavy alcohol use and that moderate drinkers have a reduced risk of cardiovascular mortality compared to non-drinkers. _____

10. True or false: Boffetta's and Garfinkel's study showed that at three or more drinks per day there is an increased risk of death for drinkers compared to non-drinkers, particularly for liver cirrhosis. _____

11. True or false: Although Dr. Marton's review of the research literature showed a 50% increase in breast cancer for moderate drinkers compared to non-drinkers, there are a number of reasons why our understanding of the relationship between moderate drinking and breast cancer is less certain than it is for cardiovascular disease. _____

12. True or false: About 90% of women who are active alcoholics during pregnancy will deliver a child who clearly suffers from FAS. _____

13. Briefly explain why women must weigh more than one risk when considering whether or not to drink. _____

_____

_____

_____

ANSWERS TO REVIEW QUESTIONS

1. False. At that time, wine was the drink of the priesthood and of the wealthy.
2. False. These scholars believe that the Italian pattern of introducing children to diluted wine at an early age in a family setting coupled with an overall social disapproval of drunkenness is one of the most effective ways to prevent alcohol abuse.
3. True
4. C
5. B
6. False. A survey of U.S. urban hospitals found that wine was used as an appetite stimulant, for its general therapeutic value, and as an aid to sleep in place of tranquilizers.
7. True
8. B
9. True
10. True
11. True
12. False. About one in ten or 10% of women who are active alcoholics during pregnancy will deliver a child who clearly suffers from FAS.
13. Women have to weigh the increased risk of breast cancer against the cardioprotective effect of moderate drinking as well as possible effects on the fetus if they are pregnant.

ENDNOTES

[1] Quoted in Peynaud, Emile, THE TASTE OF WINE, The Wine Appreciation Guild, San Francisco, 1987, p. 4.

[2] Johnson, Hugh, VINTAGE: THE STORY OF WINE, Simon and Schuster, New York, 1989, p. 10.

[3] Vaillant, G., THE NATURAL HISTORY OF ALCOHOLISM, Harvard University Press, Cambridge, 1983, p. 105, and D. Agarwal, and W. Goedde, ALCOHOLISM: BIOMEDICAL AND GENETIC ASPECTS, Pergammon Press, New York, 1989, p. 323.

[4] Klein, Hugh, and David J. Pittman, "Social Occasions and the Perceived Appropriateness of Consuming Different Alcoholic Beverages," *Journal of Studies on Alcohol,* Vol. 51, No. 1, 1990, pp. 59-67, and Marvin R. Shanken, and Thomas Matthews, "What America Thinks about Wine," *The Wine Spectator,* February 28, 1991, p. 27.

[5] *Wine and Spirits Buying Guide,* July 1982, p. 9.

[6] Peynaud, Emile, THE TASTE OF WINE, The Wine Appreciation Guild, San Francisco, 1987, p. 231. Translated by Michael Schuster.

[7] Vogler, Roger E., and Wayne R. Bartz, THE BETTER WAY TO DRINK, Simon and Schuster, New York, 1982, p. 33. This book contains many useful ideas about successful drinking.

[8] Peynaud, Emile, THE TASTE OF WINE, p. 4.

[9] Darby, William, and Agnes Heinz, ALCOHOL: DEFINING THE PARAMETERS OF MODERATION, ACSH, New York, 1991, p. 9.

[10] McDonald, J., "Nutritional Aspects of Wine Consumption," *Urban Health,* March 1982, p. 23.

[11] Bezwoda, W. R., et. al., "Iron Absorption from Red and White Wines," *Scandinavian Journal of Hematology,* Vol. 34, 1985, p. 126.

[12] A SURVEY OF WINE SERVICE IN HOSPITALS IN THE TOP METROPOLITAN AREAS OF THE UNITED STATES, Matheson and Matheson, Inc., 1985, San Francisco, p. 1.

[13] Halpern, G. M., et al., "The Effect of White Wine upon the Pulmonary Function of Asthmatic Subjects," *Annals of Allergy,* Vol. 55, No. 5, 1985, pp. 686-690, and W. S. Tichenor, "Sulfite Sensitivity — Minor Problem Proves Major Hazard for Some," *Postgraduate Medicine,* Vol. 78, No. 5, October 1985, pp. 320-325 and "The Role of Sulfur Dioxide in Winemaking," *SIMI Newsletter,* No. 3, Fall 1986.

[14] Finkel, Harvey E., "Perspective on Lead and Wine," *Society of Wine Educators Alert,* Number 2, 1991, p. 1.

[15] Marton, Keith, "The Impact of Moderate Use," *Wines and Vines,* May 1990, pp. 29-30, and Keith Marton, "Alcohol, Longevity, and Lifestyles, A Summary of Scientific and Epidemiological Findings," *Report from the American Wine Alliance for Research and Education,* Vol. 1, No. 3, August 1, 1989, pp. 2-6. A bibliography of Marton's article is available from the American Wine Alliance for Research and Education, 244 California Street, Suite 300, San Francisco, CA 94111.

[16] Shaper, A. G., "Alcohol and Mortality: A Review of Prospective Studies," *British Journal of Addiction,* Vol. 85, 1990, pp. 837-847, "Commentaries on Shaper's Alcohol and Mortality: A Review of Prospective Studies," *British Journal of Addiction,* Vol. 85, 1990, pp. 849-857, and A. G. Shaper, "Commentary: A Response to Commentaries: the Effects of Self-selection," *British Journal of Addiction,* Vol. 85, 1990, pp. 859-861.

[17] Rimm, Eric B., Edward L. Giocannucci, Walter C. Willett, Graham A. Colditz, Alberto Ascherio, Bernard Rosner, and Meir J. Stampfer, "Prospective Study of Alcohol Consumption and Risk of Coronary Disease in Men," *The Lancet,* Vol. 338, August 24, 1991, pp. 464-468, Arthur L. Klatsky, Mary Anne Armstrong, and Gary D. Friedman, "Risk of Cardiovascular Mortality in Alcohol Drinkers, Ex-Drinkers, and Nondrinkers," *The American Journal of Cardiology,* Vol. 66, November, 1990, pp. 1237-1242, and Paolo Bottetta and Lawrence Garfinkel, "Alcohol Drinking and Mortality among Men Enrolled in an American Cancer Society Prospective Study," *Epidemiology,* Vol. 1, No. 5, 1990, pp. 342-348.

[18] American Wine Alliance for Research and Education, published in AWARE Bulletin, July/August 1991, p. 2; a similar but less complete graph appeared in Curtis R. Ellison, Editorial, "Cheers!" *Epidemiology,* Vol .1, No. 5, September, 1990, pp. 337-339.

[19] Marton, Keith, "The Impact of Moderate Use," *Wines and Vines,* May 1990, p. 31.

[20] Marton, Keith, personal communication, November 12, 1991.

[21] AWARE Bulletin, Vol. 1, No. 1, Fall 1990, p. 9.

[22] Marton, Keith, "How Doctors Could Deal with the Drys," *Wines and Vines,* June 1990, p. 66.

[23] Frezza, M., C. DiPadova, G. Pozzato, M. Terpin, E. Baraona, and C. Lieber, "High Blood Alcohol Levels in Women: The Role of Decreased Gastric Alcohol Dehydrogenase Activity and First-pass Metabolism," *New England Journal of Medicine,* Vol. 2, 1990, pp. 95-99.

[24] Marton, Keith, "How Doctors Could Deal with the Drys," *Wines and Vines,* June 1990, pp. 64-67, and "Wine and Health: A Doctor Speaks Out, An Interview with Dr. Keith Marton," *Grand Cru Vineyards Newsletter,* Spring 1989, pp. 1-2.

[25] Klatsky, Arthur L., Mary Anne Armstrong, and Harald Kapp, "Correlates of Alcoholic Beverage Preference: Traits of Persons Who Choose Wine, Liquor, or Beer," *British Journal of Addiction,* Vol. 85, 1990, pp. 1279-1289.

[26] Wagner, David C., "The French Paradox," *The Wine Spectator,* June 30, 1990, p. 8.

[27] Siemann, E. H., and L. L. Creasy, "Concentration of the Phytoalexin Resveratrol in Wine," *American Journal of Enology and Viticulture,* Vol. 43, No. 1, 1992, pp. 49-52, and M. Seigneur, et al., "Effect of the Consumption of Alcohol, White Wine, and Red Wine on Platelet Function and Serum Lipids," *Journal of Applied Cardiology,* Vol. 5, No. 4, 1990, pp. 215-222.

[28] Leighton, Terrance, C. Ginther, L. Fluss, W. K. Harter, J. Cansado, and V. Notario, "Molecular Characterization of Quercetin and Quercetin Glycosides in *Allium* Vegetables, and their Effects in Malignant Cell Transformation," in PHENOLIC COMPOUNDS AND HUMAN HEALTH, American Chemical Society Symposium Series, (In Press 1992), and Terrance Leighton, "Quercetin as a Cancer Preventative," *Bulletin of the Society of Medical Friends of Wine,* Vol. 32, No. 1, June 1990, pp. 5-6.

[29] Schmitz, Anthony, "How to Spot Front Page Fallacies" in "Food News Blues," *In Health,* November, 1991, pp. 41-47.

[30] American Council on Science and Health, 1995 Broadway, 16th Floor, New York, NY 10023-5860, Telephone (212) 362-7044, Fax (212) 362-4919.

THE THEORY AND PRACTICE OF SENSORY EVALUATION
An Owner's Manual for Winetasters

As a first step toward enabling you to become proficient in the analytical approach to sensory evaluation, this chapter will serve as a kind of owner's manual for your sensory evaluation tools: the senses of sight, smell, taste, and touch. It will then explain how to systematically examine wines and the terms to use to describe them. Just about any of us can become expert winetasters if we increase our understanding of how to use our senses and then gain experience with that heightened awareness. Acquiring attentive experience with wines of different qualities — which will begin with this book's tasting exercises — and reflecting on the attributes of great wines (discussed below) will help you develop your skills in the hedonic aspect of sensory evaluation as well.

OUR SENSES ARE REMARKABLE ANALYTICAL TOOLS
There Is a Common Working Model for All Our Senses

Sensation refers to an organism's immediate neurological response to a stimulus in the environment, while perception involves the brain's interpretation of the information gathered by the senses. A sensory stimulus in wine is any chemical, physical, or thermal activator that can produce a response in a sense receptor. There is a common mechanism of sensory perception and evaluation that mediates between stimuli such as those found in wine and receptors for all our senses. As shown in Figure 2.1, an effective stimulus (one strong enough to be perceived) in the wine excites a sense receptor to create an impulse that is transmitted to the brain via nerve cells. The brain evaluates the information it receives, measuring the intensity of each sensation, weighing it against others, and comparing it to previous experiences. It then searches for the appropriate word(s) to describe the sensations experienced so that we can note and/or discuss them. As you will see in the discussion of the individual senses below, we are just beginning to understand how some of these steps work, especially for the winetaster's critical senses of smell and taste.

Figure 2.1
Sensation and Perception in Wine Evaluation

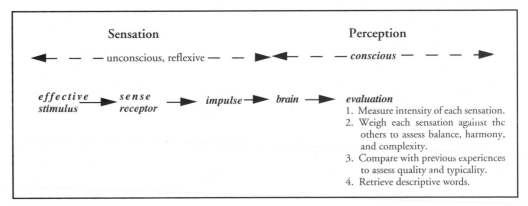

When our brains recognize and interpret a sensation, we perceive or become consciously aware of that sensation. Unknown (new or unnamed) sensations cannot be interpreted and may be missed or confused with known sensations. Stimuli that are not strong enough to be perceived are not noticed consciously, even though one or more of our sensory organs may respond to them reflexively (perhaps at low levels of stimulant not enough receptor sites or cells are excited or are excited enough to trigger the entire chain of events that carries nerve impulses all the way to the brain). Two threshold concentrations can be identified for sensory stimuli: a threshold of sensation — also called the absolute threshold or detection threshold — which is the smallest amount of the stimulus that can produce a general but unidentifiable sensation, and, at a higher concentration, a threshold of perception — also called the recognition threshold — which is the smallest amount that can be accurately described or named.[1] For example, the average threshold for people to perceive — or recognize or correctly name — sweetness from sugars is 1 gram per 100 ml. When a threshold of perception is defined quantitatively — that is, as a certain number of grams per liter or parts per million — that means that at that concentration 50% of the people who were tested were able to identify the sensation correctly as sweet. People with higher and lower thresholds of perception make up the other 50% of the population, and for sweetness from sugar these individuals' thresholds of perception can vary from about 0.5 to 2.5 grams per 100 ml.[2] A third threshold phenomenon is the differential or difference threshold, defined as the quantity of stimulus that needs to be added to an existing and perceptible amount for the change to be recognizable. All three kinds of thresholds also exist for odor stimuli. You might not think that subthreshold amounts of sensory stimuli would matter, but in winemaking sugar concentrations below the threshold of perception are often used to make wines seem "smoother" and more full-bodied.

Becoming a skillful winetaster requires practice in identifying the sensations that visual, chemical, and physical stimuli produce. The tasting exercises in this book will introduce you to the most essential odor, taste, and tactile stimuli in wines so that you can begin to match them with the correct words to describe the sensations they produce.

Sight, the First Sense

The first sense we use to examine a wine is sight. Our sight receptors are located in the retina which lines the eye and where millions of receptor cells respond to the stimuli of light waves — which enter through the cornea and are focused by the lens — and transform them into nerve impulses which go to the brain for interpretation. Figure 2.2 shows the location of the cornea, lens, and retina.

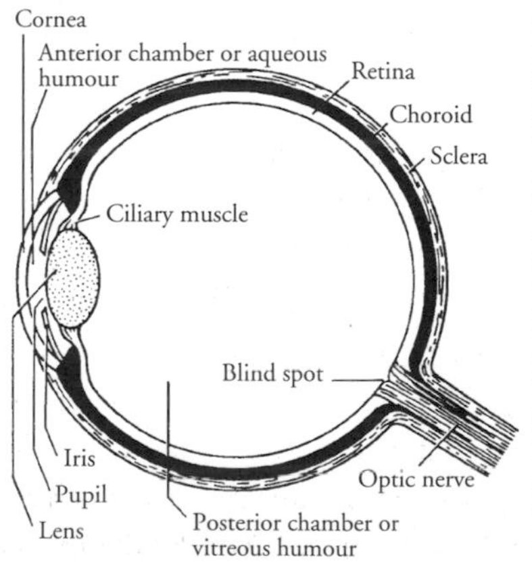

There are three kinds of color receptor cells, and each specializes in receiving stimuli from a different part of the color spectrum. By integrating the information received from these specialist cells, the brain makes it possible to discriminate several hundred different hues.[3] In winetasting we take advantage of a large part

Cross-section of the eye.

*Figure 2.2
Cross-Section
of the Eye*
THE TASTE OF WINE
Emile Peynaud

of this capacity to distinguish a wide range of colors from yellow-greens to brick reds and purples. In addition to evaluating hue, the winetaster is also interested in the intensity of color, which ranges from the low intensities of the very pale yellow-greens in young white table wines from cool growing regions to the medium intensities of the brick reds of maturing Bordeaux to the intense, deep purples of freshly fermented Port.

Apart from these two aspects of color, clarity is the other principal visual sensation that is evaluated in wine. Other visual features include the bubble display of sparkling wines; wine tears or legs; and, occasionally, surface films.

The visual stimuli in wine have a hedonic quality; that is, they are able to evoke pleasure in and of themselves. For me, this is especially true for the golden colors of late-harvest, *Botrytis-*affected White Rieslings and Sauvignon Blancs — rich, complex, sweet wines made from grapes infected with the "noble rot," *Botrytis cinerea.*

An experienced taster can derive valuable clues from the visual aspects of a wine alone that will alert him or her to what smells and tastes will follow. Visual clues allow us to anticipate both good and bad odors and tastes, much as the color of an apple or pear may suggest its level of ripeness and the smell, taste, and texture we will experience when we bite into it. A very pale, nearly colorless white wine suggests that the grapes were picked very early and perhaps were unripe. If the clue is correct, the wine will be low in alcohol, light- or thin-bodied, and high in acid, giving it a "green" taste. Dark colors in red wines are clues to intense fruit aromas and high tannin levels.[4]

Overall quality in red wines is correlated with total color and pigment content.[5] This correlation has been put to practical use by a wine merchant in northern Italy whom I heard about from Paolo DeMarchi, a fine Chianti vintner and a beguiling storyteller. Paolo explained that this négociant selected wines to buy, bottle, and sell by tossing glassfuls against a whitewashed wall behind his desk. Using this straightforward method to evaluate color intensity and, of course, predict wine quality, the merchant bought the wines that left the darkest stains- and, we presume, from time to time repainted his wall.

Our sense of sight is our most familiar and often used sense. Because they are comfortable with their sense of sight, beginning winetasters often spend a lot of time contemplating the color and appearance of a wine, trying to get more information from its visual aspects than they can, in fact, yield. Although we know how to use it well, our sense of sight gives us the least accurate information about wines.

Smell, the Most Important Sense

Our appreciation of wines is mainly due to their odors, and our sense of smell is our most important, sensitive, and versatile sensory evaluation tool. If sensory evaluation were given a common name that reflected its most important aspect, my students would refer to their class as "The Winesmelling Course" and you might get an engraved invitation to a benefit wine-smelling to raise funds for your favorite charity. Because the sense of smell is so important, a large part of this owner's manual will be devoted to it.

The sense of smell is our key sensory tool for winetasting because the rich, complex odors and flavors of wines cannot be experienced in any other way. As this suggests, we are using our sense of smell both when we actively inhale the odors of a wine and when we hold wine in our mouths to "taste" it. This is because the flavors that are experienced in our mouths are actually odors that reach our noses when we hold the wine in our mouths.

The sensitivity of our sense of smell for some molecules is astonishing. We can recognize the off odor of hydrogen sulfide (which is responsible for the characteristic smell of hard-boiled egg yolks) in concentrations of three parts per billion — the equivalent of locating a particular family of three in China.[6] We can perceive even smaller amounts of the compound that ac-counts for the bell pepper aroma in Cabernet Sauvignon: one to five parts per trillion.[7] That can be compared to sniffing out a one-cent error in your ten-billion-dollar checking account.

Our versatile sense of smell can detect an enormous range of scents — an estimated 10,000 different odors. A normal person can be trained to identify about 1000 odors, and for some of these odors several different intensities or concentrations can be discriminated. Wines are estimated to contain around 200 odorous compounds. The specificity of our sense of smell is such that it can respond to the most subtle variations in the structure of odorous molecules. Sometimes the tiniest alteration of molecular structure can create a dramatic change in the perceived odor, making it difficult to classify odor stimuli by their chemical configurations.

The sensory organ for the sense of smell is a small patch of special tissue called the olfactory epithelium. It is located at the top and rear of the nasal cavity, above and behind the nose. The olfactory epithelium is about the size of a dime and contains millions of nerve cells, each of which has one end that protrudes into the nasal cavity and reacts with odorous molecules and another end that is in the olfactory bulb of the brain. Airborne odorous molecules land on the moist surface of the olfactory epithelium and are dissolved in its mucous coating, where they make contact with the hair-like cilia that protrude from the nerve cells. (These cilia enormously enlarge the receptive surface area and ability of these critical cells to contact odor molecules.) The connection of molecule and cell surface sets off the swift transmission of a nerve impulse through the cell to the nearby olfactory area of the brain, where this and other impulses are then relayed to high-level processing regions of the brain for evaluation.[8]

The brain responds so quickly and strongly to odor sensations that biologists have speculated that the powerful hedonic and aversive qualities of odor stimuli reflect the importance of odor information in the early survival of our species. Our olfactory nerve cells are regenerated about every 30 days and it is not yet clear exactly how odor-sensing capabilities — which seem to be capable of modification by our odor experiences — are passed on to the new cells.[9] Another focus of current research in odor recognition is to determine if there is a specific receptor cell or molecule for each one of the 1,000 or so odors we can learn to recognize or whether there are fewer receptors in some sort of pattern that allows information to be combined in the brain (as with color vision) so that we can distinguish 1,000 odors with a smaller number of receptors. Recent evidence suggests that lower mammals have enough hereditary material for from 100 to several hundred different odor receptor molecules, so at this moment we do not know if the olfactory system groups odors or their reception in some manner or not. [10]

Figure 2.3 shows the location of the olfactory epithelium and its relationship to the nose, nasal and oral cavities, and the olfactory center of the brain. Knowing the location of the olfactory sense organ and its surrounding anatomy will help us better use our most important organ for sensory evaluation of wine.

In normal breathing, not very much air reaches the olfactory epithelium — an estimated 5-10%. Therefore, when tasting wines we must sniff deeply to direct more air with its dissolved odor molecules up onto the olfactory epithelium. About a tenfold amplification of stimulant at the receptor site is possible with sniffing.[11]

Air gets to the olfactory epithelium via two routes: directly though the nostrils — route 1, shown in Figure 2.3 — and indirectly through the mouth and rear nasal passages (the retro-nasal route) as we hold the wine in our mouths to savor its flavor or as we exhale after swallowing — route 2 in Figure 2.3. When we eat and drink, most of us think of the odors that we experience when we sniff through our noses as "smells"

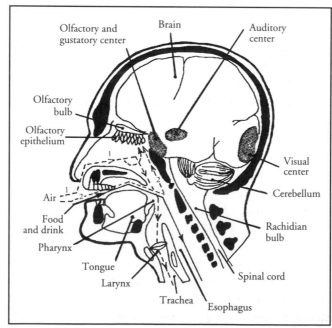

Figure 2.3
A Cross-Section of the Human Head
MAKING SENSE OF WINE,
Alan Young © 1986

and the odors we experience indirectly through the retro-nasal route as tastes, even though they are really smells. We may differentiate these "in-mouth smells" by calling them "flavors," according to one definition in the complete OXFORD ENGLISH DICTIONARY. Flavor is "the element in the taste of a substance which depends on the cooperation of the sense of smell." For two stunning demonstrations of this see the sensory homework for Exercise 4.1.

Odorous molecules can only be delivered to the olfactory epithelium in air, and thus we can only smell the ones that can evaporate from the surface of a wine at the temperature at which it is served. The molecules that are able to become airborne are called the volatile components of wine or "odorants" in some of the literature. The greater the surface area or the higher the temperature of a wine sample, the more volatile molecules will evaporate. Winetasting techniques take advantage of these facts in the following ways:

1. Because fewer components will be volatile when wines are excessively chilled, winetasters may hold the bowl of a glass of cold wine in their hand (rather than holding it by the stem) to warm the wine and release more odorous molecules.

2. Winetasters swirl wine in the glass to increase its surface area so that the concentration of volatile molecules in the air above the wine will be higher when they put their noses into the glass to sniff.

3. Wine aromas often seem more intense when the wines are in our mouths than when we sniff them. This is because wines that have been warmed up in our mouths (and held at 98°F, compared to serving temperatures from 40° to 68°F, or even as low as 32°F straight out of an ice bucket!) release more volatile components.

4. When winetasters draw air through the wine as they hold it in their mouths, they are increasing the surface area of the warmed wine and enabling more odor-saturated air to reach the olfactory epithelium through the back of the mouth and the nasal cavities.

The techniques that we use to increase the concentrations of volatile wine components can actually give us different odor sensations. The same odor stimulus can smell different at lower and higher concentrations, so that when we first smell a glass of wine without swirling it, then swirl the glass and later warm the wine in our mouths, we may have the impression of smelling different odors during each step of this process. I recently had an experience that reminded me of this phenomenon. My husband and I had rented a cabin in the woods, and while taking a post-hike shower, I noticed the unmistakable odor of skunk wafting down the hallway into the bathroom. I immediately wondered if my unfortunate spouse had met one of those cute little black and white fellows on a trip to the woodpile. Certain that he needed at least my sympathy if not immediate first aid, I quickly dried off and went out to investigate. I found Dick sitting contentedly in front of the fire sipping a cup of coffee. The "skunk" I had smelled was the faint aroma of freshly-ground Sumatran coffee beans — a vastly better companion for an afternoon by the fireside than a real skunk!

Simply putting some wine in our mouths alters our perception of its odors. It's not an uncommon experience for winetasters to find that a wine's odors are stronger and more pleasant when they are experienced in the mouth as flavors rather than as odors in inhaled air. A more extreme — and opposite — example of how perception is altered in the mouth is the case of Limburger and other strong cheeses: many people who enjoy their taste find their odors repulsive. With the volatile components of wine, one might think simply that the warmer temperatures of the mouth could cause more and different volatile molecules to reach the olfactory epithelium via the retro-nasal route, thus creating an odor sensation that is different in both intensity and quality. Psychologist Paul Rozin has suggested some additional explanations. The odors of wine or food might be modified in the mouth: perhaps some molecules selectively adhere to or become absorbed by parts of our mouths when we chew. (Maybe the stinky Limburger molecules are trapped in our oral cavities so we can't smell them while chewing a bite of cheese.) Of more interest to Rozin is the possibility that our brains process olfactory information from the same object differently when the object is in the outside world than when it is held in our mouths. As a first step in investigating this hypothesis, Rozin is attempting to determine how we figure out where an odor is coming from. He will soon report the results of investigations designed to answer two questions: Does the direction of airflow through the nose tell the brain where an odor originates? and does the tactile sensation of food in the mouth influence the perception of the source of odor stimuli?[12]   Rozin's work may, in time, tell us why we experience different odors when we sniff and when we hold wine in our mouths.

Taste, the Limited Sense

Our sense of taste can give us information about only four sensory properties of wines: sweet, sour, bitter, and salty. Saltiness is very rare in wines, so tasting a wine primarily tells us about its concentrations of sweet, sour, and bitter substances. Our brains then interpret that information and tell us how well-balanced a wine is for these tastes. As noted above, most of what we commonly call the taste of a wine is, strictly speaking, due to the complex flavors that we actually perceive with our sense of smell. If this seems like a technical use of the idea of taste, you're right. In everyday life we commonly confuse smell and taste, even though almost everyone has had the experience of losing the ability to "taste" foods when they have a head cold or allergies that block their nasal passages and prevent the delivery of odor stimuli to their olfactory receptors. Most people, nonetheless, use taste to describe all the sensations — taste, odor, thermal, and tactile — that come from an object in the mouth. Winetasters must distinguish between all these sensations. In this regard, it's fortunate that we speak English because our language gives us the ability to mirror our sensory experiences: it has words to distinguish between flavor and taste. Interestingly, not all languages make this distinction, and that makes it harder for winetasters to describe their sensory experiences.[13]

The mechanism of taste starts with our humble spit: for solids to be tasted they must dissolve. Without saliva — or another fluid such as wine — to dissolve the substances that produce taste stimuli, we could only experience touch sensations with our mouths. Because saliva coats our entire oral cavity it efficiently delivers taste stimuli to the 10,000 or so taste buds located on the tongue, the roof of the mouth, the back of the epiglottis, and even on the tonsils. On the tongue the taste buds are in papillae found on the tip, along the side edges, and on the back. Very few taste buds are in the numerous papillae that are on the tongue's top surface. (You can see the papillae when you stick out your tongue and look at it in a mirror. On the tip and in the back they look like bigger-than-average bumps, and on the sides they are gill-like vertical slits. The vast majority of the little bumps you see all over the top of your tongue are the kind of papillae with few taste buds.) There are several taste buds in each of the large papillae. Taste-receptor cells in the taste buds can respond to all four basic tastes, and each taste is recognized through a separate biochemical mechanism.[14]

If taste buds on the tips, sides, and backs of our tongues can respond to all four taste stimuli, what does that mean for the "taste bud map" that tells us that certain areas of our tongues specialize in tasting sweet or sour or bitter or salty? In fact, that map seems to correspond pretty well with our everyday taste experiences when we are eating: the bitterness of a not-quite-ripe persimmon or very strong coffee does hit us at the backs of our tongues. However, when carefully tasting something less bitter — perhaps while savoring a mouthful of tonic water on a hot summer day — you may have noticed that you can experience taste sensations "where they aren't supposed to be" according to the map. You were probably aware, for example, that you were tasting the bitterness of that refreshing tonic water on the tip of your tongue, even though the bitter taste was stronger at the back. What was happening?

Although taste receptor cells may not strictly specialize in receiving just one stimulus, the neural processing of taste stimuli from different parts of the tongue can be quite different, so our brains receive stronger information about specific tastes from different parts of the tongue. We know the most about the bitter taste mechanism in this regard: although the perception threshold for bitterness is actually lower in receptor cells on the tip of the tongue — making those cells sensitive to bitterness at lower concentrations — other receptor cells at the back of the tongue get more excited than tip-of-the-tongue receptors do by high levels of bitter stimuli and send more nerve impulses about that bitterness to the brain. This difference between the information that the tip-of-the-tongue receptors and the back-of-the-tongue receptors send to the brain about bitterness is triggered at bitter concentrations that are well above the threshold of perception — more like the amounts of bitter stimuli we encounter in foods and upon which we base our everyday experiences.

So what about the taste bud map? It is wrong on two counts: 1. we don't taste sweet or sour or bitter or salty in just one place; and 2. we don't taste much of anything on the top surface of the tongue because there are hardly any taste buds there. Many, though not all, tongue maps indicate that tartness can be tasted there. When we experience a strong localized taste sensation — which often happens with strong bitterness — it is because the signals from those taste-receptor cells are processed differently en route to our brains. One excellent reason to throw out the incorrect map of the tongue — or at least take it with a grain of salt (sorry, I couldn't resist) — is that it can lead us to question the accuracy of our own perceptions if they do not occur where the map says they should be.[15]

You probably won't be surprised to learn that at a gross level we are most sensitive to bitterness and least sensitive to sweetness: our threshold for the bitterness of quinine sulfate is an estimated 1,000-10,000 times lower than our threshold for the sweetness of table sugar.[16] Our sensitivities to sourness and saltiness are intermediate.

Touch

There are sensors in the mouth and nose which allow us to respond to the tactile stimuli in wines. These include viscosity, dissolved gas, serving temperature, astringency, heat from alcohol, and sulfur dioxide content.

Winetasters refer to the thickness or viscosity of wine as "body." For example, wines with relatively high sugar concentrations have more body and seem more mouth-filling. The bubbles of carbon dioxide in a sparkling wine bounce around in our mouths and tickle our touch receptors there and in our noses. We can even detect a "prickly" sensation in wines that have just a little dissolved carbon dioxide from being bottled shortly after a cold fermentation. Wines with intermediate levels of CO_2 can be called frizzante, pétillant, or spritzy, depending on your preference for adopting an Italian, French, or "German" word. Young red wines with high tannin levels are astringent and create a rough sensation: their tannins react with proteins in our saliva and on the surfaces of the cells lining our mouths and on the surfaces of our tongues to dry them out and create a puckery, rough sensation as our now-unlubricated mouth parts chafe against each other. Moderate astringency can nicely offset the richness of a fatty meal, but higher levels make wines unpalatable and call for patience: during bottle aging the astringency will diminish. White wines that are aged in oak barrels pick up small amounts of tannin, but they will seem smooth because the tannin levels are low. A wine with high alcohol content will produce a hot tactile sensation as well as a sweet taste. In fact, alcohol is unique among sensory stimulants: it is a pure substance that can stimulate three sensory systems — the tactile (a hot sensation), gustatory (a sweet taste), and olfactory (a penetrating, pungent odor).

Touch sensors in our noses make our noses wrinkle or may even make us sneeze in response to a wine that has too much sulfur dioxide. This compound is a commonly used aroma and color preservative which smells like the heads of matches and is normally used in amounts very much below our perception thresholds. If the smell of sulfur dioxide can be perceived in wine it is considered an off odor. Somewhat higher concentrations are required to evoke the touch sensation.

Hearing

Our sense of hearing would be more important if this were a book on the sensory evaluation of celery or potato chips. Although hearing is important for the discussion of wines, which in turn is essential for learning, it more often interferes with sensory evaluation: tasters commenting on wines as they evaluate diminishes the ability of other people in the group to concentrate on the wines and form their own impressions. Figure 2.4 suggests another role of hearing in learning about winetasting.

Figure 2.4
One Possible Role of
Hearing in Winetasting

PITFALLS IN WINETASTING—An Owner's Guide to Troubleshooting the Senses

It may seem from the discussion so far that winetasting theory assumes that we all perceive things in the same way. However, we know that winetasters differ from one another in their sensory responses due to differences in genetic and biological traits, such as in thresholds or anosmias for specific chemicals; personality and intelligence factors, which influence their interest, motivation, and understanding; differences in experience or language usage, such as the beginning taster's confusion between sour and bitter; and personal and cultural factors that influence the taster's hedonic response to a wine.[17] Training in the association of tastes and odors with appropriate descriptive words, setting up tastings to favor concentration, and the fact that professional winetasters learn to set their personal tastes aside when they taste wines can minimize some of this variability. However, we need to know about some fixed biological differences because we need to accommodate them in our tasting techniques. This section describes those differences as well as some other interesting physiological and psychological factors that can affect winetasting.

Physiological Factors
Adaptation

Adaptation is a change in sensitivity that occurs in response to different levels of stimulation. We experience adaptation countless times each day as we move from room to room, indoors and out, and our sense of smell adjusts to the background odors in each new location. Adaptation occurs in all sensory areas, but for winetasting it is most important for smell and taste, where winetasters experience it as a temporary loss of the ability to recognize an odor or taste.

Adaptation of the sense of smell can be frustrating especially for beginning winetasters who are, for example, intently searching for the fresh-ground pepper odor their teacher has just announced is to be found in the higher-alcohol Cabernet Sauvignon they are investigating. Winetasters learn to work with olfactory adaptation by resting 15-45 seconds between sniffs when evaluating wines. During these breaks they concentrate on the impressions they received in the last sniff and may associate words or pictures with the odors to help remember them.

Adaptation of the taste buds occurs in about 40 seconds if we hold our tongues still. Winetasters move wines around in their mouths with a sort of chewing motion that avoids taste adaptation. A ubiquitous example of taste adaptation is the fact that we are unaware of the taste of our own saliva. Because we are adapted to it, it has no taste, to us, yet when we kiss someone we will notice that their saliva has a taste because its composition is different.[18] In fact, it has been suggested that kissing is our civilized way of selecting a mate by taste![19]

Adaptation of the senses of smell and taste is sometimes also called palate fatigue, but the latter is actually a somewhat different phenomenon. If during a tasting you find that all the wines seem alike, take a break and let your mind become refreshed. Current research indicates that you've probably lost your ability to concentrate. It's your brain that's tired, not your nose and taste buds.[20]

Thresholds

One source of differences between individual tasters is in their thresholds for the various stimuli in wine. Let's take the sugar threshold as an example. If two people with very different perception thresholds are tasting and discussing a wine, one person could be convinced that the wine was sweet and the other could be equally sure it was dry (without perceptible sweetness) — and they both could be right. If the wine has a sugar concentration of 0.8 grams/100 ml, the taster who perceives the wine as sweet is more sensitive to sugar and has a perception threshold that is less than 0.8 grams/100 ml. The taster who is sure that the wine is not sweet is less sensitive to sugar and has a perception threshold that requires concentrations greater than 0.8 grams/100 ml for a wine to seem sweet. Both tasters' perceptions are correct. Their thresholds are different.

We also differ in our thresholds for odorous compounds. A discussion similar to the imaginary debate about sweetness in the last paragraph could result if a group of eight to ten people were asked to smell a weak sample of phenethanol — a chemical present in all beverages fermented by yeast from sugar and which plays a minor role in the rose odor of Gewürztraminer, Muscats, and White Riesling. Sensory scientists would predict that in a group of that size there would be a greater than 100,000-fold difference in sensitivity to phenethanol between the most and least sensitive sniffers.[21] That means that there would have to be 100,000 times more phenethanol in a sample of Gewürztraminer wine for the least sensitive member of the group to "smell the roses" compared to the most sensitive member. Variations of this magnitude probably exist for many of the estimated 200 odorous compounds in wine.

Given that our thresholds can differ dramatically and that we have thresholds for at least the sweet and bitter tastes and for many wine odors, it is amazing that winetasters can agree on wine descriptions at all, or that you and your date can agree on one wine to order with dinner! One of the goals of the sensory evaluation exercises in this book is to give you a better understanding of your senses so that you will become a better winetaster. In the exercise "Focus on Taste and Touch: Structural Components of White Table Wines" you will be able to estimate your perception threshold for sweetness from sugar in wine and your differential threshold for total acidity. After doing this exercise, some of my students are always a little disappointed if they discover they have relatively high sugar thresholds, but I reassure them that being less sensitive to sugar is actually an economic asset. Because many inexpensive table wines are slightly sweet, those of us with higher sugar thresholds can drink them, perceive them as dry and therefore find them compatible with a wider range of foods, and be blissfully unaware that they are sweet to more sensitive palates. Unfortunately for their pocketbooks, this state of relative insensitivity to sugar in cheaper wines seems to diminish as my students' interest in the more flavorful dry varietal wines grows. Their thresholds also appear to decrease as they begin to attend more carefully to their sensory impressions.

Many threshold differences are probably inherited, although the exact mechanisms are not known. Sensory and genetic research has shown that the ability to taste one bitter substance called PTC (phenylthiocarbamide) is inherited. Many of us have experienced the "PTC taste test" in high school science classes. Our teachers distributed innocent looking pieces of a sort of blue tissue paper and we tasted it. Those of us who could not taste the bitter PTC were amazed at the grimaces that appeared on the faces of our classmates who could taste it. People who can taste PTC have a gene that enables their taste receptor cells to respond to this bitter substance. About two-thirds of Americans are tasters. PTC tasting is a well-documented example of how dramatically people can vary in their ability to taste something bitter; but PTC tasting ability may or may not predict our sensitivity to other bitter compounds. There are weak correlations that show that PTC tasters experience coffee, saccharin, and potassium chloride, a salt substitute, as more bitter than do non-tasters.[22] This means that non-tasters perceive less bitterness in coffee and may like it better for that reason. The connection between PTC tasting and perception of bitterness in red wines has not been examined. Since there are PTC-related compounds in wine, it was thought that tasters might experience some red wines as more bitter than would non-tasters, but it now appears that we sense the bitterness in wine and the bitterness of PTC through separate systems.

Odor Blindness

Odor blindness (anosmia) can refer to the loss of a person's ability to smell all odors or just the ability to smell a certain odor. The term "specific anosmia" is used when someone cannot detect a particular scent but otherwise has a normal sense of smell. There are over 30 specific anosmias known in humans, and some are relatively common.

When data from the more than one million responses to the National Geographic Smell Survey were analyzed, it was discovered that there was a much higher incidence of inability to detect two of the smell samples than was expected: for U.S. respondents, 35% could not smell androstenone (a component of human sweat) and 29% were insensitive to galaxolide (musk).[23] Furthermore, the inability to smell these two odors appears to be linked. Given the high frequency of these two specific anosmias, it may be that odor blindness plays a more important role in winetasting than we have imagined.

The specific anosmias may give us some clues as to how our sense of smell works. First, some sensory researchers have speculated that there may be parallels between the immune and olfactory systems and that the ability to recognize an odor may be induced in a manner analogous to the way our immune systems are induced to make antibodies in response to an invasion by foreign molecules. One piece of evidence on which this exciting idea is based — in addition to the facts that both systems recognize molecules with extraordinary precision and that their cells are replaced regularly — is the result of an investigation performed at the Monell Chemical Senses Center — a facility for scientific research on taste and smell. This study showed that individuals with specific anosmia to androstenone can develop a modest degree of sensitivity to it if they are exposed to it repeatedly and frequently over several months (they carry around a little squeeze bottle with androstenone in it and smell it often).[24] Second, because there are around thirty specific anosmias, some odor researchers think that this may be the approximate number of human odor receptor systems and that there is not a separate receptor system for each of the 1,000 odors we can learn to recognize.[25]

Taste Modifiers

Taste modifiers are substances that alter our ability to respond to specific taste stimuli. The leaves of the African plant *Gymnema sylvestre*, for example, contain a taste modifier that blocks the mechanism that allows us to perceive sweetness. After chewing the leaves of this plant or drinking a tea made from them, one can no longer taste sugar and saccharin; their crystals can only be perceived by touch and feel like tasteless grains of sand in the mouth.[26] I witnessed a dramatic demonstration of this effect when a sommelier from a prestigious Boston hotel volunteered at a tasting seminar to sample a tea made from *G. sylvestre* leaves. I can still see his horrified expression when he realized that he could not taste sweetness after holding the tea in his mouth. The reaction of this man whose highly trained palate had just been rendered insensitive to sugars was very convincing evidence that taste modifiers exist. The fact that his tasting abilities did return — although I'm sure the recovery was not fast enough for him — illustrates that the effects of taste modifiers are reversible.

Winetasters, or anyone else for that matter, don't often sip *G. sylvestre* teas. However, they are likely to encounter the "orange juice effect" — the result of common taste modifiers we use at about the same time of day as we customarily drink orange juice. Mouthwash and toothpaste contain detergents that modify the lipid-containing membranes of the receptor cells in the taste buds so that incorrect messages about taste are sent to the brain. Wines — or orange juice — tasted when residues of oral-hygiene detergents are present in your mouth will taste more sour and bitter and less sweet than they would if you had rinsed your mouth thoroughly to remove any detergents before tasting.[27]

The sequence in which we taste samples also modifies our perceptions, perhaps partly because of adaptation to the earlier tastes, and the rules for the order of tasting wines described later in this chapter are designed to compensate for this effect. When, for example, a sweet wine is tasted before a dry wine, the tartness of the dry wine will be exaggerated by contrast with the sweetness of the wine tasted first. Dry wines are always tasted before sweet wines for that reason. Probably the most dramatic demonstration of the influence of tasting solutions in sequence may be performed with pure water: it can take on any of the four taste qualities depending on which taste the tongue has been adapted to before the water is tasted.[28] A sort of taste modification is also what we are after when we combine wines and foods according to the principles explained in Appendix C and choose a spaghetti sauce with a little sweetness and richness from tomatoes and meat to go with a tannic red wine. In this example the taste modification goes both ways: the slight sweetness in the sauce decreases our perception of the astringency of the tannins in the wine, and those tannins in turn diminish our perception of the fat in the sauce.

Serving Temperature and The Perception of Wine Components

The main effect of temperature is on the sweet taste of sugar: we are more sensitive to sweetness from sucrose (but not from saccharin) in wines served at higher temperatures. The other tastes are not affected as much. However, colder serving temperatures do decrease our perceptions of body — as well as sweetness — and increase our perception of acidity. The volatile, odorous components of wines are more noticeable at higher temperatures, so colder serving temperatures mask wine odors, both good and bad. (So please don't serve that $80.00 bottle of Montrachet right out of the refrigerator![29])

Pregnancy, Allergies, Smoking, and Smelling

Another interesting result of the National Geographic Smell Survey is that there were substantial discrepancies in the ways some people rated themselves on smell performance and how they actually performed on the survey's test. Pregnant women felt that they were more sensitive to smell but were not, and survey data suggested that olfactory sensitivity actually is reduced during pregnancy. Allergy sufferers rated themselves low, but on average they could detect and identify smells as well as allergy-free people. Perhaps their lower self-rating was based on past temporary loss of odor sensitivity during an allergy attack.

Some other findings were less surprising: smokers perceived some of the test odors as stronger and some as weaker than non-smokers did, and they had a blunted response to odor quality, finding unpleasant odors not as unpleasant and pleasant odors not as pleasant as non-smokers did. The study also documented a decline in odor perception during human aging that varied greatly between individuals and with odors, with the ability to detect the unpleasant odor of mercaptans — the generally repugnant odor added to natural gas — beginning to fall off starting in the fourth decade. If that piece of information made you feel older than you thought you were, how about the finding that after age 30 our ability to recall the names of all odors begins to decline![30]

Odor research has also discovered that the young learn new odors faster and the blind surpass the sighted at odor identification. Women are significantly better in all aspects of odor recognition and learning than are men.[31]

Psychological Factors

There are several psychological factors to watch out for when you are tasting wine. Some of them can fool you into making mistakes, and others can set the stage for more effective use of your sensory tools.[32]

Stimulus errors occur when irrelevant criteria are used to judge wines. I demonstrate this error to my students by switching a fine Zinfandel into a bottle with a screw cap and letting them serve themselves from that bottle at the same time as they pour the same wine from a cork-finished bottle. The results are predictable — and embarrassing — for these fledgling wine connoisseurs: they use the irrelevant criterion of the container to prejudge the wine before they taste it. Other commonly encountered irrelevant criteria are the opinions of others about the wine and how much it cost. Blind tastings — in which the wines are identified only by a letter or numerical code — help eliminate stimulus errors.

Another common error you will encounter when tasting a group of wines is called time-order error and refers to the prejudicial preference for one wine over another based on its place in the order of tasting. The first and sometimes the last wine is typically preferred over the others. You might listen carefully to the discussion following a tasting of six 1990 Chardonnays by the members of your local wine club, for example, to see if the first sample presented is preferred. You could also try testing for the time-order error by placing the same wine in a tasting in both the first and fourth positions and seeing what people have to say about it. It has been suggested that the reason the first sample is preferred is that when it is tasted there is no immediate point of reference by which to judge it, but for all subsequent wines the first wine becomes the point of comparison. The time-order error is impossible to avoid when several wines are served with a multiple course meal, but it can be eliminated in professional tastings by tasting wines more than once in different orders.

Contrast error refers to the distortion of the sensory impression of a wine caused by the quality of the wine that was tasted just before it. If a great wine precedes a wine of average quality, our impression of the second wine will suffer by contrast; however, if a defective wine is served before a wine of average quality, our impression of the second wine would be better than it was in the first pairing.

Finally, I should mention the psychological factors that can make us better tasters: a high level of motivation, good powers of concentration, and a retentive memory. Whatever you can do to enhance your motivation, concentration, and especially your memory will help you learn faster and use what you have learned more effectively.

LEARNING WINE ODORS
Odors and Remembering

There is a lot of lore about the relationship between odor and memories. Most of us have a story about how an odor has triggered a vivid, detailed memory from the distant past. Mine tells how the odor of cellophane — yes, it does have one — propels me back 40 years to an afternoon snack at the top of the stairway of my second-grade school building in Ohio and a clear recollection of drinking from little bottles of milk whose tops were covered with — you guessed it — squares of red cellophane. (I can almost taste the milk and graham crackers as I write this!) Such memories can occasionally help us remember wine odors or identify wines. I encountered one such occasion during my last sabbatical leave in Seville when I presented a bottle of fine Spanish Cabernet Sauvignon in a blind tasting and it was immediately identified correctly by a young professor who exclaimed, "Christmas dinner! It must be Vega Sicilia." Her family always served Cabernet Sauvignon produced by the Vega Sicilia winery with that holiday meal. Tales of odor-triggered memories are dramatic and delightful and they give us a clue about remembering odors: we will remember odors best if we can encode them into our brains with elaborate visual, emotional, and verbal symbolism — the more symbols and the more vivid the better — and practice remaking the association between the odor and the encoding structure. Let's take a systematic look at what else psychological research can teach us about remembering odors.

Dr. Marcia Pelchat of the Monell Chemical Senses Institute and Dr. Gregg Solomon of Harvard University have recently summarized in separate presentations what research into the psychology of memory has revealed about odor memory and learning wine odors.[33] A summary of their main points follows.

Recognition Is Easier than Naming

Our ability to recognize an odor we have learned is better than our ability to retrieve the name of the odor when we encounter it again. This is true with other sensory stimuli as well. We've all seen someone we met at a party and remembered their face but not their name, or have recognized a familiar tune on the radio and not been able to retrieve its name for a few minutes (meanwhile, someone else called the station and won the free trip to Hawaii). When we search for the name of an odor and that name is on the "tip of our nose," we often come up with associations we have made with similar odor sources: when presented with a lemon odor, for example, we might guess orange — a similar citrus odor — or pine — which is also used to scent cleaning products (see Appendix D, Exercises 4.1, 6.1, and 6.2, for similar examples of associations my students have made with common wine odors). When recalling the name of an odor, our brains don't search for the name systematically by using a mental classification like they do when a word or a person's name is on the "tip of our tongue." You have probably noticed that to come up with a particular name or word, your memory presents you with words beginning with the same letter, words with the same number of syllables, or words that rhyme with the word it is searching for, giving you clues until you can guess correctly what the word is that you're after. It has been suggested that it is hard to retrieve memories of odors because, unlike words, odors do not have inherent structures — first letters, syllables, ability to be rhymed — and we have no mental classification system for them, although our performance in recalling odors can be improved if we are given clues.[34] This also suggests how we might improve our ability to remember odors.

How To Improve Your Performance in Odor Memory

1. Add Structure to Odors

   We can improve our odor memories by using our imaginations to give odors the structures they lack. We can do this by associating verbal descriptions — such as lists of words or dictionary-style definitions, and imaginary or real events — with them as we experience new odors. People who are able to write precise descriptions of odors can improve their recognition performance, but with unfamiliar odors this is more difficult and takes a long time.[35] Subjects who were invited to write definitions or describe a life episode that the odor reminded them of were better able to recognize odors than were subjects who were given no particular memory-enhancing strategy or were instructed to form visual images while smelling the odors.[36] It seems that the more elaborate the processing or encoding tasks we do while learning odors, the better we are able to remember them. How well we remember an odor also depends in part on how well we name it with a list of words, a definition, or an event.

2. Practice

   Training can improve our performance in remembering odors, but because our ability to conjure up odor imagery in our minds is poor — it's easy to imagine a square or triangle, but impossible to completely imagine the complex odor of chocolate or mint — we cannot rehearse odor memories mentally and have to practice remaking the original associations between the actual odors and our personal encoding labels. This makes once unusual odors familiar to us and speeds up the process of retrieving their names when we smell them again.[37] Thinking of the name of an odor when we smell it facilitates making the odor-to-word connection. Experienced winetasters — who have lots of practice making word-to-odor associations with many wines — have also been shown to be more able to write meaningful wine descriptions and then to correctly match each other's written descriptions to wines than are naive consumers.[38]

   Of course we all know that "practice makes perfect," right? But just how much practice does a good winetaster need? I asked judges at the Los Angeles County Fair and learned that to be skillful enough to judge there a winetaster needs to evaluate between 200 and 300 wines per week on a regular basis!

3. Checklists Help

Studies comparing experienced winetasters with naive consumers have also found that the disciplined, systematic approach to tasting used by experts helped them differentiate and describe more aspects of the wines than did the "sip-and-swallow" approach of the inexperienced tasters whose response to the wines was a simple hedonic reaction. The performance of both the expert and inexperienced tasters was improved when a list of cues was presented.[39] The sections of this chapter on "What to Look for in Wines" and "Techniques for the Sensory Evaluation of Wines" will introduce you to the experts' methods. Lists of descriptive terms for wine odors like those found on the wine aroma wheel and in the Varietal Wine Profiles of this book are examples of helpful cues or mental checklists that suggest a limited range of odors we can expect to encounter.

4. Develop More Odor Awareness

Serious winetasters are always enlarging their mental library of reference odors for describing wines. They are curious about the odors in their everyday world. During introductory winetastings I encourage my students to explore their olfactory worlds systematically, starting with odors they have at hand — from the smells of spices in the kitchen cabinet to those of the fruits and vegetables in the supermarket and the flowers in the campus gardens. This suggestion and the two "Focus on Olfaction" exercises for white and red table wines will help you improve your facility in labeling and remembering wine odors.

A Summary

The winetaster's traditional practice of describing wine odors in terms of familiar fruit or flower scents is consistent with our current understanding of the psychology of learning odors as well as with the fact that many of the same odorous chemicals are found both in wines and in flowers, fruits, and vegetables. The list of familiar odors (grapefruit, peaches, roses, and jasmine tea, for instance) that a group of tasters might assemble to describe the scent of a young Gewürztraminer wine constitutes the label given to that odor to help encode it in their minds. Because each one of us has had different experiences with odors, we will each construct a slightly different encoding label for each odor we want to remember. For instance, based on my odor experience, the description "roses" is more meaningful to me and therefore a more helpful encoding label for Gewürztraminer than is "jasmine tea."

To improve our ability to name and recall odors we need to expand our odor awareness, practice forming complex associations with odors, and think about the name of the odor each time we smell it.

The Wine Aroma Wheel Is An Important Learning Tool

Without Training, We All Describe Odors Differently

When I lecture about sensory evaluation, I pass out little pieces of paper which have been soaked in a dilute solution of linalool (an aromatic aroma component of Gewürztraminer, Muscat, and Riesling wines) and ask the students to tell me what they smell. Their responses cover the gamut from rose water to floor wax and mothballs.[40] Although we don't know exactly why a number of people who smell a purified aroma extract give it different names, there seem to be a wide variety of reasons ranging from inherent differences in the ability to sense the odor to variations in life experiences.

To Talk about Wines, We Need to Agree on Odor Terms

One thing that teachers and students can do to improve their understanding of and communication about wine odors is to experience a group of specific odors of known origin together, talk about how they perceive them, and agree on some common vocabulary for future

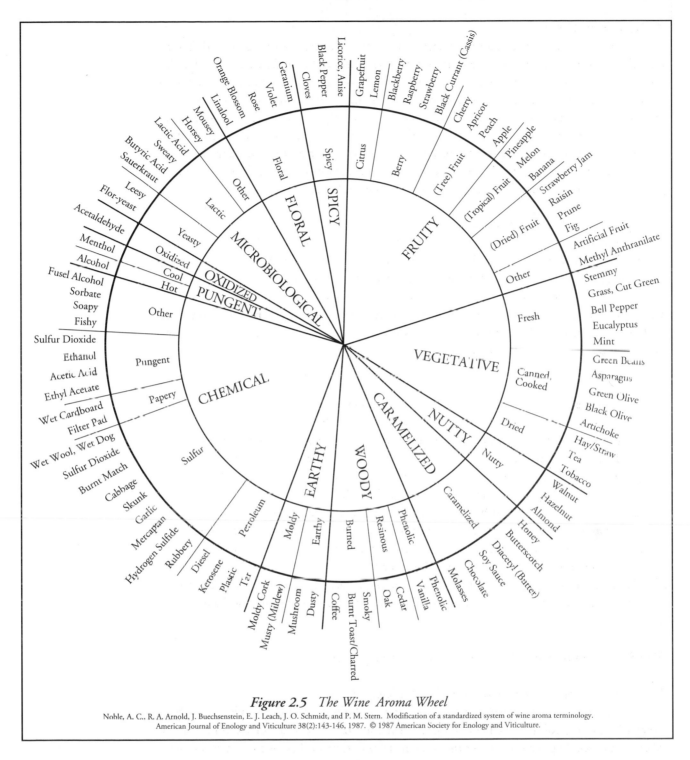

Figure 2.5 *The Wine Aroma Wheel*

Noble, A. C., R. A. Arnold, J. Buechsenstein, E. J. Leach, J. O. Schmidt, and P. M. Stern. Modification of a standardized system of wine aroma terminology. American Journal of Enology and Viticulture 38(2):143-146, 1987. © 1987 American Society for Enology and Viticulture.

Colored, laminated copies of Wine Aroma Wheel may be obtained from A.C. Noble, Dept. of Vit & Enology, U.C. Davis, Davis CA 95616
FAX: (530) 752-0380
Phone: (530) 852-0387
Email: ACNOBLE@ucdavis.edu

discussions. The wine aroma wheel provides reference odors of known origin and a construct within which to understand them. It is reproduced in Figure 2.5.[41]

The wine aroma wheel was developed in the 1980s under the guidance of Professor Ann Noble of the University of California, Davis, and is modeled after similar tools used by the beer and scotch whiskey industries. Although it was designed to enhance the accuracy of communication about wine odors among members of the wine industry, it quickly became popular with a much broader group of wine enthusiasts. Members of the wine industry worked with Professor Noble to create a catalog of commonly used odor terms, which were then organized into groups by origin and/or similarity of smell and displayed in the circular format you see in Figure 2.5.

The wine aroma wheel is a superb learning tool not only because it shows common aroma terms in relation to one another but also because there are recipes — some of which are reproduced in Appendix D — for making reference standards for each of the most precise aroma terms on the outer edge of the wheel. This means that anyone wanting to learn to describe odors precisely can make up demonstration wines showing the herbaceous, grassy qualities characteristics of Sauvignon Blanc wines or an array of bouquet components found in Cabernet Sauvignon such as tobacco, vanilla, and toasted almonds. Many of the most useful reference standards can be made at home, and each can be made stronger or weaker as your skill in identifying them improves.

Work on the development of reference standards for special groups of wines is continuing. Professor Noble has recently collaborated with producers of méthode champenoise sparkling wines to develop a set of descriptive terms for the character produced in such wines during aging on the yeast. These and other useful terms for describing sparkling wines have been incorporated into a sparkling wine aroma wheel.[42]

So, After All That, What Makes a Great Winetaster?

Sensory researchers believe that most of us have the same sensory equipment within the limits of variability of different thresholds. What sets the excellent winetaster apart is not an extraordinarily acute set of sensory organs, but a disciplined concentration and memory. It is the amount of practice in tasting, the breadth and depth of exposure to different wines, and the concentration brought to the tasting task that puts the excellent taster on a different level from the rest of us.

WHAT TO LOOK FOR IN WINES

The great variety of sensory experiences wines can provide is one of the reasons for their fascination. This section introduces some basic vocabulary for describing wines.[43] In the tasting exercises I'll describe the specific characteristics you can expect to find in the particular wines you will taste.

Appearance
Clarity

Wines should be brilliantly clear — that is, free of any visible particles. Dull wines with distinct haze or cloudy wines with suspended particles or a film on the surface may have off odors

and flavors and should be approached with caution for the rest of the tasting. Professional tasters would determine the nature and cause of the haze. The three wine samples on the left in Figure 2.6 were taken directly out of the barrels in

Figure 2.6
Examples of hazy and brilliantly clear wines

which they were aging and had not been clarified. They show a distinct haze. The two wine samples on the right were poured from bottles and are brilliantly clear.

Bubbles

The absence or presence and amount of carbon dioxide bubbles is considered in the evaluative process under appearance. When evaluating sparkling wines, the size of the carbon dioxide bubbles and their persistence are noted. Because they are associated with the traditional méthode champenoise technique of sparkling wine production, and its longer retention of carbon dioxide, small bubbles and a long-lasting bubble display are positive attributes. Young still table wines sometimes show a few bubbles around the edge of the glass: this is carbon dioxide that dissolved in the wine during the alcoholic fermentation process and was retained because the wine was stored at cool temperatures and bottled relatively soon after fermentation. These bubbles will disappear when the glass is swirled.

Legs

Figure 2.7
Streams of wine
flowing down the
sides of a wine glass
containing a 12%
alcohol solution
WINES, THEIR SENSORY
EVALUATION
Maynard A. Amerine
and Edward B. Roessler

Figure 2.8
Streams of wine
flowing down the
sides of a wine glass
containing an 18%
alcohol solution
WINES, THEIR SENSORY
EVALUATION
Maynard A. Amerine
and Edward B. Roessler

In a glass of wine that has been left undisturbed for a few minutes a liquid film can be seen creeping up the side and then forming droplets which fall back unevenly into the wine. These are called "legs," "tears," or, in the technical literature, "arches." Tears form because wines contain a mixture of water and alcohol, chemicals which differ in two properties: they evaporate at different rates and have different surface tensions (the ability of their molecules to stick to each other and to surfaces such as glass). Alcohol evaporates faster than water from the surface of the wine, causing the surface layer to have a higher concentration of water than does the wine below. Because the alcohol evaporates fastest where the air and the glass meet at the edge of the meniscus (the concave upper surface of the wine), there will be the least alcohol, the most water, and the highest surface tension (greatest ability of the liquid to stick to the glass) at that point. Thus the liquid will creep up the side of the glass until it can no longer overcome the force of gravity and then it will form drops that flow back down into the wine. A wine's tears are mainly water. The more alcohol in the wine the more tears it will generate.

A related phenomenon occurs when a glass of wine is swirled and the wine divides into streams as it runs down the sides of the glass. The higher the alcohol content of the wine, the thinner the streams it will produce when the wine falls back down the side of the glass. To observe this for yourself, try comparing a White Zinfandel table wine (about 10% alcohol) to a Zinfandel Port (around 20% alcohol). Be sure to use very clean glasses. This is also illustrated in Figures 2.7 and 2.8 — note the thinner legs in Figure 2.8.

Inconsequential Imperfections of Clarity

There are some sources of imperfect clarity that should not overly concern the winetaster. Crystals of potassium bitartrate may appear especially in young white and pink wines when they are stored at low temperatures. These crystals are normally clear and will sink to the bottom of the glass; they are harmless and can be quite lovely. The wine can be decanted off the crystals.

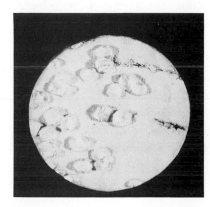

Figure 2.9
Crystals of
potassium
bitartrate on
a wine cork

Figures 2.9, 2.10, and 2.11 show three different forms tartrate crystals can take. The most common form is the clear cubical crystals in Figure 2.9. In Figure 2.10 the sample on the bottom shows a flaky tartrate deposit which was removed by chilling and filtering to produce the clear wine in the top bottle. Figure 2.11 shows a granular red sediment from on older Cabernet Sauvignon. The sediment in such wines can also occur as flakes that formed during years in the cellar and sometimes these can sneak into your glass. Forgive your butler for somewhat careless decanting if such sediments appear in your glass and go on to enjoy the fabulous complexity of the bottle bouquet of the wine. Cork floating on your wine is harmless, if unappetizing. Consider reprimanding the butler for this infraction or showing him the description of suggestions for opening wine bottles and decanting wines in the appendix on wine and food combining.

Figure 2.10
Two samples from different batches of a young White Zinfandel wine

Color
White Wines

Colors can be considered in a range of categories: colorless; light yellow-green; light straw yellow and light yellow; medium yellow through light gold and medium gold; and finally to brown hues. With experience you will learn what color to expect for the wines you are tasting.

1. Colorless: Very low color in a white wine can mean either that the fruit was immature or that the color has been bleached by the use of too much of a common wine aroma preservative, sulfur dioxide. If the latter were the case, the wine would have a characteristic off odor that would make you think of matches.

2. Light yellow-green is the color of young white table wines from cool regions. The green is from residual chlorophyll and is rare in wines from warmer areas.

3. Light straw yellow and light yellow are typical of the majority of dry white table wines.

Figure 2.11
Sediment left in the bottle after decanting an older California Cabernet Sauvignon

4. Medium yellow through light gold and medium gold are encountered in sweeter table wines such as *Botrytis*-affected late-harvest wines. Golden hues reflect some years of bottle aging.

5. Brown is to be expected in "white" dessert wines such as cream sherries, but in table wines it is a sign that the wine has been exposed to too much air in production or has been bottle aged too long. Such wines may also have an oxidized off odor.

Within the normal color range for white table wines (items 2-4 above), darker color is associated with oak barrel aging and/or later harvest dates that yield riper fruit that can be vinified to produce wines of higher residual sugar content or, in dry wines, higher alcohol content. Some "white" wines made from red-skinned grapes, such as Zinfandel, can have a distinctly pink color.

Red Wines

The color intensity of red table wines ranges from pink to light red, medium red, and dark red. At any color intensity, the wine may have a brick red or purple hue. The purple hue is associated with young red wines and the brick red or tawny hue is acquired as the wine ages in the bottle. When the red fades completely and brown takes over, the wine is likely too old and will have taken on a greater resemblance to sherry than to, say, Cabernet Sauvignon. As red wines age they lose color.

1. Pink is appropriate for rosé wines and white wines made from red grapes (Blanc de Noirs).

2. A dark purple indicates an extremely young, immature wine — for example, a cask sample. There are some grape varieties with purple juice that are used to add color to blends; Alicante Bouschet and Rubired are examples. Young bottled red wines will be red with a purple tint.

3. Light red is found in lighter-bodied red wines such as Pinot Noir and Gamay Beaujolais.

4. Medium red is the typical color of the majority of red table wines. The wines should take on a tawny hue as they mature in the bottle.

5. Dark red is the color of Ports and late-harvest red table wines.
6. Red-brown and mahogany are color terms used for red wines that have matured in the bottle for long periods. When they are all brown, it's all over, as noted above.

You can find color photographs of examples of wine colors in some wine texts, including MAKING SENSE OF WINE and the ACADEMIE DU VIN COMPLETE WINE COURSE.[44]

Odor

The total content of volatile compounds in wine is about one gram per liter or about one percent of the alcohol concentration: these compounds are tiny in concentration but very large in their impact on wine because they account for its odors and flavors, the most important factors in enjoying wine.[45]

When evaluating wine odors, a systematic check should be made for undesirable (off) odors; odors associated with the grapes (aroma); and odors originating during winemaking (bouquet). The odors in each category should be named, if possible, and their concentration or intensity noted. If the taster does not know the names of the odors — if, for example, she has never before experienced a Sauvignon Blanc varietal wine or the off odor imparted to wine by a yeast-infected cork — she should note the associations she has with the unrecognized odors and describe them as well as possible as an aid to remembering them and learning their correct names.

As you read the paragraph above, you may have realized that the wine aroma wheel isn't just an "aroma" wheel but also contains off odors and other odors most accurately called bouquet (in the dried vegetative, caramelized, and woody sections). In much of the winetasting literature aroma is used as a catch all term for aroma and bouquet, and even off odors. When learning about winetasting and making a systematic sensory evaluation, however, it is important to distinguish between these three odor categories.

Off Odors

These are undesirable odors which are foreign to the smell of a sound wine. The odors in the microbiological, oxidized, pungent, chemical, and earthy/moldy segments of the wine aroma wheel are off odors. Because their detection and prevention is of central concern to winemakers, a very large number of off odors have been linked to particular diagnostic chemicals that can be found by laboratory analysis. These include the sulfur off odors sulfur dioxide, hydrogen sulfide, and mercaptans. Being able to trace bacterial off odors by their telltale chemicals is particularly important to the prevention of wine disease: finding butyric or acetic acid or ethyl acetate in wines alerts a winemaker that sanitation practices need to be improved or that buying a particular batch of bulk wine to blend into her Château Noplace Burgundy is not a good idea. There are also some complex off odors whose precise chemical identity is not known. Horsey and wet dog are among these and also are my nominees for the most visually provocative off odors.

Aroma

The pleasant and desirable odors that come from the grape are called aromas. With experience you will be able to describe wine aromas as varietal, distinct, or vinous.

Varietal aromas are characteristic of particular grape varieties grown under proper conditions and made carefully into wine. Some of these odors are present in the fresh fruit itself (in Gewürztraminer and Zinfandel grapes, for example), while others are brought forth during the fermentation of the particular grape (as in Cabernet Sauvignon and Chardonnay). Varietal character is not just a function of using a specific variety of grapes to make the wine but also depends on the growing climate (cooler regions normally produce more varietal character), cropping level (lower yields are often associated with more varietal character), and good winemaking techniques that preserve the aromas in the fruit. Varietal aroma descriptions are included in the tasting exercises. When tasters recognize a varietal aroma they write down the name of the grape it came from.

Distinct is the term for aromas that are individual in character but not intense enough to permit varietal identification. If you smell a wine and find yourself asking, "Is this a Riesling or a Gewürztraminer or a blend containing some Muscat?" its aroma would be best described as "distinctive."

Vinous is the appropriate description when no varietal or distinct aroma is detectable. It is the term to use when your reaction is "Yes, this is wine," but not much more.

Bouquet

This is the term used for odors that are added to wines as they are made. Unlike varietal aromas, these odors are common to wines made from all types of grapes. There are several kinds of bouquet.

Fermentation bouquet is the term for the background odors common to all wines that have undergone an alcoholic fermentation. When wines are young, their fermentation bouquet is very yeasty and reminds me of the smell that pops out of a bottle of beer as it is opened. During the tasting of White Riesling and Gewürztraminer in Exercise 4.4 you will have a chance to experience fermentation bouquet and write your own personal definition by comparing a Gewürztraminer grape juice with a Gewürztraminer wine.

Oak-aging bouquet describes the odors produced by the reaction of the grape aromas and substances produced during fermentation with the components extracted from oak-aging containers, with small quantities of oxygen, and with each other. In Exercise 4.5 you will taste two styles of Chardonnay, one that was aged in oak barrels and one that was not, so that you will be able to experience directly oak-aging bouquet and the other sensory changes that oak-barrel aging produces.

The term **bottle bouquet** designates the greatly increased harmony, complexity, and mellowing of a wine's odors that are produced during aging in the bottle. In the tasting Exercise 6.7 you will experience the effect of bottle aging on Cabernet Sauvignon and have a chance to write a personal definition of bottle bouquet.

Champagne bouquet describes the characteristic toasted, yeasty character which is produced in sparkling wines made by the méthode champenoise, which includes a long period of aging the wine in the bottle on a thin film of yeast. You will meet this character in Exercise 8.1, which compares the sensory characteristics of sparkling wines made by the Charmat and méthode champenoise processes.

Other bouquets are created by special processing. Sherry, for example, acquires a characteristic oxidized or "nutty" odor by deliberate exposure to air, and vermouth gets its wonderfully complex bouquet from added herbs. You will learn the characteristic bouquet of sherry in Exercise 10.3.

Specific Stimuli for Off Odors and Aromas

The chemicals for some of the odor stimuli in wines have been identified. For off odors, this makes it possible to screen wines — perhaps in a government lab monitoring wines for export — for odor defects with simple chemical tests that are much less expensive than sensory evaluation. Knowing the chemicals for key aroma components has been useful in sensory research and could — if a quick and cheap method for their analysis were available — enable winemakers to follow the ripening of grapes in terms of the development of varietal character rather than by estimates of sugar content (the common current practice — see Chapter 3).

Table 2.1 shows some examples of these odor stimuli in wines and the sensations that are produced when they are present in concentrations above the perception threshold. Although the precise chemical stimuli for the vast majority of the varietal odors in wine remain unknown, a

Table 2.1
*Examples of Wine
Odor Stimuli in
Table Wines*

		Words that describe the stimulus	
	Odor Stimulus	for a careful but inexperienced taster	for an experienced winetaster
Varietal Aroma	linalool	floral	Gewürztraminer and Riesling varietal aromas
	2-methoxy-3-isobutylpyrazine	bell pepper	Cabernet Sauvignon varietal aroma
Off Odors	ethyl acetate	nail-polish remover	wine spoiled by vinegar bacteria
	lactic acid	sauerkraut	wine spoiled by lactic acid bacteria
	acetaldehyde	musty, swampy, like tide pools	wine exposed to too much air (oxidized)
	ethyl mercaptan	like garlic or onion	wine in which hydrogen sulfide was allowed to react with ethanol

few have been identified: two examples are listed in the table. The opposite is true for off odors: a large number of the unpleasant odors associated with wine disease and spoilage processes have been linked to specific chemical compounds.[46]

In-Mouth Impressions

It is at this point when we are examining a wine that we observe and distinguish between the flavor, taste, and tactile sensations we perceive when the wine is in our mouth. To distinguish them from flavor and odor, I will use the collective term "structural components" for the compounds responsible for a wine's taste and tactile sensations. These include the organic acids tartaric, malic, citric, and lactic (tartness); the sugars glucose and fructose (sweetness and body); tannins (bitterness and astringency); alcohol (sweetness, body, and hot); and carbon dioxide (bubbles that touch). After taking note of the flavors, winetasters consider each structural component in turn.

Flavor

The flavors of a wine should correspond to its odors, and winetasters take note of analogous aspects in odor and flavor.

A wine made with care from grapes grown in the right climate with reasonable yields should have a varietal flavor recognizable by experienced tasters. When tasters recognize a **varietal** flavor, its name is recorded. If the tasters cannot name the varietal flavor with certainty but recognize that the wine's flavor is something considerably more than "merely wine," they call the wine **distinctive**. This leaves the term **vinous** for unmemorable beverages that are, indeed, "merely wine."

If there are special flavors such as those characteristic of *Botrytis*-affected wines (the honey/mushroom/apricot smell and taste of wines made from late-harvested, mold-infected fruit) they should be noted. Also under the heading of flavor, winetasters will also make rather general notes about a wine's apparent age: **young** (fresh, tart, and grapey, perhaps with too much roughness for optimum enjoyment); **mature** (bottle-aging character has developed, tannins are moderated, and the wine is ready to drink); or **over-aged** (oops! the oxidation process has gone on too long here, creating unappealing odors and flavors and a brown color).

A wine should not have any off flavors (undesirable odors which are experienced when the wine is in the mouth), but if it does they should be described or named with as much precision as possible. Often the same terms will be used for off flavors as have been used for off odors. See the left side of the wine aroma wheel for many examples.

Taste
Acidity

Acids taste **tart**. When describing acidity, winetasters are concerned with the amount of tartness in the wine and its relationship to the wine's sugar content (see "Balance" below).

Flat wines do not have enough acid. They don't cleanse or refresh your palate and may bring to mind the image of reaching for a lemon to put a little more zip into your lemonade. **Tart** is the word for the pleasant sour taste we find in wines with the right amount of acid. **Green** wines have too much acid (you're reaching for the sugar in the lemonade-making picture). They may remind you of the taste of unripe fruit.

Sweetness

Winetasters estimate the level of sweetness in a wine and judge its appropriateness for the wine type.

Dry wines have no taste of sweetness. Sweet stimuli such as sugars may be present in the wine and detectable by chemical analysis but are in concentrations below your threshold of perception. **Low**, **medium**, and **high sugar** refer to increasing degrees of sweetness above your threshold of perception. Wines that are too sweet are described as either **sweetish** (a bit too sweet) or **cloying** (much too sweet).

Balance

A good balance between sugar and acid is just as important as the amount of either sensation. If there is too little or too much acid relative to the amount of sugar — or too much or too little sugar relative to the amount of acid — the wine is unbalanced. In practice, you may find that "unbalanced" is your first impression of a wine and then go on to determine exactly why the wine is "unbalanced" in terms of its sugar and acid content.

Bitterness

Unlike sweetness — whose absence is noted by the term "dry" — bitterness is not usually recorded in a winetaster's notes or on a score card unless it is present. It is most common in young red wines, where it is not considered a defect in small amounts. When it is found in other wines it is noted as an off flavor.

Touch
Astringency

Winetasters assess whether or not a wine dries out their mouths and describe wines in terms of the presence of various levels of this tactile sensation or its absence.

The tactile sensation **smooth** is produced by wines of low astringency. Properly made white, rosé, lighter-style red, and aged red table wines are smooth. Rough, drying tactile sensations result from wines of increasing degrees of astringency. Young red wines in the barrel are often **very rough**. Even when vinified for bottling, red wines destined for long periods of bottle aging remain **rough**. Aging diminishes roughness, and cellar treatments such as fining are often used to decrease roughness. You will learn more about astringency and the effects of fining in Chapter 5 and in Exercise 6.3, "Structural Components of Red Table Wines."

Body

Body refers to the viscosity or mouth-filling property of wines. Winetasters assess the amount of body in a wine and its appropriateness for the wine's type. Increased body in dry wines is associated with higher contents of alcohol and extract (everything in the wine that is left after the alcohol and water are boiled off). Periods of oak aging also increase body because large molecules from the wood dissolve in the wine and increase its viscosity. Residual sugar can also increase body: the higher the sugar, the heavier the body.

Thin wines do not have enough body for their type. They are watery. **Low** or **light body** describes the viscosity of most dry and low-sugar white and rosé table wines. Most red table wines as well as white table wines of medium sugar content have **medium body**. Winetasters use the term **high** or **heavy body** for late-harvest *Botrytis*-affected wines and fortified dessert wines.

Carbon Dioxide Bubbles

Bubbles will already have been evaluated under appearance, but they also produce a tactile sensation. At this point in a serious sensory evaluation they can be a nuisance, as our taste buds and touch receptors must sort among them to taste and feel the liquid part of the wine, even though they are a refreshing asset to the wine.

Alcohol

Warm, hot, and even "ouch!" are tactile sensations corresponding to increasing amounts of alcohol, from an appropriate level to way too much.

Overall Impression — Assessing Typicality and Quality

To complete the sensory analysis we add a note about our overall impression of the wine to the separate visual, olfactory, gustatory, and tactile impressions we have assembled. We sit back and think about how well the parts of the wine relate to each other, make a judgement of how good the wine is, and consider whether the wine is typical of, for example, the type, region, producer, or vintage year.

Typicality

Experienced tasters will make an evaluation at this point of the typicality of the wine for its region, variety, vintage year, producer, and price range. They will also make a kind of authenticity check for claims of uniqueness implied by label terms such as Private Reserve and Special Selection. Is this "Private Reserve Syrah" more intensely flavorful, structured for longer bottle aging (although too rough to enjoy now), or set apart in some other pleasant way from the regular bottling of that wine? It is considerably more difficult, of course, to answer questions such as "Is this Chardonnay like the rich, complex wines we have come to associate with the Burgundian village of Puligny-Montrachet, the producer Etienne Sauzet, or white Burgundies costing $40.00 per bottle?" which require knowledge of the grapes and winemaking techniques of a region as well as a great deal of experience in tasting and remembering a large number of wines. This is clearly a skill worthy of our aspirations!

Quality

The precise concept of quality or the degree of excellence of a wine — or anything else we are judging — is adjusted to the nature of the object or performance being evaluated: we do not use the same criteria to gauge the quality of the high school drama department's production of "Macbeth" which stars our favorite nephew as we use for the Royal Shakespeare Company's performance with Sir Laurence Olivier; nor do we judge ordinary wines and great wines by the same standards. Inexpensive, ordinary "jug" wines are judged acceptable when they are simply free from defects, and standards of quality for such wines are typically associated with the statutory enforcement of minimal standards. When we define quality in fine wines, we move out of the laboratories where wine defects are monitored and touch the realm of aesthetics — the branch of philosophy concerned with the nature of beauty, art, and taste.

Among the attributes that distinguish great wines from ordinary wines are complexity, harmony, and the power to stimulate the emotions.[47] Wines can be interesting, be well-made, possess varietal character, evidence aging bouquet, and be typical of their origins without creating a sense of awe in the mind of an experienced judge. Such wines are good and are expected to be somewhat complicated as well as harmonious, but they are not great.

Complexity means that the wine has a very large number of pleasing odors and flavors. I vividly remember my first experience of a wine with great complexity. This occurred when I tasted a fine, well-aged Napa Valley Cabernet Sauvignon while dining at a colleague's home. The wine surprised me with its intricacy and subtlety. Its vast array of odors and flavors aroused my curiosity and compelled me to smell and taste it again and again. With each sampling the wine rewarded me with a new nuance of aroma, bouquet, or flavor. I began to wonder about its history: where the grapes had been grown, exactly how this excellent wine was made, what weather prevailed during the vintage year, and how my host had stored it. As I searched for words to describe this Cabernet, I realized that I needed a new batch of adjectives to describe my new discoveries each time I tasted. Most of my dinner companions were not wine-lovers, so I eventually interrupted my private sensuous and intellectual journey and returned to the non-vinous conversation — after a conspicuous absence which they attributed to my eccentric fascination with wines. This is how I learned that complex wines have many intriguing odors and flavors and can be savored repeatedly without losing interest. They can stimulate your palate, mind, and heart, but you should be warned that enjoying them without the company of other wine enthusiasts may give you a reputation for bad table manners.

Great wines must have a harmonious, well-balanced combination of sensory elements: each component belongs and is present in the correct amount relative to the other components. As we taste a harmonious wine we find that as each sensory feature is revealed to us it is congruous with the ones that preceded it. We encounter no inconsistencies in the wine's complexity and intensity of color, odor, flavor, and aftertaste. We experience the wine as a well-integrated whole. In white table wines, for example, a harmonious balance between sweetness and tartness is particularly important. Refreshment of the taster's palate is the criterion for judging the balance of sugar and acid in white table wines, and even very sweet wines can be refreshing if they have adequate acidity. For another example, consider this description of a harmonious young red table wine: clear, deep red color, intense varietal aroma and flavor complemented by oak-aging bouquet, tart acid, very low sugar (dry in taste), and slightly rough to rough astringency, which reflects the presence of enough tannins to carry the wine to maturity in the bottle — at which time its potential for greatness should be realized. A wine made from the same grape variety would be unharmonious — and therefore not great — if, for example, the varietal aroma and flavor of the fruit were not recognizable, or the varietal flavors were overpowered by too much oak aging, or all the sensory properties were as described except that the wine was smooth or slightly sweet. Another example of the sort of harmonious combination of sensory elements I associate with fine wines is their continuity of aroma, flavor, and aftertaste: after I have sniffed a wine and have gauged the intensity and pleasantness of its aroma and bouquet, I expect that when I taste I will find the flavors to be equally intense and pleasing — even if they are of a somewhat different composition — and that an aftertaste of a similar nature will linger after I swallow.

A great wine also makes an impact on our emotions and will be remembered for the sense of awe it creates in us. If a wine cannot excite us enough to be remembered pleasurably, it cannot be great. Furthermore, we must learn to articulate the sense of awe — convert it into specific impressions — so that the object of our contemplation can be properly appreciated, accurately remembered, and discussed. No matter what I am judging greatness in — music, drama, fine wine, sculpture, architecture, or paintings — I must pay attention with a kind of receptive, quiet concentration that will allow an internal dialogue to develop in my mind. While I watch a play, listen to an opera, taste wine, or look at art, I take in the sights and sounds, odors and flavors, or colors and design — following the plot and the music, systematically exploring the wine or the painting. If what I am hearing, seeing, smelling, or tasting is particularly interesting, I will notice that something special is happening. Something in the wine or artwork has triggered my "WOW" response and invites my attention to linger with it. I will begin to realize things like

"I really like the way the symbolism of the costumes and sets subtly reinforces the actors' lines!" or "The performance of that aria was perfect — her voice, gestures, and emotional expression all worked together to carry the poignant sadness of the music right into my heart" (reaching for a handkerchief) or "WOW! This Cabernet Sauvignon is exciting! Just look at how its deep, delicious aroma carries through into its intense flavor and aftertaste. It also has enough acid and tannin so it will mature well. I can't wait to try it again in 20 years!" My emotional and aesthetic impressions are recorded in my memory by means of the internal dialogue they stimulated. Becoming a skilled and articulate observer — that is, a connoisseur — of wine or the arts requires both learning how to notice their important features and a vocabulary to describe them as well as your perceptions. This takes time — to attend plays and learn the elements of drama, to listen to music and learn its formal structure, to taste wines systematically and learn to describe them accurately — and many internal conversations. Reading the opinions of critics or discussing art or wine with more knowledgeable connoisseurs can help us put our experiences into perspective (maybe the performance of that aria wasn't so great after all, Marian) and sparks us to hone our observational skills and deepen our knowledge. The training in winetasting technique and vocabulary you will receive from this book and its sensory evaluation exercises will help you begin to do both.

Figure 2.12
The Perception of Quality Depends in Part on a Trained Judge
MAKING SENSE OF WINE
by Alan Young © 1986

If, after we have had some experience, we find ourselves searching for words when faced with a complex wine, we are probably also confronting greatness. Ordinary wines are fleeting and can be described adequately with a few words which readily come to mind, whereas even trained and experienced tasters will have trouble finding enough words to describe adequately the finest wines.

Figure 2.12 from Alan Young's book MAKING SENSE OF WINE reminds us of the importance of training and experience for the perception of quality in wines — and the fellow on the left looks like he's ready to attend the opera.[48]

TECHNIQUES FOR THE SENSORY EVALUATION OF WINES

The winetasting event begins as soon as you get up on the morning of the day that you are going to go to a tasting and ends when you walk out of the tasting room. The following guidelines are for professional and serious amateur tastings. While I know that you will not be able to insist that your tasting club meets at 10:00 on Saturday morning, I think it is important to understand the optimum conditions for tasting and the likely effects of fatigue. If we always go to tastings when we are tired, for example, we may find that our results are inconsistent — that is, we may give the same wine different ratings on different occasions. If we recognize the importance of being alert, we may be able to adjust our schedules so that we can arrive fresher at an evening tasting.

Setting Up the Winetasting
Tasters

- are fresh, well rested, and healthy
- are willing to work and highly motivated to do their best
- are not rushed (having arrived punctually)
- are not wearing perfume, after-shave, or other decorative odors that will interfere with everyone's ability to smell the wines
- have eaten and brushed their teeth 1-2 hours before the tasting.

Scheduling

Tastings are optimally held in the morning to help ensure freshness of the tasters' minds and palates.

The Tasting Room
- is illuminated with natural light
- is conducive to concentration — that is, it should have no extraneous odors
  (NO SMOKING), no noises, and no visual distractions.

My experience with a group of students who were challenged by a particularly obnoxious "extraneous" odor leads me to believe that the power of concentration can over-come even a serious distraction. One semester one of my colleagues was teach-ing a taxidermy class and had stored a skunk specimen in the freezer at the back of the tasting lab's classroom. People would come into the room, sniff the faint skunk bouquet, and then open the freezer to verify the source. Among the best winetasters that semester were the four students who sat at the table nearest the skunk-containing freezer. I think that was because they must have been able to concentrate remarkably well, but perhaps the skunk's odors somehow stimulated their olfactory receptors to more efficiently find alternate stimuli!

Figure 2.13
Student tasting in the classroom at California State University, Chico

Tasting Glasses
- are tulip-shaped, to trap the wine odors
- are thin, so that the wine can be warmed if necessary
- are clear, to show color accurately
- are large, holding 8-10 ounces or more so that they can be filled one-quarter full with a 2-ounce serving and tasters can swirl and splash the wine about with impunity
- have been washed using an unscented detergent, rinsed thoroughly, and drained dry
- have been stored so they do not pick up odors.

Wines
- are tasted at the same temperatures at which they would be served with a meal. The approximate temperatures are:

sparkling wines & sweet white wines	40-45°F
dry white and rosé table wines	50-60°F
light-bodied red table wines	50-65°F
red table wines	65-68°F

  (Note: within the categories of dry white table wines and red table wines, the better the wine the higher its optimal serving temperature.)
- are tasted in an order designed so that no wine will be placed at a disadvantage by its spot in the tasting sequence. This order is similar to that in which several wines would be served with a traditionally constructed meal of several courses.

1. white before red	4. modest before fine
2. dry before sweet	5. light-bodied before full-bodied
3. young before old	6. light young red before full-bodied, sweet white

- are tasted in related groups whenever possible.
- are always tasted blind — that is, identified by code only.

Approaching the Wine

This section describes how to make a systematic sensory evaluation of a wine. When you are tasting several wines, evaluate the color and appearance of all the wines first, then quickly smell them all to get a fresh impression, then smell in detail, making notes, and finally taste and feel each one. Be sure to rest as needed to avoid adaptation and fatigue.

Each sensory evaluation exercise in this book has a form for systematically recording your observations of each wine and for taking notes on the impressions of other tasters. Once you've worked with this system for a while you will have its elements memorized and will probably switch, as I have, to a more compact system for note-taking, especially at more informal tastings. I make short notes on 3 x 5 cards and file them by wine type for future reference.

Appearance

To inspect for clarity, hold the wine up to a bright source of light such as a clear light bulb or candle. For the dedicated enophile, the best tool for evaluating clarity is a small flashlight with a narrowly focused beam. Turn on the flashlight and hold it against the wineglass. If you see the beam of the light in the wine (like the beam of your headlights when you are driving in the fog or following another vehicle through the dust on a dirt road), the wine is cloudy. Small flashlights can easily be carried in tuxedo pockets or handbags for impressing dates or intimidating the restaurant wait staff. Evaluating other aspects of appearance such as the bubble display of sparkling wines requires only a well-lighted work space.

Color

Hold the wine glass up against a white surface. Tip the glass to view the edge of dark red wines. To compare the colors of several wines, place the glasses on a white surface, fill them to equal depths, and inspect the wines from above.

Odor

1. Focus your best concentration skills on the task at hand. You're now starting the hardest part.
2. Before swirling the wine, put your nose into the glass above the wine and sniff quickly and deeply. Reflect on the odors and note your impressions on paper. Repress the urge to tell everyone within earshot what you have (or perhaps have not) discovered.
3. Hold the glass by the stem unless the wine in it has been served too cold and you want to warm it. Swirl the wine in the glass 1 or 2 quick revolutions. Put your nose back into the glass and take 1 or 2 quick, deep sniffs. Record your impressions.
   - Trust your first impressions. They are the most accurate, since your sensory organs and brain are both at their best initially: fresh and alert. Pay attention to what they are telling you before they get tired.
   - Note any associations you make with the wine's odors. These will help you file and recall the odors of this wine and others like it. Each time you taste, you are adding to a mental "reference library" of standards with which to compare other wines of this type when you taste them.
4. Rest 15-45 seconds as you reflect and record your impressions.
5. Swirl the glass briefly and sniff again. Once again, note your impressions.
   - As you smell the wine, check systematically for
     - off odors
     - aroma (is the wine made from a recognizable grape variety?)
     - bouquet (was the wine aged in oak? aged on yeast? aged in the bottle?).
   - Record the intensity of all these odors.
   - You may find it helpful to look at the wine aroma wheel or other descriptions of the wine after you have recorded your first impressions to see if any of the descriptive terms used by other tasters trigger your imagination.

6. A lot of vigorous swirling can change the odors in a wine, so you'll want to pour another sample of wine if you need to investigate it further rather than continuing to swirl the same sample.

In-Mouth Impressions — Flavor, Taste, and Touch

1. Place a small amount of wine — about a tablespoon — in your mouth. Move the wine all over your tongue and the inside of your mouth with a chewing motion so that all your taste buds can come into contact with the wine and the tactile receptors in your mouth can sense it.
2. Allow the wine to warm in your mouth so that more of the volatile compounds can escape. If you hold the wine in your mouth a little longer, you will be able to appreciate more of its flavors.
3. Draw some air through the wine to extract the volatiles and force them up to your olfactory epithelium through the opening in the back of your mouth. Discretion may dictate that this step be eliminated in polite company or in public places, but it's fine in a serious winetasting.
4. Reflect on the flavors and record your impressions — associations, varietal identifications, any off flavors, etc. — much as you have for odors.
5. Note acidity, dryness, or the level of sweetness, balance, body, astringency, presence of bubbles, and hotness. Think about the balance, especially between tartness and sweetness, and about the apparent age of the wine. A note for the less experienced: if you are tasting wine in the morning or without much food you will probably have to learn to adjust your impressions. Often wines that are perceived as "a little too tart" under such circumstances are perfect with meals.
6. Spit out the wine. Consuming alcohol will alter your perceptive abilities and you want to keep them sharp. It could be that the tenth wine in the tasting will be the most interesting, and if you have consumed 18 to 27 ounces while tasting wines one through nine you may miss its delights altogether. (Nevertheless, see the note in number 3 above about discretion in public places.)
7. Repeat steps 1-5 and swallow a **small** amount of wine. Note the aftertaste.
8. Cleanse your palate with water, crackers, or bread between wines.

Summing Up

The prerequisites for performing this last step in the sensory evaluation are the acquisition and application of experience. To acquire experience we must taste and remember many wines, and in the optimal situation we would taste with an experienced mentor who would tell us whether or not a particular wine is a good example of its type — a great Australian Chardonnay, for instance, or the finest Chianti Classico Riserva — and, if it is not, where it is deficient and what it would take to make it great. If we don't have that sort of opportunity, we can use published tasting notes — such as those in Appendix D — to tutor ourselves while saving our impressions and evaluations in our memories and notes until we can converse with an expert.

Since assessing the quality and typicality of a wine requires a qualified judge, how can we even attempt this task if we are inexperienced — before we are "qualified"? The answer is that we must simply do the best we can with what experience we have and keep our limitations in mind. Our memory of wines plays a most important role here, and it is also here that our inexperience — with wines in general or with the wines of a new region, variety, or producer — becomes apparent. Even experienced tasters will be able to make only the most tentative quality and typicality judgments about wines they are not acquainted with without the guidance of information about what to expect from a certain variety or region. They have their experience with other wines to aid them in evaluating the new wines, but they are novices nonetheless when it comes to the new region and will need to rely on their memories to retain information about the new wines for later discussion or reading — much as beginning tasters must do for all wines. Here are some specific suggestions for summing up which are intended to help beginning winetasters to acquire experiences systematically, think about complexity, harmony, and balance, and be receptive to awe:

1. Take Time. Reflect upon and integrate your impressions of the individual sensory components of the wine. Ask how well those components relate to each other; evaluate the wine's complexity; and reflect upon how typical the wine is of its region, grape variety, producer, and vintage if you are familiar with them.

2. A Checklist May Help. A checklist like the following can help remind us about what we want to evaluate.

    • Is the wine complex? Does it have a lot of odors and flavors or just a few?
    • How well do the individual parts fit together? Is anything exaggerated or missing?
    • How well-balanced are the sweetness and acidity, acidity and tannin?
    • Is the intensity of the aroma and bouquet matched with an equal depth of flavor?
    • How does the wine's richness and complexity compare with that of good examples of this type of wine you've already tasted?
    • Is the wine attractive? Does it please you?

3. Open Your Mind. The items on the above checklist will jump out at you after you have had some experience with wines. Apart from remembering great wines once we've been introduced to them, is there a technique for recognizing greatness? A great wine will excite you and you will experience a sense of awe, just as I did the night I tasted my first really great Cabernet Sauvignon (as described in the earlier discussion of assessing quality). I assure you that you will — as I have — recognize this experience when it hits you, even if there is nobody standing at your elbow to say "This is a really fine wine."

HOW IS SENSORY EVALUATION USED PROFESSIONALLY?

Winetasting is an irreplaceable tool for developing new ways to grow grapes and make wines as well as for learning about wines. Here are some examples to illustrate the range of uses made of sensory evaluation in the wine industry.

A sensory examination of wines is a fundamental part of any research project that attempts to answer questions like "What is the effect of _____ on wine quality?" For example, vineyard researchers might be studying a modified viticultural (grape growing) practice, such as irrigation timing, pruning, or thinning of leaves; or, at a winery, an improved piece of equipment, a new source of oak wood for barrels, or a novel grape variety in a blend might need to be evaluated. Sensory examination is used in such projects because it goes beyond chemical and physical laboratory analysis: our senses are more precise in some cases, and, more importantly, our brains

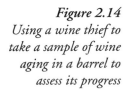

Figure 2.14
Using a wine thief to take a sample of wine aging in a barrel to assess its progress

are more useful than laboratory instruments because they can simultaneously analyze and integrate information about the many components that make up a wine. They are also well-suited for answering very complicated questions such as "Is the quality of the wine improved by the new irrigation scheduling in Vineyard A?" or "Is this new blend of 20% Merlot and 80% Cabernet Sauvignon better than our old blend with only 10% Merlot?"

In wine production, sensory examination is used to maintain standards of quality and to assure uniformity where that is desired (for example, in cases where this week's batch of Chateau Ordinary Burgundy must be exactly the same as last week's and last year's batches). There are also specific wine-production decisions that cannot be made by evaluating biological, chemical, or physical analyses and must be based on sensory evaluation. Some examples are: choosing oak for barrels whose flavors will complement those of the wine; deciding when a wine has spent enough time aging in oak cooperage; making blends of wines; and selecting the wine spirits for fortifying Port or choosing the spices for vermouth.

In the wine trade sensory evaluation is used to assess the quality of wines. Groups of similar wines are tasted together and compared to each other. For example, a California winery might pick a group of Chardonnays in the $10.00 to $12.00 price range and ask: "Where does our 1991 Chardonnay fit in with this group of 1991 Chardonnays made by our competitors?" or "Is our wine priced properly for its quality relative to the competition?" A wine buyer travelling in France might inquire: "What is a fair price to offer the producer for these casks of fine Burgundy?" or "How much should futures cost for this Bordeaux chateau's most recent vintage?"

An interesting example of the use of sensory evaluation in research and marketing is a research report by Guinard and Cliff.[49] These investigators were attempting to answer the question, "Do Pinot Noir wines from the Carneros district have characteristic aromas and flavors that distinguish them from Pinot Noir wines from Napa and Sonoma?" Their first task was to make up reference standards for Pinot Noir aromas and flavors and to test prospective members of the winetasting panel. Panel members had to be able to identify consistently a set of reference standards such as cherry, prune, and leather, and some willing and otherwise expert volunteers flunked the test. Tasters who passed the test were then asked to evaluate Pinot Noirs from Carneros, Napa, and Sonoma. The result of the research was that the Carneros wines consistently had more fresh berry, berry jam, cherry, and spicy aromas than the Pinot Noirs from Sonoma and Napa. This research gave winemakers in the Carneros district a clear definition of the characteristics that set their wines apart. They were then able to blend a highly typical wine to teach marketers and consumers about the uniqueness of the region's Pinot Noir.

Use of the techniques of sensory evaluation is not confined to the wine industry: governments use them to enforce trade laws and prevent fraud. The German wine laws, for example, require that wines be tasted by an expert panel to determine whether they are typical of the region noted on the label. In restaurants sommeliers use sensory evaluation to choose wines for their wine lists, waiters taste critically to familiarize themselves with the wines so that they can advise diners about appropriate wines for particular dishes, and chefs use sensory evaluation to choose wines for preparing dishes.

A SENSORY CLASSIFICATION OF WINES

The everyday categories we use to discriminate between different kinds of wines — categories like red or white, sweet or dry — are based on organoleptic properties. Even when we speak of district or vintage differences we are really discussing sensory properties rather than simply geographic or weather-related variations. This is because the influences of climate and weather on the composition of grapes grown in a particular locale or growing season are reflected in the organoleptic properties of the wines. In this section I will describe the organoleptic classification of wines upon which the overall organization of the rest of this book is based and define some of its key terms. Table 2.2 shows this classification of the basic wine types available in the United States based on five sensory attributes: added flavor, alcohol content, carbon dioxide content, color, and varietal aroma.[50]

Added Flavors

In the added flavor category we find only a few wines with either herb or fruit flavors added. The best-known herb-flavored wines are the dry and sweet vermouths, which are made by

Table 2.2 *An Organoleptic Classification of Wines for Sale in the United States*

Sensory Categories							
Added Flavor	Alcohol Content	CO$_2$ Content	Color	Varietal Aroma	Species	Label Name	Examples
No	14% or Less (Table Wines)	None (Still)	White	Yes	*Vitis vinifera*	Varietal	Muscats, Gewürztraminer, White Riesling, Sauvignon Blanc, Chardonnay, Sémillon, Chenin Blanc
						District	Sauternes, France; Mosel, Germany; Alto Adige, Italy; Penedès, Spain; and districts in Portugal, Greece, South Africa, Chile, etc.
					Non-*V. vinifera*	Generic Varietal District	Native American species (*V. labrusca, V. rotundifolia*) and hybrids (Catawba, Niagara, etc.)
				No		Generic Varietal District	Blends in which no variety dominates, areas with no distinctive varietals planted, and off years in districts with or wines made from normally distinctive grapes
			Red	Yes	*Vitis vinifera*	Varietal	Cabernet Sauvignon, Merlot, Zinfandel, Syrah, Pinot Noir, Gamay, etc., & Muscats
						District	Médoc, Burgundy, France; Chianti, Piemonte, Italy; Rioja, Spain; etc. as above
					Non-*V. vinifera*	Same as for white	Alicante Bouschet, Concord, Rubired, etc.
				No		Same as for white	Same as for white
			Pink	No		Generic Varietal District	Rosés Blush varietals and some White Zinfandels Tavel
		High (Sparkling)					Champagne or other districts and methods; colors; Muscats
	Over 14% (Fortified)	Dry					Sherries only: baked or yeast process (fino etc.)
		Sweet					Cream Sherry, Port, Muscatels, etc.
Yes	Herb Flavors						Dry and Sweet Vermouths; Byrrh & Dubonnet
	Fruit Flavors						Apple, peach, & berry wines; Thunderbird

soaking a blend of herbs in fortified wines or adding herb extracts to them. Fruit-flavored wines are made either by adding flavorings or by fermenting the fruit itself. Although there are many interesting features of their production and sensory evaluation — did you know, for example, that a vermouth maker must consider annual variation in the spices and herbs that are blended to flavor these wines? — they will not be considered further in this book.

Natural or Fortified Wines

Wines with no added flavors may be divided into those with 14% alcohol or less and those with over 14% alcohol. Because wines with 14% alcohol or less are produced by fermenting only the naturally occurring grape sugars, they are called natural wines. They are also referred to as table wines because of their customary use "at table" with meals. Alcohol content of more than 14% usually must be achieved by adding wine spirits to natural wines to create fortified wines. These can be dry or sweet, but the latter is more common. The category of dry fortified wines includes only the sherries, a most interesting group of wines characterized by the pungent odor and flavor of acetaldehyde — the result of deliberate oxidation. The production and sensory evaluation of both types of fortified wines will be discussed in Chapters 9 and 10.

Sometimes the alcohol content of a natural wine can exceed 14% when it is made from very ripe healthy grapes with high sugar content, as is the case with some of California's late-harvest Zinfandels. These wines are still classified as table wines but they are taxed at the higher rate by the U.S. Government.[51]

Table Wines With and Without Bubbles

Wines of 14% alcohol or less are subdivided according to their carbon dioxide content: the **still wines** have none and the **sparkling wines** have a high concentration. Sparkling wines originated in the Champagne district of northeastern France. Both the méthode champenoise and other widely used methods of producing sparkling wines will be described in Chapter 7; their sensory evaluation will be treated in Chapter 8.

Still Table Wines — The Majority

The majority of the wines for sale in the United States fall into the category of still table wines, which is subdivided according to wine color in Table 2.2. White and red table wines are further classified according to whether they exhibit the characteristic aroma of a particular grape variety or not. A **grape variety** or cultivar is a subgroup of a grape species and is distinguished from other varieties by economically important hereditary traits, such as the color of its fruit, its suitability for winemaking, its disease resistance, or its climatic adaptation. Some grape varieties suitable for winemaking can, under the right conditions, produce wines whose aromatic components have a distinctive, recognizable character, while others cannot. **Varietal wines** are made mainly from a single variety of the former type that should impart a characteristic aroma and flavor to the wine.

A grape variety, especially one that has been cultivated for many centuries, may be subdivided by natural mutations into **clones:** subgroups distinguished by inherited differences in traits important for cultivation or vinification. Pinot Noir is one of the most notoriously variable grape varieties: many clones have arisen in its region of origin (Burgundy, France) and have been exported to other growing areas. The wide variability in Burgundian wines made by different producers and the problems often experienced in making Pinot Noir varietal wines elsewhere seems to be attributable at least in part to this clonal variation.

Varietal Aroma

You will notice in Table 2.2 that pink wines are not subdivided on the basis of varietal aroma. This is because, even if they were to be made only from suitably mature grapes of a single distinctive variety, their method of production would rarely result in a wine with varietal aroma and flavor characteristics. Among red and white table wines with varietal aromas a distinction can easily be made, even by inexperienced winetasters, between the subtle aromas of wines made from *Vitis vinifera* grapes and the simpler, stronger odors of wines produced from the grapes of non-*Vitis vinifera* species. Chapter 11 will discuss the very important role of non-*Vitis vinifera* species in growing *Vitis vinifera* grapes, but wines made from these species are not covered in this book.

There are several reasons why red and white table wines sometimes lack varietal character: 1. they may be blends in which no single variety is present in sufficient concentration to give the wine a recognizable aroma; 2. they may be made from grape varieties such as Burger or Carignane that lack distinctive aromatic chemicals in their juice or skins; 3. the weather in a particular growing season may have prevented normally distinctive grapes from fully developing their varietal aroma constituents (for example, in a rainy fall grapes may have to be harvested before they are fully mature to avoid losing them to diseases); and 4. the wine may have been made from grapes grown in an overcropped or otherwise mismanaged vineyard.

Naming Wines from Distinctive Grapes

Among the wines shown in Table 2.2 that are not only made from distinctive varieties of *Vitis vinifera* but also have varietal aromas, we find wines with both varietal and district names. Whether a distinctive varietal wine will be named after the grape from which it is principally made (common among wines made in U.S. *vinifera* areas and now being seen more often on imported wine labels) or after the district in which the grapes were grown (common among the well-known Italian, French, and German wines) depends on the traditions of the region and whether or not the district name itself has been used long enough to have any significance in the market. Clearly, if a wine with a district name shows a distinguishable varietal aroma, the mixture of grapes from which it was made must reflect a high proportion of the variety that has left its mark on the wine's odor.

As noted above and illustrated in Table 2.2, wines from both *Vitis vinifera* and non-*Vitis vinifera* species may fail to exhibit characteristic varietal aromas. Wines that lack varietal character may have generic, district, or (misleadingly) varietal names on their labels. Generic wines are those named after famous wine-growing areas in Europe (Rhine, Sauternes, Burgundy, Chablis, Chianti) or European wine types (hock, claret — the British terms for white wines from the Rhine and reds from Bordeaux) as well as those that just candidly admit their nonspecific nature — as in Adelsheim Vineyards' "Red Table Wine," whose label prominently and whimsically features a large red dining table.[32] In an off year, a winery may use a generic name for a wine that is legally eligible to carry a varietal designation so that consumers will not associate a lower-quality wine with its varietal line. For the same reason, France has an elaborate system of obligatory "demotions" that governs the naming of wines in off years to protect the most prestigious vineyard and village names in wine districts such as Burgundy.

Figure 2.15
Red Table Wine Label

Wine Styles

For any wine type — from Alicante Bouschet to Zinfandel — you will encounter a wide range of wines of distinctive styles in the market. Style refers to a winemaker's characteristic way of combining and balancing the sensory features that distinguish a particular type of wine to create an individualistic expression of that type. The wine type is analogous to a musical score or photographic negative, while a wine style is analogous to a particular performance of a musical score or a print made from a negative. In performing or printing, the musician or photographer makes her own interpretation of the notes on the page or the pattern of light-sensitive chemicals on the negative.

To define the style desired for a particular wine is to decide what emphasis to give to each of its characteristic sensory features — which ones should be brought out and which suppressed, and in what degree. The definition of a wine's style could include: the overall simplicity or complexity of its odors and flavors, the intensity of its varietal aroma and flavor, the predominance of fruit aromas or oak bouquet, the balance of its sugar and acid content (whether it will tend toward sweetness or tartness), and the amount of tannin the wine will contain when released to the market.

To create the defined style requires a mastery of grape growing and winemaking. Each feature of the style definition dictates a decision in the vineyard and winery. For example, to create "intense varietal character" requires planting a particular clone of that grape variety in the climate to which it is best adapted, training and pruning the vines for a moderate-sized crop, vigilant disease control, and optimum harvest timing, followed by juice extraction, fermentation, aging, and finishing operations at the winery conducted so that the varietal character is brought out and preserved in the wine.

Types and Styles in This Book

You will be better equipped to understand how wine styles are created after you read the chapters of this book that discuss winemaking and grape growing. The sensory evaluation exercises will introduce you to two dozen varietal wine types, including two styles of Chardonnay (one aged in oak and one aged with yeast but without oak) and two styles of Zinfandel (lighter- and heavier-bodied). The instructions in Appendix D for buying the wines for each tasting will describe the styles you need to shop for. To review and reinforce what you have learned about the sensory characteristics of varietal wines, at the end of each chapter and as a grand finale to the book you will classify the wines you have tasted and develop a systematic way to distinguish between them.

REVIEW QUESTIONS

Instructions: You might want to use a separate sheet of paper to answer the following review questions. In that way you can use the questions to check your knowledge of this chapter more than once. You may, for example, want to re-test yourself on items that you have missed or use the "Review Questions" to test your knowledge before you read a chapter. For the True or False items, answer "True" if the statement is accurate or "False" if the statement is incorrect. If you determine that a statement is false make a note explaining why. For the multiple choice items pick the best alternative. Check your answers after you have completed all the questions.

1. True or false: Perception refers to an organism's immediate neurological response to a stimulus in the environment. __F__ (SENSATION)

2. True or false: Sensory stimuli in wine are restricted to being either chemical or physical "activators." __F__ (CAN ALSO BE THERMAL)

3. The smallest concentration of a wine component required for a taster to name it — "By jove, that's **sweet**! — is called the _____ .
   A. difference threshold
   B. recognition threshold
   C. stimulus concentration
   D. sensation threshold
   E. jovial concentration

4. Refer to the label De Loach Vineyards Estate Bottled Russian River Valley Gewürztraminer 1987 Early Harvest. Given that "residual sugar 1.2% by wt" is about 1.2 grams per 100 ml, this wine would taste sweet to
   A. nearly everyone
   B. about 50% of people
   C. almost nobody
   D. 2.5% of people
   E. the information needed to answer this question is unknown to modern science

DE LOACH VINEYARDS

ESTATE BOTTLED
RUSSIAN RIVER VALLEY
GEWÜRZTRAMINER
1987 EARLY HARVEST

PRODUCED & BOTTLED BY DE LOACH VINEYARDS, INC.
SANTA ROSA, SONOMA COUNTY, CALIFORNIA
ALCOHOL 12.9% BY VOLUME   RESIDUAL SUGAR 1.2% BY WT.

5. True or false: Winetasting focuses on a relatively narrow range of existing colors. __F__

6. True or false: Wine sensory components such as color which evoke pleasure in and of themselves are said to have a hedonic quality. __T__

7. What sensory quality would **not** be expected from the clue "A white wine is very pale and nearly colorless?"
   A. intense fruit aromas
   B. low in alcohol
   C. light or thin-bodied
   D. high in acid, giving it a "green" taste
   E. possible sulfur dioxide off odor

8. True or false: Overall quality in red wines is correlated with total color and pigment content. __T__

9. True or false: Our appreciation of wines is mainly due to their odors. __T__

10. True or false: Flavors are actually odors — or "in-mouth smells" — that reach our olfactory epithelium when we hold the wine in our mouths. __T__

11. True or false: The maximum sensitivity of our sense of smell has been estimated at one part per 10,000. __F__ (ONE PART PER MILLION)

12. True or false: It has been estimated that the average person can learn as many as 200 odors. __F__ (1,000 ODERS)

13. True or false: The sensory organ for the sense of smell is located at the top and rear of the nasal cavity and about 5-10% of the air reaches it in normal breathing. __T__

14. What is the "retro-nasal route?" __PASSAGE WAY FROM BACK OF MOUTH TO OLFACTORY.__

15. True or false: We can only smell volatile molecules that can evaporate from the surface of a wine at the range of temperatures at which it is customarily served. __T__

16. Which of the winetasting activities listed below is not done to enhance a taster's ability to experience the wine's odors?
    A. sniff deeply
    B. swirl the wine in the glass
    C. hold the wine against a white background
    D. warm the wine in the mouth
    E. draw air through the wine
    F. sneeze

17. True or false: Winetasters may find that a wine's odors are stronger and more pleasant when they are experienced in the mouth as flavors rather than as odors entering the olfactory area in inhaled air. __T__

18. Which taste quality is very rare in wines?
    A. sweet   B. sour   C. bitter   D. salty   E. fruity

19. When is the mechanism of taste dependent on saliva? __SOLID SUBSTANCE MUST BE DESOLVED TO BE TASTED.__

20. Where are the papillae located that have very few taste buds in them?
    A. on the tip of the tongue
    B. along the side edges of the tongue
    C. on the tongue's top surface
    D. on the back of the tongue
    E. on the roof of the mouth

21. True or false: We should question the accuracy of the taste bud map of the tongue because we don't taste sweet or sour or bitter or salty in just one place. __T__

22. At a gross level we are most sensitive to which taste quality?
    A. sweetness   B. sourness   C. saltiness   (D.) bitterness   E. volatility

23. Which item on the list below is not perceived in wine with your sense of touch?
    A. bubbles of carbon dioxide
    B. high amounts of alcohol
    C. thickness or body
    (D.) acidity
    E. astringency

24. When the stimulus alcohol is present in high amounts in a wine, you can expect to experience both a taste and a tactile sensation. These sensations are
    A. green, smooth
    (B.) sweet, hot
    C. flat, rough
    D. hot, sweet
    E. hot, dry

25. True or false: Adaptation is a change in sensitivity that occurs in response to different levels of stimulation. Winetasters learn to work with olfactory adaptation by resting 15-45 seconds between sniffs when evaluating wines. __T__

26. True or false: An example of taste adaptation is the fact that we are unaware of the taste of our own saliva. __T__

1989
WILLAMETTE VALLEY
OREGON
DRY WHITE RIESLING

PRODUCED & BOTTLED BY
WILLIAM HILL WINERY
NAPA, CALIFORNIA
TABLE WINE

27. Refer to the label William Hill 1989 Willamette Valley Oregon Dry White Riesling. Which statement below is an accurate prediction of how you would expect this wine to taste and smell to most people?
    A. sweet
    B. without perceptible sweetness
    C. sweet and with an aroma which has an element that is like roses
    (D.) without perceptible sweetness and with an aroma which has an element that is like roses
    E. The label does not give enough information to make any prediction.

28. True or false: PTC tasting is a well-documented example of how dramatically people can vary in their ability to taste something bitter and it accurately predicts a person's sensitivity to bitterness in wines. _____

29. True or false: Anosmia can refer to the loss of a person's ability to smell all odors and the term "specific anosmia" is used when someone cannot detect a particular scent but otherwise has a normal sense of smell. _____

30. The "orange juice effect" is an example of
    A. a specific anosmia
    B. threshold enhancement
    C. odor adaptation
    D. a taste modifier
    E. stimulus error

31. You just served two glasses of De Loach Vineyards Estate Bottled Russian River Valley Gewürztraminer 1987 Early Harvest to a friend. One glass is colder and the other is warmer. When she tastes them, the warmer wine will seem
    A. less sweet   B. sweeter   C. the same

32. True or false: The NATIONAL GEOGRAPHIC Smell Survey found that olfactory sensitivity is reduced during pregnancy and that odor perception declines during aging. _____

33. True or false: Women are more able to learn to identify odors than men. _____

34. True or false: Blind tastings — in which the wines are identified only by a letter or numerical code — are designed to eliminate stimulus errors which occur when irrelevant criteria are used to judge wines. _____

35. True or false: Our ability to recall wine odors can be reduced by giving the odor a verbal structure, such as our associations with the odor and dictionary-style definitions. _____

36. True or false: The wine aroma wheel was designed to enhance the accuracy of communication about wine odors among members of the wine industry. _____

37. When judging the appearance of wines, the taster evaluates their
    A. Color   B. Clarity   C. Off odors   D. Taste sensations   E. Texture

38. True or false: The higher the alcohol content of a wine, the thicker the streams produced when the wine falls back down the side of the glass after it is swirled. _____

39. In white table wines, this color is a sign that the wine has been exposed to too much air in production or has been bottle aged too long
    A. very pale yellow-green
    B. pale yellow
    C. medium yellow
    D. gold
    E. brown

40. True or false: Within the normal color range for white table wines, darker colors are associated with oak barrel aging and/or later harvests. _____

41. True or false: Among red wines, a purple hue is associated with older, bottle-aged wines and the brick red hue is characteristic of young wines. _____

42. True or false: Because their detection and prevention is of central concern to winemakers, a very large number of off odors have been linked to particular diagnostic chemicals — such as acetic acid and ethyl acetate — which can be found by laboratory as well as sensory analysis. _____

43. In wine usage, _____ refers to the odors which come from the grape and _____ is used for smells that come from fermentation and aging in oak and bottle.
    A. grape volatiles, aging volatiles
    B. aroma, bouquet
    C. bouquet, aroma
    D. aromatics, volatiles
    E. romantics, volatiles

44. True or false: For a wine to have perceptible varietal aromas requires a particular grape variety, proper growing conditions, and careful winemaking. _____

45. True or false: The term "flavor components" is used for the chemicals responsible for a wine's taste and tactile sensations. _____

46. True or false: A wine with inadequate body would be correctly described as flat. _____

47. What sensation would you expect in your mouth when the stimulus tannin in the wine is low or absent?
     A. dry   B. flat   C. frizzante   D. still   E. smooth

48. True or false: You are tasting two White Riesling wines. They are identical except for sugar content. Wine A has three times as much sugar as wine B. When you taste the two wines, you expect wine A to have more body than wine B. _____

49. True or false: Great wines are distinguished from ordinary wines by their greater complexity, harmony, and the power to stimulate the emotions. _____

50. True or false: Serious wine tasters do not smoke during tastings and do not come to them wearing perfume, after-shave, or with recently-brushed teeth. _____

51. The glasses for winetastings are not
    A. funnel-shaped
    B. thin
    C. clear
    D. able to hold 8-10 ounces
    E. washed and stored so they do not pick up odors

52. This group of wines is served at the coldest temperature both in the restaurant and tasting laboratory:
    A. sparkling and sweet white
    B. dry white table
    C. light red table
    D. rose
    E. red table

53. Which tasting order would place the second wine at a disadvantage?
    A. white before red
    B. sweet before dry
    C. young before old
    D. modest before fine
    E. light-bodied before full-bodied

54. True or false: To inspect a wine for color, hold it up to a bright source of light such as a clear light bulb or candle. _____

55. True or false: Winetasters begin the olfactory stage of evaluating a wine by swirling the wine in the glass 6 or 8 quick revolutions and putting their noses into the glass and taking 4 or 5 quick, deep sniffs. _____

56. True or false: Winetasters draw some air through the wine so that all their taste buds can come into contact with the wine and the tactile receptors in their mouths can sense its sweetness and tartness. _____

57. True or false: A winetaster who is evaluating the quality of a wine will take time to notice — among other things — if the wine has a lot of odors and flavors or just a few, how well the individual parts fit together, and if it pleases him or her. _____

58. True or false: Table wines are also referred to as natural wines and contain 14% alcohol or less. _____

59. True or false: A clone is a subgroup of a grape species and is distinguished from other clones by economically important hereditary traits such as its climatic adaptation. _____

60. True or false: Varietal wines are made mainly from a single variety of grapes that should impart a characteristic aroma and flavor to the wine. _____

61. True or false: The wine type refers to a winemaker's characteristic way of combining and balancing the sensory features that distinguish a particular wine to create an individualistic expression of that wine. _____

62. True or false: You would expect a warmer glass of a wine to have more intense aromas compared to a colder glass of the same wine. _____

ANSWERS TO REVIEW QUESTIONS

1. False. Sensation does that.
2. False. Stimuli can also be thermal.
3. B
4. B. 1.2 grams per 100ml is close enough to the perception threshold of 1 gram per 100ml that the best answer on the list is B.
5. False. In winetasting we take advantage of a large part of our capacity to distinguish a wide range of colors from yellow-greens to brick reds and purples.
6. True
7. A
8. True
9. True
10. True
11. False. It's one part per million to several parts per trillion.
12. False. The estimates suggest we can learn about 1000 odors. Wine has about 200 odors.
13. True
14. It's the passageway from the rear of the mouth and rear nasal passages to the olfactory epithelium.
15. True
16. C. (F is not a common winetasting activity, although it can be a taster's response to the sulfur dioxide off odor.)
17. True
18. D
19. To be tasted a solid substance must be dissolved in the saliva. Without saliva to dissolve the substances that produce taste stimuli, we could only experience touch sensations with our mouths.
20. C
21. True
22. D
23. D
24. B
25. True
26. True
27. D
28. False. PTC tasting does not predict a person's sensitivity to bitterness in wines.
29. True
30. D
31. B
32. True, although the first part is contrary to many womens' perceptions of their individual experience.
33. True
34. True
35. False. Giving an odor a verbal structure, such as our associations with the odor and dictionary-style definitions, enhances our ability to recall its name.
36. True
37. B
38. False. The streams are thinner in higher alcohol wines.
39. E
40. True
41. False. Purple wines are younger and get more brick red with age.
42. True
43. B
44. True
45. False. The term "structural components" is used for the chemicals responsible for a wine's taste and tactile sensations.
46. False. A wine with inadequate body would be correctly described as thin.
47. F
48. True
49. True
50. True
51. A
52. A
53. B
54. False. To inspect a wine for color, hold it up to a white background.
55. False. Winetasters begin the olfactory stage of evaluating a wine by sniffing the wine without swirling and swirl 1-2 revolutions and sniff 2-3 times in the second stage.
56. False. Winetasters "chew" the wine so that all their taste buds can come into contact with the wine.
57. True
58. True
59. False. A grape variety is a subgroup of a grape species and is distinguished from other varieties by economically important hereditary traits such as its climatic adaptation. Clones are "sub-varieties."
60. True
61. False. Style refers to a winemaker's characteristic way of combining and balancing the sensory features.
62. True

ENDNOTES

[1] Peynaud, Emile, THE TASTE OF WINE, Wine Appreciation Guild, San Francisco, 1987, p. 23.

[2] Amerine, Maynard A., and Edward B. Roessler, WINES, THEIR SENSORY EVALUATION, W. H. Freeman and Co., New York, 1983, p. 82.

[3] Levine, Michael W., and Jeremy M. Shefner, FUNDAMENTALS OF SENSATION AND PERCEPTION, Brooks Cole Publishing Co., Pacific Grove, CA, pp. 65-114.

[4] Amerine, Maynard A., and Edward B. Roessler, WINES, THEIR SENSORY EVALUATION, W. H. Freeman and Co., New York,1983, pp. 27-28 and Emile Peynaud, THE TASTE OF WINE, Wine Appreciation Guild, San Francisco, 1987, pp. 332.

[5] Amerine, Maynard A., and Edward B. Roessler, WINES, THEIR SENSORY EVALUATION, W. H. Freeman and Co., New York, 1983, p. 29.

[6] Amerine, Maynard A., and Edward B. Roessler, WINES, THEIR SENSORY EVALUATION, W. H. Freeman and Co., New York, 1983, p. 42.

[7] Allen, Malcolm S., Michael J. Lacey, Roger L. Harris, and W. Vance Brown, "Contribution of Methoxypyrazines to Sauvignon Blanc Wine Aroma," *American Journal of Enology and Viticulture*, Vol. 42, No. 2, 1991, pp. 109-112.

[8] Reed, Randall, "How Does the Nose Know?," *Cell*, Vol. 60, 1-2, January 12, 1990.

[9] Wysocki, Charles J., Kathleen M. Dorries, and Gary K. Beauchamp, "Ability to Perceive Androstenone Can Be Acquired by Ostensibly Anosmic People," *Proceedings of the National Academy of Science, USA,* Vol. 86, pp. 7976-7978, October 1989.

[10] Buck, Linda, and Richard Axel, "A Novel Multigene Family May Encode Odorant Receptors: A Molecular Basis for Odor Recognition," *Cell*, Vol. 65, April 1991, pp. 175-187.

[11] Winetasters and dogs sniff repeatedly to get a better picture of their odorous surroundings, but recent research in human odor perception by D. G. Laing suggests that this may not be the optimum method and that a single, natural sniff may produce better results. Winetasters will probably continue to sniff more often, perhaps as an aid to concentration rather than perception. This work is cited in Avery N. Gilbert and Morley R. Kare, "A Consideration of Some Psychological and Physiological Mechanisms of Odour Perception," PERFUMES: ART, SCIENCE, AND TECHNOLOGY, P. Müller and D. Lamparsky, editors, Elsevier Applied Science, 1991, Chapter 5, pp. 127-149.

[12] Rozin, Paul, "Taste-smell Confusion and the Duality of the Olfactory Sense," *Perception and Psychophysics,* Vol. 3, No. 4, 1982, pp. 397-401 and personal communication February 20, 1992.

[13] Paul Rozin found that seven out of nine languages he investigated by testing and interviewing bilingual English speakers do not distinguish between flavor and taste. In addition to English, the languages that have different words for taste and flavor are French ("gout" and "saveur/parfum") and Hungarian ("iz" and "zamat"); those he studied that did not make the distinction were Spanish (sabor), German (geschmack), Czech (chut), Hebrew (ta'am), Hindi (svad), Tamil (ruci), and Mandarin Chinese (wei). This work is described in Rozin, Paul, "Taste-smell Confusions and the Duality of the Olfactory Sense," *Perception and Psychophysics,* Vol. 3, No. 4, 1982, pp. 398-399.

[14] Kinnamon, Sue, "Taste Transduction: A Diversity of Mechanisms," *Trends in Neurosciences*, Vol. 11, No. 11, 1988, pp. 491-496.

[15] Linda Bartoshuk, and Beverly Cowart, personal communications, February 14, 1992 and February 17, 1992, and Levine, Michael W., and Jeremy M. Shefner, FUNDAMENTALS OF SENSATION AND PERCEPTION, Brooks Cole Publishing Co., Pacific Grove, CA, pp. 573-586.

[16] Beverly Cowart, personal communication, February 17, 1992. The estimates she presented for human thresholds for sweet, salty, sour, and bitter were .01 Molar for sucrose, .001 M for sodium chloride, .0001 M for citric acid, and .00001 M to .000001 M for quinine sulfate. The threshold for other bitter substances is lower and may vary for other sweet, salty, and sour stimuli.

[17] Pangborn, R., "Individuality in Responses to Sensory Stimuli," and R. Harper, "The Nature and Importance of Individual Differences," in CRITERIA OF FOOD ACCEPTANCE, J. Solms and R. I. Hall, editors, Forster Publishing Ltd., Zurich, Switzerland, pp. 177-219 and 220-237.

[18] Bartoshuk, Linda M., "Separate Worlds of Taste," *Psychology Today,* September 1980, p. 58.

[19] Wolsk, David quoted in Young, Alan, MAKING SENSE OF WINE, p. 85.

[20] Steiman, Harvey, "The Mystery Of Taste," *The Wine Spectator,* July 31, 1988, p. 19.

[21] Pelchat, Marcia, "Examining the Senses," Society of Wine Educators Conference, August 2, 1991.

[22] Bartoshuk, Linda M., "Separate Worlds of Taste," *Psychology Today,* September 1980, pp. 48-57.

[23] Gilbert, Avery N., and Charles J. Wysocki, "The Smell Survey Results," *National Geographic*, October 1987, pp. 514-525.

[24] Wysocki, Charles J., Kathleen M. Dorries, and Gary K. Beauchamp, "Ability to Perceive Androstenone Can Be Acquired by Ostensibly Anosmic People," *Proceedings of the National Academy of Science, USA,* Vol. 86, pp. 7976-7978, October 1989.

[25] Amoore, J. E., "Specific Anosmia and the Concept of Primary Odors," *Chem Senses Flavor*, Vol. 2, 1977, pp. 267-281.

[26] Levine, Michael W., and Jeremy M. Shefner, FUNDAMENTALS OF SENSATION AND PERCEPTION, Brooks Cole Publishing Co., Pacific Grove, CA, p. 579.

[27] Heintz, Christi, "Toward Understanding the Interaction Between People and Wine: Humans as Sensory Instruments," Society of Wine Educator's Professional Seminar, August 7, 1986.

[28] McBurney, D. H., and T. R. Schick, "Taste and Water Taste of Twenty-six Compounds for Man," *Percept. Psychophys.*, Vol. 10, 1971, pp. 249-252, quoted in Lawless, Harry T., Gustatory Psychophysics, Chapter 17 of NEUROBIOLOGY OF TASTE AND SMELL, Thomas E. Finger and Wayne L. Silver, editors, John Wiley and Sons, New York, 1987, pp. 401-420 (quote on p. 409).

[29] Keehn, Karen, THE STRUCTURE OF WINE, A TREATISE ON WINE AND ITS INTERACTION WITH FOOD, McDowell Valley Vineyards Food and Wine Series IV, McDowell Valley Vineyards, Hopland, CA, p. 10.

[30] Gilbert, Avery N., and Charles J. Wysocki, "The Smell Survey Results," *National Geographic*, October 1987, p. 520.

[31] Engen, Trygg, "Remembering Odors and Their Names," *American Scientist*, Vol. 75, 1985, pp. 497-50.

[32] Amerine, Maynard A., and Edward B. Roessler, WINES, THEIR SENSORY EVALUATION, W. H. Freeman and Co., New York, 1983, pp. 59-64.

[33] Pelchat, Marcia, "Examining the Senses," Society of Wine Educators Conference, August 2, 1991, and Gregg Eric Arn Solomon, "Psychology of Novice and Expert Wine Talk," *American Journal of Psychology*, Vol. 103, No. 4, Winter 1990, pp. 495-517.

[34] Reviewed in Lawless, Harry and Trygg Engen, "Associations to Odors: Interference, Mnemonics, and Verbal Learning," *Journal of Experimental Psychology: Human Learning and Memory* 177, Vol. 3, No. 1, pp. 52-59.

[35] Rabin, Michael D., and William S. Cain, "Odor Recognition: Familiarity, Identifiability, and Encoding Consistency," *Journal of Experimental Psychology: Learning, Memory, and Cognition*, Vol. 10, No. 2, 1984, pp. 306-325.

[36] Lyman, Brian L., and Mark A. McDaniel, "Effects of Encoding Strategy on Long-Term Memory for Odors," *Quarterly Journal of Experimental Psychology,* Vol. 38A, 1986, pp. 753-765.

[37] Rabin, Michael D., and William S. Cain, "Odor Recognition: Familiarity, Identifiability, and Encoding Consistency," *Journal of Experimental Psychology: Learning, Memory, and Cognition,* Vol. 10, No 2, 1984, p. 317.

[38] Lawless, Harry T., "Psychological Perspectives on Wine-etasting and Recognition of Volatile Flavours," ALCOHOLIC BEVERAGES, edited by G. G. Birch and M. G. Lindley, Elsevier Applied Science Publishers, New York, 1985, pp. 97-113.

[39] Lawless, Harry T., "Psychological Perspectives on Wine-tasting and Recognition of Volatile Flavors," ALCOHOLIC BEVERAGES, edited by G. G. Birch and M. G. Lindley, Elsevier Applied Science Publishers, New York, 1985, p. 102.

[40] For more associations see Table D.3 in the discussion of how to do Sensory Evaluations Exercise 4.1 in Appendix D.

[41] Noble, A. C., R. A. Arnold, J. Buechsenstein, E. J. Leach, J. O. Schmidt, and P. M. Stern, "Modification of a Standardized System of Wine Aroma Terminology," *American Journal of Enology and Viticulture,* Vol. 38, No. 3, 1987, pp. 143-146.

[42] The Sparkling Wine Aroma Wheel and Wine Aroma Wheel can be obtained in a very useful laminated form from Ms. Lee Curtis at The Wordmill, P.O. Box 1817, Healdsburg, CA 95448.

[43] Anonymous, DESCRIPTIVE WORDS FOR WINES, The Wine Institute, San Francisco, 1962, and various pages from Amerine, Maynard A., and Edward B. Roessler, WINES, THEIR SENSORY EVALUATION, W. H. Freeman and Co., New York, 1983.

[44] Young, Alan, MAKING SENSE OF WINE, Greenhouse Publications, Richmond, Australia, 1986, and ACADEMIE DU VIN COMPLETE WINE COURSE, by Steven Spurrier and Michel Dovas, G. P. Putnam's Sons, New York, 1983.

[45] Rapp, A., and P. J. Pretorius, "Foreign and Undesirable Flavors in Wine, Flavors and Off-Flavors," PROCEEDINGS OF THE 6TH INTERNATIONAL FLAVOR CONFERENCE, RETHYMNON, CRETE, July 5-7 1989, G. Charalambous, editor, Elsevier Science Publishers, Amsterdam, pp. 1-21.

[46] See the glossary of WINES, THEIR SENSORY EVALUATION, for many examples.

[47] Amerine, Maynard A., and Edward B. Roessler, WINES, THEIR SENSORY EVALUATION, W. H. Freeman and Co., New York, 1983, pp. 3-11; Peynaud, Emile, THE TASTE OF WINE, Wine Appreciation Guild, San Francisco, 1987, pp. 220-223; Young, Alan, MAKING SENSE OF WINE, Greenhouse Publications, Richmond, Australia, 1986, pp. 15-23.

[48] Young, Alan, MAKING SENSE OF WINE, Greenhouse Publications, Richmond, Australia, 1986, p. 19.

[49] Guinard, Jean-Xavier, and Margaret Cliff, "Descriptive Analysis of Pinot Noir Wines from Carneros, Napa, and Sonoma," *American Journal of Enology and Viticulture,* Vol. 38, No. 3, pp. 211-215.

[50] This table is based on the work of Maynard Amerine. A more detailed discussion of the organoleptic classification of wines can be found in Amerine, Maynard A., and Edward B. Roessler, WINES, THEIR SENSORY EVALUATION, W. H. Freeman and Co., New York, 1983, pp. 87-138, and Amerine, M. A., and V. L. Singleton, WINE, AN INTRODUCTION, University of California Press, Berkeley, 1977, pp. 75-88.

[51] Natural wines of alcohol contents in excess of 14% are taxed at the higher rate of $3.15 per gallon — instead of $1.57 per gallon — by the U.S. Government. The tax on fortified wines — still wines with alcohol contents between 21% and 24% — is $3.30 per gallon. These tax rates went into effect in 1991, replacing the earlier rates of $0.17, $0.67, and $2.25 per gallon for still wines with alcohol contents of not over 14%, 14 to 21%, and 21 to 24%, respectively.

[52] In Appendix B you will learn that, according to U.S. wine labelling law, there are only two generic wines — sake and vermouth — and that the wines I've named here are technically "semi-generic." This means they require the use of the name of the place where the grapes were grown to distinguish them from their European counterparts: New York Chablis or Missouri Hock, for example.

3

THE SCIENCE OF WINEMAKING
White Table Wine Production

Grape growers and winemakers manage natural processes both to grow grapes and to convert them into wine. The ability to grow the kind and quality of fruit needed and to produce wines with the desired characteristics requires an intimate understanding of how grapes grow and respond to their environment and of the biological and chemical events of wine production. The sciences of viticulture and enology play crucial roles in our ability to make good wines.

In this chapter I will explain how white table wines are typically made in California. At each step I will define key terms and briefly explain the underlying biological and chemical processes. The goal of this and the other winemaking chapters in this book is to provide you with enough basic scientific and technical knowledge so that you can 1. understand the sequence of winemaking steps described on winery tours; 2. interpret the technical information on wine labels and in winery educational materials and newsletters; and 3. understand how some of the most important sensory features of wines arise in their production. Chapter 11 on grape growing will discuss how vineyard practices influence wine quality.

MAKING TABLE WINES —THE OVERALL PROCESS

The following is a general sequence of the steps used in all table wine production.

1. Envision the type and style of wine to be made.
2. Choose the most suitable grape varieties.
3. Contract for grape production in the appropriate climatic region.
4. Consult with growers on critical cultural practices.
5. Follow the grapes' ripening closely.
6. Pick the fruit quickly at its optimum ripeness.
7. Remove the juice from the grapes.
8. Conduct the fermentation.
9. Clarify and stabilize the new wine.
10. Age the wine in bulk.
11. Blend and finish the wine.
12. Bottle the wine.
13. Age the bottled wine.
14. Release the wine into the market for sale.
15. Protect against spoilage at all times and follow the process with sensory evaluation and laboratory analysis.

This chapter will discuss each of these steps and follow that general discussion with some specific examples of how winemakers can combine these steps and vary their execution to create white table wines of different types and styles.

STEP 1. ENVISION THE TYPE AND STYLE OF WINE TO BE MADE

The types and styles of white table wines that are available in the United States today are based largely on the white wines of France and Germany. They range in type from simple, inexpensive, usually generic "jug" wines for the mass market to premium varietal wines with special aromas and bouquets. A typical winery will make many types of wines, each in a distinctive, unique style whose creation requires the imagination and skill of the winemaker and grape growers and reflects the position of that winery's products in the market.

In Chapter 2 the discussion of Table 2.2 considered some examples of the sensory factors that are involved in defining various styles of table wines. Each factor — from the distinctiveness of the aroma to the sugar and alcohol concentrations and whether or not the wine should contain the bouquet of oak aging — in turn determines a step in grape growing, winemaking, or both. For example, wines that are to have a recognizable varietal character need to be made from certain grape varieties grown in cooler climates. If the wine does not require varietal character, the grapes can be from any one of a wide range of varieties grown in any climate or may be a blend of several varieties. Usually warm climates are chosen in such cases for their ability to produce larger crops. Because non-grape sugars cannot be added to wines in California, the decision to produce a dry or a sweet wine can determine how the alcoholic fermentation is managed, just as a requirement for oak-aging bouquet will dictate the choice of aging vessel. These and many other ways to vary the steps in winemaking to create wines of different styles will be discussed below.

STEPS 2 AND 3. THE GRAPES — VARIETIES AND CONTRACTS

Picking the right combination of grape variety and climate is one of the most critical decisions affecting quality in winemaking. For premium white table wine production in California cooler growing regions are preferred, and the grape varieties considered most desirable are Chardonnay, Sauvignon Blanc, Sémillon, White Riesling, and Gewürztraminer. Chenin Blanc, French Colombard, Grey Riesling, and Sylvaner grapes are also used for premium wines occasionally, and when grown in warmer climates, for ordinary, often generically labelled, white wines. Thompson Seedless, a neutral-flavored grape variety grown for raisins and fresh fruit, is also used for jug wine production in California, although it diminishes in importance every year.[1]

Wineries that wish to assure themselves of a stable supply of high-quality grapes will enter into long-term contracts with independent grape growers or will grow grapes themselves on their own land. In California, contracts are more common, and payments to growers are based on the composition of the grapes at harvest measured in terms of their sugar and acid concentrations and the strength of the acids (pH). Growers also may be asked to modify their cultural practices to produce the exact characteristics a winery desires.

STEP 4. CONSULT WITH GROWERS ON CRITICAL CULTURAL PRACTICES

Growing grapes for premium wine production has been described as "farming for flavors."[2] It has long been known that the match between grape variety and climate is important for proper development of varietal aromas and flavors in wine grapes and that lower yields per acre correlate with higher-quality fruit and wine. Now grape growers are beginning to understand more clearly how other factors in site selection and vineyard management can influence the flavors of the resulting wine. Precisely which factors are the most important depends on the particular grape variety being cultivated. I'll use the example of Sauvignon Blanc to describe some of these factors briefly at this point so that you can get a feeling for the relationship between farming practices and wine aroma and flavor. Grape growing methods will be discussed in more detail in Chapter 11.

The composition of grapes is influenced by factors that modify their temperature and light-sensitive physiological processes, including those that produce color, sugars, acids, and aroma and flavor chemicals. Some of the aroma- and flavor-modifying factors cannot be altered very much by cultural practices and have to be decided upon when the vineyard is planted. Grape variety, soil depth and texture, and climate are examples of these more fixed factors. Climate refers to the generally prevailing weather conditions in a region — temperature, wind speed, rainfall, etc. — averaged over a series of years. Climatologists recognize three levels of climate, depending on the size of the area involved. A macroclimate is the overall climate of a particular region — the Rhine Valley or the Sauternes region, for example; a mesoclimate exists on a smaller scale and differs from the macroclimate of its region due to variations in altitude, aspect, topography, soil type, distance from a river, etc.; and a microclimate exists immediately within and around the grapevine canopy.[3] When a site is selected and the vineyard is planted, its macroclimate and mesoclimate are fixed. The canopy microclimate, in contrast, is one of the most important manageable factors that affects the aroma and flavor of the grapes and wine.

Fixed factors such as grape variety, soil, and climate as well as cultural decisions concerning variable factors such as irrigation and fertilization influence how vigorously a grapevine will grow. A vigorous vine will produce an abundance of leaves and shoots but relatively few flowers and fruit, and its canopy will be very dense and shady. Controlling vine vigor is one of the most important goals of wine grape cultivation and is accomplished by carefully matching the variety to vineyard soil and mesoclimate, giving the vines just enough water and nutrients, and controlling their size and shape. Once the overall vigor level of the vines is established, their canopy microclimate — specifically, the degree to which foliage and fruit are exposed to light — can be fine-tuned during each growing season by the positioning of shoots and especially by the removal of leaves around the fruit at critical periods during the summer. Canopy management is extremely important for influencing wine flavor: viticultural researchers in British Columbia, Canada, for example, have found that Gewürztraminer, Riesling, and Muscat fruits have more of their distinctive flavor compounds when exposed to the sun.[4] Leaf removal after fruit-set to increase exposure to sunlight was mentioned most frequently when a group of California and Washington State Sauvignon Blanc growers was asked to name the vineyard practices they used to influence the aroma and flavor of their gold medal-winning wines.[5]

The aroma and flavor of Sauvignon Blanc can range from a fruity quality to a celery/fresh vegetable, herbaceous, or grassy character. It is the presence of unimaginably tiny amounts of methoxypyrazines — the odor threshold is 5 parts per trillion! — that give Sauvignon Blancs these aroma notes. (If you have a good memory and have already read Chapter 2, you may recall that a related compound gives Cabernet Sauvignon its "bell pepper" varietal aroma.[6]) If the amounts of these methoxypyrazines are reduced in grape growing, fruity flavors of grapefruit, pineapple, melon, and fig emerge. The surveyed grape growers manage both soil and vine canopy factors to reduce the grassy characteristics of their Sauvignon Blanc grapes and the resulting wines. The four factors and practices they named, in order of frequency, and how they generally influence grassiness are summarized in Table 3.1.

Table 3.1
Vineyard Factors and Viticultural Practices Influencing Grassiness in Sauvignon Blanc Grapes and Wines

Vineyard Factor	Promotes Grassy Flavors	Encourages Fruity Flavors
Canopy	heavy, dense, shady	open, sunny
Soil	heavy, rich	shallower, less fertile
Fertilization	more	less
Irrigation	apply more water	apply less water

Among the survey respondents, as noted above, canopy management was considered the single most important management tool available to influence the nature of Sauvignon Blanc flavor. Removing the leaves next to the fruit exposes the fruit to more sunlight, allowing the fruit to ripen with a more golden color and fruity flavors; leave these leaves and grassy flavors result. It's not clear how this works, but Professor Ann Noble offers the tantalizing fact that the chemical responsible for the bell pepper odor in Cabernet Sauvignon can be broken down by light.

The other three factors influencing Sauvignon Blanc character can be considered together. Soil characteristics and management practices that increase vine vigor all increase grassiness. This includes heavier and richer soils that naturally hold more water and contain more nutrients, as well as irrigation and fertilizer regimes that add more water and nutrients. Grassiness will be limited when nature and management limit vine vigor by growing vines in shallow, naturally less fertile soils that cannot hold as much water in reserve and by adding limited amounts of fertilizer and irrigation water. Winemaking techniques can also influence the amount of grassiness. This will be discussed at the end of the chapter.

For premium wine production the importance of close cooperation between wineries and grape growers to identify and use the cultural practices that will produce the best possible fruit cannot be overemphasized. The increasing use of the term "winegrowing" by some of California's most progressive premium wineries reflects the tight linkage between grape and wine quality. A grape grower who thinks of herself as a winegrower will understand the relationship between cultural practices and wine quality and work closely with the winery that buys her grapes. From the winery's perspective, winegrowing means more attention to this same relationship between wine quality and viticulture, close relations with growers, longer-term contracts, and, probably, research to define more closely the parameters affecting grape quality. This kind of research is exemplified by the work being done at Robert Mondavi Winery to define with greater precision such cultural practices as leaf removal to modify Sauvignon Blanc flavor.[7]

STEP 5. FOLLOW THE GRAPES' RIPENING CLOSELY
What Chemical Changes Are Occurring in the Grapes?

When grapes ripen, they get bigger and softer, their green color fades, aromatic compounds increase, sugars increase, and both total acid concentration and acid strength decrease. The concentration of red pigments increases in the skins of red grapes. For winemaking purposes, the ripening process is followed by measuring the total sugar and acid contents of the grapes and determining the strength of the acids. During ripening, photosynthesis and storage of the sugar it produces increase the sugar content of the grapes; at the same time dilution through increased water storage and respiration decrease both acid content and acid strength. The concentrations of aroma components also increase. Because they are each important for wine quality, I will discuss each of these aspects of ripening further and explain how each is measured.

Aroma Components Increase

Among the grape components most critical for high-quality varietal wines are the aroma components, but, as you learned in Chapter 2, the key aroma chemicals have been identified for only a handful of grape varieties. Even if more aroma chemicals were known, it probably would not be of practical use because these elusive compounds occur in tiny amounts that cannot be measured quickly on a routine basis with present technology. We do know that for most grape varieties there is a rough correlation between increasing amounts of sugar and higher concentrations of aroma components, so winemakers rely on that relationship and on experience with each grape variety to estimate optimum ripeness.

Sugars Increase

For winemaking the most important sugars in grape juice are the simple compounds glucose and fructose. (Table sugar, sucrose, is a molecule of glucose joined to a molecule of fructose.) The amount of glucose and fructose in grape juice is estimated by measuring the density of the grape juice, expressed in units called "degrees Brix" (°Brix — pronounced "Bricks") that correspond to the percentage by weight of sugar in the juice. One degree Brix is a density corresponding to about one percent sugar. In early summer, before ripening begins, the sugar content of grapes is about one degree Brix. Their sugar content increases as ripening proceeds because glucose produced by photosynthesis in the green parts of grapevines is stored in the fruit. An enzyme converts some of the glucose into fructose. These two simple sugars are present in grape juice in about equal proportions.

The correct ripeness for harvest depends on the type and style of wine for which the grapes will be used. It takes about two degrees Brix in grape juice to make one percent alcohol in the finished wine, and winemakers decide when the grapes are ripe on that basis. Other important sensory characteristics are also related to the °Brix at harvest; the following table shows some examples.

Table 3.2
Optimum Harvest Ripeness for Four Wine Types

Wine Type	Desired % Alcohol	Optimum °Brix at Harvest	Other Important Sensory Characteristics of Ripened Grapes
Sparkling	9-10 (of 12*)	17-19	Tart, low varietal aroma
White Table	10-13	21-23	Varietal aroma, tart
Red Table	11-13	22-24	Varietal aroma, medium color
Dessert	Fortified to 17-22	23-24	Deep color, high sugar

*An additional fermentation is carried out in making sparkling wines, raising the alcohol content by 1-2%, so the sugar in the fruit needs to produce only 9-10% of the final 12% alcohol content.

Total Acid Content Decreases

In June and July before grapes start to ripen, their total acidity is between two and four percent — or 2.0 to 4.0 grams of total acid per 100 milliliters (ml) of grape juice — and consists primarily of two organic acids, tartaric and malic. The total acidity drops sharply to about half its original amount when the grapes undergo a dramatic mid-summer burst of growth, and it declines further as ripening continues because grapevines metabolize some of their malic acid each night to create energy in a process called respiration. On cool nights the grapes need less energy and use up less malic acid. That is why grapes from two vineyards with the same hot daytime temperatures can have different acid compositions: mountain locations with cooler nighttime temperatures produce fruit that is higher in malic acid than that produced in valley sites where it stays warm all night. The total acidity at harvest ranges from 0.4 to 1.4 grams per 100 ml depending on the grape variety, temperatures during ripening, and date of harvest. The total acidity of finished wines will normally be lower.

Acid Strength Weakens

More important for wine quality than the decrease in the total amount of acid in grapes is the weakening of acid strength. The strength of acids is measured in pH units, where the p stands for power and the H for hydrogen ion concentration, the property that gives a solution, such as grape juice or wine, its acidity. The lower the pH, the stronger the acid. Grape juices and wines are moderately strong acids, with pH values in the range of 2.5 to 4.0. For every decrease of 1.0 unit in the pH scale, the strength of the acidity increases ten times.[8] Grape juice samples from different vineyards or vintages can have the same total acidity but vary in their acid strengths as reflected in different pH values.

At the beginning of ripening, typical pH values will be around 2.5-2.8, but the strength of the acids decreases about ten fold during the ripening process so that the final pH values at harvest will be 3.4-3.8. Grape juice acid strength weakens because hydrogen ions are lost during the ripening process. Whenever a grapevine takes in potassium, a required mineral nutrient, from the soil and moves it from the roots into a leaf or berry cell, the first root cell and each cell through which a potassium ion moves loses a hydrogen ion for each potassium ion taken in. Every time a grape berry cell gets a needed potassium ion it must give up a hydrogen ion, thus weakening its acid strength. The amount of potassium a grape berry takes in during ripening depends on the length of the maturation period and the size of the crop (number of berries per vine), and it varies a great deal between varieties and growing seasons.[9]

The optimum harvest pH depends on the grape variety and winemaking purpose, but values of 3.5 or less are preferred. The acidity of finished wines will usually be a little stronger than the grape juices from which they were made, giving them somewhat lower pH values. Wines with higher acid strengths have brighter colors, require smaller amounts of sulfur dioxide to protect them (see below), and, most important, more easily resist oxidation and the attacks of spoilage-causing microbes.

How Do We Find Out What's Happening in the Grapes? Measuring Maturity
Our Senses Can't Keep Up With the Crush

The sugar and acid contents of grape juice can be measured organoleptically, but sensory evaluation is rarely used for routine maturity estimates, because as the harvest approaches, very large numbers of samples need to be analyzed and even the best palates couldn't keep up with the volume. Refractometers — sturdy little instruments that look like small telescopes — are employed in the field to estimate degrees Brix by measuring the ability of a juice sample to bend light. Delicate glass hydrometers similar to the ones used to determine if your car battery has a full charge are also used for this purpose, usually in a lab: the more sugar in the grape juice sample, the denser the juice and the higher the hydrometer floats in the sample. Hydrometers can also be used to measure the disappearance of sugars during fermentation. Total acidity is estimated by determining how much of a basic solution is necessary to neutralize the acid in a sample of grape juice, and acid strength is measured with a pH meter.

Figure 3.1
A hydrometer in use by a student doing a home-winemaking project. Note the sediment of lees in the jar of juice in the background. This is the sediment that is partially removed by settling and racking, filtration, or centrifugation in a winery.
Photo: Richard Meade.

It's the Sample That Matters

No matter what method is used to determine the maturity of grapes — from organoleptic evaluation to measurements with the newest laboratory instruments — the analysis can only be as good as the sample of fruit from the vineyard. Great care should be taken to collect a representative sample of grapes that will accurately predict the ripeness of the harvest from the whole vineyard. Grapes in parts of the vineyard that are a little cooler — for example, areas with clay soils, on north-facing slopes, or where fog lingers — will ripen more slowly and need to be sampled separately.

Years ago a former University of California at Davis enology classmate who was working in the Napa Valley told me a story that drove home the importance of proper sampling. A grower brought in a couple of clusters of his prize Zinfandel grapes for my friend to analyze for maturity. Ben cautioned him that the sugar and acid measurements for just two clusters might not accurately predict the ripeness of his whole vineyard, but he went ahead to determine that in that sample the maturity was nearly ideal: the sugar was at 22.7 degrees Brix and the total acid was 0.8 grams/100 ml. With this "good news" and ignoring Ben's cautions, the soon-to-be-less-happy grower went home and harvested his entire (and, thankfully, relatively small) acreage. When the maturity of the whole harvest was determined at delivery, the sugar was a meager 19.7 and the acid very high at 1.3 grams/100 ml — a juice composition suitable, at best, for blending wine and making the grape crop worth a whole lot less than it would have been if picked at the proper maturity.

STEP 6. PICK THE FRUIT QUICKLY AT ITS OPTIMUM RIPENESS
The Decision to Harvest Must Take into Account Whether Ripening Can Continue

During the fall when their fruit is ripening, grapevines are becoming dormant and wet winter weather is approaching. This means that questions about the vines' capacity to go on ripening

Figure 3.2
Delivering grapes
into a receiving
hopper — not to
be confused with the
crusher, into which
the helical conveyer
at the bottom of the
hopper will deliver
the clusters

*Figure 3.2
Delivering grapes
into a receiving
hopper — not to
be confused with the
crusher, into which
the helical conveyer
at the bottom of the
hopper will deliver
the clusters*

the grapes must be considered along with the chemical composition of the grape berries. In deciding when to pick the fruit at a particular site, grape growers and winemakers ask, "Are these grapevines healthy and active enough to continue ripening their fruit further, weather permitting?" To answer this question, they would consider, for example, whether the soils have enough stored water to support more ripening and whether photosynthesis is still actively producing sugars or has slowed down because shortening days have signalled the onset of winter dormancy. They must also consider whether rain is threatening that would dilute the grape sugars and foster mold growth. Sometimes the decision to harvest at less than optimum maturities is forced upon vintners by cool or wet autumn weather.

Hands or Machines?

When the decision to pick has been made, a rapid harvest and prompt delivery of the fruit is essential to minimize browning and other undesirable changes. Harvesting by hand usually begins in the earliest morning hours so that cool fruit can be delivered to the winery. Mechanical harvesting also may be used to speed up the process of getting cool grapes off the vines. The grapes of some fragile varieties are broken and juice is released by mechanical harvesting so they have to be hand picked or machine harvested very carefully. To eliminate the difficulty and expense of mechanical harvesting, some wineries have experimented with illumination systems to enable harvest crews to work at night.

STEP 7. REMOVE THE JUICE FROM THE GRAPES

*Figure 3.3
A Simplified
Diagrammatic
Cross-Section of
a Grape Berry*

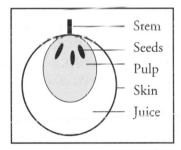

Stem
Seeds
Pulp
Skin
Juice

The process of juice removal — involving crushing and pressing the fruit — normally initiates the winemaking process at the winery, though it can be done in the field with or without mechanical harvesting. For some varieties there may be an interval of skin contact between crushing and pressing to extract more varietal character, and sulfur dioxide is often first added at this point. Let's take a look at each of these phases of juice removal.

Crushing Just Breaks the Skins

*Figure 3.4
A typical stemmer-crusher
located in a pit outside a
California winery so that
grapes can be fed into it
by gravity from the
receiving hopper located
to the left and above:
grape clusters are fed into
the crusher at the left,
must is pumped out from
the bottom by the large
pump in the foreground,
and stems exit on the right.*

Although some white wines — especially the base wines for sparkling wine production —

are made without crushing, this step typically initiates the winemaking process, whether in the field or at the winery. Crushing ideally involves only breaking the skins of the grape berries to allow the juice to flow out without any damage to the seeds, stems, and skins. Because these parts of the grape contain high concentrations of tannin, injury to them can add astringency and bitterness to the juice and wine. For this reason the well-padded but firm human foot makes a nearly ideal — if hard to mechanize — crushing apparatus. Most wineries use machines that combine crushing with destemming and locate them outside, adjacent to the winery. **Must** is the term used for the mixture of juice, seeds, stems, and skins produced by crushing. This term may also refer to the juice produced by pressing; thus in its broadest usage, "must" is the ferment-

Figure 3.5
View inside the stemmer-crusher in Figure 3.4 if the panel at the right end is removed: grape clusters fall into the center of the crusher and the berries are rubbed off the stems by the curved blades attached to the central shaft and then pushed through the holes in the stainless-steel cylinder. Crushing occurs at whatever point in this process the skin is broken.

able material produced by crushing or pressing. If the must is not already cool, it may be pumped through a heat exchanger to chill it to 50-60 degrees F as it is transferred to the press or into a tank for skin contact. The must may be sent to the press via a juice separator to remove the free-run juice so that the press will be filled efficiently with a less juicy mixture. ("Free-run" is the winemaking term for the juice that flows naturally from crushed grapes and from must that is squeezed gently rather than pressed.)

Adding Sulfur Dioxide

Sulfur dioxide (SO_2) is typically added to the whole fruit or must at crushing. It is a chemical that has been added in various forms to wines since the ancient winemakers of Egypt and Rome learned of its ability to prevent wine spoilage. In addition to slowing down the growth of microbes that can spoil wines, sulfur dioxide is also able to protect the juice and wine from reactions with oxygen that can lead to both browning of pigments and deterioration of aroma and flavor. SO_2 is normally introduced in the crusher to inhibit the off-odor-producing fermentations of wild yeast and bacteria that are naturally present on the skins of the grapes. Winemakers like to maintain SO_2 at very low levels (35-125 parts per million) and, because SO_2 gradually becomes inactivated when bound to certain wine components or combined with oxygen, they monitor and adjust its level by adding small amounts of it at intervals during the winemaking process.

Winemakers want to use as little SO_2 as possible for two reasons: it can add a pungent off odor (like that of match heads) to wine; and attention has been drawn to SO_2 use in all food products by concern over allergic reactions to it in a small proportion of consumers who are sulfite-sensitive.[10] From this point of view zero parts per million would be desirable, but because the yeast will release around 5 to 10 ppm during fermentation it is impossible to make a wine completely free of any SO_2.[11] However, research is ongoing to discover ways to make fine wines with little or no added SO_2. For example, good disease control in the vineyard can reduce mold on the fruit, making it possible to use less SO_2 at the winery. Cooling the must retards both reactions with oxygen and the growth of microbes so that less SO_2 is required to protect aroma and flavor. Some wineries have stopped using SO_2 to prevent browning, instead allowing the colorless pigments of white juices to turn brown and then removing the brown pigments. I think it is safe to predict that SO_2 levels in California wines will continue to drop from their already very low levels, but it is extremely unlikely that SO_2 use can be eliminated completely, especially in later stages of winemaking.[12]

Figure 3.6
Refrigerated tanks for skin contact outside the Chateau St. Jean Winery: note the cooling jackets and large valve-controlled outlets at the bottoms of the tanks for transferring the must into the press located below.

Skin Contact Adds More Flavor

If a premium varietal wine is being made, some wineries will send the chilled must into a tank for several hours of skin contact. If this step is managed properly — that is, done at low temperatures and for a minimum amount of time — the concentration of varietal aroma and flavor compounds will be increased and significant amounts of tannin will not be extracted. In California, skin contact is used most commonly in making Chardonnay and occasionally in making Sauvignon Blanc and White Riesling as well.

Pressing Considerations

After skin contact or directly after crushing, juice separation is followed by **pressing**: the must is squeezed to extract more juice. In the winepress more and more force is applied to the must, and separate fractions of juice are extracted at increasing pressures. The earliest fractions, extracted with very gentle pressure, are called free-run juice; all the later fractions are referred to as press juice. Free-run and press juices have very different compositions because the parts of the grape from which the juice is being extracted are different at higher and lower pressures. Free-run juice has more sugar and less acid and tannin than press-run juice. Press juice is extracted

Figure 3.7
Filling the Willmes press with white must at Freemark Abbey Winery

at higher pressures from must containing a higher proportion of stems, skins, and seeds, and it therefore contains less sugar and more acid and tannin. Wineries may blend all or part of the press juice back into the free-run juice to improve its balance or may ferment the press juice separately for later blending or sale. Sometimes press juice is fermented and then distilled to make a pungent high-alcohol liquor called grappa or marc. In the press shown in Figure 3.7 a big rubber balloon inside the press will be inflated to squeeze juice from the must. The balloon may be deflated while the cylinder is rotated to rearrange the squeezed grape solids and then inflated again. At the end of the pressing cycle the press is opened and the cylinder is rotated so that the pomace falls out.

How Much Juice Will We Get?

Yields of free-run juice are much higher than yields of press juice. Figures reported recently by California coastal wineries were 50-170 gallons of free-run juice per ton of grapes, 10-120 gallons of press juice per ton, and total juice yields of 135-185 gallons per ton for a range of premium white grape varieties.[13] The substantial variation is due to differences in yields between varieties and differences in the equipment used by the wineries surveyed.

The Pomace Is What's Left

The grape solids in the must are called **pomace**. After pressing, the pomace or "press cake" is often returned to the vineyard along with the stems separated at the crusher and incorporated into the soil to improve its texture.

STEP 8. CONDUCT THE FERMENTATION
Fermentation Fundamentals — A Definition and Its Implications

A broad variety of fermentations are important but normally unnoticed parts of our daily lives. They are involved in processes ranging from the production of pharmaceuticals, such as penicillin and insulin, to that of foods and beverages, like cheese, bread, beer, yogurt, sauerkraut, and wine, to recycling plant nutrients in backyard compost or in the stems and pomace from wineries. If we look for the common components in these seemingly widely divergent processes, we will discover that fermentation includes all processes in which chemical changes are brought about in organic substances by the metabolism of microorganisms. The microorganisms involved, mainly yeast and bacteria, live in the organic substances — from cabbage to milk and grape juice — and through their life processes transform them into very useful by-products for humans, from Amoxicillin to Zinfandel.

Let's Get Specific — The Alcoholic Fermentation

Let's take a look at the alcoholic fermentation used in winemaking in terms of the general definition of fermentations. The organic substance that the process starts with is the glucose in grape juice. The chemical change brought about is the conversion of that glucose into ethyl alcohol and carbon dioxide gas, with heat as a by-product. The microorganisms involved are yeasts, primarily from the genus *Saccharomyces,* which can produce this particular transformation of glucose only in the absence of oxygen. For each molecule of glucose fermented, two molecules of ethyl alcohol and CO_2 are produced. Because one molecule of glucose weighs about four times as much as a molecule of alcohol, the alcohol yield by weight should be about one-half of the weight of the sugar fermented. This is the basis for the rough approximation mentioned earlier: two degrees Brix in the grape juice (corresponding to about two percent sugar) will yield about one percent alcohol in the wine.

What can we learn about the alcoholic fermentation in winemaking from the definition we've just made? First, because the organic substance that the process starts with is glucose, fruits such as grapes that are naturally high in glucose will ferment easily. Other fruits or grains that are high in starch but low in glucose will be hard to ferment unless glucose is added (raisins are often called for in fruit wine recipes for that reason) or their starchy materials are converted to glucose (as in the germination of barley seeds to make beer or the chewing of corn by Andean Indians to make Chícha — saliva contains an enzyme that breaks starch into glucose). Second, because the chemical change produces both gas and heat, these have to be managed in winemaking. Fermentation tanks — from the home winemaker's gallon jugs to 60,000-gallon commercial-scale monsters — are equipped with fermentation locks: one-way valves that allow CO_2 to escape while preventing oxygen-bearing air from entering. Heat is another major enemy of wine because its delicate aroma and flavor chemicals are easily destroyed at higher temperatures; furthermore, uncooled fermentations can easily reach temperatures in excess of 100 degrees F, where concern over the loss of aromatic compounds is replaced by worry over killing the fermenting yeast and producing off odors. Wine tanks can have cooling jackets in their walls, and heat exchangers are also used to cool fermenting musts that are pumped through them. Third, because the microorganisms that transform glucose into alcohol are yeasts, but not all yeasts are alike, the particular strains that are chosen to catalyze the fermentation must be carefully selected. Wild species of yeasts are frequently present on the skins of grapes and produce unwelcome off odors when they ferment glucose to alcohol. Moreover, they cannot tolerate the alcohol levels in wine and stop fermenting at around 6-9% alcohol, leaving lots of unfermented glucose in a very unstable, easy-to-spoil wine. For these reasons, winemakers add sulfur dioxide during crushing to inhibit the growth of these wild yeasts and later inoculate the grape juice with selected strains of purified wine yeasts. Fourth, because alcoholic fermentation requires the absence of oxygen, outside air must be prevented from entering the fermentation vessel. With oxygen present, yeast cells do not produce alcohol but break down the glucose molecules completely (in much the same way we do in our muscles), producing

Figure 3.8
A double row of fermentation tanks at the Chateau St. Jean Winery: notice the cone-shaped fermentation lock on the top of each tank.

water and carbon dioxide and a lot more energy for cell growth. Yeasts grow more efficiently with this kind of metabolism and automatically switch to it when O_2 is available. In winemaking this results in lower alcohol yields, which can endanger the stability of the wine. An oxygen-free environment is produced as the small amount of oxygen initially in solution in the grape juice is used up and replaced by CO_2, which either dissolves in the grape juice or escapes through the fermentation locks.

An Aside — Grapes, Yeast, and History

Although in modern winemaking the wild yeasts on the skins of grapes are mostly a nuisance, their natural association with grapes and the high natural concentrations of glucose in this highly valued fruit probably set the stage for the ancient discovery of winemaking. The following story from the Epic of Gilgamesh recounts one mythical version of that event: "Wine was first discovered by a woman. King Jemsheed, so runs the story, was fond of grapes and was accustomed to storing them in jars so that through the year there should always be grapes for him to eat. On one occasion, however, he found that the grapes were no longer sweet — they had fermented — and, imagining that the liquid in the jar was poisonous, he labelled the jar accordingly. One of the ladies of his harem noticed the label on the jar. Having been distracted by the pain of 'nervous headaches' and desiring death in preference to this continual pain, she drank some of the 'poison.' She was overpowered by the wine, fell asleep, and awoke refreshed. With pleasure she returned to the 'poison' and finished the jar. She was forced, however, to communicate her secret to the King, upon which 'a quantity of wine was made; and Jemsheed and all his court drank of the new beverage.'"[14] And, we studious enophiles might add, all this and many later centuries of festivities were made possible by the proximity of glucose in the juice and *Saccharomyces* on the skins of *Vitis vinifera* berries!

Fermentation Fundamentals — Negotiating the Curves

Because glucose is heavier than ethyl alcohol, winemakers can follow the progress of a fermentation by measuring the drop in the density of the fermenting juice, using a hydrometer periodically to estimate the degrees Brix of the solution. If you look closely at the fermentation tanks when you visit wineries during the fall, you may see charts like the one reproduced in Table 3.3. Here the cellar crew has recorded the daily temperature and degrees Brix measurements for a batch of wine. Such measurements can be graphed to create a fermentation curve like the one shown in Figure 3.9, plotting the degrees Brix measurements from Table 3.3 over time.

Table 3.3
Fermentation Record for Belle Terre Vineyards' Chardonnay fermenting at Chateau St. Jean Winery, October, 1980

Date	Degrees Brix	Temp Degrees F	Days from Inoculation and Cellar Notes
10/18	23.8		added Champagne strain yeast, nutrients, and PVPP to remove brown pigments, day 0
10/21		51	3 days
10/22	24.0	54	4 days
10/23	22.9	57	5 days
10/24	19.3	60	6 days
10/27	16.3	56	9 days
10/28	4.0	56	10 days
10/29	3.2	52	11 days
10/30	1.8	52	12 days
10/31	1.3	53	13 days

The shape that results is characteristic of all fermentations. At the beginning of the fermentation (days 0-4 after inoculation with yeast), the degrees Brix does not drop because at this stage, while the yeast cells are metabolizing with the aid of the dissolved oxygen in the grape juice and increasing in number, they have not consumed enough glucose to change the density of the juice. In the second stage the degrees Brix fall rapidly as the fermentation goes into full swing and the density of the liquid drops, reflecting increasing amounts of alcohol and decreasing amounts of the heavier glucose (days 5-11 after inoculation). Finally, in the third stage the fermentation rate slows as the last of the food supply (glucose) is depleted and the yeast metabolize these scarce molecules more and more slowly (days 12 and later). The density of the wine will eventually reach -1.0 to -2.0 degrees Brix

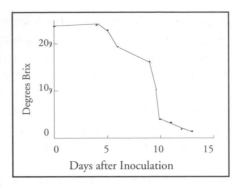

Figure 3.9
Belle Terre Vineyards' Chardonnay Fermentation Curve from Chateau St. Jean, October 1980

when fermentation is finished — that is, when all the glucose has been converted to alcohol.[15] This could take another 10 to 14 days. Another indication of the increased fermentation activity of the yeasts during the rapid drop in degrees Brix of days 5-11 and their diminished activity from day 12 is the warming of the fermenting juice to 60 degrees F on day 6 and its cooling to 52 degrees F on day 12, as seen in Table 3.3.

Fermentation curves allow us to talk in terms of degrees Brix about times during fermentation when various winemaking tasks are performed. This can be more accurate than referring to those times in hours or days because these can vary, for example, when fermentations are conducted at different temperatures. In making Chardonnay some or all of the alcoholic fermentation is often carried out in barrels. Some wineries start the fermentation in large tanks and only after it is safely under way transfer the fermenting juice to barrels to complete the process (since it is easier to fix any problems when all the wine is in one batch than after it is in barrels). Two winemakers discussing when they made the transfer for their 1990 wines might refer to the timing as "at 20 degrees Brix" or say that "we had to wait until 17 degrees Brix." I will use references in degrees Brix throughout this book when I discuss winemaking.

When Things Don't Go Right — Stuck Fermentations

Fermentation curves help monitor the progress of fermentations and can alert the winemaker to any problems that might be developing. One possible problem is a stuck fermentation — one that stops by itself before all the glucose has been used up (and may have been sluggish from the start). A fermentation can get stuck if the yeast cells are killed by natural inhibitors or high fermentation temperatures or if the yeast uses up some needed nutrient. (When grapes get very ripe they may lack adequate quantities of certain nutrients

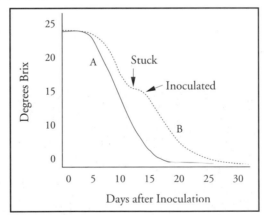

Figure 3.10
Hypothetical Normal (A) and Stuck (B) Fermentation Curves

required for yeast growth.[16]) Figure 3.10 shows two hypothetical fermentation curves: one A representing a normal fermentation and the other B showing a fermentation that began slowly, became stuck around day 11, and had to be restarted the next day, perhaps by the addition of a new batch of actively growing yeast and some nutrients.

Getting fermentations "unstuck" without lowering the quality of the finished wine is tricky, but not all stuck fermentations are disasters. During the 1980s there were several years when many California North Coast Chardonnay fermentations became stuck, leaving residual sugars of 0.5-2% and resulting in fuller-bodied wines, some of which won competitions even though they were not true to the expected dry style. It has been speculated that weather conditions during these years created conditions for ripening that resulted in high-sugar grape juices that were, perhaps, missing some essential nutrient. Without doubt the most famous stuck fermentation success story is that of Sutter Home White Zinfandel. In 1972, winery owner Bob Trinchero began to produce and market a dry, full-bodied, oak-aged white wine from Zinfandel grapes. The fermentation of the 1975 vintage became stuck, but Trinchero decided to market 26,000 cases of the sweet, 9% alcohol wine anyway. The rest is marketing history. Sales of Sutter Home White Zinfandel have grown from 25,000 cases in 1980 to 2.5 million cases in 1990, and Sutter Home and its imitators have made White Zinfandel the number 1 California varietal wine: it made up one-third of the domestic varietal wine market in 1990. One out of every ten bottles of table wine opened in America is White Zinfandel.[17]

How Do Wineries Do It? Commercial Practices of White Table Wine Fermentation
Juice Clarification and Correction

Between pressing and the beginning of fermentation, the grape juice is prepared by chilling it to about 45 degrees F and clarifying it (allowing it to settle overnight, passing it through a lees filter, or centrifuging it) to remove pieces of broken grape skins, soil from the vineyard, etc. Clarification at this stage can be overdone, and winemakers must be careful to leave enough particles in the grape juice so that yeasts can attach and grow during fermentation. If it is necessary to adjust the acidity of the grape juice — a possibility in very warm or very cold years, or with juices from warmer or colder areas, or from certain naturally low-acid grape varieties — that is best done before fermentation. In California problems with lower than desired acidities are more common, so that acid correction will most often involve the addition of tartaric acid to achieve a final concentration of 0.7 to 0.9 grams of total acid per 100 ml.

Pure Yeast

Following this preparation, an actively growing pure yeast culture of *Saccharomyces cerevisiae* or *S. bayanus* is added to the juice to make up 1-10% of its volume. A dry form of yeast is usually added to a small batch of the grape juice several hours before the whole tank is inoculated, allowing initial active growth in the presence of air and creating a dense population of healthy cells (just as is done in bread making). Wineries may choose a single yeast strain that they find easy to work with or they may have several strains on hand to match to the particular wine type or style being made: Geisenheim for White Riesling, Épernay or Champagne for Chardonnay, etc.

Figure 3.11
A Chardonnay barrel fermentation at Simi Winery: the plastic glasses are filled with a sulfur dioxide solution and are the fermentation locks for these barrels.

Where To Do It?

For the fermentation of white table wines, premium wineries use stainless steel tanks of 5,000- to 60,000-gallon capacity equipped with fermentation locks and jacketed walls in which coolant is circulated. Barrel fermentations are done in air-conditioned rooms.

To Make It Good, Keep It Cool

The most striking feature of the commercial fermentation of white wines is their low temperature. As a general rule, the cooler the fermentation temperature, the higher the quality of the wine. The actual temperatures used are between 50 and 60 degrees F, allowing the fermentations to finish in two to six weeks. Successful home producers of white table wines will work as close to these commercial temperatures as possible and have been known to commandeer the family bathtub and fill it with jugs of fermenting white grape juice bathed in ice water (having also taken over the freezer to make mountains of ice cubes).

If the preservation of delicate aroma and flavor components is not as important as finishing the fermentation quickly to get on with the next step in winemaking and make the tank available for the next batch of grape juice — as might be the case in the production of inexpensive generic wines — fermentation temperatures up to 80 degrees F may be used.

Let It "Go Dry" or Stay Sweet?

The alcoholic fermentation is over when the appropriate amount of sugar has been consumed for the style of wine that is being made. For dry wine styles such as Chardonnay, Fumé Blanc, and Dry Chenin Blanc, the fermentation is allowed to go to completion — that is, to stop naturally at minus 1 to minus 2 degrees Brix when all the glucose molecules have been converted to alcohol. Even these wines with no glucose remaining will have 0.2 to 0.3% residual sugar detectable by chemical analysis. This is mentioned on some wine labels and represents the small fraction of exotic grape sugars that yeast cells cannot ferment.

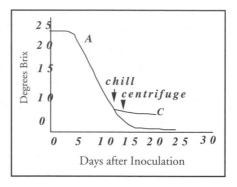

Figure 3.12
Fermentation Curves for A Dry Table Wine (A) and A Table Wine with Residual Sugar (C)

Some wines are allowed to retain enough residual sugar so that they will taste sweet. This can be desirable for a variety of reasons: White Rieslings are often made with residual sugars in order to balance their acidity, for example, and even "dry" Gewürztraminers may be made faintly sweet to offset the slight natural bitterness of this variety. Fermentations of these wines can be slowed down before all their glucose has been metabolized by "deep chilling" them to, say, 25 degrees F, when the fermentation has reached 4-8 °Brix. The wine can then be centrifuged or filtered to remove the cold-inactivated yeast without further loss of sugar during these processes. In this way wines of 2-3% residual sugar can be made. The effect of this procedure on the fermentation curve is shown in Figure 3.12. In the normal curve (A) the grape juice has fermented to dryness; in curve (C) the fermentation has been stopped by chilling and the wine has been centrifuged to remove the yeast, leaving some residual sugar in the wine.

Figure 3.13
A centrifuge like this would be used to remove the yeast cells and sediment from a fermentation that had been arrested with some residual sugar remaining and would see service in other wine-clarification processes as well.

Photo: James Pearson

Wines with residual sugar can also be made by adding some "sweet reserve" (grape juice, perhaps from the original batch, that has been sulfited, chilled, and stored) or grape juice concentrate (not recommended for premium wines).

To Rack or Not to Rack

When the alcoholic fermentation is finished, the yeast cells settle out and form a sediment at the bottom of the tank. Sediments in wine tanks are called **lees,** and the lees that form at different stages of the winemaking process are distinguished by naming their contents, as in yeast lees, gelatin lees, etc. Typically, the new wine is promptly transferred off of the yeast lees into a clean tank where clarification and stabilization are begun. When wines are transferred from tank to tank the process is called **racking**. In some cases, most commonly for Chardonnay, the winemaker may want to add a yeast character similar to champagne bouquet to the wine and will allow the wine to remain in contact with the yeast for weeks or months; this is called *"sur lie"* aging. Winemakers who use this method to add odor and flavor complexity and body to their white table wines monitor the process vigilantly, tasting each barrel at least weekly to make sure off flavors do not develop.

Another Fermentation, Mainly for Chardonnay

At the same time that the alcoholic fermentation is proceeding, some winemakers will inoculate tanks of Chardonnay (and occasionally Sauvignon Blanc) with bacteria that catalyze a second fermentation, converting malic acid from the grape juice to lactic acid and carbon dioxide gas. This process, which requires an oxygen-free environment, is known as the malolactic fermentation (MLF). Because the lactic acid (also found in milk) is less tart than the malic acid it replaces, it reduces the acidity in the fermenting grape juice and finished wine. Grape varieties differ in their content of malic acid, and in different vintages the malic acid content of their juice will vary depending on how much was consumed by respiration during ripening. The actual acid reduction produced by the MLF depends on how much of the juice's acidity was due to malic acid. In addition to reducing acidity, the MLF causes other organoleptic changes: it produces gas and causes the wines to be less fruity and to have transient cheesy off odors, but it also allows them to develop greater complexity — including a buttery flavor — with aging. It is thought that this increased complexity is created because the by-products of the MLF include new odor and flavor molecules that enter into the chemical reactions that produce bouquet during bulk and bottle aging. Because more kinds of reactions are possible in an MLF wine, the bouquet of these wines is more complex. This fermentation may also be used to reduce the acidity of cool-region or cool-season grape juices that are too tart.

It is critical for winemakers to control the timing of the MLF and to be sure that it is completed before bottling: the bacteria that cause this fermentation can grow without air and can tolerate the levels of alcohol found in wines, so the process can continue in the bottle and spoil the wine (as well as the winery's bank account and the winemaker's reputation). To make sure that the MLF will not occur in the bottle, wines that have undergone this fermentation are carefully tested to be sure all the malic acid has been consumed. The process is more complicated when a winemaker wants to create a wine of greater complexity by blending a wine that has undergone the MLF with one that has not (and hence still contains some malic acid). Such a wine — usually a Chardonnay — must be filtered to remove all bacteria and bottled under aseptic conditions.

Because most of the world's white table wines emphasize the aroma of the grapes and the MLF reduces fruitiness, most winemakers take precautions to **prevent** the MLF altogether, through prompt acid adjustments before and after fermentation, early racking off the yeast lees, filtration, maintenance of SO_2 levels, and cool storage conditions. However, the malolactic fermentation is sometimes as hard to encourage as it is to prevent. One winter I was visiting the Ridge Winery and noticed an electric blanket draped lovingly over a rather large oak wine cask. When I asked what the blanket was for, I was told that the wine had not finished the MLF and was being warmed to encourage the bacteria to grow and complete the conversion of malic to lactic acid. Warming the wine, leaving it in contact with the yeast lees, and maintaining low acid and SO_2 levels are all ways of encouraging the MLF. If you visit smaller, cool-region wine cellars during the winter months, you may see a variety of brilliant improvisational efforts being made to warm up the wines. Don't be surprised if you see heaters of various kinds — including those you would expect to see in a vineyard — cuddling up to wine tanks.

STEP 9. CLARIFY AND STABILIZE THE WINE

Once the fermentation is complete, the new white table wine begins its transformation from a cloudy, yeasty, unstable, and perhaps bitter liquid that cannot be stored very long to the familiar clear, appetizing beverage we love to drink with hors d'oeuvres, beef Stroganoff, and light entrées. The processes of clarification and stabilization can proceed while the wine is aging in bulk but are often completed before this step if the wine is to be placed in small oak barrels. During this stage sulfur dioxide is maintained at the minimum level required to protect the wine during normal cellar operations, which inevitably expose the wine to some air. It may also be necessary to readjust the acidity after fermentation.

Clarific
Wi
ing, cen
pended
form ha
each oth
handlin
oxygen

Rad
lees and
contain
the win
to move
designe
analogc
uses a f
but bec
collecti
before t
simply
help cla
moderi
contem

In
variety
particle
chunks
from g
cloth o
organis
by filte
passing
"tightr
and to
steriliz
to prov
Filters
a parti
two or
micro
T
as mud
are mi
formin
more
run sn
amou
"Focu
astring

tried to develop alternatives to oak barrel-aging. Oak flavors can be added to wine by mixing in oak chips or granules, placing a structure made of oak inside a stainless steel tank, or blending in some commercial oak extract. However, even though these alternatives add oak character to wines, they cannot have the same effect on their other sensory properties because the wines will not be concentrated by the evaporation of water the way they are in wooden cooperage. The fact that barrels remain the method of choice for aging wines is reflected in the sale of 90,000 barrels (55,000 of French oak and 35,000 of American oak) to U.S. wineries in 1989.[27]

STEP 11. BLEND AND FINISH THE WINE
Blending

Wines are blended either to improve them by enhancing their complexity or balancing their sensory components or to correct defects. Blending can be done at several stages in winemaking, starting in the vineyard — as in Bordeaux — where several varieties may be interplanted, harvested, and crushed together. Alternatively, after separate crushing and pressing, different musts can be blended and fermented together; or, after clarification, stabilization, and aging, nearly finished wines can be combined prior to bottling. Wines that are blended can be from different grape varieties, from the same variety but of different vintages or vineyard locations, or from separate lots of a particular batch of wine.[28]

When making a blend, winemakers must keep in mind the laws that govern the labelling of wines. In the United States, for example, a table wine must have an alcohol content of 7-14%. A wine may carry a vintage date only if 95% of the grapes were harvested in the year named on the label, so only 5% may be blended from another vintage. To carry a varietal name on its label, a wine must consist of at least 75% of that variety. Additional rules apply to making blends from grapes of different origins.

Many producers follow certain conventions based on flavor and structural compatibility when making varietal blends. For example, Chardonnay and Pinot Blanc are often blended as they are in Burgundy, while Sauvignon Blanc and Sémillon are combined to make the white wines modeled after those of Bordeaux, including California's proprietary white "Meritage" wines. (Sémillon adds complexity to Sauvignon Blanc and helps tame its "wild" varietal character.) Neutral varieties such as French Colombard and Thompson Seedless are versatile blenders in generic or varietal wines.[29]

As noted above, wineries may handle two or more batches of a wine separately for fermentation or aging and blend them later. To achieve the desired residual sugar level, or oak flavor, or malolactic fermentation effect, or *sur lie* aging character in the bottled wine batches of wine that have different levels of sweetness or were made with different fermentation or aging regimes are combined. For this process the winemaker must have a clear idea of the final product in mind and must make and critically taste many trial blends to achieve the desired result. Blends are always made well in advance of their bottling dates to allow flavors to marry and to provide time to correct any unforeseen problems caused by combining the wines.

In addition to differences between wines that are created intentionally, separate lots of a wine can develop differently in the cellar and may require blending to improve them. Problems such as volatile acidity, off odors or flavors, and bitterness can be corrected by blending, but the winemaker always has to be concerned that a good batch of wine may be ruined by trying to "hide" even a little of a problem batch in it.

Racing Cautiously to the Finish

The finishing stages of winemaking will include a last fining and filtrations on the way to the bottling line. These filtrations often end with a sterilizing stage to eliminate the possibility of spoilage organisms entering the bottles. When sterile filtration is used, bottling must be done under aseptic conditions to ensure that no spoilage microbes are introduced. Because bottling ends the winemaking process and the winemaker's ability to control what happens to the wine, all wines are carefully double-checked for stability before this stage and the sulfur dioxide level is also adjusted to protect the wine through its last handling at the winery.

STEP 12. BOTTLE THE WINE

The Bottles

The bottle shape and color that is chosen for a particular wine is based on the traditional shapes and colors used in the European wine districts where that wine type or style was originally made. Sauvignon Blanc and Sémillon varietal wines will be poured into clear Bordeaux bottles— the ones with the straight sides and square shoulders — in honor of their origins in the vineyards of Sauternes and Graves. Because Chardonnay is the best white-wine grape in Burgundy, wines made from that variety will appear in light green "Burgundy" bottles that are the same height as Bordeaux bottles but with more rounded shoulders. The tallest, thinnest, and sometimes brown bottle (the one that never fits in your refrigerator) hails from the Rhine and is called the hock or Alsace style; it is used for White Riesling and Gewürztraminer. Chenin Blanc and Pinot Blanc often are seen in bottles of the Burgundy shape. The 750 ml size is the most commonly used.

The Bottling Line

Bottling is a highly mechanized process at most wineries, large or small. If you visit wineries, you will often find the tour guide, especially if she or he is also a working member of the production staff, lingering at the bottling line and extolling the virtues of the new labeller or filling machine or telling stories about glue while you are noticing that your feet hurt and wondering what all the fuss is about. There are two reasons for pausing reverently to admire a smoothly functioning bottling line. First, the careful attention to quality during the entire

Figure 3.22
Filling bottles at McDowell Valley Vineyards
Photo by John Bucchenstein

preceding process of winemaking can be nullified by malfunctioning bottling-line machines — fillers that admit oxygen or filters that allow spoilage microbes into the bottles. Second, break-downs can be costly in another way: bottling lines, though mechanized, are labor intensive and if they malfunction, a lot of frustrated people find themselves sitting around with nothing to do except collect their wages while the equipment is being fixed.

Empty wine bottles arrive at the bottling line in the same boxes that are refilled with the full bottles at the other end. The bottles are washed and rinsed to sterilize them and filled with an inert gas, often purified nitrogen, before being filled with wine and corked. Corks come from the bark of yet another oak, *Quercus suber,* and must be pre-treated with SO_2 because they can carry spoilage yeasts that can cause even the finest wines to smell like your most used, least laundered gym socks. Many premium wineries blow inert gas onto the wine's surface and draw a vacuum in the headspace as the bottle is corked to minimize the addition of air. The bottles are then decorated with their labels, their corked mouths are covered with protective capsules, and they are put back in their boxes upside down or on their sides for bottle aging. The date the bottles were filled is stamped on the box and can be useful for estimating the age — and therefore the approximate drinkability — of wines without vintage dates. Sometimes the unlabeled bottles are stacked in bins in the winery's cellar to await custom labelling as orders are received for export. This is especially the case if the winery sells to several countries with different label requirements.

How Long Does All This Take?

The overall process of making white table wine can take as little as 3-4 weeks; however, it normally takes three to four months from harvest to the first sales of the average white table wine. In the Northern hemisphere this means that you will find wines of that year's vintage in the markets in November and December. Barrel-aged Chardonnays can take 12 to 18 months to reach the market, so you will notice that they are typically one or two years older than the other white wines on the shelves.

STEP 13. AGE THE BOTTLED WINE

Bottled wines are stored at the winery until they are ready to be released for sale — an average of four months for California's coastal wineries, with Chardonnay being kept longer. Bottle aging may last for only a few days or for several months — even years for wines that are stored for future reference or sale in a producer's "wine library." Wineries are careful to store their wines in the best possible conditions: in the dark, with constant, cool temperatures (55 to 68 degrees F) and no vibrations.

Figure 3.23 shows the typical shape of a wine-aging curve. All wines will improve with age after bottling (sometimes simply because slight transitory off odors can be produced during bottling and wines improve as they recover from this so-called bottling sickness), reaching a plateau of maximum tastiness — implying greater complexity and less apparent tartness, but varying greatly with the taste of the consumer — and then decreasing rapidly in drinkability.

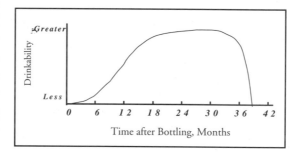

Figure 3.23
Drinkability of a Hypothetical California White Table Wine After Bottling [30]

The white table wines most likely to improve with from one to five years of bottle aging are Chardonnay, Fumé Blanc, Pinot Blanc, Gewürztraminer, and White Riesling; those less likely to improve — and whose drinkability curves will resemble Figure 3.23 — are French Colombard, Sylvaner, and Chenin Blanc; white wines made from red grapes, such as White Zinfandel, are intended to be drunk without bottle aging. Wine from cooler growing regions age longer than those from warmer areas.

Some white wines can age much longer than five years. I recall my surprise in 1977 at experiencing the refreshing qualities of a 1959 Alsatian Gewürztraminer — a wine that nicely illustrated the rule that cooler regions tend to produce wines that can age longer in barrel and bottle — and my astonishment at enjoying a white Rioja wine from a vintage estimated around 1915 and that had been left undisturbed for approximately 60 years in a cold cellar that apparently slowed the aging process.

STEP 14. RELEASE THE WINE INTO THE MARKET

Because wines can be in distribution channels an average of three to six months (and sometimes up to 15 months!) before you buy them, wineries will release their wines as soon as possible after bottling to minimize the risk of retailers selling you wines that are "over the hill." This means you should be prepared to age wines yourself to enjoy the increased complexity and moderated tartness of well-aged White Rieslings, Fumé Blancs, Pinot Blancs, and Chardonnays. The aging does not necessarily have to be very long: one or two years will often be enough to bring out some added nuances of bottle bouquet. When you are shopping for white wines to cellar for longer periods, look for wines from good vineyards in cooler regions (Appendix B has a list for California) and ask your wine merchant to point out producers who make a style that is intended for aging. Such wines for aging may seem a little "too tart" right after you've bought them, but that tartness is necessary for successful bottle aging and the wine will taste less tart after one or two years of aging. Many of these wines can age much longer.

"STEP" 15. FOLLOW THE PROCESS WITH LABORATORY ANALYSIS AND SENSORY EVALUATION

California coastal wineries maintain extensive laboratory control over their wines, performing two dozen different analyses, of which half a dozen are typically repeated several times.[31] For example, adjustment of sulfur dioxide levels during winemaking requires analysis for this compound four times in the average white table wine production cycle, and preventing spoilage necessitates the earliest possible detection of traces of ethyl acetate given off by vinegar bacteria. Laboratory tests are also run to determine the minimum effective amounts of fining agents to be used and to check heat and cold stability before and after fining or chilling.

Sensory evaluation is important in these wineries as well. The average tasting situation involves five tasters examining 30 wines in the course of one to three sessions per day. Panel members are likely to have chemical analyses of the wines at their disposal, and in about half the wineries panelists discuss the wines during the tasting. Virtually all of the wineries conduct regular and frequent blind tastings to compare their wines with their competitors' products.

HOW THE ORGANOLEPTIC PROPERTIES OF WHITE WINES ARE CREATED IN THE WINECELLAR

Table 3.6 summarizes how the sensory components of white table wines are created. All of these changes except the MLF and oak aging can be observed by comparing a Gewürztraminer wine to a Gewürztraminer grape juice (Exercise 4.4). The organoleptic changes that are produced during oak aging of Chardonnay can be experienced by tasting Chardonnays made with and without barrel aging (Exercise 4.5).

Table 3.6
Sources of the Sensory Components of White Table Wines

Component	Source	Sensory effect
After fermentation:		
Residual Sugar	From the grapes	Sweetness
Aroma Components	From the grapes or created during the alcoholic fermentation, may be reduced by the malolactic fermentation	Varietal character
Ethyl Alcohol	Fermentation end product	Sweetness, heat
Carbon Dioxide	Fermentation end product	Bubbles
Fermentation Bouquet	A variety of by-products of the alcoholic fermentation	Complex odors that say "This is wine!"
Color	Pigments dissolved from the skins	Pale yellows to gold and pink (Gewürztraminer & Blanc de Noirs)
Acidity	From the grapes, may be reduced by the malolactic fermentation	Tartness
After bulk aging:		
Aging Bouquet	Malolactic fermentation and/or oak barrel and/or *sur lie* aging, time for reaction between these and aroma components	Less fruity aroma but greater odor complexity, specific yeast and/or wood odors
Clarity	Settling, filtering, fining, etc.	Appealing appearance
Off Odors and Flavors	Moldy fruit, too much SO_2, too much exposure to air, and other mismanagements	Odors and flavors like mold, matches, sherry, and many others

HOW TO MAKE A HYPOTHETICAL CHABLIS, WHITE RIESLING, AND CHARDONNAY

So that you can get a sense of the flow of steps in the winemaking process and compare how each step is handled in the making of different types of white table wines, Table 3.7 summarizes the steps that would be used to make three very different types of California white table wine: a generic, jug wine for the mass market (Château Most Ordinary Mountain Chablis); a typical

White Riesling varietal wine (Pretty Good Wine Cellars White Riesling); and the currently reigning queen of white table wine production, a specially created select batch of Chardonnay varietal wine suitable for maturation in the bottle (Very Prestigious Wine Estate Reserve Chardonnay). You can also get a sense of how a winery handles different varietal wines by looking at the summary calendar of winery operations in Table 5.4, page 143.

SAUVIGNON BLANC REVISITED — WINEMAKING AND GRASSINESS

Let's return briefly to an earlier topic in this chapter — cutting the grass in Sauvignon Blanc. The survey described on pages 65-66 collected information on the winemaking practices that can determine whether a Sauvignon Blanc wine is grassier or fruitier style. Winemakers could **favor** grassiness by harvesting fruit at 21 degrees Brix or less, allowing skin contact after crushing, fermenting in stainless steel tanks at cooler temperatures, and by bottling the wine without oak aging or blending. Grassiness can be **reduced** by picking grapes at 22 degrees Brix or above, avoiding skin contact, fermenting in barrels at warmer temperatures, aging in oak, and by blending the Sauvignon Blanc wine with Sémillon or Chardonnay.[32] *Sur lie* aging can also be used to add complexity and reduce the assertive fruit character of Sauvignon Blanc.[33]

IMPORTANCE OF WHITE TABLE WINES IN THE U.S. MARKET

In 1990, white table wines made up 53% of the grape wines shipped from California to the U.S. market. If rosés and blush varietals are added, these three organoleptically similar wine types together constituted 85% of the shipments from California wineries to domestic markets.[34] Red, pink, and white varietal wines made up 40% of all shipments, and the leading white varietal wine in 1990 was White Zinfandel, whose sales of 14.5 million cases made up one-third of the domestic varietal wine market. Chardonnay followed with 8.9 million cases, up 22 % from 1989, and Sauvignon Blanc was third at 5.4 million cases and 16 % growth compared to 1989.[35]

Table 3.7   A Summary of Winemaking Steps for Three Hypothetical California White Table Wines

Step	Producer and Wine Type		
	Château **Most Ordinary** **Mountain Chablis**	**Pretty Good** **Wine Cellars** **White Riesling**	**Very Prestigious** **Wine Estate** **Reserve Chardonnay**
1 Envision type and style	Simple, fruity, slightly sweet, not tart, drink as soon as released — no bottle-aging potential	Distinctive varietal character, near threshold sweetness, tart; bottle age 1-2 years	Intense distinctive varietal character, lots of oak bouquet, dry, tart, richly flavored; bottle age 3-5 years
2 Grape variety	High-yielding, neutral — French Colombard or Thompson Seedless	White Riesling	Chardonnay
3 Climate	Warmest OK	Coolest	Cool
4 Example of cultural practices	Irrigate for maximum yields	Open canopy to prevent *Botrytis* rot.	Protect from spring frosts
5 Grape ripening	Follow sugar, total acid, pH, weather, & vine health	Follow sugar, total acid, pH, weather, & vine health	Follow sugar, total acid, pH, weather, & vine health
6 Ripe at	20-21 degrees Brix	20-21 degrees Brix	22-23 degrees Brix
7 Remove the juice	Crush, add SO_2, press, clarify juice, correct acidity	Crush, add SO_2, chill must, 2 hours skin contact, separate juice, press, clarify juice, correct acidity	Crush, add SO_2, chill must, 6 hours skin contact, separate juice, press, clarify juice, correct acidity
8 Alcoholic fermentation	Inoculate, ferment at 80° F for 4 days in 60,000-gallon stainless steel tanks, remove from yeast lees immediately	Inoculate, ferment in two lots at 50° F for 3 weeks in 5,000 gallon stainless steel tanks; chill one lot at 3-4° Brix, remove yeast, check sugar; chill the other lot also or ferment to dryness	Inoculate with yeast, ferment to dryness at 60° F, half in 60-gallon oak barrels also inoculated with MLF bacteria and half in 5,000-gallon stainless steel tanks
9 Stabilize and clarify	Prevent the MLF, filter, fine, and stabilize quickly	Prevent the MLF, filter, fine, and stabilize quickly	Prevent the MLF in the half that was fermented in stainless steel: filter, fine, stabilize quickly; rack to 80% French oak 20% American oak hogsheads to age in a *chai* for 8 months
10 Age in bulk	Hold in large stainless steel tanks during step 9	Hold for a short time in large oak ovals or stainless steel tanks during step 9	Leave the barrel-fermented half of the wine in barrels to age *sur lie* for 6 months in a cave, rack off yeast, clarify and stabilize as needed
11 Blend and finish	Blend in 4% Muscat sweet reserve, verify stability	Blend lots 1 & 2 as needed to achieve 0.8% residual sugar, verify stability	Blend MLF, *sur lie*-aged wine with stainless steel fermented and barrel-aged wine, verify stability
12 Bottle	Sterile filtration and aseptic bottling	Sterile filtration and aseptic bottling	Sterile filtration and aseptic bottling
13 Age bottled wine	Hold minimum time necessary for quality control	Hold for quality control and perhaps 1-2 months bottle age	Hold for quality control and 12 months bottle age
14 Release for sale	1-2 months after crush	2-3 months after crush	18 months after crush

REVIEW QUESTIONS

Instructions: You might want to use a separate sheet of paper to answer the following review questions. In that way you can use the questions to check your knowledge of this chapter more than once. You may, for example, want to re-test yourself on items that you have missed or use the "Review Questions" to test your knowledge before you read a chapter. For the True or False items, answer "True" if the statement is accurate or "False" if the statement is incorrect. If you determine that a statement is false make a note explaining why. For the multiple choice items pick the best alternative. Check your answers after you have completed all the questions.

1. Which grape variety below would be most consistently used for premium wines rather than jug wines?
    A.   Chenin Blanc
    B.   Sylvaner
    C.   Grey Riesling
    D.   Gewürztraminer
    E.   French Colombard

2. True or false: Weather refers to the generally prevailing weather conditions in a region — temperature, wind speed, rainfall, etc. — averaged over a series of years. _____

3. The climate of the vineyard is called a
    A.   macroclimate
    B.   mesoclimate
    C.   microclimate
    D.   miniclimate
    E.   monoclimate

4. True or false: The degree to which a grapevine's foliage and fruit are exposed to light can determine the amount of distinctive flavor compounds in its grapes. _____

5. True or false: If the amounts of the chemicals responsible for the celery/fresh vegetable, herbaceous, or grassy character of Sauvignon Blanc are reduced, fruity flavors of grapefruit, pineapple, melon, and fig emerge. _____

6. According to the grape growers surveyed, which vineyard factor below does **not** promote grassiness in Sauvignon Blanc?
    A.   dense canopy
    B.   heavy soil
    C.   less fertilization
    D.   more irrigation water
    E.   rich soils

7. True or false: When grapes ripen, they get bigger and softer, their green color fades, aromatic compounds increase, sugars increase, and both total acid concentration and acid strength increase. _____

8. True or false: For winemaking the most important sugar in grape juice is sucrose. _____

9. True or false: The amount of sugar in grape juice is estimated by measuring its density in units called "degrees Brix," which correspond to the percentage by weight of sugar in the juice. _____

10. If you were buying Chardonnay grapes for your winery, what composition listed below would you like them to have?
    A. 22.9 degrees Brix, .80 total acid
    B. 22.9 degrees Brix, 8.0 total acid
    C. 2.29 degrees Brix, .80 total acid
    D. 13.9 degrees Brix, .80 total acid
    E. 17.9 degrees Brix, 2.80 total acid

11. Why can grapes from two vineyards with the same hot daytime temperatures have different acid compositions? _____
    _____
    _____

12. True or false: The weakening of acid strength during ripening is more important for wine quality than is the decrease in the total amount of acid, because wines with stronger acid strengths have brighter colors, require smaller amounts of sulfur dioxide to protect them, and more easily resist spoilage. _____

13. True or false: Refractometers are used to estimate degrees Brix of a properly collected vineyard sample and can also be used to measure the disappearance of sugars during fermentation. _____

14. This winemaking step ideally involves only breaking the skins of the grape berries to allow the juice to flow out without any damage to the seeds or stems.
    A. mechanical harvest   B. crushing   C. pressing   D. breaking   E. destemming

15. The mixture of skins, seeds, stems, juice, and pulp produced when the skin of the grape is broken and the juice flows out is called
    A. lees   B. must   C. juice mix   D. pomace   E. sweet pomace

16. True or false: Sulfur dioxide is added at the crusher to slow down the growth of microbes that can spoil wines and to protect the juice from reactions with oxygen that can lead to both browning of pigments and deterioration of aroma and flavor. _____

17. A typical sulfur dioxide in wine would be _____.
    A. 0 parts per million
    B. 35-125 parts per million
    C. 1000 or more parts per million

18. True or false: Sulfur dioxide is only added once during winemaking, at the crusher-stemmer. _____

19. True or false: For premium white varietal wine production skin contact means that the chilled must is pumped into a tank to sit for several hours. _____

20. True or false: Free-run juice has more sugar and less acid and tannin than press-run juice because press juice is extracted at higher pressures from must containing a higher proportion of stems, skins, and seeds. _____

21. True or false: Grappa can be produced when press juice is fermented and then distilled. _____

22. True or false: Modern premium winemaking equipment allows the extraction of about 135-185 gallons of juice per ton of grapes. This is made up of about 3 times as much press-run juice as free-run juice. _____

23. True or false: The grape solids in the must are called pomace. _____

24. True or false: A juice with about 20 degrees Brix will yield a wine with about 10% alcohol through fermentation by yeasts, primarily from the genus *Saccharomyces*. _____

25. True or false: Because carbon dioxide gas is produced during fermentation, fermentation tanks are equipped with one-way valves that allow CO_2 to escape while preventing air from entering. _____

26. True or false: Wild yeasts are not used by most wineries because they can produce off odors and typically will stop fermenting at around 6-9% alcohol. _____

27. Why does the degrees Brix not drop much during the early stages of a white wine fermentation? _____

_____

_____

28. What additional evidence of yeast growth and metabolism besides the drop in degrees Brix do wineries measure during the active stage of fermentation? _____

_____

_____

29. True or false: A stuck fermentation is one that cannot be started. _____

30. Which procedure listed below would you not expect to be done before fermentation of Chardonnay?
    A. Skin contact
    B. Cold stabilization
    C. Juice clarification with a centrifuge
    D. Adjust total acid
    E. Inoculation with pure yeast cultures

31. A probable fermentation temperature for premium quality white table wines would be about _____ degrees Fahrenheit.
    A. 35   B. 42   C. 55   D. 75   E. 85

32. True or false: Wines of 2-3% residual sugar can be made by slowing down their fermentations before all the sugar has been used up by chilling them at about 4-8° Brix and then centrifuging to remove the cold-inactivated yeast. _____

33. True or false: Sediments in wine tanks are called lees. _____

34. You are having dinner at a friend's house and drinking a delicious bottle of white wine. You pick it up and notice that the label says "CALLAWAY Vineyard and Winery 1990 'CALLA-LEES®' Chardonnay. 'IN THE CLASSIC *SUR LIE* STYLE.'" Your friend asks you what "the classic *sur lie* style" means. You explain . . . _____

_____

_____

_____

35. True or false: The malolactic fermentation reduces the acidity in the fermenting grape juice and finished wine because it converts the malic acid from the grape juice to lactic acid, which is less tart. _____

36. What additional changes (besides those mentioned in question 35) occur in wines that undergo the malolactic fermentation? _____

_____

_____

37. True or false: The malolactic fermentation is most often used to reduce the acidity of warm-region or warm-to-hot-season grape juices. _____

38. True or false: It is critical for winemakers to control the timing of the MLF to be sure that it is completed before bottling. _____

39. True or false: Because most of the world's white table wines emphasize the aroma of the grapes and the MLF reduces fruitiness, most winemakers take precautions to **prevent** the MLF altogether in these wines. _____

40. The process of transferring wine from one vat containing lees to another vat which is clean is called:
    A. siphoning   B. pumping over   C. racking   D. vat exchange   E. punching

41. If wine can be made perfectly clear simply with settling and racking, why do few wineries rely on these methods? _____
    _____
    _____

42. True or false: In filtering, the wine is forced through media that vary in "tightness" from those that trap and remove just the very largest particles (chunks of grape skins) to those that take out tiny malolactic bacteria. _____

43. True or false: Fining is a clarification process that is used as much to alter other important organoleptic properties of wines as to clarify them. _____

44. True or false: Fining agents (such as gelatin and egg albumen) react with the specific wine components (tannins in this case) that are to be removed and form particles that can be removed. _____

45. True or false: A wine is neither heat- nor cold-stable if it becomes cloudy when exposed to high temperatures and it forms crystals when subjected to temperatures around 32 degrees F. _____

46. True or false: Making sure wines are microbiologically stable is designed to prevent gassiness and the development of off odors and flavors from bacteria and yeast growth during barrel aging. _____

47. True or false: Sterile filtration followed by aseptic bottling are key strategies in creating microbiological stability. _____

48. True or false: Because vinegar bacteria can spoil wine only in the presence of oxygen, winemakers minimize air contact with wines in bulk storage. _____

49. True or false: Because nearly all white table wines are valued principally for their youthful, fruity characteristics, the vast majority of white wines are aged in neutral containers only for as long as it takes to clarify and stabilize them. Only a tiny minority of the world's white wines are candidates for aging in oak containers. _____

50. What three things happen when wines age in oak barrels?
    1. _____
    2. _____
    3. _____

51. Why has oa

_____

_____

_____

52. True or fal
will Europ

53. True or fal
same. ___

54. True or fal
barrels. __

55. Under whi
concentrat
   A. th
      w
   B. in
   C. th
   D. o;
   E. th

56. Describe t
want to ac

_____

_____

57. You are g(
Chenin Bl

_____

_____

_____

58. True or fa
added to
aging pro

59. True or fa
that are fc
Chardonr

60. True or fa
traditiona
often use

61. True or f;

62. True or f;
useful for

63. You have
the first y
process, y
wines co
   A.

ANSWERS TO REVIEW QUESTIONS

1. D
2. False. The definition is for climate.
3. B
4. True
5. True
6. C
7. False. Both total acid concentration and acid strength decrease.
8. False. The most important sugars in grape juice are glucose and fructose.
9. True
10. A
11. On cool nights the grapes need less energy and use up less malic acid. Locations with cooler nighttime temperatures produce fruit that is higher in malic acid than that produced in sites where it stays warm all night.
12. True
13. False. Hydrometers can do both of these measurements.
14. B
15. B
16. True
17. B
18. False. Sulfur dioxide levels are monitored throughout winemaking and small amounts are added whenever they are needed.
19. True
20. True
21. True
22. False. It's (about) three times more free-run than press-run.
23. True
24. True
25. True
26. True
27. The degrees Brix does not drop because at this stage; while the yeast cells are metabolizing with the aid of the dissolved oxygen in the grape juice and increasing in number, they have not consumed enough glucose to change the density of the juice.
28. Another indication of the increased fermentation activity of the yeasts in addition to the rapid drop in degrees Brix is the warming of the fermenting juice.
29. False. It's one that stops by itself before all the glucose has been used up.
30. B
31. C
32. True
33. True
34. If you were quoting Chapter 3 directly, you would say, "In some cases, most commonly for Chardonnay, the wine-maker may want to add a yeast character similar to champagne bouquet to the wine and will allow the wine to remain in contact with the yeast for weeks or months; this is called *sur lie* aging."
35. True
36. In addition to reducing acidity, the MLF causes other organoleptic changes: it produces gas and causes the wines to be less fruity and to have transient cheesy off odors, but it also allows them to develop greater complexity — including a buttery flavor — with aging.
37. False. The MLF is used in cool-regions or cool-seasons.
38. True
39. True
40. C
41. Wineries do not use these slower, "natural" methods because the wine would be too old for contemporary tastes by the time it reached the market.
42. True
43. True
44. True
45. True
46. False. Microbiological stability is designed to prevent cloudiness as well and also to avoid undesirable changes other than off odor and flavor such as drop in the acidity of a hot-region wine. It is also very (more, actually) important to prevent changes in the bottle than in the barrels. Problems that occur when the wine is in the barrels can be fixed. After the wine is bottled, they cannot be remedied.
47. True, even when other measures are taken as well.
48. True
49. True
50. Three things happen: alcohol and water evaporate through the sides of the container, concentrating the wine; some oxygen dissolves in the wine, allowing oxygen-dependent maturation reactions to occur slowly; and substances — color, odor, and flavor components and tannins — from the wood are extracted into the wine.
51. Oak has become the traditional wood for aging premium wines because the trees are large enough to make wine containers of useful sizes, the wood is tight-grained,

strong, and resilient and can be worked into the curved shapes needed for barrels, and the flavors extracted are desirable in wines.

52. True

53. False. Winemakers find significant differences in oak from various forests in France: the trees in the warmer Limousin forest produce a more open-grained wood that contributes oak extract to wines relatively quickly, while slower-growing trees in the more central forests of Nevers and Troncais produce tight-grained woods that give up their flavors and tannins to wines more gradually.

54. False. Smaller barrels give wines more oak flavor.

55. A

56. Such wines are either aged in stainless steel tanks or large, typically oval-shaped oak barrels of 500-2000 gallons capacity.

57. You could begin by fermenting Chenin Blanc juice in oak barrels and add more oak by aging the wine for several months in new 60-gallon American oak barrels. A note of caution: you and your family may have to drink it all if you add too much oak flavor.

58. False. Even though these alternatives add oak character to wines, they cannot have the same effect on a wine's other sensory properties because they will not be concentrated by the evaporation of water the way they can be in wooden cooperage.

59. False. Chardonnay and Pinot Blanc are more often blended.

60. True

61. True

62. True

63. D

64. C

65. False. Blends are made well in advance of their bottling dates to allow flavors to marry and to provide time to correct any unforeseen problems.

66. True

67. E

68. False. Sadly, all wines will improve only up to a certain point and then deteriorate— except for the publicity that they can bring their buyers.

69. White Zinfandel.

70. True — and for all other areas too, not just California.

71. You can expect increased complexity and moderated tartness.

72. False. The average tasting situation, involves five tasters who examine 30 wines per day in one to three sessions.

73. 1. color, sugar, acidity, varietal aroma and flavor; 2. alcohol and carbon dioxide; 3. malolactic fermentation and/or oak barrel and/or *sur lie*-aging flavors

74. See the steps for Château Most Ordinary Chablis in Table 3.7.

75. Harvest at 22 degrees Brix or above, no skin contact, ferment in barrels and at warmer temperatures, age in oak *sur lie*, and blend with Sémillon or Chardonnay.

76. False. They made up 85% of the shipments.

ENDNOTES

1 Cooke, G., and H. Berg, "A Re-examination of Varietal Table Wine Processing Practices in California, I: Grape Standards, Grape and Juice Treatment, and Fermentation," *American Journal of Enology and Viticulture*, Vol. 34, 1983, pp. 249-256.

2 Benziger, Mike, as quoted by James Laube, "Farming for Flavors," *The Wine Spectator*, October 15, 1990, p. 16.

3 Zoecklein, Bruce, "Méthode Champenoise—Viticultural Considerations," *Practical Winery*, May/June 1985, p. 66.

4 Reynolds, Andrew G., "Monoterpenes, Key to Gewürztraminer Winegrape Quality," *Practical Winery and Vineyard*, May/June 1990, pp. 33-37, and Reynolds, A. G., and D. A. Wardle, "Impact of Viticultural Practices on Monoterpene Flavorants of British Columbia Grape Berries and Juices — A Review." Abstract of a presentation at the American Society of Enology and Viticulture, Eastern Section, Annual Meeting, July 1990, published in the *American Journal of Enology and Viticulture*, Vol. 42, No. 1, 1991, p. 81.

5 Stare, David, "David Stare on Sauvignon Blanc, That Other White Grape," *Wines and Vines*, June 1990, p. 29 (article spans pp. 26-31).

6 Allen, M. S., M. J. Lacey, R. L. N. Harris, and W. V. Brorn, "Sauvignon Blanc varietal aroma," *Australian Grape Grower and Winemaker*, Vol. 292, 1988, pp. 53-54.

7 Arnold, R. A., and A. M. Bledsoe, "The Effect of Various Leaf Removal Treatments on the Aroma and Flavor of Sauvignon Blanc Wine," *American Journal of Enology and Viticulture*, Vol. 41, No. 1, 1990, pp. 74-76.

8 Like the Richter scale for measuring the strength of earthquakes the pH scale is logarithmic. This means that every 1.0 change in either scale measures a 10-fold change — in the power of an earthquake in the earth's crust or of the acids in wine.

9 Anonymous. "What is pH?" *Simi News*, Vol. 7, No. 2, Summer 1983. Simi Winery, Healdsberg CA, and Boulton, Roger, "Total Acidity, Titratable Acidity and pH for Winemakers and Grape Growers," Wine Grape Day, University of California, Davis, February 20, 1982.

10 Anonymous, "The Role of Sulfur Dioxide in Winemaking," *Simi News*, Vol. 3, No. 3, Fall 1986.

11 Ough, Cornelius, "Determination of Sulfur Dioxide in Grapes and Wines," *Journal for the Association of Official Analytical Chemists*, Vol. 69, No. 1, pp. 5-7.

12 Ough, C. S., and E. A. Crowell, "Use of Sulfur Dioxide in Winemaking," *Journal of Food Science*, Vol. 5, No. 2, 1987, pp. 386-388.

13 Cooke, G., and H. Berg, "A Re-examination of Varietal Table Wine Processing Practices in California, I: Grape Standards, Grape and Juice Treatment, and Fermentation," *American Journal of Enology and Viticulture*, Vol. 34, 1983, pp. 249-256.

14 Younger, William, GODS MEN AND WINE, The Wine and Food Society, Cleveland, OH, 1966, p. 27.

15 The density is negative because alcohol is less dense than pure water, which has a density of zero.

16 Fugelsang, K. C., Vickie L. Wahlstrom, and Kevin McCarver, "Stuck Fermentations," *Practical Winery and Vineyard*, May/June 1991, pp. 49-59.

17 Hall, Kevin, "Zin Prices Propel Sutter Home Into More Vineyards" and "Sutter Home's Meteoric Rise Began With 'Stuck' Fermentation," *California Grape Grower*, September 1988, pp. 4-10, and Matthews, Thomas, "Varietals Boom as Jug Wines Fade," *The Wine Spectator*, August 31, 1991, p. 12.

18 Hock, Stan, "Coping with Brettanomyces," *Practical Vineyard and Winery*, January/February 1990, pp. 26-33.

19 Singleton, V. L., "Some Aspects of the Wooden Container as a Factor in Wine Maturation," ADVANCES IN CHEMISTRY, Vol. 137, 1974, pp. 254-277.

20 Peterson-Nedry, Judy, "Oak and Cool Climate Wines," *Eastern Grape Grower and Winery News*, February/March 1975, pp. 32-34, and René Naudin, "A French View of Barrel Aging," *Wines and Vines*, November 1990, pp. 48-55.

21 Schahinger, Geoff, "American Oak Cooperage," *Practical Winery and Vineyard*, November/December 1990, pp. 10-13.

22 Blazer, Richard M., "Wine Evaporation from Barrels," *Practical Winery and Vineyard*. January/February 1991, pp. 20-22.

23 Stare, David, "That Other White Wine," *Wines and Vines*, June 1990, pp. 26-31.

24 Anonymous, "Chardonnay Vinification Techniques Surveyed," *Practical Winery*, November/December 1986, pp. 39-40.

25 Shon, G. M., "U.S. Oak: A Match for Chardonnay?" *Wines and Vines*, November 1991, pp. 44-47.

26 Robert Mondavi Winery Oak Aging Seminar brochure.

27 Steffy, Kay, "What You Should Know Before Buying Barrels," *Wines and Vines*, March 1991, pp. 26-30.

28 Margalit, Yair, WINERY TECHNOLOGY AND OPERATIONS, The Wine Appreciation Guild, San Francisco, 1990, p. 98.

29 Heald, Eleanor, and Ray Heald, "Taming and Complexing the Sauvage," *Practical Winery and Vineyard*, March/April 1991, pp. 13-18.

30 Peterson, Richard, *Winemaker Notes,* The Monterey Vineyard, Gonzales, CA, October-November 1978.

31 Cooke, G., and H. Berg, "A Re-examination of Varietal Table Wine Processing Practices in California, II. Clarification, Stabilization, Aging, and Bottling," *American Journal of Enology and Viticulture*, Vol. 35, 1984, pp. 137-142.

32 Stare, David, "David Stare on Sauvignon Blanc, That Other White Grape," *Wines and Vines*, June 1990, p. 30 (article spans pp. 26-31).

33 Anonymous, "Sauvignon Blanc: The Taming of a Wild Varietal," *Simi News*, Vol. 7, No. 2, Autumn 1990, pp. 1-3.

34 "Shipments of California Grape Table Wine to U.S. Markets, by Color," 1990, a chart in *Wines and Vines*, July 1991, p. 28.

35 Matthews, Rhomas, "Varietals Boom as Jug Wines Fade," *The Wine Spectator*, August 31, 1991, p. 12.

4

SENSORY EVALUATION OF WHITE TABLE WINES

This chapter contains five white table wine tasting exercises, a "design-it-yourself tasting," and a review tasting. The first exercises focus on the fundamental odors and tastes that you will encounter in white table wines, and the other three consider premium white varietal wines. In addition to becoming acquainted with the wines themselves you will be introduced to fermentation bouquet by tasting a Gewürztraminer grape juice and a Gewürztraminer wine together; you will also be introduced to oak-aging bouquet by comparing two Chardonnays, one that was aged in oak and another that was not. Please refer to the brief section on tasters in The Setting for Winetasting in Chapter 2 to review how to prepare yourself to get the most out of these tastings. Exercises 4.1, 4.2, and 4.3 have sensory homework assignments that you should look over to be sure you have the necessary supplies on hand. If you want to set up these tasting exercises yourself, there are detailed instructions in Appendix D.

SENSORY EVALUATION EXERCISE 4.1
Focus on Olfaction I — White Table Wine Aromas and an
Introduction to the Wine Aroma Wheel

Most of us would agree that one of the things that sets an expert apart from a novice in any field is the ability of the expert to perceive more and to describe her perceptions more precisely. Harvard psychologist Gregg Solomon is interested in this relationship between language, perception, and expertise, and specifically in the extent to which the language of experts actually reflects a more differentiated and precise apprehension of the physical world. He has chosen to explore this relationship in the field of winetasting.

In one experiment in a recent investigation Solomon compared the language used by uncoached novice and expert winetasters to describe several wines. The wine experts — who were either professionally involved with wine or members of a wine club — were able to identify and name more attributes of wines than novices could in their descriptions and paid significantly more attention to describing the odors and flavors of the wines. All the experts described the odor and flavor of each of the 15 wines presented to them, using an average of 2.33 descriptive terms per wine, but only two of the 15 novice winetasters made any reference at all to odor or flavor. Experts also showed greater agreement on their wine descriptions and in their use of wine terminology compared to the novices.[1]

With the following exercise you will begin your formal transition into the realm of the wine experts studied by Solomon as you become familiar with some common aromas found in white varietal table wines. In a sense, you will be making a deposit of known aroma terms in your memory bank so that you will have access later to a defined aroma memory to go with words such as "peach" and "cut green grass" when you use them to describe wines. You will smell and identify nine reference standards for white table wines, each of which represents a descriptive aroma term from the thir—or outermost—tier of the wine aroma wheel. Through later tasting exercises and by gaining additional experience tasting wines, you will learn to associate each of these reference standards with a particular aroma component in wines.

Objective: The goal of this tasting is to improve your ability to talk about wines accurately and to teach you to use a common set of terms for white table wines from the wine aroma wheel so that you and your tasting companions will be able to agree on wine descriptions better than the pompous cat and his companions in Figure 4.1.

Figure 4.1
A Pompous Cat
and His Companions
Illustrate Poor
Agreement on
Wine Descriptions
Wallace Tripp's Wurst Seller
Jaffrey NH: Sparhawk Books Inc., 1981

What to Do Before This Exercise:

Reading: Review the following sections in Chapter 2: Smell, the Most Important Sense (pp. 21-24); Adaptation (p. 26); and Learning Wine Odors (pp. 30-34). You should also read the section about Odor in Approaching the Wine (pp. 45-46). Study the wine aroma wheel on page 33 closely and pay special attention to the third-tier terms (on the outside of the wheel) in the floral, spicy, fruity, and vegetative areas. (If you wish, you can order a laminated — and therefore spill-proof, color-coded version of the aroma wheel.[2])

Sensory Homework — for Fun and Preparedness: You will perform better on this exercise if you take time to do these demonstrations and odor previews beforehand.

1. Flavor is Odor

    Choose one of the following demonstrations to convince yourself of the fact that flavor is odor. You'll need to have someone help you with both and you can try them on your assistant to see their reaction. Hold your nose — no cheating or it won't work — tightly closed and have your helper put a little ground cinnamon on you tongue. What do you perceive? Most people can, at best, sense something sort of warm and granular. Open your nose and experience "Ahah! It's cinnamon!" This is more fun if you try it on someone who doesn't know what you are putting on their tongue. The expression that goes along with the "Cinnamon Ahah!" is priceless. Make up a solution of 1 teaspoon of vanilla extract in a quart of water. Hold your nose and taste it. Repeat the tasting with your nose open. I think you will be convinced that vanilla is an odor, not a taste. (Thanks to Linda Bartoshuk and Marcia Pelchat for these two demonstrations.)

2. Preview the Reference Standards

If you have easy access to some of the third-tier items in the floral, spicy, fruity, and vegetative segments of the aroma wheel — for example, maybe you have a bouquet of roses on the table or a jar of strawberry jam or peaches in the cupboard — reacquaint yourself with their odors.

Instructions:

1. Before tasting — smelling, actually, in this case — you will need to wash your hands thoroughly to make sure they do not have any distracting odors on them.

2. Working quietly to facilitate concentration, close your eyes and smell each sample, A through I. Then swirl each sample and sniff it again. To help you focus on the added odors, alternate between smelling one of the aroma samples and the base wine sample — a glass of the neutral white wine to which the reference materials were added to make the samples.

3. Record two kinds of impressions you have when smelling the samples. First, write down the associations, if any, that you make with each wine's odors, no matter how outrageous or mundane the images or memories that you connect with the samples may seem. (For example, sample A might remind you of walking through a garden. I often have images of playing softball in the sixth grade when I smell the "cut green grass" reference standard.) Second, write down your best guess as to which third-tier aroma wheel term applies to that sample. (Upon further sniffing and reflection, for example, Sample A might be revealed to you as the odor of soil or flowers, a specific floral odor such as in that garden or even roses.) If you cannot identify the aroma that specifically, use a more general first- or second-tier term or a combination of terms from the third tier.

4. After everyone has had a chance to make and record a first guess at the identity of each aroma, the set of aromas that you are actually working with will be revealed. At this point your task changes from retrieving unknown odor names from your memory bank to the simpler one of matching a known set of third-tier odor terms to the samples. Of course, if a particular odor is new to you, knowing its name won't help, unless it's the only one you haven't positively identified and you can name it by a process of elimination! Swirl and sniff the unknown samples again, alternating with the base wine.

5. After everyone has had a chance to match the odors to the samples, the identity of each sample will be revealed. The last step in this exercise, then, is to learn the aromas you did not identify correctly and to match your associations with the third-tier aroma-wheel terms. Smell the odors again and think of their names as you perceive their odors. This is especially important for those that you did not correctly name. To help encode them in your memory, describe their unique features — how they differ from the other odors, record any associations you have with them, and write a definition of each odor which incorporates these features and associations.

6. After each sample has been identified, your instructor will explain — or you can look up in Appendix D — where each aroma is found in white varietal table wines.

7. Here is some (unedited) advice on learning aromas provided by five students from a recent Introduction to Wine class at Chico State.

   Dan: *By smelling the base wine frequently, I can associate the aromas more quickly. I first take a short sniff, then swirl the glass and take a deep sniff. As I am looking at the aroma wheel, I then associate as best I can.*

   Dave: *I think that to make this exercise successful one must shut off outside distractions and focus all of one's attention on the sample at hand. Also, not hurrying will help.*

   Sally: *When I do this exercise I really need to close my eyes to "visualize" the aroma. I also seem to need to smell a few of the different aromas before I start to be able to apply specific identifications. The longer or more times I smell them the more distinctly I notice differences.*

Matthew: *I think in terms of word associations: a linguistic smell connection. I work best with a fixed system of possibilities such as the aroma wheel. After identifying a first-tier term I allow my mind to wander and then glance at the second-and third-tier terms to really connect.*

Jody: *I try to use a lot of associations. The vanilla smelled exactly like vanilla extract. The black pepper made my nose twinge, just like pepper does.*

8. When you have completed this exercise, write down a few key notes of advice for yourself about how to learn wine odors. You might want to think in terms of answering the question, "What advice would you give to future tasters doing this exercise?"

_____

_____

_____

_____

_____

_____

_____

_____

_____

_____

_____

_____

_____

_____

Sensory Evaluation Exercise 4.1. Focus on Olfaction I: White Table Wine Aromas and an Introduction to the Wine Aroma Wheel

Sample	Association(s) ①	Aroma Identity — First Guess ②	Aroma Identity — Second Guess ③	Actual Aroma ④	Where this aroma is found in white table wines and your definition of any odors that were new to you ⑤
A	FLORAL	GERANIUM	CLOVE PEACH		
B	CITRUS	GRAPEFRUIT	GRAPEFRUIT		
C	CITRUS	ORANGE	MELON		
D	FRUIT	MANGO	PEACH		
E	FLORAL	ROSE	ROSE		
F	CITRUS	LEMON	GREEN GRASS		
G	PINEAPPLE	PINEAPPLE	PINEAPPLE		
H	LICORICE	ANISE	PEACH CLOVE PEACH	LINALOOL	
I	EARTHY	MOLDY CORK	BELL PEPPER		

Number of aromas correctly identified on your first attempt: _____

Questions raised by this tasting:

SENSORY EVALUATION EXERCISE 4.2

Focus on Taste and Touch I — Structural Components of White Table Wines

A wine's structural components are sometimes referred to as its backbone and can be just as important as its odors and flavors in determining its greatness, successful use with food, and aging potential.

Taking another look at the research of Harvard Professor Gregg Solomon, we find that the novice winetasters described only two salient features of the (red) wines he presented to them: sweetness and an "undifferentiated superdimension" that combined acidity, bitterness, and astringency. Novices did not discriminate between these three structural features. Expert winetasters, in contrast, did differentiate acidity, bitterness, and astringency and also described the wines structurally in terms of sugar-to-acid balance and body, giving them five descriptive dimensions to work with. The experts also were able to describe these structural features more precisely.[3] This exercise will help your wine descriptions become more multidimensional.

Objectives: You will learn to describe the acidity, balance, bitterness, and astringency of wines by doing the following exercise and Exercise 6.3.

What to Do before This Exercise:

Reading: Review these parts of Chapter 2: Taste, the Limited Sense (pp. 24-25); Thresholds (pp. 26-27); the entry on Taste in What to Look for in Wines (p. 40); and In-Mouth Impressions in Techniques for the Sensory Evaluation of Wines (p. 46).

Sensory Homework: You will be able to perform this exercise more accurately if you first become reacquainted with tart and sweet tastes and how your mouth responds to them. The following homework exercises will enable you to do that. I have adapted most of them from the work of French enologist Emile Peynaud and Australian wine educator Alan Young and a suggestion by American psychophysicist Linda Bartoshuk.[4]

1. Tart Homework: Where Do You Taste It?

   Collect some juice from a lemon and use some to moisten a cotton-tipped applicator or swab such as a Q-Tip®. Look in the mirror and stick out your tongue or have a helper touch the juice-dipped swab to various parts of your tongue — the tip, the sides, the underside, and the back — the insides of your cheeks, your gums, and the roof of your mouth. Where do you perceive the tart taste of the lemon juice? You can make a mental note or a map of your tart perception zones.

2. Tart Homework: A Green Apple

   Apples contain malic acid which, as you know, is also found in wines. Buy a nice green — as in not ripe — apple (or an example of a naturally more tart variety such as Granny Smith), bite into it, and consider the effect on your mouth: where do you perceive its tartness? Are there any other clues to the fact that you are eating something high in acid besides the tart taste itself? Does your mouth start to water? Bite into a riper apple for comparison — or one of a less tart variety such as a yellow-gold Golden Delicious, which we assume will be of a lower malic acid content. (You should probably buy this second apple as well, actually.)

3. Alternative or Supplementary Tart Homework: Acid Solutions

   Buy some citric or tartaric acid from your friendly home brewing or home winemaking supply store. The mixtures of ascorbic and citric acids that you can buy in the grocery store for keeping canned fruit fresh won't work because they also contain sugar. Make up a set of four solutions of increasing acid concentration as follows: Mix a half teaspoon of the acid crystals in a little warm water, then add cold water to make up a liter. This is solution #1. Take one half of this solution and add an equal amount of water for solution #2. Then take half of solution #2 and add an equal amount of water for solution #3. For each person doing this exercise, pour two or three ounces of each solution into a glass. The fourth glass should be a blank water sample. Do not keep the acid solutions overnight. Taste the solutions from #4 to #1, rest, and then taste them again in reverse order. Rinse your mouth between tastes. You will probably notice that the perception of the taste sensations will move from one area of the mouth to another when you taste the strongest vs. the weakest acid solution (#1 vs. #3). Alan Young comments, "In my own case, the strong solution of acid registers on the teeth, gums and lips…the weak solutions may register on more conventional areas…of the tongue" — that is, along the sides and on the underside. Your experience may be different.

4. Sweet Homework: Sugar Solutions

   Make a strong sugar solution — solution #5 — by dissolving a heaping tablespoon of table sugar in eight ounces of water. Moisten a cotton swab with some of this solution and test your tongue and other areas of your mouth for their ability to perceive sweetness — as you did with the lemon juice for tartness — and make mental or paper notes of the sweet-perceiving zones you discover. Take one half of solution #5 and add an equal amount of water for solution #6. Then take half of solution #6 and add an equal amount of water for solution #7. "Solution" #8 is a glass of water. Taste the solutions from #8 to #5 and then taste them again in reverse order, rinsing your mouth between tastes. Where do you perceive the sweet taste in your mouth? Notice the difference in viscosity or density between solutions #5 and #8. Many people perceive sweetness on the tip and back of the tongue and solutions with higher sugar concentrations as more viscous.

5. Sweet and Tart: The Balancing Act

   To experience the interaction of sugar and acid, squeeze ½ teaspoon of lemon juice into 2-3 ounces of solution #5 and taste it. The acidity of the lemon juice should decrease the perceived viscosity of solution #5 and make it seem more tart and refreshing — just as lemonade does when you adjust it by adding another squirt of lemon juice.

6. Temperature and the Perception of Sweetness

   A trick that may come in handy if you are serving wine with food and the wine you have is too sweet is to reduce the wine's perceived sweetness by chilling it. You can try this on the sugar solutions you have made for this homework exercise by chilling them in the refrigerator for a couple of hours.

Instructions:

1. You will taste four wines in this exercise. One is a commercial dry white table wine, the "base wine," to which sugar or acid has been added to create three "component" wines. These will differ from the base wine in either sugar or acid content but will have the same aromas and flavors. They are called component wines because they differ from the base wine in just one sensory component — acid or sugar in the case of this exercise.

2. Taste each of these wines by placing a small amount in your mouth and moving your mouth in a chewing motion to distribute the wine over the entire surface of your tongue as well as between your tongue and palate and lips and teeth to contact all your taste buds and allow you to perceive the tactile sensations stimulated by the wine.

3. Rank the wines from the sweetest (=#1) to the most tart (=#4). One way to approach this task is to taste the wines in pairs. Determine which one is the sweeter and place that cup or glass of wine to the left of the less sweet member of the pair; then repeat the process with other pairings. Rinse your mouth between tastes. Arrange all four wines in order, then rinse your mouth again and taste your arrangement from least sweet to sweetest and see if your order is confirmed. Taste the wines again that seem out of order.

1. ___D___   2. ___B___   3. ___C___   4. ___A___
Sweetest   Most Tart

4. Describe the acid, sugar, balance, and body of the wines on the wine evaluation form for this exercise. Use the terms listed below. (Refer to Chapter 2, "What to Look for in Wines," for their definitions.) Don't worry about describing any other aspect of the wines; just focus on their sugar and acid contents, balance, and body.

    Acid: flat, tart, green

    Sugar: dry; low, medium, or high sugar

    Balance: OK (neither acid nor sugar is too high), too tart, too sweet

    Body: thin; low/light, medium, heavy/high

5. As you are tasting, answer these questions.

    A. What is the effect of sugar on the acid taste? _____

    +SUGAR INCREASES BODY

    ↑ SUGAR   *↓ ACID TASTE*

    _____

    _____

    B. How is the body of the wine affected by the level of sweetness? _____

    _____

    HIGH SUGAR INCREASED BODY

    _____

    C. Why is it recommended that dry wines be tasted before sweet wines? _____

    IF TASTE SWEET BEFORE DRY, SWEET WILL SEEM MORE BITTER.

    _____

6. After you have worked alone tasting and answering the questions, your instructor will reveal the correct ranking of the wines, the base wine's identity, and the compositions of the component wines, or you can look them up in Appendix D if you are working teacher-less.

    1. _____   2. _____   3. _____   4. _____

    Sweetest   Most Tart

    Wine A = _____

        Composition, grams/100 ml: acid _____ sugar _____

    Wine B = _____

        Composition, grams/100 ml: acid _____ sugar _____

    Wine C = _____

        Composition, grams/100 ml: acid _____ sugar _____

    Wine D = _____

        Composition, grams/100 ml: acid _____ sugar _____

7. What the ranking you made may say about your sugar threshold is discussed in the section on Threshold Estimates in Appendix D (pp. 356-357). Tasters with better concentration and more experience will make fewer errors in this exercise, so if your "threshold" seems high it probably could be improved with attention and practice.

Sensory Evaluation Exercise 4.2. Focus on Taste and Touch I: Structural Components of White Table Wines

Fill in your impressions of wines B, C, and D only for acid, sugar, balance, and body. The tasting notes for wine A outside the box are for your information — these characteristics are essentially the same for all 4 wines.

Sensory Features	Base Wine	Component Wines		
	Wine A	*Wine B*	*Wine C*	*Wine D*
Color	light straw yellow	CLEAR	GOLDEN	CLEAR
Clarity	brilliantly clear			
Off Odors	none			
Aroma	fruity, simple			
Bouquet	none			
Flavor	simple, young, fruity			
Acid	tart	SWEET	SWEET, TART	SWEET
Sugar	dry	LOW	MED	HIGH
Balance of Acid and Sugar	OK	+ ACID	OK	+ SUGAR
Body	light	LIGHT	FULL	LIGHT
Astringency	smooth			
Age Until?	next week (drink now)			
Overall Impression	good for an inexpensive white table wine			
Serving and Food Ideas	chill well and serve at picnics			

Questions raised by this tasting:

SENSORY EVALUATION EXERCISE 4.3
Applying the Techniques for the Sensory Evaluation of Wine to the Extremes of the White Table Wine Flavor Spectrum — A Tasting of Chenin Blanc and Muscat Blanc

Wine writer Harvey Steiman has developed a spectrum of flavor strengths for white varietal table wines designed to help make successful wine and food combinations.[5] Wines with more neutral flavors — that is, flavors at the weaker end of Steiman's spectrum — are more versatile for accompanying a meal since neutral flavors are less likely to overwhelm mild food flavors or to clash with distinctively flavored foods. Thus, wines like Chenin Blanc and Chardonnay will combine more successfully with a wider range of foods than will Muscats and Gewürztraminers, which are stronger, more distinctively flavored wines.

Strongest					Weakest
Muscat	Gewürztraminer	White Riesling	Sauvignon Blanc	Chardonnay	Chenin Blanc

Table 4.1
Harvey Steiman's White Wine Flavor Spectrum

This exercise uses Muscat Blanc and Chenin Blanc for odor and flavor contrast and to give your senses, memories, and imaginations both the chance to describe the aroma of the most floral and fruity of the white varietals and the challenge of describing one of the most neutral.

Objectives: To introduce you to two very different white varietal table wines and to the application of the techniques for sensory evaluation of wines described in Chapter 2.

What to do Before this Exercise:

Reading: Review the following parts of Chapter 2: Approaching the Wine, in Techniques for the Sensory Evaluation of Wines (pp. 45-47) and What to Look for in Wines (pp. 34-43). Look over the varietal wine profiles of Chenin Blanc and Muscat Blanc in Appendix A (pp. 301 and 303).

Sensory Homework: Do the following homework exercise as a preview of how winetasters enhance their ability to detect wine odors.[6]

1. Pick out a bottle of wine you enjoy and pour two ounces into each of three glasses.
2. Cover each glass with a take-out cup lid or some plastic food wrap.
3. Remove the lid and smell glass #1. Replace lid. Describe the odors and record your impressions of their intensity.
4. Revolve glass #2 in a circular movement, swirling the wine up along the sides of the glass. Place the glass under your nose, remove the lid and smell. Describe the odors and record your impressions of their intensity as you did for glass #1.
5. With the lid firmly held on glass #3, shake the glass vigorously. Smell as for #2 and describe the odors and record your intensity impressions.

You will observe that both swirling and shaking make more wine odors available to your nose. Odors you noticed when you sniffed without swirling become more intense and new odors become evident. Shaking is particularly helpful in detecting certain off odors: some professional tasters will cover the glass containing a suspected spoiled wine with their hand, shake it, rub their palms together, and then smell the wine evaporating off their palms to search for odors of bacterial spoilage, for example.

Instructions

1. You will learn more if you taste these two wines "in parallel" rather than making a complete sensory evaluation of one wine and then the other. Examine the color and clarity of both wines, compare one to the other, and make notes; then follow the same procedure when smelling and tasting them. Consider your overall response to each wine. Refer to the readings in Chapter 2 to refresh your memory of the steps in tasting.
2. Remember to work quietly to foster concentration; take your time and refer to the aroma wheel and your notes for Exercises 4.1 and 4.2.
3. When you are finished tasting join the discussion of the wines with your fellow tasters as a contributor and careful listener.

Wine Evaluation Form for Sensory Evaluation Exercise 4.3. Applying the Techniques for the Sensory Evaluation of Wine to the Extremes of the White Table Wine Flavor Spectrum — A Tasting of Chenin Blanc and Muscat Blanc

WINE INFO (4/2)	WINE A: Observations	WINE A: Notes	WINE B: Observations	WINE B: Notes
Type	CHENIN BLANC	~~MUSCAT CANELLI 2003 SIERRA FOOTHILLS LAVA CAP~~ (5)	MUSCAT CANELLI	
Vintage	2004		2003	
Appellation	STAION BASCH		SIERRA FOOTHILLS	
Producer	SIMAN SIG		LAVA CAP	
Cost/Other				
Clarity	BRILLIANTLY CLEAR		BRILLIANTLY CLEAR	
Color	STRAW YELLOW (LIGHT)		LIGHT STRAW YELLOW	
Off Odors	NONE		NONE	
Aroma				
Associations	PEAR, GRAPEFRUIT		FLORAL, FRUIT LOOPS	
Descriptors			HONEY	
Intensity	LOW		SARDINA	
Varietal?	YES			
Bouquet	ALCOHOL		ALCOHOL	
Flavor	GRAPEFRUIT, PEACH		SWEET HONEY!, STRAWBERRY, ORANGE, GUAVA	
Acid, Sugar, Balance	TART, TOO SWEET!		TOO, SWEET, TART?	
Body	THIN, LIGHT - MED.		HEAVY BODY (HIGH SUGAR)	
Astringency	SMOOTH		SMOOTH	
Aging Potential	2-3 yrs		2-3 yrs	
Overall Quality	SEAFOOD (ANGEY PLAWN) CHEESE COMPLEMENT / CONTRAST		FOR DESSERT & ALONE	

Questions raised by this tasting:

EYE
NOSE
TASTE
BRAIN

109

SENSORY EVALUATION EXERCISE 4.4
Contrasting Aroma and Fermentation Bouquet — A Tasting of White Riesling,
Gewürztraminer, and Gewürztraminer Grape Juice

Objectives: In this exercise you will practice the tasting techniques introduced in the Chenin Blanc and Muscat Blanc tasting, look for aroma components from the Focus on Olfaction for White Table Wines, and investigate fermentation bouquet.

What to Do Before This Exercise: Read the section of Chapter 3 (pp. 72-76) on alcoholic fermentation, Table 3.6 "Sources of the Sensory Components of White Table Wines" (p. 87), and the varietal wine profiles of White Riesling and Gewürztraminer in Appendix A.

Instructions: Taste the two wines in parallel, making notes about each aspect on the evaluation form. Pay particularly close attention to comparing the odors of the Gewürztraminer wine and grape juice. Smell the juice first, but wait to taste it until after you have completed your sensory evaluation of both wines. Answer these questions.

1. What odors does fermentation add to wine? ADDS A FLORAL, FRESH ODER, ALCOHOL, CITRUS ADDED / STRONGER AROMA THAN JUICE
CLARITY IN APPEARANCE
-MORE COMPLEX

2. How would you describe fermentation bouquet (present in the Gewürztraminer wine, absent in the Gewürztraminer grape juice)? CRISPER BONQUET, CITRUS, FLORAL, ALCOHOL, NOT AS SWEET...

3. Can differences in the density of liquids (body of wine, for example) be perceived before they are tasted? How? YES, BY SWIRLING THE GLASS

Sensory Evaluation Exercise 4.4.
Contrasting Aroma and Fermentation Bouquet — A Tasting of White Riesling, Gewürztraminer, and Gewürztraminer Grape Juice

WINE INFO	WINE A: Observations	WINE A: Notes GRAPE JUICE	WINE B: Observations	WINE B: Notes GEWÜRZTRAMINER
Type	SANTA CRUZ ORGANIC		GEWÜRZTRA,	
Vintage			2004	
Appellation			VALLEY OAKS, CA	
Producer	— BOTTLED IN CHICO		FETZER	
Cost/Other				
Clarity			BRILLIANTLY CLEAR	
Color			LIGHT STRAW	
Off Odors			NONE	
Aroma				
Associations	PRUNE		FLORAL, CITRUS, SPICY	
Descriptors	FRUITY, EARTHY		NOT AS SWEET	
Intensity	MILD		GEWÜRZT,	
Varietal?	NO			
Bouquet	LIGHT, MILD, BLAN SIMPLE		ALCOHOL, COMPLEX	
Flavor			SWEET! SPICY! ROSE	
Acid, Sugar, Balance			GOOD /W SUGAR	
Body			MED → THICK	
Astringency				
Aging Potential				
Overall Quality			FAIR	

Questions raised by this tasting:

Sensory Evaluation Exercise 4.4.
Contrasting Aroma and Fermentation Bouquet — A Tasting of White Riesling, Gewürztraminer, and Gewürztraminer Grape Juice

WINE INFO	GRAPE JUICE: Observations	GRAPE JUICE: Notes
Type	WT. REISLING	
Vintage	2001	
Appellation	WASHINGTON STATE	
Producer	BONNY DOONE	
Cost/Other		
Clarity		BRILLIANTLY CLEAR
Color	LESS	LT. STRAW YELLOW
Off Odors		NONE
Aroma		
Associations	GRAPEFRUIT, FLORAL	HERBACIOUS EARTHY
Descriptors	DRY	
Intensity	MED — MILD	
Varietal?	WT REISLING (YES)	
Bouquet	ALCOHOL!	
Flavor	TART, DRY, ALCOHOL, HOT PINEAPPLE/GRAPEFRUIT	
Acid, Sugar, Balance	ACIDIC (SLIGHTLY TART!)	
Body	LIGHT — MED/SMOOTH	
Astringency		
Aging Potential	2-3 YRS	
Overall Quality	GOOD/PERFECT	

Questions raised by this tasting:

SENSORY EVALUATION EXERCISE 4.5
Comparing Aroma, Fermentation Bouquet, and Oak-Aging Bouquet —
A Tasting of Sauvignon Blanc and Two Styles of Chardonnay

Objectives: In this exercise you will look for the aroma components from the Focus on Olfaction that are present in Sauvignon Blanc and Chardonnay, two wines which are less fruity than those tasted so far. You will also become acquainted with the oak-aging bouquet and flavors and the effect of oak aging on the perception of other wine components and find out how apples and cheese influence the perception of wine components.

What to Do Before This Exercise: Read Chapter 3, To Rack or Not to Rack (p. 76) and about Oak Aging (pp. 80-84); Chapter 8, Champagne Aging Bouquet (p. 200); and the varietal wine profiles of Chardonnay and Sauvignon Blanc in Appendix A.

Instructions: Taste the three wines in parallel and

1. Write a description of the oak-aging bouquet by smelling and thinking about the odors of the OAK-MOR® samples and by comparing the Chardonnays made without oak (Callaway Vineyard's Callalees) and with oak. _____
    _____
    _____
    _____

2. Record what you perceive to be the effect of oak aging on the acidity and body by comparing the two Chardonnays. DECREASES ACIDITY & INCREASES
    BODY
    _____
    _____

3. To learn the effect of two foods on the perception of wine components and the flavor of wines, take a **small** bite of apple and sip some Chardonnay at the same time. Think about the following questions and record your observations in the table below: Is your perception of any wine structural component altered? What about the flavor? If so, which component is altered, and how? Repeat the exercise with the baby Swiss cheese. Then, if time, food, and wine permit, repeat with the Sauvignon Blanc.

FOOD	EFFECT ON WINE(S)	COMPONENT AFFECTED
Apple	- w/ OAK - REDUCES SMOKEY REDUCES BUTTERY REDUCES OVERALL FLAVOR OF WINE.	- TASTE, FLAVOR
Baby Swiss Cheese	- w/ OAK - BALANCES OUT SWEETNESS, BUTTERY - BRINGS OUT SWEETNESS IN WINE.	- TASTE

Sensory Evaluation Exercise 4.5.
Comparing Aroma, Fermentation Bouquet, and Oak-Aging Bouquet — A Tasting of Sauvignon Blanc and Two Styles of Chardonnay

WINE INFO	WINE A: Observations	WINE A: Notes	WINE B: Observations	WINE B: Notes
Type	SAV. BLANC		CHARDONNAY (W/OUT AGE)	→ WITHOUT OAK
Vintage	GROVE MILL (2002)		2004	
Appellation	MARLBOROUGH, NEW ZEALAND		MENDOCINO COUNTY, CA	
Producer	GROVE MILL		TOAD HOLLOW	
Cost/Other				
Clarity	BRILLIANTLY CLEAR		BRILLIANTLY CLEAR (BUBBLE)	
Color	LT. STRAW YELLOW		STRAW YELLOW	
Off Odors	NONE		NA	
Aroma				
Associations	– BELL PEPPER, SHORT		– HONEY, MELON, CITRUS,	
Descriptors	BREAD, GRAPE FRUIT,		→ BUTTER ???	
	CUT GREEN GRASS			
Intensity	– LIGHT / LOW INTENSITY		– LIGHT INTENSITY	
Varietal?	YES!		YES!	
Bouquet	MILD ALCOHOL			
Flavor	TART ↑ DRY	.13% ALCOHOL	– SLIGHTLY BUTTERY	13.9% ALCOHOL
	– BELL PEPPER		DRY / HONEY	(HIGH ALCOHOL!)
	– CITRUS		(GENTLE SPICE	
			(TART AFTER TASTE)	
Acid, Sugar, Balance	– SLIGHT ACIDITY			
	TART!			
Body	– LIGHT		– LIGHT – MED.	
Astringency	– SMOOTH		– SLIGHT	
Aging Potential	– 3–4 YRS.		– 3–4 YRS	
Overall Quality	SLIGHTLY BELOW		YES! I'D BUY IT!	
	PAR / LOWER QUALITY			

Questions raised by this tasting: ↳ BEST W/ SPICY FOODS FISH, ETC...

© 1993 Marian W. Baldy
THE UNIVERSITY WINE COURSE

Sensory Evaluation Exercise 4.5.
Comparing Aroma, Fermentation Bouquet, and Oak-Aging Bouquet — A Tasting of Sauvignon Blanc and Two Styles of Chardonnay

WINE INFO	WINE C: Observations	WINE C: Notes
Type	CHARDONNAY	
Vintage	2002	
Appellation	RUSSIAN RIVER, SONOMA	
Producer	(CALUSA OF SONOMA	
Cost/Other	—	
Clarity	BRILLIANTLY CLEAR	
Color	STRAW YELLOW	
Off Odors	NA	
Aroma		
Associations	—SMOKEY! SAWDUST, CARAMEL	
Descriptors	WOODY!	
Intensity	VANILLA, NUTTY	MED INTENSITY
Varietal?	YES	
Bouquet	SMOKEY/OAK!	
Flavor	OAKY, BUTTERY, BOURBON, VANILLA	→ CITRUS APPLE TASTE
Acid, Sugar, Balance	SLIGHTLY HIGHER SUGAR THAN ACID / (RESIDUAL SUGAR LOW!)	OAK PROCESSING → HAS CHANGED FLAVOR... 13.9% ALCOHOL
Body	MEDIUM	
Astringency	SMOOTH	
Aging Potential	3-4 YRS	
Overall Quality	GOOD!	

MUSTY! (OAK)

Questions raised by this tasting:

SENSORY EVALUATION EXERCISE 4.6
Your Turn — Creating Your Own Tasting of White Table Wines

Objective: To design and conduct a sensory evaluation exercise that explores some additional aspect of white table wines that interests you.

What to Do Before This Exercise: Think about what you have learned about white table wines and make a list of things you would like to know more about. If you're stumped, look over your sensory evaluation notes to see what questions were raised for you in these tastings. If you're desperate, see Appendix D for suggestions. Also, be sure to review the information about the setting for a winetasting in Chapter 2 (pp. 43-44).

Instructions:
1. Define the objective(s) of your tasting.
2. Decide on the general characteristics of the wines you will need to use. What will you need to tell the wine merchant or winery you contact about the wines you want to buy for your tasting? This is pretty easy if you are curious about other varietal white wines or inexpensive Chardonnays, for example: you will need "wines made from Pinot Blanc grapes" or "Chardonnays for $7.00 per bottle or less." If your tasting will examine the sensory changes that occur during bottle aging of Chardonnays or White Rieslings, you will need "older and younger Chardonnays or White Rieslings"; more specific details can be settled in your conversations with your supplier. Examples of wine characteristics you may need to discuss include: region of production, vintage year, grape varieties used, producer, price, and style (level of residual sugar, for example).
3. Who's tasting? How many wines will be needed? After you have chosen your topic and selected the kinds of wines you want to use, you will need to decide how many wines to taste. You will want to consider how long the tasting will last, how experienced the tasters are, and what your budget is. Obviously, a longer time period, more experienced tasters, and a bigger budget will allow you to include more wines.
4. Consult your supplier(s). When you know how many wines you plan to taste, you will want to consult with your instructor, with a particularly knowledgeable member of your club, with a wine merchant, or directly with the wineries to pick the particular wines you will use (although the budget for wines may be slightly diminished by long-distance telephone charges). Be sure to buy the wines in plenty of time to transport and refrigerate them.
5. Define a tasting strategy. For the actual tasting session you will need to decide how much background you want to give about the wines. Do you want the tasters to approach the wines blind and make an objective assessment, or will you tell them a lot about the wines and taste more for enjoyment than analysis?
6. You will need background or reference material. What information should be available at your tasting? If you have in mind the kinds of material you would like to use, you will be able to ask your wine merchant or the wineries if such information is available and where to find it.
7. Will you need special note-taking aids? Will the tasters need any tables to fill out or questions to answer besides the wine evaluation forms on pages 118 and 119?
8. Does the regular tasting procedure need to be modified? On the day of the tasting you will also want to make sure the tasting environment is conducive to a successful sensory evaluation.
9. Have fun!

Worksheet for Creating Your Own Winetasting

1. Objective:

    _____
    _____
    _____
    _____

2. Wine characteristics:

    _____
    _____
    _____
    _____

3. Number of wines, budget:

    _____
    _____
    _____
    _____

4. Supplier(s) and the specific wines:

    _____
    _____
    _____
    _____
    _____
    _____
    _____
    _____

5. The tasting strategy:

    _____
    _____
    _____
    _____

6. Background or reference material:

    _____
    _____
    _____
    _____

7. Note-taking aids:

    _____
    _____
    _____
    _____

8. The setting:

    _____
    _____
    _____
    _____

Sensory Evaluation Exercise 4.6.
Your Turn — Creating Your Own Tasting of White Table Wines

WINE INFO	WINE A: Observations	WINE A: Notes	WINE B: Observations	WINE B: Notes
Type				
Vintage				
Appellation				
Producer				
Cost/Other				
Clarity				
Color				
Off Odors				
Aroma				
Associations				
Descriptors				
Intensity				
Varietal?				
Bouquet				
Flavor				
Acid, Sugar, Balance				
Body				
Astringency				
Aging Potential				
Overall Quality				

Questions raised by this tasting:

Sensory Evaluation Exercise 4.6.
Your Turn — Creating Your Own Tasting of White Table Wines

WINE INFO	WINE C: Observations	WINE C: Notes	WINE D: Observations	WINE D: Notes
Type				
Vintage				
Appellation				
Producer				
Cost/Other				
Clarity				
Color				
Off Odors				
Aroma				
Associations				
Descriptors				
Intensity				
Varietal?				
Bouquet				
Flavor				
Acid, Sugar, Balance				
Body				
Astringency				
Aging Potential				
Overall Quality				

Questions raised by this tasting:

SENSORY EVALUATION EXERCISE 4.7
Mystery Wine Identification — A Review Tasting

Objectives: In this exercise you will create your own system of classification by reviewing and organizing your sensory impressions of white table wines. Using your classification system and sensory evaluation skills, you will identify some of the wines you have tasted in the other exercises in this chapter.

What to Do Before This Exercise:

1. Look over your notes for Exercises 4.3, 4.4, and 4.5 — the three white varietal wine tastings — to identify the key sensory factors that are unique to each wine.

2. Organize these factors into a sorting system that will allow you to identify each of the seven wines. This sorting can begin by first dividing the wines into the broadest sensory categories and then narrowing sorting categories within these broad classifications. Alternatively, you could think of constructing your sorting system as a process of elimination in which the wine with the most unique sensory properties is taken out of the group first, then the rest are classified for further sorting, and then the most unique wine in that subset is eliminated, etc. Under the first approach you would start sorting white table wines by asking whether they are generally fruity or herbaceous in aroma. That would group together Muscat, White Riesling, Gewürztraminer, and Chenin Blanc in one category and Sauvignon Blanc and Chardonnay in another. The latter could be further subdivided by the presence or absence or amount of oak flavor in these wines. An example of the "process of elimination" method might be something like the following, which is related to Harvey Steiman's flavor spectrum:

> Step #1. sensory factor: strength of flavor and aroma
>> if very strong, floral and fruity, the variety is Muscat
>> if less strong, may or may not be fruity, go to step #2

3. Once you have your sorting system figured out, jot it down in the worksheet for this tasting and bring it along to refer to when you taste the wines. The actual white table wine sorting system that you come up with will depend on two factors: the styles of the wines that were used in these exercises and your personal perception of them. I've included a generalized classification system for this exercise in Appendix D (p. 362), but it may not work perfectly for you or for the particular varietal wines you've experienced. Take a look at it if you'd like to see an example of one approach.

Worksheet for the White Table Wine Review Tasting

The worksheet is intended to help you draft a sorting system using either method mentioned in #2. For this reason, each step contains in its first alternative ("if _____ , . . .") spaces for the variety name (if it has been identified at that point: "the variety is _____ ") or for instructions to go to another step ("or go to step _____ "). Cross out the alternative that does not apply to your sorting system.

Step #1. sensory factor: _____
    if _____ , the variety is _____ or go to step _____
    if _____ , go to step _____

Step #2. sensory factor: _____
    if _____ , the variety is _____ or go to step _____
    if _____ , go to step _____

Step #3. sensory factor: _____
    if _____ , the variety is _____ or go to step _____
    if _____ , go to step _____

Step #4. sensory factor: _____
    if _____ , the variety is _____ or go to step _____
    if _____ , go to step _____

Step #5. sensory factor: _____
    if _____ , the variety is _____ or go to step _____
    if _____ , go to step _____

Step #6. sensory factor: _____
    if _____ , the variety is _____ or go to step _____
    if _____ , go to step #7

Step #7. sensory factor: _____
    if _____ , the variety is _____
    if _____ , the variety is _____

Instructions:

Taste the wines presented, refer to your worksheet, and apply your memory to correctly identify them. Have fun and good luck!

Sensory Evaluation Exercise 4.7.
Mystery Wine Identification — A Review Tasting

WINE INFO	WINE A: Observations	WINE A: Notes	WINE B: Observations	WINE B: Notes
Type Vintage Appellation Producer Cost/Other				
Clarity				
Color				
Off Odors				
Aroma Associations Descriptors Intensity Varietal?				
Bouquet				
Flavor				
Acid, Sugar, Balance				
Body				
Astringency				
Aging Potential				
Overall Quality				

Questions raised by this tasting:

Sensory Evaluation Exercise 4.7.
Mystery Wine Identification — A Review Tasting

WINE INFO	WINE C: Observations	WINE C: Notes	WINE D: Observations	WINE D: Notes
Type				
Vintage				
Appellation				
Producer				
Cost/Other				
Clarity				
Color				
Off Odors				
Aroma				
Associations				
Descriptors				
Intensity				
Varietal?				
Bouquet				
Flavor				
Acid, Sugar, Balance				
Body				
Astringency				
Aging Potential				
Overall Quality				

Questions raised by this tasting:

REVIEW QUESTIONS

Instructions: You might want to use a separate sheet of paper to answer the following review questions. In that way you can use the questions to check your knowledge of this chapter more than once. You may, for example, want to re-test yourself on items that you have missed or use the "Review Questions" to test your knowledge before you read a chapter.

Match each statement (1-12) with the grape or wine it describes. For the True or False items, answer "True" if the statement is accurate or "False" if the statement is incorrect. If you determine that a statement is false make a note explaining why. For the multiple choice items pick the best alternative. Check your answers after you have completed all the questions.

Use the following answers for items 1-12. Each statement describes only one wine or grape variety.

    A. White (Johannisberg) Riesling
    B. Gewürztraminer
    C. Chenin Blanc
    D. Sauvignon Blanc
    E. Chardonnay

1. White varietal wine on the list with the strongest flavor. _____

2. White varietal wine on the list with the weakest flavor. _____

3. White varietal wine whose grapes predominate in the vineyards of the Rhine and Mosel valleys of Germany. _____

4. White varietal wine most likely to be fermented and aged in oak. _____

5. White varietal wine whose neutral-flavored grapes are highly susceptible to *Botrytis cinerea.* _____

6. White varietal wine whose grapes are used to make Champagne and White Burgundy wines in France. _____

7. Aroma and flavor descriptors for this white varietal wine include bell pepper, green olive, and herbaceous. _____

8. White varietal wine blended with Sémillon to make Sauternes-style, *Botrytis*-affected late-harvest wines. _____

9. Grapes for this white varietal wine rank with French Colombard as one of the most commonly planted varieties in California. _____

10. You would have to pay the highest price per ton for grapes to make this white varietal wine. _____

11. Dry white varietal wine most likely to improve with bottle aging. _____

12. White varietal wine whose wines acquire "subtle, oily scents" as they age. _____

13. You are preparing a plate of appetizers for dinner. You will serve a dry Gewürztraminer with the appetizers. You do not include green apple slices on the plate because _____.
    A. eating the apple will bring out the spicy flavors in the wine
    B. eating the apple will reduce the tannins in the wine
    C. eating the apple will bring out the sugar in the wine
    D. eating the apple will bring out the acid in the wine
    E. eating the apple will cover up the acidity of the wine

14. True or false: Mild cheeses such as baby swiss are enjoyed with wines because they reduce the perception of the wines' acidity. _____

ANSWERS TO REVIEW QUESTIONS

1. B
2. C
3. A
4. E
5. C
6. E
7. D
8. D
9. E
10. E
11. E
12. A
13. D
14. True

ENDNOTES

[1] Solomon, Gregg Erin Arn, "Psychology of novice and expert wine talk," *American Journal of Psychology*, Vol. 103, No. 4, Winter 1990, pp. 495-517, p. 503.

[2] My students have long desired an aroma wheel that would resist wine spills and cheesy fingerprints, and Ann Noble and collaborators have put it on the market. It is available from Howe Noble Lee Designed, P.O. Box 1817, Healdsburg, CA 95448, (707) 433-0427. The 1991 price was $5.00 plus sales tax, shipping, and handling. There is also a sparkling wine aroma wheel available from the same source.

[3] Solomon, Gregg Erin Arn, "Psychology of novice and expert wine talk," *American Journal of Psychology*, Vol. 103, No. 4, Winter 1990, pp. 495-517, pp. 512-513.

[4] Peynaud, Emile, THE TASTE OF WINE, The Wine Appreciation Guild, San Francisco, 1989, pp. 207-211, and Young, Alan, MAKING SENSE OF WINE, Greenhouse Publications, Richmond, Australia, 1986, pp. 94-95 for the acid exercise and p. 99 for sugar.

[5] Steiman, Harvey, "Note: Wine with Food," in THE BOOK OF CALIFORNIA WINE, Doris Muscatine, Maynard A. Amerine, and Bob Thompson, editors, University of California Press, 1984, pp. 461-464.

[6] Adapted from Young, Alan, MAKING SENSE OF WINE, Greenhouse Publications, Richmond, Australia, 1986, p. 81.

5

RED TABLE WINE PRODUCTION

Red wines have more intense aromas and flavors than white wines, and these are extracted—along with color and tannins — from the grapes' skins during fermentation. The management of this extraction determines in large part the style of the wine and is the most important step in red-wine production. The tannins extracted protect red wines during the longer aging periods that allow them to develop complex bouquets. Building on the principles of winemaking introduced in Chapter 3, this chapter will describe the general steps used to make red wines in California and their specific application to the production of Pinot Noir and Cabernet Sauvignon. It will also outline the steps involved in carbonic maceration, a technique used to make light, very fruity red wines for early consumption.

STEP 1. ENVISION THE TYPE AND STYLE OF WINE TO BE MADE [1]

The types and styles of red table wines made in California range from the blushes and rosés (which are closer in their method of production and sensory properties to white table wines) to dark, richly flavored wines that require long bottle aging and are modeled primarily on French red wines. This similarity is reflected in the use of the French varietal names Pinot Noir and Cabernet Sauvignon for California's most important premium red table wines and in the choice of the names Claret and Burgundy for generic red wines. The most important exceptions to these French-defined wine types and styles include varietal wines made from Zinfandel, Barbera, Grignolino, and Sangiovese grapes — varieties that originated in Italy — and the higher-alcohol late-harvest styles of Zinfandel made possible by California's warmer climate.

Often the decision to make a particular style of wine dictates the choice of grape variety because the inherent nature of the variety limits its versatility. For example, Pinot Noir is a relatively light-colored, delicately flavored red grape variety that would not be a good candidate for making a late-harvest style wine or for aging in American oak. In contrast, highly flavorful Zinfandel grapes have a tendency to shrivel on the vine and concentrate their sugars; this makes them good candidates for late-harvest style "table" wines with alcohol concentrations in excess of 14% and some residual sugar. And the rich, full aromas and flavors of Cabernet Sauvignon have been successfully married with the bouquet and flavor of American oak by respected producers in both Bordeaux and California.

STEPS 2 AND 3. VARIETIES, CLIMATES, AND CLONES

The California coastal wineries surveyed by Cooke and Berg (in the study referred to in Chapter 3) preferred to make red wines from the varieties Cabernet Sauvignon, Merlot, Pinot Noir, Gamay, Petite Sirah, Barbera, and Zinfandel and wanted these varieties to be grown in moderate climates (California's viticultural regions II and III; see Chapter 11). The exception was the very early-ripening variety Pinot Noir, which was considered best — with the most desirable flavors and color — when grown in the coolest area region I.[2]

The proper match between grape variety and climate is crucial for all fine wine production. This association of the coolest climates with the highest-quality Pinot Noir grapes was supported by the results of the recent California study mentioned in Chapter 2 in which researchers compared the aromas of wines from Pinot Noir grapes grown in the warmer region II areas of Napa and Sonoma counties and in the neighboring Carneros viticultural area, one of California's coolest grape-growing regions (classified as region I). Pinot Noir wines from Carneros typically had cherry, fresh berry, berry jam, and spicy characters and were low in the less desirable vegetal, leather, and smoke/tar aromas that were found in moderate to high levels in most of the Napa and Sonoma wines investigated.[3]

It has also long been known that the very cool ripening conditions typical of areas like Carneros are required for the best color in Pinot Noir: a dark, pure, red. As it turns out, this color is not only inherently pleasing but also constitutes a signal that the grapes ripened under the very cool conditions required to produce the most desirable wine aroma and flavors. The pigments in grapes and wines change their colors in response to variations in pH, which in turn is affected by temperature. Grapes ripened under cool conditions will have lower pHs and the wines made from them will be of a more reddish tint whereas grapes that ripen in warmer temperatures will have higher pHs and the wines derived from them will be more purple.[4]

Another important choice for growing grapes for all wines and which especially applies to Pinot Noir concerns which clone to use. As mentioned in Chapter 2, Pinot Noir is known for its mutability and it is estimated that there are 150 different clones grown in Burgundy, which vary in berry size, intensity of color and flavor, and tannin content — factors that can significantly affect a winegrower's production decisions and the quality of the finished wine. A variety of clones have been imported to the U.S. since the mid-nineteenth century, most of them at a time when there was little interest in producing fine wines from Pinot Noir grapes. Because making fine Pinot Noir wines has been identified by many highly accomplished winemakers as one of their major challenges for the 1990s, research is now being conducted in cool winegrowing regions throughout the world to better understand the viticultural and enological differences between Pinot Noir clones.

STEP 4. CONSULT WITH GROWERS ON CRITICAL CULTURAL PRACTICES

Adding to our Chapter 3 heading of "farming for flavors," recent studies of the effect of leaf and cluster shading and leaf removal in Cabernet Sauvignon have shown results similar to those discussed in Chapter 3 for Sauvignon Blanc: shaded berries ripen more slowly and have less color. They are also more susceptible to infection by *Botrytis* molds. In one study, improved wine quality was associated with leaf removal around clusters, while another found that differences in the shading of berries produced significant differences in the aromas of both fruit and wine.[5] For the best quality red wines, growers need to manage the Cabernet Sauvignon vines canopy to promote the development of varietal character, avoid grassy odors and flavors, and reduce the incidence of *Botrytis* infections which can lead to premature aging of wine.[6]

A preliminary report of an investigation concerning the effect of soil on the sensory properties of Cabernet Sauvignon wines from the Napa Valley found that younger, finer soils with greater water-holding capacities produced greater crop yields and wines with more vegetative, grassy flavors. Older soils with a higher percentage of gravel and less ability to hold water were associated with smaller crops and fruitier wine flavors. The notion that valley floor locations — which typically have younger, finer soils — produce more vigorous vines and more vegetative Cabernet Sauvignon wines while hillsides with scant, rocky soils are associated with smaller vines and concentrated wines with more cherry or berry flavors has long been a working rule for Napa-area winemakers and grape growers. Younger vines, vines with larger crops, and grapes harvested at lower maturity will also yield Cabernet Sauvignon wines with more vegetative and less fruity characteristics.

Color is very important for red wines and the same cultural practices that give the best flavors also give the most pleasing colors. Careful management of the vine canopy is necessary for color development: grape berries require light in order to develop pigment, but too much sun can cause them to burn and their color to break down. The amount of fruit on a vine and the vigor of its vegetative growth also affect the color of the fruit: both too much fruit (overcropping) and excess vigor (which diminishes crop size) reduce color production. The ratio of skin to juice is highest in small berries, giving their wines a greater concentration of color and flavor. For this reason, viticultural factors that determine berry size also influence the intensity of wine color. These include irrigation timing, the amount of water applied, attention to vine nutrition, disease control, and the choice of clone.[7]

Climate and Canopy Management for Cabernet Sauvignon

California winemaker Tom Peterson has summarized the combined effects of the vineyard mesoclimate and the density of the vine canopy on some important sensory characteristics of Cabernet Sauvignon wines.[8] His summary (reproduced in Table 5.1) indicates that the best results — a complex flavor that combines vegetative, fruity, and spicy elements, high color and tannins, firm (pleasantly astringent) but not bitter tannins, and a moderate to low pH — are obtained in a warm mesoclimate with an open canopy. The effects on other varieties, particularly white grapes, would differ slightly, but the trend would be the same: the best wines are achieved in the optimum mesoclimate with an open canopy. In Chapter 11 you will learn the reasons for this.

Table 5.1
The Influence of Vineyard Mesoclimate and Density of Vine Canopy on the Character of Cabernet Sauvignon Wines

		MESOCLIMATE		
		Cool	Warm	Hot
CANOPY	Dense	vegetative/green/stemmy moderate color soft tannin high pH	vegetative/fruity moderate color lower tannin level, bitter moderate pH	neutral flavor poor color high pH
	Open	vegetative moderate to high color soft tannin, bitter moderate to high pH	vegetative/fruity/spicy high color high levels of "firm" tannin moderate/low pH	neutral flavor moderate color moderate pH

(WINE CHARACTER)

STEPS 5 AND 6. FOLLOW RIPENING CLOSELY AND PICK AT OPTIMUM RIPENESS

Red-wine grapes are allowed to ripen longer and are harvested at higher sugar and lower acid levels than white-wine grapes: an average of 23.1 degrees Brix, pH of 3.4, and total acid of 0.7 grams per 100 ml were reported by the wineries surveyed by Cooke and Berg.[9] The higher sugar levels are associated with wines of greater aroma and flavor intensity, varietal character, and complexity — perhaps because they allow fermentation reactions to produce higher alcohol concentrations, which aid in the extraction of color, flavor, and tannins. These higher alcohol contents are more compatible with the strong flavors and high tannin contents of red wines than they are with the more delicate flavors and very low tannin levels of white table wines. Their high tannin contents also enable red table wines to taste well balanced at lower total acid levels, since tannins and acids accentuate each other's taste and touch sensations.

Figure 5.1
Crushing Zinfandel grapes at Butte Creek Vineyards

STEP 7. REMOVE THE JUICE

At the winery, the grapes are crushed and sulfur dioxide added. Often less sulfur dioxide is required for making red wines than white wines because their tannins take over the antioxidant function of the SO_2. If necessary the total acidity is adjusted before fermentation by adding tartaric acid. For

Blanc de Noir or blush red wines the must is pumped directly to the press to minimize skin contact — also called maceration — and color extraction; the juice collected at the press is subsequently handled as for white wine production. For all other types of red wine the must is pumped into a fermentation tank and inoculated with a pure yeast strain to begin the alcoholic fermentation.

STEP 8. CONDUCT THE ALCOHOLIC FERMENTATION

In this stage of red wine making, color and flavor components and tannins are extracted from the skins. The concentrations of these three

sensory components define the most important parameters of red wine styles, and the tannin level also determines to a large degree how long the wines will need to be aged before they are most pleasurable to drink. The most important winemaking-determined differences between a Rosé made from Cabernet Sauvignon grapes, an early-maturing Cabernet Sauvignon made for immediate drinkability or a few years' aging, and a late-maturing Cabernet Sauvignon that will

Figure 5.2 Winemaker Julia Iantosca adding potassium metabisulfite to red grapes before they are crushed at William Wheeler Winery

require 15 to 20 years of cellaring before being ready to drink are established during maceration in the alcoholic fermentation.

What choices do winemakers have for managing the extraction during maceration? The most important of these involve managing the cap — the mixture of grape solids (seeds, stems, and pulp) that rises to the top of the juice once fermentation is underway. When the yeast is first mixed into the must, the grape solids — which make up 7 to 23 percent of the must — are

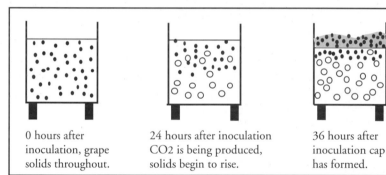

| 0 hours after inoculation, grape solids throughout. | 24 hours after inoculation CO_2 is being produced, solids begin to rise. | 36 hours after inoculation cap has formed. |

*Figure 5.3
An Example of Cap Formation in a Red Wine Fermentation*

dispersed throughout the fermentation tank.[10] After production of carbon dioxide gas begins, the solids float to the top of the juice and form a layer which can become quite thick and tightly compacted (Figure 5.3).

If the cap is not mixed into the juice, extraction from the skins will be minimal because maceration will occur only at the interface between the juice and the cap. Moreover, the top of the cap is exposed to air and can provide an ideal place for vinegar bacteria to grow. To enhance extraction and reduce the danger of spoilage, winemakers keep the cap covered with CO_2- saturated juice that discourages the growth of vinegar bacteria. This procedure also serves to discourage the growth of heat-loving spoilage organisms by making the temperature more even between the cap and the fermenting juice beneath. If the temperature difference between the juice and the cap is not enough to sufficiently cool the cap, the juice can be cooled by pumping through a heat exchanger.

*Figure 5.4
The cap on a Zinfandel fermentation at Butte Creek Vineyards: note the large carbon dioxide bubble in the lower left hand corner.*

Pump Over It, Punch It, Sink It, or Spray It

Figure 5.5
Stirring the cap
THE WINEMAKERS OF THE
PACIFIC NORTHWEST[23]

The main ways of moistening the cap in California are to pump juice over it — drawing juice out of the bottom of the fermenter, pumping it through a hose, and spraying it on the cap with enough force to break it up and submerge it — or, for small batches, to "punch it" — breaking up the cap and shoving it down to re-mix with the juice below using a canoe paddle or other high-tech apparatus. In pumping over, from 10 to 100 percent of the juice will be sprayed over the cap one to three times a day depending on the wine style, grape variety, and how much the winemaker wants to promote extraction. If it is necessary to cool or warm a fermentation, the juice can be circulated through a heat-exchanger during a pump-over. Some wineries use tanks that trap the cap in the middle of the juice for "submerged cap fermentation"; others have experimented with nozzles that continuously spray the cap; and a few have tried special fermentation tanks with hydraulic devices to punch the cap. Pumping over is a more vigorous method of wetting the cap than punching or submerged-cap fermentation.

Open-top fermenters are used for red wine production to provide access to the cap — and you might wonder, after all the discussion in Chapter 3 of the need to protect white wines from air, how red wines avoid being turned into vinegar during fermentation. Because the fermentations are not cooled very much they are rapid — often complete in a few days — and CO_2

Figure 5.6
Pumping over the cap at Louis M. Martini Winery

evolution protects the juice from oxidation. In fact, oxygen is needed for the optimum development of red wines. It is not uncommon to aerate them after fermentation. Exposing them to air does not harm their stronger flavors and helps to remove off odors such as hydrogen sulfide that are produced during fermentation. Air-exposure also begins the barrel aging process, which can involve a controlled exposure to oxygen as well as incorporation of wood odors and flavors.

How Long Will This Go On?
What's In Those Skins?

The skin and the fruit layers immediately beneath it contain most of the grape's aroma, flavor, and color constituents, while the juice of most red-wine grapes is "colorless" — a very light pink or yellow. The skins of red grapes are also rich in tannins (3.0 to 6.5 percent). Color and tannin compounds are related to each other: tannin molecules are polymers containing from two to ten smaller molecules which are closely related to the color molecules.

An eno-trivial aside: You may have wondered what's **on** grape skins. That thin, sort of white layer is a wax-like, protective material called the bloom. Some lay-people think the bloom consists of the wild yeast cells that are associated with grape berries, and it is true that the yeast cells do stick to the waxy bloom — but they would never become so numerous themselves as to create a visible haze or white layer on the skin.[11]

What Kind of Wine Are We Making, Anyway?

The choice of when to separate the juice from the skins by drawing the juice off and pressing the pomace depends on the style of wine we want to make. The longer the extraction goes on, the more color and tannins from the skins end up in the juice. Because the color molecules are smaller they are extracted faster than the larger tannin polymers. Wines containing different amounts of color and tannin can be produced depending on when the skins are separated from the fermenting must.[12] More varietal flavor will be extracted with longer maceration as well. Timing the end of extraction also takes into account the fact that red wines will lose color — up to 50% — during bulk aging.

If we are making a fruity, early-maturing red wine, it will not require a lot of tannin, but it will need to have a recognizable red — not pink — color. Such a wine might be fermented with the skins for 2-4 days or until the degrees Brix dropped into the range of about 5 to 10. If we wish to create a red wine that will be dark in color, intensely flavored, rough when young (having enough tannins to improve with extended aging in barrels and in the bottle), the maceration should last around 5-10 days and reach a degrees Brix reading of 1 to -1.

Some examples of average maceration times used by California wineries for red varietal wines are shown in Table 5.2.[13] As a general rule, the lower the degrees Brix and the more days on the skins before pressing, the more tannins, flavor, and color will have been extracted

Variety	Degrees Brix	Days On Skins
Cabernet Sauvignon	1.3	7.5
Napa Gamay	4.7	4.1
Pinot Noir	1.4	6.1
Zinfandel	1.7	6.1

Table 5.2
Average Degrees Brix and Days on Skins for Four Red Varietal Wines in California

into the fermenting juice. This table shows that the typical extraction is managed in California Cabernet Sauvignon, Pinot Noir, and Zinfandel so that these wines will be relatively high in color, tannin, and flavor and will need to be aged before bottling to reduce the astringency of its tannins. Only Napa Gamay, among these wines, is typically made in a low-tannin, early-maturing style.

After the maceration is ended by separating the juice and pressing the solids, the free-run and press juices are kept in separate batches and fermented to dryness if all the sugar has not already been consumed during the maceration of the skins. The free-run and press wines may be blended later, and the wines from very hard pressings may be distilled to make wine spirits.

Draining the Tanks and Pressing

The actual management of the maceration of a particular batch of red must will depend on the natural intensity of color and tannin in the fruit, which will vary with the grape variety and with the nature of the growing season, particularly the ripening period. Cabernet Sauvignon, Zinfandel, Syrah, and Petite Sirah are varieties that are naturally high in pigments and tannins. Pinot Noir has low concentrations of lighter pigments and is low in tannins. Winemakers have experimented with collecting the stems at the crusher and adding them to Pinot Noir fermentations to increase the tannins, but they found that peppery, green flavors can result. Warmer, drier years tend to produce grapes that are higher in tannin and color than those produced in cooler, wetter seasons.

Figure 5.7
Solids beginning to be drained from a red wine fermenter at Freemark Abbey Winery

Figure 5.8
Pressing the skins from a red fermentation at Freemark Abbey Winery (the doors of the press have been removed to show the press cake before the bladder was deflated)

When the Red Wine Isn't Really Red

Blush red varietals are Blanc de Noirs wines. They can be made without any skin contact except what occurs during crushing by separating the juice from the must immediately afterward. Some blush and rosé wines are made with up to 24 hours of pre-fermentation skin contact or by separating the skins after 24 hours of fermentation. Each of these methods will give a pink wine, and the longer the skin contact, the darker the pink. The skins recovered from any of these three procedures can be added to another red wine fermentation to enhance the extraction by increasing the proportion of skins in the mix.

What If We Don't Stop This When the Fermentation Is Dry? Extended Maceration

Maceration begins when the grapes are crushed and in certain cases can extend for several weeks beyond the completion of the alcoholic fermentation. Continuing skin contact beyond dryness — the point when all the sugar in the juice has been consumed by the alcoholic fermentation — is called extended maceration. This is not a traditional red wine making practice in California, but it is used widely in Bordeaux and is becoming more common among premium Cabernet Sauvignon producers in the U.S. because it produces highly desirable organoleptic changes in the color, aroma, bitterness, and astringency that make the wines more palatable at an early age yet do not diminish their ability to improve with bottle aging.

The difference between conventional California red wine fermentations and extended maceration begins at the stage of winery design: because fermentation tanks will be tied up for weeks rather than days, a winery planning to use extended maceration will need more space and more tanks. The first stages of extended maceration look just like a conventional red wine fermentation: the inoculated must forms a cap which is pumped over several times each day. It is when the fermentation has reached dryness that the differences in processing become apparent. In conventional fermentation management, the new wine is drained from the tank at this point and the pomace is pressed; but in extended maceration, instead of draining the new wine, the pump-overs continue for two more days to reduce excess CO_2 content and settle the cap deeper into the wine. When the cap is sunk, the tanks are hermetically sealed until maceration is finished — an average of 35 days at California's Vichon Winery.[14] During maceration the wine is checked daily to monitor changes in color and tannins. The decision to end maceration is based completely on taste and color. After the maceration is complete, the wine is drained from the tank, the pomace is pressed, and the clarification, stabilization, and aging processes proceed.

What are the organoleptic changes that are being monitored during the extended maceration? At the end of fermentation, when the Cabernet Sauvignon has reached dryness, it is bitter and has a mild astringency experienced as a coarseness on the palate. These sensations are caused by the nature of the new wine's tannins, whose drying sensation is accentuated by their bitterness. The wine's red pigments show a purple hue and the aromas are very fruity and pungent. Extended maceration changes the character of the tannin molecules and also modifies the wine's aroma. In the early stages of maceration the harshness of the young wine appears to intensify, but after the first week the softening of tannins begins. It is thought that during the first week more small tannins — which cause the wine to taste more bitter and feel very astringent — enter the wine until there are so many of them that they start reacting with each other, linking together to form long polymers. More red pigment molecules are also extracted into the wine, and these too join with each other to create larger and more stable color molecules. The small pigments begin to join with the growing tannin polymers as well to create structures so large that some of them precipitate out of the wine. As the bitterness of the wine is reduced by tannin- and color-molecule polymerization during maceration, an impression of softness on the palate is created because longer tannin molecules are both less bitter and less astringent. The polymerization of color molecules also causes the color to shift from its earlier purple hue toward the red of a more mature wine. In addition, the aroma becomes more complex, typically with the addition of "vanilla" or "cinnamon-stick" odors.[15] Until this point maceration appears to have sped up the aging process, yet after pressing the wines appear to age at a more normal pace.

Summary of the Options for Maceration of Red Wines

Figure 5.9 shows a theoretical red wine fermentation curve. Note the relatively rapid drop in degrees Brix associated with the higher fermentation temperatures of red wines (compare to Figures 3.9 and 3.10 on page 74 which contain typical fermentation curves for white table wines) and the points on the fermentation curve at which the juice would be drained off to end the extraction of color, tannins, and flavors for three

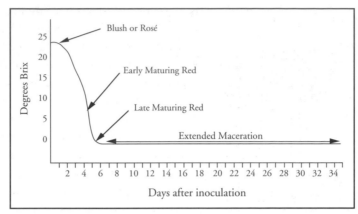

Figure 5.9
When Maceration Ends for Pink, Early-maturing, and Late-maturing Red Wines

kinds of wine: blush or rosé, early-maturing red, and late-maturing red. The figure also shows how the extended maceration process would appear on a fermentation curve.

Juice Yields

Depending on the type of pressing equipment used, yields of 80-185 gallons of free-run juice and an additional 10-80 gallons of press-run juice are recovered by California wineries. The total juice yield from 160 to 195 gallons per ton for red wines is higher than the yield for white wines because the skins are softer and yield up more juice after they have been macerated during the fermentation.[2]

How Hot and How Big Does This Get?

Depending on the grape variety used and the style of wine being produced, California wineries ferment the must for red wines at temperatures ranging from 60 to 95 degrees F. Because red wines are more strongly flavored, the cooler temperatures required to preserve the delicate aromas of white wines are not needed, as a rule. However, cool temperatures are used for Blanc de Noirs and fruitier red wines such as Gamay Beaujolais. Temperatures in the 80-87 degree range are typical for Cabernet Sauvignon. The higher the fermentation temperature, the faster the extraction during maceration. If the temperature is moving toward the high end of the desired range — say 85 degrees in a Cabernet Sauvignon — the fermentation can be cooled by routing the juice through a heat exchanger during a pump-over, or cold water or glycol can be circulated in the tanks' cooling jackets. Of course, as with white wines, temperatures over 100 degrees that can kill yeasts and result in a stuck fermentation must be avoided.

In California's coastal wineries red-wine fermenters range from 500 to 60,000 gallons capacity. Open-top concrete or redwood tanks not suitable for white wine making as well as jacketed stainless steel tanks are used.

The Malolactic Fermentation

The malolactic fermentation is much more common in premium red table wines than it is in white wines. As with white wines the MLF may occur spontaneously or may be initiated by the inoculation of the fermenting must or wine with pure strains of bacteria. It plays a more important role in the development of complexity during the aging of red table wines: it is necessary for the normal aging premium red wines, especially those from cooler growing regions. As with white table wines, the MLF is often discouraged in wines from warmer growing regions because their acid levels are naturally low.

STEP 9. CLARIFY AND STABILIZE THE NEW WINE

The end of the alcoholic fermentation phase is marked by the separation of the wines from their fermentation lees. At this point their acidities and SO_2 contents are adjusted if necessary and the simultaneous processes of stabilization, clarification, and bulk aging begin. Immediately after fermentation and during the earlier stages of tank and barrel aging, red wines are deliberately exposed to air to avoid the elaboration of off-odors (such as mercaptans from hydrogen sulfide) and to provide the oxygen needed for normal aging in tanks and barrels.

Figure 5.10
Richard Ponzi fines a barrel of wine.
THE WINEMAKERS OF THE PACIFIC NORTHWEST [24]

Red wines may be clarified before, during, and/or after bulk aging by means of filtration and/or fining with gelatin, isinglass, or egg whites. These fining agents not only clarify the wines but also reduce their tannin contents and color by reacting with the tannin and color molecules and removing them from the wine. Racking, centrifugation, or filtration typically follows fining to remove the lees of the compounds that reacted with the fining agent.

To ensure microbiological stability, wineries will follow the progress of the malolactic fermentation in each batch of wine with careful laboratory analysis to be sure that the malolactic fermentation has not become stuck and has been completed before bottling. The growth of undesirable microbes is discouraged by keeping the storage tanks and barrels full, or blanketing the wine with an inert gas such as nitrogen or carbon dioxide, carefully monitoring the wines' organoleptic properties, being vigilant about sanitation, and adjusting SO_2 levels.

Because red wines will age longer at the winery before bottling — through one or two winters — producing cold stability immediately after fermentation is not a concern. Testing for heat stability at this stage is not necessary either, since the proteins that create heat instability will often be removed from the wine during bulk aging when they react with tannins. Cold and heat stability are simply verified before bottling, and if necessary the wines can be stabilized by chilling and fining with bentonite.

STEP 10. AGE THE WINE IN BULK

Aging in oak, controlled exposure to air, and long periods of aging are more common for red wines than for white wines as a group, and American oak is used more often for red than white wines.[16] As explained in Chapter 3, the winemaker can control a number of variables to determine the amount and quality of oak character added to a particular wine and the extent to which the wine becomes concentrated during barrel aging. For example, French oak is more typically used to age delicate Pinot Noirs, while more flavorful red wines such as Cabernet Sauvignon, Syrah, and Zinfandel can be successfully aged in American oak. In California, 60-gallon barrels are increasingly popular for red-wine aging, but oak containers up to 6000 gallons capacity also may be used in combination with redwood and stainless-steel tanks to achieve the desired level of oak character in red wines. California's premium Cabernet Sauvignon producers may give their wines six to eight months of aging in large tanks to lose their yeasty/fruity fermentation character and

Figure 5.11
Julia Iantosca putting wine into barrels at William Wheeler Winery

then move them to small oak cooperage in a *chai* for another 12-18 months of aging to express their typical varietal character, stabilize their color, decrease their bitterness and astringency, and become more concentrated. The extent to which wines are exposed to air can be determined by the way they are racked and whether or not they are stored in barrels that are closed and sealed or barrels that are periodically opened and refilled. To minimize a wine's exposure to air it could be racked into a tank that has been filled with inert gas. For more air exposure the inert gas can be omitted, and for still more aeration the wine can be splashed into the receiving tank. The amount of air a wine is exposed to also depends on the way it is handled during barrel aging. Delicately flavored red wines, such as Pinot Noir, would be exposed to minimum amounts of air during barrel aging: after filling, their barrels might be sealed tight, rotated 30 degrees to wet the bung and tighten the seal, and not opened until their aging is complete. More flavorful wines, such as Zinfandel and Cabernet Sauvignon, can usually benefit from more exposure to oxygen — especially during the early stages of barrel aging. To accomplish this they can be stored in barrels positioned with the bung-hole up so the bung can be removed to "top up" the barrels periodically. Topping up means adding wine of the same type to make up the ullage — the empty space created as wine soaks into the wood and as some of its water and/or alcohol evaporates. The more often the barrels are opened, the more the wine inside is exposed to air. White wines are not exposed to much oxygen during aging because they would deteriorate, since their flavors are more fragile and they lack the protection of tannins.

Figure 5.12
Barrels of red wine at Sterling Winery (note that the barrels in the center row have been sealed and rotated for aging with minimum exposure to air)

STEP 11. BLEND AND FINISH THE WINE — MERITAGE ANYONE?
Blending

Red wines can be improved and rosé wines created by blending. A surprisingly small amount of red wine — at least it was surprising to me when I did it as a winemaker — can be added to white wine to make it blush or to create a rosé. Whatever kind of blend is being made, the winemaker must perform a careful sensory evaluation of each wine to be mixed and then make and compare many trial blends — even hundreds — before the final blend is determined.

Figure 5.13
Zelma Long of Simi Winery tasting red wines

Pinot Noir is not usually mixed with other grapes or wines, but Cabernet Sauvignon has been blended for centuries to soften its tannins and hasten its aging. In fact, the vineyards of Bordeaux are made up of mixtures of Cabernet Sauvignon, Cabernet Franc, Merlot, Malbec, and Petite Verdot, a viticultural blending that is carried on through the harvest into the winemaking. California winemakers have recently begun creating blends of these "Bordelaise" grape varieties — both red and white (but not mixed) — and many have given their wines generic or proprietary names so that they do not have to limit their blends to the 75% or more of a single variety required by the labelling laws when a varietal name is used (see Appendix B). California proprietary or generic wines that are blends of Bordelaise varieties have been named "Meritage" by an association of their producers. (In case you were about to try out your best French pronunciation skills on that word, it rhymes with "heritage.")

Mitch Cosentino, the proprietor of Cosentino Wineries, visited my Introduction to Wine class in March 1991 and talked about the process of creating his winery's Meritage blend, which is called "The Poet." He spoke of making scores of trial blends, tasting, modifying, and re-tasting them to arrive at the best combination of wines each year, and he left us with some notes (summarized in Table 5.3) about the characteristics each grape variety contributes to his blends.

Other Meritage wine names range from Carmenet Vineyard's straightforward "Red Table Wine" and "White Table Wine" to Flora Springs' "Trilogy" and Joseph Phelps' "Insignia." Although many of these wines are in great demand, the term "Meritage" has yet to become a household word, even among enophiles.[17]

Table 5.3
Mitch Cosentino's
Guide to Blending the
Bordeaux Varietals

Grape Variety	Herbal Elements	Fruit Characteristics	Structural Features	Other Effects in a Blend
Cabernet Sauvignon	cedar mint eucalyptus green pepper green bean	currants cassis blackberries black cherry	richer mouth feel and fuller body, provides tannins	develops a big bottle bouquet
Cabernet Franc	clove dill black pepper and another unidentified spice	red cherry, raspberry, blueberry, occasionally cranberry	leaner & lighter some can be more tannic than Cabernet Sauvignon	more intensely aromatic and spicier than Cabernet Sauvignon & Merlot
Merlot	offers softer fruit and floral elements	red cherry plums	softens the tannins and mouthfeel	gives an added dimension to the aromatics and flavor profile
Petite Verdot	some black pepper	not much charm in the fruit	provides tannins, density and intensity	adds color (the darkest Bordeaux variety)
Malbec	some can provide a spice element	variable -- depends on vineyard and vintage	in some cases adds color and tannin	mostly unproven in California

Finishing

After barrel aging and blending, wineries will check their red wines for heat and cold stability and will fine, chill, and filter them as needed. Final laboratory analyses will check the SO$_2$ levels and verify that no sources of instability exist. The wines will be filtered — many wineries use sterile filtration — en route to the bottling line, where some wineries fill the bottles with inert nitrogen gas before filling them with wine.

STEP 12. BOTTLE THE WINE

Deep green straight-sided Bordeaux-style bottles are used for Cabernet Sauvignon, Merlot, Meritage blends, and Zinfandel. The Burgundy-style bottle, also in dark green, is used for Pinot Noir, Syrah, Petite Sirah, and Gamay. Although brown bottles are commonly used by Italy's Tuscan wine producers for their Chiantis and protect red wine from light damage just as well as dark green bottles do, they have never become widely used in the U.S. Some wineries will bottle their premium red wines destined for years of bottle aging in magnums — containing 1500 milliliters — and even larger sizes in addition to the common 750 ml bottles because wines aged in larger bottles mature more slowly and often reach a higher level of quality.

STEPS 13 AND 14. AGE THE BOTTLED WINE AND RELEASE IT INTO THE MARKET

California coastal wineries will bottle age their red wines from 2 weeks to 48 months before releasing them into the market.[18] After they are released, the best of California's premium red wines will improve in the bottle for many years. Cabernet Sauvignons from the best vineyards and wineries will reach their optimum drinkability about ten years after the vintage and can remain attractive for another five to ten years. The finest Zinfandels and Pinot Noirs will age much like the best Cabernet Sauvignons, but many will have shorter aging lives, reaching optimum maturity about five years after the vintage and declining in quality in another five years or so.

Red wines owe their longer aging lives to the tannins added during the maceration and oak aging, and the greater aging potential of red wines from cooler regions is at least in part a function of their lower pH values. Young red wines destined for long periods of aging in barrel and bottle are high in tannins when young. During bulk and bottle aging these tannins join with each other and with pigment molecules to form polymers — in much the same way described for extended maceration — that soften the wine's astringency and shift its color from reddish-purple to tawny or brick red. Older red wines will also be lighter in color because some of the pigment molecules precipitate, forming a sediment in the bottle. The sediment may also contain tartrate crystals. The organoleptic characteristic that wine lovers are seeking to create when they age red wines is the bottle bouquet — a very complex, many-layered array of odors and flavors created by the reaction of the varietal aroma components with each other and with the oak-aging bouquet elements. Bottle aging adds new odors and flavors to wine because the vast majority of its reactions occur in the absence of oxygen. After the wine's tannins and other components have reacted with and consumed the small amount of oxygen dissolved in the wine and in the air in the bottle's headspace — usually after about a month of bottle aging — the environment inside the bottle is anaerobic. This is the first time in the life of a red wine when chemical reactions can take place with oxygen excluded. The lower the pH, the slower these bottle-aging reactions occur and these slower reactions that lead to a more complex array of desirable end products. No wonder bottle aging can add a new dimension of complexity to wines!

So when will that great bottle of Chateau Most Excellent Reserve Cabernet Sauvignon you got as a graduation present from your uncle Henry von Winebuff be ready to drink? That is a very good question — for which the correct answer is, "It depends." It depends on how you have stored it, what the vintage was like, whether you plan to serve the wine with food, and your personal taste — do you like a little bite of tannin or do you insist on smoothness at any cost?

Wines stored at lower temperatures (optimally 55-65 degrees F), at more uniform temperatures, and in larger bottles will attain a higher degree of complexity and quality. The cooler the temperature, the slower the aging, and the greater the ultimate complexity. Warmer temperatures speed up aging and wines aged in warmer cellars do not appear to me to achieve as much variety of aroma and flavor — or perhaps the wine peaks and declines so fast I miss it! When temperatures vary, the wine expands (when it is hot) and contracts (when it is cool), and the corks are pushed out and pulled in a tiny bit and can be loosened, allowing oxygen to enter the bottle, dissolve, and lead to spoilage of the wine. The greater volume of wine in larger bottles will not fluctuate as much in response to the inevitable variations in cellar temperature as will the contents of smaller bottles, and this may help account for the observation that wines aged in larger bottles achieve greater complexity. In addition, the volume of air between the cork and the wine in the neck of a small bottle is much larger in proportion to the volume of wine than is the volume of air in the neck of a larger bottle. When a 375 ml "half-bottle" and a 1500 ml magnum are compared, the volume of air in the neck is about the same but the volume of wine is four times as great in the larger bottle. This means that there will be much less oxygen dissolved in the wine in the magnum than in the half-bottle so that reactions involving oxygen will be much less significant in the bottle-aging of wines stored in magnums. Many wineries bottle both red and white wines using nitrogen gas to flush the headspace of the bottles before inserting the cork, so in their wines the difference in the relative amount of oxygen dissolved in magnums and half-bottles would be less. In wines stored in the dark, light will not react with wine proteins to form a haze and will not be available to catalyze photo-oxidation reactions. Both slower aging reactions and a vibration-free storage area will allow a sediment to form and stick to the bottle (but, as you know, that's not the only reason you should tell your cousin Rodney to take his wine rack off the top of the refrigerator!).

Information about the aging potential of the wines of a particular vintage is available from the wineries that made them, in the critiques of wine writers, and in very general terms in vintage charts, which are available from wine merchants and in a variety of wine periodicals. If you want to know where a particular wine is in its development in the bottle, Jancis Robinson has tasted hundreds of wines — often in collaboration with their makers, with whom she discussed their stage of maturation and potential for additional aging and improvement in the bottle — and has assembled her impressions in her book VINTAGE TIMECHARTS.[19] You can use this book as a reference for checking the maturity of a particular vintage of one of the approximately three dozen wines she charts or for inquiring about the maturity of another wine by comparing it to, say, Ridge 1985 Geyserville Zinfandel or Saintsbury 1987 Pinot Noir, to cite two red California examples.

Unfortunately, since I don't know your personal taste in wines, you will have to put some venture capital into educating yourself on this subject: buy a case or two of wine that your wine merchant identifies as having the potential to improve with bottle aging, store it properly, and take out a bottle from time to time and drink it, paying attention to its odor development and softening astringency and maybe glancing at the appropriate timechart to place your impressions in perspective. Have fun getting a fix on where your personal tastes lie! Maybe your uncle Harry will help you invest in that case or two of wine for your post-graduate studies.

CARBONIC MACERATION — A DIFFERENT FERMENTATION FOR FRUITY RED WINES

The vast majority of the world's red table wines are made by the methods discussed above, but a group of popular, intensely fruity red wines, often described as being made in the Beaujolais or Beaujolais Nouveau style, are produced by creating an anaerobic environment that modifies the metabolism of the grape cells so that they form alcohol without the need for yeasts. This process is called carbonic maceration and has been an important part of the production of wines from France's Beaujolais district for years. Some winemakers will conduct partial carbonic macerations to enhance the fruitiness of their wines. This is what happens in most Beaujolais wines, where whole berries are fermented along with crushed fruit.[20] Carbonic maceration has been used in the U.S. to a limited extent to create early-maturing red wines from Pinot Noir, Gamay, Gamay Beaujolais — a Pinot Noir clone masquerading under this name in California — occasionally Zinfandel, and vinifera hybrid varieties such as Marechal Foch.

Creating the Anaerobic Environment

At the winery, the process of carbonic maceration begins by loading a tank with carefully picked whole grape clusters (the loading is called encuvage, the first step in Figure 5.14). The air in the tank may have been displaced by carbon dioxide gas or will later become saturated with CO_2 released from a standard alcoholic fermentation of the juice created as some grapes in the bottom of the tank are crushed by the weight of the grapes on top of them ("Free-run juice from damaged berries" in Phase I of Figure 5.14). Winemakers will heavily inoculate this juice to produce CO_2 quickly so that no off odors or flavors can develop in the juice and to fill the tank with CO_2.

Phase I — Two Simultaneous Fermentations, Inside and Outside the Berries

The CO_2-saturated, anaerobic environment in the tank triggers the grape cells in the intact berries to alter their metabolism and use their sugars to create energy, making alcohol — which ultimately kills them — as a by-product (the "Intracellular Fermentation" in Phase I of Figure 5.14). The tanks are allowed to heat up, because the best wines result from carbonic maceration conducted at 85-95 degrees F. Winemakers will allow the yeast-catalyzed alcoholic fermentation in the juice to proceed until the sugar in the juice drops to -1 to 2 degrees Brix and will allow the sugars inside the grapes to fall to one to four degrees Brix before draining the juice, unloading the tanks, and pressing the fruit. In this case the press wine, which has been created inside the grape cells by the carbonic maceration, is more desirable than the free-run wine. (However, the press and free-run wines are usually mixed.) The first phase of carbonic maceration will last one to two days for white or pink wines and four to ten days for red wines.

Phase II — Finishing Two Fermentations, Alcoholic and Malolactic

The second phase is a very rapid, conventional alcoholic fermentation which finishes in two to four days; often the malolactic fermentation is completed at the same time. Because the juice released by pressing the carbonic-maceration fruit is richer in nutrients than regular grape juice, the yeast and bacteria can grow rapidly and bring the wine to microbiological stability quickly by using up the organic compounds — glucose and malic acid — required for both the alcoholic and malolactic fermentations. The wines are then heat and cold stabilized and clarified rapidly, often being bottled within a few weeks of the harvest and reaching the market in mid-November — the time when the new Beaujolais wines traditionally arrived in Paris and now arrive in cities across the globe.

Carbonic-maceration wines are lower in alcohol, total acid, color, body, and residual sugar than red wines made by conventional vinification methods. They have a characteristic fruity odor which reminds some tasters of ripe cherries or raspberries. Because they are most valued for their youthful fruity characteristics, most Nouveau-style wines are drunk within three to six months after they are released, even though they can age at least into the following summer and fall to be enjoyed with picnics.

Figure 5.14
The Carbonic Maceration

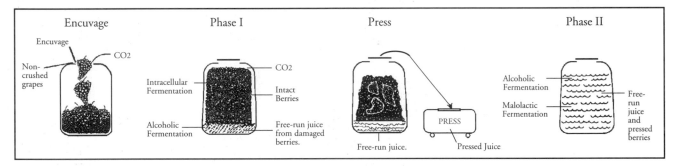

HOW TO MAKE A HYPOTHETICAL PINOT NOIR AND CABERNET SAUVIGNON

Pinot Noir

Pinot Noir producers may each have their own idea about how to forge the key to unlock the greatness of these wines — some emphasizing soils, others clones, and still others special winemaking techniques — but they would all agree that the grapes are challenging to grow and the wines unforgiving in the making. Pinot Noir grapes are difficult to vinify because their wines cannot be fixed up by blending or oak aging if something goes wrong. In a typical production sequence, Pinot Noir grapes would be harvested at 22 to 23.5 degrees Brix and crushed — although some producers will leave varying proportions of the berries whole to allow some carbonic maceration, increasing the fruitiness of the wine. The fermentation would be conducted at 80-90 degrees F, and pumping over or punching the cap would be done regularly to enhance color extraction — a difficult challenge in light-pigmented Pinot Noirs. Winemakers have a variety of tricks up their sleeves to promote color extraction from Pinot Noir grapes. For example, some wineries draw off about one-third of the juice and either add it back later during fermentation to prolong the maceration and extraction or make Blanc de Noirs out of it, effectively increasing the skin-to-juice ratio of the remaining must. To enhance tannin extraction, some producers add stems to the fermentations; others object to the stemmy flavors that accompany the tannins. Alcoholic fermentations will last seven to fourteen days, and the malolactic fermentation is encouraged during that time for the development of complexity. From this point Pinot Noir wines are handled more like white wines than like the darker, more tannic reds of the Cabernet Sauvignon, Zinfandel, and Syrah group. Aging in oak would be limited, for example, to four to eight months, and the wines would typically be bottled within a year of the harvest.

Cabernet Sauvignon

Cabernet Sauvignon is a dark-colored, intensely flavored variety that lends itself to relatively long periods of oak aging and maturation in the bottle. Cabernet Sauvignon grapes would be harvested at between 22 and 23 degrees Brix and the fruit crushed and the must inoculated with pure yeast. The fermentation temperature would be kept in the 80's and the maceration would last about eight days in the average California cellar while the juice was fermented to dryness. Some wineries might use an extended maceration to soften the tannins. After pressing of the spent skins, some of the press wine would probably be blended back into the free-run for barrel aging. The wine would be exposed to air during barrel aging, especially in the early months. The barrels used could be of American or French oak and the aging could last for around two years before the wine is bottled and aged at the winery — for up to decades if the vintage is good enough to be included in the wine library. Figure 5.15 shows an example of how California's Vichon Winery processes Cabernet Sauvignon — and Merlot.

Figure 5.15
Cabernet Sauvignon and Merlot production at California's Vichon Winery

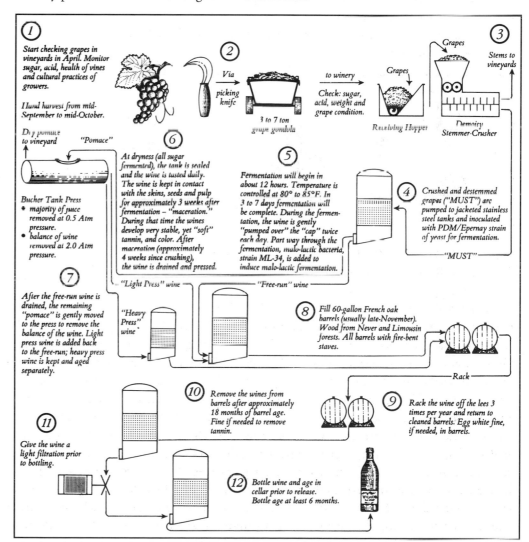

THE RED WINE MARKET IN THE U.S.

During the 1980s red wines represented a small and slowly shrinking portion of the U.S. wine market, falling from 18% in 1981 to 15% in 1991.[21] On November 17, 1991, Dr. Curtis Ellison was interviewed on a popular television program about topics discussed in Chapter 1 — including the cardioprotective effect of moderate alcohol consumption and his proposed studies of "The French Paradox." Ellison spoke about the hypothesis that substances in red wines are responsible for the alterations of serum lipid composition that lead to improved cardiovascular health. In the 30 days immediately after the show aired U.S. red wine sales climbed to 44% above the level of the previous year, with Merlot topping the list with an 82% increase.[22] This phenomenon strikes me as an "American Paradox": a society which had spurned red wine in the last decade suddenly embracing it after a 20-minute television spot. I wholeheartedly hope that this trend continues. After all, improved cardiovascular health is a boon to both individuals and society and heaven knows we can use more of the gracious living that must have increased along with those red wine sales.

RED AND WHITE WINE PRODUCTION — A WINERY CALENDAR

So that you can get a glimpse of how the production cycles of red and white table wines are managed in a commercial winery, I have summarized a fourteen-month calendar of operations for Simi Winery in Table 5.4.

You'll notice that some wines are finished in just a few months — the '87 Chenin Blanc and Rosé, for example. The Chardonnays and Cabernet Sauvignons typically take years between the harvest and bottling, with the complete production cycle for the '85 Chardonnay spanning 19-22 months and the '84 Cabernet Sauvignon requiring 33 months. The '86 Sauvignon Blanc was made in 11 months.

Wineries must plan their bottling so that tanks are empty to receive the autumn's crush. You can see that bottling the '84 Cabernet Sauvignon, '85 Chardonnay, and '86 Chenin Blanc, Rosé, and Sauvignon Blanc created space in tanks for the '87 juices and musts to ferment.

Table 5.4 does not show the details of a winery's operations, but your knowledge of winemaking basics can fill in some missing steps. For example, you can be sure that many trial blends of the '86 tank-fermented and barrel-fermented Chardonnays will be made and tasted before the wine was bottled some time later in 1988. You can also bet that during the year a lot of wine is being racked from tank to barrel and vice versa. For the details on this, I recommend a visit to the winery!

Table 5.4 A Summary of 1987 Winemaking Activities at Simi Winery[25]

Vintage and Wine	Months in 1987 and 1988
	Jan Feb Mar Apr May Jun Jul Aug Sep Oct Nov Dec Jan Feb
84 Cabernet Sauvignon	
85 Cabernet Sauvignon	
85 Chardonnay	
86 Chenin Blanc	
86 Rosé	
86 Sauvignon Blanc	
86 Chardonnay, Tank-Fermented	
86 Chardonnay, Barrel-Fermented	
86 Chardonnay Reserve	
86 Cabernet Sauvignon	
87 Chenin Blanc	
87 Rosé	
87 Sauvignon Blanc	
87 Chardonnay	
87 Cabernet Sauvignon	

Explanation of Symbols

The wine is fermenting or aging in barrels, perhaps on the yeast lees right after fermentation

The wine is fermenting (Sep-Oct), aging, being blended (especially 1-2 months before bottling), or fined in stainless steel tanks

The wine is being bottled

Part of the wine is in barrels and part is in tanks

White or red grapes are being harvested

Some of the wine is being bottled, the rest is in tanks

REVIEW QUESTIONS

Instructions: You might want to use a separate sheet of paper to answer the following review questions. In that way you can use the questions to check your knowledge of this chapter more than once. You may, for example, want to re-test yourself on items that you have missed or use the "Review Questions" to test your knowledge before you read a chapter. For the True or False items, answer "True" if the statement is accurate or "False" if the statement is incorrect. If you determine that a statement is false make a note explaining why. For the multiple choice items pick the best alternative. Check your answers after you have completed all the questions.

1. The most important step in red wine production for determining the style of a wine.
   - A. crushing
   - B. management of the extraction during fermentation
   - C. aging
   - D. fining
   - E. careful filtration

2. Which wine component protects red wines during the longer aging periods that allow them to develop complex bouquets?
   - A. alcohol   B. sugars   C. acids   D. oak flavors   E. tannins

3. Name two grape varieties of French origin and three from Italy that are used to make red varietal table wines in California. _____

   _____

4. True or false: Its inherent qualities make Pinot Noir a good candidate for Blanc de Noirs wine production. _____

5. Which red wine grape is preferred when grown in Region I? _____

6. What are the preferred viticultural regions for most red wine grapes? _____

7. Refer to the three Pinot Noir labels from The Monterey Vineyard, Buena Vista, and Inglenook wineries.

   A. In light of recent sensory research in California, which wine would be the most likely to have cherry, fresh berry, berry jam, and spicy characters?

   _____

   B. Which wine would the study predict to have more vegetal, leather, and smoke/tar aromas and less cherry, fresh berry, berry jam, and spicy character?

   _____

   C. And which wine would the study not be able to make any prediction about?

   _____

8. True or false: Cooler growing conditions produce red wines with more pleasing colors because their juices are of a stronger acidity — that is lower in pH — than hot region juices. _____

9. True or false: One thing a grower or winemaker does not have to worry about in Pinot Noir production is using the right clone. _____

10. True or false: In general, the results of canopy management studies for Cabernet Sauvignon have shown results like those for Sauvignon Blanc. _____

11. What soil conditions in the Napa area were found in preliminary studies to be associated with more cherry or berry flavors in Cabernet Sauvignon wines? _____

_____

12. True or false: In California red grapes for varietal table wine making are harvested at higher "degrees Brix" and lower total acids than are white grapes for varietal table wine making. _____

13. The juice of Zinfandel and most other red wine grapes is
    A. red   B. purple   C. green   D. colorless   E. yellow

14. During red wine fermentation the _____ on the fermenting must be kept wet by "punching down" or "pumping over" in order to prevent the growth of undesirable microorganisms and to promote _____ from the skins.

15. True or false: Pumping over circulates about 1% of the volume of juice over the solid on the top of the fermentation about once a week. _____

16. True or false: Red wines often benefit from some exposure to air after fermentation and during barrel aging. _____

17. True or false: The longer the extraction goes on during fermentation, the more varietal flavor, color, and tannins from the skins end up in the juice. _____

18. The average maceration time for California Napa Gamay is about four days and for Cabernet Sauvignon is 7-8 days. This means that the average _____ _____ is intended for more aging than the average _____ _____.

19. True or false: Pinot Noir has naturally low concentrations of lighter pigments and is low in tannins, so California winemakers commonly collect the stems at the crusher and add them to Pinot Noir fermentations to produce premium wines. _____

20. True or false: One simple, straightforward rule that can be stated for red table wine making is that the longer the skins are in contact with the wine, the harsher and more bitter and more astringent the wine will be. _____

21. Red wine fermentations are conducted at temperatures in the range _____ degrees Fahrenheit.

22. The alcoholic fermentation in red wine production is _____ than for white wine production.

23. True or false: The malolactic fermentation is both more common and more crucial in premium red table wine production than in premium white table wine production. _____

24. Why is producing cold stability immediately after fermentation not a concern for many red wines? _____

_____

25. The amount of tannin in a red wine can be reduced by adding ___ to the wine which removes tannin.
    A. salt   B. sugar   C. gelatin   D. sulfur dioxide   E. acid

26. Which red wine is most likely to be aged in French oak?
    A. Chardonnay
    B. Syrah
    C. Zinfandel
    D. Pinot Noir
    E. Muscat Frontignan

27. How would a wine be aged in barrels to minimize its exposure to air? _____

_____

_____

28. Refer to the Kendall-Jackson CARDINALE label. What grape varieties do you expect have been blended to make this wine? _____

_____

_____

29. True or false: Pinot Noir is less likely to be blended than other red wines. _____

30. Which variety is blended with Cabernet Sauvignon to "soften" its tannins? _____

31. California wineries age their red wines _____ months in the bottle before releasing them.

32. What factors are important for slower bottle aging? _____

_____

_____

33. True or false: On the average, the overall process of making red wines from grape to bottle takes longer than the overall process of making white wines.

34. Intensely fruity red wines can be produced by creating an anaerobic environment that modifies the metabolism of the grape cells so that they form alcohol without the need for yeasts. This process is called _____ .

35. True or false: The conventional, yeast-catalyzed alcoholic fermentation plays no role in the carbonic maceration method of winemaking. _____

36. True or false: In the carbonic maceration method of winemaking, free-run juice is often used for higher quality wines than press-run juice. _____

37. True or false: Pinot Noir wines are fermented at the lowest temperatures for red table wines, 60-65 degrees F. _____

38. Red wines made up about _____ % of the U.S. wine market during the 1980's.

39. What do carbonic maceration and méthode champenoise have in common? _____

_____

1987

CARDINALE™

Meritage
California
Red Table Wine

KENDALL-JACKSON

750 ML ALCOHOL 13% BY VOLUME

ANSWERS TO REVIEW QUESTIONS

1. B
2. E
3. From France: Pinot Noir and Cabernet Sauvignon (and Merlot, Cabernet Franc, Syrah, and Gamay); from Italy: Zinfandel, Barbera, Grignolino, and Sangiovese (and Charbono)
4. True
5. Pinot Noir
6. Regions II and III
7. To answer this question you need to know that the place name set in larger size type and usually located near the name of the grape variety tells us where those grapes were grown. Assuming you knew this — maybe you already browsed through Appendix B — here are the answers: A is Buena Vista because it's a Pinot Noir from the Carneros district; B is Inglenook's Napa Pinot Noir (the study compared Carneros with Napa — and Sonoma — Pinot Noirs); C is the Monterey County Pinot Noir. Wines from this region were not studied.
8. True
9. False. Pinot Noir is very mutable and there may be as many as 150 different clones used in Burgundy, France.
10. True
11. Older, typically hillside soils with a higher percentage of gravel and less ability to hold water were correlated with smaller crops and fruitier wine flavors.
12. True
13. D
14. . . . cap . . . extraction from the skins.
15. False. From 10 to 100 percent of the juice will be sprayed over the cap one to three times a day.
16. True
17. True
18. Cabernet Sauvignon for longer aging than Napa Gamay
19. False. Winemakers who tried this found that peppery, green, "stemmy" flavors can result in the wines.
20. False, because an extended maceration of Cabernet Sauvignon can produce a wine with softer tannins.
21. 60-95
22. Some possible correct insertions: shorter, hotter, messier, more labor-intensive, more likely to occur in an open-topped tank, less likely to happen in a barrel (hard to get those skins through the bung hole — going in or coming out).
23. True
24. Because they will age through one or two winters at the winery before bottling the cooling that occurs will often cause tartrate crystals to precipitate and tannins will react with and remove the heat-unstable proteins.
25. C — egg whites are also used.
26. D
27. The barrels would be sealed tight, rotated 30 degrees to wet the bung and tighten the seal, and not opened until the aging was complete.
28. Cardinale® is a red Meritage wine. This means that Cabernet Sauvignon, Cabernet Franc, and Merlot are the most likely to have been used. Malbec and Petite Verdot are possible, but less likely since they are not widely available in California.
29. True
30. Merlot
31. One-half month to 48 months.
32. Higher tannins, lower pH, lower storage temperatures, more uniform temperatures, darkness, and larger bottles.
33. True
34. Carbonic Maceration
35. False. A conventional, yeast-catalyzed alcoholic fermentation is used to create the carbon-dioxide-saturated environment into which intact clusters are loaded and is the means by which the remaining grape sugar is metabolized in the juice after pressing.
36. False. The press juice is better because it comes from inside the grapes where the carbonic maceration occurred.
37. False. Pinot Noir is fermented at 80-90 degrees F.
38. 15-18
39. Both winemaking techniques were developed in France and both start with uncrushed, whole grape clusters, an absolute requirement for carbonic maceration and a very common practice for méthode champenoise.

ENDNOTES

1 This chapter follows the outline of winemaking steps introduced in Chapter 3 and builds on basic concepts presented there.

2 Cooke, G. M. and H. W. Berg, "A Re-examination of Varietal Table Wine Processing Practices in California. I. Grape Standards, Grape and Juice Treatment, and Fermentation," *American Journal of Enology and Viticulture,* Vol. 34, No. 4, 1983, pp. 249-256.

3 Guinard, Jean-Xavier and Margaret Cliff, "Descriptive Analysis of Pinot Noir Wines from Carneros, Napa and Sonoma," *American Journal of Enology and Viticulture,* Vol. 38, No. 3, 1987, pp. 211-215.

4 Watson-Graff, Peter, "Pinot Noir: Color Extraction and Stability," *Practical Winery and Vineyard,* May/June 1988, p. 74 (article includes pp. 73-79).

5 Hunter, J. J., O. T. DeVilliers, and J. E. Watts, "The Effect of Partial Defoliation on Quality Characteristics of *Vitos vinifera* L. cv. Cabernet Sauvignon grapes. II. Skin Color, Skin Sugar, and Wine Quality," *American Journal of Enology and Viticulture,* Vol. 42, No. 1, 1991, p. 13; and Janice C. Morrison, and Ann C. Noble, "The Effects of Leaf and Cluster Shading on the Composition of Cabernet Sauvignon Grapes and on Fruit and Wine Sensory Properties," *American Journal of Enology and Viticulture,* Vol. 41, No. 3, 1990, pp.193-200.

6 Smart, Richard, and Mike Robinson, SUNLIGHT INTO WINE, Winetitles, Adelaide, Australia, 1991, p. 12.

7 Watson-Graff, Peter, "Pinot Noir: Color Extraction and Stability," *Practical Winery and Vineyard,* May/June 1988, p. 74 (article includes pp. 73-79).

8 Peterson, Tom, "The Production of Cabernet Sauvignon in California," presented at a University of California, Davis, extension course May 17, 1987, and used with permission.

9 Cooke, G. M., and H. W. Berg, "A Re-examination of Varietal Table Wine Processing Practices in California. I. Grape Standards, Grape and Juice Treatment, and Fermentation," *American Journal of Enology and Viticulture,* Vol. 34, No. 4, 1983, pp. 249-256.

10 Amerine, M. A., and M. A. Joslyn, TABLE WINES, THE TECHNOLOGY OF THEIR PRODUCTION, Second Edition, University of California Press, Berkeley, CA, 1970, p. 233.

11 Amerine, M. A., and M. A. Joslyn, TABLE WINES, THE TECHNOLOGY OF THEIR PRODUCTION, Second Edition, University of California Press, Berkeley, CA, 1970, p. 236.

12 Margalit, Yair, WINERY TECHNOLOGY AND OPERATIONS, The Wine Appreciation Guild, San Francisco, 1990, pp. 37-39.

13 Cooke, G. M., and H. W. Berg, "A Re-examination of Varietal Table Wine Processing Practices in California. I. Grape Standards, Grape and Juice Treatment, and Fermentation," *American Journal of Enology and Viticulture,* Vol. 34, No. 4, 1983, pp. 249-256 (extract from Table 13, p. 255).

14 Anonymous, "Maceration of Cabernet Sauvignon," Vichon Winery, Oakville, California P.O.S. No. V440, p. 2.

15 Ibid.

16 Cooke, G. M., and H. W. Berg, "A Re-examination of Varietal Table Wine Processing Practices in California. II. Clarification, Stabilization, Aging, and Bottling," *American Journal of Enology and Viticulture,* Vol. 35, No. 3, 1984, pp. 137-142 (citation refers to p. 140).

17 Heimoff, Steve, "What's in a Name," *The Wine Spectator,* Vol. 15, May 15, 1991, pp. 22-25.

18 Cooke, G. M., and H. W. Berg, "A Re-examination of Varietal Table Wine Processing Practices in California. II. Clarification, Stabilization, Aging, and Bottling," *American Journal of Enology and Viticulture,* Vol. 35, No. 3, 1984, pp. 137-142 (citation refers to p. 141, Table 11).

19 Robinson, Jancis, VINTAGE TIMECHARTS, Weidenfeld and Nicolson, New York, 1989.

20 Blackburn, Don, "Whole Berry Fermentation," *Practical Winery,* January/February 1984, pp. 30-36; Kenneth McCorkle, "Carbonic Maceration, A Beaujolais System for Producing Early-maturing Red Wines," *Wines and Vines,* April 1974, pp. 62-65.

21 Table "Estimated Shipments of Bottled California Table Wine to U.S. Markets, by Color Categories 1981-1990" in "Wine Shipments Down for Third Consecutive Year," *Wines and Vines,* July 1991, p. 26.

22 Study by Information Resources, Inc., cited in "Red Wine Sales Soar," *The Crush,* Vol. 18, No. 4, February 1992 (newsletter of the California Association of Winegrape Growers, 225 30th St., Suite 306, Sacramento, CA 95816).

23 Purser, Elizabeth J., and Lawrence J. Allen, photographer, THE WINEMAKERS OF THE PACIFIC NORTHWEST, Harbor House, Vashon Island, WA, 1977, p. 51.

24 Ibid. p. 55.

25 "Simi Winery News," Vol. 4, No. 1, Spring 1987.

6

SENSORY EVALUATION OF RED TABLE WINES

This chapter will introduce you to the sensory evaluation of red wines, which are more interesting in many sensory respects than white wines: they have more intense aromas and flavors and can develop very complex and subtle bouquets through bottle aging. Introductory tastings will acquaint you with red wine aromas and structural components and some common off odors. The first varietal wine tasting presents the two most accessible red wines — Pinot Noir and Gamay — and gives you a chance to relate your sensory evaluation skills to winemaking practices. You will then taste two Zinfandels made in different styles and become acquainted with Syrah. The next tasting features Cabernet Sauvignon, Merlot, and Cabernet Franc, to acquaint you with the characteristics of these wines in their youth before presenting an exercise that introduces the organoleptic changes that occur during the bottle aging of red table wines. The chapter concludes with an opportunity for you to design your own tasting and a review exercise with red wines. There are sensory homework assignments for Exercises 6.1, 6.2, and 6.3. You may want to preview them to be sure you have everything on hand that's required. To set up these exercises yourself, see the detailed instruction in Appendix D.

RED WINE TASTING TECHNIQUE

You will have to modify your sensory evaluation techniques a bit for red table wines. First, especially for the darker wines, the evaluation of color and clarity requires that you tilt the glass so that you can look through a thinner layer of wine. This allows you to examine the edge of the wine for haziness and more easily evaluate the intensity or depth of the color. If it retains its color intensity all the way to the edge of the wine, the color is very deep and you will expect other aspects of the wine to reflect this intensity. If the edge of the wine is colorless, you will find the wine to have less depth of color overall and will not expect it to be intense in odor or flavor. When making the olfactory evaluation, you will find that red wines on the whole have higher alcohol contents than do white. This means that your olfactory sense will fatigue more rapidly and you will have to pause a little longer between sniffs. In addition, when you take repeated sips of red wines, you will notice that the astringency seems to get stronger with each sip. Research has shown that this build-up of astringency is less noticeable if tasters wait 40 seconds or longer between sips.[1]

SENSORY EVALUATION EXERCISE 6.1
Focus on Olfaction II — Red Table Wine Aromas and
Aroma Wheel Descriptors for Bottle Bouquet

In Sensory Evaluation Exercise 4.1 you worked with reference standards for white table wine aromas, which are typically described by terms in the floral, spicy, and fruity segments of the wine aroma wheel and less commonly by terms from the vegetative, caramelized, and woody segments. With red table wines you will encounter fewer floral, citrus, tree, and tropical fruit odors and more odors in the berry, dried fruit, vegetative, caramelized, and woody categories.

Figure 6.1 shows how the odors you will be working with in this exercise relate to the stages in aging of a red table wine. In the early stages, aroma descriptors predominate; bottle-bouquet odors appear gradually and will dominate in the middle years of the aging cycle. The wine will begin to decrease in quality as off odors — particularly those of oxidation — begin to appear, and the wine can be pronounced dead when the acetaldehyde off odor of oxidation predominates.

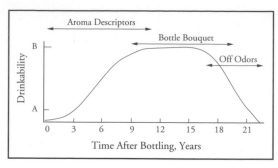

Figure 6.1
Aroma, Bouquet, and Off Odors During Bottle Aging of a Red Table Wine

Objective: In this exercise you will become familiar with some common varietal aromas of red table wines and with odors produced by bottle aging.

What to Do Before This Exercise

Reading: If you are starting with this exercise, you will need to read the introduction and reading assignment for Sensory Evaluation Exercise 4.1. If you have already completed the white table wine sensory evaluation exercises, you may want to look over any notes you made on how to perform the identification and learning of wine odors successfully. You should also review the wine aroma wheel on page 33.

Sensory Homework: If possible, reacquaint yourself with odors in the fruity-berry, fruity-dried fruit, vegetative, caramelized, and woody segments of the aroma wheel.

Instructions:

1. Refer to the instructions for Sensory Evaluation Exercise 4.1.
2. During the discussion of the aromas it will be explained where you will find them in red table wines.
3. Number of aromas correctly identified on your first attempt: _____

4. Summarize the main odor differences you've noticed between red and white table wines.

_____
_____
_____
_____
_____
_____

5. When you have finished this exercise, record what additional things you learned about identifying and learning wine odors. _____

_____
_____
_____
_____
_____
_____

6. Questions raised by this tasting: _____

_____
_____
_____
_____
_____
_____

Sensory Evaluation Exercise 6.1. Focus on Olfaction II: Red Table Wine Aromas and Aroma Wheel Descriptors for Bottle Bouquet

Sample	Association(s)	Aroma Identity — First Guess	Aroma Identity — Second Guess	Actual Aroma	Where this aroma is found in red table wines
J	RED WINE	~~BLACKBERRY~~ GRN OLIVE	GREEN OLIVE	BLACK PEPPER	SYRAH / ZIN
K	CHERRY	~~STRAWBERRY~~ RASBERRIES	RASBERRY	RASBERRY	ZIN
L	FLORAL	~~BLACK~~ ~~CASSIS~~	MOLASSES	CASSIS	CAB. SAU.
M	BLACK CHERRY	CHERRY	CHERRY	CHERRY	PINOT NOIR
N	EARTHY	EUCALYPTUS	EUCALYPTUS	RASIN	LATE HARVEST? Z.
O	BLACK PEPPER	BLACK PEPPER	BLK PEPPER	EUCALYPTUS	
P	MINT	MINT	MINT	MINT	CAB.
Q	GRAPE	MOLASSES	CABBY	GRN. OLIVE	
R	BERRY	TOBACCO	TOBACCO	TOBACCO	
S	CHOCOLATE	CHOCOLATE	CHOC.	CHOC.	BB
T	BLACK BERRY	RASIN	RASIN	MOLASSES	
U	COFFEE	COFFEE	COFFEE	COFFEE	
V					
W					

PG. 364 (SMELL ASSOCIATION) → RED WINES.

© 1993 Mar an W. Baldy
THE UNIVERSITY WINE COURSE

SENSORY EVALUATION EXERCISE 6.2
Focus on Olfaction III — When to Turn Your Nose Up
(and Your Thumbs Down) at a Wine — Four Off Odors

Objective: In this exercise you will meet four common off odors so you will be able to recognize seriously defective wines that need to be sent back in restaurants — and other places.

What to Do Before This Exercise

Reading: Look over the third-tier terms on the left-hand side of the aroma wheel (p. 33) in the earthy/moldy, chemical, pungent, oxidized, and microbiological segments to get a sense of the general nature of off odors. You should also read about off odors in Chapter 2 (pp. 37 and 38-39).

Smelly Sensory Homework: To familiarize yourself with the vinegar odor in the context of a wine's other odors, add some vinegar with an eye-dropper to a glass of ordinary wine, a drop or two at a time. Smell and taste the wine between additions until the vinegar smell becomes offensive to you. The main ingredient in vinegar is acetic acid, and it is this component that creates the off taste and off odor.

In addition to contributing a vinegar-like off odor itself, acetic acid reacts with ethanol to form ethyl acetate, which can be smelled at far lower concentrations than acetic acid.[2] If you have some nail-polish remover on hand, smell it — its main ingredient is ethyl acetate. To experience the ethyl acetate off odor in the context of other wine odors, add a few drops of nail polish remover to some wine as suggested for the vinegar.

Acetic acid forms when wines spoil as a result of the presence of oxygen **and** vinegar bacteria. Wines can also spoil if oxygen is introduced during bottle aging or cellar operations even without bacteria present. To meet the off odor produced by oxidation in the absence of vinegar bacteria, pour a sample of sherry and smell it. Sherry's prominent, pungent odor is caused by the deliberate exposure of wine to oxygen under conditions that prevent the growth of vinegar bacteria. The compound responsible is acetaldehyde — welcomed in sherries, but not in table wines.

Instructions:

1. Wash your hands.
2. Working quietly to facilitate concentration close your eyes and **smell** each sample. These samples are for smelling only, NOT for drinking!
3. Associations: Write down your impressions of what each sample smells like. If you can identify the odors from your homework, fill in the "Off Odor" column. The identity and source of each off odor will be discussed.

Sample	Association(s)	Off Odor	Source
1	NAIL POLISH REMOVER	ETHYLE ACETATE	VINEGAR BACTERIA
2	OLD BANDAID	ACATIC ACID	SPOILAGE → O_2
3	MOLDY	ACETKLDEHYDE	OXIDATION w/ BACTERIA
4	BURNT MATCH	SULFER DIOXIDE	TOO MUCH SULFER DIOXIDE IS ADDED

4. How would you describe off odors as a group? Is there a general category for them in your mind? _____

5. What has this exercise with off odors added to your understanding of wine odors and how to remember them? _____

SENSORY EVALUATION EXERCISE 6.3
Focus on Taste and Touch II — Structural Components of Red Table Wines

Objectives: In this exercise you will be introduced to the fundamental non-aromatic sensory components of red table wines. You will also become familiar with the effects of gelatin fining on astringency and the interaction of red table wines with three kinds of food.

What to Do Before This Exercise:

Reading: You may want to re-read the text pages assigned for Sensory Evaluation Exercise 4.2, and you ought to look over carefully any notes you made about sensory perception while doing or thinking about that exercise.

Sensory Homework: Red Wine Warm-Up. Some red table wines may have a slightly bitter taste and most will have an astringent feel in the mouth, bringing up one of the more difficult challenges facing beginning winetasters: learning how to distinguish between acid, bitterness, and astringency. The following homework exercises are intended to help you preview these differences and are adapted in part from Alan Young's MAKING SENSE OF WINE.[3]

1. Bitterness Revisited
   A. Bitter Foods

   Bitter salad greens include escarole, curly Belgian endive, or mustard greens. Sample a bite or two of one of these leaves. Notice the bitter taste sensations and where they occur in your mouth — typically strongest at the back of the tongue (but many people experience bitterness at the front of the tongue as well). Have some water to rinse your palate.

   B. Bitter Beverages (which are also astringent)

   We routinely taste bitterness and experience low levels of astringency in drinking cups of coffee and tea. You can remind yourself of what bitterness is by making two batches of coffee or ordinary black tea (such as Pekoe or Darjeeling), one at the normal strength and one at double strength, and then tasting them together. Notice the bitter taste sensations and where they occur in your mouth. Have some water to rinse your palate. When you begin to notice a drying effect in your mouth and a reduction or loss of its over-all feeling of smoothness which does not return quickly, that is astringency.

   Taste one of your tea or coffee samples two or three times without rinsing your mouth between tastes and concentrate on the amount of puckery sensation you perceive — a result of the tannins that are present. Most people experience the later sips as more astringent or puckery than the first. You will need to be aware of this "additive" effect of tannins and pace yourself through these homework exercises and red wine tastings, waiting at least 40 seconds between sips.

   C. Bitterness Without Food or Drink

   If you prefer a non-edible review of bitterness, buy some quinine sulfate capsules from your pharmacy or talk your friendly pharmacist out of one. The quinine sulfate capsules at my pharmacy are 200 milligrams, so I poured out about one-fifth of one to get about 40 milligrams and dissolved the powder in four ounces of water. Be sure to have a glass of water handy to rinse your mouth when you taste the quinine sulfate solution. Using the cotton swab procedure described in Exercise 4.2, test your mouth for bitter-sensing areas. You can also just taste a mouthful of the quinine solution. Note how and where you experience the bitter sensation in your mouth. If the bitterness seems too strong to you, add more water to the quinine sulfate solution.

2. Astringency
   A. Alum: It's Astringent, But Not Bitter

   Go to your pharmacist and buy some alum. Add a pinch of it to an ounce of water, and roll this around your mouth. You'll want to have something pleasant to rinse your mouth with after trying this exercise — it's important for learning, but not among the tastiest experiments. After doing this, you'll probably never forget what astringency is nor confuse it with bitterness — nor forgive me for suggesting this homework!

B. Astringency from the Grape Itself

Go to the market and buy some red table grapes, which have seeds. Peel off the skins from two or three grapes, being careful to remove as much of the juicy pulp as you can. Chew on these skins for a while. You mouth should become a little dried out. Now pop the seeds out of 1-2 grapes, again being careful to remove the pulp. Chew on these seeds. You should notice that the seeds dry your mouth faster than the skins did because they have a higher tannin content than skins. Now you know about two kinds of grape tannin — from skins and seeds — and had a grape anatomy lesson as well.

If you're game for more and want to become acquainted with the feeling of astringency produced by the tannins extracted from grapes during fermentation and in the context of wine's other sensory components, you'll need to obtain some grape tannin from a home winemaking supply store. Mix a pinch of this with a little vodka and add it to two ounces of red wine. Taste — well, feel, actually — the tannin.

3. If You Need It, an Acid Review

If you feel that your memory of the taste of acid and how you perceive it needs refreshing, repeat one of the Tart Homework exercises from Sensory Evaluation Exercise 4.2 on pages 104-105.

4. Tannic Interactions: A Preview With Tea

This exercise came to mind at breakfast one morning as I poured an ample helping of milk into my tea and watched as my friend Grace squeezed lemon juice into hers and my husband Dick dumped two packets of sugar into his. The various effects on tannin that each of us was aiming for in our tea are similar to some winemaking effects and wine and food interactions. In particular, my tea mimicked the effect that would be achieved in red wines by protein fining or by combining a red wine with foods high in fat or protein. Grace's tea approximated the effect of making red wines with low-pH/high-acid cold-region grapes and preventing the malolactic fermentation, or of eating acidic foods with red wines. Dick's tea paralleled the effect of making red wines with residual sugar, or of serving slightly sweetened sauces with them.

To find out for yourself what each effect was, brew a pot of black tea strong enough so that you can perceive the tannin clearly and pour four cups. Add some lemon juice to one, sugar to another, and milk or cream to the third. Taste them, comparing your perception of the amount of tannin in each to that in the plain tea. You will probably notice that both the milk (fat and protein) and the sugar reduce your perception of tannin, making the tea seem less drying to your mouth, and that the acidity increases your perception of tannin, making you look for a cookie (whose sugar and fat should rescue your poor, dried-out mouth from its tannic homework).

Instructions:

Describing the "ABT's": Acidity, Astringency, Bitterness, Body, and Tannins

1. Taste the white base wine, the red base wine, and small amounts of the acid and tannin component wines. Cleanse your palate between wines. Notice the effect of each wine on saliva and on the over-all feeling of smoothness in your mouth.

2. Describe the acidity, bitterness (if any), body, and astringency of each wine on the evaluation form on page 155 using the following terms. (Refer to Chapter 2, In-Mouth Impressions in What to Look for in Wines, pp. 40-41 for their definitions.) Don't worry about describing any other aspect of the wines.

Acid:	flat, tart, green
Bitterness (if present):	slightly bitter, bitter, very bitter
Body:	thin, low/light, medium, heavy/high
Astringency:	smooth, slightly rough, rough, very rough

Wine Component	Wine A White Base	Wine B Red Base	Wine C Acid Component	Wine D Tannic Component
Acid	PINO GRIGIO 2003	JA FIELDS RTW		
Body	NONE	NONE		FULLER BODIED THICKER IN MOUTH
Astringency	SMOOTH / SOME	SLIGHTLY ROUGH / SOME		ROUGH
Bitterness	NONE	TOUCH		LITTLE BIT

3. Describe the differences you perceive between acidity and astringency and between bitterness and astringency _____

_____

_____

_____

_____

4. What is the effect of tannin on your ability to perceive other aspects of the wines that are sensed in the mouth — their body and flavor, for example? _____

_____

_____

_____

_____

The Effect of Gelatin Fining on Tannin

1. Place some gelatin solution in the white base wine and in the tannic component wine and swirl each cup to distribute the gelatin. What do you see?

   White Base Wine_____ Tannic Component Wine _____

2. Let the fined wines stand for 10-15 minutes so that the gelatin can form a sediment — a wine lees, to speak technically.

3. Without disturbing the lees, taste the wines. What happened to the astringency of the tannic component wine? Did that affect your perception of any other sensory aspect(s)?

_____

_____

_____

_____

Red Wines and the Hazards of the Cheese Plate

1. Taste the Cougar Gold (or another mild, white cheddar) Cheese, Blue Cheese, and walnut with some of the red base wine. Put a bite of the food in your mouth, sip a little wine, and reflect on the effect of the food on your perceptions of the wine. Note, specifically which wine component(s) is (are) altered by each food and how.

FOOD	EFFECT ON WINE	COMPONENT AFFECTED
Cougar Gold Cheese		
Blue Cheese		
Walnut		

2. What general rules about combining red wines and foods can you derive from these results?

_____

_____

_____

_____

_____

SENSORY EVALUATION EXERCISE 6.4
"Taste and Tell" — Using Your Sensory Evaluation Skills to
Define Two Red Table Wine Styles — Beaujolais and Burgundian

Objectives: In this exercise you will practice identifying the red-wine structural components introduced in Exercise 6.3 and you will learn to look for aroma descriptors from the Focus on Olfaction exercises and for the Red Table Wines in the Pinot Noir varietal wine profile. You will also use your sensory evaluation skills to define the Nouveau and Burgundian styles of California Pinot Noir.

What to Do Before This Exercise: Read about Carbonic Maceration and the summary of Pinot Noir Production in Chapter 5 (pp. 139-140), Wine Strategies in Appendix C, (pp. 331-335), and the varietal wine profiles of Pinot Noir and Gamay in Appendix A.

Instructions:
1. Write a description of the sensory differences between Wine A, a Nouveau- or Beaujolais-Style Wine, and Wine B, a Burgundian-style red table wine (Pinot Noir). You may use the sensory evaluation form for this exercise or take notes in the following table.

Sensory Aspect	Characteristics of the Beaujolais Style	Characteristics of the Burgundian Style
Color		
Odor		
Taste		
Touch		

2. How do you think these two styles of red table wine might best be used with foods, considering the following factors about the meal:
   A. Will it be held indoors or outdoors?
   B. Is it lunch or dinner?
   C. What foods will be served? Will they be rich or simple? Consider specific foods: red meat, chicken, fish, or ham, for example.

   _____

   _____

3. Which wine seems more versatile with foods, and why? _____

   _____

   _____

   _____

   _____

4. What can you deduce about how each wine was made from its organoleptic descriptions in Question 1?

Sensory Aspect	Winemaking Deductions, Beaujolais Style	Winemaking Deductions, Burgundian Style
Color		
Odor		
Taste		
Touch		

Sensory Evaluation Exercise 6.4.
"Taste and Tell" — Using Your Sensory Evaluation Skills to Define Two Red Table Wine Styles — Beaujolais and Burgundian

WINE INFO	WINE A: Observations	WINE A: Notes	WINE B: Observations	WINE B: Notes
Type	BEAUJOLAIS	[FRENCH NOUVEAU]	PINOT NOIR 202	
Vintage	2003			
Appellation	BEAUJOLAIS			
Producer	GEORGES DE BOEFF	JM 2004		
Cost/Other	$10.00			
Clarity				
Color	PURPLE			
Off Odors	NONE			
Aroma			-SMELL FRUITIER THAN TASTE.	
Associations	(CHERRY, RASBERRY), STRAWBERRY, BLACK CHERRY			
Descriptors				
Intensity				
Varietal?				
Bouquet	ALCOHOL			
Flavor	-BLAH -LIGHT -GRAPE STEMS?	-ALCOHOL -TART AFTER TASTE	-FRUITY TASTE	
Acid, Sugar, Balance	TART (SORT OF)	SMOOTH ???		
Body	VELVET			
Astringency	???			
Aging Potential	1-3 YES			
Overall Quality				

Questions raised by this tasting:

SENSORY EVALUATION EXERCISE 6.5
Zinfandel, Syrah, and the Joys of Intensity

Objectives: The goal of this exercise is to become acquainted with two new red varietal wines and to be introduced to two stylistic interpretations of Zinfandel.

What to Do Before This Exercise: Read the varietal wine profiles of Zinfandel and Syrah in Appendix A. Review Chapter 5 on Red Wine Production.

Instructions:
1. Make a sensory evaluation of each wine.
   A. Contrast the wines on all aspects of the sensory evaluation.
   B. Select appropriate aroma wheel terms for each wine.
   C. What important differences did you notice between the Zinfandels and the Syrah?

   _____

   _____

   _____

   _____

   _____

2. Account for the differences you observe between the two Zinfandel wines by speculating on how they might have been made. Summarize your observations and speculations in the chart below.

Wine	Sensory Aspect	How Created During Winemaking
A		
B		

Sensory Evaluation Exercise 6.5.
Zinfandel, Syrah, and the Joys of Intensity

WINE INFO	WINE A: Observations	WINE A: Notes	WINE B: Observations	WINE B: Notes
Type				
Vintage				
Appellation				
Producer				
Cost/Other				
Clarity				
Color				
Off Odors				
Aroma				
Associations				
Descriptors				
Intensity				
Varietal?				
Bouquet				
Flavor				
Acid, Sugar, Balance				
Body				
Astringency				
Aging Potential				
Overall Quality				

Questions raised by this tasting:

Sensory Evaluation Exercise 6.5.
Zinfandel, Syrah, and the Joys of Intensity

WINE INFO Type Vintage Appellation Producer Cost/Other	WINE C: Observations	WINE C: Notes
Clarity		
Color		
Off Odors		
Aroma Associations Descriptors Intensity Varietal?		
Bouquet		
Flavor		
Acid, Sugar, Balance		
Body		
Astringency		
Aging Potential		
Overall Quality		

Questions raised by this tasting:

SENSORY EVALUATION EXERCISE 6.6
The Bordelais Celebrities — Cabernet Sauvignon, Merlot, and Cabernet Franc

Objectives: You will learn to identify the aroma descriptors that characterize Cabernet Sauvignon and its related varieties. You will also find out if Cabernet Sauvignon goes with chocolate.

What to Do Before This Exercise: Read the varietal wine profiles of Cabernet Sauvignon and Merlot in Appendix A; Table 5.3, Mitch Cosentino's Guide to Blending the Bordeaux Varietals; and Figure 5.15, the Vichon Winery flowchart for making Cabernet Sauvignon and Merlot.

Instructions:
1. Taste the three wines and list the key aroma and flavor descriptors you found. How do they compare with the herbal and fruit characteristics described in Mitch Cosentino's Cabernet Blending guide?

     Merlot: _____

     _____

     Cabernet Franc: _____

     _____

     Cabernet Sauvignon: _____

     _____

     Common descriptors: _____

     _____

2. Taste the three wines and note any structural differences between them. How do they compare with the structural features and other effects in a blend in Mitch Cosentino's Blending guide?

     body _____

     _____

     tannin _____

     _____

     other factors? _____

     _____

3. Try Cabernet Sauvignon with the milk chocolate and dark chocolate alone and in combination with the raspberry fruit leather.

     Does chocolate go well with Cabernet Sauvignon? _____

     _____

     _____

     _____

     Is milk chocolate or dark chocolate better? _____

     _____

     _____

     _____

     What is the effect of the raspberry? _____

     _____

     _____

     _____

Sensory Evaluation Exercise 6.6.
The **Bordelais Celebrities** — Cabernet Sauvignon, Merlot, and Cabernet Franc

	WINE A: Observations	WINE A: Notes	WINE B: Observations	WINE B: Notes

WINE INFO
  Type
  Vintage
  Appellation
  Producer
  Cost/Other				

Clarity				
Color				
Off Odors				

Aroma
  Associations
  Descriptors
  Intensity
  Varietal?				

Bouquet				
Flavor				
Acid, Sugar, Balance				
Body				
Astringency				
Aging Potential				
Overall Quality				

Questions raised by this tasting:

Sensory Evaluation Exercise 6.6.
The Bordelais Celebrities — Cabernet Sauvignon, Merlot, and Cabernet Franc

	WINE C: Observations	WINE C: Notes
WINE INFO		
Type		
Vintage		
Appellation		
Producer		
Cost/Other		
Clarity		
Color		
Off Odors		
Aroma		
Associations		
Descriptors		
Intensity		
Varietal?		
Bouquet		
Flavor		
Acid, Sugar, Balance		
Body		
Astringency		
Aging Potential		
Overall Quality		

Questions raised by this tasting:

SENSORY EVALUATION EXERCISE 6.7
Getting Older and Better — The Effects of Bottle Aging on Cabernet Sauvignon

Objectives: You will learn to describe the sensory changes that occur in red table wines as they age in the bottle and formulate a description of bottle bouquet.

What to Do Before This Exercise: Read about bottle aging in Chapters 3 and 5 (p. 86 and 137-139).

Instructions:

1. Compare the older and younger wines on all aspects of sensory evaluation. List the changes that you notice.

Sensory Component	Changes with Bottle Aging
Color	
Clarity	
Aroma	
Bouquet	
Sugar & Acid	
Body	
Flavor	
Astringency	
Overall Quality	

2. Focus on the odors of the older wines and write down as many words as you can conjure up from your imagination and the aroma wheel to describe what you perceive. Complete this statement: "Bottle bouquet is . . ." _____

_____

_____

_____

_____

Sensory Evaluation Exercise 6.7.
Getting Older and Better — The Effects of Bottle Aging on Cabernet Sauvignon

WINE INFO	WINE A: Observations	WINE A: Notes	WINE B: Observations	WINE B: Notes
Type				
Vintage				
Appellation				
Producer				
Cost/Other				
Clarity				
Color				
Off Odors				
Aroma				
Associations				
Descriptors				
Intensity				
Varietal?				
Bouquet				
Flavor				
Acid, Sugar, Balance				
Body				
Astringency				
Aging Potential				
Overall Quality				

Questions raised by this testing:

SENSORY EVALUATION EXERCISE 6.8
Your Turn — Creating Your Own Tasting of Red Table Wines

Objective: You will design and conduct a sensory evaluation exercise that explores some additional aspect of red table wines that intrigues you.

What to Do Before This Exercise: If necessary, review the instructions for Sensory Evaluation Exercise 4.6 (p. 116).

Worksheet for Creating Your Own Winetasting

1. Objective: _____
   _____
   _____
   _____

2. Wine characteristics: _____
   _____
   _____
   _____

3. Number of wines, budget: _____
   _____
   _____
   _____

4. Supplier(s) and the specific wines: _____
   _____
   _____
   _____

5. The tasting strategy: _____
   _____
   _____
   _____

6. Background or reference material: _____
   _____
   _____
   _____

7. Note-taking aids: _____
   _____
   _____
   _____

8. The setting: _____
   _____
   _____
   _____

Sensory Evaluation Exercise 6.8.
Your Turn — Creating Your Own Tasting of Red Table Wines

WINE INFO	WINE A: Observations	WINE A: Notes	WINE B: Observations	WINE B: Notes
Type				
Vintage				
Appellation				
Producer				
Cost/Other				
Clarity				
Color				
Off Odors				
Aroma				
Associations				
Descriptors				
Intensity				
Varietal?				
Bouquet				
Flavor				
Acid, Sugar, Balance				
Body				
Astringency				
Aging Potential				
Overall Quality				

Questions raised by this tasting:

Sensory Evaluation Exercise 6.8.
Your Turn — Creating Your Own Tasting of Red Table Wines

WINE INFO Type Vintage Appellation Producer Cost/Other	WINE C: Observations	WINE C: Notes	WINE D: Observations	WINE D: Notes
Clarity				
Color				
Off Odors				
Aroma Associations Descriptors Intensity Varietal?				
Bouquet				
Flavor				
Acid, Sugar, Balance				
Body				
Astringency				
Aging Potential				
Overall Quality				

Questions raised by this tasting:

SENSORY EVALUATION EXERCISE 6.9
Review Tasting for Red Table Wines

For this exercise please refer to Sensory Evaluation Exercise 4.7 (page 120) for instructions. Because you will probably have more wines to sort than in earlier review tastings, you may need to add more steps to the worksheet. Here is an example of how you might begin the sorting:

Step #1: sensory factor, color

purple, go to step 2

not purple, go to step 3

There is a sample worksheet in Appendix D (page 374) which you may refer to as long as you heed the warning that it may not apply exactly to the wines you've tasted.

Worksheet for the Red Table Wine Review Tasting

Step #1. sensory factor: _____ _____

if _____ , the variety is _____ or go to step _____

if _____ , go to step _____

Step #2. sensory factor: _____

if _____ , the variety is _____ or go to step _____

if _____ , go to step _____

Step #3. sensory factor: _____

if _____ , the variety is _____ or go to step _____

if _____ , go to step _____

Step #4. sensory factor: _____

if _____ , the variety is _____ or go to step _____

if _____ , go to step _____

Step #5. sensory factor: _____

if _____ , the variety is _____ or go to step _____

if _____ , go to step _____

Step #6. sensory factor: _____

if _____ , the variety is _____ or go to step _____

if _____ , go to step #7

Step #7. sensory factor: _____

if _____ , the variety is _____

if _____ , the variety is _____

Sensory Evaluation Exercise 6.9.
Review Tasting for Red Table Wines

WINE INFO	WINE A: Observations	WINE A: Notes	WINE B: Observations	WINE B: Notes
Type				
Vintage				
Appellation				
Producer				
Cost/Other				
Clarity				
Color				
Off Odors				
Aroma				
Associations				
Descriptors				
Intensity				
Varietal?				
Bouquet				
Flavor				
Acid, Sugar, Balance				
Body				
Astringency				
Aging Potential				
Overall Quality				

Questions raised by this tasting:

Sensory Evaluation Exercise 6.9.
Review Tasting for Red Table Wines

WINE INFO	WINE C: Observations	WINE C: Notes	WINE D: Observations	WINE D: Notes
Type				
Vintage				
Appellation				
Producer				
Cost/Other				
Clarity				
Color				
Off Odors				
Aroma				
Associations				
Descriptors				
Intensity				
Varietal?				
Bouquet				
Flavor				
Acid, Sugar, Balance				
Body				
Astringency				
Aging Potential				
Overall Quality				

Questions raised by this tasting:

Sensory Evaluation Exercise 6.9.
Review Tasting for Red Table Wines

WINE INFO	WINE E: Observations	WINE E: Notes	WINE F: Observations	WINE F: Notes
Type				
Vintage				
Appellation				
Producer				
Cost/Other				
Clarity				
Color				
Off Odors				
Aroma				
Associations				
Descriptors				
Intensity				
Varietal?				
Bouquet				
Flavor				
Acid, Sugar, Balance				
Body				
Astringency				
Aging Potential				
Overall Quality				

Questions raised by this tasting:

REVIEW QUESTIONS

Instructions: You might want to use a separate sheet of paper to answer the following review questions. In that way you can use the questions to check your knowledge of this chapter more than once. You may, for example, want to re-test yourself on items that you have missed or use the "Review Questions" to test your knowledge before you read a chapter.

Match each statement (for questions 1-9) with the grape or wine it describes. For the True or False item, answer "True" if the statement is accurate or "False" if the statement is incorrect. If you determine that a statement is false make a note explaining why. For the multiple choice items pick the best alternative. Check your answers after you have completed all the questions.

Use the following answers for items 1-9. Each statement describes only one wine or grape variety.

    A. Gamay
    B. Pinot Noir
    C. Zinfandel
    D. Syrah
    E. Cabernet Sauvignon

1.   From the Rhône Valley of France; called Petite Sirah by some California wineries. _____

2.   Grown in the best vineyards in the Burgundy district of France. _____

3.   Most vegetative/herbaceous red wine on the list. _____

4.   Most likely to be vinified by carbonic maceration. _____

5.   A fruity raspberry aroma is typical of this variety when young; originally from Italy. _____

6.   Used for sparkling wine production in California and France. _____

7.   The most commonly made blush varietal wine in California starts with this grape. _____

8.   The most commonly made red varietal wine in California starts with this grape. _____

9.   Grown in the best vineyards of Bordeaux, France. _____

10.   How is the evaluation of color and clarity modified for red wines? _____
_____
_____

11.   What might lead you to have more olfactory fatigue while tasting red wines? _____
_____

12.   What element of red wines will probably cause you to have palate fatigue? How can you
      minimize it? _____
_____

13.   True or false: Descriptors from the floral and tropical fruit segments of the aroma wheel are
      used less often for red table wines than they are for white table wines. _____

14. When is a wine "dead?" _____
_____

15. Refer to the five wines marked A, B, C, D, and E in the article "Napa Pinot Noirs Still Rank at the Top" from the *SAN FRANCISCO CHRONICLE*, May 8, 1991. Which wine has an off odor? _____

16. Refer again to the five wines marked A, B, C, D, and E in the article "Napa Pinot Noirs Still Rank at the Top" from the *SAN FRANCISCO CHRONICLE*, May 8, 1991. Which of the sound wines would you predict to have the shortest aging life in the bottle? _____

17. Which odor descriptors would you expect to find in the bottle bouquet of a fine, well-aged 1978 Napa Valley Cabernet Sauvignon?
    A. bell pepper, eucalyptus, mint
    B. rose, cassis, black pepper
    C. tobacco, coffee, chocolate, soy
    D. cherry, cedar, cut green grass
    E. acetaldehyde, ethyl acetate, geranium

18. Which odor descriptors would you expect to find in a fine bottle of 1992 Napa Valley Cabernet Sauvignon?
    A. bell pepper, eucalyptus, mint, maybe berries, cassis
    B. rose, cassis, black pepper
    C. tobacco, coffee, chocolate, soy
    D. cherry, cedar, cut green grass
    E. acetaldehyde, ethyl acetate, geranium

19. Which odor descriptors would you expect to find in a bottle of Napa Valley Cabernet Sauvignon that was spoiled by vinegar bacteria?
    A. strong bell pepper, eucalyptus, mint
    B. rose, cassis, black pepper
    C. tobacco, coffee, chocolate, soy
    D. cherry, cedar, cut green grass
    E. acetaldehyde, ethyl acetate

20. A California wine made from Pinot Noir grapes with warmer fermentation temperatures and oak aging would be?
    A. a Beaujolais-style wine
    B. Pinot Noir Blanc
    C. Gamay Nouveaux
    D. a Burgundian-style wine
    E. Pinot Oakeaux

21. Which red table wine on the list below would you predict would have the darkest color and most tannin? It also can have an aroma of fresh ground black pepper. All are from the same vintage.
    A. Zinfandel
    B. Pinot Noir
    C. Gamay Beaujolais
    D. Syrah
    E. Merlot

22. Which sensory change on the list below would you **not** expect as a fine bottle of Cabernet Sauvignon ages?
    A. The red color becomes more tawny.
    B. The tannins polymerize and the wine feels less rough.
    C. The total acid content increases.
    D. The odors and flavors become more complex and subtle.
    E. A sediment forms.

NAPA PINOT NOIRS STILL RANK AT THE TOP

BY STEVE PITCHER

Special to the Chronicle

During the last few months, the Vintners Club has held two separate tastings of new-release Pinot Noirs.

Twenty-four wines—12 at a time—were sampled and evaluated.

The appellations included Napa Valley, Russian River Valley, Santa Barbara County, Carneros, the Central Coast, Oregon, Mendocino's Anderson Valley, plus Idaho (its Pinot finished a respectable seventh).

Most were from the 1988 vintages. Four were '87s, and one was an '85.

The results provided plenty of food for thought.

Four out of four Napa Valley Pinots placed in the top six of their respective tastings, casting doubt on the popular notion that Napa Valley has been displaced as prime Pinot Noir territory by cooler-climate areas.

One Napa Valley Pinot in particular was absolutely stunning: the '88 Signorello "Founder's Reserve" Pinot Noir.

A very impressive showing by a new winery, the Signorello has won praise from critic Robert Parker, the "California Grapevine" and Norm Roby of the "Wine Spectator," among others. The only sour note came from Connoisseurs' Guide, whose tasters thought the wine had "pushy oak."

Two back-to-back vintages of Calera Jensen Vineyard Pinot Noir ('87 and '88) finished among the top six in their respective tastings, upholding Calera's unparalleled success in Vintners Club Pinot Noir tastings.

Here are the top-ranked wines out of the 24 tasted:

FIRST PLACE

(A) **1988 Dehlinger Pinot Noir**, Russian River Valley ($16.50). Complex aromas of plummy, black cherry fruit, vanilla, pleasant earthiness and cedar. Nicely balanced on the palate, exhibiting rich fruit and mild herbaceousness. Medium tannins and good texture.

(B) **1988 Signorello Founder's Reserve Pinot Noir**, Napa Valley ($25). Complex and inviting aromas of ripe strawberry/black cherry fruit, moderately toasty oak, cloves and vanilla. Full-bodied, with medium tannin. Bottled unfined and unfiltered, it was supple, offering lots of ripe fruit, plus sweet oak.

SECOND PLACE

(C) **1988 Cambria Pinot Noir**, Julia's Vineyard, Santa Maria Valley ($16). Medium-high char oak dominated the nose, which also showed some fruit, coffee and tobacco. Rounded and silky, with flavors focusing on ripe cherry-berry fruit and light spice. Lingering finish.

(D) **1988 Westwood Winery Reserve Pinot Noir**, Haynes Vineyard, Napa Valley ($20). Forward aromas of jammy, black cherry/raspberry fruit, plus spice and some mint that soon blew off. Complex flavors of berries and violets with some depths. Medium tannins.

THIRD PLACE

(E) **1988 Calera Pinot Noir**, Jensen Vineyard, San Benito County ($30). Forward, fragrant aromas of ripe fruit, with a hint of VA (volatile acidity: a slightly vinegary note). A big wine with generous, delicious flavors of ripe, plummy raspberry fruit that were almost Zinfandel-like. Medium tannins.

1988 Rex Hill Pinot Noir, Dundee Hills Vineyards, Willamette Valley, Oregon ($14). Soft, seductive nose of cherries, light oak, cloves, and chocolate. Medium-bodied, with pleasant flavors of spicy cherries, black pepper, and mild herbaceousness.

FOURTH PLACE

1987 Calera Pinot Noir, Jensen Vineyard, San Benito County ($30). Complex nose of ripe, black cherry fruit, truffles and vanilla. Concentrated flavors. Medium high tannins. Excellent aging potential.

1988 Meridian Pinot Noir, Riverbench Vineyard, Santa Barbara County ($13). Wonderful aromas of cloves and lots of cherry-strawberry fruit. Delicious flavors replicate the nose; elegant. Round, east tannins. Good drinking now.

FIFTH PLACE

1988 Carneros Creek Pinot Noir, Los Carneros ($15). Jammy, spicy, strawberry scents that were pleasant and appealing. Flavors replicated the nose and opened up over time. Medium tannins.

1987 Robert Stemmler Pinot Noir, Sonoma County ($21). Intriguing aromas of rose petals, cherries, mushrooms, leather and anise, with a slightly smoky component. Cherry-berry fruit on the palate, along with substantial oak. Tannic.

SIXTH PLACE

1987 El Molino Pinot Noir, Napa County ($30). Burgundian nose of charred oak, strawberries, violets, coffee and a whiff of mature (brown) stems. Raspberry fruit plus oak on the palate. Tannic. Needs time.

Wines are evaluated by each participant ranking the wines from 1st place to 12th place. The identities of the wines are not known until the scores have been handed in.

Steve Pitcher is vice president of the Vintners Club, a nonprofit educational organization. For information concerning tastings and membership, call 485-1166.

Reprinted from
THE SAN FRANCISCO
CHRONICLE,
May 8, 1991.

ANSWERS TO REVIEW QUESTIONS

1. D
2. B
3. E
4. A
5. C
6. B
7. C
8. E
9. E
10. You tilt the glass so that you can look through a thinner layer of wine.
11. Their higher alcohol contents and stronger odors.
12. The astringency from tannins seems to get stronger with each sip and that tires the palate. If tasters wait 40 seconds or more between sip the effect is lessened.
13. True
14. When off odors, particularly the acetaldehyde odor of oxidation, predominate.
15. E has a "slightly vinegary note"
16. C is described as "round and silky" while all others have "medium tannins."
17. C
18. A
19. E
20. D
21. D
22. C

ENDNOTES

[1] Guinard, Jean-Xavier, Rose Marie Pangborn, and Michael J. Lewis, "The Time-Course of Astringency in Wine upon Repeated Ingestion," *American Journal of Enology and Viticulture,* Vol. 37, No. 3, 1986, pp. 184-191.

[2] Young, Alan, MAKING SENSE OF WINE, Greenhouse Publications, Richmond, Australia, 1986, p. 94.

[3] Young, Alan, MAKING SENSE OF WINE, Greenhouse Publications, Richmond, Australia, 1986, p. 101 and p. 120.

7

MAKING THE WINES WITH STARS
The Production of Sparkling Wines

WHAT *IS* CHAMPAGNE?

American enologist Bruce Zoecklein opens the first article in his series on méthode champenoise with the following quotation from a market survey conducted several years ago in Britain in which people were asked what the word champagne suggested to them: "Few answered [that it meant] sparkling wine. The responses were mostly associated with abstract concepts such as pleasure, luxury, success, and love."[1] By now that market survey is over a decade old, but the mystique surrounding champagne is still even more powerful than its bouquet. This chapter explores the production of sparkling wines, including champagne; I hope you will be able to concentrate on the enological facts even as luxurious and romantic images infiltrate your imaginations.

THE BUBBLES MAKE THE WINE AND
THERE ARE SEVERAL WAYS TO ADD THEM

Sparkling wines are table wines that contain large amounts of dissolved carbon dioxide gas which bubbles up and forms a layer of foam or "mousse" on the surface of the wine. Carbon dioxide can become dissolved in wines in several ways, and the production method chosen can dramatically affect the other sensory traits of the wine, as well as the customer's pocketbook.

The most common methods of making sparkling wines use two alcoholic fermentations and trap the gas produced by the second. The first fermentation produces a dry, still table wine; sugar and yeast are added to it for a second fermentation conducted under conditions that prevent the carbon dioxide gas from escaping. Sparkling wines can also be made by trapping the carbon dioxide gas from a single alcoholic or malolactic fermentation or by carbonation — charging a wine with carbon dioxide gas artificially instead of by fermentation. These last two methods are less common.

Two distinct techniques can be used to conduct the second alcoholic fermentation that produces sparkling wines: tank fermentation and bottle fermentation. These two processes typically create very different products. Tank fermentation is chosen for less expensive wines that are intended to reach the market quickly and whose aroma and flavors emphasize the fresh, fruity character of the grapes. Bottle fermentation can also yield young, fruity wines, but it is normally chosen when more complex wines are desired because it allows the wine to be aged for years with the second fermentation's yeast, producing a complex, characteristic champagne bouquet.

This chapter will discuss three methods of producing sparkling wines: bottle fermentation based on the traditional French méthode champenoise; a variation of bottle fermentation called the transfer process; and tank fermentation, also known as the Charmat bulk process (after the inventor of a widely used fermentation tank). You will encounter many French words in this chapter because they are used by méthode champenoise sparkling wine producers all over the world to describe the steps in this process.

WHY "THE WINES WITH STARS"?

The title of this chapter refers to sparkling wines as "The Wines with Stars" because, according to tradition, this is how they were first described by their legendary discoverer, the monk Dom Pérignon. From 1668 to 1715 Dom Pérignon was the cellarmaster at the Benedictine Abbey in Hautvilliers, a town in France's Champagne District, where he was famous for his innovations in winemaking and his blending skills.[2] His interest in blending may have developed because the abbey received tithes of wine from its parishioners and the good cellarmaster learned that by mixing some of these wines a better beverage could be created; and his tasting ability may have been sharpened as a result of his blindness later in life. Dom Pérignon was one of the first winemakers to use corks instead of cloth or wooden plugs to seal wine bottles, and he preferred bottles of a stronger glass which had recently become available from England.

As the discovery story goes, one spring Dom Pérignon was following the good winemaking practice of tasting the wines that had been fermented and bottled from the preceding fall's harvest. During this tasting, he is reported to have discovered some bottles of wine with lots of bubbles and to have called out to his brothers, "Come quickly, I'm drinking stars!" Thus we now have "the wine with stars," and stars decorate many sparkling wine and champagne labels as well as this enological discussion.

How might Dom Pérignon's discovery of champagne have come about? We can apply our knowledge of winemaking (perhaps recently acquired in a previous chapter of this book) to develop a plausible explanation for these "historic" events. Perhaps the weather was cooler than normal the fall before the discovery of sparkling wines and the fermentations were slower than usual. As a result, based on the time elapsed, the apparent cessation of CO_2 evolution and, perhaps, the settling out of the yeast, the wines appeared to have finished their alcoholic fermentations and were bottled even though some sugar remained unfermented. Because modern methods of clarification and stabilization did not exist in the late 17th century when Dom Pérignon's "discovery vintage" was bottled, some yeast cells must have been included with the wine. As the alcoholic fermentation slowly finished in the bottles during the cool winter months, the resulting carbon dioxide gas became dissolved in the wine and created the "stars" that danced on Dom Pérignon's palate the following spring. By using sturdy bottles and sealing them tightly with corks, Dom Pérignon had created exactly the right conditions to trap the carbon dioxide that was produced when the prematurely bottled wine continued to ferment.

Dom Pérignon is said to have worked more on ways to "encourage the natural tendency of wine to sparkle," but the modern commercial production of sparkling wines using a second alcoholic fermentation probably dates from the early 19th century. The first reference tables that correlated the amount of sugar added to still table wines with the carbon dioxide pressure developed after this sugar was fermented were published in France in 1829.[3] Such tables were of obvious utility to sparkling wine producers, who did not want bottles of their product to explode in the cellar or at their customer's table.

MÉTHODE CHAMPENOISE — FERMENTATION IN THE BOTTLE

Exactly what is meant by "méthode champenoise" is a bit hard to pin down because a variety of pro-

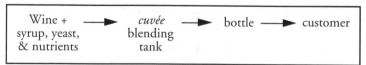

Figure 7.1
Summary of Sparkling Wine Production by Bottle Fermentation

duction techniques are employed in France's Champagne district. However, the term at least implies that you are going to drink the wine from the same bottle in which the second fermentation occurred, even if it does not prescribe precisely how the wine will be blended, fermented, aged, and clarified. The term "méthode champenoise" does not have a clear legal definition in either the U.S. or France, although the French are presently trying to restrict its use by Spanish producers of bottle-fermented sparkling wines, just as they campaigned to restrict the use of the term "champagne" by other sparkling wine-producing regions in France and in other countries. The effort was successful in most countries, the U.S. being a notable exception. In this book, "sparkling wine" and "champagne" will be used interchangeably.

Grape Varieties, Growing Conditions, and When to Harvest

The preferred grape varieties for méthode champenoise sparkling wine production are Chardonnay and Pinot Noir, and it is these varieties, along with Pinot Meunier, that are most often used in France's Champagne district.[4] In California, Pinot Blanc is used instead of Pinot Meunier along with Chardonnay and Pinot Noir. A number of other varieties are used in very cool grape-growing areas where *Vitis vinifera* varieties cannot be cultivated successfully. There is considerable clonal variation within both Chardonnay and Pinot Noir, and California sparkling-wine producers are now experimenting to discover which clones are most suitable for their winemaking programs.[5]

With the exception of the Mosel region of Germany, the Champagne district is the northern-most significant grape producing region in the world. Its grapes ripen slowly under these very cool conditions, making them relatively high in both total acid and proportion of malic acid and low in pH, sugar content, and varietal character — the perfect composition for sparkling wine production. To emulate the characteristics of the grapes produced in France, the coolest grape-growing conditions are preferred wherever bottle-fermented sparkling wines are produced.

Recognizable varietal aromas and flavors are not necessary in sparkling wines because they could mask the wines' most important odors — the champagne bouquet   which comes from long aging on the yeast after the second fermentation, so champagne grapes are harvested early. This early-harvest requirement must be balanced against the need to avoid the green, grassy character of immature fruit, however. Typical sugar and acid values at harvest for Chardonnay, Pinot Noir, and Pinot Blanc grapes under California growing conditions (which are warmer than those in Champagne) are shown in Table 7.1.

Table 7.1
Average Fruit Composition of California Grapes for Méthode Champenoise [6]

	Chardonnay	Pinot Noir	Pinot Blanc
° Brix	17.8-21.4	17.0-20.0	16.5-17.5
grams/100 ml of acid	0.85-1.5	0.9-1.7	1.05-1.1
pH	2.85-3.3	2.9-3.3	3.1-3.2

As you can see, these sugar and pH values are lower and the acid values higher than desirable for fine table wines (compare Table 3.2, for example), and table wines made from them would be low in fruit character, very tart, and low in alcohol content, probably best used for blending to improve the balance of flat, warm-region wines. However, grapes of this composition are ideal for sparkling wines that will acquire champagne bouquet, need tartness to balance their *dosage* sugar, and whose alcohol level will be raised by the second fermentation. When determining maturity, some producers supplement chemical analyses with sensory evaluation, which they use to assess the quality and intensity of the juice aroma: in warmer areas mature fruit flavors can be noticeable even at low sugar concentrations. Of course, they must also take into account the condition of the grapes (diseased or healthy) and vines (their ability to ripen the fruit further) when deciding when to harvest.

In addition to a cool regional climate for grape-growing, what vineyard management practices appear to be critical for quality in sparkling wines? Bruce Zoecklein has been investigating this question since the mid-1980s by surveying sparkling-wine producers about their viticultural practices. Apart from growing the most desirable cultivars in a cool climate, harvesting the fruit with plenty of crisp acidity, and avoiding deep, fertile soils that would encourage the vine to grow too vigorously, Zoecklein's research did not uncover a particular pattern of vineyard design or cultural procedures that sparkling-wine producers followed to produce the optimal grapes for quality wine. He believes that gaining more specific insight into the relationship between viticultural practices and wine quality is one of the major challenges facing winegrowers in the 1990s. It may be more difficult to discover these relationships for sparkling wines than for table wines, since sparkling wines are blended from many different vineyard lots and vintages and are fermented twice — procedures that would obscure the effects of the cultural practices in any one vineyard.

In California, harvesting grapes for sparkling wines typically begins in early August and may be done by hand or machine depending on the vineyard terrain, the grape varieties to be picked, the importance of speedy collection of the fruit, and the producer's philosophy and financial condition. Because cool vineyard conditions during the harvest assist the delivery of cool fruit to the winery, mechanical harvest at night has been used successfully for some of California's best sparkling wines.

Making the Base Wines

The "base wines" for sparkling wine production are small batches of dry white table wine which are blended to create the *cuvée* wine, or *vin de cuvée:* the wine that will be bottled for a second fermentation and aging. Many of the methods used to make the base wines come from practices that originally evolved to handle Pinot Noir grapes in France's Champagne district. In that area, Pinot Noir is favored because it ripens more reliably from year to year than do other grape varieties under the area's very cool growing conditions. Although it is a "black" grape with a deep blue skin and red pigment cells just below the skin, its juice is colorless, and white wines can be made from it (and many other black or "red" grape varieties) by using special techniques that minimize the extraction of color from the skins and pulp: harvest less-mature fruit, pick under the coolest conditions, inspect the fruit and remove moldy berries (with damaged skin than leaks color), and press whole grapes without first crushing them. These methods are used for all grape varieties intended for champagne because they minimize the extraction of tannins as well as color from the skins.

The most common first step in méthode champenoise sparkling-wine production is pressing whole grape clusters, stems included. Very gentle presses are used and the juice that comes from them is carefully tasted and divided into free-run juice and two classes of press-run juice. It is the free-run juice that is fermented to create the *vin de cuvée* — an average of 110 gallons per ton of grapes. The first class of press-run juice is produced in several increments by gentle pressing; these will be fermented into the so-called cut wines or *vins de taille* (about 20 gallons per ton), which may be subdivided into first, second, and even third cuts, also known as *première, deuxième, and troisième tailles*. Finally, the second class of press-run juice — that from the final pressing — will be fermented to yield the *"vin de presse"* of about 7 gallons per ton.[7] The free-run juice is nearly colorless, has little varietal character, and tastes very fresh and tart. The *vin de cuvée* and the best *première taille* wines are typically used in blends for sparkling-wine production, with the finest *vin de cuvée* being reserved for a producer's driest and most prestigious wine known as the *tête de cuvée*. The *première tailles* may also be used for sweeter "extra-dry" or "demi-sec" wines.[8] The wines made from the later cuts and the *vins de presse* are sold for blending or, following the French tradition, may be distilled to produce strong wine spirits called *marc* or made into a fortified aperitif.

Minimal amounts of sulfur dioxide are added to the juices as they leave the presses and go to refrigerated stainless-steel tanks for chilling and pre-fermentation clarification by settling or centrifugation. The three or more batches of juice from each pressing, juices from different grape varieties and vineyards, and

Figure 7.2
The Shallow Basket Presses at Moët Chandon in Épernay, France

juices from grapes picked on different dates may all be kept separate during fermentation; thus, in contrast to a table-wine production facility, a winery that makes sparkling wines will have many small fermentation tanks. Each batch of juice is inoculated, typically with the champagne strain of *Saccharomyces* yeast, and fermentation is conducted at 65-70°F in stainless-steel tanks or sometimes in French oak barrels. Because varietal character is not desired, warmer fermentation temperatures that allow the volatile aroma components to escape are used, and the first alcoholic fermentation is completed rapidly — in seven to ten days. The newly fermented wines are then chilled, filtered to remove yeast and other solids that could contribute off flavors, clarified by racking or centrifugation, and cold stabilized.

The principle goal of most producers of méthode champenoise sparkling wines is to create a particular proprietary style of non-vintage wine that is consistent from year to year. To help minimize the variation in fruit composition between vintages and insure stylistic consistency, some producers will mix reserve wine — a blend of the still base wines from previous years — into the juice before fermentation; others will add it when preparing the *cuvée* blend.[9] As much as 20-30% of the *cuvée* may be made up of reserve wine. Thus, for reasons of stylistic consistency and legal requirements for labelling — to qualify for a vintage date under U.S. law only 5% of a wine may come from another harvest — vintage-dated méthode champenoise sparkling wines are much rarer than vintage-dated still table wines.

The malolactic fermentation is encouraged during the alcoholic fermentation by some méthode champenoise producers, who believe that it improves the sugar-to-acid balance of their drier wines by reducing acidity and that it adds a more complex and longer aftertaste to their wines.[10] However, other méthode champenoise winemakers believe that malic acid is important for the freshness and tartness of their wines, especially those with higher sugar contents, and they take care to prevent the MLF.

Creating the *Cuvée*

A *cuvée* is a blend of wines. In champagne-making, *cuvées* are the many batches of base wine that will be converted into sparkling wine by means of a second fermentation. The selection of the *cuvée* is the most critical step in sparkling-wine production and involves five to seven weeks of intensive blending and tasting — typically in the late fall or spring.

The ideal base wines for blending into the *cuvée* are clear, light in color, free of off odors or flavors, of delicate aroma and flavor, dry, moderate in alcohol content, high in acidity, and light in body. These base wines are not balanced and pleasant to drink as table wines, but they become well-balanced sparkling wines after they are blended and the second fermentation has added bubbles, increased their alcohol by one to two percent, decreased their acidity slightly, and added richness and complexity to their odors and flavors.

The winemakers making the blends have to envision what the *cuvée* wines will be like after the second fermentation and two to four years of aging in the bottle with the yeast. Experience counts for a lot here: the better the quality and range of desirable styles of wines to blend, the better the *cuvée*, so a méthode champenoise producer may press more than the minimum amount of grapes needed to produce their *cuvées* in order to ensure a good selection.[11] To make the *cuvées* the base wines that have been kept separate by variety, press cut, vineyard, and harvest date are all tasted and then blended with each other and with reserve wines from earlier years. The resulting blends are then tasted, adjusted by further blending, and tasted again. This process is repeated until a satisfactory series of *cuvées* has been created for the range of styles of sparkling wines — from dry to sweet, white to salmon color, etc. — made by that particular producer. A *cuvée* may contain up to 70 different wines.

Grape varieties will be used in a *cuvée* in varying proportions depending on the style of wine desired. Each variety adds unique qualities to the *cuvée*: Pinot Noir is used for body and depth of flavor, Chardonnay for acid and aging potential, and Pinot Blanc to lengthen the aftertaste.[12]

It is unusual for a *cuvée* to contain a large enough proportion of a single grape variety (75% in California) to be labelled as a varietal wine. If the *cuvée* is blended from white grapes only, the resulting wine is called *Blanc de Blancs:* a white wine from white grapes. If red (black) grapes are used in the blend, the wine is called *Blanc de Noirs* and should have an attractive light-bronze or salmon color.

After the *cuvées* are made they may be heat and cold stabilized and filtered again before the second fermentation is begun.

The Second Fermentation — *Prise de Mousse*

To start the second fermentation — called *prise de mousse,* which means "catch the foam" — the *cuvée* is placed in a large tank, and liqueur (cane sugar dissolved in some *cuvée* wine), yeast nutrients, and an actively growing yeast culture are mixed in. Sugar and other yeast nutrients are commonly added because all or nearly all of the natural grape sugar has been consumed during the first fermentation and sometimes other nutrients are also depleted. This mixture of wine, yeast, and sugar is ready for *tirage* (rhymes with garage): drawing the mixture from the tank into the bottles for fermentation and aging. The *tirage* bottles are closed with stainless steel bottle caps and placed on their sides in tall stacks or bins (big boxes that can be stacked by forklifts).

The second fermentation takes about 30 days to complete and gives birth to the sparkling wine by using up the added sugar to produce dissolved carbon dioxide gas and alcohol as by-products. The yeast used for the second fermentation is often a different strain or species from the one used for the first fermentation because the second fermentation occurs under very different conditions: higher alcohol (9-11%), lower sugar (about 2-3°Brix), increasing carbon-dioxide gas pressures (up to 6-7 times atmospheric pressure at the end of fermentation), and cooler temperatures (50-55°F). The yeast strain must also be one that will cooperatively die after fermentation, clump up and settle out of the wine into a thin film on the inside of the bottle, give off desirable odors and flavors as it breaks down during aging, and not stick to or stain the side of the bottle.[13]

Figure 7.3
Sparkling Rosé wine in a tirage *at Schramsberg Winery — note the thin film of yeast that has settled out in each bottle*
Photo: Curtis Wentworth

How Many Bubbles?

I bet you are ready for a little méthode champenoise trivia after so many pages of serious enological talk, especially with all those French words thrown in. OK, here we go. After years of agonizing controversy among enological numerophiles (a word I just made up for people who like numbers), the Grande Marque House of Bollinger of Ay, Champagne, France, has determined that a bottle of Bollinger R. D. 1979 contained 56,000,000 bubbles. This was many more than the "7,000 to 45,000 effervescent bubbles" which a group of survey respondents thought were in the "average bottle of Champagne," but then, is Bollinger R. D. 1979 an **average** bottle of Champagne?[14] Alas — or fortunately? — the debate and research on this topic may have to go on! Happy counting!

Aging with the Yeast — *Sur Lie*

The bottles are left stacked in a horizontal position to age for two to four years on the thin film of yeast that collects after fermentation. During aging two processes occur: the wine matures as the reactions of bottle aging occur, and the dead yeast cells break open (a process known as autolysis) and release amino acids and other compounds into the wine. These autolysis products add

Figure 7.4
Bottle of Sparkling Wine removed from the tirage *at Schramsberg, showing the yeast sediment*
Photo: Curtis Wentworth

Figure 7.5
Bottles of sparkling wine in pupîtres *at Schramsberg*
Photo: Curtis Wentworth

to the development of the "toasty" champagne bouquet and help keep the carbon dioxide dissolved in the wine, aiding in a slow release of small bubbles from the wine after it is opened and a prolongation of our enjoyment of the display. When the winemaker decides that the wine has developed an appropriate amount of champagne bouquet the yeast is collected and removed.

Collecting the Yeast — *Rémuage*

Rémuage or "riddling" is the process — invented in the early nineteenth century by the famous and enviably successful champagne entrepreneur, the widow Nicole-Barbe Clicquot-Ponsardin — of helping gravity collect the yeast cells in the neck of the bottle for removal. For hand riddling the bottles are removed from the stacks or bins where they have been lying on their sides for two or three years, perhaps shaken to loosen the yeast, and placed in A-framed racks called *pupîtres*. Their punts (the indented portion of the bottom) may be marked with white paint to guide the riddlers. In 10-12 days, riddling begins: a skilled riddler turns each bottle a quarter or eighth turn each day, changing the angle slightly so that the bottle moves closer to standing upright on its cap each time it is riddled. The riddler may also shake the bottles as they are turned to loosen the yeast. The sediment slowly moves down the side of the bottle onto the cap. A skilled riddler can turn 20,000 to 50,000 bottles a day.

Hand riddling takes from one to twelve weeks to complete, depending on a number of variables, many of which are poorly understood.[15] Because each batch of wine has its own pattern of clarification, the riddler must determine the best method to handle each *cuvée*. A variety of machines to automate riddling have been devised in every sparkling-wine region of the world. Machines can reduce riddling times because they can work continually, moving the bottles twice or three times each day. Hand riddling is often used on a small batch of wine to determine how best to program the machines.

Figure 7.6
Bottle showing the yeast sediment that has been collected into the neck after rémuage

When riddling is complete all the yeast sediment is collected in the neck on the stainless steel cap. Corks rather than stainless-steel caps are used for the second fermentation of small batches of prized wines. The bottles are carefully taken off the riddling racks and placed in bins neck down *(sur pointe)*, where they will remain until it is time to remove the yeast.

Removing the Yeast — *Dégorgement*

Figure 7.7
Very large machines to automate the riddling process at Domaine Chandon

Before removing the yeast sediment, the bottles may be chilled to 25 degrees F and held for 1-2 weeks to precipitate any tartrate crystals. During disgorging *(dégorgement)*, the wine is held at around 45 degrees F to reduce the carbon dioxide gas pressure and minimize the loss of gas when the bottles are opened. The chilled bottles are then placed neck down in a subfreezing bath. As the neck of the bottle is frozen the collected yeast sediment and tartrate crystals are trapped in a small "ice cube" of wine. At this point the bottle is turned up at about a 45-degree angle and the bottle cap removed. The carbon dioxide pressure pushes the frozen wine and sediment out of the neck of the bottle, leaving the wine brilliantly clear.

When disgorging is done quickly, very little wine or

carbon dioxide pressure is lost (about one atmosphere — around 15 pounds per square inch — out of an average of 6.5 atmospheres — 100 pounds per square inch — in a bottle). Any wine that is lost will be replaced from a bottle of the same *cuvée* as the *dosage* is added. Disgorging is commonly automated both in France and California — followed quickly by *dosage* and recorking in an assembly line where the rhythmic "pops" of the caps flying off the bottles are added to the other machinery noises.

Figure 7.8
Freezing the necks of the bottles at Windsor Vineyards

Adjusting the Sugar — *Dosage*

After disgorging, the *dosage* — a mixture of cane sugar, wine, and perhaps cognac or brandy — is added. The *dosage* is blended to match the style of the wine and may have been matured by bottle aging. The amount of sugar it contains determines the sweetness of the finished sparkling wine. A few sparkling wines are made without any sugar in the *dosage,* but most require some sugar to balance their tartness.

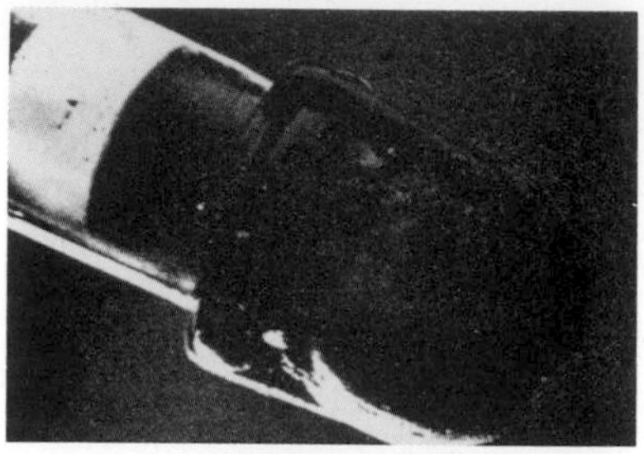

After the *dosage* is added the bottle is quickly closed with a cork and the cork is wired onto the bottle. The bottles may then be stored in the cellar as is or they may immediately be washed, dried, and decorated with labels and foil and placed in boxes before bottle aging.

Figure 7.9
Close-up of the neck of a bottle removed from the freezing bath to show the frozen wine with the yeast cells trapped inside

Bottle Aging

The minimum bottle-aging period for a méthode champenoise sparkling wine is a few months, and ideally this time elapses before the winery releases the wine into the market. During these three to nine months of initial bottle aging the *dosage* marries with the wine and some additional complexity develops in the bouquet.

How long will sparkling wines improve in the bottle? Because they have large amounts of dissolved carbon dioxide gas, sparkling wines do not undergo the same kinds of oxidative changes that occur in table wines during bottle aging; however, high-quality sparkling wines will improve for several years in the bottle. Generally it is recommended that sparkling wines be kept no longer than ten years, and many are best when drunk two or three years after release — which would be five to six years after the vintage date for vintage champagne and even later for some special bottlings.[16] The approximate timing of steps in the process of méthode champenoise sparkling wine production, bottle aging, and consumption is summarized in Table 7.2.

Figure 7.10
The actual disgorging step in which the cork or crown cap is removed and the pressure in the bottle forces out the frozen plug of wine and yeast

Figure 7.11
Hand dosage *machine on display at Domaine Chandon: bottles to receive the* dosage *are on the bottom. One bottle on the top contains the* dosage, *the other a bottle of wine to top up the occasional bottle when necessary.*

Méthode Champenoise Production Has Dramatically Increased in the U.S.

During the last two decades there has been a virtual revolution in the production of bottle-fermented sparkling wine in the United States. Production volume has skyrocketed as many small producers have entered this premium wine market and many world-famous

Figure 7.12
Bottles of sparkling wine leaving the line at Schramsberg

Table 7.2
A Sample Time Line
for Méthode Cham-
penoise Sparkling
Wine Production

Crushing & 1st Fermentation	*Cuvée* Bottled for 2nd fermentation	Aging with yeast	Riddling, Disgorging, *Dosage* added	Wine First Ready to Drink	Drink Wine before
Fall 1992	Spring or Summer 1993	2 to 4 years	Spring 1995 to Spring 1997	Fall 1995 to Fall 1997	2005 to 2007

sparkling wine firms from France, Germany, and Spain have planted vineyards and built wineries in California.[17] In 1965 an estimated 55,000 cases of méthode champenoise sparkling wine were produced in the United States.[18] By 1987 this production had increased to 2,113,000 cases, accounting for 17% of all U.S.-made sparkling wine.[19] The 1990 production of 1,922,000 cases, which again represented 17% of domestic production, reflects the stability of this strong segment of the sparkling-wine market.[20] This is good news for consumers, who now have a greater variety of quality bottle-fermented sparkling wines to choose from, and which are produced with enough competition to keep the prices moderate.

Why Are Méthode Champenoise Wines the Most Expensive Sparklers?

More costly grapes, time to bottle age, and lots of hand labor combine with mystique and tradition to make bottle-fermented sparkling wines more expensive than their transferred or tank-fermented shelfmates. The following example illustrates the effect of time and the cost of raw materials, on the price of méthode champenoise wines.

Given that a ton of grapes yields around 110 gallons of high-quality juice and that Chardonnay grapes cost an average of $1200 per ton in California in 1989 and 1990, we can estimate the cost of a gallon of grape juice for Blanc de Blancs sparkling wine at $10.91, or about $2.18 per bottle of wine.[21] The cost of aging this grape juice, without considering the costs of turning it into wine, depends on the prevailing interest rates. Let's use 10% for simplicity. In two years, the value of the grape juice will have increased to $2.64 and in three years, if we want more champagne bouquet, to $2.90. Add to this the cost of paying skilled workers to perform the estimated 120 hand operations on this bottle of méthode champenoise bubbly and the cost of keeping the winery open and you quickly have several dollars invested per bottle before the wine is marketed. Before a bottle of méthode champenoise sparkling wine leaves the winery its producer has an amount invested that approximates the retail price of a typical bottle of Charmat bulk-process wine.

THE TRANSFER PROCESS — FERMENTATION IN A BOTTLE, THEN CLARIFICATION IN A TANK

Figure 7.13
Summary of
Sparkling-Wine
Production by the
Transfer Process

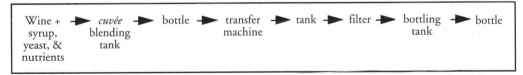

The transfer process combines bottle fermentation — to produce sparkling wines with a champagne bouquet — with bulk clarification to reduce bottle-to-bottle variation and production costs. The *cuvée* is bottled and the second fermentation and aging on the yeast are conducted in about the same way as for the méthode champenoise. Then instead of riddling to collect the yeast sediment, the bottles are emptied using a special transfer machine and their contents are blended. The wine can now be handled in bulk as it is clarified by filtration, the *dosage* is added, and the wine is rebottled — the fermentation bottles having been freshly washed in the meantime. A counterpressure of carbon dioxide is maintained from the transfer machine to the filling of the bottles so that the wine does not lose its sparkle.

Only a few medium-sized producers in the United States have adopted the transfer process — using equipment introduced from Germany in the 1950s — and the proportion of transfer-process sparkling wine has declined from 29% in 1965 to about 7% in 1990. It appears that American producers who conduct bottle fermentation are choosing to use the méthode champenoise, perhaps because it has become more mechanized since the 1950s and because consumers may perceive that wines produced by that method are of higher quality.

BULK-PROCESS SPARKLING WINES — FERMENTATION IN A TANK

Figure 7.14
Summary of Bulk-Process Sparkling Wine Production

The Charmat bulk process is used to make relatively simple sparkling wines which have the young, fruity characteristics found in white and pink table wines just after they are released into the market. Yeast character is not emphasized and aging of the wine is not desired: the whole process can be completed in as little as two weeks.

With the exception of Muscats, the grape varieties chosen for bulk-process sparkling wines do not have distinctive varietal characters: French Colombard, Chenin Blanc, Sylvaner, and many other varieties are used in California. Grapes from high-yielding vineyards in warm growing regions are chosen to keep costs down. As with méthode champenoise production, the grapes are harvested early to maintain their acidity and fermented at relatively warm temperatures.

The base wines that will be blended into the *cuvées* for bulk-process sparkling wines must meet roughly the same criteria as those for méthode champenoise. In fact, if you use a bottle-fermented wine that had only been aged on the yeast a short time for comparison, the main difference in quality between California méthode champenoise and Charmat process sparkling wines would come from the quality of grape varieties used rather than from the processes themselves. Why don't bulk-process sparkling-wine producers use better — but also more expensive — grape varieties? I believe the answer lies in the market: the typical consumer of bulk-process sparkling wine probably does not care too much about better quality but is most interested in low price; and, if he did want to spend more money on bubbly wine, he would buy one of the cheaper méthode champenoise products.

After the *cuvées* have been blended, they are cold and heat stabilized, clarified, inoculated with yeast (accompanied by cane sugar and nutrients), and racked into special small (500- to 1,500-gallon) temperature-controlled glass or stainless-steel tanks that will withstand pressures of up to 200-250 pounds per square inch. In these tanks the second fermentation takes place at about 55 degrees F and carbon dioxide gas is trapped in the wine.

After fermentation the wine is quickly removed from the thick yeast lees: unlike the complex bouquet that comes from the thin yeast sediment in bottle-fermented wines, sulfurous off odors are more likely to result from contact with the thick yeast sediment in a tank. The now-sparkling wine is cold stabilized to remove tartrate crystals and sterile filtered to remove all the yeast cells, given a *dosage* that may include some sulfur dioxide, and bottled aseptically to guarantee that the *dosage* sugar does not ferment — all under counterpressure to preserve the sparkle.

At this point you may have paused to wonder why winemakers are not concerned about yeast cells remaining to ferment the *dosage* of bottle-fermented wines. Perhaps you are thinking: "Surely *rémuage* and *dégorgement* cannot remove **all** the yeast cells from each bottle!" Yes, you are right. There are probably some yeast cells left in every bottle of méthode champenoise wine, but they are most likely dead, having expired during the many months of *sur lie* aging. So, even though yeast cells are present, they are corpses which cannot threaten to ferment the *dosage* (a fermentation which would, in any case, be an extraordinary microbiological feat, challenging even the most robust and vital yeast cells, given the high CO_2 pressure in all naturally-fermented sparkling wines and lack of nutrients in the wine at this final stage of production).

Tank-fermented sparkling wines have the great advantage of relatively low production costs.

If, for example, we estimate the cost per bottle for wines made from French Colombard grapes, we get $0.19 per bottle (based on juice yields of 150 gallons per ton and a cost of $142 per ton in California in 1990).[22] As for the wine processing itself, handling wine in bulk is less expensive than dealing with the individual bottles; moreover, tank-fermented wines are not aged.

During the last two decades tank-fermented sparkling wines have been made by as many as ten large-scale U.S. producers and have consistently accounted for around 75% of American sparkling-wine production.[23] Most German sparkling wine, called *sekt,* is also made by the bulk process (and is often sweet). Speaking of imports, sparkling wines from France, Germany, Spain, and Italy together make up about 29% of the sparkling-wine market in the United States at this time.[24]

SPARKLING MUSCATS — SINGLE-FERMENTATION SPARKLERS

Italian Asti Spumante and a Moscato Amabile made by California's Louis Martini achieve their sparkle of dissolved carbon dioxide by stopping the first alcoholic fermentation before it is complete and filtering the wines while they are still saturated with carbon dioxide from their initial fermentation. Wines made this way always taste sweet because of their unfermented grape sugar rather than sugar added in a *dosage.*

COMPARING THE TWO MAJOR METHODS OF
SPARKLING WINE PRODUCTION: CHAMPENOISE AND CHARMAT

Table 7.3 summarizes the differences between the production of sparkling wines by bottle fermentation and tank fermentation. Note that these differences ranges from the choice of grape varieties to overall time to complete the process.

Table 7.3
Two Major Methods of Sparkling Wine Production

Winemaking Step	Bottle Fermentation: "La Méthode Champenoise"	Tank Fermentation: The "Charmat Bulk Process"
Grape varieties preferred	Chardonnay and Pinot Noir	French Colombard and Chenin Blanc
Best climate	coolest	warm is OK
Select and prepare the *cuvée*	blend the base wines, clarify, stabilize and add yeast & sugar	same
Second fermentation	in bottles	in a pressure tank
Aging on yeast lees	1-3 years	most likely avoided
Clarification: collect the yeast sediment	riddling	filtering
Clarification: remove the yeast sediment	disgorging	filtering
Adjust sweetness	add *dosage* to each bottle	add *dosage* to the tank of wine
Bottling	recork same bottle in which fermented	add SO_2, bottles filled using a machine
Bottle aging potential after release	up to ten years	for a few months to reduce odor of SO_2
Time to complete the process	2-4 years	0.5 to 2 months
A U.S. label will say:	Naturally Fermented in THIS bottle ("in THE bottle" indicates that the transfer process was used)	Naturally Fermented Charmat bulk process

ENJOYING SPARKLING WINES
How Much Do the Labels Tell Us?
About How the Wine Was Made

Although there are no standards for label terms that describe the levels of sweetness in sparkling wines made in the U.S.A., the label terms that tell us how the wines were made are subject to regulation. These are described in Appendix B.

About Sweetness

Label terms such as brut, extra-dry, etc., give us a rough idea of the sweetness we'll perceive in the glass; and Table B.2 of Appendix B gives the sugar concentrations for these and other label terms. Remember that within each sweetness category, mass-market wines made by tank fermentation will usually be sweeter than bottle-fermented wines carrying the same designation. In most cases, for example, a wine whose label

Figure 7.15
Members of the CSU, Chico Wine Seminar class toast their teacher who had to stay home with the flu (Domaine Chandon Restaurant — circa 1980)

reads "Brut Sparkling Wine, Naturally Fermented Charmat Bulk Process" will be noticeably sweeter than a wine labelled "Brut Sparkling Wine, Naturally Fermented in This Bottle."

A Word About Glasses

Many of us have had the experience, usually at a wedding reception or other important social occasion, of trying to keep a serving of sparkling wine inside one of those little flat glasses that appear to have been modeled after a 1937 Chevy hubcap. With such a glass, called the "saucer-shaped *coupe*" or birdbath, it is impossible to enjoy a wine's bubble display, which anyone who has read this far knows has taken the winemaker a lot of trouble to produce and is an important sensory aspect of fine sparkling wines. In my opinion, the most interesting thing about these

glasses is the story of their origin: they were created at the request of Marie Antoinette, who wanted to drink Champagne from a glass modeled after her own breast (which one we are left to guess).[25] It is clear that this style of glass became popular because of its association with her, not because it displays sparkling wines to advantage.

Figure 7.16
Champagne flute

The preferred glass for sparkling wines is the flute. Go out and buy enough flutes so that you and your friends can appreciate the delicate streams of small bubbles that emanate from fine sparkling wines. In the convivial atmosphere created by consuming an exhilarating glass of wine with good friends you can all speculate about exactly which part of whose anatomy this glass design is based upon (just try to be polite).

One last note about glasses: whatever shape they are, glasses for sparkling wine must be scrupulously clean and free of detergent residue which can cause excess foaming and strip the wine of its bubbles.

How Do I Get the @#*! Bottle Open?

Perhaps the best thing that can be said about opening a bottle of sparkling wine is that it does not require a corkscrew. In fact, most of us ordinary mortals find it a daunting task, and who can blame us for quivering a bit before the prospect of removing the stopper from a bottle that is under about 100 pounds of pressure — around three times that of our automobiles' tires. Here are some suggestions for successful openings:

1. Chill the wine thoroughly in the refrigerator for two or three hours or in a mixture of ice and water for 30 minutes to reduce the carbon dioxide pressure — after all, the wineries do this when they open the bottles for *dégorgement,* right?

2. Bring the bottle to the table for opening with minimum agitation — no cartwheeling or jogging in from the kitchen. Place a champagne flute nearby to receive the first wine, under whatever conditions follow.

3. Remove the top of the foil and untwist the wire cage, keeping your thumb on the cork for detecting an early warning if the cork starts to launch from the bottle of its own accord.

4. Grab the cork firmly with one hand. Weaklings like me may find it helpful to wrap a towel around the cork to have something bigger and softer to grab.

5. Twist the bottle and pull it downward so it slides off the bottom of the cork. The bottle opens with a gentle "sigh" instead of a raucous "POP!" and the cork remains safely in your hand and does not ricochet off the ceiling or Aunt Bertha's forehead.

6. Fill the waiting flute one-third to one-half full, letting the mousse foam up to the top of the glass. Fill the other glasses at the table like this, and then add more wine to each glass in turn so that all are at least two-thirds full and the bubble display can be enjoyed. Don't be stingy, just grab your towel and confidently open another bottle.

7. As you are about to finish each pour, turn the bottle about a quarter turn to catch any drops of wine that might fall on the tablecloth or Aunt Bertha's sleeve.

REVIEW QUESTIONS

Instructions: You might want to use a separate sheet of paper to answer the following review questions. In that way you can use the questions to check your knowledge of this chapter more than once. You may, for example, want to re-test yourself on items that you have missed or use the "Review Questions" to test your knowledge before you read a chapter. For the True or False items, answer "True" if the statement is accurate or "False" if the statement is incorrect. If you determine that a statement is false make a note explaining why. For the multiple choice items pick the best alternative. Check your answers after you have completed all the questions.

1. True or false: Sparkling wines are a kind of table or natural wine which contain large amounts of dissolved carbon dioxide gas. _____

2. Which is the most common method of producing sparkling wines?
    A. Trap the CO_2 from a malolactic fermentation.
    B. Carbonation with compressed, pure CO_2.
    C. Trap the CO_2 from a second alcoholic fermentation.
    D. The CO_2 infusion method.
    E. Trap the CO_2 from a single alcoholic fermentation.

3. You have just inherited a vineyard of Grenache grapes — a red variety which has been used for mass-market blush varietal wines by some producers — and you want to make an inexpensive, fresh, fruity sparkling wine. You hire a consulting enologist who recommends you build a winery for the _____ process.

4. According to the legend, the méthode champenoise was discovered by _____ sometime during the period _____ to _____ .

5. True or false: The term "champagne" may be used on the label for a wine made in any part of France as long as the precise steps that are prescribed by the French law for the méthode champenoise process are followed. _____

6. Which grape variety below is **not** likely to be used for méthode champenoise sparkling wine production in France or California?
    A. Chardonnay
    B. Pinot Noir
    C. Pinot Blanc
    D. Sauvignon Blanc
    E. Pinot Meunier

7. To emulate the characteristics of grapes produced under conditions in France's Champagne district, _____ grape growing regions are preferred and the grapes are harvested _____ wherever méthode champenoise wines are made.

8. True or false: Recognizable varietal aroma is not usually sought in grapes to be used for the méthode champenoise. _____

9. The blended wine that will be bottled for a second fermentation is called the *vin de* _____ .

10. True or false: Pressing whole clusters is one fruit-handling procedure which was originally developed to minimize color extraction from dark skinned Pinot Noir grapes. _____

11. Why are the fruit-handling techniques developed to minimize color extraction from Pinot Noir also used to handle Chardonnay for méthode champenoise? _____
_____

12. True or false: In sparkling wine production, as in white table wine production, the wines produced from the free-run juices are of higher quality and those from the harder pressings are distilled. _____

13. The most prestigious wine of a sparkling wine producer may be called _____ .

14. What is reserve wine and how is its used in méthode champenoise sparkling wine production? _____
_____
_____

15. About how much of a *cuvée* would be made up of reserve wine?
    A.   no more than 5%
    B.   10-60%
    C.   as much as 20-30%
    D.   at least 35%
    E.   75%

16. True or false: You would expect to see about the same proportion of vintage-dated wines among the sparkling wines as among the varietal table wines on the shelves of your wine shop. _____

17. Which producer would encourage the malolactic fermentation?
    A.   Tart Pére et Fils which is well known for its fresh, fruity, crisply tart, slightly sweet sparkling wines.
    B.   Domaine Longtaste whose vineyards are in the coldest regions and who specialize in the driest, longest-aged, most complex sparkling wines.
    C.   Chateau Bas-Malic whose grapes come from the warmest region and are unusually low in malic acid.
    D.   Almost every sparkling wine producer encourages the MLF.
    E.   Virtually all sparkling wine producers assiduously avoid the MLF.

18. True or false: The wines to be blended into a *cuvée* would not be very attractive as still table wines because they would seem too tart, too low in alcohol, and lacking in varietal character. _____

19. Why is experience particularly important for winemakers who are blending the wines for a *cuvée?* _____
_____
_____

20. A *cuvée* blended from white grapes only is called _____ and if only red grapes are used, it is _____ .

21. Why are sugar and yeast nutrients added along with an actively growing yeast culture to start the *prise de mousse?*_____
_____
_____
_____

22. The term for drawing off the *cuvée* with its yeast, sugar, and nutrients into bottles for the second fermentation is: _____
    A. *moussage*   B. *tirage*   C. *barage*   D. *dosage*   E. *prisage*

23. True or false: Because the conditions are so different — low sugar, high alcohol, increasing CO_2 pressure — from those of the first alcoholic fermentation, yeast for the *prise de mousse* are often of a different strain or species. _____

24. In méthode champenoise, the wine ages with the yeast for about:
    A. 3-7 months
    B. 8-18 months
    C. 2-4 years
    D. 4-6 years
    E. 5-10 years

25. What are the two processes that occur during aging of the champenoise *sur lie?* _____
    _____
    _____
    _____

26. The process of collecting the yeast for removal is:
    A. *tirage*   B. *clicage*   C. *dosage*   D. *riddling*   E. *fiddling*

27. After the yeast cells are collected, the bottles may be stored neck down until the yeast cells are removed during:
    A. *disgorging*
    B. *engorgement*
    C. *remuage*
    D. *dosage*
    E. *sur pointe*

28. The sugar is adjusted in the méthode champenoise after the yeast is removed. The step is called:
    A. *sucrage*
    B. *douxage*
    C. *disgorging*
    D. *dosage*
    E. *ajoustage*

29. The neck of the bottles are frozen in the _____ step in order to _____ collected by _____ .

30. True or false: You should wait 6-9 months after the yeast removal and sugar addition steps to drink méthode champenoise wines. This period is recommended to allow the added sugar to become integrated into the wine. _____

31. True or false: After the re-corking that follows the removal of the yeast and adjustment of sugar, sparkling wines develop in the bottle in much the same way as do white table wines. _____

32. True or false: Most méthode champenoise sparkling wines are best if drunk within 2-3 years after they are released. _____

33. About _____ % of sparkling wine made in the U.S. is produced by the méthode champenoise process.

34. Describe the transfer process. _____
    _____
    _____
    _____
    _____
    _____

35. True or false: Sparkling wines made by the Charmat process reflect the fruity, youthful characteristics of the grapes they are made from because the process can be completed relatively quickly. _____

36. Charmat process wines have _____ yeast character compared to méthode champenoise wines.

37. One of the great advantages of tank fermentation for sparkling wines is low production costs. This is one important basis for the fact that about _____ % of U.S. sparkling wine is made by this method by about _____ large-scale producers.

38. Imported sparkling wine makes up about _____ % of the U.S. market.

39. An example of a sparkling wine made up by trapping the CO_2 from only one alcoholic fermentation is:
    A. Sekt
    B. Premiére Cuvée
    C. Asti Spumante
    D. Tête de Quick
    E. Moscato Uno

40. True or false: A Brut Charmat Process wine will probably be drier than a Brut sparkling wine made by the méthode champenoise. _____

41. True or false: Scrupulous rinsing of glasses is important to avoid accelerated bubble dissipation while tasting sparkling wines. _____

42. True or false: To fully enjoy a sparkling wine it should be served in a flute so its bubbles will be displayed properly, and, unlike table wine, the glasses would be filled nearly all the way to the brim. _____

SENSORY EVALUATION EXERCISE 8.1
Méthode Champenoise and Charmat Process Sparkling Wines

Objectives: You will learn to practice making sensory evaluations of sparkling wines, to compare the sensory differences produced by the méthode champenoise and tank-fermentation processes, and to describe champagne bouquet using the descriptors in Table 8.1.

What to Do Before This Exercise: Read the introductory information for this chapter.

Instructions

1. Taste the two wines, evaluating the Charmat process wine first. Pay particular attention to your tasting technique, the odors of the aromas and bouquets, and the special features of sparkling wines described in the introduction to this chapter.

2. During the discussion we will summarize the sensory differences between méthode champenoise and Charmat process sparkling wines in the table below.

Sensory Aspect	Charmat Process (BULK)	Méthode Champenoise (BLANC DE BLANC)	BLANC DE NOIRS
Visual	-LIGHT STRAW YELLOW -BRILLIANTLY CLEAR -FAIRLY SMALL BUBBLES -MED. BUBBLES -NO MOUSSE	-LIGHT STRAW YELLOW -GOOD MOUSSE -MORE, SMALLER BUBBLES -PEARS/POPCORN	-PINK, BRILLIANTLY CLEAR -DECENT BUBBLE DISPLAY
Olfactory	OAK, BURNT TOAST CITRUS, GREEN APPLE	-PEAR, POPCORN -CARMEL -GOLDEN APPLES -MELON	-FLORAL BLACK CHERRY STRAWBERRY, CHERRY
Taste	-GREEN APPLE TARTS → TO A → TART/SWEET FINISH CRISP	-SWEETER, MELON -PEAR -PEPPER & LEMON -MORE COMPLEXITY-	-BLACK CHERRY -SWEET! BUT BALLANCED COMPLEX!
Touch	-FIZZYNESS ON TOUNGE/ -IN MOUTH BUBBLE EXPLOSION -FIZZY/LIGHT ON TOUNGE	-MORE FIZZ	-LIGHT IN MOUNTH ON TOUNGE —SMOOTH—
Aftertaste	TART! → APPLE (GREEN) -LACK OF COMPLEXITY SIMPLE	-TART - FRESH LEMON	-STRAWBERRY!

(TOTB)   (MUMM)   (MUMM)

BRUT → DRY
EXTRA DRY → A LITTLE SWEET

Sensory Evaluation Exercise 8.1.
Méthode Champenoise and Charmat Process Sparkling Wines

WINE INFO	WINE A: Observations	WINE A: Notes	WINE B: Observations	WINE B: Notes
Type Vintage Appellation Producer Cost/Other				
Appearance Bubbles, Mousse				
Color				
Off Odors				
Aroma Associations Descriptors Intensity/Varietal?				
Bouquet				
Flavor				
Acid, Sugar, Balance				
Body				
Astringency				
Aging Potential				
Overall Quality				

Questions raised by this tasting:

SENSORY EVALUATION EXERCISE 8.2
Blanc de Blancs and Blanc de Noirs Sparkling Wines

Objectives: You will practice making sensory evaluations of sparkling wines, describing champagne bouquet, and comparing Blanc de Blancs and Blanc de Noirs Méthode Champenoise sparkling wines.

What to Do Before This Exercise: Review your notes from Exercise 8.1.

Instructions:
1. Taste the two wines.
2. During the discussion we will summarize the sensory differences between Blanc de Noirs and Blanc de Blancs in the table below.

Sensory Aspect	Blanc de Noirs	Blanc de Blancs
Visual		
Olfactory		
Taste		
Touch		
Aftertaste		

Sensory Evaluation Exercise 8.2.
Blanc de Blancs and Blanc de Noirs Sparkling Wines

WINE INFO Type Vintage Appellation Producer Cost/Other	WINE A: Observations	WINE A: Notes	WINE B: Observations	WINE B: Notes
Appearance Bubbles, Mousse				
Color				
Off Odors				
Aroma Associations Descriptors Intensity/Varietal?				
Bouquet				
Flavor				
Acid, Sugar, Balance				
Body				
Astringency				
Aging Potential				
Overall Quality				

Questions raised by this tasting:

SENSORY EVALUATION EXERCISE 8.3
Natural to Doux — Sparkling Wines of Different Levels of Sweetness

Objectives: You will continue to learn to describe champagne bouquet and the sensory differences between sparkling wines of different sugar contents.

What to Do Before This Exercise: Review your notes for the two preceding exercises and the section "Sparkling Wines" under "Special Rules for Special Wines" in Appendix B (pp. 316-317), which discusses the sugar levels of sparkling wines.

Instructions:
1. Taste the wines — in the order drier before sweeter — and give particular attention to the levels of sweetness in the wines and their effect on other sensory components.
2. Summarize the sensory differences between the drier and sweeter sparkling wines.

Sensory Aspect	Drier Wine	Sweeter Wine
Visual		
Olfactory		
Taste		
Touch		
Aftertaste		

Sensory Evaluation Exercise 8.3.
Natural to Doux — Sparkling Wines of Different Levels of Sweetness

WINE INFO Type Vintage Appellation Producer Cost/Other	WINE A: Observations	WINE A: Notes	WINE B: Observations	WINE B: Notes
Appearance Bubbles, Mousse				
Color				
Off Odors				

Aroma
  Associations
  Descriptors
  Intensity/Varietal?				

Bouquet				
Flavor				
Acid, Sugar, Balance				
Body				
Astringency				
Aging Potential				
Overall Quality				

Questions raised by this tasting:

SENSORY EVALUATION EXERCISE 8.4
Your Turn — Creating Your Own Tasting of Sparkling Wines

For this exercise please refer to Sensory Evaluation Exercise 4.6 (p. 116) for the Objectives, What to Do . . ., and Instructions.

Worksheet for Creating Your Own Winetasting

1. Objective:

_____

_____

_____

_____

2. Wine characteristics:

_____

_____

_____

_____

3. Number of wines, budget:

_____

_____

_____

_____

4. Supplier(s) and the specific wines:

_____

_____

_____

_____

_____

_____

_____

5. The tasting strategy:

_____

_____

_____

_____

6. Background or reference material:

_____

_____

_____

_____

7. Note-taking aids:

_____

_____

_____

8. The setting:

_____

_____

_____

Sensory Evaluation Exercise 8.4.
Your Turn — Creating Your Own Tasting of Sparkling Wines

WINE INFO	WINE A: Observations	WINE A: Notes	WINE B: Observations	WINE B: Notes
Type Vintage Appellation Producer Cost/Other				
Appearance Bubbles, Mousse				
Color				
Off Odors				
Aroma Associations Descriptors Intensity/Varietal?				
Bouquet				
Flavor				
Acid, Sugar, Balance				
Body				
Astringency				
Aging Potential				
Overall Quality				

Questions raised by this tasting:

Sensory Evaluation Exercise 8.4.
Your Turn — Creating Your Own Tasting of Sparkling Wines

WINE INFO	WINE C: Observations	WINE C: Notes	WINE D: Observations	WINE D: Notes
Type Vintage Appellation Producer Cost/Other				
Appearance Bubbles, Mousse				
Color				
Off Odors				
Aroma Associations Descriptors Intensity/Varietal?				
Bouquet				
Flavor				
Acid, Sugar, Balance				
Body				
Astringency				
Aging Potential				
Overall Quality				

Questions raised by this tasting:

SENSORY EVALUATION EXERCISE 8.5
A Review Tasting of Sparkling Wines

For this exercise please refer to Sensory Evaluation Exercise 4.7 (p. 120) for the Objectives, What to Do . . ., and Instructions. Depending on how you organize your classification and sorting system, you may not need all the steps provided in the worksheet. Here is an example of how you might begin:

    Step #1. sensory factor: color
            peach = Blanc de Noirs
            not peach = go to step #2

There is a sample worksheet in Appendix D (p.377) which you may refer to as long as you heed the warning that it may not apply exactly to the wines you've tasted.

Your Worksheet for the Sparkling Wine Review Tasting

Step #1. sensory factor: _____
    if _____ , the variety is _____ or go to step _____
    if _____ , go to step _____

Step #2. sensory factor: _____
    if _____ , the variety is _____ or go to step _____
    if _____ , go to step _____

Step #3. sensory factor: _____
    if _____ , the variety is _____ or go to step _____
    if _____ , go to step _____

Step #4. sensory factor: _____
    if _____ , the variety is _____ or go to step _____
    if _____ , go to step _____

Step #5. sensory factor: _____
    if _____ , the variety is _____ or go to step _____
    if _____ , go to step _____

Step #6. sensory factor: _____
    if _____ , the variety is _____ or go to step _____
    if _____ , go to step #7

Step #7. sensory factor: _____
    if _____ , the variety is _____
    if _____ , the variety is _____

Sensory Evaluation Exercise 8.5.
A Review Tasting of Sparkling Wines

WINE INFO	WINE A: Observations	WINE A: Notes	WINE B: Observations	WINE B: Notes
Type Vintage Appellation Producer Cost/Other				
Appearance Bubbles, Mousse				
Color				
Off Odors				
Aroma Associations Descriptors Intensity/Varietal?				
Bouquet				
Flavor				
Acid, Sugar, Balance				
Body				
Astringency				
Aging Potential				
Overall Quality				

Questions raised by this tasting:

Sensory Evaluation Exercise 8.5.
A Review Tasting of Sparkling Wines

WINE INFO	WINE C: Observations	WINE C: Notes	WINE D: Observations	WINE D: Notes
Type Vintage Appellation Producer Cost/Other				
Appearance Bubbles, Mousse				
Color				
Off Odors				
Aroma Associations Descriptors Intensity/Varietal?				
Bouquet				
Flavor				
Acid, Sugar, Balance				
Body				
Astringency				
Aging Potential				
Overall Quality				

Questions raised by this tasting:

REVIEW QUESTIONS

Instructions: You might want to use a separate sheet of paper to answer the following review questions. In that way you can use the questions to check your knowledge of this chapter more than once. You may, for example, want to re-test yourself on items that you have missed or use the "Review Questions" to test your knowledge before you read a chapter. For the True or False items, answer "True" if the statement is accurate or "False" if the statement is incorrect. If you determine that a statement is false make a note explaining why. For the multiple choice items pick the best alternative. Check your answers after you have completed all the questions.

1. Why is it not necessary to swirl sparkling wines when making a sensory evaluation?

   _____

   _____

   _____

2. Why is it detrimental to sparking wines to swirl them while making a sensory evaluation?

   _____

   _____

   _____

3. True or false: Under appearance, the bubble display of sparking wines is evaluated and tasters look for small bubbles that evolve from the wine over a long time and form a smooth, white foam on the surface of the wine. _____

4. True or false: Because they're called Blanc de Noirs, we expect all sparkling wines made from red grapes to be white, that is a very pale straw yellow to yellow color. _____

5. True or false: When the sparkling wine aroma wheel is compared to the more general wine aroma wheel, we find more spicy, floral, and fruity odors suggested for sparkling wines and fewer vegetative and herbaceous odors. _____

6. Which spice would you not expect to find in sparkling wines but would be anticipated in (red) table wines?
   A. cinnamon
   B. nutmeg
   C. cloves
   D. black pepper
   E. anise

7. Descriptive terms for champagne bouquet would be found in all but which one of these categories on the sparkling wine aroma wheel?
   A. fruity
   B. yeasty
   C. creamy
   D. caramelized
   E. nutty

8. True or false: If you come upon a group of winetasters uttering the descriptive terms "fresh bread, sour cream, burnt chocolate, cocoa, hazelnut, and toasted grains," you have probably stumbled onto a tasting of tank-fermented sparkling wines. _____

9. True or false: Among the positive structural organoleptic elements of sparkling wines are tart acidity, soft finish, freshness, and dryness. _____

ANSWERS TO REVIEW QUESTIONS

1. It's not necessary to swirl sparkling wines to increase the release of volatile odor components because the CO_2 rising from the wine carries these odorants out of the wine and into the air.

2. Swirling makes the dissolved CO_2 leave the wine prematurely and makes a proper evaluation of the bubble display and mousse impossible.

3. True

4. False. Although some Blanc de Noirs sparkling (and still) wines are a very pale yellow, many are appreciated for their light bronze, peach, or salmon colors.

5. True

6. D

7. A

8. False. These terms describe the champagne's bouquet and you've more likely come upon a sampling of bottle-fermented sparkling wines.

9. True

ENDNOTES

[1] Noble, A. C., and Patricia Howe, "Sparkling Wine Aroma Wheel," The Wordmill, Healdsburg, CA, and A. C. Noble, R. A. Arnold, J. Buechsenstein, E. J. Leach, J. O. Schmidt, and P. M. Stern, "Modification of a Standardized System of Wine Aroma Terminology," *American Journal of Eonology Viticulture*, Vol. 38, No. 2, 1987, pp. 143-146.

[2] "Sparkling Wine Aroma Wheel," © copyright A. C. Noble and Patricia Howe, The Wordmill, P.O. Box 1817, Healdsburg, CA. Excerpts reprinted with permission of the authors.

[3] Rosengarten, David, and Joshua Wesson, "The Best Champagnes for Your Holidays," *Wine and Food Companion*, Vol. 1, Issue 1, November/December 1988, p. 4.

9

THE PRODUCTION OF DESSERT WINES
Naturally Sweet *Botrytis*-Affected Wines and Fortified Wines

Dessert wine is a functional category that includes a wide range of wines that are sweet and, therefore, suitable for accompanying or replacing the customarily sweet final course of a meal. Among the types of sweet wines that can be used successfully with desserts are sweet table wines (a White Zinfandel with 2% residual sugar or a Muscat Canelli with 6-10% residual sugar, for example); demi-sec or doux sparkling wines; naturally sweet wines made from grapes affected by a mold called *Botrytis;* and fortified wines such as port and sherry. This chapter will focus on the production of wines made from *Botrytis*-affected grapes and take a quick look at how port, sherry, and fortified Muscats are made. Because fine dessert wines are somewhat unfashionable at the moment, they represent some of today's best bargains in quality wines.

BOTRYTIS-AFFECTED WINES

Botrytis-affected white wines are golden, sweet, and full-bodied with complex, concentrated aromas and flavors suggesting apricots, honey, nuts, and mushrooms. Most *Botrytis*-affected wines made in California are modelled after French and, more commonly, German wines: the Sauternes of Bordeaux and the late-harvest wines of the Mosel and Rhine regions. Sauternes are produced from blends of Sauvignon Blanc and Sémillon grapes and contain 12-13% alcohol and 6-8% residual sugar. The finest German late-harvest wines are made from White Riesling grapes and are typically lower in alcohol (7-10%) and higher in sugar (12-15%) than Sauternes. Making *Botrytis*-affected wines requires a mold, *Botrytis cinerea;* the cooperation of Mother Nature in providing a specific, relatively rare sequence of fall weather; risk-taking grape growers and winemakers; and appreciative, sweet-toothed connoisseurs to create a market. This chapter will describe the *Botrytis cinerea* mold, the vineyard climate and weather conditions that are required for it to infect grapes and produce the raw material for exquisite wines instead of rotten fruit, and the winemaking challenges presented by botrytised grapes. Appendix B, "Decoding Wine Labels," explains how you can tell a *Botrytis*-affected wine by its label.

Botrytis cinerea — The (Sometimes) Noble Rot

Botrytis cinerea is a common fungus that belongs to the same group as mushrooms and truffles. It can grow on nearly any plant material, living or dead, and is found virtually everywhere. In my refrigerator it produces a fuzzy grey growth on the celery I've mistakenly left behind during Christmas vacation. In forests and compost piles it helps recycle nutrients needed by other plant life. *Botrytis cinerea* thwarts food production throughout the world by spoiling fruits and vegetables both in the field and after harvest. It even attacks cut flowers destined for bouquets and corsages. Grapevines are one of this ubiquitous plant pathogen's favorite hosts.

It is not known who was the first to make wines from *Botrytis*-infected grapes, but all of the European regions famous for making such wines have stories dating from the sixteenth, seventeenth, or eighteenth centuries about how an apparently disastrous delayed harvest of moldy grapes resulted in a wine that not only lacked the expected spoiled character but also, to everyone's great relief and amazement, turned out to be extraordinarily delicious. Not only was a spectacular success snatched from the jaws of an impending regional economic disaster, but in addition a wonderful new kind of wine — and, perhaps, clues about how to make it again — were discovered, in Transylvania, on the Rhine, and in Sauternes.[1]

In California, botrytised wine production had no such romantic, mythical beginnings. Experiments on the biology of *Botrytis cinerea* and winemaking with *Botrytis*-infected grapes were conducted in the 1950s at the University of California, Davis. At the same time, at Livermore's Cresta Blanca Winery, the innovative winemaker Myron Nightingale created small batches of exquisite sweet wines from grapes he intentionally infected with *Botrytis* after harvest.[2] In the late 1960s and early 1970s a few Northern California winemakers became fascinated by the challenges and rewards of creating these rich and rare wines and began to make *Botrytis*-affected wines whenever the weather cooperated. Today most California producers of *Botrytis*-affected wines still rely on fall weather to provide the correct conditions for a favorable *Botrytis* infection, but interest persists in bypassing the risks of letting nature take its course, and experiments with induced *Botrytis* infections continue.[3]

To honor its role in the production of these luscious sweet wines under just the right circumstances, a complimentary common name has been bestowed upon *Botrytis cinerea*. It is known in German as "Edelfäule" and in French as "pourriture noble"; both terms mean "noble rot." Under other circumstances, a *Botrytis* infection produces just plain rot.

Botrytis in the Vineyard
Botrytis Can Be a Serious Disease

Botrytis is found in all vineyards and can be a serious disease of grapevines. It can infect the plants at any time during the growing season, attacking the soft tissues (shoots, leaves, and fruit) and leaving them dried and shrivelled or burnt as the disease progresses. *Botrytis* spores can survive over the winter months in plant debris, and the omnipresence of grapevines typical of all wine regions encourages their spread. In a typical disease cycle, the overwintering spores germinate and grow after spring rains. The mold then infects the soft, young plant parts, spreading to the berries later in the season and forming more spores that transmit the disease to other parts of the same plant and to nearby grapevines. Grape berries are the best site for the mold to multiply extensively because they contain nutrients that the mold can easily reach through a wound in the skin or with its own special structures that can attach to and penetrate the skin of an undamaged berry. When unbroken berries are infected, cracks quickly appear in their skins due to the action of *Botrytis*'s enzymes, and secondary infections such as vinegar bacteria and other molds or infestations of pests such as fruit flies can become established. A vineyard can lose up to 40% of its crop to *Botrytis*.[4]

Until a few wineries became interested in buying *Botrytis*-infected fruit for sweet wine production, California grape growers regarded this mold simply as a serious pest to be eradicated. Now that a market has developed, however, some grape growers are modifying their disease-management practices to allow *Botrytis* to grow on the fruit if their vineyards are located in a favorable mesoclimate. The general vineyard conditions that encourage a *Botrytis* infection are a moist mesoclimate (for example, one of lingering summer fogs near an ocean, lake, or river) and soils that can hold moisture and later release it into the air. Cultural practices can be modified to encourage *Botrytis* growth. This would include the limited use of specific disease-control practices such as the removal of leaves to aerate and dry the vine canopy and the precisely timed application of minimal amounts of fungicide to protect the leaves and shoots early in the growing season while allowing *Botrytis* to infect the fruit toward the end of the ripening period.[5] There are just a few mesoclimatic areas in California where *Botrytis* development is favored — mainly in cooler coastal viticultural regions.

If the Weather Is Right, the Disease Cycle Is Interrupted

The decision to modify normal vineyard management practices to encourage *Botrytis* growth is one a prudent grape grower makes only in cooperation with a winery that is willing to share the risk of total crop loss. Growers know that if the weather pattern in the fall is not right, the *Botrytis*-infected grapes will not be transformed into the concentrated White Riesling, Sémillon, or Sauvignon Blanc essences required to make sweet wines. Instead, in typical fall weather the normal disease cycle will prevail and the grapes will split open, become infected with other molds (ignoble rots!) and vinegar bacteria, decay, and fall off the vine, taking the grower's income with them. Wineries typically will share this risk with their growers and guarantee payment for the estimated crop if the fall weather does not allow a successful *Botrytis* infection.

What fall weather pattern does such an infection depend on? The ideal weather cycle for a successfully arrested infection includes a small amount of rainfall to enable the *Botrytis* spores to germinate on the skins of the grape berries when the grapes have matured to at least 18-19°Brix, followed by warm, dry days to concentrate the grape constituents. The rainfall is necessary to enable the spores to germinate: optimal conditions for germination include nearly 100% humidity and temperatures of 65-75°F for 20 to 35 hours.[6] As the germinated spores grow in humid conditions the mold's web-like mycelia cover the surface of the grapes and penetrate the skins, creating millions of microscopic holes through which water can evaporate. A subsequent period of cool to warm (but not hot) dry weather is also crucial for creating a **successful** — that is, limited — *Botrytis* infection. Such weather slows the mold's growth to a moderate rate and allows the concentration of the juice without destruction of the berries. A limited infection does not progress to the next stage of the cycle in which the berries crack and secondary infections develop. The intact skin is preserved, but the microscopic holes created by the mold allow evaporation of water and the consequent concentration of the juice. The resulting shrivelled, delicate, whole berries remain in the cluster and can be harvested. Figure 9.1 shows the effects of four fall weather patterns on the course of a *Botrytis* infection, the consequences for the appearance of the grape clusters, and what sort of wine — if any — could be made from them.

Figure 9.1
A Summary of the Effects of Fall Weather Patterns on the Course of a Botrytis *Infection and the Consequences for Cluster Appearance and Winemaking*

The Starting Point	Fall Weather Pattern Is	Botrytis Infection	Cluster Appearance	Wine Produced
healthy Fruit at 18-19° Brix growing in a vineyard with a moist mesoclimate				
	normal for California: warm and dry	is absent or very limited on a few berries	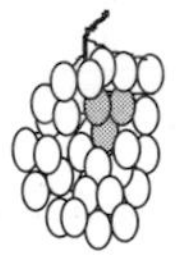	early harvest or regular dry or very slightly sweet table wines
	rain followed by more rain	spreads rapidly, fruit splits, and secondary infections develop; crop is lost		none
	rain followed by very warm weather	spreads rapidly, fruit splits, and secondary infections follow; crop is lost		none
	rain followed by dry, cool to warm weather	is slow and limited so grapes shrivel and juice is concentrated		sweet, late-harvest wines

The infection of the skin and drying of the grapes is shown in microscopic cross-section in Figure 9.2.[7]

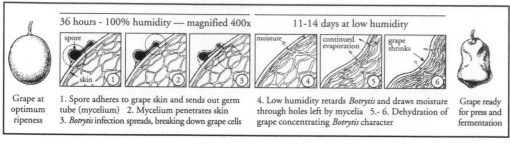

Figure 9.2
A Microscopic Cross-Section of a Grape Infected with Botrytis
Reprinted by permission of
Beringer Vineyards

What does a *Botrytis*-infected grape cluster look like? The first signs of infection are transparent spots on the grape skins. A grey fuzzy mold may become visible as the grapes shrivel, collapse, and eventually begin to look like raisins. Usually not all the berries in a cluster are infected at once; rather, the mold radiates from an infected site to involve more and more berries as shown in Figure 9.3. Within a single cluster berries will be found in all stages of infection, from turgid but spotted to completely dehydrated.

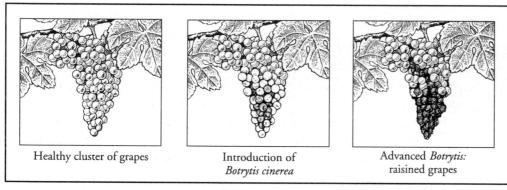

Figure 9.3
Progress of a Botrytis *Infection in a Grape Cluster*
Reprinted by permission of
Sebastiani Vineyards

A *Botrytis* infection can spread very rapidly: under hot, humid conditions the extent of infection can increase from 10% of the berries to 90% in two days, which is too rapid to avoid the development of ignoble secondary infections. Under optimal conditions of warm, dry weather it will take about two weeks after the initiation of infection for all the moisture in the grapes to evaporate. The sooner the rain that initiates the infection is succeeded by temperate dry weather, the healthier the resulting grapes and the better the wine. Not surprisingly, these conditions rarely prevail in California, where *Botrytis* infections more often develop during a series of moist, foggy nights and dry days.

Some Grape Varieties Are More Vulnerable

Grape varieties differ in their susceptibility to *Botrytis*. Table 9.1 shows the relative susceptibilities of some common California grape varieties.[8] Several factors influence this: some grapes, like Zinfandel and Chenin Blanc, grow in tight clusters that retain moisture; thick-skinned varieties like Cabernet Sauvignon present a physical barrier to mycelial penetration; and some red varieties contain mold-inhibiting compounds.

Highly Susceptible	Susceptible	Moderately Susceptible	Least Susceptible
Chenin Blanc	Chardonnay	French Colombard	Cabernet Sauvignon
White Riesling	Pinot Noir	Gewürztraminer	Merlot
Zinfandel	Sauvignon Blanc	Sémillon	

Table 9.1
Susceptibility of Some Premium Wine Grape Varieties to Botrytis cinerea *Infection in California*

It is evaporation of water from the infected berries that causes the changes important for winemaking to take place inside the fruit: all of the dissolved components of the grape juice

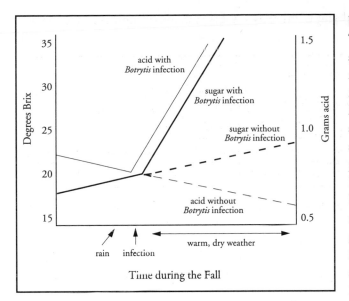

Figure 9.4
Theoretical Changes in Sugar and Acid Concentrations of Grapes During Normal Ripening and After a Successful Botrytis *Infection*

become highly concentrated. This can occur quite rapidly and completely: increases of as much as 15 degrees Brix (from 30 to 45 degrees) in four days have been reported and final sugar and acid concentrations as high as 51 degrees Brix and 1.55 grams per 100 ml can be reached.[9] Because the concentrations of both acid and sugar increase, the ripening of *Botrytis*-infected grapes is not like normal ripening in which sugars increase and acids decrease in concentration. Figure 9.4 shows this difference between normal ripening and a successful *Botrytis* infection. Because *Botrytis* uses up some of the tartaric and malic acids from the grape juice for food, the acid concentration does not actually increase at exactly the same rate as the sugar concentration does, as implied in the figure.

Harvesting *Botrytis*-Infected Fruit — Slow Picking and Low Yields

Experience has shown that wines made from grapes harvested at 35 to 45 degrees Brix show recognizable *Botrytis* character and are balanced in sweetness and acidity. The longer a grower and winemaker wait for such sugar levels to develop, the greater risk they take that the crop will be totally lost to an infection accelerated by fall rains, so they may decide to harvest the *Botrytis*-infected clusters selectively over a week or two. Selective harvesting of infected fruit is also common in both France and Germany and requires willing workers and plenty of supervision. Unlike a normal harvest in which pickers sweep though a vineyard once, cutting clusters at the backbreaking pace of one and-a-half tons per picker per day, selective harvesting requires up to a dozen slow, watchful trips through the vines. Members of the harvest crew visually inspect and smell each cluster, then pick only those *Botrytis* infected clusters that have not developed a secondary infection of vinegar bacteria. The infected clusters that are selected are very fragile and the pickers must take extra time to handle each one carefully so that the infected berries don't drop off. These factors combine to make the harvest of *Botrytis*-infected vineyards much slower than typical harvests. To save time some wineries sort the fruit after it has been harvested.

Because water evaporates from the *Botrytis*-infected fruit as it shrivels, the yield by weight of grapes in a vineyard with an extensive, successful *Botrytis* infection can decrease to about one-third its normal size: for example, a vineyard that typically produces 22 tons of White Riesling fruit for dry table wine yielded 8.5 tons of highly infected fruit (at 48 degrees Brix and 1.3 grams of total acid per 100 ml of juice) in 1978.[10] The following figures for two years when *Botrytis* infection was induced deliberately on harvested fruit at Beringer Winery show that the higher the sugar concentration, the lower the yield of fruit.[11]

Table 9.2
*Yield Reductions in Induced-*Botrytis *Infections: Grape Weight and Sugar Content before and after Inoculation and Drying of Sémillon Grapes*

	1980 Before/After	1981 Before/After	1992 Before/After
Grape Weight (tons) Weight Reduction	6.01/4.18 31%	2.53/1.21 53%	4.17/2.53 39%
Sugar Content (°Brix)	23.0/33.1	21.6/41.0	20.9/31.7

Winemaking with Botrytised Grapes

Because they are very hard to make and, glorious though they are, their market is limited, *Botrytis*-affected wines are made in small amounts as a sort of enological tour de force by a few California wineries in favorable years; a winery making *Botrytis*-affected wines is like Daimler-Benz building and racing a few Formula 1 cars to show off what its engineers and technicians can do. A California winery will typically process no more than 10 tons of *Botrytis*-affected fruit, making about 700-900 gallons of wine (about 300-400 cases).

The first problem winemakers must solve to make *Botrytis*-affected wines is how to remove the juice from the raisined fruit. Since most crushers are designed to pop open fresh, firm, juicy grapes, crushing may be skipped altogether and the fruit emptied directly into a press from small picking boxes. If crushing is done before pressing, the winemaker must assure — perhaps by re-checking the clusters as they are dumped into the crusher — that any pre-fermentation skin contact is restricted to fruit with clean *Botrytis* infections — where no secondary invasions of other molds or vinegar bacteria have occurred — so that the population of such spoilage organisms does not increase. Handling the musts from crushed *Botrytis*-infected grapes has been compared to "pumping mincemeat pie without the crust."[12]

Pressing is slow and produces small amounts of a dark amber syrup: the higher the sugar concentration at harvest, the lower the juice yield because more water has evaporated. At Sebastiani Vineyards a batch of *Botrytis*-infected White Riesling grapes harvested at 34.8 degrees Brix during the "*Botrytis* blizzard" vintage of 1982 yielded 76 gallons of juice per ton compared to 195 gallons per ton for White Riesling grapes harvested at 24 degrees Brix.[13] At Château St. Jean in 1973 and 1975, juices in excess of 40 degrees Brix yielded 33 gallons per ton.[14] Improvements in equipment and must-handling techniques had raised juice yields from *Botrytis*-affected fruit to 75-90 gallons per ton by the late 1980s.[15]

Once the thick syrup has been extracted from the shrivelled grapes, it is chilled and clarified to reduce the suspended solids and remove the browned pigments. Winery equipment designed to handle grape juices with the thickness of cream is severely challenged by the very concentrated botrytised grape juices, whose density falls somewhere between that of molasses and honey.

Fermentations of botrytised grape juices can be hard to start, both because the *Botrytis* growing in the grape juice has used up some of the nutrients needed by the yeast cells and because the high sugar concentrations that are desired in these juices also have the effect of slowing down or killing microorganisms, including wine yeasts. (This anti-microbial action is the basis of the preservative effect of the high sugar concentrations in jams, jellies, honey, and molasses.) To overcome this inhibition of fermentation, winemakers may add yeast nutrients, inoculate the juices with larger than normal amounts of special sugar-tolerant yeast strains, warm the juices to 65-75 degrees F, or dilute a small portion of the juice with water, inoculate, then build up the sugar content and add this sugar-acclimated batch of yeast to the rest of the juice. Even with these measures, the fermentation will progress more slowly than in the case of normal white table wine juices of 20 to 23 degrees Brix.

Fermentations of *Botrytis*-affected juices of 35-45 degrees Brix could theoretically produce dry wines with very high alcohol contents, but they are stopped by chilling followed by centrifugation or filtration to remove the yeast cells at alcohol contents of 8-13% and with substantial residual sugar remaining. The exact timing of the end of fermentation depends on two factors: 1. whether a Sauternes-style or German-style late-harvest wine is being made; and 2. the progress of a race between two processes occurring in the fermentation tanks: the conversion of sugar into alcohol and the production of volatile acidity (a mixture of acetic acid and ethyl acetate — see Table 2.1) by vinegar bacteria that may have begun to grow undetected on the grapes in the vineyard. A winemaker trying to keep the volatile acidity of a batch of white wine below the legal limit of 0.12 grams/100 ml may have to stop the fermentation with a little less alcohol and somewhat higher residual sugar than was originally planned.

After clarification and stabilization, aging in small oak barrels is common for the *Botrytis*-affected wines of Sauternes and California late-harvest Sauvignon Blancs and Sémillons. Late-harvest wines made from White Riesling grapes are more likely to be aged briefly in very large oak barrels or stainless steel tanks and will reach the market sooner than the Sauternes and late-harvest Sauvignon Blancs and Sémillons of the same vintage.

French and German *Botrytis*-affected wines can improve with age in the bottle for 10 years or more, acquiring a deeper golden color and a perfumed bouquet and seeming to be less sweet as they age. Because relatively few *Botrytis*-affected late-harvest white table wines have been made in California, the verdict is still out on the ability of these wines to improve with years of bottle aging.

Does *Botrytis* Add Special Flavors to the Wine?

One of California's pioneer producers of *Botrytis*-affected late-harvest wines, Walter Schug, believes that there is no *Botrytis* character per se but that *Botrytis* infection simply produces a concentration of fruit character. Schug argues that simple concentration of fruit flavors explains why good botrytised wine cannot be made from poor grape varieties, as well as why, when winemaking starts with the best varieties, great wines can be produced. Schug emphasizes that *Botrytis*-affected wines display the richness and complexity of concentrated fruit flavors, especially honey and apricot. In contrast, Myron Nightingale and Richard Arrowood hold that by growing on and in the fruit, *Botrytis* gives the grape juice a flavor of its own, which is reminiscent of nuts, mushrooms, spices, and, yes, honey. The exact source of the delicious odors and flavors of these wines is still being investigated.

Induced *Botrytis*

Beginning in the 1950s, Myron and Alice Nightingale pioneered and perfected techniques for producing a natural *Botrytis cinerea* infection of wine grapes outside the vineyard and independent of weather conditions. Their approach included: 1. selecting a vigorous strain of

Figure 9.5
Beringer 1988
Nightingale
Sémillon

Botrytis cinerea; 2. growing large numbers of spores of this pure strain in the laboratory; 3. picking Sémillon grapes at 23 degrees Brix and spreading them one cluster deep on fruit-drying trays; 4. inoculating the grapes with the concentrated spores; and 5. placing the trays of grapes in the precise environment required for a successful *Botrytis* infection — first warm, moist conditions for spore germination and then warm, dry conditions for evaporation of water and concentration of fruit components. Beginning with the 1980 harvest, the Nightingales made several vintages of botrytised Sémillon and Sauvignon Blanc in this way at Beringer Vineyard, and since then other California wineries have been experimenting with their methods.[16] Beringer still uses the name Nightingale to distinguish their induced-*Botrytis* wines, and they commemorated Myron Nightingale's life and work on the label of their 1988 Napa Valley Sémillon (Figure 9.5).

FORTIFIED DESSERT WINES — A BRIEF INTRODUCTION

Fortified wines are produced by the addition of wine spirits — a concentrated alcohol created by the distillation of wine. California's fortified dessert wines are modeled after some of Europe's most famous fortified wines — port, sherry, Marsala, Málaga, and Madeira. Many of these wines were originally created in Spain and Portugal with an eye to the British market, if not

Figure 9.7
Summary of Port
Production Methods

Figure 9.8
Special Porcelain Bowl
Used in Portugal to Help
Evaluate Port Color

depending on the intended market; in Spain the sugar level depends on whether the wine is going to the domestic market, to Britain (sweeter), or to Germany (still sweeter). Very high-sugar-content blending wines made from grapes that have been partially raisined by sun drying are used for sweetening.

Fortified Muscats

Among the dessert wines, fortified Muscats are the most closely linked to the grapes from

Figure 9.15
Summary of Fortified Muscat Production

which they are produced, emphasizing the richly fruity and intensely floral aromas characteristic of the Muscat grape varieties. They also have a somewhat lower alcohol content than other fortified wines — around 16%. The variety Muscat Hamburg is used for red fortified wines, which are made the same way as ruby ports. Orange Muscats are made into dessert wines by fortifying fermenting grape juice. The wine spirits chosen to fortify Muscat dessert wines will often have fruity elements in their aromas and may also have been distilled from Muscat wines. If the finished wines are aged in oak, large containers are used that will add minimal oak character to the wines.

ENJOYING DESSERT WINES
Using *Botrytis*-Affected, Late-Harvest Wines

The concentrated flavors and high sugar concentrations of these wines make them ideal dessert wines. They should be served slightly chilled in small portions and can be successfully accompanied by simple palate-cleansing foods. You'll get a chance to try some in the tasting exercises in the next chapter. There are more ideas about combining foods with *Botrytis*-affected, late-harvest wines in Appendix C.

Fortified Dessert Wines

Because they are strongly flavored, very sweet, and can be quite high in alcohol, fortified dessert wines are served in smaller portions than are table wines: they are meant more for contemplative sipping than for quaffing to refresh the palate as with table wines. The higher-alcohol wines — *Olorosos*, cream sherries, and ruby and tawny ports — can be left in partially full containers without deterioration, but the more delicate *Fino* sherries, vintage ports, and muscats will lose quality after opening. *Finos* and Muscats are chilled before serving, while *Amontillado* and cream sherries and ports are served at cool room temperature. A note on the serving temperatures of port: since room temperatures in the U.S. are higher than in England, you may want to put your ports into the refrigerator for half an hour before serving to duplicate the serving conditions in their principal market. If you want to serve port chilled, according to the custom in Portugal, put the bottle into an ice bucket for 15 minutes.

How old should a vintage port be when you drink it? Since this is ultimately a very personal matter of taste, the answer has to be, when it tastes good to you. While conducting a vertical tasting of Portuguese ports for the Society of Wine Educators, Bartholomew Broadbent, son of the renowned British wine authority J. Michael Broadbent, described the rich, harmonious bottle bouquet of a well-aged port as "a mixture of old sofas and horse's hairs, like toffee." Another port at a later stage of bottle aging that he said was "old, but not off," he found to be like "old cabbages." Broadbent further observed that "Americans drink wine too young and the English drink wines too old." So, if your tastes run to cabbages, keep your ports in the cellar a bit longer. If you prefer their fruity, youthful intensity, or will settle for hints of toffee, drink them sooner.

In Appendix C you will find ideas about combining fortified dessert wines and foods.

REVIEW QUESTIONS

Instructions: You might want to use a separate sheet of paper to answer the following review questions. In that way you can use the questions to check your knowledge of this chapter more than once. You may, for example, want to re-test yourself on items that you have missed or use the "Review Questions" to test your knowledge before you read a chapter. For the True or False items, answer "True" if the statement is accurate or "False" if the statement is incorrect. If you determine that a statement is false make a note explaining why. For the multiple choice items pick the best alternative. Check your answers after you have completed all the questions.

1. True or false: Dessert wines are all sweet and the category includes still and sparkling natural wines as well as fortified wines. _____

2. True or false: *Botrytis*-affected dessert wines made in California are modelled after Hungarian Tokai. _____

3. True or false: *Botrytis cinerea* is a widely-occurring destructive disease organism that can attack grapevines and many other plants. _____

4. A typical disease cycle of *Botrytis* begins with the germination of spores that have overwintered in _____ following _____ and can produce shoots and leaves that look like they have been scorched.

5. Because they contain plenty of nutrients, the _____ are the best site for *Botrytis* to multiply.

6. True or false: A *Botrytis* infection cannot develop in the fruit unless the skins of the grapes are first cracked or broken by some other agent. _____

7. Which item on the list below is **not** a general vineyard condition or cultural practice that would encourage *Botrytis* growth on grape berries?
    A. limited use of fungicide
    B. removal of leaves to aerate the canopy
    C. lingering summer fogs
    D. soils that hold moisture
    E. carefully timed fungicide applications early in the season

8. The difference between a normal *Botrytis* disease cycle in which a grower could lose a large proportion of his crop and a limited infection that produces fruit suitable for making exquisite sweet wines is determined, in part, by _____ , but hinges upon _____ .

9. A successful *Botrytis* infection requires limited fall _____ or a series of foggy days to initiate the germination of spores.

10. When *Botrytis* grows on the surface of a grape it penetrates the skin enabling water to evaporate during a period of _____ weather.

11. True or false: A successful *Botrytis* infection — from the point of view of the wine-makers, if not the mold — is one in which the disease cycle is interrupted before the berries are broken and secondary infections develop. _____

12. True or false: In a typical *Botrytis* infection all the berries in a cluster become infected at the same time. _____

13. Which grape varieties are most susceptible, and which are the least susceptible to *Botrytis?*
    A. Merlot
    B. Chenin Blanc
    C. Sauvignon Blanc
    D. Zinfandel
    E. White Riesling
    F. Cabernet Sauvignon

14. True or false: The change in sugar and acid composition following a *Botrytis* infection differs from the changes of normal grape ripening because acid and sugar **both** increase in concentration. _____

15. True or false: Both growers and wineries feel that, for *Botrytis*-infected fruit, the higher the sugar, the better. _____

16. Why is harvesting *Botrytis*-infected fruit slow? _____
    _____
    _____
    _____
    _____

17. True or false: The water evaporation that occurs in a vineyard successfully infected with *Botrytis* can reduce yields to as little as ⅓ to ½ of normal. _____

18. True or false: Even though vineyard yields are reduced by a *Botrytis* infection, in the winery, the juice yield per ton of grapes is the same as for non-infected fruit. _____

19. True or false: Fermentations of the high-sugar juices of *Botrytis*-affected fruit are hard to start and slow to progress. _____

20. *Botrytis*-affected wines made from _____ are more likely to be aged in small oak barrels.

21. True or false: Although the cultivation of a vineyard can be modified to encourage or discourage the growth of *Botrytis*, a successful infection cycle has never been completed on harvested fruit. _____

22. The concentrated alcohol used to fortify wines is called _____ .

23. True or false: For ordinary fortified wines hot growing regions are beneficial for both high vineyard yields and high sugar content grapes. _____

24. About _____ the fruit for dessert wine production goes to produce the alcohol for fortification, making the per ton yield of finished wine _____ gallons.

25. More distinctive grape varieties — many from Portugal— and cooler growing regions are associated with this group of fortified dessert wines.
    A. Muscat
    B. Sherry
    C. Port
    D. Madeira
    E. Marsala

26. Winemakers taste the fortifying alcohol and match it to the wine being made because

_____

_____

27. Which style of port takes on its important sensory characteristics during long barrel aging?
    A. Tawny
    B. Ruby
    C. Vintage
    D. Portuguese
    E. Zinfandel

28. Because producers of port must maximize color extraction during fermentation so that there will be enough color extracted by the time the must is fortified (after 24-48 hours to preserve a substantial amount of sugar), procedures have been developed to enhance color extraction. They include _____ and _____ .

29. What are two purposes for blending port? _____

_____

_____

30. True or false: Port production from Portuguese grape varieties is being done on a small scale in California — only a little over 200 tons of the most-utilized variety were crushed in 1990. _____

31. In California, ruby and vintage ports are aged in _____ barrels that do not contribute much wood flavor.

32. Which type of sherry is oxidized in the absence of *flor* yeast?
    A. *Fino*
    B. *Manzanilla*
    C. *Amontillado*
    D. *Oloroso*
    E. Tawny

33. Sherries referred to as _____ will have 7.5-10% sugar.

34. Light brown sherries made with *flor* yeast and ranging from dry to medium sugar are called by their Spanish name, _____ .

35. True or false: Sherries are fortified before oxidation and their sugar content is adjusted afterwards. _____

36. Oxidation without *flor* by _____ rather than aging for long periods in barrels is a common procedure for low-priced sherries and inexpensive fortified wine products called "Málaga," "Marsala," and "Madeira."

37. What do the processes of méthode champenoise and sherry making have in common?

_____

_____

_____

_____

38. The system for blending a new vintage of sherry with older wines so that variations from year to year are minimized is called a _____ .

39. The flavors of this group of fortified dessert wines are closest to those of their grapes: _____ .

40. Dessert wines are served in _____ portions than table wines.

ANSWERS TO REVIEW QUESTIONS

1. True
2. False. They are modelled after French Sauternes and German late-harvest Rieslings.
3. True
4. Plant debris; spring rain
5. Grape berries
6. False. *Botrytis* can penetrate an intact grape skin.
7. B. Leaf removal is done to prevent *Botrytis* infection (and early-season fungicide use prevents the young shoots — but not the fruit that forms later — from becoming infected).
8. Vineyard climate, soils, and cultural decisions; the proper pattern of fall weather.
9. Rainfall
10. Warm, dry
11. True
12. False. A typical *Botrytis* infection spreads from one site to infect adjacent berries. A cluster with an advanced infection will contain berries in all stages from shrivelled to healthy.
13. Most: Chenin Blanc; White Riesling; Zinfandels. Least: Merlot; Cabernet Sauvignon. Sauvignon Blanc is intermediate.
14. True
15. False. Even though higher sugars can be obtained, harvest sugars between 35 and 45° Brix are optimal for well-balanced wines.
16. Because each cluster must be smelled to be sure it does not have a secondary infection and handled carefully so it doesn't fall apart. In addition, because not all fruit is infected at once, a vineyard is selectively harvested several times over several days or even weeks.
17. True
18. False. The yield of juice per ton is reduced to 75-90 gallons per ton.
19. True
20. Sauvignon Blanc and Sémillon.
21. False. See "Induced *Botrytis*" for the details of how an infection is carried out on harvested fruit.
22. Wine spirits
23. True
24. Half; 75-110
25. C
26. Wine spirits can vary in their flavors depending on the starting wine and the method of distillation, and those flavors need to be compatible with the wine being fortified.
27. A
28. Choose 2: Double the frequency of pump over to 2-4 times a day, pump over continuously, heat the must, or use red-pulped varieties.
29. Ports of different sugar contents can be combined to give the desired final sugar concentration and varietal ports can be mixed to enhance complexity.
30. True
31. Neutral
32. D
33. Cream
34. *Amontillados*
35. True
36. Baking
37. There are five common features: 1. Yeast autolysis during aging; 2. varietal grape character not desired; 3. blending to create a wine which is modified during a special aging — the *cuvée* or *shermat* — process; 4. vintage-to-vintage variation is reduced by blending older and younger wines — including the reserve wines for champagne and using the *solera* for sherry; 5. both the processes originated in regions of climate extremes for grape growing: very cold for méthode champenoise and hot for sherry.
38. *Solera*
39. The Muscats
40. Smaller

ENDNOTES

1   Nightingale, Myron S., and Anonymous, "Botrytis Cinerea," *Beringer Vineyards Report*, Beringer Vineyards, St. Helena, CA, Vol. 6, No. 1, August 1984, p. 1.

2   Nelson, K. E., and M. S. Nightingale, "Studies in the Commercial Production of Natural Sweet Wines from Botrytised Grapes," *American Journal of Enology and Viticulture*, Vol. 10, No.3, 1959, pp. 135-141.

3   For example: Anonymous, "Grand Cru gets Its Botrytis the Hard Way: Inducing Noble Rot in the Lab," *Wines and Vines*, May 1980, pp. 63-64, and Nightingale, Myron S., and Anonymous, "Botrytis Cinerea," *Beringer Vineyards Report*, Beringer Vineyards, St. Helena, CA, Vol. 6, No. 1, August 1984, pp. 1-4.

4   Marois, James J., "Botrytis Bunch Rot of Grapes," presented at "Issues in Wine Production: Late Harvest Dessert Wines," course sponsored by University Extension, University of California, Davis, July 18, 1987.

5   Marois, James J., "Botrytis Bunch Rot of Grapes," presented at "Issues in Wine Production: Late Harvest Dessert Wines," course sponsored by University Extension, University of California, Davis, July 18, 1987.

6   *Beringer Vineyards Report*, p. 2.

7   *Beringer Vineyards Report*, p. 2 and p. 3.

8   Marois, James J., "Botrytis Bunch Rot of Grapes," presented at "Issues in Wine Production: Late Harvest Dessert Wines," course sponsored by University Extension, University of California, Davis, July 18, 1987, and *Beringer Vineyards Report*, p. 2.

9   Richard Arrowood, Winemaker for Chateau St. Jean, and Walter Schug, Northern California Chapter of the Society of Wine Educators, April 30, 1979.

10 Walter Schug, Winemaker for Joseph Phelps Vineyards, Northern California Chapter of the Society of Wine Educators, April 30, 1979.

11 Nightingale, Myron S., and Anonymous, "Botrytis Cinerea," *Beringer Vineyards Report*, Beringer Vineyards, St. Helena, CA, Vol. 6, No. 1, August 1984, p. 3.

12 Arrowood, Richard, panelist on California Production Techniques at "Issues in Wine Production: Late Harvest Dessert Wines," course sponsored by University Extension, University of California, Davis, July 18, 1987.

13 Sebastiani, Sam, *"Botrytis cinerea*—The Noble Rot," *Sebastiani Vineyards Newsletter*, Vol. 11, No. 1, February/March 1983, p. 3.

14 Richard Arrowood, Winemaker for Chateau St. Jean, and Walter Schug, Northern California Chapter of the Society of Wine Educators, April 30, 1979.

15 Arrowood, Richard, panelist on California Production Techniques at "Issues in Wine Production: Late Harvest Dessert Wines," course sponsored by University Extension, University of California, Davis, July 18, 1987.

16 Nightingale, Myron S., and Anonymous, "Botrytis Cinerea," *Beringer Vineyards Report*, Beringer Vineyards, St. Helena, CA, Vol. 6, No. 1, August 1984, pp. 1-4.

17 Heald, Eleanor, and Ray Heald, "California Vintners Go Port side," *Practical Vineyard and Winery*, January/February 1992, pp. 10-11 and p. 41.

18 There is a fourth kind of port, white port, used as an appetizer wine in Portugal, which will not be discussed.

19 Heald, Eleanor, and Ray Heald, "California Vintners Go Port side," *Practical Vineyard and Winery*, January/February 1992, pp. 10-11 and 41, and Robinson, Jancis, VINES, GRAPES, AND WINES, Knopf, NY, 1986, pp. 215-219.

20 Heald, Eleanor, and Ray Heald, "California Vintners Go Port side," *Practical Vineyard and Winery*, January/February 1992, pp. 10-11 and 41.

21 Amerine, M. A., and V. L. Singleton, WINE, AN INTRODUCTION, University of California Press, Berkeley, CA, 1977, pp. 167-168.

22 Amerine, M. A., and V. L. Singleton, WINE, AN INTRODUCTION, University of California Press, Berkeley, CA, 1977, p. 166.

23 Webb, A. Dinsmoor, and Ann C. Noble, "Aroma of Sherry Wines," *Biotechnology and Bioengineering*, Vol. 18, 1976, pp. 939-952.

24 Posson, Philip, "The Submerged Sherry Process," *Wines and Vines*, December 1991, pp. 30-32.

10

THE SENSORY EVALUATION OF DESSERT WINES

DESSERT WINE TASTING TECHNIQUE

When tasting dessert wines you will need to pace yourself more carefully than when you taste table wines because the stronger flavors and high sugar contents of all dessert wines and the higher alcohol contents of the fortified dessert wines will tire your palate more rapidly. You should take smaller sips, or, if you take big sips, plan to do a lot of spitting, cleanse your palate more often, and take more breaks. Exercise 10.3 has a sensory homework assignment you should preview in case you'll need to go shopping.

SENSORY EVALUATION EXERCISE 10.1
The Sauternes Style — A Tasting of Early-Harvest and Late-Harvest
Botrytis-Affected Sauvignon Blanc or Sémillon Wines

Objectives: You will begin to learn to define the sensory properties of *Botrytis*-affected, late-harvest wines by comparing a late-harvest, *Botrytis*-affected Sauvignon Blanc or Sémillon with an early-harvest wine of the same variety. In this exercise you will become acquainted with the Sauternes style. You will also test the dessert wine and food combining principle: "The food should always be less sweet than the wine."

What to Do Before This Exercise: Review the section "Does Botrytis Add Special Flavors to the Wine?" on page 223.

Instructions:

1. Taste the two wines, sampling the early-harvest wine first. Record your observations of each sensory feature, and list the key sensory features of *Botrytis*-affected wines below.

_____

_____

_____

_____

_____

_____

_____

_____

_____

_____

_____

_____

_____

_____

_____

_____

_____

2. Complete this table.

Grape Varieties	Alcohol & Sugar	Summary of Your Sensory Impressions of the Sauternes Style
Sauvignon Blanc and/or Sémillon	12-14% & 6-8 g/100 ml	

3. Sample the three foods with the *Botrytis*-affected wine. Place a small bite of food in your mouth, sip the wine, concentrate and
   A. Record the effect of combining the wine and food on your perception of each. Did the food alter your perception of some component of the wine, or vice-versa?
   B. Note your reaction to the wine and food together, and think about why it occurred.
   C. What do you think about the principle that the food should be less sweet than the wine?

Food	Sensory Effect	Your Reaction	Why?
Plain Almond			
Butter Cookie			
Hershey's Kiss			

Sensory Evaluation Exercise 10.1.
The Sauternes Style — A Tasting of Early-Harvest and Late-Harvest *Botrytis*-Affected Sauvignon Blanc or Sémillon Wines

WINE INFO	WINE A: Observations	WINE A: Notes	WINE B: Observations	WINE B: Notes
Type Vintage Appellation Producer Cost/Other				
Clarity				
Color				
Off Odors				
Aroma Associations Descriptors Intensity Varietal?				
Bouquet				
Flavor				
Acid, Sugar, Balance				
Body				
Astringency				
Aging Potential				
Overall Quality				

Questions raised by this tasting:

SENSORY EVALUATION EXERCISE 10.2
The *Auslese/Beerenauslese* Style — A Tasting of Early-Harvest and Late-Harvest *Botrytis*-Affected White Riesling Wines

Objectives: The goal of this exercise is to write a sensory definition of *Auslese/Beerenauslese*–style wines, to compare your sensory impressions of the Sauternes and *Auslese/Beerenauslese* styles, and to eat more cookies, nuts, and milk chocolate.

What to Do Before This Exercise: Look over your notes from Exercise 10.1.

Instructions:

1. Taste the two wines, analyzing the early-harvest wine first. Record your observations, and summarize them in the table below.

Grape Varieties	Alcohol & Sugar	Summary of Your Sensory Impressions of the *Auslese/Beerenauslese* Style
White Riesling	7-10 % & 12-15 g/ 100 ml or more	

2. What are the important sensory differences between the Sauternes and Auslese/ Beerenauslese styles? _____
_____
_____
_____

3. Taste the foods again in combination with each wine.

Food	Sensory Effect	Your Reaction	Why?
Plain Almond			
Butter Cookie			
Hershey's Kiss			

4. Did you notice any differences compared to tasting these foods with the Sauternes-style wine? _____
_____
_____

Sensory Evaluation Exercise 10.2.
The *Auslesel/Beerenauslese* Style — A Tasting of Early-Harvest and Late-Harvest *Botrytis*-Affected White Riesling Wines

WINE INFO	WINE A: Observations	WINE A: Notes	WINE B: Observations	WINE B: Notes
Type				
Vintage				
Appellation				
Producer				
Cost/Other				
Clarity				
Color				
Off Odors				
Aroma				
Associations				
Descriptors				
Intensity				
Varietal?				
Bouquet				
Flavor				
Acid, Sugar, Balance				
Body				
Astringency				
Aging Potential				
Overall Quality				

Questions raised by this tasting:

SENSORY EVALUATION EXERCISE 10.3
An Introduction to Port and Sherry

Tips on Tasting Port

Wine importer and port expert Bartholomew Broadbent offered these suggestions for tasting port during a presentation at the Society of Wine Educators national meeting in 1986.

First, to evaluate the intensity of color, look down into the glass from above. Next, tilt the glass to check the clarity and intensity of color at the rim. Look at the edge of the wine: does the color go all the way to the rim of the glass or is the rim of the wine colorless? A colorless rim indicates a less intensely pigmented wine, usually of lower overall quality. Color that extends all the way to the rim reflects deeper color intensity and is associated with greater overall flavor concentration and quality in the wine. Is the color purple, red, brick red, or amber?

Take shallow sniffs from a reasonable distance and catch your first impressions. You **must** catch these first impressions because with repeated sniffing the alcohol will begin to interfere with your ability to smell. Look for off odors, aroma (name the fruit components), and bouquet, and assess the overall intensity of the odors. Does the apparent age agree with the color?

Take a big mouthful and expect to spit it out. Move the wine all over your mouth but don't let it warm in your mouth like a table wine. Spit. Consider all the taste and touch sensations and the aftertaste. The wine should be sweet, possess zesty, mouth-watering acidity if young, and be full-bodied. A young port should possess tannins for longevity and an older wine should be velvety smooth. The flavor should be intense — fruity, clean, and crisp in a young wine; rich, subtle, and complex in an older port — and the aftertaste should linger.

The flavor and structural components should be balanced and harmonious and tie in with the intensity of odors, especially in a young wine if it is to age well. In an older wine in particular, the palate impressions should echo and confirm what you observed with your nose.

Objectives: In this exercise you will become acquainted with two classic fortified dessert wines and sample some foods with them.

What to Do Before This Exercise:

Sensory Homework: This homework assignment will acquaint you with the sensory properties of alcohol and its relationship to your perception of other wine odors.[1]

Alcohol: Warm, Sweet, and Pungent

Take two glasses, pour four ounces of water into one, and make a solution of ethyl alcohol and water in the other by adding a tablespoon of vodka to three ounces of water. Taste and compare the two samples. Note any differences in sweetness, texture, body, and warmth in the alcohol mixture compared to the water.

The alcohol solution should seem sweeter, smoother, and heavier, and should create a warmth on your tongue that will grow to an overall warmth in your whole mouth as you move the solution around. This warmth will remain after you spit out or swallow a bit of this homework. You may also notice an irritation in your nose that may take a moment to register. If you don't notice these sensory differences, add more vodka by teaspoon measures until you are able to perceive the warmth and irritation and further changes in viscosity and sweetness. Be sure to rest your palate between samples.

High Alcohol Content and Odor Perception

Pour an ounce of brandy into a wine glass, swirl it around, and take a sniff. Brandy is around 80 proof, or 40 % alcohol by volume, and you probably won't smell very much besides this alcohol. Dilute the brandy with an ounce of water and smell it again. You will probably be able to notice a variety of oak and wine odors with the alcohol content lowered to around 20%. Add another two ounces of water and smell the solution again to see if you detect still more odors.

Brandy has complex odors that are masked by its high alcohol content; this masking effect is increased if the brandy is served over ice. If you felt that the higher alcohol content of the red wine samples was a problem in the Focus on Olfaction II and other exercises in Chapter 6, this brandy exercise will have confirmed your impression that higher alcohol content can interfere with odor perception. It is also an illustration of how the spectrum of perceptible odors changes as a solution with a high concentration of alcohol is diluted. This explains why winemakers tasting several samples of wine spirits to select the one most appropriate to fortify a particular dessert wine, will dilute the spirits with water to approximate the alcohol content of the finished wine. It is only in this way that they can clearly assess the array of odors that will be present in the final product.

Instructions:

1. Taste and record your observations of the port and sherry.

    A. What are the most striking sensory differences between table wines and fortified wines?

    _____

    _____

    _____

    B. What are the defining sensory properties of port and sherry?

    _____

    _____

    _____

2. Try the port and sherry with Stilton Cheese, walnuts, and the other foods and record your observations.

Food	Effect with Port	Effect with Sherry
Stilton Cheese		
Walnuts		
Almond		
Butter Cookie		
Hershey's Kiss		

    A. Which foods do you prefer with each wine? Why?

    _____

    _____

    _____

    B. Do the last three foods seem different with the fortified wines than they did with the *Botrytis*-affected wines? Why?

    _____

    _____

    _____

Sensory Evaluation Exercise 10.3.
An Introduction to Port and Sherry

WINE INFO	WINE A: Observations	WINE A: Notes	WINE B: Observations	WINE B: Notes
Type				
Vintage				
Appellation				
Producer				
Cost/Other				
Clarity				
Color				
Off Odors				
Aroma				
Associations				
Descriptors				
Intensity				
Varietal?				
Bouquet				
Flavor				
Acid, Sugar, Balance				
Body				
Astringency				
Aging Potential				
Overall Quality				

Questions raised by this tasting:

SENSORY EVALUATION EXERCISE 10.4
An Introduction to Orange and Black Muscats

Objectives: The goal of this exercise is to become acquainted with two varieties of fortified Muscat dessert wines and sample some foods with them.

What to Do Before This Exercise: Look over your tasting notes for the other sensory evaluation exercises for dessert wines.

Instructions
1. Taste the Orange Muscat and then the Black Muscat wine.
   A. What are the most important points of contrast between the Muscat dessert wines and Muscat varietal table wines? _____
   _____
   _____

   B. How do the Muscat dessert wines differ from port and sherry? _____
   _____
   _____

   C. How do the Muscat dessert wines differ from the *Botrytis*-affected dessert wines?
   _____
   _____
   _____

2. Sample these foods with the wines.

Food	Result with Orange Muscat	Result with Black Muscat
Shortbread		
White Chocolate Biscotti		
Almonds		
Dark Blue Cheese		
Dark Chocolate		

   A. Note the foods you prefer with the Orange Muscat and with the Black Muscat.

   B. Is there a pattern to your food-wine preferences? _____
   _____
   _____
   _____
   _____
   _____

Sensory Evaluation Exercise 10.4.
An Introduction to Orange and Black Muscats

WINE INFO	WINE A: Observations	WINE A: Notes	WINE B: Observations	WINE B: Notes
Type Vintage Appellation Producer Cost/Other				
Clarity				
Color				
Off Odors				
Aroma Associations Descriptors Intensity Varietal?				
Bouquet				
Flavor				
Acid, Sugar, Balance				
Body				
Astringency				
Aging Potential				
Overall Quality				

Questions raised by this tasting:

SENSORY EVALUATION EXERCISE 10.5
Your Turn — Creating Your Own Tasting of Dessert Wines

For this exercise please refer to Sensory Evaluation Exercise 4.6 (p. 116) for the Objective, What to Do . . . , and Instructions.

Worksheet for Creating Your Own Winetasting

1. Objective:

2. Wine characteristics:

3. Number of wines, budget:

4. Supplier(s) and the specific wines:

5. The tasting strategy:

6. Background or reference material:

7. Note-taking aids:

8. The setting:

Sensory Evaluation Exercise 10.5.
Your Turn — Creating Your Own Tasting of Dessert Wines

WINE INFO	WINE A: Observations	WINE A: Notes	WINE B: Observations	WINE B: Notes
Type Vintage Appellation Producer Cost/Other				
Clarity				
Color				
Off Odors				

Aroma
    Associations
    Descriptors
    Intensity
    Varietal?				

Bouquet				
Flavor				
Acid, Sugar, Balance				
Body				
Astringency				
Aging Potential				
Overall Quality				

Questions raised by this tasting:

Sensory Evaluation Exercise 10.5.
Your Turn — Creating Your Own Tasting of Dessert Wines

WINE INFO	WINE C: Observations	WINE C: Notes	WINE D: Observations	WINE D: Notes
Type				
Vintage				
Appellation				
Producer				
Cost/Other				
Clarity				
Color				
Off Odors				
Aroma				
Associations				
Descriptors				
Intensity				
Varietal?				
Bouquet				
Flavor				
Acid, Sugar, Balance				
Body				
Astringency				
Aging Potential				
Overall Quality				

Questions raised by this tasting:

SENSORY EVALUATION EXERCISE 10.6
A Review Tasting of Dessert Wines

For this exercise please refer to Sensory Evaluation Exercise 4.7 for the Objectives, What to Do . . . , and Instructions. Depending on how you organize your classification and sorting system, you may not need all the steps provided in the worksheet. Here is an example of how you might begin:

Step #1: sensory factor, color

golden, go to step 2

not golden, go to step 3

There is a sample worksheet in appendix D (p. 382) which you may refer to as long as you heed the warning that it may not apply exactly to your perceptions of the wines you've tasted.

Worksheet for the Dessert Wine Review Tasting

Step #1. sensory factor: _____

if _____ , the variety is _____ or go to step _____

if _____ , go to step _____

Step #2. sensory factor: _____

if _____ , the variety is _____ or go to step _____

if _____ , go to step _____

Step #3. sensory factor: _____

if _____ , the variety is _____ or go to step _____

if _____ , go to step _____

Step #4. sensory factor: _____

if _____ , the variety is _____ or go to step _____

if _____ , go to step _____

Step #5. sensory factor: _____

if _____ , the variety is _____ or go to step _____

if _____ , go to step _____

Step #6. sensory factor: _____

if _____ , the variety is _____ or go to step _____

if _____ , go to step #7

Step #7. sensory factor: _____

if _____ , the variety is _____

if _____ , the variety is _____

Sensory Evaluation Exercise 10.6.
A Review Tasting of Dessert Wines

WINE INFO	WINE A: Observations	WINE A: Notes	WINE B: Observations	WINE B: Notes
Type				
Vintage				
Appellation				
Producer				
Cost/Other				
Clarity				
Color				
Off Odors				
Aroma				
Associations				
Descriptors				
Intensity				
Varietal?				
Bouquet				
Flavor				
Acid, Sugar, Balance				
Body				
Astringency				
Aging Potential				
Overall Quality				

Questions raised by this tasting:

Sensory Evaluation Exercise 10.6.
A Review Tasting of Dessert Wines

	WINE C: Observations	WINE C: Notes	WINE D: Observations	WINE D: Notes
WINE INFO				
Type				
Vintage				
Appellation				
Producer				
Cost/Other				
Clarity				
Color				
Off Odors				
Aroma				
Associations				
Descriptors				
Intensity				
Varietal?				
Bouquet				
Flavor				
Acid, Sugar, Balance				
Body				
Astringency				
Aging Potential				
Overall Quality				

Questions raised by this tasting:

REVIEW QUESTIONS

Instructions: You might want to use a separate sheet of paper to answer the following review questions. In that way you can use the questions to check your knowledge of this chapter more than once. You may, for example, want to re-test yourself on items that you have missed or use the "Review Questions" to test your knowledge before you read a chapter. For the True or False items, answer "True" if the statement is accurate or "False" if the statement is incorrect. If you determine that a statement is false make a note explaining why. For the multiple choice items pick the best alternative. Check your answers after you have completed all the questions.

1. True or false: Tasting dessert wines requires careful pacing because these wines are all higher in alcohol content than table wines. _____

2. True or false: When tasting dessert wines, take small sips to avoid palate fatigue. _____

3. You would expect a Sauternes-style California late-harvest wine to be made from which grape varieties?
   A. Gewürztraminer and Sylvaner
   B. Sauvignon Blanc and/or Sémillon
   C. White Riesling
   D. Chardonnay and Pinot Blanc
   E. Pinot Noir and Chardonnay

4. True or false: Color that extends all the way to the rim reflects deeper color intensity and is associated with greater overall flavor concentration and quality in ports. _____

5. Why is it especially important to catch your first impressions when tasting port?
   _____
   _____

6. What textures should you expect in a young port and an old port? _____
   _____
   _____
   _____

7. True or false: Compared to a glass of plain water, an alcohol solution should seem sweeter, smoother, heavier, and warm. _____

8. Why do winemakers dilute wine spirits with water when they taste them? _____
   _____
   _____
   _____

ANSWERS TO REVIEW QUESTIONS

1. False, on two counts: first, only the fortified dessert wines are higher in alcohol content than table wines, and second, the stronger flavors and high sugar contents of dessert wines are also fatiguing to the palate — in addition to the alcohol content of the fortified wines.
2. False. You can take big sips if you spit, cleanse your palate more often, and take more breaks.
3. B
4. True for ports and wines in general.
5. It's because with repeated sniffing the alcohol will begin to interfere with your ability to smell.
6. A young port — or young red table wine for that matter — should be astringent because it possesses tannins for longevity and an older wine should be velvety smooth because the tannins have polymerized, softening the texture and, very likely, forming a sediment.
7. True
8. For two reasons: 1. The high alcohol content of wine spirits can interfere with a winemaker's — or anyone else's — odor perception. 2. Diluting a solution that has a high concentration of alcohol changes the spectrum of perceptible odors. The spirits will be diluted in the wine and must be diluted for tasting to observe the "new odor spectrum" that will be part of the wine.

ENDNOTE

[1] Young, Alan, MAKING SENSE OF WINE, Greenhouse Publications, Richmond, Australia, 1986; alcohol exercise, p. 118, bitterness exercise, p. 101, and astringency exercise, p. 120.

GREAT WINES ARE MADE IN THE VINEYARD
Growing Wine Grapes — Principles and Practices

by
Richard W. Baldy, Ph.D.
Professor of Plant Science
California State University, Chico, California

"When I was younger I used to believe I could make good wine from anything. Now I realize that 80% of winemaking happens in the vineyard." — Daryl Groom, winemaker [1]

"Wine is still the best utilization of solar energy we have found." — Emile Peynaud [2]

It seems to me that many New World winemakers are like young cooks who keep wondering if their pies will ever equal those their parents make. At holiday family dinners the younger generation expectantly waits for the complement, "Oh, this is just as good as your Mom makes!"

The enological equivalents of such holiday scenes are international wine tastings. Californian, South African, Australian, and New Zealand winemakers bring their Cabernet Sauvignons and Chardonnays to these events and hope their creations measure up to Mother Europe's standards. Occasionally they do and chauvinistic newspapers then tout the maturity of the nascent industries on their front pages. A proud reader apprised of this New World triumph may infer that her region has finally duplicated the grape growing and winemaking conditions of France or Germany. But if she picks up a coffee-table book on the world's wine districts and studies its beautiful color plates she will see striking differences between the New and Old World vineyards.

Figure 11.1
Columnar Vines
Typical of the Mosel

Wine grape growers in different areas employ distinctly different growing practices. These differences are reflected in even such basic factors as the vine density — the number of vines per acre. Premier French and German vineyards have 2000 to 3000 vines per acre, while New World vineyards have only 360 to 1200 vines per acre. Vine shapes differ as well. Pictures of the German Mosel region show steep, rock-strewn vineyards where each vine is a slender column of foliage supported by a pole. See Figure 11.1.

Mosel-like vines will not appear in the California section of the coffee-table book. Most of the Golden State's growers plant the vines in widely spaced rows and support them with a system of stakes and wires called trellises. The trellis system positions the leafy shoots of the canopy — the vine's collection of leaves, shoots, and fruits — so they create an appearance of curtains or walls of foliage. Some growers with vigorous vines will train their plants to form two curtains per row — a so-called double curtain system. Figure 11.2 illustrates the single-curtain and double-curtain designs.

Vineyardists of the Bordeaux and Burgundy regions utilize a third design. Their plant densities often equal those of their Mosel

counterparts — 2000 to 3000 vines per acre — but these French growers utilize the curtain design later adopted in New World vineyards. However, the curtains in Bordeaux and Burgundy are lower and closer together than those found in California vineyards (Figure 11.3).

Finally, the drier climate of the Châteauneuf-du-Pape region in the Rhône Valley of France reduces the vigor of the vines and leads growers there to use still another vine-management technique. They do not trellis their vines, but let the vines develop into round bushes with shoots that droop to form an umbrella-shaped canopy. California's Sierra Nevada foothill vine districts share the dry climatic conditions of Châteauneuf-du-Pape. As in France the foothill growers employ this Old World model of low, widely spaced, umbrella-shaped canopies (Figure 11.4).

The differences between New World and Old World vineyards appear to contradict the winemakers' belief that great wines are made in the vineyard. If vineyards play such a dominant role, then how can vineyards that look so different produce wines of similar quality? The answer lies in the fact that these vineyards share a key hidden element that is crucial for wine quality: leaf arrangement. Premium wine grape growers whose vines appear distinctly different all control the development of their vines' canopies to optimize both light interception and wine quality. They do this by managing the canopies so they remain thin and open rather than allowing them to grow to become thick and dense.

Vineyard researchers have only recently recognized this key feature of leaf arrangement. A thin, open canopy exposes nearly all leaves to sunlight. When photographed, about 40 percent of the canopy surface appears as light patches. Figure 11.5 illustrates the light patterns within an optimal canopy. Photographed in New Zealand, the light penetration in this canopy is illustrative of premium wine vineyards worldwide. Adequate light penetration within the canopy correlates with premium wine production. Premium wine vineyards in Bordeaux, Burgundy, Germany, Châteauneuf-du-Pape, California, and other fine wine regions feature thin, open canopies; lower quality vineyards generally do not. Dense foliage is associated with shading within the canopy and produces grapes which present major problems in the production of quality wines. Figure 11.6 illustrates a thick canopy.

Figure 11.3
Narrow Rows of Low Curtains Typical of the Bordeaux Region

Figure 11.4
Umbrella Shaped Vines Typical of Unirrigated Mediterranean Climates

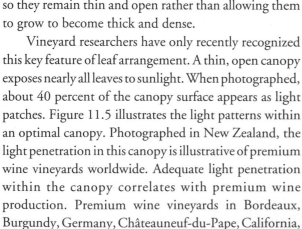

Figure 11.5
Example of Thin, Open Canopy

Figure 11.6
Example of Thick, Dense Canopy

WHY THIN CANOPIES ARE GOOD

The essence of grape growing is to arrange leaves so they intercept light, use its energy to make sugars from carbon dioxide and water, and then export the sugars to the developing fruit. Of course, there are lots of ways of configuring the canopy of leaves. What is the best way?

A designer of photovoltaic solar panels who was thinking about canopy design would likely start with the facts that leaves need sunlight in order to make and export sugars to grapes, shoot tips, etc. She probably would conclude that canopies, like other solar collectors, should maximize light absorption. So, this engineer's canopy would not let any light reach the vineyard floor. However, growers who have tried this reasonable-sounding design have found with these canopies that the grape yields and quality for winemaking have been less than from more "sunlight-wasting" canopies. Let us see why grape vines are not analogous to solar panels.

How Leaves Use Light to Make Sugars

Leaves make sugars from carbon dioxide gas which enters the leaf through tiny pores and from water which enters the plant's roots and moves through its conduit system to the leaves. The process of utilizing the sun's energy to combine carbon dioxide and water into sugars is termed photosynthesis.

As you might expect, the more intense the sunlight, the more the leaf photosynthesizes. However — and this is where the analogy between leaves and solar panels begins to break down — increasing light intensity does not lead to proportionally more photosynthesis. Additional light stimulates additional photosynthesis until the light is one-third to one-half as intense as full sun on a clear summer day. Figure 11.7 plots the response of photosynthetic rate to increases in light intensity and shows that the photosynthetic rate plateaus at about one-third to one-half full sun intensity. In the plateau range more intense light is not accompanied by an additional increase in the rate of photosynthesis.

What Figure 11.7 reveals is that a canopy with one layer of leaves held perpendicular to the

Figure 11.7
Relationship Between Rate of Photosynthesis and Sunlight Intensity

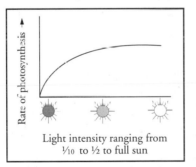

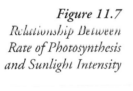

Light intensity ranging from ¹⁄₁₀ to ½ to full sun

sun — the orientation that intensifies the light per unit of leaf surface area — only uses about one-third to one-half of the light. A better leaf arrangement is one that tips the leaves —as you might tip window blinds — to reduce the light intensity on the leaves by about two-thirds. These leaves photosynthesize almost as well as they did when exposed to the full intensity of the sun, but now light "spills" on to another layer of leaves so they too can photosynthesize. As a result, the vine's photosynthetic efficiency greatly increases.

Extra Leaves Hurt Wine Quality

This line of reasoning for adding leaf layers could be extended to a third and fourth layer of leaves. One can even imagine so many leaf layers — so thick and dense a canopy — that even the wild fluttering of leaves in a strong wind would not let any flecks of light reach the ground. Obviously, there is a point of diminishing returns for the vine and for the grower, when adding more layers starts to hurt the vine. That point comes quickly for a couple of reasons. First, even though leaves in full sunlight do tip somewhat to share their excess sunlight with lower leaf layers, their ability to change their orientation is limited, so the grower cannot count on the community of leaves to work out some optimal light-sharing strategy. Canopies could be thicker with more leaf layers, if leaves were better light sharers, but they are not. The second reason is that leaves in the interior of a thick canopy receive so little light that they do not even photosynthesize enough to meet their own needs for sugar.

Nevertheless, winds do occasionally rustle outer leaves and let light flashes reach inner canopy leaves, so why not have leaves just to capture these flashes? There are four reasons why not. First, it costs the plant energy and resources to make them, so the extra "leaves on standby" are a poor investment for the vine. Secondly, leaves that are in deep shade most of the time do not, as I mentioned above, photosynthesize enough to even meet their own sugar needs. They are parasites that divert sugars from the illuminated leaves! Those sugars could better be used in producing grapes. Thirdly, shading shoots reduces the size of the following season's crop. Finally— and this brings us back to the relation of canopy thickness to wine quality — shaded leaves and fruit are associated with poor wine quality.

Dr. Richard Smart, a world leader in canopy research, summarized the results of experiments covering cool to hot climates and several grape varieties. He listed these effects of shade: [3]

Shade increases fruit:	Shade decreases fruit:
potassium	sugar
pH	tartaric acid
malic acid	phenols
Botrytis bunch rot	anthocyanins (the pigment in red grapes)
herbaceous (grassy) character	monoterpenes (flavor components of Gewürztraminer)

Table 11.1
A Summary of the Effect of Shade on Grapes

These effects of shade on fruit composition emphatically announce to growers that their objective is not to maximize light interception, but to increase light interception just to the point where within- and between-vine shading begins to compromise yields and wine quality.

Quantifying Canopy Dimensions

After much study, researchers have concluded that wine quality is not compromised if vine canopies meet two conditions: they should not be more than 1.5 leaves thick and should not be taller than the space between vine rows.[4] A vineyardist can determine leaf layer number — the measure of canopy "thickness" — by randomly selecting a number of sites at fruit cluster height along the vine row, pushing a rod through the canopy curtain at each site and recording the number of leaves it contacts.[5] The average number of leaf contacts is the leaf layer number. The grower can establish adequate illumination of each leaf if she maintains canopies with a leaf layer number of 1.5 or lower. The second condition for premium wine grape canopies limits canopy height to the spacing between rows. Taller curtains shade each other, even if they are oriented north to south to assure both curtain sides receive direct sunlight during the day. Figure 11.8 illustrates this between-canopy effect.

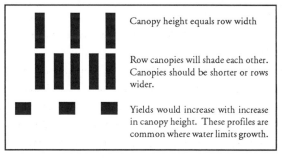

Canopy height equals row width

Row canopies will shade each other. Canopies should be shorter or rows wider.

Yields would increase with increase in canopy height. These profiles are common where water limits growth.

Figure 11.8
The Relationship Between Canopy Height and Row Spacing

To see how canopy height and row spacing affect shading between-canopies, set a couple of breakfast cereal boxes on their long edge on a table (See Figure 11.9). Start with the boxes facing each other and with a small distance between them. Imagine the long axes of the boxes are oriented north-south, the orientation that favors direct light interception by both vine curtain sides during a day. Then pass a flashlight's beam in an arc over the boxes and notice the extent of shading of one box by the other and the amount of light that reaches the table top between the boxes. Repeat the experiment with the boxes farther and farther apart as well as with taller boxes. You will discover that increasing the box height and/or decreasing the distance between the boxes increases light interception and decreases the amount of light reaching the table. But as light interception increases so does between-

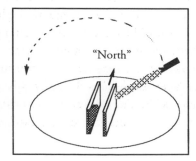

"North"

Figure 11.9
Cereal Box "Simulator" to Study Relationship Between Canopy Height and Row Spacing

box — between-canopy — shading. Viticulturalists have learned that between-canopy shading is not excessive if the canopies are no taller than the rows are wide. Canopies that are so proportioned have a surface area (the area of the top and both canopy sides) about twice the vineyard floor area. If they establish their vineyard with rows wider than the canopies are tall, growers "waste" light without receiving a compensatory increase in wine quality. In this case the grower could narrow the row spacing or increase canopy height so the vines would convert more light into grapes while maintaining grape quality.

The German, French, and New World Vineyards Revisited

The premium Mosel, Bordeaux, Burgundy, and New World vineyards described earlier conform to the thickness and height guidelines. In the Mosel, for example, the column-shaped vine canopies are about 4 ft. high and 1.5 ft. in diameter and form a cylinder with an outside surface of about 25 ft.² for each vine. With the common density of 3000 vines per acre the total canopy surface area reaches 75,000 ft.² per acre. An acre measures 43,560 ft.², so such a Mosel vineyard's canopy surface area is 1.7 times its soil surface area. This is close to the ratio achieved by curtained vines whose curtain height equals row spacing. (If one takes the top and both curtain side areas of thin canopies, the total canopy surface area is twice the soil surface area.)

Thus the Mosel vineyardists operate vineyards that are well-designed in terms of light interception. Also, several factors check the shoot growth — the means by which additional leaves are created — to limit the leaf layer number to 1.5 or less and thus prevent excessive between-canopy shading: the Mosel is a cool region and its soils are thin — both factors that inhibit shoot growth. In addition, vineyardists remove extra shoot growth during the summer.

The Mosel vineyards are so steep that they are not suitable for tractors. In areas where mechanization is possible columnar canopies give way to curtain canopies like those of the Bordeaux, Burgundy, and New World vineyards. The curtains of the Bordeaux and Burgundy vineyards are shorter and closer together than those of most New World vineyards. These differences are not very significant from a biological perspective, because light interception may be nearly equivalent between widely-spaced, tall curtains, and closely-spaced, short curtains. Tradition largely accounts for the difference in spacing: long-standing practices have been codified in Bordeaux prohibiting a change to more economically managed vineyards with wide between row spacings. Within-row spacing is also less in Bordeaux than in most New World vineyards. Sandy soils such as the sandy and gravelly ones of Graves limit shoot growth. Nevertheless, even if the Bordeaux vineyardist plants on less vine-invigorating soils, he may still have to remove extra shoot growth — extra leaves — several times during the growing season.

New World vineyardists who plant in fertile, deep soils that stimulate vigorous growth may divide the resulting thick canopy into two thinner canopies. If excess vigor still plagues the grower, he may divide each curtain into two tiers, one above the other (refer to the Ruakura Twin Two Tier or "RT2T" canopies in Figure 11.16). Such vines are elaborately trellised and appear radically different from the short, single-curtain vines of Bordeaux and Burgundy. However, all these curtains have very similar leaf layer numbers.

The umbrella-shaped canopies of Châteauneuf-du-Pape and the Sierra Nevada foothills have low yields, but no shade problems. Ironically, the "umbrellas" signal the passerby that the vines have insufficient water for high yields. The grower must plant his vines far enough apart so each will have a sufficient volume of soil to tap for water. If the grower gets the distance between vines right, shoot growth will slow as the vines extract the soil water. The vineyardist need not intervene further to control excess shoot growth and its accompanying wine-quality-reducing shade. For the vineyardist's low expenditure of time, trellising, and irrigation he gets low yields. The vines are too short and too far apart to capture enough sunlight per acre for high yields. Wine quality, though, can be excellent.

What Other Grape Growing Factors Affect Wine Quality?

There are three other crucial factors for wine quality: 1. the grower must match the grape variety to the climate at the vineyard site; 2. the grower must protect the vines from weather hazards and pests; and 3. the grower must understand vineyards as systems of interconnected parts, and vineyards as parts of larger systems. After describing how thin canopies are created I will discuss each of these wine-quality determining factors.

HOW GROWERS ACHIEVE THIN CANOPIES

Growers use a trial-and-error process of adjusting the vine's shape and checking to see if their canopies are thin. A vineyardist starts with his best guess of the vines' growth potential, which is determined by the vines' genes as well as soil and climatic factors. Based upon his evaluation of growth potential, he chooses a trellis design. Next he draws from his "toolbox" of growth management techniques those that he hopes will complement the trellis design and assure enough leaves to mature the crop, but not so many as to create the shade that detracts from grape and wine quality. In other words, he seeks to balance leaf area and crop size to maintain thin canopies.

Of course, in traditional premium wine districts, vineyard management practices have evolved over centuries. If the grower has followed his region's established practices for variety selection, trellis design, and vine management, his vines will probably produce premium quality grapes. However, if he deviates from tradition by irrigating, for example, or if he plants vines in a new, unproven region, then he needs to check if his vines conform to the guidelines for optimal canopies. If he finds that his canopy is too thick he will need to adjust his management practices, or the trellis, or — if he is replanting his vineyard — the variety and/or rootstock.

Growers have developed a number of canopy sculpting techniques. I will explain how they use some of the more common ones, including:
- dormant pruning
- shoot removal and shoot trimming and flower cluster removal
- shoot orientation
- canopy division
- changing the distance between plants within the row — the "big vine" effect
- soil management (water and mineral nutrition)
- cover crop management
- variety and rootstock selection

Dormant Pruning — Shaping the Vine and Balancing the Crop Size
Pruning and the Vine's Annual Cycle

Each spring, shoots with leaves and flower clusters emerge from nodes — swollen regions on shoots — on the dormant vine to initiate a new growth cycle. If flower clusters appear in late

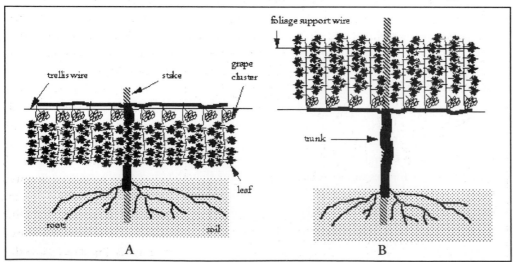

Figure 11.10
Single Curtain Vines with Leafy Shoots that Droop or are Positioned Vertically

March or early April, as they commonly do in California's premium wine districts, the tiny grape flowers will bloom in May. The flowers, if fertilized, will become a cluster of fruits. Leaves provide the fruit with the sugars they store, consume for energy, and modify to assemble into new fruit tissue. During fermentation, yeast will convert the stored sugar to alcohol. The leaves also supply the grapes with sugar derivatives such as malic and tartaric acids which the grapes consume for energy through respiration. In late summer or fall the fruit ripens and people or machines pick it. Later the leaves drop and the vine settles into deeper dormancy during which the vines become resistant to low temperatures, and little visible change occurs. Although the fruit is gone and the leaves are on the ground, the shoots remain and the vine is much larger than it was when spring growth began. It's time for pruning.

Figure 11.11
Growing Shoot

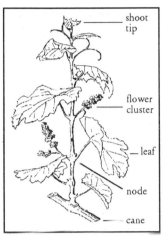

Dormant pruning — the annual, winter removal or shortening of shoots when the vine is dormant — prevents a vine from overgrowing its allotted space and also helps prevent overcropping — the loss of quality associated with excess yield. Usually pruners remove 90 percent or more of last year's shoot growth. Pruning methods vary with the vine form. Most growers train or shape their vine to one of two forms; "head-trained" or "cordon-trained." You will need to learn a little grapevine anatomy before you can understand pruning.

Shoots, Canes, Spurs, Etc. — Some Grapevine Anatomy

During the spring and summer shoots grow vertically until their increasing weight bends them over (Figure 11.10A). Some growers position the shoots between parallel foliage support wires to hold them vertical (Figure 11.10B).

Figure 11.12
Section of a
Dormant Cane
CHARDONNAY YOUR
INTERNATIONAL GUIDE,
Alan Young [30]

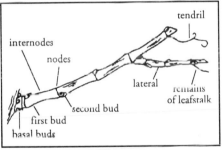

Shoots that grew in summer are termed canes after they lose their leaves in winter. Spaced at about 2.5 to 3-inch intervals along a cane are nodes where last summer's leaves attached and where next season's embryonic shoots of leaves and flowers continue to develop. Figure 11.11 illustrates a young shoot with flower clusters and Figure 11.12 shows a winter view of a cane that grew the previous spring and summer.

Head-Trained Vines

With the head-trained vine, growers develop the above-ground, permanent portion of the vine into a trunk with short branches (arms). Figure 11.13 shows a double-curtain head-trained, vine with pendant canes. The far side of the vine is not yet pruned; the near side is.

Figure 11.13
A Double Curtain,
Head-Trained,
Partially Pruned Vine

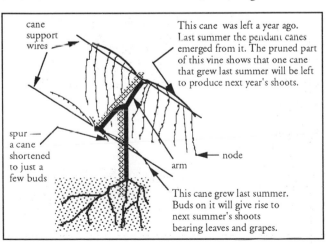

Pruners of head-trained vines remove all two-season old canes that gave rise to the last season's fruit bearing shoots. (In Figure 11.13 there were four such canes. Two have been removed from the near side.) Then the pruner selects some of the canes that grew the previous season from spurs. (Spurs are canes that are shortened to one to five nodes.) He shortens the selected canes to the desired number of nodes (usually eight or more), and secures them to the trellis. These canes, which replace the two-season old canes, will produce the next season's fruit-bearing shoots. (In Figure 11.13 two such canes on the near side have been selected.)

The pruner also leaves some spurs on the arms. Although spurs produce fruit-bearing shoots, they mainly function to produce canes near the ends of the arms. Next winter the pruner will retain these canes, rather than those that develop further from the arms. By selecting such canes the vineyardist insures that vine's permanent structure will not expand very much from year to year.

Cordon-Trained Vines

Growers utilize cordon-training as an alternative to head-training. Figure 11.14 illustrates a double-curtain, cordon-trained vine with spurs. This figure features downward growing spurs, but vineyardists select upward growing spurs if they do not intend to force shoot growth downwards. (Contrast the thick, spur-bearing cordon in Figure 11.14 with the thinner, fruiting canes without regularly spaced spurs shown in Figure 11.13.)

Each winter the pruner either removes the canes or shortens them to spurs. A recommended spur spacing of every 5 inches along the cordon with two nodes retained per spur gives an average shoot spacing of 2.5 inches — an adequate distance between shoots. In summary, head-trained vines are spur- and cane-pruned while cordon-trained vines are just spur-pruned.

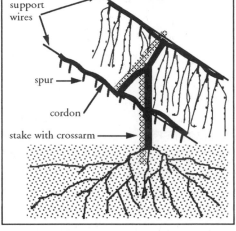

Figure 11.14
Partially Pruned,
Double-Curtain,
Cordon-Trained Vine

Balancing Leaf Area to Crop Size Through Pruning

Dormant pruning provides the grower with her first chance to adjust next summer's leaf area so it will be adequate to mature the next season's crop. If she prunes too severely, she leaves too few nodes and the vines will grow too few fruit-bearing shoots next spring and as a result the crop will be light. In addition, each shoot will produce more leaves than it needs to nourish its flower and grape clusters. This is because the limited number of shoots do not compete for stored sugars, light, water, and minerals, and so they grow excess leaves. They do not, however, produce extra flower clusters. The reason for the failure of these shoots to produce extra clusters to match the extra leaves is that the flower clusters start to develop the previous summer — months before pruning and nearly a year before they appear on a growing shoot.

In short, severe pruning results in an unnecessarily small crop and an excess of leaves per shoot, but not necessarily an excess of leaves per vine. The canopy may not be too thick but the yields are low! Figure 11.15A illustrates the high ratio of leaf area to crop size resulting from severe pruning.

In contrast, leaving too many nodes may produce more shoots than the vine — especially a young one — can support. Even if this multitude of shoots is well illuminated, each shoot's share of the resources will not support enough leaf growth. With a low ratio of leaf area to crop size, the leaves take longer to "charge" the grapes with sugars and the vine is "overcropped" (Figure 11.15B). While the grapes slowly accumulate sugar, they continue to respire and thereby lose acid. The ratio of sugar to acid goes out of balance and wine quality suffers. Yet, overcropping increases yields per acre. When growers are paid for quantity and not for quality, they are tempted to overcrop their vines.

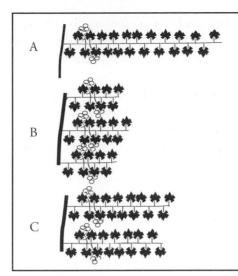

Figure 11.15
The number of nodes the
pruner retains partially
determines the leaf area
to crop size.

A. If the pruner leaves too few nodes, the shoots developing from them will experience minimal competition for light, water, and minerals and will grow excessively. More nodes could have been left to produce more fruit, as in example C.

B. The pruner leaves too many nodes. Intershoot competition reduces individual shoot growth and reduces the ratio of leaves to fruit to the point that the completion of ripening is delayed. Too much acid is respired and the sugar - acid ratio is too high for balanced wines. The grower should remove some flower clusters in the spring as a way of reaching an adequate leaf area-to-crop size ratio.

C. Leaf-to-fruit ratio is optimum. Yield is not as high as in example B, but quality is better.

Fine Tuning After Pruning — Shoot Removal, Shoot Trimming, and Flower Cluster Removal

In some growing regions winter pruning alone usually balances leaf area and crop size (Figure 11.15C). Often, though, vines require additional adjustments of leaves and crop during the growing season to avoid an excess of leaves which leads to shade problems or to avoid an excess of crop which leads to overcropping. If the average distance between shoots is less that 2.5 inches, excessive shading is likely; many vineyardists will remove extra shoots when they are about 6 inches long.

If the remaining shoots continue to grow beyond the 10 to 20 leaves necessary to properly mature the crop, many growers trim them to control canopy shading and promote wine quality. Vigorous vines may need several trimmings during the course of the growing season. Reducing shading has the added benefit of increasing the number of clusters on next year's shoots.

Some vines, especially young ones, will not produce enough leaves per shoot to establish the proper ratio of foliage to crop load (Refer to Figure 11.15B). A young vine or a sick vine may be unable to supply each shoot with enough mineral nutrients and water to nourish both the developing fruit and the shoot tip where new leaves are produced. This condition leads to a stunting of the shoot. The grower can remove some flower clusters to balance leaf area to crop size by directing more resources toward shoot tips and less toward grapes. This practice will improve crop quality, because it prevents overcropping.

Shoot Orientation — For Better Illumination and Fruitfulness

Pendant shoots grow more slowly than upright ones and therefore produce less leaf area. Some growers make use of this orientation response to avoid excess shading by directing shoot growth downward. An additional benefit of downward shoot positioning is better basal node illumination. (Basal nodes are those at the shoot base. Pruners keep them to produce next year's fruit-bearing shoots.) Illuminating these nodes increases cluster number per shoot and with vigorous vines helps bring leaf area and crop size into balance.

Canopy Division — A Strategy for Fertile Soils

Growers also manage excess growth by limiting vine access to mineral nutrients and/or water. However, vineyardists with deep, fertile soils that are watered with summer rains cannot adequately control growth by restricting mineral nutrient and water availability. In many such vineyards neither downward shoot positioning nor lighter pruning sufficiently constrains growth. The grower's first response may be to leave more nodes when he prunes. He reasons that more nodes will send forth more cluster-bearing shoots and the added clusters will compete for resources with the shoot tip and slow its production of leaves. But this reasoning is sound only if the added shoots do not create excess shade. However, if his vines are trained to a single curtain, the extra shoots that grow from the nodes may crowd and shade each other and decrease wine quality. Moreover, the shading reduces the number of clusters forming at nodes. Thus, there will be fewer clusters per shoot and shoot growth will not be constrained by the competition for sugars and mineral nutrients between the processes of shoot growth and fruit growth. The unrestrained shoot growth worsens the shading problem.

Double Curtains

The grower in this situation can divide his single thick-curtain canopy, if the distance between rows will accommodate twice as many curtains. Figures 11.13 and 11.14 illustrate double-curtain canopies. This curtain division doubles the distance between shoots — if shoot number per vine is unchanged — and increases fruit, basal node, and leaf illumination. In addition, thin double curtains expose more leaf surface to light which promotes sugar synthesis, and thus, increases the vine's yield potential. The grower recoups his investment in the extensive trellises required for double curtain vines by "trading" excessive shoot growth for additional crop.

Double curtains can convert the curse of fertile, well-watered soils to a blessing. The extra growth that such soils stimulate decreases quality if the vines are trained to a single curtain. But the grower who switches to a double-curtain vineyard channels the vine's potential for producing lots of "plant mass" into extra quality fruit instead of excessive foliage.

The double-curtain canopies illustrated in Figures 11.13 and 11.14 are similar to those which Cornell University Professor Nelson Shaulis designed. He converted single-curtain vigorous Concord grapes to his double-curtain system, controlled shoot growth, and increased yields by 40% — a noteworthy trade of extra shoot growth for crop![6]

Going to (Vertical) Extremes: The Vineyard of the Future?

If doubling the distance between shoots by switching from a single curtain to a double curtain does not sufficiently relieve shoot crowdedness, the grower can resort to another canopy division. She can again double between-shoot spacing by dividing each curtain into two fruiting tiers — one above the other (some growers first divide a single curtain into two tiers, decrease vine spacing per row, and then, if necessary, divide the single curtain to form a double curtain). Dr. Richard Smart designed the double-curtain, two-tier-per-curtain system. Its name — the Ruakura Twin Two Tier (RT2T) — reflects its New Zealand origins. Figure 11.16 incorporates some of his more recent ideas for modifying the RT2T and should still be considered experimental.[7,8] Growers with vigorous varieties planted in fertile, well-watered soils will closely follow reports about this trellis. If vines on it yield as well as early results indicate, growers will invest in this elaborate trellis to obtain high yields of quality grapes.

Smart reported that Cabernet Franc grown in New Zealand on an RT2T trellis

Figure 11.16
The Twin Two Tier Trellis

produced better quality grapes and twice the yield of single-curtain vines.[9] These results contradict the common notion that an increase in yield is offset by a drop in quality! His original version of this trellis directed all shoots upward, but other versions "devigorate" shoots of the bottom tier or both tiers by directing their growth downward.

The "Big Vine Effect"— The Bigger the Vine, the Shorter the Shoots

A vineyard row's canopy can be formed from widely-spaced big vines or from narrowly-spaced small vines. Michelle Gandell's research in New Zealand suggests that growers who anticipate excess shoot vigor should consider the big vine alternative: she found that shoot vigor declined when vines were planted farther apart[10]

Soil and Water Management — Sculpting Vines by Controlling their Diets

In most cases, soil affects wine quality mainly by provisioning vines with the nutrients and water that influence shoot growth. Soils, therefore, have the potential to indirectly exert important effects on wine quality. However, drainage of excess soil water, irrigation, mineral nutrient additions — fertilization — and the growth management practices I have discussed can counterbalance the effects of soil on important canopy characteristics. There are growers who plant vines in a range of soil types. In each soil type these vines produce premium wine grapes. Management of mineral nutrition, soil water, and cover crops — the plants grown between the vine rows — decisively influences vine growth and grape quality.

Mineral Nutrient Management

Grape shoots grow faster than teenage boys if provided with warm temperatures and plenty of light, mineral nutrients, and water. However, a shortage of any one of these factors slows the growth rate. Often, vineyardists effectively limit mineral nutrients and/or water and thereby regulate vine growth.

To grow and reproduce, plants need 17 essential elements: carbon, hydrogen, oxygen, nitrogen, phosphorus, potassium, sulfur, calcium, iron, copper, zinc, manganese, magnesium, nickel, boron, molybdenum, and chlorine. Air supplies carbon as carbon dioxide, which as you now know enters the leaf and with the aid of sunlight combines with water to form sugars in a process known as photosynthesis. The vine's roots absorb water, which is made of hydrogen and oxygen, from the soil. Roots also mine the soil for all other essential elements. If the soil lacks sufficient levels of a nutrient, the vines grow poorly and yield few grapes of low quality, unless the grower adds the needed nutrient in the form of fertilizers. "Organic" vineyardists fertilize with "natural," chemically-unaltered materials such as manure, which provides nitrogen, and pulverized rock phosphate which supplies phosphorus. Legume cover crops — for example, clovers — are another "organic" source of nitrogen. "Non-organic" growers generally apply nitrogen fertilizers synthesized in chemical factories. If phosphorus is lacking, non-organic growers utilize superphosphate which is produced by treating rock phosphate with sulfuric acid. Whether supplied though organic or synthetic fertilizers, the vine absorbs the same chemical compounds or elements from the soil. Organic sources such as manures or spent skins from the wine presses may improve the soil's physical properties, but they are often in short, irregular, or seasonal supply and their bulk makes them expensive to transport and apply. Nitrogen must be managed with special care. It is easy to apply excess nitrogen which stimulates excessive shoot growth and shading.

Soil Water Management

The notion that irrigation detracts from grape quality is probably as common as the notion that increasing yields always brings poor quality. I already cited Smart's experiment, which showed that, under the right conditions, crop yield and quality can increase together. In this section you will learn that in some cases irrigation improves quality.

Water vapor escapes through the same pores that let carbon dioxide into the leaf for photosynthesis. If the water lost in one season from a vineyard in a hot, dry summer climate were replaced all at once, the grower would have to cover his vineyard with 30 inches of water. On the other hand, a grower in a cool, dry summer climate where less water evaporates might apply about 16 inches of water.

Growing season temperatures, rooting depth, humidity, and rainfall determine the need for irrigation in the vineyard. Vines can extract 1 to 2 inches of soil water for each foot of rooting depth. Roots, if uninhibited, will grow to a depth of eight or more feet. Consider a vineyard soil that can store 16 inches of available water in an 8-foot-deep root zone — the depth of soil the roots grow in. If the vineyard is in a cool, summer rain-free region, its growth may follow an ideal pattern. In the spring, water from the winter rains that has been stored in the soil is readily available. The shoots grow quickly and fill the allotted canopy space with sun-capturing leaves. As the vines use the soil water, the remaining moisture becomes increasingly hard to get. The vines begin to suffer from water stress. Shoot growth stops, since this process is sensitive to water stress. However, photosynthesis, which is less sensitive, continues and the leaves keep furnishing the grapes with sugars and acids so they mature normally. Great fortune! The grower need not irrigate. If she does she may stimulate excessive shoot growth and detract from wine quality.

On the other hand, if our vineyard soil is in a hot region, or even a cool region with shallow soils, shoots will grow rapidly until checked by decreasing water availability in early to middle summer. To conserve water the vine closes its leaf pores. But its water-conserving strategy brings a cessation of photosynthesis, because the necessary carbon dioxide cannot enter through the closed leaf pores. The leaves do not make and transport the sugars to the developing fruit. In this case irrigation can improve both yields and grape and wine quality. The vineyard manager strives to irrigate with just enough water to maintain photosynthesis without stimulating excessive shoot growth.

In areas with summer rains or deep soils, the vines may never experience water stress. Vineyardists in these regions may yearn for shallower soils that dry out enough so they could manage the vines' water status and thereby control shoot growth.

Cover Crops — Competitors or Fertilizers?

Many vineyardists grow other plants called cover crops between the vine rows. For growers coping with excessive shoot growth these plants compete with the vines for water and mineral nutrients and may slow the vines' growth. The species mix in the cover crops varies with soil type and climate. Growers who wish to promote rather than restrict vine growth may choose to enrich the soil with nitrogen via plant legumes such as clovers. Legumes form a mutually beneficial relationship with special bacteria that allows them to change atmospheric nitrogen into nitrogen-rich plant tissue. In time, these legumes die and their decaying tissues become nitrogen-rich organic fertilizer. In contrast, a vineyardist will avoid legumes and plant a nitrogen-consuming cover crop if his vines are too vigorous.

Cover crops have other benefits. On hillsides, they stabilize the soil and help control erosion. Also, they can create favorable conditions for beneficial insects.

Variety and Rootstock Selection — Matching or Modifying Natural Vigor

Varieties differ in their innate growth potential. For example, Cabernet Sauvignon grows more vigorously than Pinot Noir. A vineyardist planning to grow both might plant Cabernet Sauvignon in less fertile soils and Pinot Noir in more invigorating soils. If he reverses the positions of the varieties his grape yields and/or quality may suffer.

Growers can join two vines of different varieties or species so the fruit-bearing portion of the vine is genetically different from the root portion — the rootstock. This practice — called grafting, described in more detail later — allows the grower to select among rootstocks that differ in the amount of shoot growth they promote. For example, the rootstock St. George stimulates shoot growth more than the rootstock known as Selection Oppenheim No. 4 (SO 4).

MATCHING VARIETY TO CLIMATE — ANOTHER KEY TO GRAPE AND WINE QUALITY

The climate that affects the vine is the mesoclimate — climatic conditions such as temperature, wind, humidity, etc., that are unique to the vineyard site. Climatic differences, especially temperature differences, between two vineyards of the same variety often lead to significant wine differences. Grape varieties differ in their sensitivity to temperatures. Some varieties, for example White Riesling, are suited only to cool regions, whereas others, such as Sauvignon Blanc, perform well over a wider range of temperatures. A vineyardist must select the varieties that perform best under the temperature conditions of his or her specific vineyard.

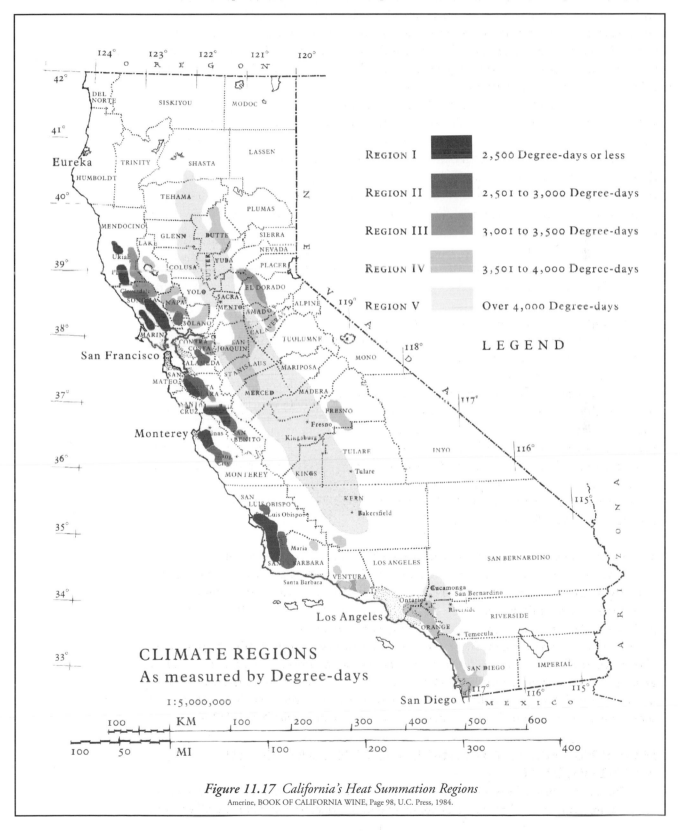

Figure 11.17 *California's Heat Summation Regions*
Amerine, BOOK OF CALIFORNIA WINE, Page 98, U.C. Press, 1984.

Heat Summation and Regions I-V

For a number of decades, the University of California has maintained vineyards with many identical varieties in several diverse viticultural areas. Using data from these vineyards, Professors Amerine and Winkler established a relationship between growing temperatures and grape composition and wine quality. When they summed average daily temperatures above 50 degrees F over the growing season — April through October — for each vineyard site they found that "heat summation" correlated well with wine quality. (They choose 50 degrees F because vines don't grow at lower temperatures.) To calculate heat summation values for different locations, they first subtracted 50 degrees from each day's average temperature to obtain its number of "degree-days," a measure of heat summation. For example, if a day's average temperature ([maximum temperature + minimum temperature]/2) is 60°, subtracting 50° gives that day a value of 10 degree-days. They then added up the degree-day value[5] for each day from April through October.

Amerine and Winkler used the April through October degree-day totals to determine five distinct heat summation regions. They defined the regions as follows:

Region I   less than 2500 degree-days.
Region II   2501-3000 degree-days.
Region III   3001 to 3500 degree-days.
Region IV   3501 to 4000 degree-days.
Region V   4001 or more degree-days.

Figure 11.17 maps heat summation regions in California.[12]

Matching Grape Varieties to Heat Summation Regions

Amerine's and Winkler's study finds its practical application in their recommended variety-region matches. Table 11.2 presents these matches in a very abbreviated form.[13] Growers calculate their vineyard site's heat summation region, go to the table of recommended varieties, and select those that will produce quality wine grapes at that site.

	Production[1]	Flavor[2]	Region[3]		
	Tons/Acre		I & II	III & IV	V
White Varieties					
Chardonnay	L	D	HR	NR	NR
Chenin Blanc	M+	N+	R	R	QR
French Colombard	H	D-	QR	R	HR
Gewürztraminer	L	D+	R	NR	NR
Sauvignon Blanc	M	D	HR	QR	NR
White Riesling	M-	D-	HR	NR	NR
Red Varieties					
Barbera	L+	S	NR	R	QR
Cabernet Sauvignon	M-	D	HR	QR	NR
Merlot	M	D	R	QR	NR
Petit Sirah	M+	S	R	QR	NR
Pinot Noir	L	D	R	NR	NR
Zinfandel	M	D	R	QR	NR

Table 11.2 Recommended Varieties for Table Wine Production in California

Source: Adapted from Amerine et al. (1980)
[1] L for 1 to 3, M for 4 to 6, H for over 6
[2] N for neutral, S for slightly distinctive, and D for distinctive
[3] HR is for highly recommended, R for recommended, QR for a qualified recommendation, and NR for not recommended

Regions, Yields, and Quality

Table 11.2 includes most of the premium wine grape varieties grown in California. A clear pattern emerges from the table: with the exception of French Colombard, varieties with distinctive flavors have moderate yields, and they are recommended for Regions I and II, recommended with qualifications for Regions III and IV, and are not recommended for Region V. Let us see how this information matches your knowledge of the origins of fine wines. Table 11.3 aligns some better known wine districts with heat summation regions.[14]

Table 11.3
Classification of Selected Locations by Heat Summation

Trier,[1] Germany; Burgundy, Champagne, and Bordeaux, France; Geneva, New York; Willamette Valley, Oregon; Santa Cruz, Anderson Valley, Carneros, and Santa Maria, California	Region I
Asti,[2] Italy; Budapest, Hungary; Auckland, New Zealand; Yakima, Washington; Napa, Sonoma, and Santa Barbara, California	Region II
Milan,[3] Italy; St. Helena, Oakville, Healdsburg, Livermore, and Sierra Foothills, California	Region III
Florence, Italy; Mendosa, Argentina; Capetown, South Africa; Sydney, Australia; Clarksburg, Davis, and Lodi, California	Region IV
Palermo, Italy; Fresno and Modesto, California	Region V

[1] Trier and the entire Mosel and Rhine River Valleys. [2] In the Piemonte District. [3] Chianti district.

You probably noted that the world's most famous table wine producing areas — Germany's Rhine and Mosel, Burgundy, Champagne, Bordeaux, Asti, and Napa — are clustered in the cooler regions. The next section explains why.

Temperature and Grape Ripening

Premium wine grapes produce more intense pigments and flavors if they ripen under cool, fall temperatures rather than warm, late summer conditions. Figure 11.18 gives an example of the relative changes in sugar, pH, acid and anthocyanin — the pigments of red grapes — during grape maturation. Note that sugar, pH, and anthocyanin increase along with berry size, whereas acid decreases.

In a hotter region, the grapes of Figure 11.18 would reach desired sugar levels earlier than in a cooler region. However, higher temperatures diminish pigments and flavors and reduce acid.

Figure 11.18
Changes in berry diameter, pH, percent soluble solids (mainly sugars), titratable acidity, and anthocyanins (milligrams per square centimeter of berry dermal tissue) for Cabernet Franc growing on a hillside near St. Helena, California
Adapted from Mathews, Anderson and Schultz [15] and Mathews and Anderson [16]

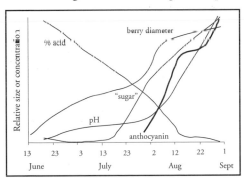

(Grapes respire more malic acid if temperatures are high during ripening.) Premium varieties generally have an excessively high sugar to acid ratio and little or no varietal character when grown in hot regions. Vineyardists who choose quantity over distinctive varietal character will grow highly-productive varieties such as French Colombard and Chenin Blanc in Regions IV and V. These regions have a long growing season. Heat summation correlates with length of growing season and the longer the growing season the greater the yield potential. Growers striving for grapes with varietal character, in contrast, will select varieties such as Gewürztraminer, Chardonnay, and Cabernet Sauvignon, and grow them in cool regions where the vines can realize their genetic potential for converting sunlight into both sugars and distinct flavors.

Wind can be added to our list of climatic factors affecting grape growing. Whereas slight air movement is beneficial in reducing humidity and controlling grape rots, a steady wind is harmful because it stimulates leaf pores to close. As mentioned earlier, water loss from the leaf nearly ceases with leaf pore closure; but so does photosynthesis, because the carbon dioxide needed for photosynthesis enters though the same pores that the water exits. The nearly daily "shut down" of photosynthesis in the windy Salinas Valley of California markedly delays sugar accumulation in the grapes.[17] Although some of California's most experienced enologists and viticulturists had predicted — based on heat summation — that Cabernet Sauvignon wines could be made from Salinas Valley grapes, the grapes that matured very slowly in the wind produced wines that were too vegetative to be great.

QUALITY FRUIT COMES FROM HEALTHY VINES — PROTECTING VINEYARDS FROM WEATHER HAZARDS AND PESTS

The vineyardist may have matched variety to mesoclimate and managed his vines' canopies so they are thin, but his challenges continue, thanks to the fickleness of nature. Nature provides the vineyardist the raw material which he attempts to manage to produce quality grapes. But his control is always tentative, because nature delights in weather and pest surprises. For this section on plant protection I have selected examples of how growers respond to typical weather and pest challenges you might see when you visit a vineyard.

Spring Frost Protection

Dormant *V. vinifera* vines will survive temperatures as low as 5 degrees F.[18] Where winters are severe, determined vineyardists can grow *V. vinifera* if they bury the vines each fall. In Northern China, for example, workers prune elaborately trellised vines, then untie them from the trellis, push them into shallow trenches, and cover them with soil. The following spring just before shoot emergence they uncover the vines and retie them on the trellis.

Although dormant vines can survive 5 degrees F, growing shoots often die from more than a half-hour exposure to 31 degrees F. There are up to three growing points in a node, and if one shoot freezes, another growing point will elongate to form a replacement shoot. However, these new shoots may have a reduced number of flower clusters or none at all, depending on the variety. Therefore, growers in areas with spring frosts try to protect their vines.

Growers rely on wind machines and sprinklers to protect against radiation frosts — those frosts that occur on still, clear nights and that are most severe in low-lying areas such as valley floors where cold air collects. Radiation frosts are so named because on clear nights heat quickly radiates from the vineyard which, as a consequence, cools. As an alternative to using frost control methods, some growers avoid planting on valley floors (where cold air collects, since it is heavier than warm air) and opt instead for warmer hillside locations.

Wind Machines

In some, but certainly not all, growing regions, a layer of cold air at vine level is accompanied by a layer of warmer air above the vines. Wind machines (see Figure 11.19) mix the two air layers and warm air near the vines by one to two degrees F — not much, but often enough to save the shoots and the crop. Some growers combine wind machines with oil-burning heaters to protect against lower temperatures.

Figure 11.19
Wind Machine

Over-the-Vine Sprinklers

It is a startling sight to pass a vineyard on a clear, cold spring morning and see ice-encased vines and tall, rotating sprinklers squirting water over the vine tops. (See Figure 11.20.) Neoprohibitionists are not sabotaging the vineyard and the grower is not intent on economic suicide. Instead, she has reasoned as follows: As the water cools and then freezes, it releases heat. If the rotating sprinklers distribute 50-80 gallons per minute per acre, and if the temperature low is in the mid to upper 20's,

Figure 11.20
Ice Encrusted Shoot, Resulting from Overhead Sprinkling

then each shoot's casing of ice will never be without a coating of water. The shoot with its covering of ice and water will remain at 32 degrees F. Once the sun comes up, the air warms, but the vineyardist continues to sprinkle until all ice melts. If there have not been any lapses in sprinkling, the shoots and clusters will have survived without frost injury.

Soils and Cover Crops in Frost Protection

Valley vineyardists prepare for the frost season by testing the wind machines and sprinklers. They either bury the winter cover crop and then smooth and firm the soil, or they cut the cover crop very short so the soil will absorb as much solar energy as possible during the day. The soil releases the accumulated heat at night. A vineyard with smooth, firm, and moist soil will be 1 to 3 degrees F warmer than a vineyard with an unmowed cover crop. Fortunately, grapes are usually the last fruit plants to begin spring growth, so their shoots avoid many cold spring nights that damage other fruit plants that begin to grow earlier in the spring.

Pest Control — Managing the Ecosystem to Favor the Vines

Modern vineyardists use natural pest controls. They husband "good" bugs that eat "bad" bugs. They also employ mechanical controls, such as plowing, to control weeds. In addition, they manipulate the vineyard environment. For example, growers change the grape clusters' micro-climate by removing leaves near the clusters, a practice which controls grape rots. Pesticides — agents that control harmful organisms — are a last resort. Vineyardists know they are managing a complex ecosystem, so when they must use a pesticide they try to choose one that will bring the pest population into balance with its natural controls without destroying those controls or creating new pest problems.

What About Organic Pest Control?

Many people have the incorrect impression that organic growers do not use any pesticides. They do; and, of course, so do non-organic growers. Organic growers rely on biological and botanical pesticides and on chemical pesticides such as sulfur that are not chemically altered in their preparation. Biological pesticides are preparations of beneficial viruses, bacteria, nematodes, or fungi that control pests. Botanical pesticides are plant extracts with pesticidal properties such as strychnine, a rodent poison, and pyrethrum, an insecticide. Non-organic growers may use the same pesticides as organic growers, but they may also use synthesized pesticides such as malathion and synthesized pyrethrums.

What's Going On Here?

In this section I will discuss pests whose presence or controls create enough commotion or interest in the vineyard to spark an observant visitor to California's wine country to ask, "What's going on here?"

Why is That Guy Kneeling in Front of That Little Grapevine?

You're probably asking this in late summer. The trellis may or may not be in place, but in either case, the young vines are just growing along the ground. What you are witnessing is grafting, the joining of a small piece of cane from a *V. vinifera* wine grape variety to another vine of a different species whose roots resist phylloxera. Phylloxera is a soil insect that kills *V. vinifera* roots. Resistant rootstocks are also used to control some types of plant attacking nematodes — microscopic round worms.

Phylloxera is indigenous to the Mississippi Valley, where it coexists with native American grapes such as *V. rupestris* and *V. riparia*. In the middle of the last century plant collectors introduced phylloxera to Europe, and it quickly killed most *V. vinifera* vines there. The control of phylloxera is a classic example of biological control — using a beneficial organism to control a pestiferous one. Researchers found they could continue to grow *V. vinifera* vines by grafting them onto native American rootstocks which resist phylloxera. The choice of which of the many phylloxera-resistant rootstocks to plant hinges on the rootstocks' performance in specific kinds of sites. As mentioned earlier, vineyardists are particularly interested in the amount of shoot growth a rootstock stimulates.

Phylloxera was introduced to California at about the same time it was introduced to Europe. In the Napa and Sonoma Valleys, California's most famous premium wine areas, most vines are grafted to a rootstock known as AXR#1. Growers knew from European reports that AXR#1 was a gamble in regard to some phylloxera strains, but its good characteristics and its tolerance to the phylloxera strain in California led growers to use it in about 80% of the Napa and Sonoma vineyards. In the mid-1980s many of these vines started dying, and investigators discovered they were being attacked by a new strain or biotype of phylloxera. This virulent strain, which is either a mutant of the old strain or a new introduction, is spreading and necessitates widespread vine removal, replanting with resistant rootstocks, and grafting. When lost wine sales are added to the actual cost of vine removal and replanting, estimates of the per-acre cost to reestablish a Napa vineyard reach $70,000.[19] In the long run, grape yields and grape and wine quality will improve in the Napa and Sonoma valleys as new replanted vineyards come into production. Growers will plant virus-free plants of accurately-identified clones and will space and trellis them to facilitate the achievement of thin canopies and the production of quality grapes.

The most common type of grafting, termed budding, joins a node and underlying wood of a wine grape variety to a rootstock. Chip budding is the most popular budding technique in California. The budder starts his knife cut just above the node and continues it down through the node to separate it from the cane. He makes a second cut, at a 45-degree angle to the first, to complete the node removal. Then he cuts a "chip" of wood the same size as the severed node from the young trunk of the rootstock plant. Finally, he replaces the chip with the node, ties it into place, and covers the vine with soil to prevent drying of the inserted node. (See Figure 11.21.) Both the wood under the node and the rootstock generate cells at the graft to unite the two pieces. By spring this process is complete, and the grower removes the remaining rootstock shoots. The resulting plant is not a hybrid of its two components, since the hereditary information of each component is not shared with that of the other.

Figure 11.21
Chip Budding V. Vinifera *Onto a Phylloxera Resistant Rootstock* [31]
Courtesy of Richards Lyon

Why Is That Field Covered with Plastic?

As you drive through a California viticultural area in the fall, you may see the shimmering clear plastic wrapping bare soil. You are not witnessing another of Cristo's enormous and ephemeral art projects. The plastic is in place to retain a fumigant that has been injected into the soil to control nematodes and/or a fungus, *Armillaria melea*. The fungus will slowly but steadily kill vines unless the soil is treated before planting. (If the preplanting fumigant is the last "non-organic" pesticide used, the first grapes harvested three or four years later can be sold as "organic.") Growers cannot use rootstocks to control *A. melea*. Rootstock trials since the 1930s have yet to discover significant resistance to this pest.

Why Are Plants Growing Between the Vine Rows but Not in the Rows?

That's because this vineyardist considers plants in the row (other than vines) to be weeds — plants out of place. If they grow tall enough they will compete with the vines for light and will make harvesting, shoot positioning, and leaf removal difficult. The organic tool for keeping the row free of weeds is a special plow that uproots the weeds between vines. Before the plow reaches the vine it swings out from the row and then, when past the vine, swings back to plow the next row section. The conventional grower may use the same method or may control the weeds by spraying the vine row with herbicides — pesticides for weeds. You may see both row plowing and herbicide application during late winter and the first part of the growing season. Once the mature vine produces sufficient foliage to shade vine-row weeds and slow their growth, the grower will seldom need to spray or plow again in that season.

Isn't It Pretty in the Fall When the Grape Leaves Turn Red?

Yes, it is, but the vineyardists know that this beauty comes at a high price. Red leaves with rolled-down leaf margins announce the presence of leaf-roll virus. White-fruited varieties display the leaf-rolling symptoms but not the intense red leaf color of infected red-fruited varieties. Leaf-roll virus slows sugar accumulation in the grapes, and while the vineyardists wait for the grapes finally to acquire enough sugar for harvest, the grape acid levels and quality keep dropping. This virus is transmitted by grafting. The grower with leaf-roll virus-infected vines should have purchased plants that were certified by the state to be free of known diseases.

If the grower was so careless about the origins of his or her plants, you might wonder if he or she was careful to get the best clone of, say, Pinot Noir. A vine's genetic makeup sets its yield and grape quality potential. A clone is a group of genetically identical, asexually propagated plants that in principle can be traced back to a single plant. Over time, some members of a clone mutate (the genetic makeup changes) and become new clones. Unfortunately, growers may call these mutants and the old clone by the same name. The grower who is unaware that several clones may be identically named can easily select the "wrong" clone and be disappointed in the yields and wines that his vineyard produces.

Why Are They Just Picking Off the Leaves and Not Even Saving Them?

Look more closely — they aren't picking all the leaves, just those near the flower clusters. This is a pest-control measure directed at a number of humidity-loving fungi, such as *Botrytis cinerea,* that share a propensity for infecting and spoiling grapes. For a disease to take hold the environment must be right for infection. In Mediterranean climates, summer precipitation is minimal and humidity low, so grape diseases caused by fungi and bacteria seldom become serious unless a thick, dense canopy creates a humid microclimate. The vineyardist can rectify the humid microclimate "mistake" by removing leaves near the clusters. Since the air around leaves is humidified by the evaporation of water from the leaf surfaces, removing leaves reduces the moisture source and allows drying by the sun and wind. Furthermore, if it does rain, clusters dry faster, because the air freely circulates around them. California researchers controlled grape rots equally well with leaf removal or with fungicides! [20] In addition, they found leaf removal altered fruit composition. Removing leaves from Sauvignon Blanc increased fruit sugars and lowered titratable acidity, pH, potassium, and malic acid.[21]

What's That Tractor Driver (or Pilot) Doing? It Looks Like She Is Just Creating a Cloud of Dust.

She is — and it's a cloud of sulfur dust, a finely ground mineral used as an "organic" pesticide to control the fungus that causes powdery mildew disease.[22] Even though low humidity thwarts many fungal diseases in dry Mediterranean climates, it doesn't prevent powdery mildew infections. This pest and many other fungi are propagated by spores — microscopic, durable structures analogous to the seeds of higher plants that disperse, germinate, and grow into a new fungus organism. Fungal spores generally require free moisture or at least very high humidity to germinate and grow. Powdery mildew spores, however, pack enough water so they can germinate and grow even in low-humidity conditions. The fungus grows over the surface of leaves, fruit, and shoots, and sends nutrient-absorbing structures into these plant parts. If untreated, it can destroy the crop. Powdery mildew is the most commonly treated pest in both organic and non-organic California vineyards. Sulfur deposited on the plants inhibits powdery mildew spore germination. Sulfur dustings commence when the shoots are about 6 inches long, and applications are repeated when the shoots are 12 inches and 18 inches long and then at two-week intervals until the fruit begins to ripen. Computer models of powdery mildew's development provide growers an alternative to a rigid biweekly treatment schedule. In many years growers who follow the treatment schedule suggested by the model will treat less frequently than those growers adhering to a calendar schedule.

If too much sulfur remains on the fruit, wines made from it may develop an off odor. Under the low oxygen conditions of fermentation, the sulfur will be converted to hydrogen sulfide, the same chemical that gives rotten eggs their memorable smell. Some wineries insist that their growers limit sulfur dustings to the spring and then switch to "non-organic" fungicides.

THE VINEYARD SYSTEM

You can think of a vineyard as a system of interrelated elements. When these are diagrammed, the resulting scheme looks like a web; webs are, in fact, good analogies for systems. For example, consider a grower with an unirrigated vineyard. It may produce quality grapes over a narrow range of yields — expressed in tons of grapes harvested per acre — before the vines are overcropped and quality declines. Figure 11.22A illustrates such a quality–yield relationship. If the vineyardist disturbs the water thread by installing an irrigation system, she inescapably repositions all the other threads to form a different web, a different vineyard. If she makes no other changes, it is possible that yields will increase somewhat because water no longer limits growth, but that the increase in shading from the extra foliage will decrease grape quality (Figure 11.22B). If the vineyardist is experienced and familiar with viticultural research, she will know that only rarely can she make just one change. To realize the benefit of the extra growth the irrigation system affords, she may also change the single-curtain, thick canopy to double, thin curtains which produce more than the thick canopy and maintain the quality of the original unirrigated vineyard (Figure 11.22C).

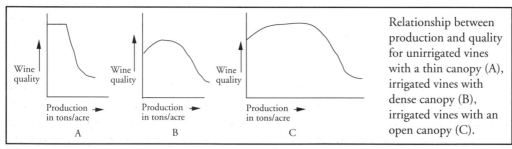

Relationship between production and quality for unirrigated vines with a thin canopy (A), irrigated vines with dense canopy (B), irrigated vines with an open canopy (C).

Figure 11.22
The change in wine quality with increasing yield for: A, unirrigated vines with limited growth and a thin canopy; B, vigorous, irrigated vines with a thick canopy; and C, irrigated vines with a thin canopy.

I do not mean to imply from this example that viticultural knowledge is refined enough to eliminate the need to test changes on a small scale before applying them on a large, expensive scale. Vineyards, as economic systems, are complicated, and viticulturists, as economists, still lack models which can accurately predict the consequences that a change will cause. Nevertheless, viticulture researchers can be proud of their progress in understanding vineyards. Nearly all of that progress has occurred in the last 100 years.

The Vineyard System — Research

The following anecdote exemplifies the level of viticultural knowledge one hundred years ago. Leland Stanford, the founder of Stanford University and owner of the world's largest winery, did not know how markedly vineyard temperatures affect grape and wine quality. He had hoped to duplicate great French wines, but he unknowingly made the mistake of bringing French varieties and vintners to Vina, California, a hot Region V site about 110 miles north of

Sacramento. Stanford did not realize the futility of his Region V venture, because University of California researchers had not yet demonstrated that heat summation should be used to match variety to vineyard site.

We can stretch the analogy of the web of interrelated vineyard elements to include new ideas and research results. This chapter's topics of heat summation regions and canopy management serve as an example. New knowledge changes vineyard practices and in turn prompts refinement of older "knowledge." Amerine's and Winkler's "heat summation – variety match" research preceded intense study of canopy management by two decades.

While canopy researchers have been specifying the features of optimal canopies, they have also been learning that canopy design affects the climate the grapes and leaves experience — the microclimate. Within the same mesoclimate, microclimates vary according to canopy characteristics. So, growers and researchers need to refine the "heat summation–variety match" knowledge. They will again compare each variety's grape quality when each variety's vines are grown in different heat summation regions. But now they will make sure the canopies at each site are optimal in terms of such factors as leaf layer number. Such studies, coupled with ongoing attempts to refine grape-growing region classifications, promise even more felicitous marriages of growing sites and varieties.

We still do not have (and probably never will have) the final answer to the question "What explains the excellence of premium wine grape vineyards?" Nevertheless, canopy researchers have an answer. For years vineyardists and winemakers have offered simple explanations for various premium wine vineyards' excellence — "It's the clay soil"; "It's the chalky soil"; "It's the rocky, steep site"; "It's the plant spacing"; "It's the pruning method"; "It's the trellising method"; "It's the viruses." However, canopy researchers have discovered that soil composition, soil water, summer rains, irrigation, cover crops, between-row and within-row spacing, pruning, shoot removal and trimming, cluster removal, trellising, latitude, and continent all can differ and yet the vineyards can produce similar wines — if their canopies share the critical characteristics you have learned about in this chapter. This is like saying that spider webs of many designs can catch flies as long as the holes don't exceed a critical size. Of course, canopy researchers hasten to add that the best clones must be planted. Also, canopy management cannot overcome wide differences in mesoclimates. The Region I-V classification is not the final word (Amerine and Winkler did not think so either), but even the best canopy manager cannot produce, say, high quality Pinot Noir in Region V.

The Vineyard Ecosystem

Many of the elements that make up the vineyard system are the other organisms that interact with the grapes, with each other, and with the environment. All of these factors constitute the vineyard ecosystem. Vineyard ecologists study this ecosystem to develop ecologically sound pest management strategies. Because the vineyard ecosystem is extremely complex, ecologists' understanding of the system will probably always remain incomplete.

One example of pest management from the San Joaquin Valley of California illustrates the complexity of the vineyard ecosystem, and shows how vineyardists with ecosystem understanding can manage pest problems with elegant fine tuning instead of using "heavy-handed" methods that may solve one problem, yet create another. The Pacific mite, a tiny (period-sized) relative of insects and spiders, feeds on grape leaves. A leaf can tolerate some mites, but not dozens of them. Fortunately, a predatory mite exists that loves to dine on Pacific mite. In some vineyards the population swings of these two species are wild: the Pacific mite population soars and causes leaf damage before the predators multiply, eat most of the Pacific mites, and then die of starvation. The next year the cycle repeats. Vineyards that suffer minimal Pacific mite damage have a third actor in this arachnid play: an innocuous mite that eats stray pollen. It serves as alternative prey for the predatory mite so that when the Pacific mite population drops, the predatory mite can survive and be "prepared" for the Pacific mite's next try at a population explosion.[23]

Vineyard managers who understand this three-mite drama will not use pesticides or practices that injure the predator and the pollen feeder. If the Pacific mite remains a problem, the manager might encourage cover-crop plants that shed pollen throughout the summer to support the pollen feeder.[24] In this example of ecologically sound pest management, cover crops become a principal factor in controlling a mite pest.

Pest and canopy management are the vineyardist's attempts to manipulate the vineyard system. But nature can always introduce new variables for the vineyardist to respond to. For example, there will be years in which a pest such as the Pacific mite becomes a problem for even the most ecologically savvy grower. To save his crop the vineyardist may use pesticides. But more and more, growers think of pesticides as tools which supplement control by predators or other natural means. Their goal is not to annihilate the Pacific mite but to adjust its numbers relative to its predators so that the latter can, once again, control the pest.

Sometimes the grower will not be able to respond successfully to nature's whims. A vineyardist may have her vines at optimal water stress for grape maturation when a heavy rain arrives just before harvest and changes grape composition. Good vintage years are those in which most growers successfully adjust to nature's challenges. (This is recognized in some wine regions such as Champagne or the Port district, where a vintage date appears on bottles only in the best years.) There will always be situations that call for more knowledge than the grower and her consultants have. The art of winemaking in the vineyard lies in bridging gaps in knowledge with intuition honed by years of vineyard experience.

The Vineyard System — The Human Element

The vineyard system also encompasses the vineyard manager and the people she coordinates. She cannot know as much as individual specialists know about soils or climatology, but she needs to understand the principles of each vineyard speciality. After reading this chapter, you have enough background to understand the following illustration of the benefits of broad knowledge. If you were a vineyard manager in a Region IV area, you might consult a climatologist to learn if there is any practical way to change your vineyard's heat summation to that of Region III so you could grow Cabernet Sauvignon with varietal character (and make big bucks!). What if your consultant suggests over-vine sprinkling or misting during hot days to lower vine temperatures? Because you understand the role of moisture in the development of grape-rot disease, you will be wary of this suggestion and will test it on only a small portion of your vineyard. If you are really savvy, you will also enlist the free help of your county's University of California Cooperative Extension Service personnel to design the test and statistically analyze the data to check if differences between your misted and non-misted vines are "real" or just due to chance.

Some of the most knowledgeable vineyardists hire consultants. They might employ a canopy-management specialist, a pest control advisor, an irrigation specialist, an accountant, and, of course, an attorney! The people who are part of the vineyard system also include men and women who carry out the field operations of pruning, harvesting, equipment operation, pest control, irrigation, etc. Figure 11.23 is a calendar of vineyard operations for the Napa and Sonoma valleys that you can refer to when you visit a vineyard to help you decipher what the vine and the vineyard crew are up to.

Vineyard managers supplement their permanent vineyard staff with temporary employees for pruning and harvesting. The vineyard location, as well as the manager's temperament, affect the treatment of staff and seasonal workers. The treatment and use of farm labor depends on the vineyard's location, because the vineyard is a subsystem of larger socioeconomic and political systems. An example from my personal experience compares California's San Joaquin Valley with Alsace, France. The San Joaquin Valley has many large farms employing many field workers. A number of social indices, such as median family income and number of people per room of housing, place agricultural workers near the bottom of society in this, one of the world's richest

Figure 11.23
Calendar of Events for California's North Coast Vineyards
Adapted from *Grape Pest Management* [25]

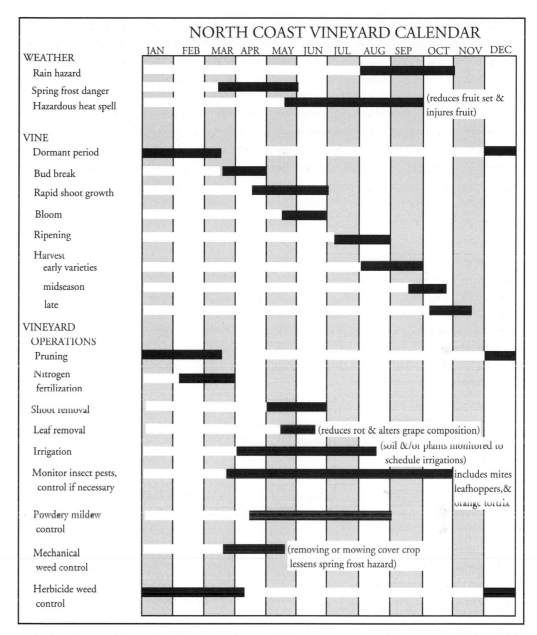

Figure 11.23
Calendar of Events for California's North Coast Vineyards
Adapted from *Grape Pest Management* [25]

agricultural areas.[26] The first language of many of the permanent and temporary field workers is not the same as the owner's first language. It is obvious that the workers and owners are from different cultures. I grew up in the San Joaquin Valley, so on my first sabbatical leave I was amazed to dine in Alsace with the grape harvesters who shared the luncheon table with the vineyard owners who had prepared the meal! The harvesters were like part of the family. Each year the same people would spend their "vacation" time away from their regular jobs to travel to Alsace for the grape harvest.

In fairness, I don't know whether that was a typical Alsatian vineyard. Furthermore, not all large California Central Valley farmers and farm managers consider laborers as just another cost of production to be treated as impersonally as a tractor. Many farm managers are very concerned with their employees' welfare. Nevertheless, even if we only compared California farmers who operate with "enlightened" farm labor policies to the Alsatian farmer I met, the differences in manager–field worker relations would be striking. The Alsace and the San Joaquin Valley vineyards may share important physical characteristics such as leaf-layer number, but they are located — maybe even trapped — in different sociopolitical and economic systems and play very different roles in those systems.

The Vineyard System — Economic and Political Factors

Vineyards are also subject to economic realities that influence manager–worker relations and force changes in vineyard practices. For example, Napa Valley grape production costs are about $2,500 per acre,[27] or $3.50 per bottle of wine. If the grower receives the average 1991 price of $1,241[28] per ton, then at two tons per acre the owner just meets production costs with nothing left to cover his annual investment costs of about $7,000 per acre.[29] (Although *Wine Spectator* columnist James Laube gives the yield of great California vineyards as 1-3 tons per acre, grapes from such vineyards fetch more than the above average prices.) If the vineyard manager can incorporate the results of the kind of viticultural research you have learned about in this chapter and increase production while maintaining or improving quality, the increased revenue may persuade the owner to remain a grower and not sell to urban developers. His decision to continue grape production is not important to just wine consumers and his employees; it is also important to the local economy and quality of life. Each year millions of wine pilgrims tour this and other premium wine districts worldwide, supporting thriving tourist industries and maintaining political support for keeping scenic lands covered with vines instead of shopping malls and townhouses.

The larger system encompasses you as well as the vineyard subsystem. When you spend your tourist dollar to visit vineyards and buy those vineyards' bottled essences, you create employment, stimulate the local economy, and thereby help thwart the ravagers of rural scenic beauty. Responsible wine drinking does have social value.

REVIEW QUESTIONS

Instructions: You might want to use a separate sheet of paper to answer the following review questions. In that way you can use the questions to check your knowledge of this chapter more than once. You may, for example, want to re-test yourself on items that you have missed or use the "Review Questions" to test your knowledge before you read a chapter. For the True or False items, answer "True" if the statement is accurate or "False" if the statement is incorrect. If you determine that a statement is false, make a note explaining why. For the multiple choice items pick the best alternative. Check your answers after you have completed all the questions.

1. The number of vines per acre in the Mosel region is about
   A. 300   B. 1000   C. 3000

2. What is the effect of a dry summer climate on the vigor of unirrigated vines? _____
   _____
   _____
   _____

3. A key factor that separates premium wine grape vineyards from mediocre vineyards is
   A. stony soil
   B. rootstock
   C. vineyard slope
   D. canopy dimensions
   E. phylloxera

4. Quantitatively distinguish between thin and thick canopies. _____
   _____
   _____
   _____

5. Thick canopies adversely affect
   A. grape composition
   B. next year's crop
   C. grape berry health
   D. all of the above
   E. none of the above

6. What is photosynthesis? _____
   _____
   _____

7. True or false: An increase in light intensity is accompanied by a proportional increase in the rate of photosynthesis. _____

8. The curve describing the relationship between light intensity and photosynthesis rate plateaus when the light is
   A. as intense as full sunlight on a clear summer day
   B. 50% as intense as full sunlight on a clear summer day
   C. 10% as intense as full sunlight on a clear summer day

9. True or false: The intensity of light per unit area of leaf is greatest if the leaf is perpendicular to the light rays. _____

10. Leaves in deep shade
    A. use sugars synthesized by illuminated leaves
    B. photosynthesize enough to meet their own sugar needs but do not export sugars to the rest of the vine
    C. hardly photosynthesize at all, but at least remain innocuous

11. True or false: Shade decreases the concentration of monoterpenes in Gewürtztraminer. _____

12. True or false: Because the essence of grape growing is converting sunlight into wine, it follows that grape growers should maximize their vines' interception of sunlight. _____

13. How does a vineyardist determine leaf layer number? _____
    _____
    _____

14. If canopy height remains constant, then increasing between-row spacing
    A. increases light interception by the vineyard
    B. decreases light interception by the vineyard
    C. does not change light interception by the vineyard

15. True or false: The canopy surface area should not exceed twice the soil surface area. _____

16. True or false: The curtains of the Bordeaux and Burgundy vineyards are shorter and closer together than those of most New World vineyards. _____

17. True or false: Leaf layer numbers differ significantly among premium wine grape vineyards. _____

18. Grape shoots emerge from
    A. leaves   B. nodes   C. roots   D. flower clusters

19. True or false: Leaves export sugars to developing grapes. _____

20. When are grape plants most resistant to low temperatures? _____

21. Define "canes." _____
    _____

22. Are spurs longer or shorter than canes? _____

23. Explain why the shoots on a severely pruned vine tend to grow very long. _____
    _____
    _____

24. Explain why severe pruning decreases crop size. _____
    _____
    _____

25. What is overcropping? _____
    _____

26. About how many leaves does a shoot need to mature its grape clusters? _____
    _____

27. What is the purpose of flower cluster removal? _____

_____

28. True or false: Upright shoots grow more slowly than pendant ones. _____

29. True or false: It is good to keep basal buds in the shade. _____

30. If canopies are thin, leaf layer numbers low, but shoot growth is excessive, the pruner should leave more nodes next year than he left last year. Explain. _____

_____

_____

_____

31. True or false: Dividing a thick, single-curtain canopy doubles the number of curtains and decreases canopy thickness. _____

32. True or false: If shoot spacing along cordons remains constant, then dividing a canopy curtain into two fruiting tiers doubles the number of shoots per curtain. _____

33. True or false: Increasing grape yields lowers grape quality. _____

34. What is the big vine theory? _____

_____

_____

35. True or false: Legume cover crops will help devigorate grapevines. _____

36. True or false: Irrigation decreases wine grape quality. _____

37. Rootstocks are used to control
    A. leaf-roll virus
    B. *Armillaria melea*
    C. powdery mildew
    D. vine size
    E. *Botrytis*

38. True or false: Strong winds stimulate photosynthesis and speed the accumulation of sugar by the grapes. _____

39. Describe the calculation of degree-days for a day. _____

_____

40. True or false: Region I is cooler than Region V. _____

41. True or false: California has more Region I acres than Region V acres. _____

42. True or false: Gewürztraminer is less suited to hot regions than is French Colombard. _____

43. True or false: During radiation frosts, the valley floors are warmer than the adjoining hillsides. _____

44. True or false: Wind may warm a vineyard if a layer of warm air exists above the vineyard. _____

45. True or false: If ice encrusts a shoot, the shoot will freeze. _____

46. True or false: "Organic growers" eschew pesticides. _____

47. Which is a botanical pesticide?
    A. sulfur
    B. strychnine
    C. malathion
    D. nematodes
    E. phylloxera

48. Growers control phylloxera by means of
    A. rootstocks
    B. botanical pesticides
    C. nematodes
    D. pesticides
    E. all of the above
    F. none of the above

49. Leaf-roll virus is spread by
    A. irrigation water
    B. grafting
    C. birds
    D. downy mildew

50. True or false: Several grape clones may share the same name. _____

51. Removing leaves from around grape clusters
    A. decreases grape rots
    B. lowers grape potassium
    C. lowers grape pH
    D. all of the above
    E. none of the above

52. In regards to winemaking, what is the hazard of treating grapes with sulfur? _____
    _____
    _____

53. True or false: Canopy management affects the vine's microclimate. _____

ANSWERS TO REVIEW QUESTIONS

1. C
2. Dry summers reduce vigor because they do not replenish soil water. As a consequence the vines deplete their water supply and stop growing.
3. D
4. When photographed, about 40 percent of the canopy surface of a thin canopy appears as light patches. The value is much lower with thick canopies. Also, the leaf layer number of thin canopies is 1.5 or lower.
5. D
6. Photosynthesis is the use of solar energy to synthesize sugar from carbon dioxide and water.
7. False. If at low light levels a one unit increase in light intensity yields, for example, a one unit increase in photosynthetic rate, then at higher light levels a one unit increase in light intensity will yield less than a one unit increase in photosynthetic rate.
8. B
9. True
10. A
11. True
12. False. If growers maximize light interception, the vine canopies will be thick and shady and grape yields and quality will be lower than if vines intercept somewhat less light.
13. A vineyardist can determine leaf layer number — the measure of canopy "thickness" — by randomly selecting a number of sites at fruit cluster height along the vine row, pushing a rod through the canopy curtain at each site, and recording the number of leaves it contacts. The average number of leaf contacts is the leaf layer number.
14. B
15. True
16. True
17. False. Leaf layer numbers are about the same in premium winegrape vineyards.
18. B
19. True
20. When they are dormant.
21. Shoots that grew in summer are termed canes after they lose their leaves in winter.
22. Shorter. They have 1-4 or 5 nodes while canes have 8 or more nodes.
23. The limited number of shoots do not compete for stored sugars, light, water, and mineral resources, so shoot growth is not restricted by shortages of these resources.

24. Severe pruning reduces the number of nodes from which will emerge the shoots bearing the next season's crop.
25. A vine's production of more crop than it can satisfactorily mature.
26. About 10 to 20, if they are well exposed to sunlight.
27. To prevent overcropping and its accompanying loss of grape quality.
28. False
29. False. Shade reduces the number of clusters on the shoots that emerge the following year from the nodes.
30. Leaving more nodes will increase the number of crop-bearing shoots the following year, and the increased competition for resources among the more numerous shoots will decrease their growth.
31. True
32. True
33. False. In some cases quality increases as yields increase.
34. The theory that increased node number per vine, but with little change in nodes per meter of row, devigorates the vine.
35. False. Legumes add nitrogen fertilizer to the soil which will invigorate the vines.
36. False. Under the right circumstances, irrigation improves winegrape quality.
37. D
38. False. Leaf pores close in strong winds and carbon dioxide, which is essential for photosynthesis, cannot enter the leaf.
39. Subtract 50 degrees from the day's average temperature.
40. True
41. False. More Region V acres.
42. True
43. False. Colder air settles in low lying areas.
44. True
45. False. Not necessarily. If water keeps flowing over the ice, the ice will remain at 32 degrees F and the grape shoot will be uninjured.
46. False. Many organic growers use pesticides.
47. B
48. A
49. B
50. True
51. D
52. If the sulfur remains on the grape, it will be reduced during fermentation to stinky hydrogen sulfide.
53. True

ENDNOTES

1 Anonymous, "New at the Peak," *Wines & Vines,* Vol. 71, 1990, p. 38.

2 Peynaud, Emile, THE TASTE OF WINE, The Wine Appreciation Guild, Ltd., San Francisco, CA, 1987, p. 258.

3 Smart, R. E., J. K. Dick, I. M. Gravett, and B. M. Fisher, "Canopy Management to Improve Grape Yield and Wine Quality – Principles and Practices," *South African Journal of Enology and Viticulture,* Vol. 11, 1990, pp. 3-17.

4 Smart, R. E., J. K. Dick, I. M. Gravett, and B. M. Fisher, "Canopy Management to Improve Grape Yield and Wine Quality – Principles and Practices," *South African Journal of Enology and Viticulture,* Vol. 11, 1990, pp. 3-17.

5 Smart, R. E., and M. D. Robinson, SUNLIGHT INTO WINE: A HANDBOOK FOR WINEGRAPE CANOPY MANAGEMENT, Australian Industrial Publishers Pty. Ltd., Underdale, SA, 1991, p. 88.

6 Shaulis, N., H. Amberg, and D. Crowe, "Response of Concord Grapes to Light, Exposure and Geneva Double Curtain Training." *Proceedings of the American Society of Horticultural Science,* Vol. 89, 1966, pp.268-280.

7 Smart, R. E., J. K. Dick, I. M. Gravett, and B. M. Fisher, "Canopy Management to Improve Grape Yield and Wine Quality – Principles and Practices," *South African Journal of Enology and Viticulture,* Vol. 11, 1990, pp. 3-17.

8 Smart, R. E. and M. D. Robinson, SUNLIGHT INTO WINE: A HANDBOOK FOR WINEGRAPE CANOPY MANAGEMENT, Australian Industrial Publishers Pty. Ltd., Underdale, SA, 1991, p. 88.

9 Smart, R. E., J. K. Dick, I. M. Gravett, and B. M. Fisher, "Canopy Management to Improve Grape Yield and Wine Quality – Principles and Practices," *South African Journal of Enology and Viticulture,* Vol. 11, 1990, pp. 3-17.

10 Gandell, M., SUNLIGHT INTO WINE: A HANDBOOK FOR WINEGRAPE CANOPY MANAGE-MENT, (R. E. Smart, and M. D. Robinson, principal authors), Australian Industrial Publishers Pty. Ltd., Underdale, SA, 1991, p. 88.

11 Smart, R. E., J. K. Dick, I. M. Gravett, and B. M. Fisher, "Canopy Management to Improve Grape Yield and Wine Quality – Principles and Practices," *South African Journal of Enology and Viticulture,* Vol. 11, 1990, pp. 3-17.

12 Amerine, M. A., "The Vine and Its Environments," BOOK OF CALIFORNIA WINE, D. Muscatine, M. A. Amerine, and B. Thompson, eds., University of California Press/Southeby Publications, Berkeley, CA, 1984, p. 615.

13 Amerine, M. A., H. W. Berg, R. E. Kundee, C. S. Ough, V. L. Singleton, and A. D. Webb, THE TECHNOL-OGY OF WINE MAKING, Avi Publishing Co., Inc., Westport, CT, 1980, p. 794.

14 Winkler, A. J., J. A. Cook, W. M. Kliewer, and L. A. Lider, GENERAL VITICULTURE, University of California Press, Berkeley, CA, 1976, p. 710.

15 Mathews, M. A., M. M. Anderson, and H. R. Schultz "Phenologic and Growth Responses to Early and Late Season Water Deficits in Cabernet Franc," *Vitis,* Vol. 26, 1987, pp. 147-160.

16 Mathews, M. A., and M. M. Anderson, "Fruit Ripening in *Vitis vinifera* L.: Responses to Seasonal Water Deficits," *American Journal of Enology and Viticulture,* Vol. 39, 1988, pp. 313-320.

17 Freeman, B. F., W. M. Kliewer, and Stern, P., "Influence of Windbreaks and Climatic Region on Diurnal Fluctuation of Leaf Water Potential, Stomatal Conductance, and Leaf Temperature of Grapevines," *American Journal of Enology and Viticulture,* Vol. 33, 1982, pp. 233-236.

18 Becker, N., "Site Selection for Viticulture in Cooler Climates Using Local Climatic Information," PROCEED-INGS OF THE INTERNATIONAL SYMPOSIUM ON COOL CLIMATE VITICULTURE AND ENOLOGY, Oregon State University Agricultural Experiment Station Technical Publication, No. 7628, 1984, pp. 20-34.

19 Anonymous, "Could phylloxera cost $70,000 per acre?" *Wines and Vines,* Vol. 2, 1991, p. 27.

20 Gubler, W. D., J. J. Marois, A. M. Bledsoe, and L. J. Bettiga, "Control of Botrytis Bunch Rot of Grape with Canopy Management," *Plant Disease,* Vol.71, 1987, pp. 599-601.

21 Bledsoe, A. M., W. M. Kliewer, and J. J. Marois, "Effects of Timing and Severity of Leaf Removal on Yield and Fruit Composition of Sauvignon Blanc Grapevines," *American Journal of Enology and Viticulture,* Vol. 39, 1988, pp. 49-54.

22 A chemist would not classify sulfur as organic because it does not contain carbon.

23 Flaherty, D. L., C. D. Lynn, F. L. Jensen and M. A. Hoy, "Correcting Imbalances — Spider Mite Populations in Southern San Joaquin Vineyards," *California Agriculture,* Vol. 26, 1972, pp. 10-12.

24 Flaherty, D. L., C. D. Lynn, F. L. Jensen and M. A. Hoy, "Influence of Environment and Cultural Practices on Spider Mite Abundance in Southern San Joaquin Valley Thompson Seedless Vineyards," *California Agriculture,* Vol. 25, 1971, pp. 6-8.

25 Jensen, F. L., A. N. Kasimatis, H. Kido and W. J. Moller, GRAPE PEST MANAGEMENT, Publication No. 4105, Division of Agricultural Sciences, University of California, Davis, CA, 1981, p. 312.

26 MacCannell, D., "Industrial Agriculture and Rural Community Degradation," AGRICULTURE AND COM-MUNITY CHANGE IN THE U.S. THE CONGRES-SIONAL RESEARCH REPORTS, L. Swanson, ed., Westview Press, Boulder, CO, 1988, p. 355.

27 Weber, E., J. Wolpert, K. Klonsky and J. Du Bruille, SAMPLE COST TO ESTABLISH AND PRODUCE WINE GRAPES IN NAPA VALLEY, University of California Cooperative Extension, 1989, p. 9.

28 Anonymous, FINAL GRAPE CRUSH REPORT 1990 CROP, California Department of Food and Agriculture, 1991, Sacramento, CA.

29 Laube, J., "The Roots of Greatness," *Wine Spectator,* December, 1985, pp. 1-15.

30 Young, A., CHARDONNAY, YOUR INTERNA-TIONAL GUIDE, 1991, Napa, CA.

31 Lyon, R., VINE TO WINE, 1985, Napa, CA.

12

SHOWING WHAT YOU KNOW WITH YOUR NOSE
Review Tastings

Well, here we are at the "final examination," the time we all dreaded in school because we had huge piles of information that we could no longer avoid coming to terms with. The time to review, sum up, and put it all together had arrived. Although I didn't look forward to finals any more than any other student, once I got over bemoaning my fate — if it weren't for finals I could be skiing, Christmas shopping, sunbathing, or otherwise leading a normal existence — and got involved with the task of looking over a large body of material, to put my own stamp of organization on it or see the teacher's overall organization for the first time, I really did discover new insights, understand some things I'd not grasped before, and — though I would never have admitted this to my fellow sufferers — truly did benefit from the time spent preparing for those comprehensive exams. It is, of course, my hope that these two exercises will give you the chance to capture your own fresh insights and understandings as you review the text and your tasting notes in preparation for the last two Sensory Evaluation Exercises: The Mystery Wine Identification and Zinorama.

SENSORY EVALUATION EXERCISE 12.1
Mystery Wine Identification

Objective: This exercise will give you a chance to find out how much you have learned about describing the sensory properties of wines and to try your skills at wine identification.

What to Do Before This Exercise: To prepare yourself to determine which of the wines you have tasted are presented in this exercise, you will want to pull together all the information from the other Mystery Wine Identification exercises into one big sorting system for all the wines you have tasted. Use the worksheet for the Mystery Wine Identification. You will probably find, as you are creating this sorting system for all the wines you have tasted, that you will reach a point when you will direct yourself to, for example, "go to the worksheet for the white or red table wine, sparkling or dessert wine review tasting" rather that to go to a step on this worksheet. After you get your key done, it may look something like Table 2.2, the Organoleptic Classification of Wines. There is a sample worksheet for a key to the mystery wines on pp. 382-383.

Worksheet for the Mystery Wine Identification

Step #1. sensory factor: _____
    if _____ , the variety is _____ or go to step _____
    if _____ , go to step _____

Step #2. sensory factor: _____
    if _____ , the variety is _____ or go to step _____
    if _____ , go to step _____

Step #3. sensory factor: _____
    if _____ , the variety is _____ or go to step _____
    if _____ , go to step _____

Step #4. sensory factor: _____
    if _____ , the variety is _____ or go to step _____
    if _____ , go to step _____

Step #5. sensory factor: _____
    if _____ , the variety is _____ or go to step _____
    if _____ , go to step _____

Step #6. sensory factor: _____
    if _____ , the variety is _____ or go to step _____
    if _____ , go to step #7

Step #7. sensory factor: _____
    if _____ , the variety is _____
    if _____ , the variety is _____

Instructions:

1. Work alone and silently. The taster who has the greatest tendency to talk may not have the best palate and can throw everyone off. You certainly don't want this to be you!
2. Make a sensory analysis of each wine presented.
   You will probably find it most effective to work in the following way:
   A. Observe the color and appearance of all the wines.
   B. Smell each wine, but do not taste it until you have smelled all the wines and made notes on them.
   C. Taste each wine, making notes but not swallowing the wine.
   D. Record your observations.
   E. Refer to the notes you made on your Worksheet for the Mystery Wine Identification and during the preceding Sensory Evaluation Exercises and match your observations about each mystery wine with the notes you took earlier.
   F. Be sure to interrupt this process to write down the name of a wine or (wines) whenever you have an "AHA !" insight about its identity.
3. Report your results. For example: I think wine A is #6, a Chardonnay made with no oak aging; I'm sure wine B is #3, a Gewürztraminer; I'm positive wine C is #14 and #28 and #35 and #40; etc. (Numbers refer to the list of possible identities of the mysterious wines.)

Possible Identities of the Mysterious Wines

1. Chenin Blanc _____
2. White Riesling — Early Harvest _____
3. Gewürztraminer _____
4. Sauvignon Blanc — Early Harvest _____
5. Chardonnay — oak-aged _____
6. Chardonnay — no oak _____
7. Pinot Noir _____
8. Gamay Beaujolais _____
9. Zinfandel _____
10. Syrah _____
11. Merlot _____
12. Cabernet Franc _____
13. Cabernet Sauvignon — recent vintage _____
14. Cabernet Sauvignon — older vintage, bottle-aged _____
15. Sparkling Wine — Blanc de Blancs — Méthode Champenoise _____
16. Sparkling Wine — Blanc de Blancs — Charmat Process _____
17. Sparkling Wine — Blanc de Noirs — Méthode Champenoise _____
18. Sparkling Wine — Doux or Demi-Sec _____
19. Select Late-Harvest, *Botrytis*-Affected White Riesling _____
20. Select Late-Harvest, *Botrytis*-Affected Sauvignon Blanc _____
21. Orange Muscat Dessert Wine _____
22. Black Muscat Dessert Wine _____
23. Port _____
24. Cream Sherry _____
25. White Base Wine _____
26. Red Base Wine _____

More Questions to Answer

Which is:

27. The youngest red wine _____
28. The oldest wine _____
29. The sweetest wine _____
30. The wine with the most tannins _____
31. The white wine with the same residual sugar as the red wines _____
32. The white wine that would go well with more kinds of foods _____
33. The red wine with the most aging potential _____
34. The red wine with the most aroma _____
35. The wine with the most bouquet _____
36. The wine with the darkest color _____
37. The wine with the most bubbles _____
38. The wine with the most alcohol _____
39. The Sauternes-style late-harvest wine _____
40. The wine you want for your birthday _____

Sensory Evaluation Exercise 12.1.
Mystery Wine Identification

WINE INFO	WINE A: Observations	WINE B: Observations	WINE C: Observations	WINE D: Observations
Type Vintage Appellation Producer Cost/Other				
Clarity				
Color				
Off Odors				

Aroma
  Associations
  Descriptors
  Intensity
  Varietal?				

Bouquet				
Flavor				
Acid, Sugar, Balance				
Body				
Astringency				
Aging Potential				
I think this wine might be				

Questions raised by this tasting;

Sensory Evaluation Exercise 12.1.
Mystery Wine Identification

WINE INFO	WINE E: Observations	WINE F: Observations	WINE G: Observations	WINE H: Observations
Type				
Vintage				
Appellation				
Producer				
Cost/Other				
Clarity				
Color				
Off Odors				
Aroma				
Associations				
Descriptors				
Intensity				
Varietal?				
Bouquet				
Flavor				
Acid, Sugar, Balance				
Body				
Astringency				
Aging Potential				
I think this wine might be . . .				

Questions raised by this tasting:

SENSORY EVALUATION EXERCISE 12.2
A "Zinorama" — Tasting Zinfandels from White to Port

Objectives: In this exercise you will become acquainted with the range of wine types that can be made from Zinfandel grapes. You will also learn to relate the sensory impressions of these wines to how they were made.

What to Do Before This Exercise: To refresh your memory of the different procedures used for making various types of wine, review each of the wine production chapters and complete the worksheet: Your Summary of Winemaking Procedures.

Instructions:
1. Taste each Zinfandel wine, making notes as usual about your observations.
2. Relate your sensory observations to the winemaking procedure used to create them.
3. Summarize your observations by checking off the winemaking procedures needed to make each wine on the Checklist of Winemaking Procedures that follows the sensory evaluation forms. Note any procedures that were omitted from the summary in the margin next to item #39, "anything else"?
4. If you find questions coming up as you taste, record them here:

_____
_____
_____
_____
_____
_____
_____
_____
_____
_____
_____
_____
_____
_____
_____
_____
_____
_____
_____
_____
_____
_____

Sensory Evaluation Exercise 12.2 — Your Summary of Winemaking Procedures

Winemaking Steps	White Table	Sparkling	Red Table
Grape growing region			
Grape varieties			
Special viticultural practices			
Harvest maturity			
Crush and press			
Fermentation temperature			
Other fermentation management			
Clarification & stabilization			
Age in bulk, in oak?			
Bottling — sterile?			
Bottle aging — how long			
Other special processes or factors			
Total time to complete			

Sensory Evaluation Exercise 12.2 — Your Summary of Winemaking Procedures, Continued

Winemaking Steps	Carbonic Maceration	*Botrytis*-Affected	Fortified Dessert
Grape-growing region			
Grape varieties			
Special viticultural practices			
Harvest maturity			
Crush and press			
Fermentation temperature			
Other fermentation management			
Clarification & stabilization			
Age in bulk, in oak?			
Bottling — sterile?			
Bottle aging — how long?			
Other special processes or factors			
Total time to complete			

Sensory Evaluation Exercise 12.2.
A "Zinorama" — Zinfandels from White to Port

WINE INFO	WINE A: Observations	WINE A: Winemaking Deductions	WINE B: Observations	WINE B: Winemaking Deductions
Type				
Vintage				
Appellation				
Producer				
Cost/Other				
Clarity				
Color				
Off Odors				
Aroma				
Associations				
Descriptors				
Intensity				
Varietal?				
Bouquet				
Flavor				
Acid, Sugar, Balance				
Body				
Astringency				
Aging Potential				

Sensory Evaluation Exercise 12.2.
A "Zinorama" — Zinfandels from White to Port

WINE INFO Type Vintage Appellation Producer Cost/Other	WINE C: Observations	WINE C: Winemaking Deductions	WINE D: Observations	WINE D: Winemaking Deductic
Clarity				
Color				
Off Odors				
Aroma Associations Descriptors Intensity Varietal?				
Bouquet				
Flavor				
Acid, Sugar, Balance				
Body				
Astringency				
Aging Potential				

Sensory Evaluation Exercise 12.2.
A "Zinorama" — Zinfandels from White to Port

WINE INFO	WINE E: Observations	WINE E: Winemaking Deductions	Additional Observations	Additional Observations
Type Vintage Appellation Producer Cost/Other				
Clarity				
Color				
Off Odors				
Aroma Associations Descriptors Intensity Varietal?				
Bouquet				
Flavor				
Acid, Sugar, Balance				
Body				
Astringency				
Aging Potential				

Sensory Evaluation Exercise 12.2 — Checklist of Winemaking Procedures

Wines					Winemaking Procedures
A	B	C	D	E	
					1. harvest at 14-15 degrees Brix
					2. harvest at 17-19 degrees Brix
					3. harvest at 21-23 degrees Brix
					4. harvest at 22-24 degrees Brix
					5. prefer grapes from Region I
					6. prefer grapes from Regions I and II
					7. prefer grapes from Regions II and III
					8. prefer grapes from Region IV
					9. prefer shrivelled, moldy grapes
					10. crush grapes as soon as possible after harvest
					11. macerate whole grapes in field gondolas for 1-2 days
					12. press without crushing
					13. press immediately after crushing
					14. crush, chill must, allow skin contact before pressing
					15. ferment immediately after crushing
					16. ferment clarified juice
					17. add yeast, ferment at 55 degrees F
					18. add yeast, ferment at 60-90 degrees F
					19. add wine spirits during fermentation
					20. draw juice and press at 1-5 degrees Brix
					21. draw juice and press at 12-14 degrees Brix
					22. draw juice and press after 12-24 hours of fermentation
					23. ferment to dryness
					24. stop fermentation with some residual sugar remaining
					25. make sure the malolactic fermentation is complete
					26. must be cold stable
					27. must be heat stable
					28. must be microbiologically stable
					29. age in stainless steel tanks
					30. age in small oak hogsheads
					31. age on old, neutral oak cooperage
					32. sterile bottling is absolutely necessary
					33. sterile bottling is not necessary
					34. process takes 6-8 weeks
					35. process takes about 3 months
					36. process takes about 18 months
					37. process takes more than 18 months
					38. wines age in the bottle at the winery

39. anything else?

Appendix A

A QUICK REFERENCE GUIDE TO VARIETAL WINES

This quick reference guide contains an informational profile for each varietal wine used in the sensory evaluation exercises. Each profile contains grape and wine information: descriptions of key viticultural characteristics of the variety, recent data on California production of grapes and wine, wine aroma and flavor descriptions, typical styles, and the number of U.S. producers, if available. I've included pronunciation suggestions for varietal wine names and key foreign terms in the Glossary.

Key viticultural characteristics are included in the varietal wine profiles because they can significantly influence the styles of wine that can be made. For example, White Riesling and Sauvignon Blanc are both susceptible to *Botrytis cinerea* and this enables them to be made into elegant, rich, naturally sweet dessert wines. The time of maturation — early-, mid-, or late-season — tells us approximately when to expect the variety to be ready for harvest and is a factor in matching grape variety and vineyard climate. Often the earliest-maturing varieties — Pinot Noir and Chardonnay, for example — perform better in the coolest climates, while later-maturing varieties such as Cabernet Sauvignon can be grown successfully in warmer areas.[1]

The information described below is intended to enable you to put the production and utilization data for each profiled grape variety into perspective within California's wine scene. All statistical information has been rounded off for the sake of simplicity.

CALIFORNIA GRAPE ACREAGE

Each varietal wine profile gives recent acreage figures for that variety in California. In 1990 there were 694,000 acres — about 1,000 square miles — of California grapes, an expanse slightly larger than the area of the state of Rhode Island and about 10% larger than the Grand Duchy of Luxembourg.[2] Wine grapes represent about 48% of California's total grape acreage, with raisin and table grapes accounting for 40 and 12% respectively. Raisin and table grapes can be crushed for wine, and when the demand for ordinary wines is high or when the yield of wine grapes has been lowered by a natural disaster, they can constitute a higher percentage of the grape crush than the 17% they contributed in 1990.

The Thompson Seedless variety is California's most commonly planted and most versatile grape, with 261,000 acres of vines bearing fruit in 1990. It is the state's number one raisin variety, a leading table grape variety, and the most likely non-wine grape variety to be crushed for wine.

Table A.1
California Grape Acreage, Selected Recent Statistics [3]

	Total Acres	Percent Bearing Fruit
All Grapes	694,000	92
Wine Grapes	330,400	88
Red Wine Grapes	151,000	85
Zinfandel	34,000	82
Cabernet Sauvignon	33,000	73
White Wine Grapes	180,000	90
French Colombard	59,000	100
Chardonnay	52,000	72
Chenin Blanc	33,000	100

Among wine grapes, French Colombard, the backbone of hot-region Chablis and inexpensive sparkling wines, is the most widely planted, with Chardonnay a close second. In terms of acreage planted, the most important red wine grapes are Zinfandel and Cabernet Sauvignon.

CALIFORNIA GRAPE ACREAGE TRENDS

From 1969 to 1974 California wine grape acreage experienced a 118% growth boom, reaching a total of 328,000 acres in 1975, with 96,000 acres yet to bear fruit. (Grapevines will not bear a commercial size crop for two to five years after they are planted or grafted in the field and for statistical purposes are considered "non-bearing" for three years.) During the 1980s premium wine grape acreage continued to increase moderately, with a 55% increase in white-wine grapes and a 40% increase in red-wine varieties from 1981 to 1990. A 175% increase in Chardonnay acreage during the same period reflects the growth in popularity of that wine, while an increase of 60% for Sauvignon Blanc mirrors a rising demand for the ingredients of everyone's favorite Chardonnay alternative. Growth was not as dramatic among the major premium red varietal grapes, but Cabernet Sauvignon, Cabernet Franc, Merlot, Malbec, Zinfandel, and Syrah were all planted at rates well above the average 40% increase for other red wine varieties. Pinot Noir acreage, for example, increased 39%, while the acreage of Gamay, Gamay Beaujolais, and Petite Sirah and non-premium red varieties did not rise.

A GLIMPSE INTO THE (NEAR) FUTURE

To get an idea of how grape growers are reading trends in the market for California wines, we can look for the varieties with a significant proportion of non-bearing acreage (vines planted within the past three years). In Table A.1 we can see that there have been virtually no new plantings of French Colombard or Chenin Blanc recently, while about one-fourth of both the Chardonnay and Cabernet Sauvignon acreage was non-bearing in 1990. This reflects the relative strength of the premium varietal wine market and the weakness of the "jug" wine market in the late 1980s.[4] Chardonnay leads the state in the number of non-bearing acres with 15,000, followed by Cabernet Sauvignon, Zinfandel, and Merlot as shown in Figure A.1.

Other varieties with significant non-bearing acreage are: Grenache (1,200 of 13,600), Cabernet Franc (490 of 1,600), Pinot Noir (1,000 of 9,500), and Sauvignon Blanc (836 of 13,400). The plantings of Grenache and Zin-fandel reflect the growth of the blush varietal wine market. Cabernet Franc and Merlot are valuable blending wines for Cabernet Sauvignon and are used in another strong area of the current wine market: ultra-premium red wines such as Reserve Cabernet Sauvignons and Meritage blends. Pinot Noir is of interest in three market categories: blush varietal wines; a premium varietal table wine in which there is a lot of current interest; and for méthode champenoise sparkling wine production by a growing number of new, often European-owned houses. Some grape growers are banking on an expanding market for Sauvignon Blanc, as more wine drinkers are switching from expensive Chardonnays and less interesting White Zinfandels.

Apart from the market forces that influence planting decisions, the renewed phylloxera threat in California requires that vineyards be replanted on phylloxera-resistant rootstocks. This is already being reflected in non-bearing acreage statistics and will continue to be a force driving new plantings at least through the year 2000.

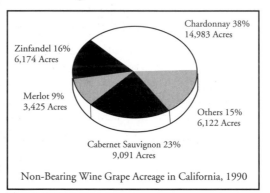

Non-Bearing Wine Grape Acreage in California, 1990

Chardonnay 38%
14,983 Acres

Zinfandel 16%
6,174 Acres

Merlot 9%
3,425 Acres

Others 15%
6,122 Acres

Cabernet Sauvignon 23%
9,091 Acres

Figure A.1
Wine Variety Acreage Coming On-Line in California
Source: California Department of Agriculture

WINE PRODUCTION — CALIFORNIA'S CRUSH STATISTICS

The "crush" refers both to the time in the autumn when wine grapes are harvested — as in "The crush was really late and long this year because of the cool summer and fall weather" — and to the common first winemaking step in which the grapes are broken, starting their conversion into wine. Table A.2 presents some excerpts from the 1990 crush report for California and Figure A.2 graphically presents the leading varieties crushed in 1990.

	Tons Crushed x 1000	Percent of Crush Volume	Average Price Per Ton
All Grapes	2,570	100	$280
Non-Wine Grapes	435	17	126
Thompson Seedless	226	9	124
Wine Grapes	2,135	83	306
White-Wine Grapes	1,330	52	277
French Colombard	685	27	143
Chenin Blanc	276	11	183
Chardonnay	170	7	1,128
Red-Wine Grapes	804	31	357
Zinfandel	185	7	391
Grenache	113	4	185
Cabernet Sauvignon	94	4	977

The 1990 crush was around two and one-half million tons, which is about average for the last decade and 17% less than the record 3.1 million ton crush of 1982. The size of the crush is influenced most significantly by weather and market factors: an April cold snap or a heat wave during pollination can drastically reduce the size of the crop, while optimal weather can make for a larger-than-average harvest. An increasing — or, as is the case now, decreasing — demand for ordinary jug wines determines how many tons of non-wine grapes are crushed.

In terms of quantity processed, French Colombard dominated the crush, comprising 27% of its volume, followed by Chenin Blanc at 11%. The premium white varieties — Chardonnay, Sauvignon Blanc, Gewürztraminer, and White Riesling — made up 22% of the white-wine grape crush and 11% of all grapes crushed. The coastal counties of Napa, Sonoma, and Monterey accounted for about 30% of the red- and white wine grapes crushed, and grapes produced in Napa County commanded the highest average price per ton, $1,241. The overall average price per ton of grapes for crushing was $280 in 1990, off 8% from 1989's

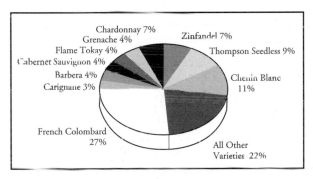

record high price but higher than the average price per ton for any other year since 1981. The most expensive grape varieties in 1990 were three relatively rare varieties that are used to blend with Cabernet Sauvignon: Petite Verdot, Cabernet Franc, and Merlot, which sold for averages of $1,406, $1,298, and $1,220 per ton respectively.

AN INTERNATIONAL PERSPECTIVE

During this discussion of how big, how much, and how many, you may have been wondering where California and the U.S. rank in wine production internationally. Preliminary data for the year 1989 for the top eleven — yes, eleven, I wanted to squeeze in Australia — wine-producing nations in the world is reproduced in Table A.3. As you can see, the U.S. ranks sixth in the world in the amount of wine produced, a position it has maintained for at least two decades. California is responsible for 85-90% of U.S. wine production, making its output comparable to that of West Germany. Depending on the weather in each country, this international ranking can vary somewhat from year to year; for example, France and Italy routinely swap positions for the top ranking, with Italy edging out France in six of the last ten years.

Country	Production, Million Gallons
France	1607
Italy	1580
Spain	765
Soviet Union	560
Argentina	537
United States	411
West Germany	349
Romania	264
South Africa	256
Portugal	203
Australia	132

THE VARIETAL PROFILES
Sources of Wine Information

The aroma and flavor descriptors and typical wine styles mentioned in the varietal wine profiles have been collected from a variety of publications on sensory evaluation as well as from my experience in the classroom.[7] An estimate of the number of wineries in the United States that produce specific varietal wines is given in some of the profiles. The source of this information is a survey conducted every two years by *Wines and Vines* magazine of the approximately 1200 wineries in the U.S.; the information in the varietal wine profiles is from the September 1990 issue.[8]

Varietal Wine Profile: CABERNET SAUVIGNON
Grape Information

Description: Small blue-black berries that taste "peppery" or "weedy"; small clusters; growth is vigorous; grows well on moderately fertile soils; bud break is late; tough-skinned berries resist rain damage and disease.

Yields:	Relatively low, 3-5 tons/acre.
Maturity:	Late (mid-October to early November).
Preferred Climate:	Cool to warm.
1990 Data:	33,200 acres (9,100 non-bearing); 94,000 tons crushed — or about 12% of the red-wine grape crush; $977/ton average price.

Other Important Growing Regions: Cabernet Sauvignon is the most important grape variety in the world because it is the primary ingredient in the most famous red wines in the world — the fine, long-aging clarets made by the Châteaux of Bordeaux's Médoc. These wines have long been recognized for their quality and are the standard to which the red wines of other regions — new and established — are compared. Cabernet Sauvignon vineyards are established throughout the world in wine regions that are seeking to improve the quality of their red wines. In the 1980s it was the most widely planted premium wine grape, with an estimated 324,000 acres worldwide. Chile, France, Russia, and Bulgaria were the top-ranking Cabernet nations in terms of acreage.[9] Notable Cabernet Sauvignons have been produced in California, Spain, Italy, South Africa, and Australia, while those made in New Zealand, South America, and Eastern Europe have been of lesser quality.

Wine Information

Aroma and Flavor Descriptors: Berry, black currant, cassis, herbaceous or vegetative (bell pepper, green bean, olives), mint, black pepper.

Typical Styles: Rich, complex, highly tannic wines that need barrel and bottle aging and are normally blended with Merlot and Cabernet Franc to quicken the aging process. White, blush, and lighter styles are not typical.

Aging Potential: Long for the best examples (10-20 or more years).

Number of U.S. Producers: 466 in 1990, making Cabernet Sauvignon the second most frequently produced varietal wine after Chardonnay and the most frequently produced red table wine.

Varietal Wine Profile: CHARDONNAY
Grape Information

Description: Small berries and clusters; vigorous and adaptable to many soils; there are many clones, some of which are virus-infected; very early spring growth means potential frost damage problems. "The best wine grape in California" — Hugh Johnson.[10]

Yields:	Production variable: 2-5 tons/acre.
Maturity:	Very early.
Preferred Climate:	Cool.
1990 Data:	52,200 (15,000 non-bearing) acres = 29% of California's white-wine grape acreage; 169,700 tons crushed; $1,128/ton average price.

Other Important Growing Regions: Chardonnay originated in France, where it is blended to make Champagnes and used to produce excellent oak-aged, rich, dry white wines in the Burgundy district, which includes the Chablis region whose wines are often more tart and lighter bodied. Chardonnay is very popular internationally and is vinified successfully in Italy's northern districts, as well as in Spain and Eastern Europe. Outside Europe it has performed well in Washington, Oregon, the Eastern U.S., South Africa, New Zealand, and Australia.

Wine Information

Aroma and Flavor Descriptors: Because it is often aged in oak, it is difficult to pinpoint the varietal aroma characteristics of Chardonnay. Descriptions heard around the tasting table are fruity (apple, peach, citrus, pineapple), ripe grape, and fig, along with the bouquet terms vanilla (from oak aging) and buttery (from the malolactic fermentation).

Typical Styles: Dry wines of rich complexity, and intensity; the white wine most likely to be fermented and/or aged in small oak cooperage; cooler growing regions produce wines with greater finesse and aging potential; wines, especially White Burgundies, acquire great complexity with bottle age.

Aging Potential: 5-6 years or more.

Number of U.S. Producers: 586 in 1990, making Chardonnay the most commonly produced wine in the U.S.

Varietal Wine Profile: CHENIN BLANC
Grape Information

Description: Also called Pineau de la Loire; medium-size, tough-skinned berries; medium-size clusters, which can be tight and susceptible to rot; berries vary in color from green to straw yellow; can be very vigorous; adapted to a range of soil types.

Yields:	Consistently 5-8 tons/acre in coastal areas and 9-12 tons/acre in the Central Valley.
Maturity:	August to mid-October.
Preferred Climate:	Cool preferred for better acid balance.
1990 Data:	32,900 acres (300 non-bearing); 276,400 tons crushed; $183/ton average price.

Other Important Growing Regions: Middle Loire (Anjou-Touraine) region of France, where it is used to produce dry and naturally sweet table wines and sparkling wines. It has been very successful in South Africa as well and is also grown in Australia and New Zealand.

Wine Information

Aroma and Flavor Descriptors: Chenin Blanc wines are moderately distinct, with aromas that are less easily characterized than those of White Riesling or Sauvignon Blanc, for example; they are described as having odors of pears, melons, or peaches.

Typical Styles: Commonly made with low residual sugar; a few, usually smaller North Coast producers in California make a dry style which may be aged briefly in oak.

A Note: Jancis Robinson considers Chenin Blanc to be "One of the world's undervalued treasures."[11]

Aging Potential: 2-5 years.
Number of U.S. Producers: 137 in 1990.

Varietal Wine Profile: GAMAY (Napa Gamay)
Grape Information

Description: Large black berries form medium to large clusters, to distinguish this variety from Gamay Beaujolais; medium in vigor and adaptable; leafs out late in spring, so there is less potential for frost damage.

Yields:	5-7 tons/acre on the coast, more in the Central Valley.
Maturity:	Late (mid-October to November).

Preferred Climate: From cool to warm and hot, depending on the style desired and market targeted, from varietal- to jug-wine makers.

1990 Data: 1541 acres (24 non-bearing); 9,000 tons crushed, $418/ton average price.

Other Important Growing Regions: Gamay makes up 98% of the vines in France's Beaujolais area and is also planted in Burgundy and the Loire; there are 85,000 acres in the country as a whole, making it the sixth most widely grown variety in France. Beaujolais is France's most popular wine.[12]

Wine Information

Aroma and Flavor Descriptors: Simple, sometimes intensely fruity wines.

Typical Styles: Modeled on those produced in the Beaujolais region of France, where the Gamay grape produces refreshing fruity wines for early consumption or is used for rosé wines. Beaujolais wines are light purple, high in acid, and low in tannin. Carbonic maceration is used to emphasize the fruity character and bring the wines to market swiftly, usually within four to six weeks of the harvest, the so-called "Nouveaux" style.

Aging Potential: Very limited (1-2 years). Drink the youngest available.

Number of U.S. Producers: 18 in 1990.

Varietal Wine Profile: GEWÜRZTRAMINER
Grape Information

Description: Small, pink to reddish-brown, thick-skinned berries with typical spicy flavor; the most pungent wine grape. Small clusters; one of the earliest varieties to mature; timing of the harvest is tricky because maximum varietal character may be achieved at relatively low sugar and high acid levels.

Yields: Low, 2-4 tons/acre.

Maturity: Very early.

Preferred Climate: Coolest.

1990 Data: 1900 (20 non-bearing) acres; 7,500 tons crushed; $598/ton average price.

Other Important Growing Regions: A very important variety in Alsace, France, where 6,250 acres are planted. Small amounts are found in Germany, Austria, and Italy's Tyrol. Cooler non-European areas such as Oregon, Washington, and New Zealand have also had success with this variety.

Wine Information

Aroma and Flavor Descriptors: The fruit odor is the same as the wine aroma, which is unusual. The word Gewürz means "spicy," and this has stuck as an appropriate description for the wine's aroma even though no particular spice gives a satisfactory description of the wine. Terms used by winetasters to describe Gewürztraminer include: spicy, floral (rose petals), fruity (citrus, grapefruit, peach), lychee, cold cream, honey, jasmine tea. Muscat and Riesling have related aromas. When well-made, it is intense and distinctive.

Typical Styles: Dry to sweet; Gewürztraminers seem soft and rich even when dry. Occasionally *Botrytis*-affected Gewürztraminers are produced.

Aging Potential: 3-5 years.

Number of U.S. Producers: 169 in 1990, down from 177 in 1988 and 207 in 1986. (Maybe the name is too hard to pronounce?)

Varietal Wine Profile: MERLOT
Grape Information

Description: Reddish-black berries form medium-size clusters; relatively early budbreak and flowering; vigorous growth; does not stand rains well before harvest; susceptible to molds.

Yields: Production variable from year to year and vine to vine — about 3-6 tons/acre, but can be higher.

Maturity: Mid-season (before Cabernet Sauvignon).

Preferred Climate: Cool to warm.

1990 Data: 7,400 acres (3,400 non-bearing), 15,200 tons crushed; $1,220/ton average price.

Other Important Growing Regions: "One of the world's great underdogs" — Jancis Robinson.[13] Makes excellent wines in the St. Emilion and Pomerol districts of Bordeaux; Château Pétrus is the best-known producer. Merlot is the second most widely planted premium red-grape variety worldwide, with an estimated 216,000 total acres. France has 91,000 acres, which is more than double the amount in Italy, the second-ranking Merlot nation in the 1980s.[14] Merlot is also widely planted in eastern Europe. In the U.S., Washington state seems to be an ideal home for this variety.

Wine Information

Aroma and Flavor Descriptors: Fruit and floral, red cherry, plums.

Typical Styles: Supple and lower in tannins, Merlot plays a key role in California's Red Meritage (rhymes with heritage) blends. Christian Mouiex of Château Pétrus has been making a Merlot blend — Dominus — in the Napa Valley and his presence has spurred interest in Merlot in California.

Aging Potential: Less than Cabernet Sauvignon (5 to 10 years).

Number of U.S. Producers: 199 in 1990.

Varietal Wine Profile: MUSCAT BLANC

Grape Information

Description: Also called Muscat Canelli and Muscat Frontignan; medium-size berries and clusters; berries yellow with delicate Muscat flavor; weak to average vigor; need fertile soils.

Yields: Low, 2-4 tons/acre. Susceptible to raisining.

Maturity: Mid-September to October.

Preferred Climate: Cool for dry wines, warm also okay for dessert wines.

1990 Data: 1350 acres (20 non-bearing); 9000 tons crushed; $306/ton average price.

Other Important Growing Regions: Southern France (Muscatels) and Northern Italy (Asti Spumante Sparkling Wine) have about 7,500 acres each. Small amounts are grown in Germany, Hungary, Greece, Australia, South Africa, and Argentina. Muscat Blanc vines are thought to be among the oldest known.[15]

Wine Information

Aroma and Flavor Descriptors: Muscat wines have an intense floral/fruity odor.

Typical Styles: The original style of Muscat varietal wines was a fortified dessert wine. Recently, lower alcohol table wines finished dry or sweet (6-10% residual sugar) have become popular.

Aging Potential: 2-5 years.

Number of U.S. Producers: 53 in 1990.

Varietal Wine Profile: PINOT NOIR

Grape Information

Description: Thought to be one of the first cultivated varieties, it was described by Pliny and Columella in the first century AD; it is highly mutable, producing many clones and closely related varieties, including Gamay Beaujolais, Pinot Gris, and Pinot Blanc; small, blue-black, thin-skinned berries in small clusters; moderate vigor with early spring budbreak; virus infections can produce low color; susceptibility to *Botrytis* and bird damage are problems.

Yields: Low, 2-4 tons/acre.

Maturity: Early (late August to early September).

Preferred Climate: Coolest.

1990 Data: 9,500 acres (1000 non-bearing), 32,300 tons crushed; $846/ton average price. Figures for the Pinot Noir clone Gamay Beaujolais are 1400 (0), 5,600 and $550 respectively.

Other Important Growing Regions: There are 42,500 acres of Pinot Noir in France, where it makes up 70% of the vines in the Côte d'Or (14,250 acres), and it is used for these and other highly esteemed French red Burgundies. It is also grown for fine French Champagnes. It produces only ordinary wines in Germany and northern Italy, but the cooler districts of Australia, California, and Oregon have produced some fine Pinot Noirs.[16]

Wine Information

Aroma and Flavor Descriptors: Pinot Noir has no single recognizable flavor. Aroma descriptors include intense fresh berry (strawberry, raspberry, black currant), berry jam (strawberry, raspberry, blackberry), cherry, spicy (black pepper, cloves), with vegetal (green tea), leather, smoke/tar, peppermint, and cherry also found; bottle bouquet suggests violets, game, or truffles.[17]

Typical Styles: No typical styles. Many boring low-color, low-tannin wines with little character have given California Pinot Noirs a poor reputation. Fine California Pinot Noirs are becoming more common, however, especially from cool regions such as Carneros.

Aging Potential: 5-10 years for better wines.

Number of U.S. Producers: 241 (29 for Gamay Beaujolais) in 1990.

Varietal Wine Profile: SAUVIGNON BLANC
Grape Information

Description: Small clusters; medium-large, greenish berries with tender skin and aromatic flavor; very vigorous; yields can be lower on irrigated, fertile soils (2-3 tons per acre) than in conditions which favor less leaf growth and have proper trellising (4-6 tons per acre); spring frost can be a problem; susceptible to *Botrytis* rots.

Yields:	Variable, 2-6 tons/acre.
Maturity:	Early to mid-September.
Preferred Climate:	Cooler to warm.
1990 Data:	13,400 acres (800 non-bearing); 60,000 tons crushed; $518/ton average price.

Other Important Growing Regions: Sauvignon Blanc is well-known both in the Sauternes region of Bordeaux, France, where *Botrytis* infection can produce fine late-harvest dessert wines, and in the Loire districts of Sancerre and Pouilly-sûr-Loire, where the wines are usually dry. It is also grown in northern Italy, eastern Europe, Argentina, South Africa, New Zealand, and Australia.

Wine Information

Aroma and Flavor Descriptors: Sauvignon Blanc is described as floral, fruity (citrus, peach, apricot) to vegetative (bell pepper, asparagus), green olive/herbaceous, smoky.

Typical Styles: The name Fumé Blanc is used for dry California Sauvignon Blancs; current styles emphasize fruity rather than herbaceous character; leaf removal in the vineyard reduces herbaceous aromas (and *Botrytis* rot); some oak fermentation aging; blends with Sémillon.

Aging potential: 3-5 years or more. Seems less fruity and tart as it ages.

Number of U.S. Producers: 296 in 1990.

Varietal Wine Profile: SYRAH
Grape Information

Description: Also called Shiraz in Australia; small, oval-shaped berries; well-filled, cylindrical clusters; vigorous and performs well on poor soils; overall disease resistance good, but sensitive to *Botrytis;* canes subject to wind damage. There are several clones of Syrah grown in California, which were imported from different sources in France and at different times.

Yields:	For quality wines, must be low — about 3-4 tons/acre.
Maturity:	Mid-season.
Preferred Climate:	Cool to warm.
1990 Data:	344 acres (200 non-bearing); 586 tons crushed; $931/ton average price.

Other Important Growing Regions: Syrah may be the original grape variety imported to the Mediterranean from the Middle East, perhaps having been brought to Marseilles from Shiraz by the Phocaeans. It is known that Syrah was well-established in the Rhône by Roman times.[18] In Hermitage and Côte Rôtie in the northern Rhône Valley of France, Syrah is made into wines that rival the best Bordeaux clarets and red Burgundies; it has been planted extensively in the Midi to improve the wines of this area. Shiraz is the most important red-grape variety in Australia, where it makes up 40% of red-wine grape plantings and is blended with Cabernet Sauvignon.

Wine Information

Aroma and Flavor Descriptors: Intense blackberry, cassis, black pepper, violets, smoke, and tar.

Typical Styles: The wines are dark, dense, tannic, and capable of maturing for many years.

Number of U.S. Producers: A handful. There are a few grape growers and winemakers in California who are interested in Syrah and I think their work may bring another fine wine grape to prominence. Watch for the Syrahs of Joseph Phelps, Estrella River, Duxoup, Preston, McDowell Valley, and Bonny Doon.

Note: Syrah should not be confused with Petite Sirah, which is a different variety: higher-yielding, undistinguished, and probably the same as France's Durif, a variety which is not grown in the Rhône.[19] Petite Sirah is widely grown in California (3,072 acres in 1990) and makes a dark, tannic blending wine. There were 65 producers of Petite Sirah in 1990.

Varietal Wine Profile: WHITE RIESLING

Grape Information

Description: May also be called "Johannisberg Riesling" in California; greenish-yellow berries with aromatic flavor; small clusters; susceptible to *Botrytis cinerea* rots.

Yields:	Moderate, 4-6 tons/acre.
Maturity:	Mid- to late September.
Preferred Climate:	Coolest.
1990 Data:	5,000 acres (33 non-bearing); 20,000 tons crushed; $502/ton average price.

Other Important Growing Regions: This variety predominates in the best vineyards of the Rhine and Mosel valleys of Germany; all of Germany's greatest wines are made from White Riesling. It is also important in the Alsace district of France, Italy's Alto Adige, the Eastern U.S., Australia, and New Zealand.

Wine Information

Aroma and Flavor Descriptors: Riesling wines are floral, fruity (citrus, peach, apricot, pineapple), honey, Muscat-like when young; they acquire "subtle, oily scents" as they age — Hugh Johnson.[20]

Typical Styles: Sugar/acid balance is important; range is from dry to very, very sweet, and elegant dessert wines may be made from *Botrytis*-affected fruit; lower alcohol levels are typical. For late-harvest, *Botrytis*-affected wines, the residual sugars can be very high and the alcohols as low as 6 or 7 percent.

Aging Potential: Dry wines may be aged 3-5 years; with more residual sugar, the aging potential should be longer. However, California's late-harvest, *Botrytis*-affected Rieslings have not aged as well as their German counterparts.

Number of U.S. Producers: 312 in 1990, making it the second most commonly produced white table wine in the U.S.

Varietal Wine Profile: ZINFANDEL

Grape Information

Description: Large, reddish-black, neutrally flavored berries that form medium to large clusters; medium vigor, adapted to a variety of soils, leafs out late in spring; compact clusters susceptible to rot; fruit ripens unevenly and tends to raisin if harvest is delayed.

Yields: Very productive, 4-7 tons/acre in the North Coast, 5-9 or more tons/acre in the Central Valley; cool regions best for fine table wines.

Maturity: Mid-season.

Preferred Climate: Depends on style of wine to be made.

1990 Data: 34,200 acres (6,200 non-bearing); 185,000 tons crushed, representing 23% of the red-wine grape crush (the grapes are red, if not always the resulting wines); $391/ton average price.

Other Important Growing Regions: It has long been held that Zinfandel is unique to California; however, grape taxonomists believe it to be identical with Primitivo, a variety from Southern Italy. Tasting blending wines from that area while living on a Chianti estate makes me think the taxonomists are right.

Wine Information

Aroma and Flavor Descriptors: Raspberries, berries, black pepper, raisins. The Zinfandel varietal aroma has not been associated with specific aromatic compounds like Cabernet Sauvignon by flavor researchers.[21]

Typical Styles: Zinfandel more than any other variety defies generalization about wine styles because it can successfully serve as the raw material for every wine type from white to blush, rosé, light red, or elegant long-aging red table wines, late-harvest red dessert wines, and fine port-style wines; it can even serve as the base wine for inexpensive or fancy varietal sparkling wines. Ridge Winery has long specialized in interesting red Zinfandels from several select sites in California, and Sutter Home's white Zinfandel sparked the blush wine revolution of the 1980s.

Aging Potential: In the fine red table wine style Zinfandels approximate Cabernet Sauvignons in aging potential — from 10 to 20 or more years. Good red Zinfandels are a bargain.

Number of U.S. Producers: 185 wineries made red Zinfandel, and white Zinfandel constituted one-third of the U.S. varietal wine market in 1990.[22]

ENDNOTES

1. WINE GRAPE VARIETIES IN THE NORTH COAST COUNTIES OF CALIFORNIA, University of California Cooperative Extension, 1977.
2. INFORMATION PLEASE ALMANAC, 1991 edition.
3. *California Grape Acreage 1990*, California Crop and Livestock Reporting Service, May 1991. Statistical information has been rounded off for the sake of simplicity.
4. Fredrickson, Jon, "The 80's Didn't Deliver as Forecast," *Wines and Vines*, June 1990, pp. 32-35.
5. *Final Grape Crush Report 1990 Crop*, California Department of Food and Agriculture, March 1991. Statistical information has been rounded off for the sake of simplicity.
6. *Wines and Vines*, July 1991, p. 39.
7. See, for example: THE CONNOISSEUR'S HANDBOOK OF CALIFORNIA WINES, Charles Olken, Earl Singer, and Norm Roby, Knopf, New York, 1984; WINES, THEIR SENSORY EVALUATION, Maynard A. Amerine and Edward B. Roessler, W. H. Freeman, New York, Second Edition, 1983; various publications by Ann Noble; HUGH JOHNSON'S POCKET ENCYCLOPEDIA OF WINES; CONNOISSEUR'S HANDBOOK OF CALIFORNIA WINE; and student comments, more of which can be found in Appendix D.
8. Anonymous, "The Exclusive Wines and Vines Varietal Chart for 1990," *Wines and Vines*, September 1990, pp. 25-38.
9. Robinson, Jancis, VINES, GRAPES, AND WINE, Alfred A. Knopf, New York, 1986, p. 54.
10. Johnson, Hugh, HUGH JOHNSON'S POCKET ENCYCLOPEDIA OF WINE 1990, Simon and Schuster, Inc., New York, 1989, p. 6.
11. Robinson, Jancis, VINES, GRAPES, AND WINE, Alfred A. Knopf, New York, 1986, p. 130.
12. Robinson, Jancis, VINES, GRAPES, AND WINE, Alfred A. Knopf, New York, 1986, p. 135.
13. Robinson, Jancis, VINES, GRAPES, AND WINE, Alfred A. Knopf, New York, 1986, pp. 91-96.
14. Robinson, Jancis, VINES, GRAPES, AND WINE, Alfred A. Knopf, New York, 1986, p. 54.
15. Robinson, Jancis, VINES, GRAPES, AND WINES, Alfred A. Knopf, New York, 1986, p. 183.
16. Robinson, Jancis, VINES, GRAPES, AND WINE, Alfred A. Knopf, New York, 1986, pp. 81-86.
17. See Guinard, Jean-Xavier, and Margaret Cliff, "Descriptive Analysis of Pinot Noir Wines from Carneros, Napa, and Sonoma," *American Journal of Enology and Viticulture*, Vol. 38, No. 3, 1987, pp. 211-215, for regional differences in California Pinot Noirs wines.
18. Robinson, Jancis, VINES, GRAPES, AND WINE, Alfred A. Knopf, New York, 1986, p. 87.
19. Galet, Pierre, A PRACTICAL AMPELOGRAPHY — GRAPEVINE IDENTIFICATION, Cornell University Press, Ithaca, NY, 1979, p. 68.
20. Johnson, Hugh, HUGH JOHNSON'S POCKET ENCYCLOPEDIA OF WINE 1990, Simon and Schuster, Inc., New York, 1989, p. 8.
21. Noble, A. C., and Mark Shannon, "Profiling Zinfandel Wines by Sensory and Chemical Analysis," *American Journal of Enology and Viticulture*, Vol. 38, No. 1, pp. 1-5, 1987.
22. Anonymous, "The Exclusive Wines and Vines Varietal Chart for 1990," *Wines and Vines*, September 1990, pp. 25-38, and Anonymous, "Varietals Boom as Jug Wines Fade," *The Wine Spectator*, August 31, 1991, p. 12.

Appendix B

HOW DO I KNOW WHAT'S IN THE BOTTLE WITHOUT OPENING IT?
Decoding Wine Labels — Mostly U.S.

What you read on a U.S. wine label is the tiniest tip of a regulatory iceberg that involves both the state and federal governments. This appendix will give you a brief background about wine-label law, define label terminology, and illustrate it with some California wine labels, scattered within but mostly found at the end of the text.

WHO'S IN CHARGE HERE? WINE LABELS AND THE LAW

Federal regulation of the wine industry in the United States has evolved from the simple system of taxation that existed in the nineteenth century, through National Prohibition (1919-1933) during which wine production and trade was forbidden, to today's extensive bodies of law that encompass regulation of grape growing, wine production, and wine marketing. Government oversight of the wine industry is intended to guard public health, protect consumers, and collect tax revenue. Regulation includes wine production, labeling, and advertising, and the pertinent laws are part of the Internal Revenue Code of 1986 and the Federal Alcohol Administration Act (FAA) of 1935. They are administered by the Bureau of Alcohol, Tobacco, and Firearms (ATF, as it is known in the trade and literature) in the Treasury Department.[1]

Protecting Taxes — The Internal Revenue Code

The parts of the Internal Revenue Code that address the wine industry are designed to ensure that wineries pay their taxes. The items on a wine label that reflect this world of wine taxes are the Bonded Winery or Bonded Wine Cellar number and the wine's alcohol and carbon dioxide contents; the higher the concentration of either, the higher the taxes.

Anyone who wants to establish a facility to produce or cellar — to blend, age, finish, or just bottle — wine must qualify with the ATF as a Bonded Winery (for production operations) or Bonded Wine Cellar (for non-production operations). When the prospective vintner's or wine merchant's application is approved by the ATF and business is about to begin, a bond — usually a guarantee given by an insurance company — must be posted to cover the potential tax liability on the wines stored on the premises should the winery fail to pay its taxes. Hence, you will occasionally see the terms "Bonded Winery" and "Bonded Wine Cellar" or their abbreviations (BW and BWC) on labels, followed by a number that was assigned to the business when its application was approved, as well as, perhaps, the abbreviation of the state in which the business is located. This number is, in effect, a winery's "social security number" for keeping track of its tax payments and reports. Among the sample labels at the end of this Appendix, the Sterling Vineyards Pinot Noir, Inglenook Reunion, and Monterey Vineyards Sémillon-Chardonnay include a Bonded Winery number.

The dollar amount of the bond that must be posted to cover a winery's taxes depends on both the volume and the kind of wine sold, with taxes ranging from $1.07 per gallon for still table wines of 14% alcohol or less, to $1.57 per gallon for still wines over 14% alcohol, and $3.40 per gallon for naturally sparkling wines. The alcohol and carbon dioxide contents of a wine that are given on the label, or implied by the terms table wine, champagne, or sparkling wine, reflect the factors ATF uses to determine the applicable tax rate. That tax rate, along with the volume of wine leaving the winery premises, determine the size of a winery's bond. As you can see, a winery specializing in dessert or sparkling wine — such as Quady or Korbel — would have to post a bond from one and a half to three times larger than a winery producing the same amount of table wine.

The Internal Revenue Code also specifies extensive, highly technical regulations governing wineries' cellar operation and imposes vast and detailed record-keeping requirements on wineries to document their compliance. The ATF has the authority to enter the business premises of a winery unannounced at any time to inspect these records. Examples of the records that must be kept to substantiate information appearing on wine labels include: alcohol content and other chemical analyses, the weight of grapes of various varieties crushed, the method used to identify grape varieties, and the amounts of all wines of different regions, vintages, and varieties that have been blended.

Protecting Consumers — The Federal Alcohol Administration Act

The majority of the information required on wine labels falls under the system of marketplace controls authorized by the Federal Alcohol Administration (FAA) Act, which contains one of the most far-reaching consumer protection provisions ever adopted by the U.S. Congress (in 1935, shortly after the repeal of National Prohibition). These regulations require label information to be truthful, accurate, and specific, and they also prohibit false, misleading, or obscene statements. The ATF enforces the consumer-protection provisions of the FAA Act through a system of label approvals: a winery or importer must obtain approval of the label for a wine before that wine can be sold or removed from customs. The creation of label regulations and the label approval process are summarized in Figure B.1.

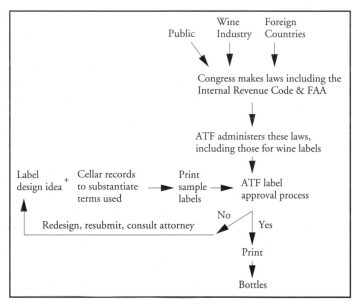

Figure B.1
A Flowchart of the Wine Label Approval Process

The vertical portion of Figure B.1 shows that the label laws that the ATF enforces are created by Congress, with foreign countries, the public, and the wine industry having input into them. For example, foreign countries are especially involved in the area of generic and semi-generic wine type names, as explained later in this appendix. A winery enters the label approval process by creating a sample label whose design is restricted by ATF requirements — and whose information must be substantiated by cellar records — and sending it to the ATF for approval. If approval is granted, the label is printed and used. If approval is denied, the winery must redesign and resubmit the label, perhaps in consultation with an attorney to help obtain clarification of, or to challenge the legal point involved in, the denial of approval.

Many wineries have tales to tell of their adventures in the label-approval process. Doris Muscatine recounts the story of Kenwood Winery's experience in winning approval of the label for their first Artist Series Cabernet Sauvignon, Vintage 1975. The label featured a vineyard scene by renowned California watercolorist David Lance Goines. In the first design submitted the vineyard was populated by "an innocent art nouveau nude female recumbent in a bucolic hillside vineyard." The ATF ruled the recumbent female obscene and rejected the label. Mr. Goines resubmitted the design with a recumbent skeleton in place of the nude female figure, and it was rejected again. The label that was finally approved shows an empty vineyard, and Goines observed good-humoredly that "we'll just have to imagine the girl is still on the hill."[2]

A more recent example involves the Robert Mondavi Winery's statement reflecting the position of wine in Western culture. This statement was first used in 1988 and is shown on the back label from his 1989 Napa Valley Chardonnay Reserve, "before" in Figure B.2. In 1990 Mondavi received a verbal warning from the ATF that when this statement was resubmitted on other labels, it would not be approved. When the winery inquired about the rationale behind the intent to deny approval, the ATF did not cite a specific legal basis for their intention and never responded to the winery in writing. After some negotiating, the statement shown as "after" in Figure B.2 on the Woodbridge 1989 Cabernet Sauvignon label won approval.

Figure B.2
Wine and Civilization
Before and After
ATF Approval

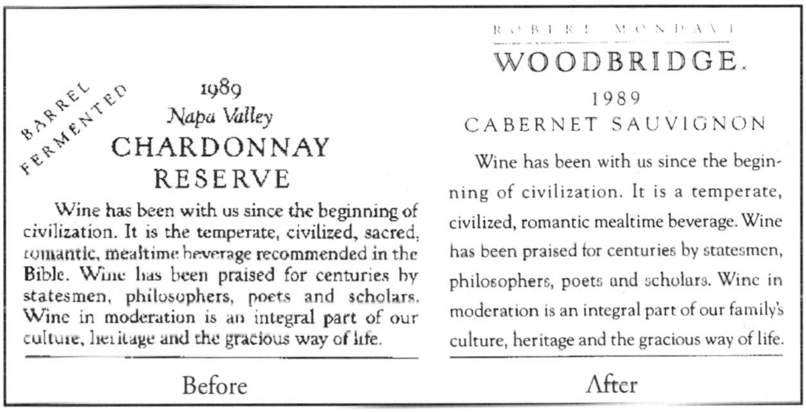

Before	After
BARREL FERMENTED	ROBERT MONDAVI
1989	WOODBRIDGE.
Napa Valley	1989
CHARDONNAY RESERVE	CABERNET SAUVIGNON
Wine has been with us since the beginning of civilization. It is the temperate, civilized, sacred, romantic, mealtime beverage recommended in the Bible. Wine has been praised for centuries by statesmen, philosophers, poets and scholars. Wine in moderation is an integral part of our culture, heritage and the gracious way of life.	Wine has been with us since the beginning of civilization. It is a temperate, civilized, romantic mealtime beverage. Wine has been praised for centuries by statesmen, philosophers, poets and scholars. Wine in moderation is an integral part of our family's culture, heritage and the gracious way of life.

The differences between the two statements, of course, involve references to religion and Western culture. It was reported in the press that ATF's concern over the Mondavi label statement arose because the Center for Science in the Public Interest had complained that positive label statements about wine did not present both sides of the issue.[3] One can only wonder exactly what the issue is (and what another point of view might be) regarding the existence of scores of references to wine in the Bible and the fact of its use as a sacramental beverage for centuries in Jewish and Christian religious celebrations.

As you have no doubt concluded, the label approval process is sensitive to how the political winds are blowing. At this moment, positive statements about wine are being discouraged through a strict enforcement of FAA provisions and wine taxes are being increased as part of what I consider a misguided federal effort to deal with our nation's alcohol abuse problems by trying to restrict access to all alcoholic beverages, regardless of their patterns of consumption and abuse, instead of treating alcoholics and their families. This will not work: our nation already carried out an unsuccessful 14-year experiment which unequivocally proved that a complete National Prohibition cannot prevent people from consuming alcohol if they want to.

WHAT'S ON A WINE LABEL AND WHAT DOES IT MEAN?

OK, that's enough of history and my opinions of the current political climate. What does the information on a wine label have to tell you that will be helpful when you buy wines?

There are seven items that must be included on a U.S. wine label: a brand name, the class or type of wine, the name and address of the bottler, the alcohol content of the wine, a sulfite statement, a health warning, and the net contents of the bottle. Let's look at each of these items.

Brand Name

The brand name is usually the most prominent item on a label. For premium wines this is usually the name of the producing winery. However, a bottler may use different brand names to distinguish its product lines of different qualities or to personalize wines bottled for other organizations or special occasions. A winery's second brand name is often referred to in the trade as its "second label." Restaurants, wine merchants, clubs, and even families celebrating weddings or other special events can order wines labeled with their own brand name. Among the sample labels, Fetzer's Bel Arbors is an example of a winery's "second label," and the 42nd St. Oyster Bar White Zinfandel was bottled for that Raleigh, North Carolina establishment by Wente Bros. Winery.

Wine Class or Type

U.S. wine law recognizes various classes and types of wines, including the classes of fruit wines, sparkling grape wines, and grape wines, and types such as table wine, dessert wine, and varietal or generic and semi-generic wine.

Generic Wines

There are only two types of generic wine recognized by the U.S. wine law: sake and vermouth. This means that the producer can use these names on a label without specifying where the grape — or the rice (for sake) — were grown to make the wine. Most of the wine names that you and I consider "generic" in everyday use are classified as semi-generic — or even as wine types such as red and white table wines — by the wine law. Semi-generic wines have an interesting history.

Semi-Generic Wines

Semi-generic terms can be applied to any class or type of wine. For example "American Chablis," "Sparkling Oregon Burgundy," and "California Port Wine" are all considered to be semi-generic. Although some wine consumers turn up their noses at semi-generic wines, wine lawyers and historians are fascinated by the questions surrounding their designation, especially those involving wine names that refer to geographic regions, many of which have been embroiled in long-standing international disputes. These international legal contests have resulted in the federal requirement that an appellation of origin (which tells where the grapes were grown) be used in conjunction with any semi-generic term on a U.S. wine label — hence, the examples *American* Chablis, etc.

As an example of how these disputes over wine names have come about, consider the case of California. In the eighteenth and nineteenth centuries, when immigrants from France, Germany, and Italy made the state's first commercial wines, they named their products after "similar" European wines, often using geographic terms such as Mosel or Chablis or even very specific names such as Saint-Julien, a small town in Bordeaux, on their labels. Needless to say, the French and Germans did not appreciate the use of their place names on inferior wines that were not made in the regions the names suggested and that could only discredit those that were, should anyone confuse them. Thus began the arguments — which continue today — between European governments and the U.S. ATF about who is entitled to use a particular place name on a bottle of wine.

Because generic and semi-generic terms cannot be protected as trademarks, the question under international discussion is "When has a 'generic' term lost its original geographic significance?" Is "Chablis," for example, just a kind of white wine, or does it still signify a hilly wine district southeast of Paris where Chardonnay grapes are grown in a very exacting, cool environment? In this context the ATF periodically reevaluates the generic or non-generic status of geographic names and then publishes lists of terms that fall into three established categories. A few names are considered to have lost their original geographic significance completely, making them truly generic (as mentioned, at present this category includes only sake and vermouth). Many more terms retain their original geographic references, but also designate wine types with generic characteristics under U.S. law; these are classified as "semi-generic" and are legally required to carry an appellation of origin to tell the consumer where the grapes were grown. Chablis, Burgundy, Chianti, Champagne, and Sherry, among others, fall into this category. A third group of terms can be applied only to wines made in the place their name indicates; these terms — including such designations as French, Mosel, Châteaux Margaux, Saint-Julien, Spanish, Rioja, Barbaresco, and Oporto — are considered non-generic. The most recent ATF list of non-generic terms included Beaujolais, the subject of a recent skirmish in the generic wine terminology war. Even though "Beaujolais" is non-generic and cannot be used as a wine type designation, the ATF has ruled that U.S. vintners can still use the term as part of the grape varietal name Gamay Beaujolais.[4]

I have chosen the Robert Sinsky Vineyard's Carneros Claret label to include among the sample labels collected here, to remind us that wine connoisseurs as well as lawyers and historians can be fascinated by certain semi-generic wines. A number of California vintners who are striving — as is Robert Sinsky — to produce fine red and white varietal blends have chosen to use semi-generic or wine type designations rather than varietal names for these wines. The mention of the percentages of Merlot, Cabernet Sauvignon, and Cabernet Franc blended to create the 1988 Sinskey Claret also sets this wine apart from ordinary semi-generic wines.

Varietal Wines

To use any wine type designation a winery must be able to document that the wine meets the relevant ATF standards, concerning, for example, alcohol content or the minimum content of carbon dioxide. Varietal wines, which bear the name of the grape (or, rarely, grapes) from which they are made, must meet two additional ATF requirements: when a single grape variety name is used, at least 75% of the wine must come from grapes of that variety, and the appellation of origin must appear on the label. If you are lucky enough to own or taste some older varietal wines, you should know that the varietal requirement was only 51% for wine bottled before January 1, 1983. Varietal names among the sample labels include Chardonnay, Cabernet Sauvignon, Gewürztraminer, and Zinfandel. The Monterey Vineyard label mentioned earlier for its Bonded Winery number is an example of the use of two varietal names on a label when the optimum blend is less than 75% of one variety or to distinguish a new kind of wine.

There is no legal requirement about the varieties that may be used to create generic and semi-generic wines, though some wineries will give that information on a back label. Kenwood's Vintage Red Table Wine is an example of a wine with a varietally revealing back label.

Proprietary Wines

Because generic and varietal names can be used by any winery or négociant, a wine producer or blender that wants to be identified as the sole source of a particularly delicious and memorable wine may register a proprietary name as a trademark for its exclusive use. Some proprietary names sound like plausible grape variety names, but you'll know for certain that you've run across a proprietary name if the producer includes the symbol ® or ™ on the label. The proprietary wine names among the sample labels are Calla-lees®, Grand Finale™, and Reunion®. The symbols ® and ™ can also appear in another place on labels: next to a registered trade name — a "doing business as" [DBA] name or the name of the winery itself. That's why you may see more than one ® or ™ on a label or find these marks on labels that are not proprietary wines. Among the sample labels, "Hard Rock Cafe"™, Sterling Vineyard®, The Monterey Vineyard®, and Inglenook® are examples of a DBA and three winery names which are registered trademarks.

Name and Address of the Bottler

The wine law uses the term "bottler" because it includes not only wineries that produce wines from grapes but also other enterprises, such as those of wine merchants or négociants, who buy wine produced by others and then cellar, blend, bottle, and market it. The name and address of the bottler typically appears in small print on the bottom of the label and tells us only where the wine was actually bottled. Other production steps may have occurred in another location. The bottler's name can be the name of the winery or another trade name or DBA that has been approved by the ATF, such as Neiman-Marcus Cellars and Hard Rock Cafe Vineyards among the examples.

Take a close look at the small print on the bottoms of the various sample labels. You will notice a variety of phrases preceding the words "bottled by" that indicate what additional involvement the bottling winery had in making the wine. For example, if the bottling winery crushed some of the grapes, the terms "produced" (for crushers of 75% of the grapes) or "made" (for crushers of 10% or more of the grapes) will be on the label. If the bottling winery crushed less than 10% of the fruit and bought the rest of the wine from another producer to blend, finish, and age, then "cellared," "selected," "vinted," or other similar terms will be used. When the bottling winery also grew the grapes, the phrases "Grown, Produced and Bottled by" and "Estate Bottled" may appear on the label. The term Estate Bottled is subject to special restrictions, which are explained below.

OK, now that you've got those percentages down, here's a short "quiz" (don't worry, it's just for fun). Refer to the sample labels:
1. Which label(s) show(s) that the bottler crushed
   A. 75% or more of the fruit to make the wine?
   B. at least 10% of the fruit?
   C. 10% or less?
2. Which label(s) show(s) that the winery also grew the grapes?

That quiz wasn't so bad, was it? Here are the answers. For question 1, part A, crushing of 75% or more of the fruit, are the "producers," including Bargetto Winery, Delicato Vineyards, Louis M. Martini, Andrew Quady, Kenwood, The Monterey Vineyard, Inglenook, Robert Sinskey, Simi, and Joseph Phelps. For question 1, part B, crushing from 10-74% of the fruit, are the "makers:" Hard Rock Cafe Vineyards and Mirassou Vineyards. And for part C of question 1, crushing 10% or less, are the "selectors" (Wente Brothers for the 42nd St. Oyster Bar), "vinifiers" (Callaway), and "cellarers" (Bel Arbors Vineyards and Neiman-Marcus Cellars). For question 2, Sterling Vineyards grew all the grapes for its Pinot Noir as did Kendall-Jackson for Grand Finale and Inglenook for its Estate Bottled Reunion and Charbono (a red varietal wine from a rare grape of Italian origin).

Alcohol Content

This information is given in percent by volume and can also be found lurking near the bottom of the label in small print. Wineries making vintage-dated wines often print the exact alcohol content. The ATF allows a variation of plus or minus 1.5% between the alcohol content printed on the label and the actual alcohol content of the wine, for wines not over 14% alcohol. This is handy if you are producing millions of gallons of Château Ordinary American Burgundy that may vary in alcohol content from batch to batch and you don't want to have to print new labels every week. If you see a label with a round figure such as 12% alcohol, that is probably an approximation taking advantage of the "plus or minus 1.5%" leeway in actual alcohol content. Figures like 12.8% or 13.7% on vintage-dated wines most likely represent the actual alcohol content of the wine. In 46 states, the designation "Table Wine" may be used in place of giving the percentage of alcohol for wines of 14.0% alcohol or less. For wines over 14% alcohol, a tolerance of plus or minus 1% applies.

Sulfite Statement, Health Warning, and Net Contents

Since January 9, 1987, wines containing more than 10 parts per million of sulfur dioxide (which means nearly **all** wines, since many wine yeast strains produce that much during fermentation) have had to carry a label statement such as "Contains Sulfites." Some labels give the name of the specific chemical added — for example, they might say "Contains Potassium Metabisulfite."

On November 18, 1989, a rule went into effect requiring the labels of all alcoholic beverages sold in the U.S. to carry the following statements: "GOVERNMENT WARNING: 1. According to the Surgeon General, women should not drink alcoholic beverages during pregnancy because of the risk of birth defects," and 2. "Consumption of alcoholic beverages impairs your ability to drive a car or operate machinery, and may cause health problems." The wine industry is concerned about these statements because it does not say anything about **how much** wine may produce these results. For example, there is evidence that some women who drink very large amounts of alcohol will have children with birth defects, but no data to suggest that drinking moderately — one to two glasses of wine per day — brings any risk to the fetus.[5] Another point of concern for winemakers is the considerable doubt among social scientists about the ability of warning labels to influence the use of wine by individuals who need the warning the most: young people and those with problems of alcohol abuse.[6]

The net contents is occasionally found on the label, but most producers rely on that information having been stamped into the glass when the bottle was made.

Where Were the Grapes Grown? The Appellation of Origin

As mentioned, appellation of origin is a geographical term that tells you where the grapes were grown that were used to make the wine. If a winery chooses to use a varietal or semi-generic wine type designation, it is required to include the appellation of origin on the label.

Depending on the appellation and other label information, 75-100% of the grapes must come from the area named. The boundaries of appellations used on wine labels must be legally defined, and in the U.S. these can be the boundaries of states, counties, or viticultural areas. If the appellation is a state, then according to federal law at least 75% of the grapes must have been grown there. However, states can pass label laws that are more restrictive than the federal law, and, for example, California requires that 100% of the grapes be grown within its boundaries. Wines made from grapes grown in more than one state are called "American." A county name may be used as an appellation of origin if 75% or more of the grapes were grown there.

Among the sample labels, the appellation of origin American is found on the Bel Arbors Chardonnay, which is blended from wines made in California, Oregon, and Washington. The appellation California can be seen on the Sutter Home Sparkler, Mirassou White Zinfandel, Kenwood Vintage Red Table Wine, Grand Finale, and others. The Sémillon and Chardonnay grapes in the Monterey Vineyard's Sémillon-Chardonnay came from Monterey County and the grapes for Quady's Port were grown in Amador County — somewhere along Shenandoah School Road. The Simi 1990 Chardonnay labels win the prize for precision in county appellations and reminds us that up to three counties can be named on a label.

Viticultural Areas

A viticultural area may be larger or smaller than a state or county and, according to federal regulations, may be established if:

Figure B.3
Sonoma County's
Viticultural Areas

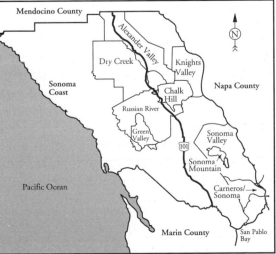
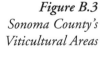

1. the name is known locally or nationally as referring to the area
2. the boundaries are established by historical or current evidence
3. the geographical features (climate, soil, elevation, physical features, etc.) distinguish it viticulturally from surrounding areas
4. the specific boundaries are based on features on U.S. Geologic Survey topographic maps.[7]

A wine may be identified with a viticultural area if 85% or more of its grapes are from the named area. About 100 viticultural areas have been approved in 25 states, ranging in size from 500 to 16 million acres. Most of the approved viticultural areas are in California.[8] Some examples include Carneros, Livermore Valley, Napa Valley, North Coast, Central Coast, Howell Mountain, Fiddletown, and Sierra Foothills, as well as the Sonoma County areas shown in Figure B.3. Note that this map shows that one viticultural area may be within another — Sonoma Mountain is inside the boundaries of Sonoma Valley (which makes for a rather lumpy valley).

Some examples of viticultural areas on the sample labels are North Coast (Louis Martini Merlot), Central Coast (Bargetto), Carneros (Gloria Ferrer Carneros Cuvée and Robert Sinskey Claret), and Napa Valley (on many examples).

When The Winery Controls the Grape Growing — "Estate Bottled" or "Grown, Produced, and Bottled By"

A winery aspiring to use the term "Estate Bottled" must meet following conditions:

1. The wine must have a viticultural area appellation.
2. The winery must be located in the viticultural area.
3. The winery must have grown 100% of the grapes used to make the wine on land owned or controlled by the winery within the viticultural area of appellation. "Controlled" means a lease of at least three years' duration.
4. The winery must have crushed the grapes, fermented the resulting must, and finished, aged, and bottled the wine in a continuous process.[9]

Linking the use of the term "Estate Bottled" to viticultural areas and requiring the winery to be located in the same viticultural area where the grapes are grown has led to some large, unusually shaped viticultural areas in California. The boundaries of the Central Coast viticultural area extend from Livermore to Monterey County, including both mountain and valley areas and, we would think, stretching the requirement that a viticultural area's "geographical features distinguish it viticulturally." Some vintners argue that viticultural areas should truly reflect the climate and soil of a homogeneous — and, therefore, rather small — unique, winegrowing region and that departures from this philosophy should not be allowed. The system of viticultural area appellations dates from the early 1980s in the U.S., and, as this fundamental dispute shows, it is still evolving. However our system turns out, I doubt that we will arrive at rules even approaching the stringent nature of the French laws of Appellation Côntrollée, which not only specify the boundaries of regions but also define grape growing practices with great precision, including such things as the allowable varieties in an area, training systems, harvest sugar contents, and maximum yields. The phrase "Grown, Produced, and Bottled By" may appear in front of the bottler's name and address if the winery meets all the conditions listed for use of "Estate Bottled" but is not located in an approved viticultural area.

The Inglenook Vineyards Charbono and Reunion are the only sample labels with the "Estate Bottled" designation. The phrase "Grown, Produced, and Bottled by" on the Sterling Vineyards Pinot Noir and Kendall-Jackson's Grand Finale labels reflect the fact that these wineries control growing the grapes but are not located in a viticultural area. If you find a wine label with a puzzling mixture of these terms — or other apparent contradictions to the labelling rules discussed here — you may have discovered an example of an allowed exception that has been negotiated between a winery and the ATF and which may apply only to a particular label or set of circumstances.

Including a Vineyard Name

Wineries may use a vineyard name in addition to an appellation of origin in order to differentiate between several wines of the same variety and appellation or to highlight a particularly well-known vineyard. If a vineyard name is used, 95% of the grapes must have been grown there.

Table B.1
California's Great
Vineyards

Vineyards	Location	Grape Varieties Grown
THE FIRST GROWTHS*		
Independent Growers		
Martha's Vineyard	Napa Valley	Cab Sauv** (Heitz)***
Bosche	Napa Valley	Cab Sauv (Freemark Abbey)
York Creek	Napa Valley	Cab Sauv, Petite Sirah (Ridge)
Robert Young	Alexander Valley	Chard, LH Riesling (Ch St. Jean)
Winery Estates		
Winery Lake Vineyard	Carneros	Chard, Pinot Noir (Mumm's, Sterling)
Chalone Vineyard	Monterey County	Chard, Pinot Noir
Hanzell Vineyard	Sonoma	Chard, Pinot Noir
Stony Hill	Napa Valley	Chard
Monte Bello (Ridge)	Santa Clara County	Cab Sauv
Diamond Creek	Napa Valley	3 Cab Sauv vineyards
THE "SECOND TIER"		
Independent Growers		
Bella Oaks Vineyard	Napa Valley	Cab Sauv (Heitz)
Belle Terre Vineyard	Alexander Valley	Chard, LHR, Gewürz (Ch St. Jean)
Cook	Yolo County	Chenin Blanc (Kenwood et al.)
Deaver	Amador County	Zin (Sutter Home Reserve)
DuPratt	Anderson Valley	Zin (Kendall-Jackson)
Eisele	Napa Valley	Cab Sauv (Phelps et al.)
Stelzner	Napa Valley	Cab Sauv
Tepesquet	Santa Maria Valley	Chard
Ventana	Monterey County	Chard
Winery Estates		
Caymus	Napa Valley	Cab Sauv
Chappellet	Napa Valley	Cab Sauv, Chard, CB
Jekel	Monterey County	Chard, Riesling, Cab Sauv
Long	Napa Valley	Chard
Jordan	Alexander Valley	Cab Sauv
Mayacaymas	Napa Valley	Chard, Cab Sauv
Stag's Leap	Napa Valley	Cab Sauv
Winery-Owned Vineyards		
Arroyo Seco (Wente)	Monterey County	LH R
Les Pierres (Sonoma Cutrer)	Sonoma County	Chard
Lytton Springs (Ridge)	Sonoma County	Zinfandel

* The term "First Growth" is a translation of the French "Première Cru," the phrase used to designate their best vineyards.
** Abbreviations: Cab Sauv = Cabernet Sauvignon, CB = Chenin Blanc, Chard = Chardonnay, R = Riesling, Gewürz = Gewürztraminer, LH = Late Harvest, Zin = Zinfandel, et al. = and others
*** winery producing wine from this vineyard

Which vineyard names are worth looking for? In 1985 *The Wine Spectator* published a list of California's Great Vineyards.[10] James Laube, the list's author, included only those vineyards with a reputation of at least ten years standing for excellent wines of distinctive, constant style and good ability to improve with bottle age. Fine vineyards throughout California made the list and were found to share some common features: they are maintained in excellent condition, often are managed by resident owners, are relatively small (averaging less than 50 acres), and tend to specialize in one or two kinds of grapes, producing small crops of intensely flavored fruit. The first two tiers of the list are reproduced in Table B.1 and I have included Laube's list of "Vineyards to Watch" in a footnote because some of my favorite vineyards are on that list.[11]

Here's another "quiz:" Which sample labels include the names of listed vineyards? Answer: The grapes for the Joseph Phelps Vineyards Napa Valley Cabernet Sauvignon were grown in the Eisele Vineyard and the grapes used for the Sterling Vineyards Carneros–Napa Valley Pinot Noir were grown in the Winery Lake Vineyard, which is located in that part of the Carneros viticultural area that overlaps the Napa Valley viticultural area.

When Were the Grapes Harvested? The Vintage Date

If a vintage date appears on a label, 95% of the wine in the bottle must have been made from grapes harvested and crushed in the year named. The 5% allows cellar practices such as topping up barrels to be done with other wine. The vintage year is normally the same year in which the grapes matured, but the grapes for some late-harvest wines mature mostly in the fall of one year (1991) but are not harvested until the following year (1992). The vintage date on the label would be 1992. If a vintner puts a vintage date on a label, she must also include an appellation of origin that must be more specific than a country. Most of the sample labels are of vintage-dated wines.

Another important date in the life of a wine is its bottling date. You will see it on a label only occasionally, but it must be stamped on all cases. This is a useful piece of information for estimating the age of non-vintage-dated wines. Cases of sparkling wines carry the date of disgorging, and it is helpful to know this date since it is advisable to wait at least six to nine months after the bottles have been disgorged before drinking a sparkling wine, so that the dosage will have had enough time to marry with the wine.

Optional Terms That Are Not Legally Defined

This category includes information about the wine's sensory attributes — dry or sweet — and advice about serving the wine — recommended temperatures and food combinations — and terms such as Reserve, Special Selection, and the like. Terms in this last category are usually associated with wines that are extraordinary in some way — made from grapes from a fine vineyard or blended from a few lots that turned out unusually well. As an informed consumer you should approach reserve wines carefully; since this and similar terms are not legally defined, their significance depends entirely on the integrity of the winery using them. Some wineries are not above completely abusing such descriptions, as Glen Ellen did when it assigned the term Proprietor's Reserve to its cheapest line. Yes, Beaulieu Vineyards Georges de la Tour Private Reserve Cabernet Sauvignon is special, and it has been for years. But all reserves are not created equal!

SPECIAL RULES FOR SPECIAL WINES
Sparkling Wines

To distinguish effervescent wines made using yeast fermentations from artificially carbonated wines, the label term "sparkling wine" is used in the United States. Wines made in this country by bottle fermentation are designated as "Naturally fermented in THIS Bottle" while those made by the transfer process will be labelled "Naturally fermented in THE Bottle." U.S. sparkling wines that get their bubbles in a tank instead of a bottle must confess their origins if they use the term "champagne," and a commonly seen phrase is: "naturally fermented Charmat Bulk Process."

French labels use the appellation "Champagne" to tell us not only that the grapes were grown in this district but also that bottle fermentation was used and that minimum *sur lie* aging requirements were met. If it's French but not from the Champagne district, it's *Vin Mousseaux* and the label may not

even mention it but use a regional appellation instead. CAVA on a Spanish sparkling wine label tells us that the wine was bottle-fermented.

Can a consumer know how sweet a sparkling wine will taste by reading its label? In common market countries, guidelines have been established for sparkling wine label terminology. In the U.S. we use the same names but are not obliged to adhere to the same — or any — standards. Nevertheless, Table B.2 can serve as a general guideline for American sparkling wines. Be sure to note that Extra Dry really isn't dry either in the E.E.C. or the U.S.A.

Table B.2
Sparkling Wine Label Terms, Perceived Sweetness, and Common Market Standards [12]

Label Designation	Perceived Sweetness	Common Market Standard
Extra Brut	none	less than 6 grams per liter (0.6%)
Brut	none	less than 15 g/L (1.5%)
Extra Dry	slight to noticeably	12-20 g/L (1.2-2.0%)
Sec	noticeably sweet	17-35 g/L (1.7-3.5%)
Demi-Sec	very sweet	33-50 g/L (3.3-5.0%)
Doux	super sweet	more than 50 g/L

The label terms listed in Table B.2 give us a rough idea about the sweetness we'll perceive in the glass. Remember that within each sweetness category mass-market wines made by tank fermentation will usually be sweeter than bottle-fermented wines carrying the same designation. In most cases, for example, a wine whose label that reads "Brut Sparkling Wine, Naturally Fermented Charmat Bulk Process" will be noticeably sweeter than a wine labelled "Brut Sparkling Wine, Naturally Fermented in this Bottle."

Late-Harvest Wines
Germany, the Model for Most American Labels

German wine law divides all German wines into *Tafelwein* and *Qualitätswein* — ordinary table wine and better-quality wine. The quality wines are further divided into regional wines (*Qualitätswein bestimmter Anbaugebiete,* or QbA) and more distinctive wines with special characteristics (*Qualitätswein mit Prädikat,* or QmP). Late-harvest, sweet table wines are considered the best wines of the QmP category and are allowed to carry additional label terms — besides *Qualitätswein mit Prädikat* — if the grapes they used meet specified minimum sugar concentrations at harvest. Table B.3 shows the sugar levels required for the various label terms, literal translations of each term, and descriptions of the wines.[13] Suggestions for pronunciation may be found in the glossary.

When I first went to Germany after learning the literal meanings of the label terms for late-harvest QmP wines, I expected to find the vineyards in the waning days of October to be full of people running around with some kind of vineyard equivalent of tweezers, meticulously selecting the "individual" dried overripe berries for Trockenbeerenauslese (TBA) wines. After all, TBA means that the individual shrivelled berries are picked out, right? Wrong. Of course, I was a little disappointed that my picturesque image was incorrect and escaped being extremely embarrassed only because I had not told my German hosts about my visions of tweezer-toting harvesters combing their vineyards. As in California, the time to harvest is determined by the average sugar level of the vineyard, and bunches are selected, not "individual berries." TBA wines are considered the crowning achievement of German viticulture, and given the location of their vineyards at the 50th parallel and their cold climate, it's easy to understand why an exceptionally warm growing season that allows naturally sweet wines to be produced is to be celebrated.

Minimum Brix at Harvest*	Label Term	Harvest and Wine Description
17.0-19.5	*Kabinett*	"cabinet" harvest fruit at normal ripeness; wines driest, lightest in QmP group
18.4-21.7	*Spätlese*	"late-harvest" of completely ripe fruit; wines have more sweetness and body than Kabinett wines
20.0-24.8	*Auslese*	"select," very ripe bunches are harvested; wines sweeter and fuller bodied than Spätlese wines
25.8-29.0	*Beerenauslese*	harvest "select berries," overripe berries or berries with noble rot; these are exceptional wines that are very sweet, heavy, and complex**
34.5	*Trocken-beerenauslese*	harvest "select dried berries," shrivelled and with noble rot; these rarely-made wines are sweeter, richer, and heavier than Beerenauslese

* No sugar may be added to the must of Qualitätswein mit Prädikat wines
** Mold is required to be present only in vintages when the weather conditions permit *Botrytis* infections to develop; otherwise just overripe berries for Beerenauslese or overripe and shrivelled grapes for Trockenbeerenauslese will do.

Table B.3
Minimum Sugar Concentrations at Harvest and Label Terms for German Late-Harvest Table Wines

California

Labels of late-harvest wines made in the United States must give the percentage by weight of sugar before and after fermentation and may not use German label terms. Unlike Germany, in the U.S.A. there is no nationwide agreement on what additional label terms may be used to tell consumers what sort of wines they are about to buy. In 1981 a dozen California winemakers who were producing late-harvest wines met to develop recommendations for industry standards for the labeling of these wines. The committee agreed "to define the label terms (shown in Table B.4) according to the sugar levels in the grapes at harvest." The table also gives the closest equivalent German label terms and an example of how one winery — Château St. Jean — relates residual sugar levels in the wine and the extent of *Botrytis* infection to each suggested label term.[14]

Suggested Label Term	° Brix at Harvest	Approximate Equivalent German Term	Wine Residual Sugar*	Incidence of *Botrytis*
Early Harvest	20.0	Trocken and Halbtrocken		none
No special designation	20.5	Kabinett	<2.6%	none
Late Harvest	24.0	Spätlese and Auslese	<11.5%	some
Select Late Harvest	28.0	Auslese and Beerenauslese	usually >11.5%	use only affected fruit
Special Select Late Harvest	35.0	Beerenauslese and Trockenbeerenauslese	usually >15%	all fruit affected and some is fully raisined

* Residual sugar values are in percent by weight.

Table B.4
Suggested Minimum Harvest Sugars and Label Terminology for Late-Harvest White Wines Produced in the U.S.A. and Used at Château St. Jean Winery

The suggested U.S. and German label terms do not match exactly because the committee felt that the much warmer growing conditions in California required that higher sugar content standards than those used in Germany be established. This complex system of proposed label terminology for *Botrytis*-affected late-harvest wines is unlikely to be implemented because it is not applicable to all U.S. wine growing regions. Late-harvest wines are required to show their degrees Brix at harvest and residual sugar in the wine and all the sugar and alcohol in the wine must come from the grape.[15]

The Delicato Late Harvest Johannisberg Riesling label illustrates both the required information for late harvest wines and the fact that not all California producers have adopted the suggested terminology — this wine might have been labelled "Special Select Late Harvest" under

those suggested guidelines. Many bottlers of late-harvest wine, like Delicato, also include residual sugar and total acid data on their labels. Kendall-Jackson's Grand Finale is a second example of a late-harvest wine label.

France

French labels give the vintage date, the name of the district (look for Sauternes — or its neighbor Barsac), the name of the Château (winery) that made the wine, information about where it was bottled (*"mise en bouteilles au château"* — means it was bottled at the winery), and the name of the exporter or importer. They do not give any information about the sweetness of the wine, which, as you now know, varies from vintage to vintage. However, you can get a rough idea of how sweet the wine is by looking at a vintage chart or the wine's color: generally speaking, the darker the wine the sweeter it will be, and Sauternes and Barsac bottles are clear to allow the color to be checked. However, to be sure about a Sauternes' or Barsac's sweetness you'll have to ask your trusty wine merchant or consult your favorite wine critic.

AFTER ALL THAT, WHAT DO I LOOK FOR ON THE LABEL TO GUARANTEE QUALITY?

Well, I don't blame you if you are a little exasperated with me for not telling you this sooner, and it goes back to the beginning, to the brand name. The name of the winery that made the wine is your best guarantee of quality. The vintage year, the appellation of origin, the wine type, and terms like "reserve" cannot help you as much as the one piece of information that ties the wine in the bottle directly to the winery that made it and to that winery's philosophy and its dedication to filling a particular market niche with a product of a particular level of quality.

Part of the fascination of wine is that each of us who loves it must learn through experience to match wines made by different producers to our tastes and pocketbooks. If you want to explore California wines, this book offers some excellent starting points. You could begin by sampling the wines of the producers whose labels I have chosen to illustrate this appendix and other parts of this book. On page 336 you will find wine writer Dan Berger's choice of California's top ten wineries for consistent quality and where to find more winery tips. These recommendations should help launch your explorations. Have a pleasant voyage!

IN SUMMARY: WHAT QUESTIONS CAN A WINE LABEL ANSWER?

Wine labels can answer some questions well, and others poorly or not at all. Table B.5 summarizes some of these questions and where to find their answers on a wine label.

Question	Where to Look
Who made the wine?	"Estate Bottled" means the bottling winery made all the wine. The phrase in front of the name and address of the bottler tells you the involvement of the bottling winery, which may range from making the wine starting from the grapes to just bottling wine from another producer.
Where was the wine made?	Most premium wines are made by the bottler whose name and address appears on the label, but the wine could have been made in another location.
What grapes were used?	Varietal wines are named after the grapes from which they were made, and some back labels will tell you the varieties used in a generic or proprietary wine.
Who grew the grapes?	Sometimes a label will tell you this if it says "Estate Bottled" or names a vineyard. Most of the time you cannot learn this from the label.
Where were the grapes grown?	Semi-generic and varietal wines must carry an appellation of origin that tells where the grapes were grown. The actual percentage of the grapes grown there may vary from 75 to 100%.
When were the grapes harvested?	Vintage-dated wines tell you the year in which the grapes were harvested.
How will the wine taste?	Except for late-harvest wines, label law does not require sensory information on labels. Some wineries include analytical data on their labels or statements about how the wine will taste. Mostly you're on your own here.
Questions the Label Won't Answer	
Is this wine good? Will I like it?	If you like other wines made by the bottler, you may like this one too. Good luck!

Table B.5
What Questions Can a Wine Label Answer?

SAMPLE LABELS

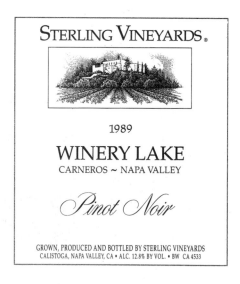

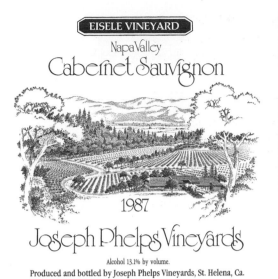

EISELE VINEYARD

Napa Valley

Cabernet Sauvignon

1987

Joseph Phelps Vineyards

Alcohol 13.1% by volume.
Produced and bottled by Joseph Phelps Vineyards, St. Helena, Ca.

R S V

1988   № 00000

PRODUCED & BOTTLED BY ROBERT SINSKEY VINEYARDS
NAPA, CALIF. USA • TABLE WINE

CARNEROS CLARET
59% Merlot 22% Cabernet Sauvignon
19% Cabernet Franc

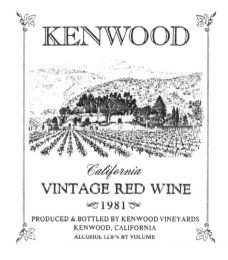

KENWOOD

California

VINTAGE RED WINE

1981

PRODUCED & BOTTLED BY KENWOOD VINEYARDS
KENWOOD, CALIFORNIA
ALCOHOL 12.8% BY VOLUME

1981
VINTAGE RED WINE

Composition:	Cabernet Sauvignon	47.2% / vol
	Zinfandel	27.4% / vol
	Pinot Noir	21.0% / vol
	Ruby Cabernet	3.9% / vol
	Petite Sirah	0.3% / vol
	Carignane	0.2% / vol
Total Acid At Bottling:		0.62% / vol
Barrel Aging:		50 gal. American Oak
Alcohol:		12.8%
Bottle Date:		June 1983

NEIMAN-MARCUS

Napa Valley
CABERNET SAUVIGNON

CELLARED AND BOTTLED BY NEIMAN-MARCUS CELLARS
ST. HELENA, CALIFORNIA • ALCOHOL 12.8% BY VOLUME
CONTAINS SULFITES

Louis M Martini

1988

MERLOT

NORTH COAST

ALC. 13.0% BY VOL.

PRODUCED AND BOTTLED BY LOU S M. MARTINI
ST. HELENA, NAPA VALLEY, CA   CONTAINS SULFITES

1985   *Charbono*

PRODUCED AND BOTTLED BY   ESTATE BOTTLED

750 ML • ALCOHOL 12.5% BY VOLUME

Inglenook
NAPA • VALLEY
RUTHERFORD, CALIFORNIA • USA • B.W. 9

NAPA VALLEY

THE
MONTEREY
VINEYARD®

19 *90*

Semillon · Chardonnay

MONTEREY COUNTY

PRODUCED AND BOTTLED BY THE MONTEREY VINEYARD
B.W. 4674 GONZALES, MONTEREY COUNTY, CA., U.S.A.

75cl (e)   PRODUCE OF THE U.S.A.   ALC. 12,0% VOL.

1989

HARVEST SUGAR:
36.0% BY WEIGHT

RESIDUAL SUGAR:
20.2% BY WEIGHT

LAWRENCE J. BARGETTO

Special Select Late Harvest
CENTRAL COAST

White Riesling

PRODUCED & BOTTLED BY BARGETTO WINERY, SOQUEL., CA, USA ALC. 9.0% BY VOL.

1989

GRAND FINALE™

Select Late Harvest

California

White Table Wine

KENDALL-JACKSON

ALCOHOL 13.7% BY VOLUME

1989 GRAND FINALE

This Select Late Harvest wine was created under a rare set of circumstances, when our estate Lakewood Vineyard experienced rain storms during the harvest of 1989. Botrytis cinerea resulted in some of the grapes, producing the intense and concentrated flavor that gives the wines of Sauterne their distinctive character. The clusters were harvested by hand, pressed, then fermented and aged in small French oak barrels. The sugar in the grapes at harvest measured 33.2° brix. The wine's 10.7 grams/100 ml residual sugar is balanced by a firm acid backbone.

Grand Finale is a special wine meant to enhance a special occasion. The wine's delicate fruit flavors of peaches and pears and its rich, satiny texture combine to add an atmosphere of elegance and celebration to the evening in which it is enjoyed. We at Kendall-Jackson hope that it will enrich a special evening for you.

Bottle number [   ] of 1,020 — 750 ml bottles.

GROWN, PRODUCED, AND BOTTLED
BY KENDALL-JACKSON VINEYARDS & WINERY,
LAKEPORT, CALIFORNIA

GOVERNMENT WARNING: (1) ACCORDING TO THE SURGEON GENERAL, WOMEN SHOULD NOT DRINK ALCOHOLIC BEVERAGES DURING PREGNANCY BECAUSE OF THE RISK OF BIRTH DEFECTS. (2) CONSUMPTION OF ALCOHOLIC BEVERAGES IMPAIRS YOUR ABILITY TO DRIVE A CAR OR OPERATE MACHINERY, AND MAY CAUSE HEALTH PROBLEMS.

CONTAINS SULFITES

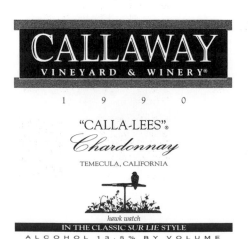

CALLAWAY
VINEYARD & WINERY®

1   9   9   0

"CALLA-LEES"®
Chardonnay

TEMECULA, CALIFORNIA

hawk watch
IN THE CLASSIC *SUR LIE* STYLE

ALCOHOL 13.5% BY VOLUME

"CALLA-LEES" CHARDONNAY 1990

CLASSIC STYLE
Callaway produces Chardonnay in the true *sur lie* style, aging the wine on its lees without the influence of oak barrels. The richness and complexity of flavor which results enhances the true varietal character of Chardonnay, unmasked by oak.

HAWK WATCH
Since 1969, we at Callaway have been committed to conscientious stewardship of our environment. We've built nesting boxes and perches for red-tail hawks and owls to provide rodent control. And we avoid using insecticides by encouraging grasses to grow in the vine rows, providing a home for beneficial insects which prey on pests.

From the vineyard to the bottle, we hope you will find Callaway's wines among the most carefully nurtured.

Dwayne Helmuth
Dwayne Helmuth
Vice President & Winemaker

GOVERNMENT WARNING: (1) ACCORDING TO THE SURGEON GENERAL, WOMEN SHOULD NOT DRINK ALCOHOLIC BEVERAGES DURING PREGNANCY BECAUSE OF THE RISK OF BIRTH DEFECTS. (2) CONSUMPTION OF ALCOHOLIC BEVERAGES IMPAIRS YOUR ABILITY TO DRIVE A CAR OR OPERATE MACHINERY, AND MAY CAUSE HEALTH PROBLEMS.

VINIFIED & BOTTLED BY CALLAWAY VINEYARD & WINERY®
TEMECULA, CA • PLEASE RECYCLE THIS BOTTLE

CONTAINS SULFITES

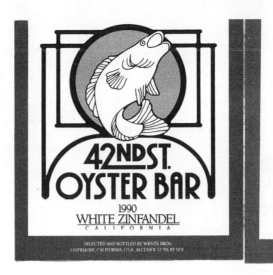

42ND ST. OYSTER BAR

WHITE ZINFANDEL
CALIFORNIA

42nd Street is a Raleigh tradition. Once a grocery, then an Oyster Bar, it was dubbed "42nd St." by Dr. Louis "Tick" West, a prominent physician, and his friends to commemorate an evening on 42nd St. in New York. It became the fashionable place for Raleigh's famous and not-so-famous, a curious blend of fine dining downstairs and a beer hall above. This Raleigh tradition was reborn when Thad Eure, Jr., purchased and renovated the premises in 1987. 42nd Street is once again a meeting ground for all of Raleigh. Fresh seafood and shellfish are served in a convivial atmosphere where echoes of the past can still be heard.

Our White Zinfandel was selected because Wente shares our commitment to quality and tradition. Light, fruity, and zesty, we recommend it as a refreshing aperitif or with our light entrees.

GOVERNMENT WARNING: (1) ACCORDING TO THE SURGEON GENERAL, WOMEN SHOULD NOT DRINK ALCOHOLIC BEVERAGES DURING PREGNANCY BECAUSE OF THE RISK OF BIRTH DEFECTS. (2) CONSUMPTION OF ALCOHOLIC BEVERAGES IMPAIRS YOUR ABILITY TO DRIVE A CAR OR OPERATE MACHINERY, AND MAY CAUSE HEALTH PROBLEMS.

CONTAINS SULFITES   750 ml

S I M I

MENDOCINO COUNTY 29%
SONOMA COUNTY 58%
NAPA COUNTY 13%

1 9 9 0

750 ml   ALC. 13.4%
                          BY VOL.

S I M I

PRODUCED & BOTTLED BY SIMI WINERY INC.
HEALDSBURG, SONOMA COUNTY, CA USA

GOVERNMENT WARNING: (1) ACCORDING TO THE SURGEON GENERAL, WOMEN SHOULD NOT DRINK ALCOHOLIC BEVERAGES DURING PREGNANCY BECAUSE OF THE RISK OF BIRTH DEFECTS. (2) CONSUMPTION OF ALCOHOLIC BEVERAGES IMPAIRS YOUR ABILITY TO DRIVE A CAR OR OPERATE MACHINERY, AND MAY CAUSE HEALTH PROBLEMS.

CONTAINS SULFITES

0 88415 78405 0

America's Oldest Winemaking Family

Mirassou

1990
California

White Zinfandel

MADE AND BOTTLED BY
MIRASSOU VINEYARDS, SAN JOSE, CALIFORNIA
ALCOHOL 10.0% BY VOLUME, 750 ML

Mirassou

White Zinfandel

Style: Off-dry, lighter-bodied
Aroma: Ripe berries, slightly floral
Taste: Fresh and fruity "nouveau" style

Serve chilled as an apéritif or with delicate poultry and seafood dishes, ham, semi-soft to firmer style cheeses.

At Mirassou we combine the latest winemaking techniques with five generations of experience in a constant effort to bring you the finest wines available.

America's Oldest Winemaking Family
Since 1854

GOVERNMENT WARNING: (1) ACCORDING TO THE SURGEON GENERAL, WOMEN SHOULD NOT DRINK ALCOHOLIC BEVERAGES DURING PREGNANCY BECAUSE OF THE RISK OF BIRTH DEFECTS. (2) CONSUMPTION OF ALCOHOLIC BEVERAGES IMPAIRS YOUR ABILITY TO DRIVE A CAR OR OPERATE MACHINERY, AND MAY CAUSE HEALTH PROBLEMS.

CONTAINS SULFITES · 750 ML

0 858153 3

Bel Arbors

CASK 90
CHARDONNAY
AMERICAN-GROWN

ALC. 12.5% BY VOL.

Our American-grown Chardonnay is a unique wine-making concept: Selected grapes from preferred vineyards in specially chosen grape-growing regions of Washington, Oregon, and California were blended to create a classic Chardonnay of superior varietal character and drinkability.

Our Chardonnay is a wonderful and exciting wine with velvety depth and smoothness. Enjoy it with food, friends and fun.

CELLARED & BOTTLED BY
BEL ARBORS VINEYARDS
REDWOOD VALLEY, CA.

CONTAINS SULFITES 750 ml

GOVERNMENT WARNING: (1) ACCORDING TO THE SURGEON GENERAL, WOMEN SHOULD NOT DRINK ALCOHOLIC BEVERAGES DURING PREGNANCY BECAUSE OF THE RISK OF BIRTH DEFECTS. (2) CONSUMPTION OF ALCOHOLIC BEVERAGES IMPAIRS YOUR ABILITY TO DRIVE A CAR OR OPERATE MACHINERY, AND MAY CAUSE HEALTH PROBLEMS.

EST. LONDON JUNE 14, 1971

CALIFORNIA WHITE WINE

ALCOHOL 12% BY VOLUME

GOVERNMENT WARNING: (1) ACCORDING TO THE SURGEON GENERAL, WOMEN SHOULD NOT DRINK ALCOHOLIC BEVERAGES DURING PREGNANCY BECAUSE OF THE RISK OF BIRTH DEFECTS. (2) CONSUMPTION OF ALCOHOLIC BEVERAGES IMPAIRS YOUR ABILITY TO DRIVE A CAR OR OPERATE MACHINERY, AND MAY CAUSE HEALTH PROBLEMS.

CONTAINS SULFITES 750 ml

MADE & BOTTLED BY HARD ROCK CAFE VINEYARDS REDWOOD VALLEY, CALIFORNIA, U.S.A.

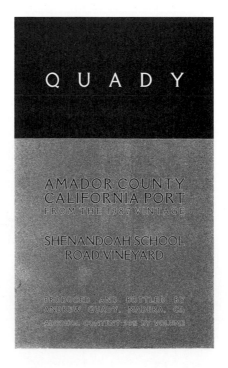

QUADY

AMADOR COUNTY
CALIFORNIA PORT
FROM THE 1983 VINTAGE

SHENANDOAH SCHOOL
ROAD VINEYARD

PRODUCED AND BOTTLED BY
ANDREW QUADY, MADERA, CA.

ALCOHOL CONTENT 20% BY VOLUME

ENDNOTES

[1] Attorneys John Manfreda and Richard Mendelson have written an accessible summary of U.S. WINE LAW, 1988. At the time of publication, Mr. Manfreda was Assistant Chief Counsel of the BATF and Mr. Mendelson was with the law firm of Dickenson, Peatman, and Fogarty, Napa, California.

[2] Muscatine, Doris, "Understanding a California Label," THE BOOK OF CALIFORNIA WINE by Doris Muscatine, Maynard Amerine, and Bob Thompson, University of California Press, Berkeley, CA, 1984, pp. 329-331.

[3] Anonymous, *Wines and Vines*, April 1991, pp. 15 and 32.

[4] Marcus, Kim, "US Seeks Truth in Wine Labelling," *The Wine Spectator*, June 30, 1988, p. 7, and anonymous, "ATF Label Rules," *Wine and Vines*, June 1990, p. 32.

[5] See Chapter 1 of this text.

[6] Mendelson, J., M.D., et al., "Hospital Treatment of Alcoholism; A Profile of Middle Income Americans," *Alcoholism: Clinical and Experimental Research*, Summer 1982, Vol. 6, No. 3, p. 379 (of patients admitted to proprietary hospitals for alcoholism treatment, over 80% described themselves as daily drinkers; these patients did not prefer wine) and Heath, D. B. "Beyond the Controversy: Education and Practical Sociocultural Alternatives," *Adolescent Counselor*, August/September 1989, Vol. 2, No. 3, p. 39 (social controls exerted by one's peers tend to have more lasting and pervasive impact than legal or regulatory controls).

[7] 27 C.F.R. Section 4.25a(e)(3) quoted in John Manfreda and Richard Mendelson, U.S. WINE LAW, 1988.

[8] All of California's viticultural areas are shown on the handsome map "Vineyards and Wineries of California," Donald Holtgrieve, 1989. This map can be obtained from Raven Maps and Images, (800) 237-0798.

[9] 27 C.F.R Section 4.26(a) quoted in John Manfreda and Richard Mendelson U.S. WINE LAW, 1988.

[10] Laube, James, "In Other Words: The Roots of Greatness," *The Wine Spectator*, December 1-15, 1985, p. 15, and a telephone conversation with Mr. Laube on January 9, 1992. Since "The Roots of Greatness" was published, Laube has authored exhaustive studies of both California Cabernet Sauvignon and California Chardonnay which include more detailed ratings of vineyards and wineries for these two varieties: Laube, James, CALIFORNIA'S GREAT CABERNETS, Wine Spectator Press, San Francisco, CA, 1989, and CALIFORNIA'S GREAT CHARDONNAYS, Wine Spectator Press, San Francisco, CA, 1990.

[11] The rest of Laube's list included the following "Vineyards to Watch": Alexander Valley (Sonoma Co., C & CS), Batto Ranch (Sonoma Co., CS), Calcaire (Alexander Valley, C), Diamond Mountain (Sterling Napa, CS), Dunn (Napa Valley, CS), Eagle (Sebastiani Sonoma Valley, CS), Edna Valley (San Luis Obispo, C & PN), Laurel Glen (Sonoma Mountain, CS), Lee (Los Carneros, PN), Newton (Napa Valley, CS & Merlot), Lytton Springs (Ridge Winery, Sonoma Co. Zinfandel), St. Clair (Los Carneros, PN), William Hill (Napa Valley, CS), Matanzas Creek (Bennett Valley in Sonoma Co., CS), Preston (Dry Creek Valley in Sonoma Co., Zinfandel & Sauvignon Blanc), Marlstone (Clos du Bois, Alexander Valley, CS & Merlot); proprietary label = vineyard name.

[12] Anonymous, A USER'S GUIDE TO SPARKLING WINE, Domaine Chandon, Yountville, CA, 1987, p. 25.

[13] Movius, John D., "A Short Guide to the German Wine Law," *The Wine Scene*, Vol. 5, No. 5, Los Angeles, CA, 1978, pages 2, 3, and 7, for sugar minimums in Brix and wine descriptions; GERMAN WINES, A CORRESPONDENCE COURSE, The German Wine Institute, Mainz, pp. 17-19 and 54-55, for the fantastical harvest descriptions and the pronunciation suggestions that follow the Table; and "Reform of the Wine Act, Article 12" in GEOGRAPHIC DESIGNATIONS OF ORIGIN FOR GERMAN WINES, Federal Republic of Germany, Bonn, p. 62.

[14] Gustafson, Dan, "Standards for Late Harvest White Wines," Château St. Jean Vineyards and Winery, P.O. Box 293, Kenwood, CA, (one-page document).

[15] Conversation with Richard Gahagan, Wine Technical Advisor, U.S. Treasury Department, Bureau of Alcohol, Tobacco, and Firearms, December 9, 1991.

Appendix C

GETTING THE CHEMISTRY RIGHT
Matchmaking With Wine and Food

This appendix is a guide to help you explore wine and food combinations based on the knowledge of wine styles you have acquired from the text and the winetasting exercises. It contains advice from my students on experimenting with wine and food, an explanation of wine and food combining concepts, an outline of what you should expect when you order wine in a restaurant, suggestions for further reading, and some special reference material for combining sparkling wines and food.

ADVICE FROM MY STUDENTS

I collected the ideas in this appendix to help my students with homework assignments that require them to choose a wine and food combining principle, select wine and food to test that principle, observe and report the effect of the food and wine on each other and on their palates, and tell me — based on this experience — what they would do differently the next time they match wine and food. In their final homework assignment, I ask them to reflect on their experience in matching wine and food and to give some advice to future students. Here are some typical suggestions:

- *Just do it. Try anything. If it doesn't work, it will only give you an excuse to try another idea. Have fun.*
- *Keep it simple, and above all be true to your taste!*
- *Use foods you know you'll like and you will be at least 50% happy with your meal! Have fun and experiment!*
- *Go ahead and try the "no-no's" of wine and food rules and decide for yourself.*
- *You don't have to rely on a bunch of rules if they clash with your tastes. They are handy to know, though, because you might have to make a choice for a person without your tastes. If you like it, drink it!*
- *I would advise other students to rely on their instincts to decide what is best for them. They should experiment because they might find a really great combination that had been previously condemned by wine connoisseurs.*

As you can see, after a semester under my tutelage, these students are a compliant and rule-bound bunch who slavishly adhere to traditional rules for wine and food combinations.

In light of their advice, I thought you might like to know their favorite wine and food "principle" for homework testing: "Dry wine may be better enhanced by foods that are not artificially sweetened . . . or high in natural sugars."[1] I'm certain the appeal of this particular idea is the great range of options it gives for experimentation!

If you like, you can stop reading here and just go out and experiment. You need no further information to follow my recommended overall strategy for matching wine and food: try a lot of combinations and decide for yourself what you like! Keep in mind that the objective is to enjoy yourself, and then experiment, observe, and remember. And, after all, the penalty for making a bad combination is not as harsh as suggested in Figure C.1, but as one of the students notes, it will only give you an excuse to try another. And, as she also said, have fun.

Figure C.1
The consequences of
experimenting with
wine and food are not
usually so harsh!
© 1990 by King Features Syndicate,
Inc. World rights reserved.

If you choose to read on, you will find that the rest of this appendix sets forth some concepts I give my students to keep their experimentation from repeating past disasters (but as you can see from their comments, even these "no-no's" offer fertile ground for testing). If you do continue reading, don't forget to follow the basic strategy and to pay attention, above all, to your own tastes.

WHY DO WE LIKE TO DRINK WINE WITH FOOD? — A LITTLE BACKGROUND IN PHYSIOLOGY AND AESTHETICS

Peynaud reminds us that the fundamental, physiological reason we drink liquids with food is to quench the thirst that comes with eating, to moisten our mouths and the food, to facilitate swallowing, and to rinse our mouths between bites.[2] Thirst motivates us to meet our daily water needs — about one milliliter per calorie of food consumed in temperate weather (the food provides about half the water we need and we make up the rest with drinks).[3]

We can also acquire a physiologically useless desire to drink when we learn that it is pleasurable to cleanse our palates after particular tastes or tactile sensations — think of the refreshment that comes after eating meat or cheese when we drink a mouthful of tart or slightly astringent wine, for example. When we add the elements of aroma and flavor to the taste and tactile refreshment — by, for example, serving a Sauvignon Blanc with a dish containing dill or red bell peppers, or sip a smooth Pinot Noir with a silky filet mignon — we have even more clearly extended the discussion to one of "gourmet thirst," and only those liquids whose odors and tastes have an affinity for the textures, odors, and tastes of foods can satisfy it. Enter wine, the beverage whose organoleptic qualities — especially its acid and tannin — most successfully complement foods. To remind my class that wine should be drunk with food, Chef Fred Morgan suggested this rule: "Never drink wine standing up — unless you are cooking!" Sitting down to dine, we venture into the realm of carefully considering wine and food together. Complementary or contrasting combinations of taste, flavor, and texture become the goal rather than quenching thirst — which is just as well, since alcoholic drinks do not satisfy our physiological thirst but actually increase our need for water because they are mild diuretics.

WHY CONCEPTS AND ODDS-MAKING, BUT NO "RULES"?

The purpose of presenting the following concepts is to help you understand why choosing wines with certain properties and avoiding certain foods will improve your chances of creating pleasing wine and food combinations. You should keep in mind that, because everyone's tastes are different, there are no real "right answers" for wine and food combinations — something you may already have learned from having a group of friends to dinner and noticing that everyone preferred a different wine and food match-up. As a result of this variation, you will have to modify the concepts offered here according to your unique tastes and preferences. As you do this you will develop your own personal principles for successful wine and food matching.

Another reason for evaluating potential wine and food combinations in terms of "odds of success" is that the large number of variables involved make it impossible to guarantee success every time. All wine and food combinations are gambles, so looking into the underlying concepts will improve your odds of success, although it can't guarantee against occasional failures. Rest assured, however, that almost any food will taste better with nearly any wine than it would by itself, and it **can** be guaranteed that serving wine will help create a more congenial atmosphere — so, in the balance, the risk is clearly worth taking!

I have also found that my students benefit most when I approach wine and food combining from a food chemistry angle. In this way their knowledge of wine and food interactions is anchored in concepts that will not change with new food fads or as they travel in search of new culinary delights. As you will learn, it is the overall style of a wine (the sum of **all** its organoleptic components) rather than interesting but irrelevant characteristics (like the grape variety, producer, or region of production) that is most important in matching wine and food. The more you know about the organoleptic (chemical) properties of a wine and how they interact with food, the better you will be able to predict successful wine and food matches. Rather than presenting you with a series of rules for specific dishes and wines — which would be useful only as long as you stuck to those particular foods — this chapter will show you how to evaluate whether a particular wine's style gives it a good or bad chance of matching foods well. This approach will allow you to venture into unexplored culinary territory with confidence and enable you to adapt easily to new situations. You will also be able to appreciate why the traditional wine and food matches of particular regions are successful.

STRATEGIES FOR IMPROVING YOUR ODDS OF SUCCESS AT WINE AND FOOD MATCHING

Wine writer and cooking teacher David Rosengarten has summarized current wine and food matching wisdom in the following brief list of food, wine, and producer strategies to maximize the chances of a successful wine and food pairing.[4] We'll consider them in that order because that is the way most of us think about putting wine and food together, especially in a restaurant: we listen to the day's specials, select our meal, think about the kind of wine(s) we want to drink, and then consult the wine list.

Food Strategies
Foods with the following sensory properties decrease your odds of success, so avoid them or approach them with caution when holding a glass of wine:

  salty foods
  very sweet foods
  acidic vegetables
  strong, raw, or fermented flavors
  food with vinegar
  foods with hot, spicy tactile sensations

Wine Strategies
Wines with the following sensory attributes have a greater probability of combining well with foods:

  crisp acidity
  dry or slightly sweet
  light or medium body
  low to moderate alcohol
  smooth or slightly rough tannins
  neutral flavor

(Note: the wines that you enjoy alone are often not the wines that you will enjoy most with a meal.)

The Producer Strategy
Choose a consistent winery, merchant, or importer, preferably one whose brands you have personal experience with.

To explain why Rosengarten's recommendations work, we'll take a closer look at each of these strategies in light of Karen Keehn's exploration of the chemical basis for successful food and wine combinations. Finally, we'll discuss a list of consistent California wineries that will help you navigate wine shops and restaurant lists.[5]

FOOD STRATEGIES — THE DETAILS

Almost any food will be improved by serving a good wine with it. (By the way, if you have to compromise on quality, save on the food, **not** on the wine — quoth the wine teacher!) There are, however, some foods that clash badly with wines. To introduce this topic in my class, we take a break in the lecture to write a quick list of our favorite foods, and then we check them for "wine friendliness." Last semester I listed:

1. Snickers bars
2. Chips and salsa
3. Guinness Stout
4. Rare lamb chops
5. Espresso and cappuccino
6. Scallops poached in Fumé Blanc (a microwave favorite)
7. Pasta with pesto
8. Gelato (chocolate, of course)
9. Spinach salad
10. Thai cuisine

As you can see, my favorites will give us plenty to discuss in terms of "foods to avoid." I'll also mention some of the ways I "cheat" and drink wine with some of these low-odds-of-success foods.

Let's check my list. The first and eighth items would be eliminated in the "very" sweet category, and item five would be the recommended beverage rather than wine. My second item — salsa — would be wine unfriendly on three counts: vinegar, salt, and hot, spicy tactile sensations, which would also suggest item three or a lighter brew, well-chilled, as an accompaniment. Even if a wine-friendly citrus juice were substituted for the vinegar in my salsa, the dominant tastes of the chilis, cilantro, and the raw onion and garlic would make it an extremely hard dish to combine with wine. If I chose my Thai food (item 10) carefully to avoid "hot, spicy tactile sensations" I could create a wine-friendly meal in spite of the challenge of the spicy, lemony, and fishy ingredients; but the reason I've gone to that Thai restaurant is to enjoy those very hot, spicy tactile sensations, so I'll probably be sipping ice water or Thai beer to quell the invited fires — though chilled sparkling wines can be a successful combination for some people. Item nine is one of those acidic vegetables — containing oxalic acid, in this case — that are generally wine unfriendly, but I think I'll order a light, refreshing, chilled brut sparkling wine or a glass of cold and very slightly sweet rosé to enjoy with it. That leaves me with three optimally wine-compatible foods on my list of favorites: lamb, scallops, and pasta with pesto, and the pesto receives a rating of "maybe" depending on how much the raw basil and garlic flavors come through. If I'm lucky and they are strong — the way I like them best — I'll just order a simple, fruity, less tannic red like Gamay Beaujolais or a lighter style Zinfandel to wash down those little green-coated rotini.

Let's take a closer look at why my favorite foods that are salty, sweet, hot, spicy, strong, raw, fermented, vinegary, or made with acidic vegetables are not good companions for the wines I love.

Salty Foods

Salt in small amounts does not clash with wines, and it can even soften a red wine's astringency for some people. However, in larger quantities salt is not compatible with wines — especially red wines, since for many tasters it reinforces their bitterness and astringency — and it can produce a metallic taste with more acidic wines. Can any wines be used successfully with the Easter ham? Yes, you can drink wine with ham, and the best bets for success will have some residual sugar, full fruit flavors, moderate acidity, and no tannins. If that sounds like a white or rosé wine, you're right; and the rosé would get my vote for the added beauty of its color.

Very Sweet Foods

Sweet foods can have sugar contents as high as 24%. The sugar contents of sweet wines are rarely over 10%, so most wines cannot balance the sweetness of the sweeter desserts. Furthermore, such very sweet foods make even well-balanced wines seem sour and many people prefer to drink a slightly bitter beverage like coffee with them to cut through their richness. The best desserts with wine are only moderately sweet. Fruit-based desserts, for example, can be successful with wines. Most tropical and dried fruits need to be avoided because their sugar levels are too high, but ripe, sweet apricots, peaches, pears, and berries have more moderate sugar contents. These stone fruits and berries — perhaps poached in the wine or in spiced cream and served with cookies or in a tart with a nut crust — can become desserts that combine successfully with naturally sweet late-harvest wines such as White Riesling and Sauvignon Blanc.

Acidic Foods

Because wines are acidic, it is hard to combine them successfully with acidic foods. In fact, the stronger the acid in the food, the lower the odds of a successful combination. Happily, all acids are not created equally problematic: among the citrus fruits, for example, wine acidity can be combined more successfully with the acidity of oranges and lemons than with that from limes or grapefruit.[6] Another tactic to help us enjoy wines with acidic foods is to combine them in dishes made with added sweetness or fat — in cream sauces, for example — which can moderate the acids in vegetables such as spinach, asparagus, sorrel, and artichokes. (Artichokes, by the way, have another interesting effect on some people: they can make a dry wine — or glass of water, for that matter — taste sweet if you take sip after eating a petal or two.) The strong acidity of fermented foods such as sauerkraut, pickles, and other foods made or preserved with vinegar cannot be masked and is best avoided with wines.

Hot, Spicy Foods

Hot and spicy foods cry out for cool, refreshing beverages that are low in alcohol so that the warmth of a high-alcohol beverage does not add to the heat from the foods. When eating in a Mexican, Szechuan, Hunan, Indian, or Thai restaurant, for example, it's best to ignore the wine list and opt for very cold beer or ice water. If you insist upon drinking wine, a simple, **very** well-chilled sparkling wine would be the best bet — and I'd advise you not to choose a very expensive wine in case you lose your own wager! Foods with strong flavors — including vinegar, raw onions, sauerkraut, pickles, garlic, and many kinds of olives — will also overwhelm a fine wine's more subtle flavors and call for less complex, quaffable beverages such as beer, iced tea, or, for die-hard enophiles, the simplest, fruity young wines taken in well-spaced sips so that your tongue does not become the battlefield for the predicted clashes in these wine–food tactile wars. For more on this subject, see "Strategies to Salvage Sub-Optimal Gastronomic Occasions" later in this chapter.

WINE STRATEGIES

There are five strategies based on wines' structural components and one flavor strategy to follow when choosing a wine to increase your odds of a successful match. I will consider each structural strategy in turn before discussing the flavor strategy.

Structural Strategy #1 — Crisp Acidity

Acid, alcohol, and tannin are the key wine components involved in a wine's fundamental sensory function at a meal — refreshing the diner's palate. The acidity of white wines is their most important attribute for palate-cleansing and food matching; in red wines, however, the astringency of their tannins is more important. Because the perceived acidity of a wine increases with its astringency, red wines with their lower acid concentrations seem similar in acidity and will have the same palate-cleansing effect as white wines of higher acid content.

The higher acidity of younger wines makes them a good match for rich foods (those high in fat and protein content), which require more acid in the wine to refresh the diner's palate. They should not, however, be combined with "rich" sweet foods because they will taste too acidic. Foods that are less rich are better enjoyed with wines of lower acid content or lower apparent acidity. Because the apparent acidity of wines decreases with residual sugar and barrel and bottle aging, wines with these characteristics combine well with foods that are lower in fat content, such as broiled fish or chicken. For example, suppose the wine list you are perusing features two styles of Chenin Blanc: one is dry, and the label reproduced in the wine list tells us that it was aged in oak for two months and describes it as "austere"; the other has a residual sugar of 1.0 gram/100 ml and is described as fruity. Both wines are available for sale by the glass in this restaurant. Following your low-fat diet carefully, you have ordered a plain grilled halibut steak, while your perennially slender cousin has requested a chicken breast with a light herb-cream sauce — the specialty of the house. Following the strategies suggested above, you would order the slightly sweet Chenin Blanc for yourself and the dry one for your cousin — unless she insists on the sweeter wine because she likes it better. Remember, personal taste always wins in this game!

A final note: wine acidity may create a problem if it is very high, making the wine itself taste sour — not a good bet for either dining or sipping — and causing an unpleasant metallic taste with salty foods. Wines with very high acidities are relatively rare in the U.S. market, so this problem should not arise often.

Structural Strategy #2 — Dry or Slightly Sweet

Dry wines are the most versatile with foods and, as mentioned in my students' favorite wine-and-food-combining principle, they taste better with foods that are not sweet. This is because sweet foods — cashew and macadamia nuts, fruits, many barbecue sauces, and desserts, for example — will make them taste sour and feel thin. Wines that are slightly sweet can be a good choice when you want to reduce the perception of saltiness, tartness, or bitterness in a food. Slightly sweet wines can make more successful combinations than dry wines with ham, salty cheeses, vegetables, and nuts with some astringency in their skins (walnuts or almonds). When considering the relative sweetness of the wine and food, be sure to take into account all the food's ingredients: sweet herbs and spices, nuts, and ripe fruit.

Going beyond "slightly sweet," dessert wines, with their high levels of sugar, are particularly hard to match with sweet foods, and I think they are best with foods that are less sweet than the wine, such as pound cake, cheeses, unsalted nuts, and fruit. In such cases the food serves to refresh the palate between sips of the wine. However, to illustrate the variability of taste in this area, I must mention the instructor who took over my wine class when I was on my last sabbatical leave: he likes to drink *Botrytis*-affected, late-harvest wines with the richest available cheesecakes. For more about serving dessert wines and specific food suggestions, see the section "Dessert Wines and Foods" later in this chapter.

To salvage the occasion when you have nothing but a bottle of sweet wine to serve with dinner, remember that cold serving temperatures decrease our perception of sweetness and chill the wine as much as possible before serving. Wine in a standard 750 ml bottle drops five to ten degrees F per hour in a standard 42 degree refrigerator.

Structural Strategy #3 — Light to Medium Body

A couple of years ago I called a local radio station to ask the wine-savvy chef who hosts the Saturday morning cooking show what advice he could give my students for their wine and food homework. He responded: "Match the weight of the wine to the weight of the food." If you are intent upon streamlining your learning and want to remember just one wine- and food-matching concept that covers all wines and all foods, this is it.

A dry wine's weight or body increases with increasing concentrations of tannin, alcohol, and grape extract — a collective term for everything that is left in a wine after the water and alcohol are evaporated. As you will have deduced, red wines in general will have more body than white wines, and it is the match between the body of the wine and the weight of the food that constitutes a large part of the rationale for the familiar rule: "red wine with meat and white wine with fish."

The strategy of selecting wines of light to medium body reflects the fact that white wines and most red wines will combine well with the majority of foods we eat these days (**my** list in an earlier section notwithstanding). This is because we just don't eat rich, strongly flavored game or similar dishes very often — but that has not always been the case. If, for example, we stepped back to 450 AD and were slogging through the remains of the Roman Empire in the army of Attila the Hun and "dining" off the land, we'd have a different strategy for increasing our odds of success in wine and food combinations: "serve only the heaviest red wines with fresh venison, game birds, or rodents, served raw or hastily roasted over an open fire."

Beyond the generalizations about red vs. white, what can we say about the body of specific wines? I have summarized the relative weights of some dry California varietal wines in Figure C.2. The only truly heavy-bodied wines shown are some Cabernet Sauvignons and Syrahs and the late-harvest Zinfandels. There is an overlap in the relative weights of the white and red wines: both Chardonnay and Pinot Noir fall in a transitional area between the generally lighter-bodied white wines and the generally medium- to heavy-bodied red wines. Because I'm certain that you will be able to find cases in which one winery's Zinfandel is heavier than another's Syrah, take the relationships in this figure with a grain of salt.

Figure C.2
Relative Weights of
Some California
Table Wines

Lighter					Heavier
White Riesling Chenin Blanc Sparkling Wines	Gewürztraminer Sauvignon Blanc Chardonnay, no oak	Chardonnay, barrel-fermented or aged			
	Gamay Beaujolais Nouveau	Pinot Noir	Zinfandel Merlot Cabernet Franc	Cabernet Sauvignon Syrah	Late-Harvest Zinfandel

Here are some examples of matching the weights of wines and foods: lighter-bodied wines should be paired with foods of delicate texture such as filet of sole or red snapper á la microwave (a staple chez Baldy), and heavier-bodied wines are best matched with chewier, richer foods that have a sturdier texture and/or higher fat or oil content — lamb, duck, salmon, cheeses, and foods prepared with butter and cream. Matching a spectrum of white varietal wines with a range of fish also uses this concept, with wines of increasing body suggested with fish of increasing fat content: dry, tart Chenin Blanc with sole or perch and richer-style Chardonnay with salmon.

If you cannot get the exact match you want or find out it needs adjustment, you might be able to save the day by taking advantage of the fact that colder serving temperatures decrease the perception of body in wine — just be sure to drink it before it warms up.

Structural Strategy #4 — Low to Moderate Alcohol

Alcohol content is correlated with wine body — the higher the level of alcohol, the heavier the body — and produces a slightly sweet taste as well as, in high concentrations, a hot tactile sensation. With foods, low or moderate alcohol helps cleanse the palate, as do a wine's tannins and acids. As the strategy suggests, however, the hotness of higher-alcohol wines makes them harder to combine with foods. A high level of alcohol is an overpowering perception in itself and can transform pleasant food flavors into tastes that aren't pleasant at all. As already mentioned, the hotness of high-alcohol wines adds to the hot spiciness of peppery food. This concept was brought home to me one evening as I sweated through a notably unsuccessful combination of my favorite Zinfandel (alcohol content 13.5%) with a "spicy" tomato sauce on pasta — a chilled Gamay Beaujolais would have been a much better choice. Fortunately, there were no dinner guests present to add embarrassment to my lesson! A cooking note: nearly all of a wine's alcohol will evaporate with about 10 minutes of simmering.

Structural Strategy #5 — Smooth or Slightly Rough Texture

Only red wines and barrel-fermented and barrel-aged white wines have significant amounts of tannin, with the red wines having very much higher levels. These tannins are vital to the complexity and longevity of such wines, but they constitute a defect if their levels are too high or if they are noticeably bitter. High levels of astringent tannins can make it hard to perceive a wine's flavors and other tastes. Other structural components can mitigate or reinforce this effect: residual sugar in a wine can mask tannins, while high acid levels can increase the perception of both their astringency and bitterness.

Fats, proteins, and sweetness in foods can reduce the perception of tannin — so, for example, cream sauces, cheeses, and spaghetti sauces with meat that have a little natural sweetness from the vegetables and richness from the meat's fat can work well with red wines. Acids and saltiness in foods reinforce the astringency in wines, so order an off-dry Chenin Blanc instead of a young Syrah with your Caesar Salad! Some vegetables have their own tannins: the hot peppers in my disastrous spicy pasta sauce had tannins as well as heat, which accentuated both the pucker and the hotness of my yummy-in-other-circumstances Zinfandel. The strategy of choosing a wine with low to moderate tannin levels — one that is smooth to slightly rough — avoids the potential pitfalls presented by combining the acidity, salt, and tannins in food and wine.

A note for cooks: when reducing a red-wine-based sauce, keep in mind that the wine's tannins will become concentrated, creating an increased perception of astringency. Stock is often added to red wine sauces to diminish their astringency.

A Flavor Strategy — Neutral Flavors

Although they may not be the optimum for the ultimate gastronomic experience of the mutual flavor enhancement that can happen with wine and food, neutral wine flavors are the best bet for raising our odds of success because they avoid potential flavor clashes. Even with relatively neutral wines, however, you will still need to consider whether the overall strength of the wine's flavor matches that of the food or seasonings. This often turns out to depend on the age of the wine: younger wines are usually coarser in structure and stronger in flavor and combine well with more strongly flavored foods, while older wines are more delicate in structure and flavor and are best with milder foods.

Flavor similarities between wine and food can sometimes complement each other brilliantly, but they can also compete or clash, and such combinations need to be approached with caution and in the context of other considerations about the wine's sensory properties. For example, plum-scented Syrah can work well with a plum sauce for roast duck, but if the grapefruit aroma note in Gewürztraminer suggests fresh grapefruit with this wine for Sunday brunch you should remember that the acidity in fresh grapefruit is very difficult to harmonize with wine. Flavor contrasts also can spark a wine and food pairing. Here are some examples of flavor affinities between wines and ingredients with contrasting flavors (more of Karen Keehn's affinity suggestions are reproduced in the reference section of this Appendix):

Chardonnay with orange
Sauvignon Blanc and mustard
Chenin Blanc with dill
Cabernet Sauvignon with nutmeg
Zinfandel with sage
Syrah with tomatoes[8]

A Strategic Question — What About Color?

The color of wine is an important contribution to the overall aesthetic pleasure of a meal, and I believe that, in general, it should harmonize or contrast tastefully with the colors of the food. Glasses of a brilliantly clear, light-colored Fumé Blanc will blend better with the colors of a meal of sole or swordfish than do servings of inky Syrah, but a cranberry-red Gamay could create a pleasant color contrast and be structurally compatible with a meal of fish. Sauces and garnishes can also play an important role in the area of color harmony or contrast between wine and food.

Speaking of color, what about the hackneyed idea of drinking "white wine with fish and red wine with meats"? As it turns out, this is a useful rule, but not just because of the aesthetic role of color in a meal. You may be a little disappointed that your arduous journey through the chemistry of wine- and food-matching concepts has led you to nothing more than the conventional wisdom — but now you know that the rule works, because many important characteristics of wine may frequently (though not always) be predicted based on the wine's color. White color in wine is typically associated with lighter body, smooth texture, and less intense flavors (perfect with most fish), and red color in wine goes along with heavier body, rough texture from tannins, and greater intensity of flavor (which is what we are looking for in a wine that can combine well with rich dishes, including red meats).

David Rosengarten's and Joshua Wesson's apparently iconoclastic book, RED WINE WITH FISH, is actually based on the same concepts of wine and food combining outlined here: it tells you what the conventional rules are and then how to "break" them based on the principles that underlie the rules. For example, they suggest that you serve red wines that are young, fruity, high-acid, very light-bodied, and have low or no tannin (sound like white wines to you?) with fish that have "something brown in the preparation — grilling, broiling or meat juices" to help them match the red wine.[10] In addition, if you want to "break the rule in the other direction," most of their suggested white wine with meat combinations feature meats that are white — chicken, veal, or pork.

THE PRODUCER STRATEGY — CHOOSE A CONSISTENT WINERY

Some guidance in this aspect of the strategies is very important when you are operating in the most intimidating arena for wine and food matching: at a restaurant with important guests. This setting has the smallest allowable margin of error and brings out the most conservative behavior in even the most adventurous matchmakers. Somehow, the philosophies of *"Just do it, Have fun; Try the 'no-no's'"* and *"Be true to your taste!"* all fade from consciousness in the presence of a waiter or wine steward, the limits of the menu (Is *"the food I know I'll like"* even on here?),

Figure C.3
Restaurant Wine Pricing

"There's a bottle of wine on here that's more than our mortgage payment!"

your guests, a restaurant wine list with prices approximating your recollection of the national debt (or your mortgage payment, as in Figure C.3), and a list of wineries notable for their obscurity as well as their costly products. It is here that we are all in danger of reverting to the gastronomic equivalent of the fetal position: turning the wine list toward the waiter, pointing to the name of the least expensive white wine, and whispering "We'll have a bottle of this."

What to do? Well, it's time to take several deep breaths and remember 1. the strategies for a successful wine and food match (*"they are handy to know, though, because you might have to make a choice for a person without your tastes"*), and 2. that you have a voice with which to converse with the well-informed wine steward standing at your side, to learn what you need to know about the wines on the list to put your strategies to work. So, after everyone has made their choice from the menu, just go back to "dry or slightly sweet" and work through the list of strategies. And, if you're stuck in the gastronomic fetal position, remember that Gamay Beaujolais is the odds-maker's favorite wine because it fits every strategic criterion and most budgets.

Ten Wineries to Bet On

If the wine list features California wines, you are in luck. In 1989 syndicated wine columnist Dan Berger put together this list, which he characterizes as "highly personal," in response to a question he is frequently asked: what wineries would you pick for consistency, regardless of the kind of wine you wanted to drink? Berger first established two criteria: a winery must make at least three wines and must have released at least five vintages. He then evaluated all of a number of wineries' products and gave extra credit for value. Here is his list of the top ten California wineries, which he updated in a December 1991 conversation.

Dan Berger's Top Ten California Wineries for Consistency.[11]

1.	Silverado Vineyards	6.	Château Montelena
2.	Sterling	7.	Beringer
3.	Navarro	8.	Fetzer
4.	Chappellet	9.	Clos du Val[12]
5.	Iron Horse	10.	Kenwood

Because Berger insisted that a winery produce three or more wines, some notably consistent specialists did not make his list, including Jordan, Hanzell, Dunn, Silver Oak, Laurel Glen, and Grace. What is the key to these wineries' consistency? For most of them the consistent style and quality of their wines are based on California's overall good weather, which reduces vintage-to-vintage variation, and a reliable source of good grapes, either grown by the winery itself or purchased from the same growers year after year.

Going Beyond the Top Ten: Where to Find More Winery Tips

If you want more than ten recommendations, I have included the "runners up" to his top ten in the endnotes. You could also consult the wine-buying suggestions for the tasting exercises in Appendix D for wines I like to use in class. Another resource for learning about consistent California wineries is CALIFORNIA WINE WINNERS, an annual publication that lists the medal winners at wine competitions.[13] You can also assemble your own list of locally available wines by interviewing your wine merchant, wine stewards, and knowledgeable friends.

WHEN SHOULD I USE SPARKLING WINES WITH FOODS?

The Champenoise would answer, "All the time!" — and, perhaps, "Who needs food to drink Champagne?" As aperitifs, sparkling wines, because of their legendary mystique and light, refreshing character, both heartily welcome guests and prepare their palates for the meal to come. With a meal, sparkling wines can be combined with lighter dishes or used to cleanse the palate between heavier courses. Sparkling wines are often good combinations with spicy and fishy foods. Sweeter sparkling wines — those with an extra dry, demi-sec, sec, or doux finish — add elegance as well as sweetness to a dessert course. See "Champagne goes Well with . . ." and "Ten Strategies for Matching Champagne and Food" in the reference section of this appendix for some specific suggestions, from whimsical to elegant.

DESSERT WINES AND FOODS
Using *Botrytis*-Affected, Late-Harvest Wines

Simple foods such as plain roasted almonds, ripe Bartlett or Comice pears, or slightly sweet baked goods containing apricots or peaches pick up the flavors in these wines. They can even combine well with entrées — even beef — for the adventuresome.[14]

Fortified Dessert Wines

Dry *Fino* sherries and *Manzanillas* are traditional apéritif wines and are used in their native habitat, southern Spain, to accompany *tapas* of air-cured ham, almonds, seafood, or humble, but delicious, fresh potato chips. I enjoy *Amontillado* and *Oloroso* sherries with light desserts of fruit and toasted almonds, walnuts, or hazelnuts, and port with its classic partners — Stilton Cheese and walnuts. For more imaginative suggestions, winemaker Andrew Quady publishes a newsletter for dessert wine aficionados and even sponsored a contest recently to devise entrées to accompany his orange Muscat dessert wine.[15]

TWO SHORT NOTES ON THE NON-GUSTATORY ASPECTS OF WINE AND FOOD MATCHING
Strategies to Salvage Sub-Optimal Gastronomic Occasions

If you absolutely cannot avoid participating in an inevitable gastronomic disaster — if, for example, you must eat a strong vinegar-rich food and drink wine with it, because you are the ambassador who is being honored at a state occasion in a strategically important, cabbage-producing country whose most important export product is sauerkraut — you can always cleanse your palate with bread or converse at length between well-spaced bites of food and sips of wine. When confronted with wine-unfriendly foods, simply insert time, water, or bland food between the sips and the bites. In fact, that is how we eat most of the time anyway, taking several sips of wine between bites of food. The sips of water you substitute for wine will have the added benefit of diluting the wine in your stomach and slowing the rate at which alcohol is absorbed into your blood, thus keeping your mind sharp for your after-dinner negotiations of world sauerkraut prices with the powerful members of the international cabbage cartel.

The key to enjoying yourself under such circumstances is flexibility. If the wine won't cleanse your palate between bites of a wine-unfriendly food, use something else, like a bite of bread or plain baked potato, and drink the wine for its own sake — and for the sake of international relations and prolonging the pleasures of good company (remember, it's only the gastronomy that is sub-optimal in this example).

Another Note — Psychological Considerations

In the above example, the diplomatic considerations of being a gracious guest can be more important than the wine and the food. At home, being a thoughtful host who makes guests feel comfortable may mean that you have to compromise your principles — of wine and food combining, that is. For example, my mother-in-law loves lamb and beef, but she does not like red wine, so we always have a bottle of White Zinfandel for her, along with a bottle of Cabernet Sauvignon or Pinot Noir for us (compromising does not necessarily have to include suffering for the hosts!).

The careful choice of wine and food can add a range of important psychological elements to a meal, including the recollection of the pleasant memories of a special occasion, the warmth of holiday traditions, and even the fun of a humorous mismatch. The mental stimulation as well as the gustatory pleasure of variety is part of the reason we are intrigued by matching wine and food. The psychological aspect of choosing a combination is highly personal and occasion-specific, of course, so I can really only offer one basic piece of advice: if you want to create a memorable meal, don't overlook it.

WHAT YOU SHOULD EXPECT WHEN YOU DINE OUT — WINE SERVICE IN RESTAURANTS

Let's return to the restaurant that we were just visiting when we were discussing the producer strategy of choosing a consistent winery and look at what you should expect in terms of wine service.

The Wine List

The best wine lists are put together with an eye to providing the customers with a variety of wines that are compatible with the restaurant's cuisine and fall within a wide range of prices. The list should identify the wines with precision, giving the type, vintage, and producer, and should organize them in a logical order. My favorite wine lists arrange the wines by style rather than region, making it easier for me to consider and discuss my options. Be sure to study the wine list at a leisurely pace so that you are comfortably familiar with it and don't overlook something special.

A Wine Steward?

There should be someone on the restaurant staff who is particularly well-informed about the wines and the actual preparation of menu items to help you select a wine that will make a pleasing combination with your meal. This person may have trained the waiters or may have made specific suggestions about wine and food matches on the wine list or a chalkboard. Few American restaurants have a wine steward, but if your waiter is not able to answer your questions about the wines and how the food was prepared, ask whether someone else on the staff — perhaps the manager or owner — might be more knowledgeable.

Selecting a Wine

Because we've already considered in some detail how to evaluate a wine's sensory attributes to pick a wine that will go well with food and have identified some consistent California producers, we're left with some additional non-sensory matters to consider here.

Choosing the Wine Before You Choose the Food

I've presented the strategies for improving the odds of a successful wine and food match under the assumption that we generally choose our entrées and then pick the wine. However, selecting the wine may precede the choice of foods, or even your arrival at the restaurant. Maybe there is a wine on the list that you especially enjoyed last month and tonight you want to plan your dinner around it, or perhaps you have some special wine in your cellar at home and want someone else to create the meal to show it off. In both cases, you will need to look at the menu and decide what to order based on the properties of the wine you've selected, and this will often require some additional information about the food preparation from the restaurant staff. Bringing your own wine with you can allow you to drink older wines — most restaurants do not have the space to age wines and feature only young red wines — or allow you to enjoy wines that the restaurant does not carry. That, by the way, is one thing you should check before arriving at a restaurant with your own bottle(s): is the wine you plan to bring on the wine list? If it is, leave it home.

What will the restaurant do when you've brought your own wine? Someone on the staff will greet you and admire your wines, congratulate you on your excellent taste, and ask you when and how you would like the wines to be served: in what order, with which courses; slightly chilled, at room temperature, or placed in an ice bucket, if you want only one wine poured at time; and whether you want the bottles left at the table or brought out for serving. The restaurant will charge you a "corkage fee" — which varies considerably between restaurants — for using their glasses and for serving the wines.

How Much to Spend

Don't be shy about letting your waiter or wine steward know how much you are comfortable investing, because this is part of the information they need to help you make the best wine choice. If you don't want to reveal your financial limitations to your guests you can simply point to a price on the wine list and say you'd like "something like this." Beware the "helpful" assistant who steers you to the expensive end of the wine list.

How Much to Order

Each person dining will consume, in the course of an evening, about one-half of a standard 750 ml bottle of wine. If you order more than one wine for a group of diners, you will need to specify the order in which you want them served. The "half bottle per person" approximation also means that it is perfectly reasonable to order two 375 ml bottles for two diners. This is, in fact, the most reasonable approach if each person's choice of entrée or their divergent tastes in wine make it impossible to choose a single wine that is compatible with both dishes or both palates. Remember, don't compromise on the wine! Date someone else if you don't like little wine bottles.

The Wine Service — Presenting, Opening, and Tasting Your Choice

The wine you have selected should always be brought to you unopened so that you can verify that it is actually the wine you have selected or can approve a substitution, usually of a more recent vintage than the one on the wine list. While you are waiting for the bottle to be brought to the table or opened, you will want to discretely smell the empty wine glass to be sure it has no residual soap or chlorine odors. The glass should not be chilled.

After you approve the wine, the bottle will be opened. The server will cut off the top of the capsule, check the cork, wipe it with a napkin, and deftly insert the corkpuller, withdraw the cork in a smooth, elegant, but unobtrusive motion, and wipe the lip of the bottle again, checking to see that the cork did not crumble. The cork will then be presented for your inspection — it should be firm and not cracked — and a sample of wine will be carefully and driplessly poured for you to taste.

You should follow the normal sequence of steps for sensory evaluation and not hurry the process of checking the color and clarity, aroma, bouquet, flavors, sugar, acid, body, astringency, and aftertaste. Because restaurants typically serve chilled wines too cold — right out of their cold storage unit whose temperature is typically set to the optimum for beer, not wine — be sure to let the wine warm up in your mouth to check for off odors. Retaste the wine and even ask for another sample if you have a concern and you want to re-evaluate; your first impression, especially of a cold wine, may not be enough. After you have approved the wine, it will be poured for your guest(s), the women being served before the men. As the host, you will be served last.

Sending the Wine Back

If the wine is flawed — with a corked or sulfur dioxide odor, or unbalanced in acid, sugar, or astringency, for example — or if it has been misrepresented — the 1991 vintage turns out not to be "exactly like the 1990" (which the restaurant ran out of last week) or the wine really is not a "rich, oak-aged" Chardonnay — you may reject it and choose another. Most likely the restaurant staff will cheerfully consume the wine you spurned.

There may be an occasion when it is to your advantage to accept a misrepresented wine. Several years ago, Dick and I stopped relatively late to eat lunch at a California restaurant highly recommended for both its cuisine and its extensive wine list. We were seated and a waitress who had apparently spent too much time on her feet that day presented us with the menu and wine list and tossed the silverware and bread and butter onto the table. We looked at each other and decided, given this hostile service, to make this a perfunctory meal rather than the great dining experience we had anticipated. Checking the wine list, I settled on a recent vintage of Cabernet Sauvignon listed for $6.00 per bottle. When Ms. Crabby-Sorefoot returned to the table with the bottle, I was presented not with the recent, inexpensive vintage I had chosen but with a bottle of a much older wine of a superb vintage, worth at least ten times what I was originally planning to invest in our luncheon beverage. Feeling it was fit retribution for the "service" we had been subjected to, I approved the bottle, tasted the wine to confirm that I was not just dreaming about the vintage error, and instructed the waitress to serve it. We then enjoyed this excellent wine with the bread, ate our lunch, paid the modest bill — even tipping Ms. Crabby-Sorefoot — and left feeling only moderately guilty about not pointing out her error.

Adjusting the Temperature

Ice buckets often appear automatically when you order white wines, but they are necessary only for sparkling wines that will be consumed over a relatively long time and need the cold to help retain their bubbles. White wines usually need to warm up from refrigerator temperature rather than to be chilled further. The ice bucket can be useful, however, if wines have been stored in a warm place. Unfortunately, this happens in Chico during the summer at my favorite restaurant, so if you dine there in July you may see me endangering my credibility with a bottle of fine Cabernet Sauvignon protruding from the ice bucket at my table. As mentioned earlier, the proper serving temperature for red wines is 65-68 degrees F, which is cooler than most American rooms — especially in California in the summer — so chilling red wine is not always a forbidden practice.

Breathing and Decanting

Letting a wine "breathe" means aerating it — exposing its components to air so that they can react with the oxygen. Young wines with minor sensory defects are the only wines that can benefit consistently from aeration. Allowing a wine to breathe requires pouring it from the bottle into a larger container with a lot of splashing, since just taking the cork out of a bottle does not expose the wine to a significant amount of air. Aged wines should not be aerated, but they are often decanted.

Decanting is recommended to separate a wine from its sediment. Red wines over about ten years of age are often candidates for this procedure, which involves: 1. bringing the wine carefully from the cellar so as to not disturb the sediment and then either maintaining it in a horizontal position until it is decanted or placing it upright for a couple of days before opening so that any loose sediment settles to the bottom of the bottle; 2. completely removing the capsule from the neck of the bottle so you can see the wine as it passes through the neck; 3. positioning a bright light source — such as a candle or flashlight — below the naked neck of the bottle so that it will illuminate the wine as it is poured; and 4. pouring the wine slowly without interruption from its bottle into a clean container, holding the neck over the light source, and stopping when you see the first flecks of sediment appear in the neck. To minimize aeration, pour the wine down the side of the receiving carafe without splashing.

IF ALL THAT WASN'T ENOUGH — SUGGESTIONS FOR FURTHER EXPLORATION

For ideas, recipes, and specific exercises to help you to practice the concepts of wine and food pairing, see David Rosengarten's and Joshua Wesson's book, RED WINE WITH FISH: THE NEW ART OF MATCHING WINE WITH FOOD[16] or Malcolm Hébert's WINE LOVERS' COOKBOOK.[23] For a guide to using wines when entertaining, you can consult the new edition of Barbara Ensrud's WINE AND FOOD, A GUIDE TO ENTERTAINING THROUGH THE SEASONS[17] or FAVORITE RECIPES OF CALIFORNIA WINEMAKERS.[22] The definitive word on the science of foods can be found in Harold McGee's ON FOOD AND COOKING: THE SCIENCE AND LORE OF THE KITCHEN.[18]

To keep your mouth watering and stimulate your gastronomic imagination, you could subscribe to *The Wine and Food Companion* or *Bon Appétit* or add yourself to the mailing list of *Napa Valley Tables*, a free, high-quality publication featuring recipes, menus, and informative articles on wine and food that is produced by Beringer Vineyards' Culinary Arts Center.[19] Other Northern California wineries that offer wine and food information, from charts to seminars, are McDowell Valley Vineyards, Fetzer, Simi, Robert Mondavi, and Inglenook-Napa Valley.[20]

For more on restaurant tactics, opening wine bottles, decanting, wine storage, and the like, I recommend Hugh Johnson's HOW TO ENJOY WINE. Both the book and its sometimes quite funny videotape rendition are full of good information.[21]

FOR REFERENCE — SPECIFIC WINE AND FOOD SUGGESTIONS

As specific points of departure for your food and wine explorations, some suggestions from McDowell Valley Vineyards, Korbel, and David Rosengarten and Joshua Wesson are reprinted below. Another widely available source of specific wine- and food-matching ideas — in addition to the publications mentioned earlier — is any edition of Hugh Johnson's POCKET ENCYCLOPEDIA OF WINE. This pocket-size book may be discreetly taken into an elegant restaurant more successfully than a copy of this text.

From Fruits to Nuts, and Beyond — Wine and Food Affinities

Often the composition of the sauce lovingly made to ladle onto a dish is the key to linking that dish successfully to wines. The following affinities between some ingredients used for sauces and garnishes — as well as some appetizers — are included to help improve your chances of creating pleasing marriages of wines and foods. This information was adapted from McDowell Valley Vineyards' WINE AND FOOD AFFINITIES by Karen Keehn.

Chardonnay Orange and lemon zest, orange (w/o membranes), tomato, eggplant, red bell pepper, onion, leek, chive, olive; fresh bay, thyme, tarragon, oregano, sage, ginger, dried cardamon, and paprika; walnut, pecan, hazelnut, pistachio, brazil nut; morel, truffle, chanterelle, and shitake mushrooms.

Fume Blanc Orange and lemon zest, tomato, red and yellow bell pepper, hearts of palm, onion, chive, leek, eggplant, fresh marjoram, lemon thyme, dill, sorrel, chervil and parsley, basil, tarragon, ginger, mustard, mild curry, tumeric, nutmeg; domestic or wild mushrooms (shitake, chanterelle, morel); pistachio, almond, toasted sesame seed.

Chenin Blanc Lemon zest, pear, melon, scallion, leek, hearts of palm, shallot, tomato, cucumber, caper and green peppercorn; fresh lemon thyme, dill, lemon basil, parsley and chervil, tarragon, dry curry, ginger; pistachio, blanched almond; domestic and wild mushrooms, particularly cepes (boletes), chanterelle, shitake.

French Colombard Apple, pear, peach, melon, prosciutto, grape, strawberry, cabbage; lemon thyme, fennel bulb and seeds, basil, tarragon, clove, allspice, mild curry, cardamon, mint, ginger; blanched almond, cashew, macadamia; domestic mushrooms and wild boletes or chanterelle.

Zinfandel Blanc Tropical fruits like mango and papaya, pomegranate, kiwi, prickly pear, peach, apple, grapes; fruit chutney, especially mango ginger; spinach, cucumber, chard; ginger, dry cardamon, spicy mustards; combine with cashew, macadamia, peanuts.

Grenache Rosé Apricot, orange, peach, strawberry, kiwi; onion, kidney beans, red and green bell peppers, eggplant; combine with fresh fennel bulb and seeds, mild curry dishes, fresh mint, tumeric, cinnamon, or unsweetened orange marmalade; use with walnuts or pecans; complements domestic or wild mushrooms.

Cabernet Sauvignon Apple, pear, blackberry, elderberry; shallot; domestic and wild mushrooms (bolete, shitake, chanterelle); wild rice; fresh tarragon, basil, mint, green peppercorn, cinnamon, nutmeg, allspice; nuts with stronger tannins like pecan, hazelnut, walnut; most people do not care for tomato or orange sauces with Cabernet.

Zinfandel Orange, tomato, and tomato salsas; onion, leek, mild garlic; red and green bell and anaheim peppers, eggplant, olive, brussel sprouts, cabbage, various beans, carrot; fresh sage, rosemary, basil, black, green and red peppercorns, thyme, oregano, kummel, caraway and fennel seeds, summer savory, dry coriander, tumeric, cumin, mustards; walnut, pecan, brazil, hazelnut; all domestic and wild mushrooms.

Syrah Plum, orange, kiwi; red, green, and anaheim pepper; sweet red onions, mild garlic, tomato; fresh sage, rosemary, basil, mint, cinnamon, nutmeg, clove, allspice, ground fennel, anise, kummel, caraway seeds; pecan, walnut, brazil, hazelnut, some bittersweet chocolate; all wild mushrooms, particularly morels and shitake.

The Champagne Compatibility Index

During the 1980s, Korbel Champagne Cellars commissioned a food and beverage research firm to determine which everyday, non-gourmet foods go well with champagne. The result is the following Champagne Compatibility Index. Every semester some of my students have enjoyed using one of their wine and food homework assignments to retest items on the index. For some reason, Oreos, Twinkies, Nacho Cheese Doritos, and Lay's Ruffle Potato Chips have proven particularly popular research objects.

Food	Index	Food	Index
Shrimp Cocktail	97.5	Italian Spaghetti Sauce	69.4
Smoked Salmon	96.7	Brownies (Duncan Hines)	69.3
Raw Oysters with Lemon	94.8	Chili with Beans	68.8
Beef Stroganoff	93.0	Twinkies	68.7
Shrimp Scampi	85.7	Caviar	68.2
Tuna Salad Sandwich	84.3	Vanilla Ice Cream	64.9
Lobster with Drawn Butter	84.1	Curried Chicken	64.9
Brie	82.7	Taco Filling	64.6
Mixed Nuts	80.4	Ritz Crackers with Velveeta	64.2
Veal Scallopini	80.2	Chocolate Mousse	62.7
Oreos	78.8	Barbecue Pork Ribs	60.4
Omelette	77.7	Chicken Chow Mein	60.3
Apple Pie	77.0	Peanut Butter & Jelly Sandwich	59.0
Strawberries with Cream	76.8	Meat Loaf with Catsup	58.6
Strawberry Yogurt	76.7	Sweet and Sour Pork	58.4
Chicken Cacciatori	75.6	Foie Gras	58.3
Breaded, Frozen Fish Sticks	75.5	Tuna Sashimi	56.8
Pickled Herring	74.0	McDonald's Big Mac	56.2
Beef Wellington	73.9	Grilled Beef Steak	55.0
Bacon (Oscar Mayer)	73.9	Grilled Swordfish	52.4
Oriental Pepper Steak	73.6	Nacho Cheese Doritos	51.0
Turkey with Dressing (Stove Top)	73.2	American Cheddar Cheese	50.6
Baked Ham (Honey Mustard Glaze)	72.8	Breakfast Sausage (Jones Farm)	47.6
Pork Chops (Baked)	71.6	Cheese Pizza	45.6
Kentucky Fried Chicken	70.6	Popcorn	45.4
Escargot with Garlic Butter	70.2	Banana Pudding	39.4
Hot Dogs with Mustard (Oscar Mayer)	70.2	Lamb Chops (Baked)	29.7
Duck a l'Orange	69.8	Lay's Ruffle Potato Chips	27.5

Further Ideas on Champagne's Compatibilities

A more elegant and less numerical approach to matching sparkling wines and foods was taken by David Rosengarten and Joshua Wesson in the premier issue of their magazine, *Wine and Food Companion*. I have selected parts of their article "The Best Champagnes for Your Holidays...and the Best Ways to Match Them" to reprint here for your reference. This article has also stimulated my most inquisitive students to test the myths and strategies for their homework, but has not been as fascinating to them as the above-mentioned "food" items.

Five Myths About Champagne with Food That You Must Never Believe

Myth 1: Champagne is the proper drink with caviar. Rubbish! We've tasted over a hundred Champagnes recently with caviar, and found that most of them leave a sugary-fishy taste in your mouth. Only the very driest and most acidic or the extremely rich and complex have a chance. There's a strong psychological bond between the two items — luxury food, luxury beverage — but we prefer good, iced vodka with caviar, almost every time. Don't compromise the exquisite harmony of your Champagne by pouring it over fish eggs.

Myth 2: Champagne is the proper drink with smoked salmon. Another loser. The fish oils of smoked salmon go to work just as the fish oils of caviar do, making the Champagne unpleasantly fishy. Some people like Rosé Champagne with smoked salmon, but that's just color-coding. Rosés generally have less acid than other Champagnes, and are usually even less satisfactory with smoked salmon. Give us a glass of Mosel Kabinett.

Myth 3: Champagne is the perfect compromise wine and can be drunk all through the meal. Well, it can — but, like any other wine, it's going to go well with some things and poorly with others. Champagne has special properties, and you must take special care in matching it with food.

Myth 4: Great Champagne is perfect for dessert, the climax of the meal. We shudder at the amount of great Champagne that gets consumed with wedding cakes and other confections. Yes, it is celebratory to end a meal with Champagne, but if the wine is to accompany dessert you must make sure that it's a sweeter Champagne such as an Extra Dry. Many hosts have an elegant vintage or non-vintage Brut for the dessert course. Many guests, accordingly, never get to appreciate those wines, since their delicacy is overwhelmed by the sweetness of dessert.

Myth 5: Champagne is best when it's young. If you're drinking Champagne without food, it is a good idea to drink Champagne soon after it's bottled — unless you appreciate the taste of oxidation. (Some do, notably the British.) But everything changes when you consider Champagne with food. We find young fruitiness in Champagne one of the most problematic qualities for food-matching. Older Champagnes, on the other hand, are less fruity, less sweet, a little less vigorous . . . and often easier to match with food.

So Champagne with food has a bad name, we believe, because hosts and hostesses have dutifully followed "the rules," leading to some pretty awful matches. We'd like to propose alternative strategies for Champagne with food, guaranteed to bring pleasure.

Ten Strategies for Matching Champagne and Food

Strategy 1: Serve Champagne with salty foods. The first time a Champagne producer handed us a hunk of Parmesan cheese to taste with Champagne, we were surprised. But he was absolutely right: Salty cheeses are great with Champagne. The bubbles offer a lovely, welcome refreshment after the salt. Salty foods in general are superb partners for Champagne, as long as they don't feature heavy fish oils, as do caviar and smoked salmon. This is good news for menu-planners, since so many aperitif-time goodies are salty — roasted nuts, slices of cured ham or dried sausage, puff-pastry finger food with savory stuffings.

Strategy 2: Serve Champagne with deep-fried foods. Here's more good news at aperitif time. We don't know why exactly — and maybe no one has ever noticed it before — but Champagne bubbles have a real affinity for things fried in oil. Deep-fried tiny fish, oysters, pieces of chicken, vegetable tempura — all of these items will marry well with a glass of Champagne.

Strategy 3: Serve Champagne with Oriental foods. We're not talking about Oriental cooking that's intensely-flavored, very sweet, or very spicy. But the subtler representatives of Oriental cuisine go very nicely with Champagne. The whole range of Chinese, Thai, Vietnamese and Japanese fried foods, as discussed above, is superb.

Strategy 4: Serve Champagne with sushi and sashimi. These Japanese treats are so great with Champagne, they deserve their own category. To our tastes, there is nothing better to drink with sushi. The bubbles provide the scrape that beer usually provides, and the delicacy of the fish lets the Champagne be itself. We try to serve lighter Champagnes with sashimi (just the raw fish), and heavier, sweeter Champagnes with sushi (the raw fish combined with sweetened and vinegared rice). Speaking of raw seafood, light, dry and acidic Champagne is a great partner to raw oysters. No cocktail sauce please!

Strategy 5: Serve Champagne with foods that present texture problems for still wine — vegetables, soups, eggs. Wine is not often drunk with vegetables, soups, and eggs because these foods don't provide solid, dramatic texture as a foil for the wine. A relatively thin liquid such as wine seems redundant next to a bowl of soup. But the unique texture of Champagne insures contrast. Sparkling liquid is interesting next to still liquid (soup), and next to light solids (vegetable and egg dishes). We found Champagne to be lovely, in particular, with light mushroom soup, buttered corn-on-the-cob, and egg dishes containing something salty, like ham or bacon.

Strategy 6: Avoid heavy sauces with Champagne. Champagne works surprisingly well with a range of fish dishes and light meats — but heavy sauces, especially cream sauces, destroy the harmony of the wine, making it seem coarser, sweeter, clumsier.

Strategy 7: Serve Champagne with acidic fruit. Strawberries and Champagne constitute the type of culinary cliche we usually avoid — but we'd be missing something if we did avoid it. The sugar/acid balance of acidic fruit can wonderfully engage the sugar/acid balance of Champagne.

Strategy 8: The most important factor of all in considering Champagne for food is the level of sugar in the wine. Basic Brut Champagnes can, by law, have anywhere from 0 percent to 1.5 percent residual sugar. A wine with 1.5 percent sugar tastes quite sweet to most palates — even though it is labeled Brut! A sweet Brut can ruin any dish that's crying out for a dry wine. Imagine how unpleasant oysters might be with a sweetish wine when you were expecting something tinglingly acidic. On the other hand, dishes with a bit of sweetness — say quail with a red currant reduction sauce — might need some sweetness in the wine to work.

Strategy 9: The second most important factor in choosing Champagne for food is the type of Champagne: Non-Vintage Brut, Vintage Brut, Blanc de Blancs, Rosé, Crémant, Extra-Dry. Sometimes there's surprising similarity between Champagnes of different types (read our notes carefully), but usually Champagnes are true to their label designations. Here's a brief look at what we observed in different types of Champagnes:

Non-Vintage Brut. Usually the least expensive wine from a house, and usually the sweetest-tasting (except Extra Dry, Demi Sec, etc.). Menu-planners should familiarize themselves with the various house styles for Brut, since non-vintage Brut, a blended wine, is usually any house's most consistent wine. The basic Brut is the same year in and year out, but vintage wines usually show their variations. Non-vintage Brut is usually the least expensive Champagne from any house, and often a much better value — sometimes a much better wine! — than the higher-priced Champagne styles. Choose non-vintage Bruts if you value freshness in Champagne.

Vintage Brut. Higher in price than non-vintage Brut, and not always worth it. One positive that menu-planners can count on: Vintage Brut is usually drier than non-vintage Brut. And vintage Brut, since it's older, will have less of the fruitiness that can cause trouble for food in young Bruts. But do keep in mind that vintage Brut will usually emphasize older, toastier, more oxidized flavors. This can be complex and magnificent if the wine has been well-made, but it can taste tired if not done well. We found vintage Champagne from houses without top-flight reputations to be a risky proposition. It's better to go with a non-vintage Brut if you don't know the house's reputation.

Blanc de Blancs. One of our favorite Champagne styles. Made from 100% Chardonnay, these elegant, graceful wines are at their best when they offer complexity of flavor in addition to their lightness. They are the wines to consider when you're serving anything that seems to demand a light wine.

Rosé. The most disappointing category in our tasting. There are two types of Rosé that we love: fresh ones, bursting with essence of strawberry; and aged ones, offering complex whiffs of earth, truffle, chocolate, etc. Non-vintage Brut Rosés are the ones to count on for strawberry flavors. Older vintage Rosés are best for the other style. Unfortunately, most of the Rosés we tasted fell somewhere in between: neither fresh nor complex, and with a distressingly diffuse, low-acid feel. Our advice is to gamble on the non-vintage Rosé if you don't know the house. And our only food advice on Rosés in the current market is to be careful!

Crémant. These Champagnes are made with lower pressure, so they feel much less forceful in the mouth than regular Champagne. This is valuable news for menu-planners. Poached salmon in a beurre blanc might have its silky serenity upset by a forceful Champagne, but the gentler Crémant would fit in perfectly. Generally speaking, you can think of Crémants for food more the way that you think of still wines. In the last century, many people considered Crémant the *only* Champagne to drink with food.

Extra Dry. Although this is a sweeter style of Champagne, the Extra Drys from some houses, though they're supposed to be sweet, can seem drier than the supposedly dry Bruts offered by other houses. Many of them had a burnt sugar, almost honeyed nose that's quite attractive. The slight sweetness makes them tricky to match with food. We find them to be perfect palate-cleansers after the cheese course and before dessert. And, if the dessert is not too sweet, they can serve beautifully as the dessert wine, too.

Strategy 10: The third most important factor in considering Champagne for food is the relative weight of the wine. We've had heavy Champagnes with venison — spectacular! But that same wine would wreak havoc with fluke sashimi. And we've had light Champagnes with sashimi — magnificent! But that same wine would spell trouble for venison. Use good sense in matching food weights and wine weights.

ENDNOTES

[1] Keehn, Karen, "The Structure of Wine, A Treatise on Wine and Its Interaction with Food," McDowell Valley Vineyards, Hopland, CA, 1987, p. 2.

[2] Peynaud, Emile, THE TASTE OF WINE, The Wine Appreciation Guild, San Francisco, CA, 1987, p. 235.

[3] Of course, our thirst varies tremendously with the climate as well as with exercise. This approximation is for a moderate climate, perhaps Bordeaux, where Peynaud lives.

[4] Rosengarten, David, "The Odds of Wine-Food Matching," *The Wine Spectator*, October 31, 1987, p. 56.

[5] Keehn, Karen, interview, "Matching Food and Wine Styles," in *Practical Winery and Vineyard*, July/August 1988, pp. 41-43, and Karen Keehn, "Palate Perceptions of Premium Wines and Their Interaction with Food," McDowell Valley Vineyards, Hopland, CA, 1988, and Dan Berger, "Great Wineries Are Built on a Foundation of Overall Consistency," *Los Angeles Times*, December 29, 1989.

[6] The pH values of the juices of limes and grapefruits are in the range of 1-2, while the pH of lemon juice is 2.1 and that of orange juice is 3. The lower the pH, the stronger the acidity. How much stronger? As noted in Chapter 2, one unit on the pH scale is a 10-fold difference in acid strength, so the acidity of lemon juice is about 10 times stronger than that of orange juice, and grapefruit and lime juices are 10 to 100 times stronger in acidity than orange juice.

[7] Keehn, Karen, "Wine and Food Affinities, Fish," McDowell Valley Vineyards, Hopland, CA, p. 1.

[8] Keehn, Karen, "Palate Perceptions of Premium Wines and Their Interaction with Food," McDowell Valley Vineyards, Hopland, CA, 1988, p. 7. See also Karen Keehn, interview, "Matching Seasonings and Wines," *Practical Winery and Vineyard*, November/December 1988, pp. 41-43, and Karen Keehn, "Herbs, Spices and Wine, Seasonings and Wine in Recipe Development" and "Glossary of Seasoning Groups," McDowell Valley Vineyards, Hopland, CA.

[10] Rosengarten, David, and Joshua Wesson, RED WINE WITH FISH: THE NEW ART OF MATCHING WINE WITH FOOD, Simon and Schuster, New York, 1989, p. 40.

[11] Berger, Dan, "Great Wineries Are Built on a Foundation of Overall Consistency," *Los Angeles Times*, December 29, 1989. In our conversation of December 18, 1991, Berger replaced Raymond with Clos du Val in ninth place among the top ten, and Dan Berger's Runners Up (listed alphabetically with their notable wines in parentheses): Caymus (Cabernet Sauvignon and Zinfandel), Clos du Val (Sémillon, Sauvignon Blanc, and long-lived Cabernet Sauvignon, Merlot, Zinfandel, Pinot Noir), Cuvaison (Cabernet Sauvignon, Chardonnay, and Merlot), Dehlinger (Chardonnay, Pinot Noir), Dry Creek (Fumé Blanc, Cabernet Sauvignon, Petite Sirah, and Zinfandel), Inglenook (Gravion, Cabernet Sauvignon, Charbono, and Reunion), Matanzas Creek (Chardonnay, Sauvignon Blanc), Mondavi (Cabernet Sauvignon and Pinot Noir), Preston (dry Chenin Blanc and Petite Sirah), Simi, Trefethen (Chardonnay, dry Riesling, and Pinot Noir).

[12] Because the wines of Clos du Val are made for aging, you will need to look for older vintages on wine lists.

[13] CALIFORNIA WINE WINNERS by Varietal Fair, 4022 Harrison Grade Road, Sebastopol, CA 95472.

[14] See tales of drinking Château D'Yquem — Sauternes' premiere wines — with cold roast beef in Vol. 9, No. 1 (December 1, 1990) of *The Dessert Wine Digest*, Andrew Quady Winery, Madera, CA.

[15] The address for *The Dessert Wine Digest* is P.O. Box 728, Madera, CA 93639, and the winning recipe was Smoked Grilled Pork Loin with Apple, Tasso, and Pan Fried Corn Bread. Yum.

[16] Rosengarten, David, and Joshua Wesson, RED WINE WITH FISH: THE NEW ART OF MATCHING WINE WITH FOOD, Simon and Schuster, New York, 1989.

[17] Ensrud, Barbara, WINE AND FOOD, A GUIDE TO ENTERTAINING THROUGH THE SEASONS, Simon and Schuster, Fireside Books, New York, 1991.

[18] McGee, Harold, ON FOOD AND COOKING, THE SCIENCE AND LORE OF THE KITCHEN, Charles Scribner's Sons, New York, 1984.

[19] Beringer Vineyards' Culinary Arts Center, P.O. Box 111, St. Helena, CA 94574.

[20] McDowell Valley Vineyards, P.O. Box 449, Hopland, CA 95449; Fetzer, P.O. Box 227, Redwood Valley, CA 95470; Simi Winery, P.O. Box 698, Healdsburg, CA 95448; Robert Mondavi, P.O. Box 106, Oakville, CA 94562; and Inglenook-Napa Valley, P.O. Box 391, St. Helena, CA 94574.

[21] Johnson, Hugh, HOW TO ENJOY WINE, Simon and Schuster, Fireside Books, New York, 1985, and the video by the same title and from the same vintage by Simon and Schuster Video, 60 minutes.

[22] Wine Advisory Board, FAVORITE RECIPES OF CALIFORNIA WINEMAKERS, Wine Appreciation Guild, San Francisco, CA, 1981 and 1983.

[23] Malcolm, Hébert, WINE LOVERS' COOKBOOK, Wine Appreciation Guild, San Francisco, 1983.

Appendix D

DO IT YOURSELF
How to Set Up and Conduct the Tasting Exercises at Home

This appendix explains how to conduct the sensory evaluation exercises in this book, whether you are doing this on your own, as a member of a winetasting club, or teaching a class. My goal is not to put other wine educators out of business, because the opportunity to study with an expert, not to the mention the camaraderie of a class, cannot be replaced. My intent is to help you to study independently, perhaps to supplement a class — as assigned or spontaneous homework or to continue learning after the class is over — or to pursue a personal interest, on your own, in a club, or with a group of friends, to share the cost and fun. If you are teaching a class, there are suggestions for doing these tasting exercises with larger groups in the teacher's manual, TEACHERS MANUAL FOR THE UNIVERSITY WINE COURSE. See page 402.

This appendix first describes the supplies, equipment, and resources you will need. For each exercise there are guidelines for buying and/or preparing the wines and conducting the tastings as well as information for the discussion of observations and questions that may come up. At the end of this appendix you will find the addresses and telephone numbers of wineries and suppliers mentioned in the text.

SOME BACKGROUND ABOUT MY WINE APPRECIATION CLASSES

Because this book — and especially this appendix — grew out of two wine appreciation classes I have taught, here is a brief description of them. "Introduction to Wine" was first offered in the Spring of 1972 and has enrolled about 120 students each term. The students pay a $12.00 fee that covers 80-90% of the cost of the wines they taste. I meet with them three times a week, lecturing to the assembled multitude twice for an hour each session and leading four groups of 25-35 for one hour of tasting. My students take a quiz every two weeks and a final exam at the end of a fifteen-week semester. Those who complete the course successfully earn three elective credits and, until about four years ago, could enroll in a seminar in sensory evaluation to pursue their enological interests further. The seminar class consisted of 9-26 students who were willing to cough up a $60.00 fee; many repeated the course — the record was six times. Each student investigated a topic in viticulture or enology and made a two-hour presentation to the class, including an illustrative tasting. The group also went on a two-day field trip. The wine seminar was the testing ground for many of the sensory evaluation exercises for "Introduction to Wine," which are included in this book. The "Your Turn" exercises in each sensory evaluation chapter retain the spirit of the seminar class by presenting an opportunity for tasters to look into something that intrigues them.

One of the things that has made my wine classes successful is that I always ask my students to suggest improvements. In that tradition, I'd like to ask you to help me improve this appendix. The instructions for the exercises are based on my experience teaching in a university, with the help of technicians to prepare and clean up, and as a member of a local winetasting club. Because this is the first time I've tried to put together a set of instructions like this, I'm very interested in how well they work. If you have suggestions for improving this appendix — or any other aspect of the book — please write to me at the School of Agriculture, California State University Chico, Chico, California 95929-0310. Thank you!

WHAT YOU WILL NEED TO PREPARE THE SENSORY EVALUATION EXERCISES

Money Matters: A Budget

Planning for a series of tastings with friends or in a club ought to include making a budget as well as choosing the wines everyone is eager to sample. The suggestions in this appendix will help your friends or club estimate the total cost of supplies, wines, and expenses incurred in choosing, buying, and getting information about wines to share — including long-distance phone calls to wineries, photo-duplicating the analytical and winemaking data, etc.

The Wines

1. Sources for Wine Ideas

Once you have decided which sensory evaluation exercises you want to try, you'll need to find specific wines to taste. The wine-buying guidelines for each sensory evaluation exercise describe the characteristics of the wines you need to buy and offer some specific examples of California wines I have used. If you live where California wines cannot be obtained easily, the varietal wine profiles in Appendix A name other regions where similar wines are made. This information and the characteristics of the wines required for a particular tasting will be enough to enable your wine merchant to help you find the appropriate wines for a particular exercise. When you are making your shopping list, don't forget to buy extra wine for the review tastings.

If you want wine suggestions beyond those in this book, there are many publications, including wine buying guides and winery newsletters, you could consult. Here are some that I like to use. Your wine merchant may subscribe to others.

The POCKET ENCYCLOPEDIA OF CALIFORNIA WINES by William I. Kaufman, 1993, contains descriptions of all California wineries and their wines, and all of the Orange County Fair Award winners.

Hugh Johnson's POCKET ENCYCLOPEDIA OF WINE is helpful for getting ideas about non-California wines to taste.

Practical Winery and Vineyard magazine has "varietal review" articles that profile a varietal wine and include interviews with the winemakers and tasting notes for the wines. I highly recommend these articles for planning winetastings, because they can give you an idea of how the wine's sensory characteristics were created in production, and the tasting notes will help with the post-tasting discussion.

I occasionally use publications such as *The Wine Spectator* and newsletters such as *Connoisseur's Guide* for specific wine-buying ideas. They are also a great source of supplementary tasting notes for discussions.

My wine merchant is an excellent source of information. When I have an idea of the kind of wine I want — a dry Chenin Blanc, for example, or a two- to three-year-old White Riesling with 1-2% residual sugar — I go chat with Jim and he can tell me what is available in the market in various price ranges in those styles.

2. Wineries — Key Resources for Learning

Wineries can provide analytical data, descriptions of production methods, and tasting notes for the specific wines in your tasting.

Professional winetasters have at their disposal analytical data about the wines they are tasting. This may include the percentage of alcohol, amount of residual sugar, total acid, pH, and tannin content (for red wines), as well as information about grape varieties, harvest parameters, and relevant viticultural or winemaking practices. Having analytical data available will help any taster relate his or her sensory impressions to wine characteristics, and it's well worth a phone call or letter to a winery to collect this information for your tasting group. In fact, other things being equal, I will choose a wine from a winery that can provide analytical data. You may not need to contact the winery to get some essential information: a number of wineries include some key analytical data on their labels. You can also determine the approximate sugar content of a wine yourself using a Clinitest® kit (described below and in Exercise 4.2).

In addition to analytical data, information about how the specific wines you are tasting were made can help you relate your sensory knowledge to production techniques. Wineries will typically be happy to share production information about their wines with serious tasting groups. You can find out, for example, the degrees Brix and total acid of the grapes at harvest, how the fermentation was managed (temperature, pump-overs, inoculation with malolactic bacteria, etc.), oak-aging regime, bottling date, and bottle-aging potential.

Wineries also commonly make available tasting notes, including aroma and flavor descriptions, and ideas about combining the wine with food. Your wine merchant may have descriptive information about the wines you want to taste or could help you get it. When I want to contact wineries directly I use Kaufman's POCKET ENCYCLOPEDIA OF CALIFORNIA WINES or the *Wines and Vines Buyer's Guide,* which includes the names of key personnel and the address and telephone numbers of all the wineries in North America, as well as winery and vineyard industry suppliers.

3.   Receiving Wine Shipments

Wines cannot be freely shipped or mailed everywhere in the U.S., so you will want to let the winery or other supplier know early in the conversation or correspondence where you live so that they can consult the latest regulations and determine whether and how they can get their product to you.

Equipment and Supplies
1.   Wine glasses. Everyone attending a tasting can bring their own glasses — one for each wine to be tasted — and should follow the suggestions in Chapter 2 to make sure their glasses are appropriate. They should be reminded to wash and rinse their glasses thoroughly.
2.   Measuring and mixing containers. These should include jars or bowls, funnels, eye droppers, measuring spoons, and measuring cups or a graduated cylinder (available at photo supply stores).
3.   Knives, plates, spoons, etc., for handling foods.
4.   Good corkpuller (I swear by the Screwpull model) and special caps to seal partially full sparkling wine bottles.
5.   CLINITEST ® — a home analysis kit for urine sugar testing available in pharmacies and by mail order from All World Scientific — to estimate the residual sugar in wines for tasting. See Exercise 4.2 for details.
6.   PRIVATE PRESERVE ™. You will probably want to save partially full bottles of wine. This situation could arise if your group is not large enough to consume an entire bottle of each wine or if you want to keep some wines for later reference. The best product I have found for this purpose is PRIVATE PRESERVE ™, an inexpensive can of compressed nitrogen and carbon dioxide gasses that you "squirt" onto the surface of the wine in a partially full bottle. This protects the leftover wines from oxidation with a blanket of inert gases — the same way they are protected when stored in partially-filled tanks in wineries. PRIVATE PRESERVE ™ is available at many gourmet food shops, kitchen supply stores, and wine shops, or may be ordered from The Wine Appreciation Guild or from its inventor.
7.   Chemicals to make component wines and aroma reference standards may be obtained from your local home winemaking supply store, or can be mail-ordered from the suppliers listed

on page 389-390. The chemicals you will need include tartaric or citric acid, sucrose (table sugar), and tannic acid or grape tannin. You might want to get some acetaldehyde (but you can substitute sherry), ethyl acetate (or nail-polish remover), acetic acid (or vinegar), phenethanol (also called phenethyl alcohol; or you can substitute crushed rose petals). Linalool is useful for demonstrating the Gewürztraminer aroma as is trichloroanisole for the corky off odor. You should enlist the help of someone with laboratory experience if you want to work with linalool and acetic acid, acetaldehyde, ethyl acetate, or phenethyl alcohol in forms other than vinegar, sherry, nail-polish remover, or crushed rose petals. (See the section on helpers below.)

8. Small paper cups for serving component wines and samples of food, larger paper cups for disposable spitoons, dishwashing detergent, paper towels or napkins, marking pencils.

9. Energy, enthusiasm, and imagination.

Helpers

1. A wine merchant can help you locate the wines for each exercise and, perhaps, information about them.

2. A high school chemistry or biology teacher or someone who works in a medical, quality control, or other biological or chemical laboratory can help order chemicals, measure them in small amounts, and handle those which require more experience (such as linalool, acetic acid, acetaldehyde, ethyl acetate, and phenethanol), and explain the things in this appendix that I only **think** I've made clear.

3. Someone to donate a room in their home or to schedule a place to hold the tastings — unless you are going to rotate the responsibility among the members of your group. However you arrange the tasting location, you'll need a place that has tables where people can spread out their wines, papers, and books; it should also be well-lighted and well-ventilated.

4. A cabinetmaker or hobbyist woodworker to help you make an oak reference standard for Exercise 4.1.

Information for the Post-Tasting Discussions

Many of the resources mentioned in the discussion of selecting wines and getting analytical data about them will be useful for adding other voices — through tasting notes — to your group's post-tasting discussions. Each exercise also contains my comments and/or tasting notes I've collected from my students to show how other beginning winetasters have responded to the exercises. Your group may want to order a copy of GLOSSARY OF SENSORY EVALUATION TERMS from The Wine Lab ($5.00 in 1991). Although it is somewhat technical, I have found this glossary to be a very useful adjunct to the wine aroma wheel, especially because it suggests common terms to describe off odors, and has a nice summary of where to look for specific fruit odors in wines.

A Suggested General Format for Tastings

At a typical tasting: 1. the leader or host for the tasting briefly reminds the group of the purpose of the tasting or suggests a perusal of the appropriate text pages to focus everyone on the task at hand; 2. the wines are presented blind and tasted — allowing a minimum of 5-8 minutes per wine for the sensory evaluation and to record observations; 3. after everyone has finished tasting, the leader invites the tasters to discuss their observations; 4. when group members have finished sharing their observations, the leader may want to add tasting notes from the wineries or wine critics before revealing the identities of the wines. All tasters should use the suggestions in the section on Techniques for the Sensory Evaluation of Wines in Chapter 2.

Cubes of fresh white bread — preferable crusty, fresh-baked French — or a supply of unsalted saltine crackers, water, small paper cups for the water, and larger paper cups for use as spitoons should be set out at every tasting session. Food morsels to sample with the wines can also be distributed in paper cups — though more elegant presentations are by no means prohibited.

TAILORING THE SENSORY EVALUATION EXERCISES TO SUIT YOUR GROUP

Because the content and order of the sensory evaluation exercises in this book are tailored to the 50-minute tasting sessions of my wine class, their length and arrangement may not suit your tasting group. You may, for example, meet once a month for three or four hours and have interests and objectives that differ from those of my class. For these reasons, I encourage your group to adapt this book to your needs: you might change the order of exercises or greatly expand the "Your Turn" exercises to fit your priorities. Here is an example of how this suggestion may apply to the five introductory exercises (the "Focus on Olfaction I, II, and III" and "Focus on Taste and Touch I and II").

The informal groups I have participated in are not usually interested in doing these foundation exercises right after they have formed, preferring the excitement of tasting varietal wines or champagnes or something **really** expensive. After some experience tasting together, two things happen. First, the members realize that everyone is using different terms to describe the same wine and that if they want to understand each other they will need to standardize their vocabularies for describing odors and flavors. Second, after the tasters hear one person call a wine tart while another person says that same wine is astringent, the group realizes that it needs to reacquaint itself with taste fundamentals. After these experiences, the tasters are motivated to do a little basic training in winetasting and are eager for the knowledge that can be gained in the "Focus on Olfaction" and "Focus on Taste and Touch" exercises. Of course, all groups are different, and while a new winetasting club may need to discover for itself the value of these exercises, one that has been established longer may be ready to start right off with "Focus on Olfaction I."

Another approach to using the "Focus on Olfaction" and "Focus on Taste and Touch" exercises with the varietal winetastings is to include something from these basic exercises when you taste varietal wines. For example, rather than doing a "Focus on Olfaction" exercise as written, your group might prefer to have a specific subset of aroma reference standards made for each varietal wine being tasted. If your club is tasting Cabernet Sauvignons, for instance, you could refer to the aroma descriptions in its varietal wine profile in Appendix A and prepare a set of reference standards for the descriptors listed there: berry, black currant, cassis, bell pepper, green bean, olives, mint, and black pepper. You could also divide up the "Focus on Taste and Touch" exercises and their sensory homework assignments and present, for example, the "Tart Homework" and "Sweet Homework" from Exercise 4.2 with the Chenin Blanc and Muscat Blanc sensory evaluation exercise (4.3); you might then include the ranking of component wines by sweetness with the White Riesling and Gewürztraminer sensory evaluation exercise (4.4). Given the difficulties we all encounter when learning wine odors and describing taste sensations, the optimum way to use the five Focus exercises would be to present them first in the order in which they appear in the book, before the varietal wine exercises, and then have the aroma standards and component wines available for review during the varietal winetastings.

SENSORY EVALUATION EXERCISE 4.1.
Focus on Olfaction I — White Table Wine Aromas
and An Introduction to the Wine Aroma Wheel

How to Make the Reference Standards in Your Kitchen
The Base Wine

To prepare the wines for this exercise you will need an inexpensive white table wine that is neutral in odor, free of defects, and low in odor intensity. We use Parducci Vintage White Table Wine, but there are other — usually generic — wines on the market that are satisfactory as well.

Recipes for the Aroma Reference Standards

We start with the recipes published in the wine aroma wheel article and modify them as needed.[3] Making aroma reference standards is not an exact science and you will need to let your nose be the judge of whether the samples are the right strength or not. When introducing the aromas to beginners, they should be rather strong. If you repeat this exercise when your group has become more proficient, the standards can be more subtle — more as they would be found in wine. You will notice that the reference standards become stronger if they sit with the pieces of fruit, etc., in them. To avoid their becoming too strong and to reduce the incidence of "aroma identification by peeking," we take out as much of the flavoring material as possible before presenting the wines to the students.

To make an aroma reference standard, add the material in the right-hand column in Table D.1 to a wine glass containing ⅛ cup (about 30 milliliters) of the base wine, soak until the wine has acquired the odor of the flavoring material — about 20 to 30 minutes — then remove. Start with the smaller amount of flavoring and add more if needed after 20-30 minutes. If the standard is too strong, add more wine. Note that some of the chemical additions are made to larger amounts of wine because the chemicals are very concentrated. Use 30 ml per glass.

The nine standards I always use are indicated with asterisks. If you want to make other reference standards that are not in the recipes, you can experiment with adding small pieces or drops of liquid to some wine until you can clearly smell the added material.

Reference Standard	Add to ⅛ Cup White Wine and Soak
Rose*	Crushed petals of one rose (or add one drop of phenethanol to ½ cup of wine, then take three teaspoons of this and add it to ⅛ cup of wine)
Linalool	One drop linalool in ⅔ cup of wine — add more wine if this is too strong.
Cloves*	One whole clove
Grapefruit*	One teaspoon of juice and a small piece of peel from a fresh fruit
Lemon	One teaspoon of juice and a small piece of peel from a fresh fruit
Apricot*	1-1½ Tablespoons of apricot nectar
Peach	1-1½ Tablespoons of peach nectar or syrup from canned peaches
Melon	1 piece fresh, ripe cantaloupe — 1-inch cube
Orange	One teaspoon of juice and a small piece of peel from a fresh fruit
Pineapple*	½ tsp to 1 tsp freshly opened pineapple juice
Fig	½ fresh fig or 1-2 tsp liquid from canned figs
Cut green grass*	1 shredded 1-inch blade of green grass
Bell pepper	1 piece of fresh bell pepper ¼-inch square
Green olive*	1-2 tsp brine from canned green olives
Honey*	1-2 tsp honey: smear the approximately correct amount in the bottom of a wine glass and pour the wine over it
Oak*	½ tsp of Oak Mor (an oak concentrate available from Cellulo Corporation) or a sample made from shavings**
** A cabinetmaker might supply you with oak shavings or could make some from barrel staves, which you might obtain by a visit to or correspondence with a cooperage company (see the *Wines and Vines Buyer's Guide*). To make oak extracts for the oak aroma reference standard: put the shavings into a neutral white wine and let them steep for a few weeks, smell, taste, and dilute with the same neutral wine if the wood odors and flavors are too strong.	

Table D.1
Recipes for the White Wine Aroma Reference Standards

How Much to Make? One Set of Reference Standards "Serves" Four to Eight Tasters

Four to eight tasters can share a set of nine reference standards and complete this exercise in about an hour. If you have more time, you may want to use more standards, but if you do this, the tasters may become tired and discouraged. Depending on which reference standards you choose to make, you will need about 300 milliliters or 1¼ cups of wine for a set of nine. In addition, each taster should have their own glass

Cups	Milliliters	Tablespoons	Teaspoons
1	240	16	48
½	120	8	24
¼	60	4	12
⅛	30	2	6
⅔	160	11	33
⅓	80	5.5	17
1 oz	30		
1 tsp	4		
1 Tbsp	15		

Table D.2
Some Handy Conversions for Your Kitchen

of basic wine to smell between reference standard samples. Be sure to read the recipes in Table D.1 before you decide how much base wine to buy for this exercise — and don't forget to plan for the Focus on Taste and Touch (Exercise 4.2) as well.

Presenting the Reference Standards

To present the wines to the tasters we use 10-ounce, tulip-shaped wine glasses, cover them with aluminum foil, and label them A, B, C, etc., with a paper label stuck to the foil — labels written on the bases of the glasses get rubbed off. Be sure to remind the tasters that these samples are for smelling, not drinking, and not to look at!

Information for the Post-Tasting Discussion
Aromas — Associations and Where They're Found

As you can see from steps 5 and 6 of the instructions for this exercise in Chapter 4, after this tasting the associations that tasters have made with the reference standards and where these odors are found in varietal wines are discussed. I have collected some of the associations my students have made with these reference standards into Table D.3, Associations with White Table Wine Aroma Reference Standards, which is intended as a guide and supplement to your group's discussion. When reading Table D.3 remember that aroma reference standards are "what the odor really is" — peach or bell pepper, etc.— and associations are "what the odor smells like." The column "Wines with This Aroma" names the varietal wines in which this aroma is prominent; however, as noted in the footnote to the table, each of the aromas can occur in other wines.

Table D.3
Student Associations with White Table Wine Aroma Reference Standards

Aroma Reference Standard	Selected Student Association(s)	Wines with This Aroma Note*
Rose	*Bubble bath, candle wax, perfumes, bubble gum, potpourri, rose buds, walking through a garden, Plumeria lei*	G, WR, M
Linalool	*Towelettes, floor wax, little soaps you don't use, furniture polish*	G, WR, M
Cloves	*Clove cigarettes, baked ham, gingerbread, (spiced) apple cider, Christmas (cloves in oranges), Wassail, tea, hot mulled wine, cinnamon sticks*	G, WR, M
Grapefruit	*Squirt, mandarins, being on a diet, Arizona at night in the springtime, being healthy*	G, WR, M
Lemon	*Mexico (lemons in the beer), lemonade, furniture polish (Lemon Pledge)*	G, WR, M
Apricot	*Baby food*	WR, esp BA
Peach	*Friend's peach farm, fruit nectar, peach wine cooler*	G, WR, M
Melon	*Breakfast, fruit salad, cantaloupe*	G, WR, M
Orange	*Orange juice, rotting lemons*	G, WR, M
Pineapple	*Fruit bowl, Hawaii — Dole pineapple cannery, fruit cocktail, tropical fruit punch/cooler*	G, WR, M
Fig	*Making jam, dried fruit, nutty*	C
Cut green grass	*A meadow after rain, golfing, pile of grass, mud, oregano, mowing the lawn, mint, soccer fields, weeds, parsley, coming home from school to a freshly cut lawn*	SB
Bell pepper	*Fajitas, stir-fry, jalapeños, pizza*	SB
Green olive	*Thanksgiving hors d'oeuvres, an olive grove*	SB
Honey	*Mead, toast, stale beer, honeycomb, garden with honeysuckle, throat lozenges, corn bread*	C, WR, esp BA
Oak	See student descriptions of oak-aging bouquet, Exercise 4.5	C and many red wines

*And many other notes in their aromas. The equation of a single, particular aroma descriptor with a wine's aroma is an oversimplification, which becomes obvious when tasting varietal wines; nevertheless, the reference standards do represent a prominent element of the wine's aroma. G = Gewürztraminer, WR = White Riesling, M = Muscats. These three varieties have similar aromas, with the Muscats being the most intense and Gewürztraminer often seeming more spicy and grapefruit-like. Esp BA = especially *Botrytis*-affected, that is, WR grapes that have been concentrated by an infection with the mold *Botrytis cinerea*. See Chapter 9. C = Chardonnay and SB = Sauvignon Blanc.

The point of including these typical student associations is to emphasize that it is all right for these reference standards to smell like apparently odd things such as bubble gum or baked ham. The associations each of us make are highly individual, coming from our unique life experiences and further distilled through our memories of those experiences. There is no "right" association for any reference standard, only associations that mean something to each of us. The reason to share them is to spark forgotten memories and associations in other members of a group learning these references standards together. Making associations is to take the step from not knowing an odor to learning its correct identity, and each of us takes that step a little differently.

Exercise Steps 7 and 8

The advice from Dan, Dave, and friends in Step 7 (pages 101-102) was collected from a short writing assignment like the one in exercise Step 8 (page 102). After the members of your group have completed step 8, they would probably enjoy discussing their "key notes of advice . . . about how to learn wine odors" and contrasting their ideas with those of my four students.

Information for "Number of Aromas Correctly Identified on Your First Attempt"

Your tasting group is probably too small to collect and use this information the way I do in my classes: I ask the students to report how many aromas they correctly identify and then I analyze the data to see if indeed the women — as expected from sensory research — are better at this odor recognition task than are the men.[1] I have found significant differences in the number of odors correctly identified by my male and female students, but the analysis requires large numbers of tasters to be valid, so your tasting group may or may not reflect the expected gender difference.[2]

SENSORY EVALUATION EXERCISE 4.2.
Focus on Taste and Touch I — Structural Components of White Table Wines

Preparing and Presenting the Component Wines
The Base Wine

The base wine for this exercise needs to be a dry white table wine. Many inexpensive, neutral jug wines contain perceptible residual sugar, so you may have to buy one of the less expensive varietal wines for this tasting. In any case, you must make sure that the wine you have chosen is dry. When I've found a candidate, I use Clinitest® — a home analysis kit for urine sugar testing available in pharmacies and by mail order from All World Scientific — to be sure that the wine I'm using has no more than about one-fourth to one-third of 1% residual sugar. To use Clinitest® for testing wine sugar, follow the directions in the kit for the 5-drop method.

Before you try Clinitest® on an unknown wine, I suggest you practice with a wine whose residual sugar content you know so that you can see how the test works, learn how to read the color chart, and practice diluting the wine before testing. The residual sugar content is printed on the labels of many white wines. A wine of about 1.5% residual sugar would be ideal for practice. Test 5 drops of the undiluted wine by adding one of the testing tablets. The color of the liquid after the reaction will be between brown and orange — the colors on the chart that correspond to 1% and 2% sugar, respectively. To get a more accurate estimate of the residual sugar, you will need to dilute wines whose sugar content is this high or higher. Rather than making the dilution in the kit's test tube, make it in a clean glass, using a tablespoon measure, for example, and adding one tablespoon of water to one tablespoon of wine. Test 5 drops of the diluted wine. If you started with a wine of about 1.5% residual sugar, the diluted wine will contain about 0.75% sugar, and the test reaction will produce the corresponding color on the chart: olive green. Continue adding additional tablespoons of water one at a time. When you get a reading below 1% for a dilution, you can calculate back to the actual residual sugar content of the wine. Test the practice wine after each dilution until the liquid matches the blue-green color on the chart that indicates a level of sugar between 0 ("negative" on the chart) and 0.25%. This blue-green is the color you are looking for in the dry base wine you will use for this exercise.

Because you will be using it often, you will probably want to protect the Clinitest® color chart in plastic so that you will not have to buy a complete new test set when the tablets are used up. Note that because the Clinitest® reaction measures both glucose and fructose, it gives an accurate estimate of the total residual sugar in wine, but you can't use it to verify the sugar content of the sweet component wines you will make because it cannot react with sucrose (table sugar).

If you do not want to bother with Clinitest® you can get the exact sugar — and total acid — analysis of the base wine you're thinking of using from the winery. It is very helpful — though not absolutely necessary — to know the total acid in the base wine so that you can relate the taste sensation of the base wine to a known quantity of acid and estimate the acid content of component wine B more accurately (see Table D.4).

Making the White Wine Components in Your Kitchen

Follow the recipes in Table D.4. Use **either** the teaspoons and cups **or** the grams and milliliters combination, for accurate results. Because the amounts of sugar and acid that you will be adding are small, it is better to make up a big batch of wine and throw some away than try to scale down the amount you are making. The recipes will serve 12-20 tasters enough wine to do the exercise. A glass pitcher makes a good container in which to stir the wine to dissolve the sugar and acid. The acid will be a little harder to dissolve.

Table D.4
Recipes for White
Wine Components

For Wine	Add to 2½ c. (or 750 ml)* base wine
A	Nothing
B	¼ tsp. (1.5 grams) tartaric acid
C	1 tsp. (6 grams) table sugar or sucrose
D	½ tsp. (3 grams) table sugar or sucrose
Add the number of grams in parentheses to 750 ml base wine or the amounts in teaspoons to 2½ cups base wine.	

Regular table sugar (sucrose) can be used for this exercise because it is equal in sweetness to the mixture of glucose and fructose in grape juices and wines. You can substitute citric acid if you cannot find tartaric acid. Citric acid will change the component wine more than will tartaric acid, adding a citrus flavor. Observant tasters may find the component wines reduced in fruitiness compared to the base wine. This is because the stirring necessary to dissolve the sugar and acid will oxidize and diminish their aroma compounds. You may want to ask someone who is not a member of your tasting group to make up the component wines so that nobody will know their composition.

Information for the Post-Tasting Discussion

The typical general reaction of groups to this exercise is that it was harder than they thought it would be. This is because the differences in sugar and acid in the component wines are relatively small and reflect values that will be encountered in real commercial wines. Individual reactions vary from pride in having arranged the wines correctly to dismay at having scrambled them completely. The following discussion addresses each of the items in the instructions for this exercise in Chapter 4.

Exercise Step 3. Rank the wines according to sweetness.

The correct ranking of the wines according to sweetness is: C, D, A, then B, from sweetest to least sweet/most tart.

Many people who do this exercise are curious about how well they did compared to another group of beginning tasters. If your group wants to compare its success rate with that of some of my students, you can use Table D.5 to get a rough idea of their performance. The data in Table D.5 was recorded during class; the correct placement of each wine is shown by the bold, italicized numbers. Students indicated where they had placed each wine in the ranking from sweetest to least sweet/most tart by raising their hands. For example, in the top row of data, one student thought that Wine A was the sweetest, 6 students thought Wine A was the next to the sweetest; 43 students placed it correctly as the third sweetest; and 28 students placed it as the least sweet/most tart. In addition to the data summarized in Table D.5, the following information was also collected: 29 students correctly ranked the wines according to sweetness and 32 students switched only two wines compared with the correct ranking.

Number of Students Ranking Each Wine				
Wine	Sweetest			Least Sweet
A	1	6	*43*	28
B	8	6	23	*41*
C	*56*	18	3	1
D	13	*48*	9	8

Table D.5
Class Results from
Introduction to Wine

Exercise Step 4. Describe the acid, sugar, balance, and body of the wines.

	Base Wine	Component Wines		
	Wine A	Wine B	Wine C	Wine D
Acid	tart	green	tart, but less than D	tart, but less than A
Sugar	dry	dry	low to medium sugar	low sugar
Balance of Acid & Sugar	OK	too tart	too sweet for most tastes	
Body	light	lighter than A	light to medium, heavier than all the others	still light, but heavier than A

Table D.6
Wine Descriptions for
Exercise 4.2

Exercise Step 5. As you are tasting, answer these questions:

A.   What is the effect of sugar on the acid taste? You probably noticed that sugar diminishes the perception of acid. Winemakers take advantage of this fact: wines from cooler regions such as England, Germany, or the northern regions of Italy or France will be naturally high in acid and are usually made with some residual sugar to balance or mask the acid taste and give the wines more body.

B.   How is the body of the wine affected by the level of sweetness? The more residual sugar in a wine, the thicker its viscosity and the heavier its body will be.

C.   Why is it recommended that dry wines be tasted before sweet wines? Because the tartness of the dry wines is exaggerated if they are tasted after sweet wines, the recommended tasting order is dry before sweet.

Exercise Step 6. Wine Identities and Compositions.

		Approximate	Composition
Wine	Identity	sugar g/100 ml	acid g/100 ml
A	Dry White Base Wine	0.3*	0.8
B	A + 0.2 grams per 100 ml tartaric acid	0.3	1.1
C	A + 0.8 grams per 100 ml sucrose	1.1	0.8
D	A + 0.4 grams per 100 ml sucrose	0.7	0.8
*This is the amount of sugar that cannot be fermented by yeast cells and is found in even the driest wines. It cannot be tasted.			

Table D.7
Wine Identities and
Compositions

Exercise Step 7. Threshold Estimates.

With the caveat that informal tasting conditions are far from ideal for determining exact sugar thresholds, the way each taster has ranked these samples can give some information about his or her sugar threshold (see Table D.8). The average threshold for detecting sweetness from sugars in wines is about 1.0% by weight, or approximately 1.0 gram per 100 ml, but there is wide variation around this average: Amerine and Roessler report individuals who can regularly detect 0.5% sugar and those who fail to recognize 2.5% sugar in wines.[4] Table D.8 gives the approximate relationship between your arrangement of wines A-D and your sugar threshold in white table wine. Your threshold in water or red wine would be different.

Table D.8
The Approximate Relationship Between Your Arrangement of Wines A-D and Your Sugar Threshold in White Table Wine

If you perceive these wines as dry	and these wines as sweet	your estimated sugar threshold is
A and B	D and C	0.7 grams/100 ml or less
A, B, and D	C only	between 0.7 and 1.1 grams/100 ml
all 4 wines, A, B, C, and D	none	1.1 grams/100 ml or more

If you could discriminate between Wines A and B on the basis of their acidity, that tells you something about your difference threshold for acid in white table wines. You difference threshold — for discriminating between wines with different concentrations of acid — is less than the difference in acid concentrations between the two wines, that is, less than 0.2 grams/100 ml.

SENSORY EVALUATION EXERCISE 4.3.
Applying the Techniques for the Sensory Evaluation of Wine to the Extremes of the White Table Wine Flavor Spectrum — A Tasting of Chenin Blanc and Muscat Blanc

Wine Buying Guidelines
A Reminder

Because I try to use wines that my students can buy, the wine-buying guidelines for these exercises are exclusively Californian. If you live in an area where California wines, heaven forbid, are hard to find, you can use the information in the varietal wine profiles in Appendix A under "Other Important Growing Regions" along with the sensory descriptions of the wines for each tasting (for example, "an older Cabernet Sauvignon," "a 2-3 year-old White Riesling with 1-2% residual sugar") to help you shop for alternative wines that should work well in the tastings.

Wine-Buying in General

When you consult with your wine merchant or a winery, be sure to explain that you are shopping for wines for a particular tasting exercise. Explain what the exercise is intended to accomplish. For this tasting, for example, you could briefly go over the objectives from the exercise description in Chapter 4. The more carefully you describe what you are planning as well as the individual wines you need, the more successfully your wine suppliers will be able to fulfill your needs.

Wine-Buying Guidelines For This Tasting:

I have used Kendall-Jackson Vintner's Reserve Muscat Canelli — another name for Muscat Blanc — for this exercise for years. It's very floral and has recognizable — but not overwhelming — amounts of residual sugar and low alcohol (2.4% residual sugar and 9.6% alcohol in the 1989 vintage). To contrast with the Muscat Canelli structurally as well as in odor and flavor, the Chenin Blanc you choose should be dry. Among California producers of dry Chenin Blancs are Chapellet, Hacienda, Grand Cru, Dry Creek, Kenwood, and Landmark. As mentioned in Exercise 4.2, the amount of residual sugar in wines that are "completely dry" is about 0.20 to 0.30% or 0.2-0.3 grams per 100 ml. Many of the so-called dry Chenin Blancs will contain around 0.70% residual sugar. This is satisfactory for this tasting because it is below most tasters' thresholds and will be a strong contrast to the sweetness of the Muscat Canelli. You should always test the sugar content of the wines with Clinitest® to confirm their residual sugar level before the tasting. There is nothing like leading a winetasting group to destroy your ability to detect near-threshold amounts of residual sugar. Testing the wine before the group meets can eliminate potential opportunities for embarrassment.

Procedural Suggestion

Be sure to taste the drier and less strongly flavored Chenin Blanc first, which makes it Wine A on the sensory evaluation form. Your tasters should record their impressions of the wines under "observations" and write down additional useful comments — of other tasters or from notes supplied by the tasting leader — under "notes."

Information for the Post-Tasting Discussion

Typical Tasting Notes for Exercise Step 3

To help your group discuss the wines, here are some general tasting notes for Chenin Blanc and Muscat Blanc/Muscat Canelli. If you can get them, it is much better to have tasting notes for the actual wines you are using.

Chenin Blanc: light straw yellow color; brilliant clarity; either no off odors or an odor that may strike you as "something pungent that tickles my nose" or "reminds me of opening a package of dried apricots." The odor that provokes these reactions is a very small amount of sulfur dioxide. This off odor is not uncommon in young white table wines and will diminish with two to three months of bottle aging. The aroma intensity is typically low and often described using terms from the middle of the aroma wheel such as "fruity," or as "fresh" and "neutral." You may perceive the fermentation bouquet — the alcohol and other odors added by the alcoholic fermentation — as a "coolness." Exercise 4.4 will address fermentation bouquet in more detail. You will probably notice the tartness and lack of sweetness — the dryness — of the wine and many beginning wine-tasters find a dry Chenin Blanc to be too tart without food. Body will be light, the flavor young, and the wine smooth, not astringent. If you are not sure of the difference between tartness and astringency, don't be worried about that at this stage. Typical flavor associations for Chenin Blanc include apples, lemons, and fruit in general. You may notice a few bubbles in the wine, especially if it is from the most recent vintage.

Muscat Canelli: You may find that this wine is darker than the Chenin Blanc. This is because it was harvested later so that the grapes would contain enough sugar to leave some residual sugar in the wine after fermentation. You will find the very intense aroma obvious and your description may include peaches, apricots, flowers, honey, etc. The fermentation bouquet will be less apparent, as will the acidity. Because the wine has some residual sugar, the body will be medium. You will find yourself using a variety of floral and fruit descriptors for the aroma and for the intense, fruity/floral flavor as well.

Other Topics that May Come Up

Bubbles will probably come up under the discussion of appearance. In young pink and white table wines there are often bubbles of carbon dioxide gas that dissolved in the wine during fermentation and have remained in solution during the relatively brief life of the wine in the cellar. As the wine is warmed during the tasting, the carbon dioxide cannot remain dissolved and bubbles form.

The higher sugar in the Muscat will reduce its apparent acidity and increase its body. This is an example in a commercial wine of the effect of sugar on the acid taste and the relationship between sugar and body that you observed in the component wines of Exercise 4.2.

It may be fun to brainstorm about how the members of your tasting group would use these two wines with foods. For general guidelines see the introduction to this exercise in Chapter 4 and wine and food combining principles in Appendix C.

SENSORY EVALUATION EXERCISE 4.4.
Contrasting Aroma and Fermentation Bouquet — A Tasting of White Riesling, Gewürztraminer, and Gewürztraminer Grape Juice

Wine-Buying Guidelines

I use Gewürztraminer Grape Juice from Navarro Vineyards. As for the wines, I prefer that the Gewürztraminer be dry or very low in sugar (residual sugar 0.7% or less) and from the most recent possible vintage and that the White Riesling be sweeter (residual sugar 1.5-2.0%) and one to two years older than the Gewürztraminer.

Procedural Suggestion

The grape juice can be smelled first, but must be tasted third, after the two wines. The drier wine should be Wine A.

Information for the Post-Tasting Discussion
Typical Tasting Notes

You may notice that the Gewürztraminer has a less intense aroma that could be characterized as "light and floral" in contrast to the clove, peach, and apricot aroma of the White Riesling, which may also have a characteristic faint odor of rubber bands or erasers which is — believe it or not — not an off odor but a typical scent in White Rieslings, at least the ones I've tasted in California and Germany. My students have described the Gewürztraminer varietal aroma as resembling pumpkin pie, grapefruit, fresh air in an open field, and jasmine tea, and they often mention that it has herbaceous notes. If you succeed in finding an older White Riesling you may notice that its color is darker and its odor contains hints of butterscotch, toast, and nuts, and recognize that the odor is richer, "heavier," and more complex, with "more smells," all of which — along with an overall change from fruity to perfumed — are expected when White Rieslings age in the bottle and develop "bottle bouquet." The wine-buying instructions also call for the White Riesling to be sweeter, and you will notice this taste as well as the increase in body and reduced perception of acid from the additional residual sugar.

Exercise Steps 1 and 2. What odors does fermentation add to wine? How do you describe fermentation bouquet?

To answer these two questions I have reproduced some student responses below. I must remind you that I encourage students at this early stage not to worry about using "wine correct" terminology in their answers.

    A.   *Fermentation gives the wine a floral, fresh odor, alcohol smell, a more citrus taste, an aroma that is much stronger but lighter (than grape juice).*

    B.   *When swirling the glass the juice doesn't move as much.*

    C.   *The Gewürztraminer wine has a crisper smell and creates a "tingling" sensation and the alcohol makes the wine disappear in my mouth faster than the juice does.*

    D.   *Fermentation seems to take away some of the very strong fruity smells present in the grape juice and gives the wine a lightness (complexity) compared to the dull and simple grape juice.*

    E.   *Grape juice seems boring whereas fermentation tastes young.*

    F.   *The wine has a wider range of smells. The fermentation added scents of cloves, roses, violets— many more floral smells.*

    G.   *The wine has a smoother combination of smells; the juice has a strong smell and the wine smells like there's something going on in it as compared to the sweet/mild juice.*

    H.   *Fermentation adds a dry sensation in your mouth and leaves it watering and wanting more.*

    I.   *The fermentation process to me brings the flavors up and highlights them. They "jump" at you after fermentation whereas before they seemed more laid-back.*

J.   *Fermentation increases tangyness, tartness, dryness — makes the wine more pungent — makes it seem cool, sharp, crisp, tart, alive, lingering.*

K.   *The fermentation bouquet adds a scent that smells tangy/greenish or that gives a "puckery nose feeling"; the grape juice had a very dull smell.*

L.   *It seems that fermentation gives wines the sharp smell that gets your attention.*

Exercise Step 3. Can differences in the densities of liquids be perceived before they are tasted? How?

Yes, they can. Differences in the body of wines and juices become apparent when the glasses are swirled: the grape juice is much heavier than a normal wine (see student B's observations). This can also happen with some very sweet late-harvest wines that approach 15-20% residual sugar.

Other Topics That May Come Up

1.   How is the grape juice made? According to the Navarro Vineyard's promotional material for their Gewürztraminer and Pinot Noir grape juices, premium wine grapes are crushed, pressed, and chilled immediately to 29 degrees F to prevent fermentation. After settling, the juice is filtered to remove any naturally occurring yeast and then bottled. Because they are not pasteurized by heating like many grape juices, the Navarro juices retain the delicate, heat-sensitive aroma compounds from the grapes.

2.   What do you *do* with this grape juice? Here's another chance for some brainstorming in your tasting group. One possibility is to make Gewürztraminer sorbet.

SENSORY EVALUATION EXERCISE 4.5.
Comparing Aroma, Fermentation Bouquet, and Oak-Aging Bouquet — A Tasting of Sauvignon Blanc and Two Styles of Chardonnay

Wine- and Food-Buying Guidelines

I use one of the more herbaceous-style Sauvignon Blancs, dry (often labelled Fumé Blanc), and try to find an excellent — even award-winning — oak-aged Chardonnay so that my students can have the experience of tasting a very (for most of them) expensive bottle of wine. For the non-oak-aged Chardonnay I have successfully used a wine called "Callalees" made by Callaway Vineyard and Winery. This wine is made with *sur lie*-aging so it will give your tasters a nice preview of this character for the sparkling wine tastings.

You will need one or two small pieces of crisp, tart apple (Granny Smiths are perfect) and a mild-flavored, low acid Swiss cheese. (At our local delicatessen it's called "Baby Swiss.")

Procedural Suggestions

Taste the Sauvignon Blanc first, then the Callalees Chardonnay, and finally the oak-aged Chardonnay. Taste the food samples after the wines have been evaluated.

Information for the Post-Tasting Discussion
Tasting Notes

All three of these wines should be dry and you will notice that they are much less fruity as a group than Muscats, White Rieslings, and Gewürztraminers.

You will probably find the Sauvignon Blanc to be lighter in color and body than the oak-aged Chardonnay. Here are some descriptions my students have offered of Sauvignon Blanc varietal aroma and flavor: *bell pepper, green pepper, citrus(y), grassy, cut grass, lawns, shrubs, eucalyptus, mint, floral, peaches, kitty's fur, walking around in a forest.*

You will find the Callalees Chardonnay to be similar to the Sauvignon Blanc in color and body. Its odor and flavor are marked by the *sur lie*-aging character, which is also found in greater amounts in bottle-fermented sparkling wines. Some of the champagne bouquet terms described in Exercise 8.1 for tasting sparkling wines may apply to this wine. Here are some descriptions of the *sur lie*-aging character from my students: *black licorice, burnt tortillas, charcoal, rubber bands, dust on rubber bands, earthy, latex balloons, mushrooms, musty, toasted, wet grass.*

The oak-aged Chardonnay will be the darkest and heaviest-bodied of the wines. Its odors and flavors will feature a prominent oak-aging character, described with the following terms by my students: *brandy, whiskey, Jack Daniels, toasted caramel, burnt coconut, smokey, buttery, butterscotch, caramel, spicy, gingerbread, nutmeg, honey, maple, molasses, oak panelling, sawing wood, suntan lotion, vanilla.*

Exercise Step 1. Write a description of the oak-aging bouquet.

Please refer to the student descriptions of the odors and flavors of the oak-aged Chardonnay for the answer.

Exercise Step 2. What is the effect of oak aging on the acidity and body of wines?

Like residual sugar, oak aging decreases the perceived acidity in wines and increases their body.

Exercise Step 3. Food Observations

Table D.9
The Effect of Apples and Baby Swiss Cheese on the Perception of Chardonnay

Food	Effect on Wine(s)	Component Affected
Apple	Makes both the wines seem more tart, more herbaceous	Perceived Acidity Increases
Baby Swiss Cheese	Makes the wines seem smoother, more rich; oak may be accentuated in the Chardonnay	Perceived Acidity Decreases

SENSORY EVALUATION EXERCISE 4.6.
Your Turn Creating Your Own Tasting of White Table Wines

Procedural Suggestions

Use these suggestions and the books mentioned earlier under "Sources for Wine Ideas" only if tasters in your group cannot come up with their own ideas — which seems very unlikely. The winery addresses at the end of this appendix may also prove helpful for obtaining wines.

Among the general categories of winetasting, "foundation exercises" — such as those you have just completed — are designed to investigate aromas, components of wines, types of varietal wines, the sensory effects of fermentation and oak aging, and bottle bouquet. For additional foundation tastings, members of your group could: 1. explore additional fundamentals, such as serving temperature; 2. look more deeply into the fundamentals already studied, by setting up tastings of additional aroma standards or making components with greater refinement such as several levels of sugar concentration; 3. taste additional varietal wines — perhaps some of the less common quality varietals such as Pinot Blanc or Pinot Gris; or 4. investigate bottle aging further by using a so-called vertical tasting, in which several vintages of the same wine are tasted together.

Another general category of tasting considers wines from a geographical perspective, for example, looking into regional differences in California wines or comparing California wines to their European counterparts: Sauvignon Blanc and White Bordeaux, Chardonnay and White Burgundy, White Riesling and Mosel or Rheingau wines. The members of your tasting group could study the varietal wine profiles in Appendix A for more ideas for regional comparisons. You could set up tastings to study wines from an economic perspective, comparing the first and second labels of a particular producer, looking for the best jug wine in a defined price range, or trying several Chardonnays of different prices.

SENSORY EVALUATION EXERCISE 4.7.
Mystery Wine Identification — A Review Tasting of White Table Wines

Wine-Buying Guidelines

When you are buying wines for the three varietal white table wine exercises, buy an extra supply of each wine for this tasting.

Procedural Suggestions

Select four of the seven wines tasted earlier — Chenin Blanc, Muscat Blanc, Gewürztraminer, White Riesling, Sauvignon Blanc, and two Chardonnays — for identification in this exercise. I'd suggest not using both a Gewürztraminer and a White Riesling unless the wines you bought for the exercises were very distinctive. Use the other bottles of wine as prizes for those tasters who correctly identify all the wines.

Conceal the identity of the wines. The best way to do this is to pour the wines into decanters or to dispense 30 ml samples into glasses for each taster (Many people can identify wines ahead of time by their distinctive bottle shapes and colors). Using a waterproof system — at least, waterproof until it's time to wash them — mark the decanters or glasses of wine with letters or numbers. Be sure to have paper available for the tasters to report the wines' identities. I let my students refer to all their notes during these exercises. Since this tasting will involve more wines than the tasters have previously worked with at one time, be sure to have water and crackers on hand for palate cleansing. Be sure to take time after revealing the identity of each wine to invite the tasters who have correctly identified it to discuss how they made their deductions.

A Sample Worksheet for a Key to the White Varietal Wines

Each taster should develop his or her own key, since the value in doing so lies more in the process of thinking about the wines and their differences and similarities than in creating a foolproof system for distinguishing them. Also, everyone's sensory impressions will be somewhat unique, so one person's key might not work for someone else. Here is a sample to illustrate the process.

Step #1: sensory factor: strength of flavor and aroma
      If very strong, floral and fruity, the variety is Muscat. Confirm with a complete
        odor description.
      If the aroma is less strong, and may or may not be fruity, go to step #2.
Step #2: sensory factor: nature of the aroma
      If fruity, go to step #4.
      If not fruity, go to step #3.
Step #3: sensory factor: presence and amount of oak-aging bouquet
      If prominent, the variety is probably Chardonnay. Confirm with complete odor
        description.
      If not prominent or absent, the variety is probably Sauvignon Blanc. Confirm with
        complete odor description.
Step #4: sensory factor: nuances of fruity aroma
      If aroma has peach and apricot elements, the variety is probably White Riesling.
        Confirm with complete odor description.
      If aroma has floral and spicy elements, the variety is probably Gewürztraminer.
        Confirm with complete odor description.

SENSORY EVALUATION EXERCISE 6.1.
Focus on Olfaction II — Red Table Wine Aromas and Descriptors for Bottle Bouquet

How to Make the Aroma Reference Standards in Your Kitchen
The Base Wine

The base wine for this exercise and Exercises 6.2 and 6.3 needs to be a neutrally flavored, sound, dry red table wine. Generic wines are most suitable because they are neutral in flavor, but they may contain residual sugar and need to be tested. We use Parducci Vintage Red for these exercises.

Recipes for the Reference Standards

If you are starting with this exercise, you'll want to look over the instructions for making and presenting the reference standards in Exercise 4.1. Some of the recipe ingredients for this exercise are pretty hard to get out of the wine (ground pepper and shreds of tobacco, for example), but if your group has already done Exercise 4.1, the participants will know the importance of not peeking into the glasses to look at the added aroma ingredients. The twelve reference standards I use most often are indicated with an asterisk.

Table D.10
Recipes for the Red Wine Aroma Reference Standards [5]

Reference Standard	Add to ⅛ cup red wine and soak
black pepper*	2-3 grains ground black pepper
blackberry	1-2 crushed fresh or frozen blackberries
raspberry*	1-2 crushed fresh or frozen raspberries
cassis* (black currant)	2 tsp cassis or 2 tsp liquid from canned black currants and 1 tsp Ribena® (sweetened concentrate)
cherry*	2 tsp liquid from canned cherries
strawberry jam	1 tsp strawberry jam
raisin*	5-8 crushed raisins — may need to soak overnight and may need to be pulverized before adding them to the wine
eucalyptus*	1 crushed eucalyptus leaf
mint*	1 crushed mint leaf (spearmint) or 1 drop mint extract
green bean	½ -1 tsp liquid from canned green beans
black or green* olive	1-1½ tsp liquid from canned black or green olives
tobacco*	take a cigarette apart and use ½ tsp (a pinch?) of the tobacco; tobacco should be the least aromatic available
soy	1-2 drops soy sauce
chocolate*	½ tsp powdered cocoa
molasses*	smear ½ tsp on the bottom of the glass (molasses tends to lose its flavor with storage)
vanilla	1-2 drops vanilla extract
oak	see Exercise 4.1
coffee*	2-3 grains fresh ground coffee

Procedural Suggestions

If your tasting group has been working through these exercises in order, by the time you've arrived here you'll be quite familiar with winetasting procedure and able to work with a dozen reference standards. You could combine Exercises 6.1 and 6.2, including the four off-odor examples here as well. The reference standards and off odors should be presented in foil-covered wine glasses as explained in Exercise 4.1.

Information for the Post-Tasting Discussion

Although you may be a more experienced taster by the time you work on this exercise, you may experience more fatigue smelling the red than white wine reference standards. This may be because the red wine odors are stronger and red wines have a slightly higher alcohol content and/ or because this exercise presents more samples.

Exercise Steps 1 and 2. Aromas — Associations and Where They're Found.

As I did for Exercise 4.1, I have collected and summarized some of the associations my students have made with the red reference standards into Table D.11, Associations with Red Table Wine Aroma Reference Standards. This table is intended as a guide and supplement to your group's discussion. If you have not done Exercise 4.1, please read about the use and value of these associations in "Information for the Post-Tasting Discussion" on pages 353-354.

Aroma Reference Standard	Selected Student Association(s)	Wines with This Aroma Note*
black pepper	*black tea, citrus, berry, pepper steak*	S
raspberry	*raspberry mineral water/jam/fruit leather/syrup*	Z
cassis (black currant)	*black currant mineral water/jelly/cough syrup; raspberry, cherry cough syrup*	CS
cherry	*cherry Jello, cherry Coke, box of ripe bing cherries, red lollipop, Hawaiian punch*	PN
raisin	*prune, prune juice, raisins*	LHZ
eucalyptus	*Ben Gay, tea, Stanford campus, koalas, Qantas, walking through the Berkeley Hills*	MVCS
mint	*fresh mint, after-dinner mints, gum, Morocco (mint tea), Certs, toothpaste, spearmint, Vicks*	MVCS
green olive	*martinis, appetizer plates*	CS
black olive	*pizza*	CS
tobacco	*stogies, baseball, grandpa's cigar box, my grandfather, spice, straw, tea*	PN, BB
chocolate	*candy bar, Ghirardelli, Hershey's, chocolate milk, chocolate-covered cherries*	BB
molasses	*prune juice, dairy farm (feed), gingerbread/snaps, burnt raisins, tar, soy sauce, BBQ*	BB
vanilla	*chocolate-chip cookies, vanilla car freshener, baking cookies, chocolate?*	oak-barrel aged
oak	*butterscotch, oak, vanilla, caramel, ginger, coconut meringue pie, old-fashioned attics/places, soy sauce, smoke*	oak-barrel aged
coffee	*cappuccino, Sunday morning, French roast*	BB

*That the equation of a few odor descriptors with the aroma of a varietal wine is an over-simplification should be clear from a look at Table 5.3: Mitch Cosentino's Guide to Blending the Bordeaux Varietals. You will find odors such as black pepper and mint in wines other than Syrah and Martha's Vineyard Cabernet Sauvignon, but this chart indicates where they are expected. S = Syrah, Z = Zinfandel, CS = Cabernet Sauvignon, PN = Pinot Noir, LHZ = Late-Harvest Zinfandel, MVCS = Martha's Vineyard Cabernet Sauvignon, a Napa Valley Cabernet Sauvignon noted for its mint and eucalyptus character, BB = odor found in bottle bouquet.

Table D.11 Student Associations with Red Table Wine Aroma Reference Standards

Exercise Step 3. Number of Aromas Correctly Identified on Your First Attempt.

If you have been doing these exercises in the order in which they are presented, the members of your tasting group will probably notice that they will have developed skills — such as better concentration — that enable them to correctly identify a higher proportion of these odors than they did in Exercise 4.1. Your group may or may not notice the gender differences in odor recognition ability discussed in Exercise 4.1.

Exercise Step 4. The Main Odor Differences Between White and Red Table Wines.

Red wine odors are stronger and their composition is distinct from the odors of white wines. As mentioned in the introduction to this exercise, in red wines there are fewer aromas from the floral, citrus, and tropical fruit segments of the wine aroma wheel and more from the fresh and canned/cooked vegetative, woody, and caramelized segments. The alcohol is more prominent in red wines and they are more likely to have oak odors.

Exercise Step 5. Additional Things You Have Learned About Identifying and Learning Odors.

At this point my students have had more experience with tasting wine and have done two wine and food matching homework assignments, so their advice on how to remember wine odors is different in this exercise. It contains hints such as "making associations with wines tasted before" and "imagining foods that have been or could be eaten with the wine," in addition to the suggestions I reproduced in the text of Exercise 4.1. At this stage they also frequently mention the usefulness of practice and knowing what to expect from reading about the wines.

Step 6. Questions Raised by This Tasting — One Topic That May Come Up.

You may wonder if these reference odors — soy sauce, tobacco, chocolate — are **really** in bottle bouquet. Yes, they are, and there are a lot of other odors as well, created by the reaction of the volatile wine components with each other and with other compounds in the wine. Each odor is very subtle, so you won't find sniffing a fine bottle of 1978 Alexander Valley Cabernet Sauvignon, which may have a suggestion of chocolate in its bouquet, the same as inhaling the aromas emitted by a chocolate sundae. When you encounter the elements of bottle bouquet in a wine they will be part of a very complex and subtle set of odors made up of scores of individual scents. The term "odor notes" applies nicely to the components of bottle bouquet: a chocolate "note" is just one tone in the symphony of a wine's bottle bouquet.

SENSORY EVALUATION EXERCISE 6.2.
Focus on Olfaction, III — When to Turn Your Nose Up (and Your Thumbs Down) at a Wine — Four Off Odors

Preparing the Off Odor Reference Standards

It's Parducci Vintage Red, the wine we love to abuse, that we will once again use to make the reference standards. The recipes to use depend on whether or not you have someone with lab skills to help you.

Table D.12
Recipes to Make Off Odor Reference Standards in Your Kitchen

For Wine	Add	To Wine
1	2-6 drops nail-polish remover	½ cup wine
2	½ teaspoon vinegar	½ cup wine
3	2 teaspoons sherry	½ cup wine
4	Strike one wooden match, blow it out, let it cool, and drop the head into 1 ounce of wine. Let your nose recover from smelling the match, sniff the wine to see if you can smell the pungent "burnt match/match heads" odor; if not, repeat the above.	

Table D.13
Recipes to Make Off Odor Reference Standards in a Laboratory

For Wine	Add	To Wine
1	1 drop ethyl acetate	50 ml wine
2	1 drop glacial acetic acid	50 ml wine
3	4 mg acetaldehyde	100 ml wine
4	0.5 ml of 5% SO_2 solution (To make a 5% sulfur dioxide solution, dissolve 5 grams of potassium metabisulfite in 100 ml of water.) The final desired concentration is 250 mg/L SO_2.	100 ml wine
	* use extreme caution when handling acetaldehyde	

Another Common Off Odor — Corked

Corks are cut from the outer layers of the bark of oak trees growing wild in the countries bordering the western Mediterranean. Molds that sometimes grow in the cork can spoil wines by producing a musty, moldy, dank odor and flavor. Such wines are called "corked." This corresponds to the term "moldy cork" on the wine aroma wheel. Until recently a winery might encounter only two or three faulty corks per year, but now they are as common as two or three a month and have been known to affect from three to five percent of the bottles at major wine competitions.[6] It is thought that the increased incidence of corked wines has resulted from treating corks with chlorine to disinfect them. The chlorine reacts with mold-produced compounds to produce tyrene (also called tricholoroanisole), which is responsible for the moldy cork odor and flavor. If you want to demonstrate this odor you can order vials of tyrene for $2.00 each (discounts for large purchases) from The Wine Trader.

Information for the Post-Tasting Discussion
Exercise Step 3. Associations.

This exercise is usually entered into with some trepidation about smelling bad things. Table D.14 summarizes the responses of the brave survivors.

Off Odor	Association(s)
Ethyl Acetate	*Turpentine, paint remover, nail-polish remover*
Acetic Acid	*Brake fluid, model-airplane glue, gasoline, vinegar*
Acetaldehyde	*Cool, wet, closed, moldy, freshly-painted room, shellac, dirty shower, musty/mildew*
Sulfur Dioxide	*Tide pools, exposed mud flats, matches, cigarette ashes, working in a darkroom*

Table D.14
Associations with Four
Wine Off Odors

Exercise Step 4. How would you describe off odors in general?

Typical student responses to this question include: *Bad, rancid, chemical, foreign, adulterated; flattens the normal wine smells; not fruit- or plant-oriented but man-made, offensive.* No wonder they weren't looking forward to this tasting!

Exercise Step 5. What has this tasting added to your understanding of wine odors and how to remember them?

My students note that these off odors are easier to remember and require no special techniques because they are so pungent and unusual.

SENSORY EVALUATION EXERCISE 6.3.
Focus on Taste and Touch II — Structural Components of Red Table Wines

Preparing and Presenting the Component Wines
The Base Wines

For the red base wine you will need to use a wine that is dry and relatively low in tannins. Because many red generic wines contain residual sugar you will need to call the winery for the sugar analysis or you can use Clinitest® to check the sugar content. For the white base wine for this exercise we have been known to mix together assorted leftovers, since all we want to illustrate with that wine is the absence of tannins.

Making the Red Wine Components in Your Kitchen

Follow the recipes in Table D.15. Use **either** the teaspoon and cups **or** the grams and milliliters combination. You will probably find that the grape seed tannin and tannic acid are a little hard to dissolve, so keep stirring patiently. Component Wine D should be made up right before the tasting.

For Wine	Add to 2¼ cups (or 750 ml)* red base wine
A	nothing (this is the white base wine)
B	nothing (this is the red base wine)
C	¼ tsp. (1.5 grams) tartaric or citric acid
D	¼ tsp. (0.75 grams) tannic acid or grape seed tannin
*Add .75 and 1.5 grams to 750 ml red base wine **or** ¼ tsp. to 2¼ cups of red base wine.	

Table D.15
Recipes for Red
Wine Components

Presenting the Wines

Tasters will need an average-size serving of Wines A, C, and D — about ⅛ cup or 30 ml — and a double-size serving of Wine B to taste with the cheeses and walnut. There will be plenty of spitting out of these component wines, so be sure to have spitoons available and water for rinsing your tasters' poor palates.

Gelatin for the Fining Demonstration
Because it will solidify if made up ahead of time, gelatin is dissolved when the tasters come to the point in the exercise when they need it. You can have a cup or so of hot water and an

envelope of KNOX unflavored gelatin on hand. Dissolve the gelatin in as little hot water as possible and add 2-4 drops to each taster's glass of Wines A and D. Because the wines will be tasted after the gelatin settles out, be sure to add a minimal amount of water so that the wine is diluted as little as possible. Compared to gelatin fining in a winery, this little fining demonstration adds **much** more water to the wine. It is important to minimize the water addition when doing this exercise and to emphasize to the tasters that the watery post-fining texture of the wine is not what results in wineries.

Cheese-Buying Guidelines: Buy the firmest blue cheese you can find for ease in cutting and distribution. Cougar Gold Cheese is a mild, white cheddar favored by wineries for showing off their red table wines to good advantage. It can be ordered from the Washington State University Creamery or a mild white cheese can be substituted. The walnut should be unsalted and have its skin intact.

Information for the Post-Tasting Discussion

Exercise Step 1. The effect of each wine on saliva and the overall feeling of smoothness in your mouth.

Wine A contains no tannins and should leave your mouth smooth. The low tannin levels in Wine B will be astringent and dry your mouth a little, reducing its saliva content somewhat. Wine C's acidity will accentuate your perception of the wine's astringency but the acidity itself may stimulate some saliva flow (it will be more "mouth-watering" than the other wines). Wine D will be distinctly astringent, drying your mouth more than the others by stripping it of its smooth saliva.

Exercise Step 2. Describe the acidity, bitterness, body, and astringency of each wine.

Wine A is perceived as tart, not bitter, light-bodied, and smooth. Wine B would be slightly less acidic, but still perceived as tart, not bitter, light- to medium-bodied, and very slightly rough. Wine C will probably seem green — or at least noticeably more tart than A or B, not bitter, with less perceived body and more astringency than Wine B. Tasters will recognize Wine D as tart, probably bitter to many, medium-bodied, and very rough.

Exercise Step 3. Describe the differences you perceive between acidity and astringency and between bitterness and astringency.

For your tasting group's discussion of this step, here is a collection of student responses. I like these because they are more colorful and original than my approach, which would be to simply state that bitter and tart are tastes and astringency is a tactile sensation produced by the reaction of the tannin molecules with the insides of our mouths.

A. *Bitterness is a taste perceived at the back of the tongue and astringency gives the wine a duller flavor—or maybe more mild.*
B. *Acid hits the sides and middle of the tongue leaving the taster with a tangy, biting taste while tannins dull the wine's flavor. Acid has more taste while tannin has more feel.*
C. *Tannin "shocks" the mouth, causing a loss of sensation.*
D. *Acid literally gave me shivers! It makes my mouth water or tingle. My mouth has a fizzy feeling.*
E. *Tannin tastes more bitter and feels rougher.*
F. *Tannin produces a thicker feeling in the mouth.*
G. *Tannin closes up everything in your mouth whereas acid opens everything and makes you salivate.*
H. *Tannin is leathery, chalky, like unripe persimmons or pomegranate skin, herbaceous, roughens the mouth, makes my mouth feel sticky, reminds me of "things you're not supposed to eat" — like leaves, parsley, or paper towels.*
I. *Tannin makes my mouth feel the way it does when I take aspirin without water or like when I have a nervous "dry mouth."*

Exercise Step 4. What is the effect of tannin on your ability to perceive other aspects of the wines that are sensed in the mouth?

The members of your tasting group will probably join my students in unanimous agreement that high tannin levels in wines (Wine D, for example) reduce a person's ability to sense everything about a wine that is perceived in the mouth — including its basic tastes, body, and flavors.

The Effect of Gelatin Fining on Tannin, Steps 1 and 3

You will notice that nothing happens when gelatin is added to the white base wine because it has no tannins, but when it is added to Wine D the gelatin will coagulate and form a sediment. The astringency of Wine D will be reduced and the wine may seem "sweeter" and taste more fruity. As mentioned above, both wines that receive gelatin will also seem more watery.

Red Wines and the Hazards of the Cheese Plate

Step 1: Table D.16 presents a summary of the interaction of the foods and Wine B.

Food	Effect on Wine*	Why
Cougar Gold Cheese	Smoother, less astringent	Fat and protein in the cheese reduce the perception of astringency
Blue Cheese	Rougher, more astringent	Salt and acidity increase the perception of astringency
Walnut	Rougher, more astringent	Tannins in the skin of the walnut increase the perception of astringency
* The component affected in each case is tannin.		

*Table D.16
Interaction of Red
Wine and Three Foods*

Step 2: Suggestions for combining red wines and foods that can be derived from this exercise are: red wines match better with foods high in protein and fat; wines taste better with milder flavored foods (the mild cheese is preferred to the pungent blue; wines taste better with less acidic foods (less acidic cheddar is better than acidic blue cheese); and tannic foods make red wines seem more astringent.

A Topic that May Come Up

A typical taster's reaction to this exercise will be "I don't like this tannin stuff very much." The fact that we are more sensitive to bitterness than any other taste — our thresholds for the perception of bitterness are the lowest among the four basic tastes — has led sensory scientists to speculate that our species evolved a protective distaste for bitter tastes and their associated astringent sensations because many poisonous plants that our ancestors needed to avoid were bitter and astringent.[7]

SENSORY EVALUATION EXERCISE 6.4.
"Taste and Tell"— Using Your Sensory Evaluation Skills to Define
Two Red Table Wine Styles — Burgundian and Beaujolais

Wine-Buying Guidelines

You will need to find a Gamay or Gamay Beaujolais Nouveau from the most recent vintage. Look for a carbonic maceration wine if you want to explore the sensory qualities of wines made by this process. I usually invest in a very good Pinot Noir for this exercise. It will typically be two to three years older than the Gamay or Gamay Beaujolais Nouveau. If you choose a Pinot Noir from the Carneros viticultural area of California, your tasting group can refer to the descriptive terms for these wines mentioned in the discussion of the work of Guinard and Cliff in the section "How is Sensory Evaluation Used Professionally?" in Chapter 2.

Procedural Suggestions

Depending on how your tasting group has been using these sensory evaluation exercises, this one could be used simply to become acquainted with two kinds of red varietal wines or to relate sensory impressions to winemaking methods. If your group has started with the red-wine exercises and has limited tasting experience, you'll do best with the first approach — a "get acquainted" tasting. In contrast, if your group has more tasting experience — for example, if you have been following these exercises in order — you are prepared to try the second approach, "Taste and Tell."

Procedure for a "Get Acquainted" Tasting

Identify the wines for the tasters. Wine A is the Nouveau wine; taste it first. Wine B is the Pinot Noir. Refer to the tasting notes for descriptions of the wines and suggestions for using the two wines with foods.

Procedure for a "Taste and Tell" Tasting

For this approach, don't identify the wines before they are tasted. Simply tell your taster that Wine A is a "Beaujolais-style wine" (which should be tasted first) and Wine B is a "Burgundian-style wine" and let them define these styles with their sensory impressions. During the post-tasting discussion, everyone's observations can be assembled into a description of each style and connected with the methods used to make each wine.

Information for the Post-Tasting Discussion

Exercise Step 1. A Description of the Sensory Differences Between a Beaujolais-style and Burgundian-style Wine.

These descriptions are the tasting notes for Wines A and B, the Gamay (or Gamay Beaujolais) Nouveau and the Pinot Noir.

The Gamay or Gamay Beaujolais Nouveau will have a striking light to medium purple color that may remind you of cranberry juice. The aroma will be very fruity and fresh and suggest an array of fruit descriptions, including black currant, cassis, cherries, cranberries, grape jelly, and raspberry. You will recognize that the odors on the whole are more simple and fruity than those of the Pinot Noir. This wine will have a refreshing tart acidity and fruity, young flavors.

The Pinot Noir's color will be a tawny, brick, or blood red. A recent class described the more complex odor of this wine with the following terms: *black cherry pie, cherry, cinnamon, leather, pine trees, roots, musty, silver polish, spicy, earthy, complex, tobacco, molasses, butter, smokey, soy sauce, vanilla, woody, cedar, and oak.* You will notice that the wine has less apparent tartness and is rougher.

Exercise Step 2. How do you think these two styles of red table wine might best be used with foods?

To help your tasting group brainstorm this exercise step, Table D.17 summarizes some ideas about using Beaujolais and Burgundian-style wines with foods.

Table D.17
Meal Ideas with Beaujolais and Burgundian Wines

Food or Meal Factor	Beaujolais	Burgundian
Where	outdoors OK	indoors only
When	lunch: simpler, lower alcohol (it's a work day)	dinner: more complex, higher alcohol
Kind of foods	OK with both rich and less rich; red meat, chicken, richer fish, ham	probably better with rich foods, but best with high quality, simple foods if a great Pinot Noir; avoid ocean fish and ham because the salt will increase the perception of tannin for some people

Exercise Step 3. Which wine seems more versatile with foods, and why?

The Beaujolais style is more versatile because it has virtually all the essential characteristics of a wine with high odds of combining well with foods: crisp acidity, dry, low to medium body, moderate alcohol, low tannins, and a neutral flavor.

Exercise Step 4. What can you deduce about how each wine was made from its organoleptic description?

For the Beaujolais style the color is that of a very young wine, with little or no bulk aging prior to bottling. The predominant fruit aroma suggests cool fermentation temperatures — such as those used for white table wines — or a whole berry fermentation to emphasize fruitiness. The tartness of the wine and its fruitiness suggest that the wine did not undergo the malolactic fermentation and its limited aging potential in bottle is reflected in a lack of tannins. These wines typically are bottled within four to six weeks of the time the grapes are picked.

For the Burgundian-style wine, the colors mentioned are typical of a wine aged in oak, which is also suggested by the descriptions vanilla, woody, cedar, and oak. Less fruit character implies fermentation at higher temperatures and longer bulk aging times. Oak barrel and bottle aging are reflected in the odor descriptions complex, tobacco, molasses, butter, smokey, soy sauce. The greater tannin content (rougher) suggests a longer fermentation with the skins, barrel aging, and a wine intended for bottle aging.

SENSORY EVALUATION EXERCISE 6.5.
Premium Red Varietal Wines — Zinfandel, Syrah, and the Joys of Intensity

Wine-Buying Guidelines

You will need three wines for this exercise: a Syrah, a lighter-style Zinfandel with low to moderate varietal character and tannins, and a heavier-style Zinfandel with a more intense varietal character and higher tannins. We regularly use McDowell Valley Vineyards Syrah, but this variety is also produced by Estrella River, Duxoup, Preston, Bonny Doon Vineyards, and Joseph Phelps Winery. To minimize other differences between the wines, you should buy the two Zinfandels from the same winery if possible. Ridge Vineyards and Kendall-Jackson are examples of wineries that produce Zinfandels in more than one style.

Procedural Suggestion

Taste the lighter Zinfandel first (Wine A), then the heavier Zinfandel, and lastly the Syrah.

Information for the Post-Tasting Discussion
General Tasting Notes

In contrast to the two red varietal wines tasted in Exercise 6.4, the Syrah and the heavier style Zinfandel will be darker in color, stronger in aroma and flavor, and higher in body and astringency content. They will need longer bottle aging than the Gamay Nouveau or the Pinot Noir before their tannin levels are reduced so that they are more pleasant to drink.

Exercise Step 1: A, B, and C. Contrast the wines on all aspects of the sensory evaluation, select appropriate aroma wheel terms for each wine, and note important differences between Zinfandel and Syrah.

The sensory evaluation should confirm that you bought the right wines! The lighter Zinfandel should be lighter in color, dry, and have a more raspberry aroma and flavor, lighter body, less oak character, and be smoother than the heavier Zinfandel. This wine will have a more concentrated or intense blackberry or black pepper aroma and flavor. The Syrah will be more like the heavier Zinfandel in overall sensory characteristics and will have a similar aroma, perhaps with smoky, fresh black pepper, and plum jam elements.

Exercise Step 2. Account for the differences you observe by speculating on how the two Zinfandel wines might have been made.

Table D.18 summarizes the relationship between the key sensory features of these wines and vineyard and winemaking factors.

Table D.18
Vineyard and Wine-
making Factors for
Lighter (A) and
Heavier (B) Styles of
Zinfandel

Wine	Sensory Aspect	How Created During Winemaking
A	1. lighter color 2. lower odor intensity 3. less tannic 4. less oak 5. lighter body	1. shorter time of skin contact during fermentation 2. same as 1 and 5 3. same as 1 and more gelatin used in fining 4. aged in larger, older, less flavorful barrels for shorter times 5. harvest at lower degrees Brix
B	1. darker color 2. more intense odor 3. more tannic 4. more oak 5. heavier body	1. longer skin contact during fermentation, vineyard with low crop of smaller berries 2. same as 1 3. same as 1 and less gelatin fining 4. aged in smaller, newer, more flavorful barrels for longer times 5. harvest at higher degrees Brix

A Topic that May Come Up

Many tasters wonder how long will these wines need to age before they are more palatable/less tannic. For Zinfandel in California, the answer is often "not as long as you might expect," even for some wines that are very tannic when young. In France's Rhône district the Syrah grape produces some very long-lived wines, but in California Syrah has a very limited track record, having been made by a small number of producers for a relatively short period of time, so the verdict is still out on their long-term aging performance. Jancis Robinson's VINTAGE TIMELINES is a useful reference for this question, and you could also ask your wine merchant or the winery what their experience has been with aging Zinfandels and Syrahs.

SENSORY EVALUATION EXERCISE 6.6.
The Bordelais Celebrities — Cabernet Sauvignon, Merlot, and Cabernet Franc

Wine- and Food-Buying Guidelines

You will need a Merlot, a Cabernet Sauvignon, and a Cabernet Franc for the exercise. To find wines that are typical of each variety, you should use the descriptions in the post-tasting discussion for Exercise Steps 1 and 2 to describe their flavor and structural characteristics to your wine supplier. All three wines should be from the same vintage. Many more wineries make Merlot and Cabernet Sauvignon than make Cabernet Franc, so you will have many choices for the first two varietals and only a handful for the third. California Cabernet Franc producers include Caymus, Congress Springs, Guenoc, Gundlach-Bundschu, Jekel, Konocti, Madroña, Ridge, Sebastiani, Whitehall Lane, and Wild Horse Vineyards. We usually use a Merlot and Cabernet Sauvignon from the same producer.

You will need one or two pieces of milk chocolate, dark — but not bittersweet — chocolate, and raspberry fruit leather — or a dollop of raspberry jam or puree — for each taster. The raspberry fruit leather works better than the jam because it is not as sweet and is easier to handle.

Procedural Suggestions

Taste the lighter-bodied, less complex, less astringent wine first. If you succeeded in buying typical wines, Wine A should be the Merlot and Wines B and C the Cabernet Franc and Cabernet Sauvignon.

Information for the Post-Tasting Discussion
Exercise Step 1. Aroma and Flavor Descriptors for the Bordelais Varietals.

Your tasting group will recognize both the herbaceous aromas such as bell pepper, green olives, and cut grass, and the berry characteristics resembling cassis, blackberries, and black cherries that are associated with these wines. You will want to check to see how the herbal elements and fruit characteristics in the aromas compare to the descriptions below from Mitch Cosentino's Blending Guide, Table 5.3.

Merlot: softer fruit and floral elements; red cherry, plums

Cabernet Franc: clove, dill, black pepper; red cherry, raspberry, blueberry, occasionally cranberry; more intensely aromatic and spicier than Cabernet Sauvignon and Merlot

Cabernet Sauvignon: cedar, mint, eucalyptus, green pepper, green bean; currants, cassis, blackberries, black cherry

Exercise Step 2. Structural Differences Between the Wines and How They Compare to Mitch Cosentino's Blending Guide.

The structural differences you can expect to find between Merlot, Cabernet Franc, and Cabernet Sauvignon are:

Merlot: softer tannins and softer feel in the mouth

Cabernet Franc: leaner and lighter; some can be more tannic than Cabernet Sauvignon

Cabernet Sauvignon: richer feeling in the mouth and fuller body, more tannin.

Exercise Step 3. Cabernet Sauvignon and Chocolates.

This part of the exercise usually generates a lot of lively discussion because people don't usually eat chocolates with Cabernet. The chocophiles (lovers of chocolate) in your group will probably take the position that anything goes with chocolate, but others with a more moderate affection for this delectable substance may object to its sweetness with red wines. Among my students, the dark chocolate is more often preferred and the raspberry is found to bring out the fruit flavors in the wines. This discussion is typically followed by plans to bake and taste-test a dark chocolate cake with raspberry puree or jam between the layers. Your group will probably have fun with this too!

SENSORY EVALUATION EXERCISE 6.7.
Getting Older and Better — The Effects of Bottle Aging on Cabernet Sauvignon

Wine-Buying Guidelines

For this tasting you will need to find two Cabernet Sauvignon wines made by the same producer, using grapes from the same vineyard during two vintages that are rather far apart, so that the older wine has a well-developed bottle bouquet. Your wine merchant should be able to help with this, and I have also found wineries — Louis Martini and Beaulieu Vineyards, for example— very cooperative when I have explained what I am trying to accomplish with this tasting: they have been willing to sell me older wines from their wine libraries, have suggested appropriate combinations of younger and older vintages, and have provided me with tasting notes and other information about the wines.

Procedural Suggestions

Taste the younger wine first (Wine A). When you serve the older wine you may want to decant it so that the tasters don't get a lot of sediment in their glasses, but if they do, don't worry— this is a learning situation, and your job as sommelier is not on the line. (See the wine and food appendix for instructions.) If there is sediment in the bottle, save the bottle and collect the sediment on a coffee filter to show everyone.

Information for the Post-Tasting Discussion

Exercise Step 1. Compare the older and younger wines on all aspects.

Table D.19 summarizes the changes that occur as red wines age.

Exercise Step 2. "Bottle bouquet is. . . ."

Here are some descriptions of bottle bouquet from my students: *subdued, sweet, subtle, complex, mellow, smooth, musty, potpourri, floral, oxidized, complex, intriguing, delicious, vanilla, blended, figgy, raisiny, richer, cedar closet, maple syrup, a campfire, redwood bark, buttered popcorn, well-integrated, flavors blend, more body, like brandy or very old sherry, like a dark red rose, nothing in particular stands out, like a Jeffrey pine forest on a warm day, resin/wood but not oak, French roast coffee grounds, cedar chest with wool mittens, like walking into a winery, wine softens/tastes sweeter, like a stout beer, and flavors get real mild.*

Students gave these responses when asked to describe the general nature of bottle bouquet: *It is harder to recognize distinct odors; there are a lot of odors there, but it's hard to isolate the individual odors; a wine with bottle bouquet has more toasty, smoky, and dusty odors and less fruit; wines with bottle bouquet have subtle and "sweeter" odors; the bottle bouquet odors are "strong, not sharp"; and the odor of wines with bottle bouquet reminds me of violets at the base of a redwood tree.*

Table D.19
A Summary of the Organoleptic Changes in Red Table Wines During Bottle Aging

Sensory Component	Changes with Bottle Aging
Color	Becomes browner as the pigments oxidize and lighter as the pigment molecules precipitate in the sediment.
Clarity	In the glass the wine should be clear because it has been carefully decanted; in the bottle there could be a dark sediment, perhaps stuck to the side.
Aroma	Characteristic odors of the grape typical of a young wine will diminish as they react with one another and with other wine components to form the bottle bouquet.
Bouquet	Should be in evidence as a very complex, multi-faceted, subtle, bewitching, intriguing, come-hither, hard-to-describe assortment of odors.
Sugar & Acid	The older wine may seem a bit sweeter and lower in perceived acidity.
Body	May seem lighter with age.
Flavor	Much more complex and much less strong and simple; complexity should echo the general and specific characteristics of the bottle bouquet.
Astringency	Smoother because the tannins have polymerized with each other and reacted with other wine components to form the sediment.
Overall Quality	Will increase with the added complexity up to a point and then diminish when the odors of oxidation begin to dominate — a situation that will occur, hopefully, in other bottles and long after your tasting. Refer to Figure 6.1: Aroma, Bouquet, and Off Odors During Aging of a Red Wine.

SENSORY EVALUATION EXERCISE 6.8.
Your Turn — Creating Your Own Tasting of Red Table Wines

Procedural Suggestions

Refer to Exercise 4.6, Your Turn for White Table Wines, for some overall guidelines that can apply to this exercise as well. Additional varietals that could be tasted include Sangiovese and Charbono. Bottle aging certainly represents a most inviting topic to explore further with red table wines because vertical tastings can go back over many years if your budget allows and if you can locate older wines. Studying differences between vintages is another option with red wines. You can investigate both how the weather in that year affected the wine and how well the wine is aging. There are many sources of tasting notes available in the literature and from wineries about vintages of California wines and especially those from Bordeaux and Burgundy. Of course, there is also the possibility of making regional comparisons such as between French, Californian, Chilean, Italian, and Australian Cabernet Sauvignons or between California Pinot Noirs and red Burgundies.

SENSORY EVALUATION EXERCISE 6.9
A Review Tasting of Red Table Wines

Wine-Buying Guidelines and Procedural Suggestions are the same as for the Review Tasting of White Table Wines, Exercise 4.7. If you have been working on these exercises in order, your tasters should be more experienced and will probably do better on this exercise, so you may need to have some extra prizes! For this reason, and also because you will have tasted more red wines during the exercises in Chapter 6, you may also want to include six rather than four wines in this exercise.

A Sample Worksheet for a Key to the Red Varietal Wines:

Step #1: sensory factor: bottle bouquet

   If present, it's probably the older Cabernet Sauvignon. Confirm with a complete odor analysis.

   If absent, go to step #2.

Step #2: sensory factor: color intensity

   If light, go to step #3.

   If medium to dark red, go to step #4.

Step #3: sensory factor: color hue

   If red or brick red, the variety may be Pinot Noir. Confirm with a complete odor analysis.

   If purple, the variety may be a Nouveaux Gamay or Gamay Beaujolais. Confirm with cranberry-like aroma.

Step #4: sensory factor: aroma

   If herbaceous, go to step #5.

   If berry-like, go to step #6.

Step #5: sensory factor: structural features of Cabernet Sauvignon and its relatives

   If more tannic, heavier body, the variety is Cabernet Sauvignon. Confirm with a complete sensory evaluation.

   If softer, lighter in body, the variety may be Merlot. Confirm with a complete sensory evaluation.

Step #6: sensory factor: variations in berry odors

   If raspberry, the variety may be Zinfandel. Confirm with a complete sensory evaluation.

   If blackberry/brambly/peppery, the variety may be Syrah. Confirm with a complete sensory evaluation.

SENSORY EVALUATION EXERCISE 8.1.
Méthode Champenoise and Charmat Process Sparkling Wines

Wine-Buying Guidelines

I have had good luck with Cook's Brut American Champagne (produced by Guild Winery in Lodi, CA) as an example of a typical Charmat Bulk Process wine. For the méthode champenoise example I like to use a wine with a pronounced champagne bouquet; Gloria Ferrer Non-Vintage Brut has worked well and is moderately priced, but there are many other exciting wines you could include here depending on your budget. Don't forget to buy extra wine if you plan to do a review tasting for sparkling wines.

A Thought About Food

I have not included any wine and food exercises for sparkling wines because I have not used them in my classes. If you want to include some for your tasting group, you could try some of the items from the Korbel Champagne and Food Compatibility Index, which has been reproduced in the Wine and Food Appendix.

Procedural Suggestions

Taste the Charmat Process wine first (Wine A) even though it is probably going to be sweeter. Its simplicity will be exaggerated if tasted after the méthode champenoise wine.

Information for the Post-Tasting Discussion
Exercise Step 1. Tasting Notes.

You may find the Charmat Bulk Process wine to be a more familiar wine, having tasted wines like it at weddings and brunches. Tasting it next to a méthode champenoise wine, you will be aware of its relative simplicity and sweeter finish. My students have described the fruit character as reminiscent of *cream soda, honey, cotton candy, and gummi bears.* There is usually very little champagne bouquet.

When tasting the méthode champenoise wine you will notice its bouquet and its higher-than-expected tartness. Here are some of the more notable terms my students have used to describe the bouquet: *like the back of a closet; creamy, like butterscotch or caramel; sort of burnt; woody; like wet hay; like cheese; a wet, "forest" smell; like a musty creek.* You will probably also notice the very light body of this wine.

Exercise Step 2. Summary of the Expected Sensory Differences.

The sensory differences produced by méthode champenoise and tank-fermentation processes are summarized in Table D.20.

Table D.20
A Summary of the Differences Between Méthode Champenoise and Charmat Process Sparkling Wines

Sensory Aspect	Méthode Champenoise	Charmat Process
Visual	smaller bubbles	bigger bubbles
Olfactory	complex, older, dusty, yeasty, toasted, etc.	simple, fruity
Taste	tart, complex	sweet, often cloying
Touch	very light!	heavier
Aftertaste	lingers, complex	simple, sweet

The terms from Table 8.1 and those additional descriptors named in the tasting notes above can be referred to during your group's discussion of champagne bouquet. Like the bottle bouquet that is formed in table wines as they age, champagne bouquet is very complex and each individual odor is very subtle, so that each taster will probably have an even more unique and personal list of descriptive words than for the younger varietal table wines.

SENSORY EVALUATION EXERCISE 8.2.
Blanc de Blancs and Blanc de Noirs Sparkling Wines

Wine-Buying Guidelines

I like to use méthode champenoise wines and select the Blanc de Blancs and Blanc de Noirs from the same producer. Domaine Chandon's Blanc de Noirs is reasonably priced and readily available in California and well illustrates the heavier body and fruitier aroma of that style.

Procedural Suggestions

If you like, this tasting can be combined with Exercise 8.1 into one tasting with three wines, using the Méthode Champenoise Blanc de Blancs to compare with both the Charmat Process Blanc de Blancs and the Blanc de Noirs (Wine C).

Information for the Post-Tasting Discussion
Exercise Step 1. Tasting Notes.

The Blanc de Noirs wine stands out for its lovely peach, salmon, or bronze color. You will probably notice that it seems fruitier and has more body than the Blanc de Blancs wine.

Exercise Step 2. Summary of Expected Sensory Differences.

Table D.21 contains a summary of the sensory differences between Blanc de Noirs and Blanc de Blancs sparkling wines.

Sensory Aspect	Blanc de Noirs	Blanc de Blancs
Visual	bronze, salmon color	light straw yellow
Olfactory	fruit more noticeable	fruit less prominent
Taste	fruitier here too	less fruity here as well
Touch	seems slightly thicker	thinner
Aftertaste	more fruity	less fruity

Table D.21
Summary of the Differences Between Blanc de Noirs and Blanc de Blancs Sparkling Wines

The discussion of champagne bouquet in this exercise should reveal some additional descriptions. Tasters in your group will probably find that it is less noticeable in the Blanc de Noirs wine.

SENSORY EVALUATION EXERCISE 8.3.
Natural to Doux — Sparkling Wines of Different Levels of Sweetness

Wine-Buying Guidelines

For this exercise it is best to use two wines made by the same method, preferably by the same producer. Korbel and Hans Kornell make moderately priced méthode champenoise sparkling wines of several levels of sweetness. Christian Brothers does the same for Charmat Process wines. You will want to refer to Table B.2 for sparkling wine label terms for different levels of sweetness.

Procedural Suggestions

Taste the drier wine first. Make a careful organoleptic evaluation of each wine and follow with a spirited discussion.

Information for the Post-Tasting Discussion
Exercise Step 1. Tasting Notes.

You will probably find that the sweeter sparkling wines are less complex than Brut or drier wines. You will notice the body increases with increasing sugar content as it does with other wines.

Exercise Step 2. Summary of Expected Differences.

Table D.22 summarizes the general sensory differences between drier and sweeter sparkling wines.

Sensory Aspect	The Drier Wine	The Sweeter Wine
Visual	may be lighter	may be darker yellow
Olfactory	often less fruity	often more fruity
Taste	dry, tart	sweeter (surprise!)
Touch	thinner	thicker

Table D.22
Summary of the Sensory Differences Between Drier and Sweeter Sparkling Wines

The use of these two sparkling wines with a meal can be considered in terms of how to best use any two wines of different levels of sweetness and can be another opportunity for some enjoyable brainstorming in your tasting group. The lighter, drier wines are best used as aperitifs; the sweeter wines may be used with some rich sauces but most folks prefer them with or instead of a dessert course.

SENSORY EVALUATION EXERCISE 8.4.
Your Turn — Creating Your Own Tasting of Sparkling Wines

Procedural Suggestions

You may want to design a tasting to investigate such topics as: the differences between regions (California vs. France or Spain) or between wineries within a region; the differences between varietal and blended sparkling wines; the effect of bottle aging on méthode champenoise wines. Your tasting could also be a search for the best bargain among wines of a particular type— say, Charmat wines under $5.00 per bottle or French Champagnes over $40.00 per bottle. You may want to investigate the floral aromas of sparkling Muscats, perhaps the Asti Spumantes or their California counterparts. The possibilities are limited only by your curiosity. A number of European Champagne houses have established wineries in California; these include the French firms of Moët Chandon (whose California branch is Domaine Chandon), Piper Heidsieck (Piper Sonoma), Louis Roederer (Roederer Estate), G. H. Mumm & Cie (Domaine Mumm), Tattinger (Domaine Carneros), Deutz (Maison Deutz), Pommery & Greno (Scharffenberger), and Spain's Freixnet (Gloria Ferrer), and Codorniu (Codorniu Napa). In addition, Laurent-Perrier has entered into a joint venture with Iron Horse Vineyards. If you decide to make a comparison between Californian and European sparkling wines, I'd suggest writing or telephoning one of these California wineries to ask which wines would be the most appropriate to compare in this tasting. Refer to Exercise 4.6 for some additional suggestions.

SENSORY EVALUATION EXERCISE 8.5.
A Review Tasting of Sparkling Wines

Use the wine-buying guidelines and procedures of Exercise 4.7, The Review Tasting of White Table Wines.

A Sample Worksheet for a Key to the Sparkling Wines

This sample key assumes that Exercises 8.1 and 8.2 were combined and that the wines for Exercise 8.3 were made by the méthode champenoise. If Exercises 8.1 and 8.2 were not combined or your tasting group used Charmat Process wines for Exercise 8.3, your group members will have other categories to include in their keys.

Step #1: sensory factor: color

> If salmon pink, Blanc de Noirs.
>
> If not salmon pink but yellow or light straw yellow, go to #2.

Step #2: sensory factor: Champagne bouquet

> If absent or low, the wine is a Charmat Bulk Process product.
>
> If present, go to step #3.

Step #3: sensory factor: sweetness

> If dry, the wine is Brut or drier.
>
> If sweet, the wine is Sec, Demi-Sec, or Doux.

SENSORY EVALUATION EXERCISE 10.1.
The Sauternes Style — A Tasting of Early-Harvest and Late-Harvest *Botrytis*-Affected Sauvignon Blanc or Sémillon Wines

Wine- and Food-Buying Guidelines

To minimize sensory variables other than the effect of *Botrytis* you will need to buy a late-harvest and an early-harvest Sauvignon Blanc or Sémillon made by the same winery. Since we have found that it is hard to always find pairs of wines like this in our local wine shops, we buy them directly from the wineries. We have done a lot of satisfactory business with Château St. Jean because they have been able to provide both styles of wine we need as well as background information for each wine. Their labels also contain useful analytical data as shown in Figure D.1 in the next Exercise 10.2.

For this exercise and the next you will need one or two pieces of milk chocolate (we use Hershey's kisses), two or three plain, unsalted almonds, and a plain, not very sweet butter cookie for each taster.

Procedural Suggestions

1. Taste the early-harvest wine first (Wine A).
2. The servings of late-harvest *Botrytis*-affected wines need to be somewhat smaller than average — about 25 ml is usually enough. Otherwise you will have to choose between throwing out lots of nice, expensive wine and wondering what sort of communicable disease

you might acquire if you sip up all the leftovers as you clean up after the tasting.

3. If your tasting group has time, you may want to combine this exercise with Exercise 10.2. Doing this would provide an opportunity to compare the Sauternes and *Auslese/Beerenauslese* styles directly. A warning: tasting that much sweet wine can tax your tasters' palates.

Information for the Post-Tasting Discussion

Exercise Step 1. The Key Sensory Features of *Botrytis*-Affected Wines.

The late-harvest wine will be darker in color, much more complex in odor and flavor, and much sweeter and thicker than the early-harvest wine. You will probably find the members of your tasting group enthralled with the beautiful golden colors of the *Botrytis*-affected wines, but the sensory aspect of these wines that will probably receive the most comment is their new and unusual odors. Table D.23 summarizes some descriptions of those odors by my students.

Odor Aspect	Comments and Associations
Overall	*rich, concentrated, intense, strong, thick smells*
Spice	*something curried or spicy, woody (like oak aging), orange spice tea*
Floral	*honeysuckle*
Fruit	*ripe apricots, Fig Newtons, orange blossoms, peaches, a very ripe or dried pear, orange marmalade*
Caramelized	*molasses, butterscotch, caramel, honey, nuts, brown sugar, golden raisins, Spaten beer, tobacco*
Earthy	*musty, moldy, wet hay, mushroom, dusty, earthy (not mentioned as often)*
Pungently Aromatic	*new shoes, rubbing alcohol, anise, dill, licorice, kerosene/varnish/alcohol, brandy-soaked raisins, Amaretto*

*Table D.23
A Collection of
Botrytis "Bouquet"
Terms*

Here are some additional notes about the other sensory aspects: sugar to acid balance is *"tangy after the sugar wears off,"* the flavor is *"intense like a raisin, honey, nectar, fruity, like the Gewürztraminer grape juice we tasted in lab, honey graham crackers, ultra-ripe peaches and apricots and many other echoes of the odor descriptions,"* and the body was found to be *"full, thick, syrupy, and heavy."*

Exercise Step 2. Summary of Your Sensory Impressions of the Sauternes Style.

Rich golden color, perhaps with bronze hues if the wine is very old; intense, complex, concentrated odors including a pungent note of alcohol; sweet, tart, heavy body; flavors rich, complex, and echo the odors; smooth.

Exercise Step 3. Sample the Foods.

The experience of my students with the three foods is typified by this response: *The plain almond balanced out the sweetness of the wines because the bitterness and astringency of the almond counteracted the sugar in the wine.* The butter cookie is often the most popular because it seems similar in sweetness to the wine and makes the wine seem more buttery. The Hershey's milk-chocolate kiss once again ignites the dispute between the "chocolate-at-any-cost" advocates and those with a more temperate relationship with the most prominent member of the brown food group. Many feel — and I agree — that the milk chocolate is too rich in fat and sugar to combine well with the sweet wine.

What about the idea that the food should be less sweet than the wine? Many people prefer to have the dessert less sweet than the wine so that the food can, in effect, cleanse the palate between sips of wine.

SENSORY EVALUATION EXERCISE 10.2.

The *Auslese/Beerenauslese* Style — A Tasting of Early-Harvest and Late-Harvest *Botrytis*-Affected White Riesling Wines

Wine- and Food-Buying Guidelines

Buy a late-harvest and an early- or normal-harvest White Riesling made by the same winery. (See the last Exercise, 10.1, for details.) Figure D.1 shows labels from an early-harvest (1990 Sonoma County) and a late-harvest (1989 Alexander Valley) Johannisberg Riesling made by Château St. Jean. Note the analytical data on both the front and back labels.

You will need one or two pieces of milk chocolate (we use Hershey's kisses), two or three plain, unsalted almonds, and a plain, not very sweet butter cookie for each taster.

Procedural Suggestion

Taste the early-harvest White Riesling first (Wine A) and check Exercise 10.1 for other details.

Information for the Post-Tasting Discussion

Exercise Steps 1 and 2. The Wines.

You will notice that the lower alcohol of the *Auslese/Beerenauslese*-style wine does not give the wine the same pungent odor that you found in the Sauternes-style late-harvest wine. The

Figure D.1

Labels from an Early-Harvest (1990 Sonoma County) and a Late-Harvest (1989 Alexander Valley) Johannisberg Riesling made by Château St. Jean.

higher sugar content will make the wine seem very sweet and fuller bodied than the Sauternes style. Many of the same odor and flavor descriptions in Table D.23 will fit these wines, with more comments, perhaps, reflecting odors like apricot and peach.

Exercise Steps 3 and 4. The Foods.

Because this late-harvest wine is so much sweeter, the palate-clogging problems that sweet foods bring about are accentuated with this wine. See notes for Exercise 10.1.

SENSORY EVALUATION EXERCISE 10.3.
An Introduction to Port and Sherry

Wine- and Food-Buying Guidelines

This topic can be covered at two economic levels: you can buy examples of port and sherry from one of the large, widely-distributed producers such as Gallo or Christian Brothers, or you can hunt for ports from specialty producers like Ficklin or Quady or from wineries like Shenandoah Vineyards that make a small amount of fine port as a specialty item. The second route will be more expensive but will yield wines of greater distinction and interest. Weibel has been making a nice *Amontillado*-style *flor* sherry if you want to take a drier route with this wine type.

In addition to the foods for the two previous exercises, you will need a piece of Stilton cheese and one or two unsalted walnuts which are still wearing their skins.

Procedural Suggestions

1. Taste the wine with the lower sugar content first. This may be the port if you have chosen a cream sherry or the sherry if you are tasting an *amontillado* — or *fino* — style.
2. Serve smaller portions of these rich, alcoholic wines and serve food.

Information for the Post-Tasting Discussion

Exercise Step 1A. The Most Striking Sensory Differences Between
Dessert Wines and Table Wines.

You will find that the dessert wines are, of course, higher in alcohol. This higher alcohol will add a very prominent pungent note to the odors. The wines will also taste hot. Their flavors and odors will be much stronger, more concentrated, and the wines will be very full-bodied.

Exercise Step 1B. The Defining Properties of Port and Sherry.

Port is defined by its dark red color, high sugar and alcohol contents, and intensely fruity and spicy odors. Tawny port should have the distinct odor and flavor of oak. Sherries of all sorts are defined by their nutty, acetaldehyde odor and can vary dramatically in color (from lightest yellows to brown) and sweetness (dry to very sweet). My students offer this profile of cream sherry: *odors of Kahlua, caramel, butterscotch, with burnt characteristics; tastes like a box of raisins or a handful of brown sugar; really sweet; thick and smooth.*

Exercise Steps 2A and 2B. The Foods.

You will probably find some people prefer the almond, walnut, and Stilton cheese because these foods tend to cleanse the palate more than the butter cookie and chocolate kiss. You may also find your tasters mentioning that the higher alcohol contents of these wines make the cookie and chocolate more compatible than they were with the *Botrytis*-affected sweet wines.

SENSORY EVALUATION EXERCISE 10.4.
An Introduction to Orange and Black Muscats

Wine- and Food-Buying Guidelines

I use Shenandoah Vineyards' Black Muscat and Quady's Orange Muscat "Essencia."

You will need a small piece of shortbread, half of a white chocolate-dipped biscotto (La Tempesta), two or three almonds, a piece of creamy blue cheese, and a piece of dark chocolate for each taster. If La Tempesta Biscotti are not available in your area, you can obtain them from La Tempesta Bakery Confections (see "Other Useful Addresses" at the end of this appendix). The white chocolate version recommended is called Amore. Danish Blue and Maytag Blue are recommended.

Procedural Suggestions

1. Taste the Orange Muscat first (Wine A).
2. Smaller samples served with food are advised as for Exercise 10.3.

Information for the Post-Tasting Discussion

Exercise Step 1A. Muscat Dessert Wines and Muscat Table Wines.

Your tasters' comments about the most important points of contrast between muscat table wines and muscat dessert wines will echo their notes for Exercise 10.3, Step 1A: the dessert wines will be darker in color, more concentrated in fruit odor and flavor, sweeter, and more full-bodied. The alcohol content will be higher and more noticeable to smell and taste in the dessert wine.

Exercise Steps 1B and 1C. Muscats vs. Other Dessert Wines.

You will notice that the Muscat dessert wines are a little lower in alcohol content and more fruity than the sherries and ports. You'll most likely find them more alcoholic and less complex in odor and flavor than the *Botrytis*-affected late-harvest wines. Here is a sketch of Orange Muscat from a recent class: *dark gold color; apricot, peach, orange blossom; alcohol in bouquet (tequila); alcohol not as strong-tasting as it smelled, sweet.*

Exercise Step 2. The Foods and Your Preferences.

I leave this item to your individual gastronomic introspections.

SENSORY EVALUATION EXERCISE 10.5.
Your Turn — Creating Your Own Tasting of Dessert Wines

If you are curious about how dessert wines age, for example, your tasting could focus on wines of different vintages made from the same grape variety by the same producer. If you have been wondering how French or German *Botrytis*-affected late-harvest wines compare with those made in the U.S., you could taste a Sauternes or Barsac alongside a California late-harvest Sauvignon Blanc or Sémillon of about the same vintage, or you could taste a *Beerenauslese* from a Rhine or Mosel vineyard next to a select late-harvest California White Riesling of about the same age. For a port or sherry tasting, you could compare Portuguese and California ports, or some older and younger vintage ports, or Spanish and California sherries, or you could just take a look at the various types of Spanish or California sherries. Refer to Exercise 4.6 for general guidelines.

SENSORY EVALUATION EXERCISE 10.6.
A Review Tasting of Dessert Wines.
Use the procedures for Exercise 4.6.

A Sample Worksheet for a Key to the Dessert Wines
Step #1: sensory factor: color

        If red, go to step #5.

        If not red, go to step #2.

Step #2: sensory factor: color is not red, but is

        Tan or brown, the wine is *Amontillado* or cream sherry. Confirm with a complete sensory evaluation.

        Yellow, gold, or orange, go to step #3.

Step #3: sensory factor: yellow, gold, or orange color

        If yellow and pungent (acetaldehyde), the wine is *Fino* sherry. Confirm with a complete sensory evaluation.

        If orange and very fruity, the wine is Orange Muscat. Confirm with a complete sensory evaluation.

        If gold and lower in alcohol, go to step #4.

Step #4: sensory factor: sugar and alcohol levels

        If sugar is high and alcohol is low, the wine is a *Botrytis*-affected White Riesling. Confirm with a complete sensory evaluation.

        If the sugar is lower and the alcohol is higher, the wine is a Sauternes-style *Botrytis*-affected wine. Confirm with a complete sensory evaluation.

Step #5: sensory factor: aroma among red dessert wines

        If intense fruit and flowers, the variety is Black Muscat. Confirm with a complete sensory evaluation.

        If spicy and the fruit is less intense, the wine type is port. Confirm with a complete sensory evaluation.

As mentioned in the other review exercises, you could make your key in many other ways. For example you could start sorting the wine by alcohol content into fortified wines and table wines.

SENSORY EVALUATION EXERCISE 12.1.
Mystery Wine Identification

Wine-Buying Guidelines
You bought extra bottles of six to eight of the wines you were planning to use in the earlier tastings and you have them on hand now for the grand finale.

A Sample Worksheet for a Key to the Mystery Wines
Step #1: sensory factor: alcohol content

        If very high, it is fortified wine; go to step #2.

        If low to moderate, it is a natural wine; go to step #3.

Step #2: Differentiate among the fortified wines on the basis of sugar content (only sherries are dry), presence of oxidized character (cream sherry), and Muscat varietal character (if the wine has none, it's port). Consult your key for the dessert wine review tasting exercise for the details of the wines you tasted.

Step #3: sensory factor: CO_2 content

        If very high, it is a sparkling wine. Consult your key for the sparkling wine review tasting to distinguish between the types of sparkling wines.

        If low, it is a still wine; go to step #4.

Step #4: sensory factor: color

If white, go to step #5.

If red, go to step #6.

If pink, you didn't taste it in an exercise from this book. Drink the wine and hide the bottle to eliminate it from this exercise.

Step #5: sensory factors: sweetness and *Botrytis* character

If the wine is very sweet and has *Botrytis* character, differentiate between the Sauternes-style and the *Auslese/Beerenauslese*-style using your key to the dessert wines and/or notes for Exercises 10.1 and 10.2.

If the wine is drier, with sweetness in the range expected for table wines, use your key for the white varietal wine review tasting to identify the wine.

Step #6: sensory factor: red color

Congratulations, you made it to the end of the maze. Consult the key you constructed for the red wine review tasting to differentiate the red varietals.

Procedural Suggestions

Same as for Exercise 4.7, just make sure there is enough time for the tasters to complete the exercise without feeling rushed. Be sure to take time after revealing the identity of each wine to discuss how the tasters who were able to correctly identify it made their deductions. Depending on your group's preferences, you could first do the "Zinorama," Exercise 12.2, as a review of all the wine types in the course, and then use this exercise to focus on a more refined identification of wines of one or two types, say, only table wines or table and sparkling wines. You will need to make up a key to the answers for questions 27-40 in Exercise 12.1, page 287.

Some General Ideas for the Post-Tasting Discussion

1. The discussion following this tasting can be a lot of fun. After you have revealed the identity of each wine and the answers to questions 27-40 about the wines in Exercise 12.1, be sure to ask the tasters who were able to correctly name the wines to share their "secrets of success,"

2. Some tasters will ask "Why is this still so hard?" This creates an excellent opportunity for your group to discuss the merits of continued practice together, and perhaps to begin planning the next round of tastings, including a review of selected tasting exercises, and to appoint someone else to be in charge of organizing the tastings.

SENSORY EVALUATION EXERCISE 12.2.
The "Zinorama" — Tasting Zinfandels from White to Port

A Note about What's Not Here

There is no key to the chart "Your Summary of Winemaking Procedures," because the value of the chart lies in each taster reviewing the chapters and to make it for himself or herself.

Wine-Buying Guidelines

The objectives of this tasting are to show the versatility of Zinfandel, to present in a single tasting the entire range of wine types encountered in the course, and to review how each type of wine is made. The shopper's task, therefore, is to buy a Zinfandel sparkling wine, a Zinfandel white table wine, a lighter-style red Zinfandel table wine (perhaps made by carbonic maceration), a heavier and more intense-style red Zinfandel table wine, and a Zinfandel port — a challenge the creative and resourceful wine merchant would welcome. Sutter Home has been making a Charmat Process Sparkling Zinfandel, and both Quady and Shenandoah Vineyards have made ports from Zinfandel. Finding the other Zinfandels should be less problematic.

Procedural Suggestions

Taste the Zinfandels from sparkling to white, lighter red, heavier red, then port. Food, water, and spitoons are especially advised with this tasting. Be sure to take time after revealing the identity of each wine to discuss how the tasters who were able to correctly identify it made their deductions.

Information for the Post-Tasting Discussion

Table D.24 offers a suggested key to relate sensory characteristics to winemaking procedures for the wines in the Zinorama .

Wine Types	Key Sensory Characteristics	Winemaking Deductions
Charmat Process Sparkling Wine	Bubbles, simple fruity aroma, no yeast character from Champagne bouquet, sweet, young	Bubbles with little champagne bouquet and an overall simple, fruity wine suggest the Charmat Process
White (or probably pink) Zinfandel Table Wine	Pink, fruity, simple, slightly sweet to sweet, young, smooth	Typical white table wine characteristics suggest cool alcoholic fermentation, no malolactic fermentation or oak aging, short bulk aging
Lighter-style Red Table Wine	Light to medium red, fruity aroma but more intense than for white Zinfandel, dry, tart, just slightly rough; may have oak characteristics	Fermentation at higher temperatures and with the skins to perhaps 5-10 degrees Brix; if the wine has oak bouquet and flavors, bulk aging was in oak, probable malolactic fermentation
Lighter-style Red Table Wine, Carbonic Maceration	Purple, extremely fruity — almost tropical or artificial fruit odors and flavors, no oak, smooth	The very strong fruit odors and purple color set these wines apart from other lighter-style Zinfandels.
Heavier-style Red Table Wine	Dark color, very intense, rich aroma of berries, oak, dry, rough	The darker color and higher astringency suggest longer fermentation with the skins and longer oak aging in small cooperage, probable malolactic fermentation.
Botrytis-affected late-harvest Zinfandels	Very sweet, light color, smooth, low alcohol	These are rare, but they can be found. They are made much like conventional sweet white table wines after pressing without crushing.
Zinfandel Port	High alcohol, dark color, intense fruit	Add wine spirits during fermentation.

Table D.24
Key to the Zinorama Wines: Sensory Characteristics and Winemaking Deductions

Table D.25 contains some guidelines for completing the checklist of winemaking procedures found on page 296 of the Zinorama.

Winemaking Procedures	Wine(s) Using this Procedure
1. harvest at 14-15 degrees Brix	none — this is not ripe enough for winemaking
2. harvest at 17-19 degrees Brix	sparkling wines
3. harvest at 21-23 degrees Brix	white table wines
4. harvest at 22-24 degrees Brix	red table wines and ports
5. prefer grapes from Region I	sparkling wines
6. prefer grapes from Regions I and II	white table wines
7. prefer grapes from Regions II and III	red table wines except Pinot Noir (Region I)
8. prefer grapes from Region V	most dessert wines — vintage-style ports cooler
9. prefer shrivelled, moldy grapes	*Botrytis*-affected wines only; otherwise highly undesirable
10. crush grapes as soon as possible after harvest	for all wines it is best to begin the winemaking as soon after harvest as possible by crushing (most common) or pressing

Table D.25
Sensory Evaluation Exercise 12.2: Guidelines for the Checklist of Winemaking Procedures

continued next page

Table D.25
Sensory Evaluation
Exercise 12.2: Guidelines
for the Checklist of
Winemaking Procedures
(continued from
previous page)

Winemaking Procedures	Wine(s) Using this Procedure
11. whole grapes macerate in field gondolas for 1-2 days	no wines — the fruit in the bottom of the gondola will be crushed and wild yeast and bacteria will start to ferment the juice
12. press without crushing	some méthode champenoise sparkling and *Botrytis*-affected wines; carbonic maceration wines after the intracellular fermentation
13. press immediately after crushing	white table wines that will not undergo skin contact
14. crush, chill must, allow skin contact before pressing	only for premium white table wines; unlikely for white Zinfandels
15. ferment immediately after crushing	all red wines made by conventional alcoholic fermentations
16. ferment clarified juice	white and pink table wines
17. add yeast, ferment at 55 degrees F	white and pink table wines and the second fermentation of méthode champenoise sparkling wines especially
18. add yeast, ferment at 60-90 degrees F	red table wines; for carbonic maceration too if yeast is added only to the small amount of juice in the bottom of the tank
19. add wine spirits during fermentation	fortified wines — port in the Zinorama
20. draw juice and press at 1-5 degrees Brix	very long-lived, tannic red table wines
21. draw juice and press at 12-14 degrees Brix	lighter, less tannic red table wines and fortified wines if this step is followed by fortification
22. draw juice and press after 12-24 hours of fermentation	rosé table wines
23. ferment to dryness	all dry wines, red or white
24. stop fermentation with some residual sugar remaining	all sweet wines, both when fermentation is stopped by fortification and when it is arrested by chilling and yeast removal
25. make sure the malolactic fermentation is complete	virtually all red table wines, especially those made from grapes grown in cooler regions
26. must be cold stable	all wines
27. must be heat stable	all wines
28. must be microbiologically stable	all wines
29. age in stainless steel tanks	wines that have no oak flavor — whites, rosés, and carbonic maceration red wines — most all wines probably have been aged in stainless steel tanks
30. age in small oak hogsheads	wines with oak character — red table and Chardonnay
31. age in old, neutral oak cooperage	California's vintage-style ports
32. sterile bottling is absolutely necessary	table wines with residual sugar, including most White Zinfandels, Blush, and Zinfandel Rosés
33. sterile bottling is not necessary	fortified wines and wines fermented dry except to protect from spoilage in the bottle by *Brettanomyces*
34. process takes 6-8 weeks	the fastest white table wines, rosés, carbonic maceration, and Charmat Process sparkling wines
35. process takes about 3 months	most white table wines and rosés
36. process takes about 18 months	Chardonnays and oak-aged lighter red table wines
37. process takes more than 18 months	heavier-style red table wines intended for longer bottle aging and reserve Chardonnays
38. wines age in the bottle at the winery	more common for red than white table wines, but can occur for premium white table wines; vintage-style ports
39. anything else?	disgorging and *dosage*, etc., for sparkling wines

WINERY ADDRESSES

Alexander Valley Vineyards
8644 Highway 128
Healdsburg, CA 95448
(707) 433-7209 in CA,
(800) 248-8900 out of CA

Bargettos Winery
3535 North Main Street
Soquel, CA 95073
(408) 475-2258

Beaulieu Vineyards
1960 St. Helena Highway
Rutherford, CA 94573

Beringer Vineyards
200 Main Street
St. Helena, CA 94574
(707) 963-7115

Bouchaine Vineyards, Inc.
1075 Buchli Station Road
Napa, CA 94559
(707) 252-9065

Buena Vista Winery
18000 Old Winery Road
Sonoma, CA 95476
(707) 252-7117

Callaway Vineyard and Winery
32720 Rancho California Road
Temecula, CA 92390
(714) 676-4001

Caymus
8700 Conn Creek Road
Rutherford, CA 94573
(707) 963-4204

Chalone Vineyards
P.O. Box 855
Soledad, CA 93960

Chappellet Winery
1581 Sage Canyon Road
St. Helena, CA 94574
(707) 252-7362

Chateau St. Jean
8555 Sonoma Highway
Kenwood, CA 95452
(707) 833-4134

Clos du Bois
19410 Geyserville Avenue
M/A: P.O. Box 940
Geyserville, CA 95441
(707) 857-1651

Cordorniu Napa
1345 Henry Road
Napa, CA 94558
(707) 224-1688

De Loach Vineyards
1791 Olivet Road
Santa Rosa, CA 95401
(707) 526-9111

Domaine Carneros
1240 Dunig Road
Napa, CA 94558
P.O. Box 5420
Napa, CA 94581
(707) 257-0101

Domaine Chandon Inc.
#1 California Drive
P.O. Box 2470
Yountville, CA 94599
(707) 944-8844

Domaine Mumm
8445 Silverado Trail
Rutherford, CA, 94573
(707) 963-1133

Dry Creek Vineyard
3770 Lambert Bridge Road
Healdsburg, CA 95448
(707) 433-1000

Fenestra Winery
2954 Kilkare Road
Sunol, CA 94586
(415) 862-2292

Fetzer Vineyards
1150 Bel Arbres
P.O. Box 227
Redwood Valley, CA 95470
(707) 784-7634

Ficklin Vineyards
30246 Avenue, 7 ½
Madera, CA 93637
(209) 674-4598

Firestone Vineyards
5017 Zaca Station Road
Los Olivos, CA 93441
(805) 688-3940

Fisher Vineyards
6200 St. Helena Road
Santa Rosa, CA 95404
(707) 539-7511

Freemark Abbey
3022 St. Helena Highway
St. Helena, CA 94574
(707) 963-9694

Gallo Winery
P.O. Box 1130
Modesto, CA 95353
(209) 579-3111

Glen Ellen Winery
1883 London Ranch Road
Glen Ellen, CA 95442
(707) 935-3000

Gloria Ferrer Champagne Caves
23555 Highway 121
Sonoma, CA 95476
(707) 996-7256

Grand Cru Vineyards
1 Vintage Lane
Glen Ellen, CA 95442
(707) 996-8100

Guenoc
21000 Butts Canyon Road
Middleton, CA 95461
(707) 987-2385

Hacienda Wine Cellars
P.O. Box 416, 1000 Vineyard Lane
Sonoma, CA 95476
(707) 938-3220

Iron Horse Vineyards
9786 Ross Station Road
Sebastopol, CA 95472
(707) 887-1507

Jordan Vineyard and Winery
1474 Alexander Valley Road
Healdsburg, CA 95449
(707) 433-6955

Kendall-Jackson Vineyards
421 Aviation Blvd.
Santa Rosa, CA 95403
(707) 544-4000

Kenwood Vineyards
9592 Sonoma Highway
P.O. Box 447, Sonoma Highway
Kenwood, CA 95452
(707) 833-5891

Korbel Champagne Cellars
13250 River Road
Guerneville, CA 95446
(707) 887-2294

Landmark Vineyards
101 Adobe Canyon Road
Kenwood, CA 95452
(707) 833-0053 or 833-1144

Maison Deutz Winery
453 Deutz Drive
Arroyo Grande, CA 93420
(805) 481-1763

Martini, Louis
254 S. St. Helena Highway
P.O. Box 112
St. Helena, CA 94574
(707) 963-2736

Mayacaymas Vineyards
1155 Lokoya Road
Napa, CA 94558
(707) 224-4030

McDowell Cellars
P.O. Box 449, 3811 Highway 175
Hopland, CA 95449
(707) 744-1053

Monticello Cellars
4242 Big Ranch Road
Napa, CA 94558
(707) 253-2802

Mont St. John Cellars
5400 Old Sonoma Road
Napa, CA 94558
(707) 255-8864

Navarro Vineyards
P.O. Box 47, 5601 Highway, 128,
Philo, CA 95466
(707) 895-3686

Parducci Winery
501 Parducci Road
Ukiah, CA 95482
(707) 462-3828

J. Pedroncelli Winery
1120 Canyon Road
Geyserville, CA 95441
(707) 857-3531

Phelps Vineyards, Joseph
P.O. Box 1031, 200 Taplin Road
St. Helena, CA 94574
(707) 963-2745

Piper Sonoma Cellars
11477 Old Redwood Highway
Healdsberg, CA 95448
M/A: P.O. Box 650
Healdsberg, CA 95492
(707) 433-8843

Preston Vineyards
9282 West Dry Creek Road
Healdsburg, CA 95448
(707) 433-3372

Quady Winery
13181 Road 24
P.O. Box 728
Madera, CA 93639
(209) 673-8063

R & J Cook
38045 Netherlands Road
M/A: P.O. Box 227
Clarksburg, CA 95612
(916) 775-1234

Raymond
849 Zinfandel Lane
St. Helena, CA 94574
(707) 963-3141

Robert Mondavi Winery
7801 St. Helena Highway
Oakville, CA 94562
P.O. Box 106
Oakville, Napa Valley, CA 94562
(707) 226-1395

Robert Pecota Winery
3299 Bennett Lane, Box 303
Calistoga, CA 94515
(707) 942-6625

Roederer U.S., Inc.
2000 Powell St., Suite 1205
Emeryville, CA 94608
(510) 652-4900 or (707) 895-2288

Sanford Winery
7250 Santa Rosa Road
Buellton, CA 93427
(805) 688-3300

Santa Barbara Winery
202 Anacapa Street
Santa Barbara, CA 93101
(805) 963-3633

V. Sattui Winery
1111 White Lane
St. Helena, CA 94574
(707) 963-7774

Scharffenberger Cellars
8501 Highway 128
P.O. Box 365
Philo, CA 95466
(707) 895-2065

Shenandoah Vineyards
12300 Steiner Road
Plymouth, CA 95669
(209) 245-4455

Simi Winery Inc.
16725 Healdsburg Avenue
Box 698
Healdsburg, CA 95448
(707) 433-6981

Sterling Vineyards
1111 Dunaweal Lane
Calistoga, CA 94515
(707) 942-5151

Storybook Mountain Vineyards
3835 Highway 128
Calistoga, CA 94515
(707) 942-5310

Stratford Winery
472 Railroad Avenue
St. Helena, CA 94574
(707) 963-3200

Sutter Home Winery Inc.
227 St. Helena Highway, South
P.O. Box 248
St. Helena, CA 94574
(707) 963-3104

Topolos at Russian River
5700 Gravenstein Highway
North Forestville, CA 95436
(707) 887-2956

Vichon Winery
1595 Oakville Grade
Oakville, CA 94562
(707) 944-2811

Weibel Vineyards
1250 Stanford Avenue
Mission San Jose, CA 94538
(415) 656-2340

Wild Horse Winery
2484 Templeton Road
P.O. Box 910
Templeton, CA 93465
(805) 434-2541

William Hill Winery
1761 Atlas Peak
1775 Lincoln Avenue
P.O. Box, 3989
Napa, CA 94558
(707) 224-6565

Zaca Mesa Winery
6905 Canyon Road
Los Olives, CA 93441
(805) 688-9339

OTHER USEFUL ADDRESSES

All World Scientific
5515 186th Place S.W.
Lynnwood, WA 98037
(206) 672-4228 or (800) 28WORLD
Fax (206) 776-1530

American Wine Society
3006 Latta Road
Rochester, NY 14612
(716) 225-7613

American Wine Alliance for Research and Education (AWARE)
244 California Street
San Francisco, CA 94111
(415) 291-9113

Brotherhood of the Knights of the Vine
Box 13285
Sacramento, CA 95813

Cellulo Corporation
949 East Townshend Avenue
Fresno, CA 93721
(209) 485-2692

Fisher Scientific
711 Forbes Avenue
Pittsburgh, PA 15219-9919
(800) 672-3550

International Wine Academy
38 Portola Drive
San Francisco, CA 94116
(415) 641-4767

La Tempesta Bakery Confections
439 Little Field Avenue
South San Francisco, CA 94080
(415) 873-8944

Practical Winery and Vineyard Magazine
15 Grande Paseo
San Rafael, CA 94903
(415) 479-5819

Private Preserve ™
360 Swift Avenue #34
South San Francisco CA 94080
800 231-9463

Society of Medical Friends of Wine
P.O. Box 218
Sausalito, CA 94966-0218

The Society of Wine Educators
8600 Foundry St., Box 2044
Savage, MD 20763
(301) 776-8569 FAX : (301) 776-8578   Email: vintage@erols.com

The Wine Appreciation Guild
360 Swift Ave.
San Francisco, CA 94080
(800) 231-WINE
Fax (415) 866-3513

The Wine Lab
477 Walnut Street
Napa, CA 94559
(707) 224-7903

The Wine Spectator
Opera Plaza
601 Van Ness Avenue, Suite 2014
San Francisco, CA 94102

The Wine Trader
P.O. Box 1598
Carson City, NV 89702
(702) 884-2648

University Extension
University of California
Davis, CA 95616
(916) 752-0380

Vinifera Wine Growers Association
Box P
The Plains, Virginia 22171

Washington State University Creamery
Troy Hall 101
Pullman, WA 99164-4410
(509) 335-4014

Wine Glasses
112 Pine Street
San Anselmo, CA 94969
(415) 454-0660

Wines & Vines Magazine
1800 Lincoln Avenue
San Rafael, CA 94901-1298
(415) 453-9700
Fax (415) 453-2517

Women for Wine Sense
Box 2098
Yountville, CA 94599

MAGAZINES AND NEWSLETTERS

The Beverage Communicator
5 Barker Avenue, Suite 104
White Plains, NY 10601
(914) 761-7700

California Grapevine
14315 Barrymore Street
San Diego, CA 92129

DECANTER Magazine
583 Fulham Rd.
London SW65UA
England

Friends of Wine
2302 Perkins Place
Silver Springs, MD 20910
(301) 588-0980

The Moderation Reader
4714 Northeast 50th Street
Seattle, WA 98105
(206) 525-0449

Practical Winery and Vineyard Magazine
15 Grande Paseo
San Rafael, CA 94903
(415) 479-5819

Quarterly Review of Wine
24 Garfield Avenue
Winchester, MA 01890
(617) 729-7132

Restaurant Wine
Ron Wiegand, MW
Box 222
Napa, CA 94559-0222
(707) 224-4777

The Wine Advocate
Mr. Robert Parker
Box 311
Monkton, MD 21111

The Vine
Clive Coates, MW
Lamerton House
76 Woodstock Rd.
London W41EQ
England

Vineyard and Winery Management
Box 231
Watklins Glen, NY 14891
(607) 535-7133

Wine East
620 N. Pine Street
Lancaster, PA 17603
(717) 393-0943

The Wine News
353 Alcazar Avenue, Suite 33134
Coral Gables, FL 33134
(305) 444-7250

The Wine Spectator
Opera Plaza
601 Van Ness Avenue, Suite 2014
San Francisco, CA 94102

Wine & Spirits Magazine
54 Continental Avenue
Forest Hills, NY 11375

Wine Tidings
5165 Sherbrooke Street, Suite 414
Montreal, Quebec H4A IT6
Canada

The Wine Trader
P.O. Box 1598
Carson City, NV 89702
(702) 884-2648

Wines & Vines Magazine
1800 Lincoln Avenue
San Rafael, CA 94901-1298
(415) 453-9700
Fax (415) 453-2517

SUPPLIERS

All World Scientific
5515 186th Place S.W.
Lynnwood, WA 98037
(206) 672-4228 or (800) 28WORLD
Fax (206) 776-1530

Cellulo Corporation
949 East Townshend Avenue
Fresno, CA 93721
(209) 485-2692

Fisher Scientific
711 Forbes Avenue
Pittsburgh, PA 15219-9919
(800) 672-3550

Great Fermentations
87 Larkspur
San Rafael, CA 94901
(415) 459-2520

Home Winemaking Shop

22836 Ventura Boulevard

Woodland Hills, CA 91364

(818) 884-8586

La Tempesta Bakery Confections

439 Little Field Avenue

South San Francisco, CA 94080

(415) 873-8944

Private Preserve ™

155 Connecticut Street

San Francisco, CA 94107

Washington State University Creamery

Troy Hall 101

Pullman, WA 99164-4410

(509) 335-4014

Wine Art Inc.

6800 Airport Road

Richmond, B.C.

Canada

Wine Glasses

112 Pine Street

San Anselmo, CA 94969

(415) 454-0660

Wine Supply Inc.

2758 N. E. Broadway

Portland, OR 97232

(503) 287-2624

ENDNOTES

[1] Engen, Trygg, "Remembering Odors and Their Names," *American Scientist*, Vol. 75, 1985, pp. 497-503.

[2] Baldy, Marian W., TIPS FOR TEACHERS USING THE UNIVERSITY WINE COURSE, The Wine Appreciation Guild, San Francisco, 1992.

[3] Noble, A. C., et al., "Modification of a Standardized System of Wine Aroma Terminology," *American Journal of Enology and Viticulture*, Vol. 38, No. 2, 1987, pp. 143-146.

[4] Amerine, Maynard A., and Edward B. Roessler, WINES, THEIR SENSORY EVALUATION, W. H. Freeman and Co., NY, 1983, pp. 82-83.

[5] Noble, A. C., et al., "Modification of a Standardized System of Wine Aroma Terminology," *American Journal of Enology and Viticulture*, Vol. 38, No. 2, 1987, pp. 143-146.

[6] Anonymous, "Teaching Aids: Essence of Corky," *The Wine Educator*, Vol. 1, No. 1, May 1990, pp. 32-33.

[7] Ackerman, Diane, THE NATURAL HISTORY OF THE SENSES, Random House, New York, 1990, p. 376.

Glossary

OF WINETASTING AND WINEMAKING TERMINOLOGY

The pronunciation suggestions in this glossary are rough approximations intended to give English speakers guidance in pronouncing foreign terms; however, they do not reflect the nuances of the languages represented.[1] Most words defined elsewhere in this glossary appear in italics.

Acetaldehyde A distinctive and desirable component of *sherry,* but undesirable in other wines.

Acetic The vinegar-like *off odor* of acetic acid and *ethyl acetate.*

Acetobacter The microorganism that produces acetic acid (vinegar) in wines exposed to air.

Acidity Tartness, the taste of natural fruit acids (tartaric, citric, malic, or lactic) in wine.

Adaptation A change in sensitivity of the receptor organ to adjust to different levels of stimulation. In *winetasting* most commonly experienced as a temporary loss in the ability to perceive an *odor* or a *taste.*

Aeration The deliberate addition of oxygen in winemaking or decanting.

Aftertaste The odors and flavors that linger in the mouth after swallowing or spitting out the wine.

Aging Holding wines for a period of time in barrels, tanks, or bottles.

Alcohol Ethanol, or *ethyl alcohol,* formed during fermentation. A component of the odor, taste, and tactile sensations of wines.

Alsace (*al-*zass) French wine district bordering the Rhine just north of Switzerland and known for varietally-named white wines that age well, especially *Gewürztraminers* and *Rieslings.*

Alto Adige (*ahl-*toe *ah*-dee-jay) Northernmost Italian wine district—near the Austrian border—producing varietally-named table wines and *méthode champenoise* sparkling wines. Austria and Germany are important markets.

Amontillado (ah-mon-tee-*yah*-do) An aged dry *sherry.*

Anosmia Loss of the sense of smell.

Anbaugebeite (*ahn*-bough-ge-beet-eh) See *Qualitatswein Bestimmter Anbaugebeite.*

Anjou-Touraine (ahn-*jou* too-*rehn*) Two French wine districts in central Loire Valley southwest of Paris whose table wines encompass a range of qualities and styles. Best-known wines are dry *Sauvignon Blanc* and dry to sweet *Chenin Blancs* such as *Vouvray* and light reds from *Cabernet Franc* (Chinon and Bourgueil).

Anthocyanins The pigments that provide the red colors in grapes and wine.

Aperitif (ah-pair-ee-teef) A wine generally drunk before a meal.

Appearance The first category by which a wine is judged by sensory evaluation. Includes assessment of clarity and bubble display.

Appellation of Origin Term for the label designations that indicate the geographic origin(s) of the grapes.

Aroma *Odors* in the wine that originate in the grape. To be distinguished from *bouquet.*

Aroma Wheel A classification of the characteristic *odors* of a beverage such as wine, beer, or scotch liquor organized into a circle to show odor relationships and for reference. See the *wine aroma wheel* in Chapter 2

Asti Spumante (*ah*-stee spoo-*mahn*-teh) Sweet, white, low alcohol, intensely fruity *sparkling* (spumante) wines made from Muscat grapes in one of northwestern Italy's major wine centers (Asti).

Astringent Harsh, drying, tactile sensation in the mouth caused by high *tannin* levels. The opposite is *smooth.*

Auslese (*ouse*-lay-zah) A term used on German *QmP* wines to indicate wines made from very ripe bunches. Wines are sweeter and more full-bodied than *Spätlese* wines. Literally, "select."

Autolysis The self-digestion of *yeast* by enzymes contained in it.

B.A.T.F Bureau of Alcohol, Tobacco, and Firearms. The branch of the U.S. Internal Revenue Service which regulates the wine industry.

Bacterial Term for a number of *off odors* originating with bacterial activity, including butyric, lactic, mousy, etc.

Baked The caramel odor in sweet wines, such as *Madeiras,* that have been heated at high temperatures.

Balanced A wine in which *acidity,* sweetness, and *flavor* are in pleasing proportions.

Barbera (bar-*bear*-ah) A red grape grown in the Piedmont region of Italy.

Barrel-Fermented Wine fermented in small oak casks.

Beaujolais (bo-jo-lay) A light, fruity red wine from the Beaujolais district of France. "Beaujolais-style" refers to a wine with similar sensory qualities.

Beaujolais Nouveau (bo-jo-lay noo-vo) The "new" *Beaujolais* that is marketed within a few weeks of the harvest.

Beerenauslese (*bear*-en-*ouse*-lay-zuh) A term used on German *QmP* and some other *late-harvest* wines to indicate wines made from overripe berries or berries with *noble rot*. Wines are sweeter and more full-bodied than *Auslese* wines. Literally, "select berries."

Bentonite A clay used in *fining* to react with proteins.

Berry-like Term to describe the *aroma* and *flavor* of some red wines with flavor notes reminiscent of raspberries, strawberries, blackberries, etc.

Bin To store bottled wine (before its release for sale) for *bottle aging*.

Bitter A *taste* sensation, usually sensed on the back of the tongue. Not to be confused with *sour* or *rough*.

Blanc de Blancs (blahn duh blahn) A white wine made from white grapes.

Blanc de Noirs (blahn duh nwahr) A white wine made from red grapes.

Blend To combine grapes, *musts,* or wines of different varieties or lots.

Body The viscosity or thickness of wine. Correlated with *extract* and *alcohol:* the higher the alcohol and extract content, the more *full-bodied* the wine. A tactile sensation.

Bollinger (bowl-in-jer) One of the best firms (Grande Marque—grahn'd mahr'k) in France's *Champagne* district. R.D. is the *tête de cuvée.*

Bordeaux (bore-doe) Large wine region along the Gironde and Dordogne Rivers in southwestern France best known for dry red and dry to sweet white table wines of high quality. For more wine and grape information see: *Médoc, Pomerol, St. Emilion,* and *Sauternes.*

Botrytis Cinerea (bo-*trie*-tiss sin-eh-*ray*-ah) A mold that pierces grape skins, causing dehydration. Also called *noble rot.*

Botrytised (*bot*-trah-tized) The odor of sweet wines made from sound grapes shrivelled by *Botrytis.*

Bottle-Aged The characteristics of a wine derived from its stay in the bottle.

Bottle Aging Keeping bottled wines for a time to allow some of the components to mature and bottle *bouquet* to form.

Bottle-Aging Bouquet Characteristic complex, subtle odors of wines aged in the bottle under proper cellar conditions. See Appendix D for a collection of descriptions.

Bottle-Fermented A *sparkling* wine made by the *méthode champenoise* or *transfer method.*

Bottle Sickness A temporary, unpleasant *oxidized* odor that can follow bottling.

Bouquet The *odors* in wines from *fermentation,* processing, and *aging,* especially those that develop after bottling.

Brilliant The appearance of a wine that is absolutely clear.

Brix (briks) A measure of the density of grape juice or fermenting wine.

Browning A sign of *aging,* most often if a wine has *oxidized* too much.

Brut (brute) Term for almost-dry *Champagnes.*

Bulk Process *Champagne* made by tank *fermentation* or *Charmat process.*

Bung A plug for closing a wine cask.

Bung Hole A small opening in a cask through which wine can be put in or taken out.

Burgundy A wine district in France centered around Beaune and the wines from that district. A *semi-generic* wine type on U.S. labels.

Buttery *Odor* in wine from *malolactic fermentation* and reminiscent of butter and caused by the presence of *diacetyl.*

Cabernet Franc (*cah*-bair-nay frahn) A red wine grape best known for its presence in the fine wines of *Bordeaux,* especially those of *Pomerol* and *Saint-Emilion* and also *Médoc.* Also grown in northeastern Italy and California.

Cabernet Sauvignon (*cab*-air-nay *so*-vee-n'yohn) The most important red wine grape in the world. The basis of the great red wines of *Bordeaux,* California, and outstanding wines of other districts. See also Appendix A.

Canopy The foliage of a grape vine.

Cap Layer of skins that forms on top of the juice during *fermentation.*

Capsule Plastic or metallic foil that fits over the cork and part of the neck of a wine bottle.

Caramel Prominent *odor* in heated sweet wines and a subtle component of the *champagne bouquet.*

Carbonated Wines infused with carbon dioxide to make them bubbly.

Carbonic Maceration The *fermentation* of uncrushed whole grapes which takes place inside the cells of the berries.

Chai(x) (shay) A French term for above-ground areas for wine storage.

Chablis (shah-blee) Wine from grapes (*Chardonnay* mostly) grown in the *Chablis* district of France. In the U.S. a *semi-generic* wine type.

Champagne (shahm-panyeh, if you want to approximate the French pronunciation) The region in France and the *bottle-fermented sparkling* wines produced there. Under U.S. labelling law a *semi-generic* term for sparkling wines.

Champenoise (shahm-pah-n'wahz) Something or someone from France's *Champagne* district. See *méthode champenoise.*

Chardonnay (*shar*-doh-nay) Among the world's finest white wine grapes. Widely planted and used for dry, barrel-aged white table and blends for fine *sparkling* wines. See Appendix A for more information.

Charmat Process A method to produce *sparkling* wine in which the second *fermentation* takes place in a pressurized tank instead of individual bottles.

Chateau (shah-toe) Synonymous with vineyard when referring to French wines, especially those of *Bordeaux*. Otherwise a country house, usually big and fancy.

Châteauneuf-du-Pape (shah-toe-nuff doo pahp) A *Rhône* village that lends its name to the sturdy, full-bodied red wines from nearby vineyards of *Grenache* and *Syrah*. Literally "new castle of the pope," for its fourteenth-century summer home of the Avignon popes.

Châteaux Plural of *chateau.*

Château Pétrus (shah-toe peh-truos) The most prominent wines of *Pomerol*: rich, concentrated, and very expensive *Merlots* from a 28 acre vineyard.

Chenin Blanc (shch-nan blahn) A versatile white grape variety first known for its use in dry and sweet table wines and *sparkling* wines in the *Loire* district of France and now widely used in California and South Africa. See Appendix A for more information.

Chianti (k'*yahn*-tee) Wine from the Tuscany region of Italy.

Chianti Classico Riserva (k'*yahn*-tee *klah*-see-koh ree-*sehr*-vah) Wine from the center (Classico) of the *Chianti* district that has been aged longer in casks (Riserva).

Claret A dry red wine from the *Bordeaux* region of France and a *semi-generic* wine type in the U.S.

Clarity Clearness—opposite of *turbid.*

Clone A group of genetically identical, asexually propagated plants that can, in principle, be traced back to a single plant. In grape growing these plants are sub-varieties that differ from each other in important enological traits.

Cloudy A hazy appearance.

Cloying An excessively sweet wine taste. See *Sweetish.*

Cold Stabilization Chilling wine before bottling to precipitate potassium acid tartrate crystals or other sediment.

Complex A wine with numerous *odors* and *flavors,* each one usually rather subtle.

Component Wines Wines which have had one *odor* or *taste* element exaggerated for easier recognition.

Contrast Error The distortion of the sensory impression of a wine caused by the quality of the wine that was tasted just before it.

Cooperage Containers for storing wine, usually barrels, casks, but also tanks of wood or steel.

Corked or Corky A moldy *odor* and *flavor* from a fungus-infected cork attributable to the presence of small amounts of tyrene in the wine.

Côte d'Or (coat dor) French region that includes the most important *Burgundy* vineyards: the southerly Côte de Beaune (coat dah bone—great white wines from *Chardonnay*) and northerly Côte de Nuits (coat duh nweet—famous for *Pinot Noir*). Literally, "golden slopes."

Côte Rôtie (coat roe-tee) The finest red wines of the *Rhône* from *Syrah* vineyards on the river south of Vienne. With age these deeply colored, rich, long-lived wines acquire a complexity and delicacy that has been compared to that of fine *Bordeaux* reds. Literally "roasted slope."

Cream A full-bodied, golden, and sweet dessert *sherry.*

Cream of Tartar *Potassium bitartrate*; causes cloudiness or crystalline deposits in wine.

Crémant (cray-mahn) French term for wines that are slightly *sparkling*—four atmospheres of pressure compared to six for *Champagne.* Literally, "creaming."

Crush Breaking the grape skins prior to pressing or *fermentation* and the season of the year when this occurs.

Crusher A machine that breaks open grapes and usually de-stems them as well.

Culture An actively-growing batch of micro-organisms such as yeast or *malolactic* bacteria used to inoculate juice or *must* to catalyze a *fermentation.*

Cuvée (cue-vay) A specific blend of wines, often of different *vintages* and *varieties,* combined to make *sparkling* wine. Occasionally also used for *table wine.*

Decant To pour clear wine off a sediment.

Dégorgement (day-gorje-mahn) French term for *disgorging,* the removal of collected *yeast* sediment from bottles in *méthode champenoise.*

Demi-sec (deh-mee sek) Moderately sweet to medium sweet *sparkling* wines.

Descriptors Collective term for the third-tier terms on the *wine aroma wheel.*

Dessert Wine Any sweet wine used to accompany dessert, such as high-sugar *late-harvest* and *fortified wines.*

Deuxième (duh-zyem) In *méthode champenoise,* deuxième *taille* refers to the second batch or "cut" of *press juices* collected from the wine-press after the *free-run* juice. Literally, "second."

Diacetyl A chemical by-product of the *malolactic fermentation* which adds a buttery *odor* enhancing wine complexity at lower concentrations but an *off odor* at higher concentrations.

Disgorging Using the pressure of the gas in the wine to expel the collected sediment from *bottle-fermented sparkling* wine.

Distinctive Term for the *odor* and *flavor* of wines that are more individual and *complex* than those that are simply *vinous*, but that do not display recognizable *varietal* odor and flavor.

Dom Pérignon (dohn payring-yong) Legendary discoverer of champagnization. Namesake of Moët and Chandon's *tête de cuvée.*

Dosage (doh-sajh) In the making of *sparkling* wine, the wine and sugar mixture used to adjust the sweetness of the wine.

Doux (doo) Sweet. Usually the sweetest category of *sparkling* wines.

Dry Without a sweet taste.

Dull The appearance of a wine with colloidal haze.

Durif (duh-reef) Undistinguished grape variety introduced into southern France in the nineteenth century but not grown much now. Much of what is called *Petite Sirah* in California is probably Durif.

Early-Harvest Wine made from early-harvested grapes, usually lower in alcoholic content or sweetness.

Earthy An undesirable *odor* or *flavor* suggestive of earth or soil.

Enology (also spelled **oenology**) The science of wines and winemaking. Also called viniculture.

Épernay (eh-pear-neigh) Along with *Reims,* a principlal city in France's *Champagne* district and location of the blending, aging, and bottling facilities of many *Champagne* producers. Also the name of a strain of wine *yeast.*

Ethyl Acetate Chemical responsible for vinegary *odor,* along with acetic acid.

Ethyl Alcohol, Ethanol Product of the conversion of sugar by *yeast* enzymes during *fermentation.*

Extended Maceration A process for making premium red *table wines* in which the *fermentation* tanks are sealed after the *alcoholic fermentation* and the skins are allowed to remain with the new wine.

Extra Dry A *Champagne* or *sparkling* wine that is, to contradict its name, generally sweet, containing 1.5 to 2.5 percent sugar.

Extract Those wine components that remain when the *volatiles, alcohol,* and water are evaporated and that contribute to a wine's *body.*

Fermentation Any conversion of organic compounds which is catalyzed by microorganisms.

Fermentation, Alcoholic The conversion by *yeast* enzymes of the grape sugar in the *must* or juice into *alcohol* and carbon dioxide.

Fermentation Bouquet Characteristic *odors* added to wines during the *alcoholic fermentation.* See Appendix D for descriptions.

Fermentation, Malolactic See *malolactic fermentation.*

Fermentation, Stuck See *stuck fermentation.*

Fining Clarifying wine by mixing in agents such as *gelatin* to remove specific components and suspended matter.

Finish The lingering *aftertaste* of a wine.

Finishing All the processes involved in stabilizing and clarifying wines before they are bottled.

Fino (fee-no) A kind of *sherry*, light and *dry,* produced by the *flor* method.

Flat Wine lacking a refreshing slightly *sour* taste and *sparkling* wines that have lost most of their carbon dioxide.

Flavor *Odors* perceived in the mouth.

Flor A *yeast* that produces a film on the wine's surface and gives it a distinctive flavor.

Foil See *capsule.*

Fortified Wine A wine in which the *alcohol* content has been increased by the addition of wine, spirits, or brandy.

Free-Run Grape juice that runs freely from the *crusher* and *press* before force is used.

French Colombard A white grape grown extensively in California and used to make jug wines.

Frizzante (freet-*zahn*-tay) Italian term for slightly *sparkling* wines. See *pétillant.*

Fruity The grape-like flavor and taste of refreshing young wines.

Full-Bodied A wine that is high in alcoholic content and *extract.*

Fumé Blanc (foo-may blahn) Dry *Sauvignon Blanc.*

Gamay (gam-may) A red grape variety known for its use in makeing France's *Beaujolais* wines. See Appendix A for more information.

Gamay Beaujolais (gam-may bo-jo-lay) A red grape grown in California and which is a *clone* of *Pinot Noir.*

Gelatin A protein used in *fining* wine.

Generic Wines named after general categories (red or white table wine) and place names *(Burgundy, Rhine, Sherry* [Jerez], *Champagne),* although the latter are technically known in the United States as *semi-generic.*

Gewürztraminer (geh-*vurtz*-tra-*mee*-ner) Distinctively-flavored pink grape used for fine white wines. Best known for its use in *Alsace,* France. Literally, "spicy Traminer." See Appendix A for more information.

Grappa Italian term for the high-alcohol beverage made by distilling *press* wines made from juices extracted from the *pomace.*

Green The high acid *taste* of wines made from unripe grapes. "Acidulous" is synonymous.

Grenache A red grape of the *Rhône* Valley region of France.

Harmonious Wines in which all sensory properties are in *balance.*

Hautvilliers (oh-veel-yay) A village in the *Cham-*

pagne district and the site of the monastery where *Dom Pérignon* is said to have discovered the "wine with stars."

Headspace The air space between a wine and the top of a tank or the closure of a bottle.

Herbaceous An agreeable *odor* reminiscent of herbs, and usually associated with *Sauvignon Blancs* and *Cabernet Sauvignons* when grown under cooler climatic conditions.

Hermitage (air-mee-*tahj*) A *Rhône* district south of the *Côte Rotie* and also noted for dark, rich, long-aging red wines from *Syrah.*

Hogsheads Usually 60-gallon oak barrels.

Hot High in *alcohol*, producing a slight burning sensation on the palate, generally undesirable except in *fortified wines.*

Hydrogen Sulfide Chemical responsible for the *off odor* of "rotten eggs" in wine.

Hydrometer An instrument used to estimate the degrees *Brix* of grape juice during ripening, at harvest, and during *fermentation.*

Johannisberg Riesling (yo-*hahn*-iss-bairg *reete*-ling) See *White Riesling.*

Jug Wines Generally less expensive and simple *generic* wines sold in large containers.

Kabinett (kah-bee-*net*) A German term producers use for their driest and least expensive *QmP* wine.

Lactic Acid Organic acid in milk and which is produced in wine from malic acid during the *malolactic fermentation.*

Late-Harvest Most often a white wine whose level of sugar at harvest is the result of *Botrytis cinerea;* used as a dessert wine. Also used for some *Zinfandel* wines from grapes picked at high levels of sugar.

Lees Any residue that settles out of a wine.

Legs The drops that inch up the inside surface of a glass above the wine and slowly run back down. Same as "tears."

Limousin (lee-moo-zan) A forest in Central France where oak is harvested for wine barrels.

Linalool The chemical responsible for the flowery odor associated with *Gewürztraminer, Riesling*, and *Muscat* grapes.

Loire (l'war) The longest river in France, it flows northwest from near Lyons to empty into the Atlantic near Nantes. Its best-known wine districts are based on *Chenin Blanc* and *Sauvignon Blanc* vineyards and include *Anjou, Touraine, Vouvray, Pouilly-Fumé* and *Sancerre.*

Luscious Soft, sweet, rich, fruity, round and ripe. All these qualities in harmonious balance.

Maceration In winemaking, the extraction of *aroma,* color, *flavor,* and *tannins* from grape skins usually during skin contact during the *alcoholic fermentation* or *carbonic maceration.*

Maceration, Extended See *extended maceration.*

Macroclimate The overall average weather conditions in a vineyard region such as the Rhône,

Champagne, or Napa Valley districts.

Madeira (muh-*deh*-rah) A dessert wine with a burnt, caramel flavor which originated on the Portuguese island of this name.

Malic Acid The organic acid in apples, grapes, and wine which is converted to *lactic acid* during the *malolactic fermentation.*

Malolactic Fermentation A bacterial fermentation that converts *malic* to *lactic acid* and carbon dioxide and can add complexity to wines.

Manzanilla (mahn-thah-*nee*-yah) Very light, refreshing *sherry* from San Lucar de Barrameda named for its apple-like qualities.

Marriage In the enological sense, the integration of the components of blended grapes or wines or of additions to wine such as a *dosage* or *sulfur dioxide* to form a more pleasing combination.

Mature A wine which has reached its optimum point during *aging* and has a pleasing combination of sensory properties, especially *odors.* It is neither too *young* nor too old.

Médoc (meh-doc) *Bordeaux's* biggest district famous for long-aging, *Cabernet*-based red wines of its great *châteaux.* Look for the names of the Médoc's four villages—Margaux, Saint-Julien, Pauillac, and Saint Estèphe—on the most celebrated wines. Médoc is the *appellation of origin* of wines made from grapes grown anywhere in the district.

Mercaptan Onion-like or garlic-like *off odor* of methyl and ethyl mercaptans and *sulfides.*

Merlot (mair-*lo*) Fine red wine grape widely planted in *Bordeaux*—especially *Pomerol* and *Saint Emilion*—and used there and in California in blends with *Cabernet Sauvignon.* See Appendix A for more information.

Mesoclimate The unique climate of a subsection of a vineyard region (compare to *macroclimate* and *microclimate).*

Méthode Champenoise (may-tud shahm-pah-n'wahz) The bottle-fermentation method of making champagne that is sold in the same bottle in which its secondary *fermentation* took place.

Methoxypyrazines A group of complex organic compounds that includes the chemicals responsible for the bell pepper and grassy odors of *Cabernet Sauvignon* and *Sauvignon Blanc.*

Microclimate The climate in and around the grapevine's *canopy.*

Midi (mee-dee) Vast region along the Mediterranean coast of France known for producing ordinary wine.

Mise en Bouteille au Château (meez ahn bootay oh shah-toe) French for "bottled at the winery," usually in *Bordeaux.*

Ml Milliliter, one-thousandth of a liter.

Moldy Grapes, containers, or corks that have become moldy transmit this *off odor* to the wine they contact.

Monoterpenes Group of organic compounds that include the chemicals responsible for the fruity flavors of *Gewürztraminer, Muscat,* and *Riesling.*

Montrachet (mon-rah-shay) An extraordinary 20-acre vineyard in the Côte de Beaune of the *Côte d'Or* that produces the most famous and expensive dry white *Burgundy* wines. Also a widely used strain of wine *yeast.*

Mosel (mo-z'l) The principal river of the Mosel-Saar-Ruwer wine region of Germany. Wines from the steep hillside vineyards of this coolest of viticultural areas range from ordinary *Tafelwein* to the highest quality *QbA* and *QmP White Rieslings* in dry to very sweet styles. Spelled Moselle in French and English.

Mousse (moos) The foam of bubbles that forms on the top of a glass of *sparkling* wine.

Mousseaux (moo-suh) *Sparkling,* not plural of moose **or** *mousse.*

Muscat Blanc Best of the many varieties of the universally planted Muscat family and known for its intense floral-fruit perfume and sweet wines. See Appendix A for more information.

Muscat Canelli See *Muscat Blanc.*

Muscat Frontignan (frohn-tee-n'yahn) See *Muscat Blanc.*

Must Term for the juice and pulp produced by *crushing* or *pressing* grapes. Used until the end of *fermentation* when it is called wine.

Napa Gamay California's name for *Gamay.*

Natural Wines Produced by fermenting the sugar in the grapes. Not *fortified.*

Nebbiolo (neh-b'*yoh*-lo) A red grape grown in the Piedmont district, Italy. Produces some of the finest Italian wine.

Négociant (nay-go-syahn) French for a wholesale wine merchant, blender, and shipper.

Neutral A wine lacking distinctive or recognizable flavor and odor; *vinous.* A common feature of ordinary blended wines.

Nevers (nee-vehr) Forests surrounding the town of Nevers where oak is harvested for wine barrels.

Noble Mold, Noble Rot See *Botrytis cinerea.*

Nouveau (noo-vo) French for a young wine meant for immediate drinking. May be produced by *carbonic maceration.*

Nouveaux Plural of *nouveau.*

Nutty An *oxidized,* walnut-like flavor, desirable in dessert or appetizer wines such as *sherry* and *Madeira,* but an *off flavor* in *table wines.*

Oaky Toasty and vanilla smells and flavors contributed during barrel aging by the oak.

Odors Sensations stimulated by the volatile components of wines and perceived in the *olfactory epithelium.* Includes *aroma, bouquet,* and *off odors.*

Oenology See *enology.*

Off Dry Very slightly sweet.

Off Flavors Undesirable odors perceived in the mouth.

Off Odors Undesirable odors from a variety of possible sources ranging from moldy fruit to aging the bottled wine too long. Whenever possible the specific odor and its origin should be named.

Olfactory Epithelium The sensory organ of the sense of smell. A small patch of tissue located in the top of uppermost nasal passage.

Oloroso A type of *sherry,* usually dark in color and often sweet. Produced without the use of *flor.* The sweeter styles are called *cream.*

Organoleptic Elements or Characteristics Those attributes of wine or food that we perceive with our senses of sight, smell, taste, touch, and hearing.

Organoleptic Evaluation See *Sensory Evaluation.*

Over-Aged A general breakdown of a wine kept too long in wooden cooperage or bottles; *oxidized.*

Oxidation The changes in wine caused by exposure to air.

Oxidized Wine changed by contact with air, usually producing undesirable browning and *sherry*-like flavors. Over-aged.

Perlant (pehr-lahn) French term for wines that are naturally very slightly *sparkling*—between *still* and *pétillant.* German equivalent is "Spritzig."

Pétillant (pah-tee-yahn) French term for slightly *sparkling* wines of two atmospheres of pressure or less—more bubbly than *perlant,* less than *crémant.* "Perlwein" in German; "frizzante" in Italian.

Petite Sirah (puh-tee see-rah) An undistinguished red grape grown in California. In the past it has been confused with *Syrah.*

pH The measure of acid strength: the lower the pH, the higher the acid strength.

Phenols See *polyphenols.*

Pineau de la Loire (pee-no duh l'war) A name for *Chenin Blanc* sometimes used in France.

Pinot Blanc (pee-no blahn) A white grape variety derived from *Pinot Noir.* Capable of producing fine *varietal* wines and may be blended with *Chardonnay.*

Pinot Gris (pee-no gree) A grayish-rose colored grape derived from *Pinot Noir* and capable of producing full-bodied white wines.

Pinot Meunier (pee-no mun-n'yay) A red grape variety which is the most widely planted variety in France's *Champagne* region. Related to *Pinot Noir* but does not age as well.

Pinot Noir (*pee*-no n'wahr) Great red wine grape that is the basis of the finest red wines of

France's *Burgundy* region. See Appendix A for more information.

Polyphenols A complex group of organic chemicals that include wine's *tannins*.

Pomace The solid residue left after pressing.

Pomerol (paw-meh-rawl) Smallest *Bordeaux* wine district noted for rich, flavorful wines from *Merlot* and *Cabernet Franc*. Home of *Château Pétrus*.

Port A fortified dessert wine, usually red, modelled after wines shipped from Oporto, Portugal.

Potassium Bitartrate The crystals that sometimes precipitate in bottled wine but which are normally removed by cold-stabilization before bottling. The chemical in cream of tartar.

Pouilly-Fuissé (poo-yee fwee-say) The highest quality white wine from *Chardonnay* grapes grown near Mâcon in southern *Burgundy*.

Pouilly-Fumé (poo-yee foo-may) A dry white wine from *Pouilly-Sûr-Loire*.

Pouilly-Sûr-Loire (poo-yee soor l'war) A village in France's *Loire* Valley near *Sancerre* and known for *Pouilly-Fumé*—an excellent, dry white table wine from *Sauvignon Blanc*.

Ppm Part(s) per million. One milligram per liter is one part per million.

Première (pruh-m'yay) In *méthode champenoise*, première *taille* refers to the first batch or "cut" of *press juices* collected from the winepress after the *free-run* juice. Literally, "first."

Press To exert pressure on grapes or *must* to extract their juices and the mechanical device used in the process.

Press Juice or Wine Juice or wine obtained by pressing.

Primitivo (pree-mee-tee-voh) A grape variety of southern Italy believed to be the same as California's *Zinfandel*.

Prise de Mousse (preez duh moose) French term for the second fermentation of *méthode champenoise*. Literally, "catch the foam." Also the name of a strain of wine *yeast*.

Puckery The tactile sensation in highly *tannic* wines. *Astringent* is a more precise and preferable term.

Pulp The flesh of the grape or other fruit.

Pump Over To circulate fermenting juice from the bottom of the tank over the top of the *cap* that forms during *fermentation* to ensure optimal extraction from the grape solids and prevent *bacterial* spoilage.

Puncheons (punch-ons) Larger oak barrels, usually 135 gallons.

Punch Down To push the *cap* that forms on the surface of fermenting *must* down into the juice.

Punt The indentation in the bottom of some wine bottles.

Pupître (pew-pee-truh) French term for the "A-frame" rack in which bottles of *méthode champenoise* sparkling wine are placed for *riddling*.

PVPP Polyvinylpolypyrrolidone, a synthetic protein-like material, used in removing substances that cause *browning*.

QbA A tongue-saving abbreviation for *Qualitätswein Bestimmter Anbaugebeite*.

QmP A handy abbreviation for *Qualitätswein mit Prädikat*.

Qualitätswein (kvah-lee-*tayts*-vine) Better quality German wines. See *Tafelwein*.

Qualitätswein Bestimmter Anbaugebeite (kvah-lee-*tayts*-vine be-shrimter *Ahn*-bough ge-beet-eh) Better quality German wines from recognized viticultural regions — such as the *Mosel-Saar-Ruwer*, for example.

Qualitätswein mit Prädikat (kvah-lee-*tayts*-vine mit *pray*-dee-kaht) Best quality German wines which must conform to detailed requirements of origin and composition and include dry to very sweet wines which may be designated *Kabinett, Auslese, Spätlese, Beerenauslese,* and *Trockenbeerenauslese*.

Quality The degree of excellence of a wine. Associated with complexity, harmony, and the ability to stimulate the emotions.

Racking Siphoning or pumping wine from one container to another to clarify it by leaving the sediment behind.

Refractometer An instrument for estimating the sugar content of grape juice by measuring the bending of light passing through it.

Reims (ranz) Along with *Épernay*, a principle city in France's *Champagne* district and location of the blending, aging, and bottling facilities of many *Champagne* houses.

Rémuage (ray-mew-ahje) A French term for *riddling*.

Reserve Wine In *méthode champenoise*, wine that is held to be blended into the *cuvées* of future *vintages*.

Residual Sugar Grape sugar that remains unconverted in the wine after *fermentation*.

Retro-Nasal Route One of the two pathways — the other is directly into the nose from the outside environment — through which *volatile* compounds reach the *olfactory epithelium*: through a passageway from the back of the mouth up into the upper nasal cavities.

Rhine (rine) A mighty European river that runs from Switzerland, through Germany to the North Sea. With reference to wines, the term refers to a variety of predominantly white wines produced in the several districts bordered by the river, ranging from ordinary wines of the Rheinpfalz (*rine*-fahl'tz) to the world's greatest *White Rieslings* from the Rheingau (*rine*-gao).

Rhône (rone) A great European river that rises in Switzerland and flows through France to empty into the Mediterranean near Marseilles. "Rhône wines" most commonly refers to wines from the French districts of *Hermitage, Côte Rotie, Châteauneuf du Pape,* and Tavel.

Riddling In *méthode champenoise,* turning bottles of *sparkling* wine to collect the sediment on the closure (cork or bottle cap) for removal during *disgorging.*

Riddling Rack The rack designed to hold bottles of *sparkling* wine in the proper position for *riddling.* Also called a *pupitre,* or A-rack.

Riesling (*reece*-ling) See *White Riesling.*

Rough The *astringent* tactile sensation, not to be confused with the *bitter* taste.

Ruby A style of *port,* generally on the young side and rather sweet.

Saccharomyces Cerevisiae One of the main species of *yeasts* found in grapes and wines throughout the world. Most of the strains used in wine *fermentation* are of this species.

Saint Emillion (san't eh-mee-l'yon) Small *Bordeaux* district noted for its high proportion of fine wines from the varieties *Merlot* and *Cabernet Franc.* Château Cheval Blanc is one of the best vineyards.

Sancerre (sahn-sair) A French township and popular *Loire* wine made from *Sauvignon Blanc.* Closely resembles its neighbor *Pouilly-Fumé.*

Sapid Substances that have taste.

Sauternes (saw-tairn) A sweet wine from the *Bordeaux* region of France made from *Sémillon* and *Sauvignon Blanc* grapes infected with *Botrytis.*

Sauvignon Blanc (*so*-vee-n'yohn blahn) A distinguished white grape variety. Called *Fumé Blanc* by many California producers and can be made into sweet wines after a successful *Botrytis* infection. See Appendix A for more information.

Sec French for "dry." Medium sweet to sweet *sparkling* wines.

Secondary Fermentation A *fermentation* that takes place after the completion of the primary alcoholic fermentation. It is used for both the second alcoholic fermentation in *sparkling* wine production and the *malolactic fermentation.*

Semi-Generic U.S. wines named after places which *B.A.T.F.* rules require be modified by a U.S. appellation of origin, as in California Sherry or Napa Valley Burgundy.

Sémillon (*seh*-mee-yohn) A less common white grape variety known for blending with *Sauvignon Blanc,* especially in the production of the sweet wines of Sauternes, France.

Sensory Evaluation The systematic assessment of wine by sight (color and *appearance),* smell *(aroma, bouquet, off odors,* and *flavors),* taste *(sweet, sour, bitter),* and touch (viscosity, hotness).

Settling The natural precipitation of the solid matter in wine.

Shermat The base wine used in making *sherry.*

Sherry A fortified wine made by a deliberate, controlled oxidation first practiced around Jerez de la Frontera, Spain.

Shiraz (shee-*raz*) The Australian name for *Syrah.*

Skin Contact The process of holding *must* before pressing to obtain an extraction of *aroma* and *flavor.* This occurs before *fermentation* for some white *table wines* and during *fermentation* for red wines, in which case it is called *maceration.*

Slightly Sweet Containing a barely precipitable amount of residual sugar.

Smooth The tactile sensation for a wine's lack of *astringency.*

Solera System A process used to systematically *blend* various *vintages* of *sherry.*

Sommelier (so-mel-yay) A wine steward.

Sour The acid taste of wines made from green (unripe) grapes.

Sparkling A wine containing an induced effervescence from carbon dioxide most commonly captured during a second alcoholic *fermentation.*

Spätlese (schpate-lay-zuh) A term used on German *QmP* and some other *late-harvest* wines to indicate wines made from very ripe bunches. Literally, "select."

Spicy Distinctive *odors* and *flavors* reminiscent of aromatic spices and found in wines made from certain varieties of grapes, for example, *Gewürztraminer.*

Spirits Distilled *alcohol* used to fortify wines.

Spritzy Wines with a minor amount of sparkle left over from the alcoholic *fermentation.* See *Perlant.*

Spumante (spoo-*mahn*-tay) An Italian *sparkling* wine. See *Asti Spumante.*

Stabilization The process of causing the precipitation of unwanted substances so that they will not cause haziness or form crystals in the finished wine.

Starter A batch of actively-growing *yeast* used to initiate *fermentation.*

Stemmer A machine that separates the stems from the grapes; usually combined with a *crusher,* and called a stemmer-crusher.

Still Wines All wines without effervescence.

Stimulus, Effective In wine, any chemical, physical, or thermal activator that can produce a perceptible response in a sense receptor. For chemicals, for example, their concentration must be above the *threshold of perception.*

Stimulus Error Tasters who use irrelevant criteria to judge wines make this kind of error.

Structural Components All of the *organoleptic elements* of a wine other than *flavor* which are experienced in the mouth: sweetness, *acidity, astringency,* hotness, *body,* effervescence, etc.

Stuck Fermentation An incomplete *fermentation* that stops before all the sugar has been converted to *alcohol.*

Style The characteristic combination of wine components associated with the wines of a particular winemaker, winery, or region.

Sulfide The same rotten-egg odor as *hydrogen sulfide.*

Sulfur Dioxide Compound used to inhibit the growth of undesirable microorganisms and inhibit *browning.* It gives an unpleasant "match-stick" odor to wine when present in noticeable quantities.

Sur Lie (soo'r-lee) Literally, "on the *lees.*" Most commonly used to refer to the *aging* of wines on the *yeast* deposits that form after the *alcoholic fermentation.*

Sur Pointe (soo'r pwan't) A neck-down position for storing wine bottles. After *riddling,* *champagne* bottles may be stored *sur pointe* before *disgorging.*

Sweet The taste of a wine with perceptible sugar content; the essential characteristic of any dessert wine.

Sweetish Unpleasantly sweet, cloying.

Sylvaner An uncommon white grape in California which is widely grown for ordinary wines in Germany and *Alsace.*

Syrah (see-rah) A distinguished red grape grown in the *Rhône* Valley region of France. See Appendix A for more information.

Table Wine In general, still, dry wine of 14% or less alcohol meant to accompany food.

Tafelwein (*tah*-fel-vine) German term for ordinary table wine.

Taille (tah'y) In *méthode champenoise, vins de taille* are made from *press juices* and some producers sell them rather than use them in their *Champagne cuvée.* See also *première, deuxième,* and *troisième.*

Tank-Aging Bouquet Odors of wines that have matured during bulk *aging.* Characterized by a diminution of the *yeasty* character which appears right after the *alcoholic fermentation,* a greater integration of *odors,* and a development of greater *complexity.* Obviously, more often experienced by winemakers than consumers.

Tannin A *polyphenolic* compound derived from the skins, seeds, and stems of grapes, which gives young red wine an *astringent* quality, but contributes to its longevity and normally ameliorates as the wine ages. In excess, it causes a *bitter* taste.

Tart A pleasant, sour taste in young wines. Wines with a total acidity of 0.65 to 0.85 g/100ml and a pH of 3.1 to 3.4.[2]

Tartaric Acid One of the essential organic acids in wine.

Tartrates Salts of tartaric acid that can form crystals in unstabilized wine. See *Potassium Bitartrate.*

Taste Technically limited to four categories: sour, bitter, sweet and salt (seldom in wine). Many of the terms used to describe "taste" in wine are actually *odors* which are responsible for the wine's *flavors.*

Tawny The amber or brownish color characteristic of wines, such as *port,* that have been aged in wood.

Tears See *legs.*

Tête de Cuvée (tet-duh-cue-vay) French term for a *Champagne* producer's best bottling.

Thief A tubular glass, plastic, or wooden instrument for withdrawing a sample of wine from a cask or barrel.

Thin A wine lacking *body.*

Thompson Seedless A white grape grown in California for raisins and fresh fruit and used to make jug wines.

Threshold The intensity below which a stimulus cannot be perceived and produces no response.

Threshold, Absolute See *Threshold of Sensation.*

Threshold, Detection See *Threshold of Sensation.*

Threshold, Difference The quantity of stimulus that must be added to an existing and perceptible amount for the change to be recognizable.

Threshold, Differential See *Threshold, Difference.*

Threshold of Perception The smallest concentration of a stimulus that can be accurately described or named. When defined qualitatively for a population, it is the concentration at which 50% of the people tested can correctly name or describe the stimulus. Higher than the *Threshold of Sensation.*

Threshold, Recognition See *Threshold of Perception.*

Threshold of Sensation The smallest concentration of a stimulus that can produce a general but unidentifiable sensation. Lower than the *Threshold of Perception.* Also called the absolute threshold or detection threshold.

Time-Order Error The prejudicial preference for one wine over another based on its place in the order of tasting.

Tirage (tee-rahj) In *méthode champenoise* the mixture of still *cuvée* wine, *yeast* culture, and sugar drawn off into bottles for the *secondary fermentation.*

Toasted An odor element of *Champagne bouquet* reminiscent of toasted bread.

Toasting The caramelization of the staves of barrels.

Topping A technique to control *oxidation* in wines aging in barrels by adding wine periodically to replace wine lost through evaporation and soaking into the wood.

Total Acid The measure of amount of all the acids in wine taken together.

Transfer Process *Sparkling* winemaking process that removes the wine from the bottle after *fermentation* for filtering in pressurized tanks before re-bottling.

Trockenbeerenauslese (*traw*-ken-*bear*-en-*ouse*-lay-zah) A term used on German *QmP* and some other *late-harvest* wines to indicate wines made from shrivelled berries infected with *noble rot*. Wines are sweeter and more full-bodied than *Beerenauslese* wines. Literally, "select dried berries."

Troisième (trwaz-yem) In *méthode champenoise,* troisième *taille* refers to the third batch or "cut" of *press juices* collected from the winepress after the *free-run* juice. Literally, "third."

Troncais (trohn-kay) A small forest near the French city of Moulins where oak is harvested for making wine barrels.

Unbalanced See *balanced.*

Unripe See *green.*

Vanilla Vanillin, which has a vanilla-like *odor,* is found in wines that have been aged in new oak barrels, particularly of American white oak.

Varietal Said of the *odor* and/or *flavor* of a wine that can be recognized as having been made from a particular grape *variety.*

Variety Sub-species of cultivated plants such as *Vitis vinifera* that are distinguished by economically important traits such as yield, disease resistance, or the distinctiveness of the *flavors* of their wines.

Vegemite Australian vegetable extract spread with a "toasted" flavor.

Vegetal A pronounced *grassy* or *herbaceous off odor* containing such *flavors* as bell pepper and asparagus. Adds to the complexity of a wine in small amounts, but undesirable when excessive.

Vin (van) French term for wine.

Vin de Cuvée (van-duh-cue-vay) In *méthode champenoise,* the wines that are fermented from the *free-run juice.* About 110 gallons per ton.

Vin de Taille (van-duh-tah'y) In *méthode champenoise,* the wines that are fermented from the juices produced by gentle pressing. About 20 gallons per ton. See *taille.*

Vinegary The *off odor* of acetic acid and ethyl acetate.

Vin Ordinaire (van or-dee-nahr) A French term for everyday wine.

Vinous A wine without a specific, distinguishable *odor.*

Vintage The season when wine grapes are harvested as well as the year on a wine label in which those grapes were matured for harvest.

Vintner A person who makes or sells wine.

Viticulture The science of growing grapes.

Volatile Those chemicals that can leave the surface of a liquid at a particular temperature.

Volatile Acidity A term used to describe the spoilage *odors* of *acetic acid* along with *ethyl acetate;* in noticeable amounts, this gives the wine a vinegary quality.

Vouvray (voo-vray) Very famous *Chenin Blanc* wines from Touraine. Can be dry to sweet and still to *sparkling.* See *Anjou-Touraine.*

Wine The fermented juice of grapes.

Winetasting See *Sensory Evaluation.*

White Riesling (*reece*-ling) One of the great white wine grapes. Widely planted in cool wine districts throughout the world for fine wines. Known simply as Riesling in Germany and also called *Johannisberg Riesling* in the U.S. See Appendix A for more information.

Woody The *off odor* of wines stored too long in oak barrels.

Yeast Microscopic fungi. Some species catalyze useful *fermentations* in bread and winemaking.

Yeasty The odor of the yeast used in fermentation, attractive in modest amounts in young wines.

Young A fresh, fruity, unoxidized, and possibly very slightly yeasty odor.

Zinfandel A distinguished and versatile red grape used in California for wine types ranging from *sparkling* wines to white and red *table wines,* and *port.* See Appendix A for more information.

Zinorama A winetasting featuring several *Zinfandels.*

ENDNOTES

1. Most of the pronunciation suggestions in the glossary are from THE NEW FRANK SCHOONMAKER ENCYCLOPEDIA OF WINE by Alexis Bespaloff, William Morrow & Co., New York, 1988. Suggestions for pronouncing the French terms for sparkling wine production were developed with the assistance of Dr. Cecile Lindsay, Chair, Department of Foreign Languages and Literatures, California State University, Chico, and Mary Van Steenbergh, Managing Editor, Journal of Modern History, University of Chicago.

2. Amerine, M. A., and E. B. Roessler, WINES, THEIR SENSORY EVALUATION, W. H. Freeman and Co., New York, 1983, p. 331.

3. Adams, Leon D., THE COMMONSENSE BOOK OF WINE, Wine Appreciation Guild, San Francisco, 1991.

Supplementary Reading

Adams, Leon. THE COMMON SENSE BOOK OF WINE.
   San Francisco: Wine Appreciation Guild, 1991.
___. THE WINES OF AMERICA. San Francisco: McGraw Hill, 1990.
Allen, Elizabeth & Lawrence. THE WINEMAKERS OF THE PACIFIC NORTHWEST.
   Vashon Island: Harbor House Publishing, 1977.
Amerine, M. A. & M. A. Joslyn. TABLE WINES, THE TECHNOLOGY OF THEIR
   PRODUCTION. Berkeley: University of California Press, 1970.
___. and C.S. Ough. METHODS OF MUSTS FOR ANALYSIS AND WINES.
   New York: John Wiley & Sons, 1980.
___. and Edward B. Roessler. WINES: THEIR SENSORY EVALUATION.
   New York: W. H. Freeman and Company, 1983.
___. WINE: AN INTRODUCTION.
   Berkeley: University of California Press, 1977.
Anderson, Stanley F. WINEMAKING, RECIPES, EQUIPMENT AND TECHNIQUES FOR
   MAKING WINE AT HOME. New York: Harper, Brace, Jovanovich, 1992.
   . and Raymond Hull. THE ART OF MAKING WINE.
   New York: Hawthorn/Dutton, 1970.
Ballard, Patricia. FINE WINE IN FOOD. San Francisco: Wine Appreciation Guild, 1988.
___. WINE IN EVERYDAY COOKING. San Francisco: Wine Appreciation Guild, 1981.
Berger, Dan and Richard Paul Hinkle. BEYOND THE GRAPES, AN INSIDE LOOK AT
   THE NAPA VALLEY. Wilmington: Atomium Books, 1991.
___. BEYOND THE GRAPES, AN INSIDE LOOK AT THE SONOMA VALLEY.
   Wilmington: Atomium Books, 1991.
Broadbent, Michael. THE GREAT VINTAGE WINE BOOK.
   New York: Alfred A. Knopf, 1991.
Caldewey, Jeffrey. WINE TOUR BOOK, VOL. I, NAPA VALLEY.
   St Helena: Vintage Image, 1988.
DeAvila, Edie. THE GREAT WINE ADVENTURE. Port Royal Publications, 1992.
Edgerton, William, Ed. WINE PRICE FILE. Darien: Wine Price File, 1990.
Ford, Gene. ILLUSTRATED GUIDE TO WINES, BREWS & SPIRITS.
   Dubuque: Wm. C. Brown, 1983.
___. THE BENEFITS OF MODERATE DRINKING.
   San Francisco: Wine Appreciation Guild, 1988.
___. THE FRENCH PARADOX, DRINKING FOR HEALTH.
   San Francisco: Wine Appreciation Guild, 1993.
Fulmer, Alan and Harry Hayes. BLUFF YOUR WAY IN WINE. Lincoln: Centinnel, 1990.
Galet, Pierre. A PRACTICAL AMPELOGRAPHY, GRAPEVINE IDENTIFICATION.
   Ithaca: Cornell University Press, 1979.
George, Rosemary. WINES OF CHABLIS.
   San Francisco: Sotheby Publications in association with the Wine Appreciation Guile, 1984.
Grossman, Harold J. GROSSMAN'S GUIDE TO WINES, BEERS AND SPIRITS.
   New York: Charles Scribner's Sons, 1983.
Hallgarten, Fritz. WINE SCANDAL. London: Weidenfeld and Nicolson, 1986.
Halliday, James. THE WINE ATLAS OF AUSTRALIA AND NEW ZEALAND.
   San Francisco: Wine Appreciation Guild, 1991.
Hébert, Malcolm. WINE LOVER'S COOKBOOK.
   San Francisco: Wine Appreciation Guild, 1983.
___. The Champagne Cookbook. San Francisco: Wine Appreciation Guild, 1993.

Jackson, David and Danny Schuster. PRODUCTION OF GRAPES AND WINES IN COOL CLIMATES. Wellington: Butterworths Horticultural Books, 1987.

Johnson, Hugh. THE WORLD ATLAS OF WINE. London: Simon and Schuster, 1985.

___. HOW TO ENJOY WINE. New York: Simon and Schuster, 1985.

Johnson, Robert. THE CONSUMER'S GUIDE TO ORGANIC WINE. Lanham, MD: Rowman & Littlefield, 1993.

Kaufman, William I. POCKET ENCYCLOPEDIA OF CALIFORNIA WINE. San Francisco: Wine Appreciation Guild, 1989.

___. POCKET ENCYCLOPEDIA OF AMERICAN WINE — NORTHWEST. San Francisco: Wine Appreciation Guild, 1992.

___. ENCYCLOPEDIA OF AMERICAN WINE. Los Angeles: Geremy P. Tarcher, Inc., 1984.

Laube, James. California's GREAT CHARDONNAYS. San Francisco: Wine Spectator Press, 1990.

Margalit, Phd., Yair. WINERY TECHNOLOGY AND OPERATIONS. San Francisco: Wine Appreciation Guild, 1990.

Mayson, Richard. PORTUGAL'S WINES AND WINEMAKERS. San Francisco: Wine Appreciation Guild, 1992.

Muscatine, Doris, Maynard A. Amerine, Bob Thompson. BOOK OF CALIFORNIA WINE. Berkeley: University of California Press, 1984.

___. THE TASTE OF WINE: THE ART AND SCIENCE OF WINE APPRECIATION. San Francisco: Wine Appreciation Guild, 1987.

Oregon Winegrower's Association. OREGON WINEGRAPE GROWER'S GUIDE. Portland: Oregon Winegrower's Association, 1992.

Peynard, Emile. THE TASTE OF WINE: The Art and Science of Wine Appreciation. San Francisco: Wine Appreciation Guild, 1987.

___VINTAGE: THE STORY OF WINE. New York: Simon and Schuster, 1989.

Parker Jr., Robert M. WINE BUYERS GUIDE. New York: Simon and Schuster, 1989.

Pomerol, Charles. THE WINES AND WINELANDS OF FRANCE, "GEOLOGICAL STUDIES." London: Robertson McCarta Limited, 1989.

Robinson, Jancis. VINES, GRAPES & WINES. New York: Alfred A. Knopf, 1986.

Roby, Norman and Charles Olken. CONNOISSEUR'S HANDBOOK OF CALIFORNIA WINES. New York: Alfred A. Knopf, 1991.

Rosengarten, David and Joshua Wesson. RED WINE WITH FISH. New York: Simon and Schuster, 1989.

Schoonmaker, Frank. ENCYCLOPEDIA OF WINE. New York: William Morrow and Company, Inc., 1988.

Smart, Richard and Mike Robinson. SUNLIGHT INTO WINE. Adelaide: Winetitles, 1991.

Stevenson, Tom. CHAMPAGNE. San Francisco: Wine Appreciation Guild, 1986.

Sullivan, Charles L. LIKE MODERN EDENS. Cupertino: California History Center, 1982.

Teiser, A. R. and C. Harroun. WINEMAKING IN CALIFORNIA. New York: McGraw-Hill, 1983.

Thompson, Bob. NOTES ON A CALIFORNIA CELLARBOOK. New York: William Morrow, 1988.

Waugh, Harry. WINE DIARY. San Francisco: Wine Appreciation Guild, 1987.

Wine Advisory Board. GOURMET WINE COOKING THE EASY WAY. San Francisco: Wine Appreciation Guild, 1987.

___. FAVORITE RECIPES OF CALIFORNIA WINEMAKERS. San Francisco: Wine Appreciation Guild, 1981.

Winkler, A. J., James Cook, W. Klierwer & L. Linder. GENERAL VITICULTURE. Berkeley: University of California Press, 1974.

Young, Alan. CHARDONNAY. Napa – Sonoma: International Wine Academy, 1988.

___. MAKING SENSE OF WINE. Richmond: Greenhouse Publications, 1986.

NOTE: A TEACHER'S MANUAL for The University Wine Course is available to bona fide instructors. It includes tips on planning a wine course, delivering the lectures and labs, additional sensory evaluation exercises and how to evaluate students. Homework assignments, study questions and exams are included. 78 pages. To Order: State your educational institution and address, name of course or intended course, number of students and classes per year. Cost: $12.95 plus $3.00 postage in U.S. or Canada. Overseas postage $6.00. Check or credit card number must be included, (VISA, MASTERCARD or AMEX). The Wine Appreciation Guild, 360 Swift Avenue, South San Francisco, CA 94080

INDEX

Bold numbers indicate pages where terms are defined in the text.
Numbers in parentheses identify Sensory Evaluation Exercises.

YEAR INDEX

1982, *Botrytis* blizzard, 222
1988, Napa Pinot Noirs, 177
1990,
    California crush, 298-299
    sparkling-wine market, 187
    varietal wines data, 300-306

ALPHABETICAL INDEX

A

abbreviations, wine name, 315*t*
"ABT's," describing the *(Ex.)*, 154-155, 367
abuse of alcohol, 8
acetaldehyde, 39, 150, 152, 229, 366
acetic acid, 80, 152, 366
acid content of wine, 40, 154, 269
    Botrytis-affected grapes and the, 220-221
    correction, 75
    food matching and the, 331-332
    and strength, 67-68
acidic foods, 331
adaptation of the senses, 26
added flavor wines, 48-49*t*
addresses,
    for suggestions to author, 348
    trade magazines, 389-390
    trade organizations, 388-389
    winery, 386-388
Adelsheim Vineyards, 51
aesthetics of wine with food, 328-329
affinities, food and wine. *See* food and wine
    combinations
age (human) and smell performance, 29
aging,
    barrel, 80-84, 135-136, 141, 227
    Botrytis-affected wines, 223
    bottle, 39, 86, 137-139, 149-150, 186, 227,
      373*t*
    bottle bouquet and *(Ex.)*, 166-167, 372-373
    bottle vs. bulk process, 189*t*, 316-317
    bulk, **80**-84, 87*t*, 135-136, 187-188
    cellars, 82-83, 138
    changes during, 334, 373*t*
    curve, 86
    maceration and, 130, 133-134
    in oak, 80-84, 135-136, 141, 227
    potential, 138-139
    red wine, 135-136, 371
    red wine odors and *(Ex.)*, 149-150
    rough wines, 40

aging, *(continued)*
    sparkling wine, 184-185, 186, 189*t*
    storage and, 138-139, 385*t*
    sur lie, 76, 184-185, 188, 360-361
    temperature for, 135
    transfer process bottle fermentation, 179,
      187-188, 316-317
    white wine, 80-84, 86, 87*t*
    See also bouquet; fermentation; oak-aging;
      production steps, wine
air-exposure, 131, 340
    in-bottle, 138
    See also oxidation
alcohol consumption,
    abuse, 8, 12-13
    during winetasting, 46
    the French paradox, 141-142
    research on health and, 11-14
alcohol content of wine,
    and carbonic-maceration, 140
    food matching to, 333-334
    label information and actual, 312
    legs and, 35
    odor perception and *(Ex.)*, 242-243
    red wine, 129, 140
    sensory stimulation and, 25, 242
    sugar weight ratio to, 72
    tax rate by, 50, 307-308
    of wines sold in U.S., 49*t*
    See also fermentation
alcoholism, 8
allergies and smell performance, 29
almonds, winetasting and *(Ex.)*, 238, 240, 377,
    378, 379, 380
Alsace, France, 276-277
alum, 153-154
America, United States of. *See* United States
Amerine, M. A., 268, 275
Amontillado sherries, 227-229, **228**, 380
anaerobic aging, 138
    See also maceration, carbonic
anosmia, 28
aperitif (wine), 336, 337
appearance (wine), 34-36, 45, 199, 242
    tartrate crystals in, 35-36, 79
    See also sediment, wine
appellation of origin, 310-311
    American, 177, 313, 314
    French, 314
    See also district wines; viticultural areas
appetite stimulation by wine, 9
apples, 104, 113-115, 360-361*t*

---

i, illustration or photograph *t*, table or chart

i, illustration or photograph *t*, table or chart

i, illustration or photograph *t*, table or chart

---

i, illustration or photograph *t*, table or chart

ATTENTION: Instructors, Teachers, Professors, Librarians, Department Heads, Deans and Academic Administrators.

NOW AVAILABLE: TEACHER'S MANUAL for The University Wine Course
by Marian W. Baldy, Ph.D.

The same depth of experience and knowledge that has gone into this book is also available for those planning and teaching wine classes.

The Teacher's Manual is a complete guide and handbook — Included are:

Planning – from Course Goals to Student Feedback

Lesson Planning Worksheet, sample lesson plans

Learning styles

Organizing the content

Collecting feedback

How to help your students be active participants in lectures and labs

How to set-up the labs and taste tests

How to use wine labels for review

Wine and Food matching problems

How to use slides and videos

Connecting students to the world beyond the classroom

Suggestions for Sensory Evaluation Exercises

Facilities, control of consumption, liability, equipment and supplies

Evaluating Students

Homework sequence with wine and food

Review study questions and other study guides

Suggested exams

How to keep current

Continuing education

Resources

Bibliography

And More . . .

Available by special order from the publisher. #6680M TEACHER'S MANUAL, ISBN #0-932664-68-7 paperback $12.95. Complete this order form. (**Note**: this manual is not available to students or non-qualified personnel.)

THE WINE APPRECIATION GUILD
360 Swift Ave., South San Francisco, CA 94080 USA
Phone Toll Free (800) 231-9463 FAX: (650) 866-3513

Name _____ Teaching Institution _____

Department _____ Phone _____

Address _____

Your Title _____ Degree _____

Name of Class _____ Credits _____

Number of Students per Class _____ Frequency _____

Ship to _____ Address _____

City _____ State _____ ZIP _____ Country _____

Please send the following:

_____ Copies #6680M TEACHER'S MANUAL for The University Wine Course $12.95 @ _____

_____ Copies #6680 THE UNIVERSITY WINE COURSE $35.00 @ _____

_____ Copies of VINDEX, triple-indexed catalog of over 1000 wine books and audio-visual materials. $5.00 @ _____

Subtotal _____

Check enclosed _____ or charge my MasterCard or VISA   CA residents add 8.25 % sales tax _____

_____ Exp. _____   US and Canada Shipping $4.00 _____

Signature _____   Overseas Shipping $10.00 _____

Note: Checks must be payable in US funds and drawn on an American bank.   Total _____